The Impact of Technology on the Criminal Justice System

This comprehensive volume explores the impact of emerging technologies designed to fight crime and terrorism.

It first reviews the latest advances in detecting deception, interrogation, and crime scene investigation, before then transitioning to the role of technology in collecting and evaluating evidence from lay witnesses, police body cameras, and super-recognizers. Finally, it explores the role of technology in the courtroom, with a particular focus on social media, citizen crime sleuths, virtual court, and child witnesses. It shines light on emerging issues, such as whether new norms have been created in the emergence of new technologies and how human behavior has shifted in response. Based on a global range of contributions, this volume provides an overview of the technological explosion in the field of law enforcement and discusses its successes and failures in fighting crime.

It is valuable reading for advanced students in forensic or legal psychology, and for practitioners, researchers, and scholars in law, criminal justice, and criminology.

Emily Pica is an associate professor in the Department of Psychological Science and Counseling, Austin Peay State University, USA. Her current research interests involve investigating ways in which we can improve eyewitness identification accuracy, as it is one of the leading causes of wrongful convictions. Additionally, she examines which factors may be more (or less) influential in jurors' decision making.

David Ross is a UC Foundation Professor of Psychology at the University of Tennessee at Chattanooga. He studies factors that impact the accuracy of eyewitness memory in children and adults. He has helped exonerate the wrongly imprisoned based on errors in eyewitness identification and works to prevent wrongful convictions by training law enforcement on collecting identification evidence according to research-based guidelines.

Joanna Pozzulo is Chancellor's Professor in the Department of Psychology at Carleton University, Canada, director of the Mental Health and Well-Being Research and Training Hub (MeWeRTH), and director of the Laboratory for Child Forensic Psychology. The primary goal of her research is to understand how memory in the context of witnessing crime differs across the lifespan, focusing on the young eyewitness.

The Impact of Technology on the Criminal Justice System
A Psychological Overview

Edited by Emily Pica, David Ross
and Joanna Pozzulo

NEW YORK AND LONDON

Designed cover image: © Getty Images

First published 2024
by Routledge
605 Third Avenue, New York, NY 10158

and by Routledge
4 Park Square, Milton Park, Abingdon, Oxon, OX14 4RN

Routledge is an imprint of the Taylor & Francis Group, an informa business

© 2024 selection and editorial matter, Emily Pica, David Ross, and Joanna Pozzulo; individual chapters, the contributors

The right of Emily Pica, David Ross, and Joanna Pozzulo to be identified as the authors of the editorial material, and of the authors for their individual chapters, has been asserted in accordance with sections 77 and 78 of the Copyright, Designs and Patents Act 1988.

All rights reserved. No part of this book may be reprinted or reproduced or utilised in any form or by any electronic, mechanical, or other means, now known or hereafter invented, including photocopying and recording, or in any information storage or retrieval system, without permission in writing from the publishers.

Trademark notice: Product or corporate names may be trademarks or registered trademarks, and are used only for identification and explanation without intent to infringe.

ISBN: 978-1-032-34634-2 (hbk)
ISBN: 978-1-032-34565-9 (pbk)
ISBN: 978-1-003-32311-2 (ebk)

DOI: 10.4324/9781003323112

Typeset in Sabon
by KnowledgeWorks Global Ltd.

Contents

List of Contributors   *viii*
Preface   *xii*

PART I
Advances in Detecting Deception, Interrogation, and Crime Scene Investigation   1

1 Do Automated and Virtual Interrogation and Deception Detection Systems Work?   3
KIRK LUTHER, VALERIE ARENZON, ASHLEY CURTIS, HANNAH DE ALMEIDA, JOSHUA HACHEY, AND JESSICA LUNDY

2 The Emergence of Police Real-Time Crime Centers   41
JOHNNY NHAN

3 Facial Recognition Software for Lead Generation and Lineup Construction   56
LAUREN E. THOMPSON

4 Advances and Future Prospects in Evolving Face Matching Technologies for Crime Prevention and Investigation   73
TIA C. BENNETT, HARRIET M. J. SMITH, AND HEATHER D. FLOWE

5 Insanity Evaluations in the Age of Neuroimaging   94
MICHAEL J. VITACCO AND SAVANNA COLEMAN

6 A Decade of Evolution in the Forensic Investigative Field:
A South African Overview   111
BERNADINE CAROL BENSON, JUANIDA SUZETTE HORNE, AND
GIDEON JONES

PART II
Collecting and Evaluating Eyewitness Evidence from Lay Witnesses, Police Body Cameras, and Super-recognizers   141

7 Who Are You Looking at?: Using Eye Tracking to
Understand Eyewitness Decision Making   143
JAMAL K. MANSOUR AND JONATHAN P. VALLANO

8 Understanding Eyewitness Testimony with Virtual Reality   173
MARKUS BINDEMANN AND MATTHEW C. FYSH

9 Facial Composite Technology and Eyewitness Identification   205
GRAHAM PIKE

10 Technological Advances in the Administration of Lineups   233
TIA C. BENNETT, MADELEINE P. INGHAM, MELISSA F. COLLOFF,
HARRIET M. J. SMITH, AND HEATHER D. FLOWE

11 Using Body-Worn Camera Footage to Remember Use-of-
Force Incidents   253
CRAIG BENNELL, SIMON BALDWIN, ANDREW BROWN, AND
ARIANE-JADE KHANIZADEH

12 "Super-recognizers" and the Legal System   272
EMMA PORTCH, JANICE ATTARD-JOHNSON, ALEJANDRO J.
ESTUDILLO, NATALIE MESTRY, AND SARAH BATE

PART III
Technology in the Courtroom: Social Media, Citizen Crime Sleuths, Virtual Court, and Child Witnesses   301

13 Digitally Networked Sleuthing: Online Platforms, Netizen
Detectives, and Bottom-Up Investigations   303
JAMES P. WALSH

14 The Virtual Court: Implications for Eyewitnesses
 and Beyond 330
 ERYN J. NEWMAN, BETHANY MUIR, AND NERICIA BROWN

15 The Impact of Technology on Jurors' Decisions 350
 EMMA REMPEL AND TARA BURKE

16 The CSI Effect and its Impact on the Legal System, Policy,
 and Practice 379
 KIMBERLEY SCHANZ

17 Is Facial Recognition Software a Solution to the Negative
 Effects of Social Media on Eyewitness Testimony? 397
 HEATHER M. KLEIDER-OFFUTT AND BETH B. STEVENS

18 Developmental Psychology and Law in the Digital Era:
 Emerging Trends, Challenges, and Opportunities 423
 I-AN SU AND STEPHEN J. CECI

Index 446

List of Contributors

Valerie Arenzon is currently completing her Master's in Forensic Psychology at Carleton University and starting her PhD in Psychology at University of Montreal in Fall 2023.

Janice Attard-Johnson is a Deputy Head of Department in Psychology at Bournemouth University.

Simon Baldwin is an Adjunct Professor of Psychology in Carleton University's Police Research Lab and the Manager of the Royal Canadian Mounted Police's Operational Research Unit.

Sarah Bate is Head of the Psychology Department at Bournemouth University.

Craig Bennell is a Professor in the Department of Psychology at Carleton University, where he also serves as Director of the Police Research Lab.

Tia C. Bennett is a Psychology PhD Student at the University of Birmingham, UK.

Bernadine Carol Benson is an Associate Professor at the Department of Police Practice, in the College of Law, at UNISA.

Markus Bindemann is a Professor of Cognitive Psychology at the University of Kent in the UK.

Andrew Brown is a doctoral candidate in Psychology in Carleton University's Police Research Lab.

Nericia Brown, PhD student School of Medicine and Psychology, Australian National University.

Tara Burke is an Associate Professor, and Director of the Psychology and Law Lab, at Toronto Metropolitan University.

List of Contributors   ix

Stephen J. Ceci is the Helen L. Carr Chaired Professor of Developmental Psychology at Cornell University. He is a member of the American Academy of Arts & Sciences and the recipient of numerous lifetime contribution awards.

Savanna Coleman received her Master of Science in Experimental Psychology from Augusta University in May 2023. She is currently enrolled in a doctoral program studying psychological sciences at the University of North Carolina Wilmington, and she plans to work in academia after obtaining her PhD.

Melissa F. Colloff is an Associate Professor in Psychology at the University of Birmingham, UK.

Ashley Curtis is currently completing her Master's in Forensic Psychology at Carleton University with plans to begin her PhD in Cognitive Psychology at University of Canterbury in Fall 2023.

Hannah de Almeida completely her Master's in Forensic Psychology at Carleton University, where she examined the impact of social influence techniques on information provision during investigative interviews.

Alejandro J. Estudillo is a Senior Lecturer in Psychology at Bournemouth University.

Heather D. Flowe is a Professor of Psychology at the University of Birmingham, UK.

Matthew C. Fysh is a psychology researcher for the NHS working at the Tavistock & Portman NHS Foundation Trust, London, UK.

Joshua Hachey is currently completing his masters in forensic psychology at Carleton University. His research involves the use of minimization in investigative interviews, and the effect this has on false confessions.

Juanida Suzette Horne is an Associate Professor at the Department of Police Practice, in the College of Law, at UNISA.

Madeleine P. Ingham is a Psychology PhD Student at the University of Birmingham, UK.

Gideon Jones is a private investigator with more than 3 decades of investigative experience both within the SAPS and external to it.

Ariane-Jade Khanizadeh is a doctoral student in Psychology in Carleton University's Police Research Lab and a Senior Researcher in the Royal Canadian Mounted Police's Operational Research Unit.

List of Contributors

Heather M. Kleider-Offutt is Associate Professor of Psychology at Georgia State University: Research interest is memory and decision-making in the legal context. Focus on eye-witness identification and face recognition.

Jessica Lundy is currently completing her Master's in forensic psychology at Carleton University, with plans to begin her PhD at Carleton in Fall 2023.

Kirk Luther is an Assistant Professor in the Department of Psychology at Carleton University where he conducts research on all things investigative interviewing.

Jamal K. Mansour is an Associate Professor in the Department of Psychology at the University of Lethbridge where she studies eyewitness identification decision making and confidence.

Natalie Mestry is a Principal Academic in Psychology at Bournemouth University.

Bethany Muir, PhD student School of Medicine and Psychology, Australian National University.

Eryn J. Newman is Senior Lecturer at School of Medicine and Psychology, Australian National University.

Johnny Nhan is the associate dean of graduate studies and professor in the criminology and criminal justice program at Texas Christian University.

Graham Pike works in the United Kingdom as a Professor of Forensic Cognition at The Open University's School of Psychology and Counselling, and he is a founding member of the Centre for Policing Research and Learning.

Emma Portch is a Senior Lecturer in Psychology at Bournemouth University.

Emma Rempel is a PhD Candidate at Toronto Metropolitan University. Her research explores the intersection of technology and legal judgment.

Kimberley Schanz is an associate professor of criminal justice and victimology and victim services at Stockton University in Galloway, NJ.

Harriet M. J. Smith is an Independent Research Fellow in Psychology at Nottingham Trent University, UK.

Beth B. Stevens is an MA student at Georgia State University. Her research interests focus on the intersection of psychology and the law, including eyewitness memory, legal decision-making, and face recognition.

I-An "Amy" Su is a PhD Candidate in Psychology at Cornell University. In addition to her academic pursuits, she is a qualified attorney-at-law in Taiwan with a specialization in capital cases. Amy is the founder and manager of her own legal firm, known as LegalChime Attorneys-at-Law.

Lauren E. Thompson is a recent graduate from the PhD program in psychology at Carleton University.

Jonathan P. Vallano conducts research on topics including eyewitness memory, investigative interviewing, and juror decision-making as an Associate Professor of Psychology at the University of Pittsburgh at Greensburg.

Michael J. Vitacco is a professor in the Institute of Public and Preventative Health and Department of Psychiatry and Health Behavior at Augusta University.

James P Walsh is an Associate Professor of Criminology at the University of Ontario Institute of Technology. In addition to policing and media, his research focuses on the topics of migration, border security, surveillance, terrorism, and moral panic.

Preface

Emily Pica, David Ross, and Joanna Pozzulo

Various technologies have emerged in the last thirty years to fight crime and terrorism. This book documents these developments and assesses their impact on the criminal justice system. Three historical events were the impetus for this volume.

First, on September 11, 2001, four hijacked commercial planes were used by al-Qaeda terrorists to attack the United States. A total of 2,977 people, including 383 firefighters, died in New York City from the collapse of the World Trade Center buildings. In Washington, DC, 184 people died in the attack on the Pentagon, and 40 passengers died gallantly trying to fight their hijackers, only to have their plane crash in a rural area in Pennsylvania. It was the deadliest day in the history of the United States.

Immediately following the attack, President George Bush created Operation Enduring Freedom, formed the Department of Homeland Security, and launched an international effort to prevent future terrorist attacks. These efforts resulted in technological advances in "global surveillance" designed to identify terrorists. Many of these are examined in Part I of this volume, "Advances in Detecting Deception, Interrogation, and Crime Scene Investigation." This section discusses, for example, advances in automated deception detection systems, facial identification and surveillance systems designed to spot terrorists at airports and in mass gatherings, the development of "real-time" law enforcement criminal investigation centers intended to monitor and investigate crime, software that aids police in identifying suspects, and the use of neuroimaging to evaluate the mental status of a suspect.

Second, DNA exoneration studies by the United States Department of Justice found that eyewitness identification errors are the most significant reason for wrongful convictions. As a result, the Department of Justice distributed guidelines to every law enforcement agency in the United States on collecting identification evidence and has updated them since their conception. Part II of this volume, "Collecting and Evaluating Evidence from Lay Witnesses, Police Body Cameras, and Super-recognizers," examines technology designed to increase eyewitness accuracy, including computer programs that collect lineup identification data, generate composite photographs to identify suspects, and physiological measures used to determine whether a witness has crime-relevant information. Additional topics in this section include collecting identification evidence using police-worn body cameras, biometric surveillance systems, facial recognition systems, neurotechnology, virtual reality, artificial intelligence, composite face development software, and super-recognizers—law enforcement individuals who are exceptionally accurate at facial identification.

Third, there has been a worldwide adoption of social media, the Internet, and cell phones. To date, 5.2 billion people have access to the Internet, and 4.8 billion people use social media. Social media is a public source of information about crimes, and witnesses with cell phones can record a public event they observe that has legal importance. For example, few could ever forget a bystander recording George Floyd's cries, "I can't breathe." Bystander videos of the event were instrumental, leading to inner-city rioting and pressure on the legal system to prosecute the officers.

Social media has become a tool law enforcement and the public use to help solve crimes. Police have used social media to collect evidence, encourage community policing when seeking the identity of a suspect, communicate about neighborhood crime, generate investigative leads, or ask for help locating missing people. Sometimes, the public has taken things into their own hands and used social media to investigate crimes, sometimes with mixed results. When the Boston Marathon Bombing occurred in 2013, Reddit users investigated the case. This group called themselves the Reddit Bureau of Investigation (RBI), and unfortunately, they wrongly identified several innocent suspects.

A different outcome occurred when the parents of Gabby Petito turned to the public for help finding their missing 22-year-old daughter, who was last seen with her boyfriend Brian Laundrie in the Grand Teton National Park in Wyoming. A group of citizens on social media investigated the case. It revealed clues that helped police focus their search for Gabby, saving them from having to search over 485 miles of wilderness area. A couple who traveled through the Teton area found Gabby Petito's white van on a YouTube video they posted, a tip that led investigators to the site where Gabby's body was found.

Part III of this volume, "Technology in the Courtroom: Social Media, Citizen Crime Sleuths, Virtual Court, and Child Witnesses," examines the pros and cons of citizens using social media and the Internet to investigate crimes, how recognition software can overcome the adverse effects of social media on eyewitness testimony, how technology in the courtroom is used to communicate with jurors in criminal cases, how the role of virtual courts in criminal cases, and how technology is used with child witnesses.

This volume overviews emerging technologies designed to fight crime and terrorism. Moreover, the authors are from around the world and provide an international perspective on this crucial topic. With the rapid advancement of technology in this field, we hope this volume will encourage others to monitor the evolution of global surveillance technology.

Part I

Advances in Detecting Deception, Interrogation, and Crime Scene Investigation

1 Do Automated and Virtual Interrogation and Deception Detection Systems Work?

Kirk Luther, Valerie Arenzon, Ashley Curtis, Hannah de Almeida, Joshua Hachey, and Jessica Lundy

Do Automated and Virtual Interrogation and Deception Detection Systems Work?

Obtaining high-quality information from witnesses, victims, suspects, and sources (i.e., interviewees) is integral to the successful resolution of crimes (Vrij et al., 2017). The field of investigative interviewing has seen significant advances in interrogation and deception detection practices, including the rise of advanced virtual environments and new automated technologies (e.g., artificial intelligence). To determine whether advances in automated interrogation and deception detection systems are ready for applied use, it is important to understand the roots of these systems—that is, the theories these systems are based on, and how these systems evolved over time to meet the needs of society and incorporate the latest scientific evidence. In the current chapter, we will provide information on: (i) the evolution of interrogation techniques ranging from early (and problematic) practices from the nineteenth century to today's virtual and automated systems; and (ii) the evolution of deception detection research and practice ranging from over 2,000 years ago to today's automated and artificial intelligence systems—knowing where we came from will help us better understand where we are now, and where we are headed.

The Evolution of Interrogation Techniques

Third Degree Practices

Early methods of interrogation in the nineteenth century largely consisted of "third degree" practices involving various forms of physical abuse, torture, isolation, and deprivation of basic human necessities such as food and water (Leo & Ofshe, 2008). Society was "at war" with crime and this "get tough" approach to interrogations was believed to be an effective way to elicit confessions—one of the most substantive forms of evidence for prosecuting individuals (Snook et al., 2014). The judiciary was slow to take issue with third degree interrogation tactics given the apparent success of such methods for obtaining confessions and perceiving such methods as a necessary evil to remove criminals from society (Leo & Ofshe, 2008). However, in 1929, United States President Herbert Hoover ratified a commission to undertake the first national study of crime, the criminal justice system, and law enforcement practices across the country. President Hoover's initiative, which would become known as the "National Commission on Law Observance and Enforcement" produced a series of 14 reports that highlighted deep-rooted problems with the criminal justice system. One such report released in 1931, titled "Lawlessness in Law Enforcement," is cited throughout the interrogation literature as the undoing of third-degree interviewing tactics across the United States (Waite, 1931). It was in this review that law enforcement agencies were first introduced to the prospect of false confessions and misinformation resulting from physically coercive interrogation methods. The report led to widespread public distrust in the criminal justice system and impeded efforts to "professionalize" policing (Leipold, 2020).

Accusatorial Interviews

By the mid-1960s, physical interrogation methods were all but antiquated; techniques centered on psychological persuasion became common practice (Leo & Ofshe, 2008). Polygraphist John E. Reid was largely responsible for changing the field of interrogation when he released *Criminal Interrogation and Confessions*, in which he detailed a method of interrogation known as the Reid Technique. The Reid Technique is one of the most widely taught interrogation models in North America (King & Snook, 2009); interrogations using the Reid technique are designed to elicit a confession. The Reid Technique consists of a behavior analysis interview (BAI) and a subsequent 9-step interviewing model. The BAI is the keystone of the Reid Technique and is anchored on the idea that there are behavioral cues to deception (e.g., body language, eye contact, speed of speech). The BAI consists of a 15-item questionnaire designed to help the police determine who is innocent and who is guilty and must be subjected to an interrogation. Police are instructed to use the BAI in the pre-custodial interview to determine which subjects are being deceptive and should be targeted for the subsequent Reid-based interrogation.

The first step in the Reid Model of Interrogation involves the interrogator directly confronting the suspect with a belief in their guilt, accompanied by an emphasis on the benefits of telling the truth (Inbau et al., 2013). The goal is for the suspect to believe that their guilt is known to be true by investigators. During this step, interrogators are instructed to evaluate the suspect's verbal and nonverbal responses for indicators of deception (more on deception detection later in the chapter). Kassin and Fong (1999) noted that no evidence supported the diagnostic value (i.e., the extent to which behavioral cues can accurately distinguish between deception and truth) of the behavioral cues that investigators are trained to observe. Specifically, observers were unable to reliably differentiate between true and false denials. Moreover, those that were trained in the deception cues were significantly less accurate, more confident, and more biased towards seeing deception compared to untrained observers (Kassin & Fong, 1999). A follow-up study showed taped interview clips of 14 suspects (12 male and 2 female; 4 were juvenile) to experienced police detectives, asking them to note what verbal and nonverbal deception cues they use to judge guilt, whether they believed the suspect was guilty and their confidence in their judgement (Mann et al., 2004). Researchers noted the same biased responses; police tended to have more confidence in their judgements, but were biased towards seeing guilt, making them less accurate in their judgements overall (Mann et al., 2004; Meissner & Kassin, 2002).

During the second step of the Reid Technique, the investigator is encouraged to introduce a theme—i.e., a belief about the reason for the crime's commission including moral excuses, minimizing the seriousness of the crime, or blaming another person or the circumstance, a set of practices known as minimization (Inbau et al., 2013). Minimization techniques, while deemed admissible by courts in the United States and Canada (Inbau et al., 2013) have been linked to increased incidents of false confessions (Horgan et al., 2012; Kassin & Kiechel, 1996; Russano et al., 2005). Russano and colleagues (2005) developed a novel paradigm aimed at assessing the diagnosticity (i.e., the likelihood of obtaining a true confession over a false confession) of common coercive interview practices, specifically examining how minimization techniques impact interview outcomes. In their study, undergraduate students were asked to complete logic tasks alongside a confederate, who either asked for assistance from the participant to cheat, or did not ask the participant for assistance. Participants in both conditions were accused of cheating, and interviewed using minimization (e.g., "I'm sure you didn't realize what a big deal it was"). The interviewer lessened the seriousness of the participant's offence by making statements that expressed sympathy or concern, by offering moral excuses, or by proposing an explicit deal (e.g., where participants could confess to the crime, allowing them to settle the matter quickly). Specifically, when minimization techniques or the explicit deal were used, the number of both true and false confessions increased, negatively impacting the interview's diagnosticity. The diagnosticity rating was 7.64 when no tactics were used, compared to 4.50 when minimization was used, and 2.02 when minimization techniques and the explicit deal were used (Russano et al., 2005). Higher diagnosticity ratings are desired, as such implies a particular technique is more likely to elicit a true (cf. false) confession.

Step three of the Reid technique involves discouraging denials of guilt by returning to the previously presented theme and interrupting suspects during their denial of the crime (Inbau et al., 2013). The manual notes that innocent suspects and guilty suspects will react differently to this tactic. For example, innocent suspects are believed to be forceful in their denials and maintain eye contact, while guilty suspects are believed to be more hesitant and defensive in their denials. Step four involves overcoming a suspect's secondary line of defense: reasons they would not or could not have committed the crime. Notably, Inbau and colleagues (2013) stated that the excuses are normally only offered by guilty suspects. During step five, the investigator is trained to display sincerity in what they say and increase the physical closeness between them and the suspect. Step six involves recognizing that the suspect may have a passive mood, as they weigh the benefits of telling the truth, which is supposedly reflected in changes in nonverbal behavior. In step seven, the investigator uses an alternative question, or a suggestion of a choice to be made by the suspect concerning a component of the crime. For example, the officer may state "Did you intend to kill her or was it just an accident?" (Inbau et al., 2013). Both alternatives offered are the functional equivalent of an incriminating admission. The final two steps involve the interrogator getting verbal and written confessions, respectively.

Together, it is evident that each step of the Reid Technique serves to solidify an interviewer's belief in suspect guilt. In turn, the Reid Technique leaves investigators vulnerable to the effects of tunnel vision and puts innocent suspects at risk for false confessions (Moore & Fitzsimmons, 2011).

False Confessions

Before the science of DNA in 1984, the legal community had little knowledge on false confessions. It was not until geneticist Alec Jeffreys applied DNA sequencing to identity-based testing that research on false confessions began to erupt in the academic community (Saad, 2005). Over the next several years, sobering statistics began to emerge regarding the prevalence of false confessions across North America. To date, more than 360 DNA-based exonerations have taken place across the United States alone (Cooper et al., 2019), representing 15% of the 2,359 exoneration cases documented in the National Registry of Exonerations (NRA; Saber et al., 2022). Recent data from the Innocence Project (2023) revealed that approximately 30% of the organization's exoneration cases were the result of false confessions.

There are four main types of false confessions discussed in the literature: (1) voluntary, (2) coerced-internalized, (3) coerced-compliant, and (4) coerced-reactive. First, voluntary false confessions refer to omissions that are made without prompting from law enforcement (Kassin & Wrightsman, 1980). There are several reasons why an individual may voluntarily confess to a crime they did not commit. Most explanations speak to an underlying psychopathology (e.g., desire for attention, self-punishment, guilt, delusion, mental illness). In some cases, however, voluntary confessions are made in the interest of protecting someone (i.e., friend, family member), or because of some perceived tangible gain (e.g., publicity, monetary reward).

The second and third types of false confession involve coercive interviewing methods. Coerced-internalized false confessions, for example, occur when highly coercive interviewing tactics end up being so convincing that the accused themselves eventually end up believing they committed the crime in question (Chapman, 2012). Research investigating the internalized subtype of false confessions suggests that many false confessors experience a lack of confidence in their recollection of an event, a phenomenon referred to as memory distrust syndrome (MDS; see Gudjonsson, 2017 for a detailed analysis). Antecedents such as suggestibility, lack of confidence, and undue trust in authority are found to compound one's risk of making a coerced internalized false confession. Finally, coerced-compliant false confessions occur when the accused is persuaded into an omission of guilt using coercive interrogation tactics (Kassin, 2008). Coerced-compliant false confessions differ from coerced-internalized in the sense that the accused offers the omission out of compliance instead of an internalized belief that they are guilty. Often, coerced-compliant confessions happen when an individual confesses to evade the psychological stress of an interrogation, to avoid punishment (i.e., expectation of leniency), or because of an expectation of harsh punishment if they do not confess (Kassin, 2008).

More recently, a fourth type of false confession has been proposed by scholars: coerced-reactive false confessions. Coerced-reactive confessions occur when individuals confess to avoid or escape coercive actions that come from sources outside of police and the interrogation room (e.g., pressure from criminals; McCann, 1998). For example, a gang member who confesses to a crime committed by another offender under threat of death by fellow gang members would be considered a coerced-reactive confession. These confessions are distinct from voluntary and coerced-compliant false confessions as the motivation to confess is external to the interrogation, meaning it is not related to coercive interviewing practices, nor is the confession voluntary, as the individual would not likely confess without the influence of the external pressure (McCann, 1998).

Humanitarian Interviews

In response to critical issues emerging from the accusatorial interrogation methods, some countries have seen a shift in policy for sanctioned interrogation practices. Recently, a group of academics, practitioners, and policy makers collaborated on a global set of guidelines and universal protocol for investigative interviewing (Mendez et al., 2021). These guidelines are aimed at facilitating a transition away from accusatorial, coercive interviewing practices toward humanitarian, evidence-based interviewing practices. In contrast to accusatorial interviewing, humanitarian interviewing is rooted in ethical practices, encourages rapport building, a relaxed atmosphere, and the use of empirically supported memory enhancement techniques. Ultimately, the aim of the humanitarian interview is to obtain detailed and accurate information about a crime to conduct an efficient and effective investigation.

In England and Wales, a national review of investigative interviewing practices was conducted following several high-profile wrongful convictions (e.g., the Birmingham Six, the Guildford Four), which led to the introduction of the PEACE Model of Investigative Interviewing (see Clarke & Milne, 2001; Milne & Bull, 1999 for a comprehensive overview of the PEACE Model of Investigative Interviewing). PEACE was named for the steps of the interviewing model, that include Planning and Preparation, Engage and Explain, obtain an Account, Closure, and Evaluation.

PEACE: Planning and Preparation

Before the beginning of an interview, the PEACE model requires investigators to plan and prepare for the interview. In this initial step, interviewers are encouraged to develop an extensive written plan of their questions, investigative objectives, and practical arrangements for how the interview should proceed (e.g., a route map of questions, plans for obstacles and eventualities; Snook et al., 2014). The model also recommends investigators gather as much information as possible about the interviewee (e.g., presence of mental illness, family and social ties, financial situation) to help inform the interview.

PEACE: Engage and Explain

Once a suspect interview begins, interviewers enter the Engage and Explain phase of the interview. This second phase is characterized by engaging the interviewee in a personalized conversation (e.g., building rapport, self-disclosing) and providing a breakdown of the interview process. Some key elements of this stage include a clear statement of suspect's legal rights and an explanation of reason(s) for the interview.

PEACE: Account

Following the completion of the Engage and Explain phase, interviewers are expected to enter the Account phase of the interview which aims to obtain a clarified account from the suspect. During this phase, suspects are encouraged to provide an uninterrupted account of experienced events. Open-ended (i.e., tell, explain, describe) and focused prompts (i.e., who, what, when, where, how) are encouraged so that the interviewer can obtain detailed and accurate information from the interviewee (Snook et al., 2012). The account phase also encourages interviewers to address inconsistencies and discrepancies in a respectful and ethical manner.

PEACE: Closure

The fourth phase of the PEACE model is Closure. Considered as the conclusion of the interview, the interviewer provides an overview of everything that was discussed, including explaining what will happen in the future. This phase also gives the suspect an opportunity to add or correct any information (Snook et al., 2014).

PEACE: Evaluation

The PEACE model extends beyond the end of the interaction with the suspect as it encourages interviewers to self-evaluate their performance and request feedback from colleagues.

In the past two decades, researchers have extensively studied the effectiveness and the impact of the accusatorial and humanitarian interview models. Multiple benefits have been identified regarding the use of humanitarian models, such as PEACE, for interviewing. First and foremost, such models do not contain unethical or coercive strategies that were observed in cases of false confessions (Snook et al., 2014). Thus, a humanitarian interview ensures the respect of human rights while also avoiding the risk of inadmissible statements. Secondly, multiple researchers have conducted both observational and experimental studies that provide empirical evidence supporting the use of humanitarian models. In their meta-analysis, Meissner et al. (2014) found humanitarian interviewing approaches to be more effective in eliciting information compared to accusatorial interrogations. For example, an experimental study by Evans et al. (2013) examining intelligence-gathering interrogations found that participants questioned in the information-gathering approach provided more details and confessed more frequently compared to those in the accusatorial interrogation. A third piece of evidence supporting the humanitarian interviewing approach was revealed in studies considering the offender's perspective. Specifically, an offender's decision to cooperate during an interview is influenced by the style of interviewing adopted by the officer (Snook et al., 2014). When asking offenders about their perspective regarding an experienced interrogation, research has found that offenders display increased resistance and denials when questioned in an accusatorial style (Holmberg & Christianson, 2001). Taken together, benefits for using information-gathering approaches over accusatorial approaches have been widely demonstrated. However, changes in term policy and training are still lacking in many countries (Snook et al., 2010).

Virtual and Automated Interviewing Systems

Arguably the next stage in the evolution in investigative interviewing practice is the use of virtual and automated interviewing environments and systems. Recent advances in technology—virtual reality and artificial intelligence—have created additional avenues for eliciting information in the context of investigative interviews as well as interviewer training. Further, the context of the COVID-19 global pandemic led to an increased adoption of technology and resulted in investigative interviews making their way to online virtual platforms (e.g., interviewing via Zoom or similar videoconferencing software; Vieth et al., 2020). This shift in interviewing context posed sudden and unexpected difficulties that required investigators to adjust. While very few studies have been conducted on virtual and automated interviewing prior to the pandemic, it appears we are on the cusp of the next stage of the evolution of interviewing practices.

Virtual Interviewing Benefits and Challenges

Virtual environments, or computer simulations, have been shown to be useful in contexts related to investigative interviewing. For example, computer mediated communication has demonstrated success for increasing self-disclosure (Baccon et al., 2019; Joinson, 2001) and reducing social pressure (Herrera et al., 2018) relative to face-to-face interactions. The use of virtual environments has also proven useful for gathering reliable and accurate information, albeit in other contexts than investigative interviewing (e.g., counseling, health; Kang & Gratch, 2010, 2012; Peiris et al., 2000).

The use of virtual environments for interviewing also may prove useful for investigators who are required to interview witnesses living in remote areas, as opposed to bringing them to the police station. That is, using virtual environments to conduct remote interviews has allowed investigators to save time and resources, as well as to question witnesses within shorter delays of the incident (Hager, 2020). Notably, a witness's recollection of the details of a crime can be forgotten or interfered with following significant delays. For example, people tend to mentally replay events or discuss events with others, often adding and removing details without even knowing it. This type of rehearsal only increases one's confidence about what happened, but negatively affects the accuracy of their memory (Busey et al., 2000). Therefore, conducting the interview as soon as possible after the event can have great benefit for the accuracy of witness's recollection of details. Additionally, virtual interviews remove the cost and difficulty associated with travel for interviewees (Hoogesteyn et al., 2020).

One of the potential issues associated with virtual interviewing is the ability to build rapport may be hindered. Rapport is fundamental to facilitating cooperation and disclosure during investigative interviewers (Gabbert et al., 2021). There are nonverbal cues that people typically use when building connections with others such as posture mirroring, eye contact, and physical touching (e.g., handshakes) which are difficult or impossible to replicate in virtual settings. Common techniques that investigators use to control physical distance between the interviewee and to provide practical needs (e.g., offering food, water) also are limited.

Dion Larivière and colleagues (2022) developed a study to measure the ability to build rapport in an online interviewing context. To build rapport, interviewers were instructed to start the interview with attempts to show empathy as well as with self-disclosure by asking participants about their experiences with online learning during the pandemic. Throughout the interview, the interviewer addressed the participant by their first name, used a gentle tone, smiled, and attempted to keep their gaze toward the screen and the webcam when possible. The interviewer was also instructed to sit upright in a visibly relaxed and open posture. These behaviors were to be maintained throughout the entire interview. Conversely, the interview guide for the no-rapport condition began with five close-ended filler questions that did not emphasize personal interest (e.g., "Is the webcam integrated into this computer?"). Throughout the interview, the interviewer did not address the participant by their first name—they used a flat tone of voice and made no effort to smile or attempt to keep their gaze toward the screen and the webcam. The interviewer was sitting upright and was facing slightly offscreen. The interviewer was instructed only to make comments that helped progress the interview and ask clarification questions when needed. Their results showed that in the rapport condition, the interviewer was able to successfully build rapport in a virtual environment, which led to more accurate reporting from the participants. Therefore, interviewers can build rapport effectively in a virtual environment using approaches like those found effective in in-person interviews.

A second potential issue with virtual interviewing is technology and connection-related problems. The unpredictability of technology can interrupt the flow of an interview and prevent the transmission of visual and verbal cues due to lagging and/or freezing. These technological issues also can affect the ability to record the interview, which is crucial for admissibility in court. Safety and confidentiality are also potential concerns with virtual interviewing. Virtual interviewing is often done from the comfort of one's home, which means other people may be present. The presence of other individuals could be distracting for the interviewee, but more crucially problematic in cases where the victim and suspect live in the same home (e.g., domestic abuse). For example, a suspect may be forcing the victim to say certain things in the interview.

Avatar-based Interviewing Benefits and Challenges

Researchers have also begun to examine the efficacy of avatar-based interviewing (e.g., Pompedda et al., 2022; Taylor & Dando, 2018). Avatar-based interviewing involves a virtual computer representation of a user, who can be completely customized in terms of age, tone of voice, realistic features, etc. The benefit of using avatar-to-avatar interviewing is that each avatar can be tailored to best fit the interviewee. Avatar-to-avatar based interviewing, while under-researched, is beginning to show promise for practical use. For example, research has shown that avatar-to-avatar communication results in high levels of interpersonal trust (Segal et al., 2022).

In perhaps the first study to test the efficacy of interviewing adult witnesses using avatars, Taylor and Dando (2018) examined eyewitness' memory performance for interviews conducted in a virtual environment (avatar-to-avatar) using either a virtual reality headset, or in-person (face-to-face). Specifically, participants watched a mock crime video (1 minute and 45 seconds) depicting a car theft and were interviewed about what they remembered from this event. Their results showed that those interviewed with avatars recalled more correct information about the crime and made fewer errors in their recall compared to those interviewed in-person.

More recently, Dando et al. (2022) examined participants' memory as a function of being interviewed via avatars or face-to-face, and whether rapport could be successfully built using avatars. Specifically, the authors engaged in several attentive verbal (e.g., self-disclosure) and physical (e.g., eye contact, nodding) behaviors to build rapport with the interviewees in both interviewing modalities. Their results showed that rapport was successfully established in avatar-based interviews. Further, participants interviewed in the virtual environment with rapport building practices outperformed those interviewed in-person by providing more, and more accurate information about the crime they witnessed.

Avatar-based interviewing has also proven beneficial for interviewing children. For example, in child sexual-abuse cases, the only tangible evidence police can obtain is from statements the child makes in an interview

(Elliot & Briere, 1994). Research has suggested that children stay more engaged and may feel more comfortable when talking to animated characters (i.e., puppets) versus real people (Eder, 1990). Avatar-based interviewing also has the flexibility of programming certain body language and reactions into the avatars (Pompedda et al., 2022). The ability to program certain nonverbal behaviors is especially important when interviewing children because children are highly susceptible to influence and they naturally look for cues of approval when speaking with others (Howe, 2000).

Research has also examined the utility of avatar-based interviews for training interviewers. The main advantage of this approach is that the child avatars can be programmed with pre-defined memories, which means what "actually" happened is known and therefore specific feedback can be given to the trainee (Haginoya et al., 2021). Recently, Pompedda and colleagues (2022) conducted a meta-analysis of the effectiveness of providing feedback on avatar-based interview training. Their analysis included nine studies with over 2,200 interviews. Overall, their results revealed strong support for the use and efficacy of avatar-based training—trainees showed robust effects of increasing their use of appropriate question types and decreasing their use inappropriate question types during interviews.

While the meta-analysis by Pompedda and colleagues (2022) is promising for the future of avatar-based training, researchers have argued that child avatars for interview training still requires significant development (Powell et al., 2022). For example, there needs to be development around the sets of questions that child avatars can respond to, as well as development of the range of responses that the avatars can produce (Brubacher et al., 2015; Pompedda et al., 2015). Also, current iterations of the avatars are often reported as visually primitive and lacking in realism (Wang & Ruiz, 2021). While avatar-based interview training tools certainly hold promise for significant advances in delivering investigative interview training, further research and development of these tools are required. Further information is also needed on the admissibility of such interviews in court cases.

Artificial Intelligence Interviewing

Recent developments in technology have led to the development of Spot—an online digital misconduct reporting tool (see www.talktospot.com). Spot, developed as a tool for reporting harassment in workplace contexts, is an artificial intelligence bot that conducts interviews via text-chat. Spot is designed to recognize keywords (e.g., names, dates, places) to ask relevant follow-up questions. An advantage of a tool such as Spot is its timing—individuals can access it immediately following an event, which may prevent false memories and increase accuracy of reporting. While artificial intelligence tools, such as Spot, offer a promising technological advancement to investigative interviewing, we are unaware of any research examining its efficacy or reliability.

The Evolution of Deception Detection Techniques

The ability to solve crimes quickly and efficiently, often with minimal resources, is an important issue faced by investigators. One investigative skill that has received a great deal of attention in the literature is the ability to detect deception. Deception detection research and practice has a rich history, with methods dating back to ancient times. For example, in the Medieval ages, holding onto a hot iron or being tied to a sack and submerged in cold water were commonly employed methods of deception detection. If the subject was burned by the iron or floated in the water, they were deemed dishonest (Sullivan, 2001). The use of dangerous tests was common in English Medieval courts as methods were based in theology and the belief that honesty would prevail in the person on trial (Ford, 2006). There have been several instruments developed to increase investigators' ability to detect deception (e.g., polygraph, voice stress analyzer). There are three main factors that deception detection instruments examine to accurately detect fabricated statements: nonverbal behaviors (e.g., eye movement), physiological responses (e.g., sweating), and verbal behaviors (e.g., an individual's vernacular) (Vrij & Fisher, 2016; Vrij et al., 2004). Before discussing the specific factors of deception, it is helpful to know about some theoretical approaches to deception detection.

Theoretical Approaches to Deception Detection

There are two primary theoretical approaches to deception detection—emotional theories and cognitive theories.

Emotional Theories of Deception

Ekman and Friesen (1969) developed the emotion-based approach to deception detection. This approach stated that lying causes emotions different from those experienced when telling the truth. For example, a liar may experience guilt about telling a lie, delight in fooling someone, or fear of being caught in a lie, while a truthteller may not experience any guilt or fear. The emotional approach suggests that experiencing emotions when lying can lead to a leakage of these emotions, thus giving away concealed information. This theory applies exclusively to lies of consequence, as they are more likely to produce emotional responses that can be signaled behaviorally. In early iterations of the nonverbal leakage theory, lies are signaled in different parts of the body. Because people are aware of their face and able to exercise control over their facial expressions, deception is unlikely to manifest in the face aside from fleeting signs of expressions that are being suppressed, called micro-expressions. According to Ekman and Friesen (1969), the legs and feet are a primary source of leakage and deception cues because we are less aware of what our feet or legs are doing. Leakage in the legs or feet could include behaviors such as soothing leg squeezing, flirtatious leg displays, or restless flight movements. Ekman suggested that the less aware we are of a behavior, the more likely the behavior is to signal a lie.

Subsequent research has not supported Ekman and Friesen's leakage theory (e.g., Burgoon, 2018; Vrij et al., 2019). More recent iterations of emotion theories have focused on the role of micro-expressions—involuntary emotional leakage that presents itself as fleeting facial expressions (i.e., lasting only one-quarter to one-half of a second). Research has shown, however, that there is often a disconnect between emotions that are displayed and those that are felt. As such, deception does not necessarily produce negative emotions, which, in turn, do not necessarily signal deception (Hoque et al., 2012). Researchers have found that micro-expressions do not occur often enough to be useful. For example, a study by Porter and ten Brinke (2008) found that only 2% of emotional expressions that were coded could be labeled as micro-expressions; further, they appeared equally in the expressions of liars and truth tellers (Porter et al., 2012; Porter & ten Brinke, 2008). Other studies have found that liars and truth-tellers exhibit different emotional responses than would be expected given Ekman's theory of micro-expressions. For example, Pentland and colleagues (2015) found that in a concealed information test (described in detail later in this chapter), liars showed less contempt and more intense smiles than truthful individuals, which is at odds with the fundamental assumption that it is impossible for a liar to conceal their true nature (Porter et al., 2012).

Jordan and colleagues (2019) examined whether the micro-expression training tool (METT; see Ekman, 2006 and Paul Ekman Group, 2011 for more information on this tool) could improve an individual's ability to identify micro-expressions and use them for lie detection. Their results showed that METT-trained participants performed *worse* than chance on identifying micro-expressions. Further, the METT-training individuals did not perform better than untrained or bogus trained (i.e., trained on the Interpersonal Perception Task; see Costanzo & Archer, 1989) individuals. While all individuals in the study had high confidence in their ability to detect deception, their actual ability to do so was no better than chance. Similar results have been found with other micro-expression training research (e.g., Zloteanu et al., 2021) and deception detection training in general (Driskell, 2012). While training to detect deception has very little empirical support, such training has unfortunately been implemented in practice. For example, training to recognize and identify micro-expressions is used in the Screening Passengers by Observation Technique (SPOT) program—used by airport security organizations (see Higginbotham, 2013; Smith, 2011; Weinberger, 2010 for more info on the SPOT program).

Overall, the convergence of evidence shows that micro-expressions are not a reliable indicator of deceit, and that training to detect micro-expressions does not improve veracity judgements. What is also troubling is that it appears that Ekman has yet to publish empirical data showing evidence that micro-expressions can be used to distinguish truth-tellers from liars (Vrij et al., 2014).

Cognitive Theories of Deception

Cognitive theories of deception are based on the knowledge that lying is more cognitively demanding than telling the truth as liars must maintain both internal and external consistency in their stories (Zuckerman et al., 1981). Internal consistency is when the facts line up and make sense with each other; external consistency is when the facts make sense with other people's understanding of the event. The cognitive demand thought to be associated with lying led Zuckerman and colleagues to hypothesize that liars would exhibit the following cues: longer response times to questions, more hesitations, and fewer hand movements to accompany speech. Zuckerman and colleagues developed the Four-Factor Theory of Deception, which stated: (1) arousal is greatest when lying; (2) emotional affect is associated with guilt; (3) the cognitive aspects of lying are more complex than truth telling; and (4) liars attempt to control both verbal and nonverbal behaviors to avoid being caught. For further understanding on cognitive theories of deception, see the Interpersonal Deception Theory (Buller & Burgoon, 1996), the Preoccupation Model of Secrecy (Lane & Wegner, 1995), the Activation-Decision-Construction Model (Walczyk et al., 2003), and Mohamed and colleagues' (2006) neurological model of deception.

Lying is cognitively demanding, especially during a police interview (Granhag & Strömwall, 2002; Vrij, 1998). Two cognitive theories that consider the difficulty of interviews as advantageous to detecting deception are the Content Complexity Theory and the Attempted Behavioral Control Theory. Content Complexity Theory encompasses the demands of an interview, wherein a truthful person's account will be more complex and have more detail than a liar's account (Vrij, 2000). Liars will present fewer details (cf. truth tellers) as they are better able to maintain a simple story while under the pressures of an investigative interview (DePaulo et al., 2003). To increase the pressure on liars in an interview, research has found that increasing cognitive load is effective (Vrij et al., 2006, 2008, 2012). To increase cognitive load, the interviewer gives cognitively challenging tasks to the suspect (e.g., provide an account from its end to beginning), with the goal of causing the suspect to make mistakes and deviate from their initial account (Vrij et al., 2006). Content Complexity Theory is supported by research studies that use the number of details provided by a suspect as a cue to deception, meaning liars tended to provide fewer details compared to truth tellers (DePaulo et al., 2003; Granhag & Strömwall, 2002; Nahari et al., 2019). Attempted Behavioral Control Theory rationalizes that as liars try to appear calm in an interview, their endeavors are seen as rigid and unnatural (Vrij, 1998). Essentially, liars actively try not to fidget, break eye contact, show too much emotion, or pause for too long because they believe doing so will aid in appearing innocent. However, research has found that liars' behaviors are dissimilar to that of truth-tellers: they smile, pause, blink, and avert their gaze less than truthtellers (DePaulo et al., 2003; Granhag & Strömwall, 2002).

Cues for Detecting Deception

As mentioned, there are three main factors that deception detection instruments examine when attempting to detect fabricated statements: nonverbal behaviors (e.g., eye movement), physiological responses (e.g., sweating), and verbal behaviors (e.g., an individual's vernacular) (Vrij & Fisher, 2016; Vrij et al., 2004). Each of these factors are reviewed briefly below.

Nonverbal Cues to Detecting Deception

A wealth of research has indicated that nonverbal cues are not reliable indicators of deception. Specifically, a meta-analysis by Bond and DePaulo (2006) examined more than 200 deception detection studies, finding an average lie-truth discrimination rate of 54%. The meta-analysis also noted that truthful messages were more often judged correctly compared to deceptive messages, meaning that in settings where virtually no lies are told, there are substantially higher discrimination rates compared to settings where virtually all statements were lies (Bond & DePaulo, 2006). A follow-up meta-analysis examined the role of individual differences in people's abilities to detect deception (Bond & DePaulo, 2008). The authors found similar results to their earlier meta-analysis; specifically, results accounting for the range of variance in people's abilities still produces chance levels of accurate deception detection.

Physiological Cues to Detecting Deception

The first record of using physiological cues to detect deception is from ancient China (*c*.1000 BCE), where dry rice powder was used as a lie detector mechanism (Cotton, 2014). The accused was asked to chew on the powder and if it was dry, they were determined to be a liar; conversely, if the powder was wet, they were deemed to be telling the truth (Cotton, 2014). The rice powder technique depended on physiological responses, which were mistakenly associated with deceptive persons (e.g., dry mouth and decreased salivation), yet those same symptoms may also be exhibited by anxious, fearful, or fight-or-flight states (Vicianova, 2015). Despite the misattribution of these physiological responses to deception, they gained increasing popularity in the late 1800s, which led to the development of the polygraph.

Using the assumption that certain physiological responses predicted deceit, Cesare Lombrosso invented the first recorded polygraph device in the 1880s, which measured systolic blood pressure using a simple cuff (Vicianova, 2015). William Marston improved on this technology (Marston, 1917); in the following decades, Leonard Keeler and John Larson combined galvanic skin response (the production of sweat in the fingertips), heart rate, and respiratory rate into the first modern polygraph patented in the 1930s (Saxe et al., 1985). The polygraph went through many more decades of development, all of which mapped the physiological symptoms of systolic blood pressure, heart rate, galvanic skin response and respiratory rate (Ford, 2006). The general logic behind the polygraph is that during questioning, liars would have raised blood pressure, sweat more, and show an increased heart rate and respiratory rate compared to truthtellers (Saxe et al., 1985). Overall, the combination of physiological analysis and an interview with intense questioning was thought to produce an accurate confession (Horvath, 2019; Horvath & Reid, 1971).

COMPARISON QUESTION TEST

The most frequently used polygraph test is the control question test (CQT), also commonly referred to as the comparison question test (Ben-Shakhar, 2002; Honts & Reavy, 2015). The CQT is administered in several stages (Ben-Shakhar, 2002). First, the interviewer establishes rapport and obtains basic information. During this stage, the subject is provided the opportunity to freely recall details of the incident. Based on the information provided, questions are formulated, and the examiner and the subject discuss these questions. The purpose of the formulation and discussion phase is to ensure the subject understands all the questions, and for the examiner to ensure the subject will respond to the questions with "yes" or "no"

(Vrij, 2008). Next is the question phase, which is run through in several iterations to allow for the responses to be averaged across different test instances. Questions asked fall into three categories: (1) irrelevant or neutral questions (e.g. "Do you live in Canada?"), which are not included in the analysis of the results; (2) relevant questions that are directly related to the crime in question (e.g. "Did you steal the purse?"); and (3) control questions, which are unrelated to the crime in question, but concern likely transgressions in the past (e.g. "Have you ever lied to your parents?"). The control questions are designed to force everyone to give a deceptive response, but are vague enough to cover likely transgressions, such as lying within social settings. The use of control questions acts as a baseline for establishing the subject's deceptive responses, which will then be compared to responses to the relevant questions. The premise of this comparison is that guilty subjects will react more strongly to the relevant questions compared to control questions, and the opposite will be seen for innocent subjects (i.e., they will react more strongly to the control questions than the relevant questions), as they are telling the truth for the control questions (Honts & Reavy, 2015).

Field studies have shown that the CQT is relatively good at correctly classifying guilty suspects, with an accuracy rate of approximately 80%. However, the CQT has a tendency for false positives, incorrectly classifying innocent suspects as guilty (Vrij, 2008). The validity of the CQT is hotly debated among scholars, with some stating that the test has a significant positive association with interpersonal deception detection, and that experimental studies that show the that the CQT is effective are generalizable to investigative settings (see Honts et al., 2020 for a review). However, other scholars believe that little has changed in polygraph research since a landmark report (National Research Council, 2003), which asserted that claims of the CQT's accuracy are unfounded. Researchers acknowledge that while the CQT has an accuracy above chance, its error rate is unknown and little progress has been made in polygraph research to address these concerns (Iacono & Ben-Shakhar, 2019).

GUILTY KNOWLEDGE TEST

The second type of polygraph test is the concealed information test (CIT), more widely referred to as the guilty knowledge test (GKT). Lykken (1959) developed this test originally to address concerns that practitioners had regarding the CQT. The GKT suggests that people suppress or attempt to inhibit their knowledge of details related to the event/objective in question (Lykken, 1959). As such, the GKT aims to detect concealed knowledge that only the guilty suspect will know. The GKT involves presenting suspects with multiple-choice questions (e.g., "What weapon was used in the crime: a gun, a knife, a rope?"), with the belief that the guilty suspect will recognize the correct answer and have a greater physiological response to the correct choice compared to the other responses (Meijer & Verschuere, 2015). Innocent suspects should have similar physiological responses to all options since they lack the knowledge that the guilty suspect would have (MacLaren, 2001).

Unlike the CQT that has a tendency of producing false positives and incorrectly classifying innocent suspects as guilty, the GKT is more accurate at classifying innocent suspects (Vrij, 2008). While most psychologists consider the GKT to be based on sound reasoning (75% compared to 33% who consider the CQT to be based on sound principles), researchers have serious concerns about GKT's validity (Iacono & Lykken, 1997). For example, if the correct response stands out in any way, the validity of the test can be seriously compromised. In addition, innocent suspects must not know the correct option, or they would risk providing guilty responses. An innocent individual providing a "guilty" response could occur because investigators inadvertently provide the suspect with privileged information during an investigation, or because the media released details of a crime. On the other hand, the guilty suspect must also know the answer for the test to work. Thus, if the suspect failed to perceive the targeted detail of the crime, they may provide responses indicating innocence, despite their true guilt (Honts, 2004). Moreover, recent examinations of the GKT have found gender differences in the magnitude of responses, suggesting that the GKT may not have robust effects. For example, males showed higher skin conductance and respiration than females when responding to critical GKT items; conversely, heart-rate responsivity was higher in females compared to males (Staunton & Hammond, 2011). Findings have also suggested that there are substantial variations between the psychophysiological measures used to evaluate the GKT, indicating there is a lack of equivalence between the measures (Staunton & Hammond, 2011).

CRITIQUING THE POLYGRAPH TEST

Despite its shortcomings, the polygraph is a widely used tool. For example, polygraph tests are mandatory in the UK for domestic abuse suspects and terrorists, however, the polygraph outcome evidence is not admissible in court (UK Government, 2022). In the United States, polygraph evidence admissibility varies by state and is often determined based on recommendation from *Frye v. United States* (1923), such that the results are admitted if they have gained "general acceptance" (Myers et al., 2006). In Canada, police continue to use the polygraph test for law enforcement investigations and employee screening purposes. However, according to *R. v. Béland* (1987) and much like the UK, polygraph evidence is not admissible in court. A major reason for making polygraph evidence inadmissible is the well-studied fact that jurors are highly influenced by the presentation of polygraph evidence in court, more so if accompanied by a confession (Han, 2016; Kassin, 2008; Vrij, 2008). Additional reasons for the inadmissibility of polygraph evidence include the subjectivity of the technology measuring physiological responses, and the variation in obtained responses from the test (i.e., results vary based on gender; Staunton & Hammond, 2011). Furthermore, a report published by the National Research Council's Committee to Review the Scientific Evidence of the Polygraph (National Research Council, 2003) critiqued the validity of admissions and confessions from polygraph examinations, informing interviewers of the poor accuracy of polygraph examinations. The authors warned against pairing interrogation methods designed to obtain confessions with polygraph tests, and recommended the number of false confessions obtained by the test be considered as evidence against its utility.

Verbal Cues to Detecting Deception

In the mid-2000s, researchers and practitioners began working on interviewing protocols and models to better elicit verbal veracity cues from interviewees (Vrij et al., 2022). Using language to discriminate between truthful and deceptive statements requires several assumptions to be made: first and foremost, the basic assumption is that there are distinct and observable differences in the language use of those who tell the truth versus those who lie (Smith, 2011). However, as Smith stated, this assumption is problematic as these distinct indicators do not appear to exist. There are several potential explanations for the lack of verbal indicators of deception, though the primary reason is differences in language acquisition: language development is not universal. Factors that affect language acquisition include socioeconomic status, occupation, education, and culture (Hoff & Tian, 2005; Landry et al., 2001). For example, those raised in impoverished conditions may not have the same opportunities as those raised in families with higher socioeconomic status (e.g., attend better schools). As such, an individual's vernacular is subject to diverse factors which ensure a departure from universality. Due to this departure, it cannot be assumed that people mean or understand the same thing by individual words. Language is an inherent social construct which varies among cultures, locations, and the social norms present in an individual's environment.

While there are pitfalls for verbal (linguistic) deception detection, meta-analyses reported that such cues do provide discriminability beyond chance levels (Hauch et al., 2017; Oberlader et al., 2016; Vrij et al., 2017). As mentioned in the Cognitive Theories section, the number of details provided by a suspect is a well-studied verbal cue to deception (DePaulo et al., 2003; Granhag & Strömwall, 2002; Vrij et al., 2000, 2006). Liars also are less likely to make errors when speaking or provide unusually ordered statements, both of which are common in truthtellers (DePaulo et al., 2003). Higher voice pitch, slower rate of speech, and fewer speech disturbances (e.g., umm, ah) are also verbal cues that have been associated with deception (Vrij, 2000). Interestingly, liars do not engage in spontaneous correcting, admitting they do not remember something during their recall or going back and correcting something they previously said.

Unanticipated Questions Approach

The unanticipated questions approach to eliciting verbal cues to deception is based on the finding that liars tend to spend time preparing their account prior to an interview, by predicting the questions they will be asked and rehearsing answers to those questions (e.g., Liu et al., 2010; Hartwig et al., 2007; Lancaster et al., 2013). This strategy initially showed promise as research has shown that advanced planning makes lying easier, and lies that are planned usually contain fewer cues of deceit than spontaneous lies (DePaulo et al., 2003). Interviewers can exploit liars' tendency to prepare their responses by asking unanticipated questions, specifically questions that truthtellers will be in a comparatively better position to answer when compared with liars. For example, in a study by Vrij et al. (2009), liars and truthtellers were asked about an alleged visit to a restaurant. The opening questions were anticipated (e.g., "Can you tell me in as much detail as possible what you did while you were in the restaurant?"), while subsequent questions were unexpected (e.g., "In relation to the front door, where at the table did the waiter stand when serving your food?"). Raters performed at chance when classifying the truthtellers and liars based on the opening questions. However, when classified based on the unanticipated questions, coders were able to correctly classify 60% of truthtellers and 80% of liars (Vrij et al., 2009).

While initially promising, recent studies have found the relationship between unanticipated questions and response details does not improve veracity judgements significantly above chance level (Parkhouse & Ormerod, 2018). Specifically, observers were more accurate at distinguishing between liars and truthtellers when judging transcripts of unanticipated questions, with the effect being stronger for spatial (e.g., "Please describe this room,") and temporal questions (e.g., "Please describe the task in full, but now in reverse order,") compared with planning questions (e.g., "Explain the steps you would have taken had you not been able to access Room B via the main door"). Together, the studies suggested that the unanticipated questions approach is not as robust and effective as initially believed.

Reality Monitoring

Reality monitoring (RM) refers to people's ability to discriminate between self-experienced (true) and imagined events (Johnson & Raye, 1981). RM research is based on the notion that real experiences are the result of perceptual processes, whereas imagined events are the result of reflective processes. As such, memories of real events are believed to contain more contextual information (i.e., temporal and spatial details) and perceptual information (e.g., details relating to the five senses), compared to memories of imagined events. In 1992, it was first suggested that RM could be used to distinguish between real and imagined events, and thus as a tool for distinguishing between truthful and deceptive accounts (Alonso-Quecuty, 1992). Research has examined the efficacy of RM in detecting deception, with an average accuracy of 75% and comparable efficacy for statements made by children and adults (Bogaard et al., 2019; Masip et al., 2005; Sporer, 2004).

Verifiability Approach

One of the newer approaches for interviewing to elicit verbal cues to deception is the verifiability approach. The verifiability approach relies on two assumptions; first, liars prefer to avoid mentioning details that can be verified, and second, liars often include less detail in their account than truth-tellers, though liars are aware that the level of detail is important for being assessed as truthful (Nahari et al., 2014). This approach relates to how liars attempt to navigate around this dilemma—that is, providing sufficient information but not details that can be checked for veracity. For example, a liar may state that on the way home, they chatted with a stranger, wearing a grey jacket in the park about the weather. While appearing to contain some detail, because the individual cannot be identified the veracity of this statement cannot be checked. Studies have shown that liars consistently report fewer verifiable details compared to truthtellers (Nahari et al., 2014; Nahari & Vrij, 2014; Verschuere et al., 2020).

Statement Validity Assessment

The Statement Validity Assessment (SVA) is one of the most widely used techniques for detecting deception and assessing veracity based on verbal content. The underlying premise of the SVA is that statements based on actual experience will differ in content from statements based on fabrications (Amado et al., 2015). The SVA consists of four stages: (1) case-file analysis, where hypotheses are made about the source of the statement (i.e., based on actual experience versus fabrications); (2) a semi-structured interview is conducted; (3) the statement is assessed for credibility using a criteria-based content analysis (CBCA), which is based on a set of 19 criteria (see Steller & Köhnken, 1989); and finally, (4) using a validity checklist, where alternative explanations to the CBCA outcomes are considered (Steller & Köhnken, 1989; Vrij, 2000). The criteria of the CBCA are then grouped into five categories: general characteristics, specific contents, peculiarities of content, motivation-related content and offense-specific elements. The presence of each of the 19 criteria is rated, and the stronger the presence of each criterion, the stronger the hypothesis that the memory is based on a personal experience rather than a fabrication (Köhnken, 2004). Laboratory studies on the SVA show an overall accuracy rate of 73%, performing equally well at detecting truthful and fabricated accounts (Vrij, 2008).

Strategic Use of Evidence

Strategic use of evidence (SUE) is a combination of questioning and evidence disclosure tactics that separates liars from truthtellers by their verbal differences. Guilty suspects have an information management dilemma in an interview—they must simultaneously suppress critical information while asserting innocence (Hartwig et al., 2014). SUE capitalizes on suspects' cognitive strategies, how they control information, and their conduct in the interview (Hartwig et al., 2014). An interviewer will employ the SUE technique by sequentially revealing pieces of evidence in the interview and encouraging the suspect to explain them (Granhag, 2010). The explanations can be identified as accurate or inaccurate by comparing them to the suspect's initial statement, or to other evidence known by the interviewer. Over the course of the interview, the cognitive demand on the guilty suspect accumulates, causing them to produce inconsistencies between their story and the evidence that the interviewer presents. These inconsistencies are called statement evidence inconsistencies (SEIs) or within-statement inconsistencies (WSIs) and can be used to confirm the accuracy of a suspect's statement. According to Granhag and Hartwig (2015), a proper use of the SUE technique will force suspects to continually revise their perceptions of what evidence the interviewer has and lead them to make SEIs or WSIs.

By forcing a suspect to account for evidence presented against them, SUE can be used to identify whether suspects are being avoidant with information and deceptive, or verbally forthcoming and truthful (Granhag, 2010). Therefore, SUE improves veracity judgements, unlike other deception detection techniques, by separating guilty suspects from innocent ones by identifying SEIs and WSIs (Hartwig et al., 2014). Out of all the deception detection techniques used by interviewers in the present day, SUE is likely to be the most promising. The SUE technique relies on four key principles: (i) how the suspect perceives the evidence; (ii) what counter-interrogation strategies suspects may use; (iii) whether presenting the evidence causes inconsistencies in their detailed account; and (iv) the suspect's overall perspective of the evidence (Granhag & Hartwig, 2015).

Overall, the timing of evidence disclosure is crucial to the success of the SUE technique. The most recent meta-analysis on evidence disclosure timing confirmed that later disclosure of evidence in a suspect interview produces more SEIs (Oleszkiewicz & Watson, 2021), however fourteen of the fifteen studies included in this meta-analysis included an author from the original SUE study, meaning the findings should be interpreted with caution.

Automated Deception Detection Systems

The accuracy of humans' ability to detect deception hovers around chance level (Bond & DePaulo, 2006, 2008; Bond et al., 2014; DePaulo et al., 2003; Levine et al., 2005; Zuckerman et al., 1981). Thus, researchers have recently begun studying whether machine learning methods can better discriminate between liars and truthtellers. Much like the research on virtual and automated interrogations, the research on automated deception detection systems is also in the early stages.

Automated deception detection systems typically involve researchers developing machine learning models to analyze transcripts, spoken statements, or written texts (Kleinberg et al., 2018). Various linguistic features of the text are analyzed to predict the outcome of the text being truthful or deceptive. For example, researchers have used variables from the Linguistic Inquiry and Word Count (LIWC) software (Pennebaker et al., 2015) and other classification algorithms (e.g., random forests, Naïve Bayes; Kleinberg & Verschuere, 2021) to attempt to discriminate between truthtellers and liars.

In a recent study by Kleinberg and Verschuere (2021), the authors tested whether the combination of machine learning and human judgement could improve deception detection accuracy. Following the outcome of the machine learning (automated) judgement on whether a statement was classified as truthful or deceptive, human raters had the opportunity to fully overrule the automated judgement or adjust it within a given boundary. Their results showed that humans were unable to add meaningful contributions to the automated judgements. That is, while the automated judgements produced an overall accuracy of 69%, human intervention reduced the judgement accuracy rates to chance levels. The results of their study are likely explained by the "truth bias"—that is, our tendency to assume we are being told the truth and that we experience a larger bias towards classifying messages we hear as truthful (Bond & DePaulo, 2006).

A recent study by the RAND corporation (Posard et al., 2022) examined the use of machine-learning methods for detecting deception in security clearance background investigations. Although the machine learning techniques were examined from a lens of security clearance background investigations, the techniques can still arguably apply for interrogations as well. Participants were asked to read a vignette about someone who leaked classified information and were then assigned randomly to either tell the truth during the interview about the vignette they read, or lie about the vignette they read. The machine learning models they developed used a range of model classifications including aspects such as word counts, metadata (average word length), and stance (characteristics of emotion and doubt) to attempt to discriminate between truthful and deceptive responses. The accuracy of their machine learning models for discriminating between truthful and accurate statements ranged from 62% to 75%.

Recently, the European Union (EU) began implementing an artificial intelligence program in select EU airports to detect deceit—named iBorder Ctrl (Campbell, 2020). The iBorderCtrl involves a two-phase procedure. First, passengers register with an on-line system designed to collect various pre-travel information (e.g., visa, passport, purpose of trip). Second, when crossing the border, iBorderCtrl is used to assist border guards with identifying passenger risks. Part of the second stage involves the Automatic Deception Detection System (ADDS). ADDS is purported to "quantif[y] the probability of deceit in interviews by analyzing interviewees' nonverbal micro-gestures." However, the fundamental issue, as described above, is that micro-expressions have not been proven to be a reliable indicator of deceit. Thus, a system that relies on unvalidated information to make consequential judgements will undoubtedly provide questionable decisions to border agents (for more comprehensive reviews of the potential issues associated with iBorderCtrl, see Sánchez-Monedero & Dencik, 2020; Jupe & Keatley, 2020).

Overall, the use of machine learning to discriminate between truthful and deceptive statements is still in its early stages. The current evidence suggests that the performance of automated deception detection systems ranges between 64% and 84% (Burns & Moffitt, 2014; Fornaciari & Poesio, 2013; Kleinberg et al., 2018; Mihalcea & Strapparava, 2009; Pérez-Rosas & Mihalcea, 2014).

Future Directions

Research and practice in automated and virtual systems for interrogation and detecting deception are experiencing a rapid growth due to factors such as the availability of new technologies and contexts that demand it (e.g., global pandemic, continued proliferation of online communication).

Based on the research reviewed in this chapter, we are incredibly enthusiastic about what the future holds for research and practice in advancing virtual environments and automated systems for interrogations and deception detection. We believe there are abundant opportunities to advance both research and practice in the next stage in the evolution of interrogation and deception detection. However, we strongly caution against the immediate adoption of such tools and techniques until more research is conducted, and until significant underlying issues are considered and addressed in future research.

A significant issue to address in both the interrogation and deception detection literatures is that most of the research has been conducted with Western, educated, industrialized, rich, and democratic (WEIRD) participants (Hope et al., 2021; Vrij et al., 2022). Culture—"the distinctive customs, values, beliefs, knowledge, art, and language of a society or a community" (American Psychological Association, 2020)—plays a significant role in how information is communicated (Hope et al., 2021). For example, factual, direct, and linear communication is characteristic of Western (individualistic) cultures (Gudykunst et al., 1988; Hall, 1976; Triandis & Suh, 2002). However, collectivist cultures tend to be more indirect and context-oriented in their communication, building on shared understanding, meaning, and relationships (Beune et al., 2009; Gelfand et al., 2001). Cross-cultural interviews can include communication features unlikely to occur in Western-based strategies for gaining cooperation. For example, Gelfand and colleagues (2015) noted the importance of negotiation strategies addressing "honor," an important concept in some Middle Eastern, Latin American, and African cultures, which functions as a commodity to be gained or lost within communication contexts. Failure to take account of these features results in inadequate interviewing that can directly affect the outcomes of investigations. Unfortunately, interviewing policies for cross-cultural engagement have not kept pace with basic research identifying important cultural communication dimensions, such as individualism/collectivism (Hofstede, 1984; Hofstede & Hofstede, 2001). Communication problems arising from cultural differences are an increasing contemporary challenge for investigators (Duffey, 2000). Unless investigators can navigate cultural differences, there exists a serious threat to developing generalized automated and virtual tools and techniques for interrogation and deception detection.

Another fundamental issue that needs to be addressed is the external validity of the research. Like many areas of psychological research, researchers have criticized the external validity of deception detection (i.e., the applicability to real-world situations). In standard deception detection research, participants provide truthful or deceptive statements regarding their opinions, emotions, or involvement in a past event (e.g., a mock crime).

This context represents a low-stakes situation, in that it has little to no consequences for failing to deceive the experimenter. On the other hand, the situations encountered outside of the lab (e.g., an interrogation or police interview) are high-stakes, such that the consequences for failing to convince individuals of your innocence are severe. Researchers have argued that deceptive behavior is different in high- and low-stakes situations, meaning it would not be reasonable to draw conclusions about real-world high-stakes situations, such as a police officer's ability to detect deception in an interview, using data from laboratory experiments (Miller & Stiff, 1993). Studies which have examined high stakes lies in interrogation settings have found that realistic target materials seem to slightly improve people's ability to detect lies, however the pattern is unclear (Mann et al., 2004).

The other part of the external validity criticism is that the context of assessment lacks realism. In many deception detection studies, participants watch video-clips of the target and make judgements based on those clips. Participants in laboratory studies lack background information and direct interactions with suspects, where they could ask questions that they deem necessary to determine the suspect's veracity (Hartwig et al., 2004). A meta-analysis by Hartwig and Bond (2011) examined the generalizability of laboratory results and the extent to which deception cues are robust across situations. The researchers investigated whether the detectability of lies varied depending on their accompanying emotion, the severity of perceived consequences (i.e. high- versus low-stakes situations), and whether the motivation to lie was external (e.g. instructed by the experimenter to lie) or internal (e.g. decided to lie themselves). The meta-analysis determined that the weakness of cues to deception is not exclusive to laboratory studies, and that deception detection cues fail to reliably detect deception in field studies as well (Hartwig & Bond, 2011). Alternatively, results suggested there was no basis for the belief that laboratory studies of deception detection produce unrealistic results unapplicable to real-world deception detection settings (e.g., interrogations). Instead, researchers have identified general problematic research practices in the deception detection literature—namely, low powered studies, selective reporting, and too many positive results reported within the literature (Luke, 2019). Criticisms of deception detection cite the realism of the target material (i.e., the lies and truths), and the realism of the situation, as causes for concern (Ben-Shakhar & Nahari, 2018; Hartwig & Bond, 2011).

Conclusion

Our answer to the question "Do automated and virtual interrogation and deception detection systems work?" is "not yet." However, we are looking forward to what the future holds. We urge researchers who study automated interrogation and deception detection systems to rigorously test their systems before public and widespread implementation. Premature implementation of such systems has the potential to cause severe harm—wrongfully convicted individuals or individuals deemed to be deceitful when they are being truthful. Researchers must first identify reliable and valid cues to deceit before we can automate the detection of such behaviors.

References

Alonso-Quecuty, M. (1992). Deception detection and reality monitoring: A new answer to an old question? In *Psychology and law: International perspectives* (pp. 328–332). Walter De Gruyter. https://doi.org/10.1515/9783110879773

Amado, B.G., Arce, R., & Fariña, F. (2015). Undeutsch hypothesis and criteria based content analysis: A meta-analytic review. *The European Journal of Psychology Applied to Legal Context*, 7(1), 3–12. https://doi.org/10.1016/j.ejpal.2014.11.002

American Psychological Association (2020). Culture. In *APA Dictionary of Psychology*. https://dictionary.apa.org/culture

Baccon, L., Chiarovano, E., & MacDougall, H.G. (2019). Virtual reality for teletherapy: Avatars may combine the benefits of face-to-face communication with the anonymity of online text-based communication. *Cyberpsychology, Behavior, and Social Networking*, 22(2), 158–165. https://doi.org/10.1089/cyber.2018.0247

Ben-Shakhar, G. (2002). A critical review of the Control Questions Test (CQT). In M. Kleiner (Ed.), *Handbook of polygraph testing* (pp. 103–126). Academic Press.

Ben-Shakhar, G., & Nahari, T. (2018). The external validity of studies examining the detection of concealed knowledge using the concealed information test. In J.P. Rosenfeld (Ed.), *Detecting concealed information and deception: Recent developments* (pp. 59–76). Academic Press. https://doi.org/10.1016/B978-0-12-812729-2.00003-3

Beune, K., Giebels, E., & Sanders, K. (2009). Are you talking to me? Influencing behaviour and culture in police interviews. *Psychology Crime & Law*, 15(7), 597–617. https://doi.org/10.1080/10683160802442835

Bogaard, G., Colwell, K., & Crans, S. (2019). Using the reality interview improves the accuracy of the criteria-based content analysis and reality monitoring. *Applied Cognitive Psychology*, 33(6), 1018–1031. https://doi.org/10.1002/acp.3537

Bond, C.F. & DePaulo, B.M. (2006) Accuracy of deception judgments. *Personality and Social Psychology Review*, 10(3), 214–234. https://doi.org/10.1207/s15327957pspr1003_2

Bond, C.F., & DePaulo, B.M. (2008). Individual differences in judging deception: Accuracy and bias. *Psychological Bulletin*, 134(4), 477–492. https://doi.org/10.1037/0033-2909.134.4.477

Bond, C.F., Levine, T.R., & Hartwig, M. (2014). New findings in non-verbal lie detection. In *Detecting Deception* (pp. 37–58). John Wiley & Sons. https://doi.org/10.1002/9781118510001.ch2

Brubacher, S.P., Powell, M., Skouteris, H., & Guadagno, B. (2015). The effects of e-simulation interview training on teachers' use of open-ended questions. *Child Abuse & Neglect*, 43, 95–103. https://doi.org/10.1016/j.chiabu.2015.02.004

Buller, D.B., & Burgoon, J.K. (1996). Interpersonal deception theory. *Communication Theory* 6(3), 203–242. https://doi.org/10.1111/j.1468-2885.1996.tb00127.x

Burgoon, J.K. (2018). Microexpressions are not the best way to catch a liar. *Frontiers in Psychology*, 9. Retrieved from www.frontiersin.org/articles/10.3389/fpsyg.2018.01672

Burns, M.B., & Moffitt, K.C. (2014). Automated deception detection of 911 call transcripts. *Security Informatics*, 3, 1–9. https://doi.org/10.1186/s13388-014-0008-2

Busey, T.A., Tunnicliff, J., Loftus, G.R., & Loftus, E.F. (2000). Accounts of the confidence-accuracy relation in recognition memory. *Psychonomic Bulletin and Review*, 7(1), 26–48. https://doi.org/10.3758/BF03210724

Campbell, Z. (2020, December 11). Sci-fi surveillance: Europe's secretive push into biometric technology. *The Guardian*. Retrieved from www.theguardian.com/world/2020/dec/10/sci-fi-surveillance-europes-secretive-push-into-biometric-technology

Chapman, F.E. (2012). Coerced internalized false confessions and police interrogations: The power of coercion. *Law and Psychology Review*, 37, 159–209. https://doi.org/10.2139/ssrn.2467049

Clarke, C., & Milne, R. (2001). *A national evaluation of the PEACE Investigative Interviewing Course* (p. 187). Home Office.

Cooper, G.S., Meterko, V., & Gadtaula, P. (2019). Innocents who plead guilty: An analysis of patterns in DNA exoneration cases. *Federal Sentencing Reporter*, 31(4–5), 234–238. https://doi.org/10.1525/fsr.2019.31.4-5.234

Costanzo, M., & Archer, D. (1989). Interpreting the expressive behavior of others: The interpersonal perception task. *Journal of Nonverbal Behavior*, 13, 225–245. https://doi.org/10.1007/BF00990295

Cotton, D. (2014, March 4). No sure way to spot liars. *Blue Line Magazine*.

Dando, C., Taylor, D.A., Caso, A., Nahouli, Z., & Adam, C. (2022). Interviewing in virtual environments: Towards understanding the impact of rapport-building behaviours and retrieval context on eyewitness memory. *Memory & Cognition*, 1–18. Advance online publication. https://doi.org/10.3758/s13421-022-01362-7

DePaulo, B.M., Lindsay, J.J., Malone, B.E., Muhlenbruck, L., Charlton, K., & Cooper, H. (2003). Cues to deception. *Psychological Bulletin*, 129(1), 74–118. https://doi.org/10.1037/0033-2909.129.1.74

Dion Larivière, C., Crough, Q., & Eastwood, J. (2022). The effects of rapport building on information disclosure in virtual interviews. *Journal of Police and Criminal Psychology*, 1–9. https://doi.org/10.1007/s11896-022-09535-5

Driskell, J.E. (2012). Effectiveness of deception detection training: a meta-analysis. *Psychology Crime & Law*, 18(8), 713–731. https://doi.org/10.1080/1068316x.2010.535820

Duffey, T. (2000). Cultural issues in contemporary peacekeeping. *International Peacekeeping*, 7(1), 142–168. https://doi.org/10.1080/13533310008413823

Eder, R.A. (1990). Uncovering young children's psychological selves: Individual and developmental differences. *Child Development*, 61(3), 849–863. https://doi.org/10.1111/j.1467-8624.1990.tb02827.

Ekman, P. (2006, October 29). How to spot a terrorist on the fly. *The Washington Post*. Retrieved from www.washingtonpost.com/archive/opinions/2006/10/29/how-to-spot-a-terrorist-on-the-fly/e8f5865f-1dac-4c55-990f-459c1e8b3563/

Ekman, P., & Friesen, W.V. (1969). Nonverbal leakage and clues to deception. *Psychiatry: Journal for the Study of Interpersonal Processes*, 32, 88–106.

Elliott, D.M., & Briere, J. (1994). Forensic sexual abuse evaluations of older children: Disclosures and symptomatology. *Behavioral Sciences & the Law*, 12(3), 261–277. https://doi.org/10.1002/bsl.2370120306

Evans, J.R., Meissner, C.A., Ross, A.B., Houston, K.A., Russano, M.B., & Horgan, A.J. (2013). Obtaining guilty knowledge in human intelligence interrogations: Comparing accusatorial and information-gathering approaches with a novel experimental paradigm. *Journal of Applied Research in Memory and Cognition*, 2(2), 83–88. https://doi.org/10.1016/j.jarmac.2013.03.002

Ford, E.B. (2006). Lie detection: Historical, neuropsychiatric and legal dimensions. *International Journal of Law and Psychiatry*, 29(3), 159–177. https://doi.org/10.1016/j.ijlp.2005.07.001

Fornaciari, T., & Poesio, M. (2013). Automatic deception detection in Italian court cases. *Artificial Intelligence and Law*, 21(3), 303–340. https://doi.org/10.1007/s10506-013-9140-4

Frye v. United States, 368 U.S. (1923).

Gabbert, F., Hope, L., Luther, K., Wright, G., Ng, M., & Oxburgh, G. (2021). Exploring the use of rapport in professional information-gathering contexts by systematically mapping the evidence base. *Applied Cognitive Psychology*, 35(2), 329–341. https://doi.org/10.1002/acp.3762

Gelfand, M.J., Nishii, L.H., Holcombe, K.M., Dyer, N.A., Ohbuchi, K., & Fukuno, M. (2001). Cultural influences on cognitive representations of conflict: Interpretations of conflict episodes in the United States and Japan. *Journal of Applied Psychology*, 86(6), 1059–1074. https://doi.org/10.1037/0021-9010.86.6.1059

Gelfand, M.J., Severance, L., Lee, T., Bruss, C.B., Lun, J., Abdel-Latif, A.-H., Al-Moghazy, A.A., & Moustafa Ahmed, S. (2015). Culture and getting to yes: The linguistic signature of creative agreements in the United States and Egypt. *Journal of Organizational Behavior*, 36(7), 967–989. https://doi.org/10.1002/job.2026

Granhag, P.A. (2010, November). The Strategic Use of Evidence (SUE) technique: A scientific perspective. In Washington, DC, USA: High Value Detainee Interrogation Group (HIG, FBI). HIG Research Symposium: Interrogation in the European Union.

Granhag, P.A., & Hartwig, M. (2015). The strategic use of evidence technique: A conceptual overview. In Granhag, P.A., Vrij, A., & Verschuere, B. (Eds.), *Detecting deception: Current challenges and cognitive approaches* (231–251). Wiley-Blackwell. https://doi.org/10.1002/9781118510001.ch10

Granhag, P.A., & Strömwall, L.A. (2002). Repeated interrogations: verbal and non-verbal cues to deception. *Applied Cognitive Psychology*, *16*(3), 243–257. https://doi.org/10.1002/acp.784

Gudjonsson, G.H. (2017). Memory distrust syndrome, confabulation and false confession. *Cortex*, *87*, 156–165. https://doi.org/10.1016/j.cortex.2016.06.013

Gudykunst, W.B., Ting-Toomey, S., & Chua, E. (1988). *Culture and interpersonal communication*. Sage Publications.

Hager, E. (2020). Your zoom interrogation is about to start. Retrieved from www.themarshallproject.org/2020/07/20/your-zoom-interrogation-is-about-to-start (accessed December 1, 2022).

Haginoya, S., Yamamoto, S., & Santtila, P. (2021). The combination of feedback and modeling in online simulation training of child sexual abuse interviews improves interview quality in clinical psychologists. *Child Abuse & Neglect*, *115*, 105,013. https://doi.org/10.1016/j.chiabu.2021.105013

Hall, E.T. (1976). *Beyond culture*. Anchor.

Han, Y. (2016). Deception detection techniques using polygraph in trials: Current status and social scientific evidence. *Contemporary Readings in Law and Social Justice*, *8*(2), 115–147. https://doi.org/10.22381/CRLSJ8220165

Hartwig, M., & Bond, C.F. (2011). Why do lie-catchers fail? A lens model meta-analysis of human lie judgments. *Psychological Bulletin*, *137*(4), 643–659. https://doi.org/10.1037/a0023589

Hartwig, M., Granhag, P.A., & Luke, T. (2014). Strategic use of evidence during investigative interviews: The state of the science. In D.C. Raskin, C.R. Honts, & J.C. Kircher (Eds.), *Credibility assessment: Scientific research and applications* (1–36). Elsevier Academic Press. https://doi.org/10.1016/B978-0-12-394433-7.00001-4

Hartwig, M., Granhag, P.A., Strömwall, L.A., & Andersson, L.O. (2004). Suspicious minds: Criminal's ability to detect deception. *Psychology, Crime & Law*, *10*(1), 83–95. https://doi.org/10.1080/1068316031000095485

Hartwig, M., Granhag, P.A., & Strömwall, L.A. (2007). Guilty and innocent suspects' strategies during police interrogations. *Psychology, Crime & Law*, *13*(2), 213–227. https://doi.org/10.1080/10683160600750264

Hauch, V., Sporer, S.L., Masip, J., & Bland'on-Gitlin, I. (2017). Can credibility criteria be assessed reliably? A meta-analysis of criteria-based content analysis. *Psychological Assessment*, *29*(6), 819–834. https://doi.org/10.1037/pas0000426

Herrera, F.G., Bailenson, J.N., Weisz, E., Ogle, E., & Zaki, J. (2018). Building long-term empathy: A large-scale comparison of traditional and virtual reality perspective-taking. *PLOS ONE*, *13*(10), e0204494. https://doi.org/10.1371/journal.pone.0204494

Higginbotham, A. (2013). Deception is futile when big brother's lie detector turns its eyes on you. *Wired*, *21*, 90–97.

Hoff, E., & Tian, C. (2005). Socioeconomic status and cultural influences on language. *Journal of Communication Disorders*, *38*(4), 271–278. https://doi.org/10.1016/j.jcomdis.2005.02.003

Hofstede, G. (1984). *Culture's consequences: International differences in work-related values* (Vol. 5). Sage.

Hofstede, G.H., & Hofstede, G. (2001). *Culture's consequences: Comparing values, behaviors, institutions and organizations across nations.* Sage.

Holmberg, U., & Christianson, S. (2001). Murderers' and sexual offenders' experiences of police interviews and their inclination to admit or deny crimes. *Behavioral Sciences & the Law, 20*(1–2), 31–45. https://doi.org/10.1002/bsl.470

Honts, C.R. (2004). The psychophysiological detection of deception. In *The detection of deception in forensic contexts* (pp. 103–123). Cambridge University Press. https://doi.org/10.1017/CBO9780511490071.005

Honts, C.R., & Reavy, R. (2015). The comparison question polygraph test: A contrast of methods and scoring. *Physiology & Behavior, 143,* 15–26. https://doi.org/10.1016/j.physbeh.2015.02.028

Honts, C., Thurber, S., & Handler, M. (2020). A comprehensive meta-analysis of the Comparison Question Polygraph Test. *Applied Cognitive Psychology, 35.* https://doi.org/10.1002/acp.3779

Hoogesteyn, K., Meijer, E., & Vrij, A. (2020). Examining witness interviewing environments. *Journal of Investigative Psychology and Offender Profiling, 17*(3), 238–249. https://doi.org/10.1002/jip.1549

Hope, L., Anakwah, N., Antfolk, J., Brubacher, S.P., Flowe, H.D., Gabbert, F., Giebels, E., Kanja, W., Korkman, J., Kyo, A., Naka, M., Otgaar, H., Powell, M.B., Selim, H., Skrifvars, J., Sorkpah, I.K., Sowatey, E.A., Steele, L.R., Stevens, L.M., ... Wells, S. (2021). Urgent issues and prospects at the intersection of culture, memory, and witness interviews: Exploring the challenges for research and practice. *Legal and Criminological Psychology, 27*(1), 1–31. https://doi.org/10.1111/lcrp.12202

Hoque, M.E., McDuff, D.J., & Picard, R.W. (2012). Exploring temporal patterns in classifying frustrated and delighted smiles. *IEEE Transactions on Affective Computing, 3*(3), 323–334. https://doi.org/10.1109/T-AFFC.2012.11

Howe, M.L. (2000). *The fate of early memories: developmental science and the retention of childhood experiences.* American Psychological Association. https://doi.org/10.1037/10369-000

Horgan, A.J., Russano, M.B., Meissner, C.A., & Evans, J.R. (2012). Minimization and maximization techniques: Assessing the perceived consequences of confessing and confession diagnosticity. *Psychology, Crime & Law, 18*(1), 65–78. https://doi.org/10.1080/1068316X.2011.561801

Horvath, F. & Reid, J. (1971). The reliability of polygraph examiner diagnosis of truth and deception. *Journal of Criminal Law, Criminology and Police Science, 62*(2), 276–281. https://doi.org/10.2307/1141892

Horvath, F.S. (2019). Chicago: Birthplace of modern polygraphy. *European Polygraph, 13*(2), 61–84. https://doi.org/10.2478/ep-2019-0005

Iacono, W.G., & Lykken, D.T. (1997). The validity of the lie detector: Two surveys of scientific opinion. *Journal of Applied Psychology, 82,* 426–433. https://doi.org/10.1037/0021-9010.82.3.426

Iacono, W.G., & Ben-Shakhar, G. (2019). Current status of forensic lie detection with the comparison question technique: An update of the 2003 National Academy of Sciences report on polygraph testing. *Law and Human Behavior, 43*(1), 86–98. https://doi.org/10.1037/lhb0000307

Innocence Project (2023). DNA Exonerations in the United States. Retrieved from https://innocenceproject.org/dna-exonerations-in-the-united-states/

Inbau, F.E., Reid, J.E., Buckley, J.P., & Jayne, B.C. (2013). Criminal interrogations and confessions (5th ed.). Jones & Bartlett Learning.

Johnson, M.K., & Raye, C.L. (1981). Reality monitoring. *Psychological Review*, *88*, 67–85. https://doi.org/10.1037/0033-295X.88.1.67

Joinson, A. (2001). Self-disclosure in computer-mediated communication: The role of self-awareness and visual anonymity. *European Journal of Social Psychology*, *31*(2), 177–192. https://doi.org/10.1002/ejsp.36

Jordan, S.R., Brimbal, L., Wallace, D.B., Kassin, S.M., Hartwig, M., & Street, C.N.H. (2019). A test of the micro-expressions training tool: Does it improve lie detection? *Journal of Investigative Psychology and Offender Profiling*, *16*(3), 222–235. https://doi.org/10.1002/jip.1532

Jupe, L.M., & Keatley, D. (2020). Airport artificial intelligence can detect deception: or am i lying? *Security Journal*, *33*(4), 622–635. https://doi.org/10.1057/s41284-019-00204-7

Kang, S-H., & Gratch, J. (2012). Socially anxious people reveal more personal information with virtual counselors that talk about themselves using intimate human back stories. *Studies in Health and Technology Informatics*, *181*, 202–206.

Kang, S.H., & Gratch, J. (2010). Virtual humans elicit socially anxious interactions' verbal self-disclosure. *Computer Animations and Virtual Worlds*, *21*(3–4), 473–482. https://doi.org/10.1002/cav.345

Kassin, S.M. (2008). False confessions: Causes, consequences, and implications for reform. *Current Directions in Psychological Science*, *17*(4), 249–253.

Kassin, S.M., & Fong, C.T. (1999). "I'm innocent!": Effects of training on judgments of truth and deception in the interrogation room. *Law and Human Behavior*, *23*(5), 499–516. https://doi.org/10.1023/A:1022330011811

Kassin, S.M., & Kiechel, K.L. (1996). The social psychology of false confessions: Compliance, internalization, and confabulation. *Psychological Science*, *7*(3), 125–128. https://doi.org/10.1111/j.1467-9280.1996.tb00344.x

Kassin, S.M., & Wrightsman, L.S. (1980). Prior confessions and mock juror verdicts. *Journal of Applied Social Psychology*, *10*(2), 133–146. https://doi.org/10.1111/j.1559-1816.1980.tb00698.x

King, L., & Snook, B. (2009). Peering inside a Canadian interrogation room: An examination of the reid model of interrogation, influence tactics, and coercive strategies. *Criminal Justice and Behaviour*, *36*(7), 674–694. https://doi.org/10.1177/0093854809335142

Kleinberg, B., van der Toolen, Y., Vrij, A., Arntz, A., & Verschuere, B. (2018). Automated verbal credibility assessment of intentions: The model statement technique and predictive modeling. *Applied Cognitive Psychology*, *32*(3), 354–366. https://doi.org/10.1002/acp.3407

Kleinberg, B., & Verschuere, B. (2021). How humans impair automated deception detection performance. *Acta Psychologica*, *213*, 103250. https://doi.org/10.1016/j.actpsy.2020.103250

Köhnken, G. (2004). Statement Validity Analysis and the "detection of the truth." In *The detection of deception in forensic contexts* (pp. 41–63). Cambridge University Press. https://doi.org/10.1017/CBO9780511490071.003

Lancaster, G.L.J., Vrij, A., Hope, L., & Waller, B. (2013). Sorting the liars from the truth tellers: The benefits of asking unanticipated questions on lie detection. *Applied Cognitive Psychology, 27*(1), 107–114. https://doi.org/10.1002/acp.2879

Landry, S.H., Miller-Loncar, C.L., Smith, K., & Swank, P.R. (2001). The role of early parenting in children's development of executive processes. *Developmental Neuropsychology, 21*(1), 15–41. https://doi.org/10.1207/s15326942dn2101_2

Lane, J.D., & Wegner, D.M. (1995). The cognitive consequences of secrecy. *Journal of Personality and Social Psychology, 69*, 237–253. https://doi.org/10.1037/0022-3514.69.2.237

Leipold, A.D. (2020). The puzzle of clearance rates, and what they can tell us about crime, police reform, and criminal justice. *Wake Forest Law Review, 56*, 47–95.

Leo, R., & Ofshe, R. (2008). The truth about false confessions and advocacy scholarship. *Available at SSRN 1141365.* Retrieved from http://papers.ssrn.com/sol3/papers.cfm?abstract_id=1141365

Levine, T.R., Feeley, T.W., McCornack, S.A., Hughes, M., & Harms, C. (2005). Testing the effects of nonverbal behavior training on accuracy in deception detection with the inclusion of a bogus training control group. *Western Journal of Communication, 69*(3), 203–217. https://doi.org/10.1080/10570310500202355

Liu, M., Granhag, P.A., Landström, S., Hjelmsaeter, E.R.A., Strömwall, L.A., & Vrij, A. (2010). "Can you remember what was in your pocket when you were stung by a bee?": eliciting cues to deception by asking the unanticipated. *The Open Criminology Journal, 3*(1), 31–36. https://doi.org/10.2174/1874917801003010031

Luke, T.W. (2019). Lessons from Pinocchio: Cues to deception may be highly exaggerated. *Perspectives on Psychological Science, 14*(4), 646–671. https://doi.org/10.1177/1745691619838258

Lykken, D.T. (1959). The GSR in the detection of guilt. *Journal of Applied Psychology, 43*, 385–388. https://doi.org/10.1037/h0046060

MacLaren, V.V. (2001). A quantitative review of the Guilty Knowledge Test. *Journal of Applied Psychology, 86*, 674–683. https://doi.org/10.1037/0021-9010.86.4.674

Mann, S., Vrij, A., & Bull, R. (2004). Detecting true lies: Police officers' ability to detect suspects' lies. *The Journal of Applied Psychology, 89*, 137–149. https://doi.org/10.1037/0021-9010.89.1.137

Marston, W.M. (1917). Systolic blood pressure symptoms of deception. *Journal of Experimental Psychology, 2*(2), 117–163. https://doi.org/10.1037/h0073583

Masip, J., Sporer, S.L., Garrido, E., & Herrero, C. (2005). The detection of deception with the reality monitoring approach: A review of the empirical evidence. *Psychology, Crime & Law, 11*(1), 99–122. https://doi.org/10.1080/10683160410001726356

McCann, J.T. (1998). A conceptual framework for identifying various types of confessions. *Behavioral Sciences & the Law, 16*(4), 441–454.

Meijer, E.H., & Verschuere, B. (2015). The polygraph: Current practice and new approaches. In *Detecting deception: Current challenges and cognitive approaches* (pp. 59–80). Wiley-Blackwell.

Meissner, C., & Kassin, S. (2002). He's guilty!: Investigator bias in judgments of truth and deception. *Law and Human Behaviour*, 26, 469–480. https://doi.org/10.1023/A:1020278620751

Meissner, C.A., Redlich, A.D., Michael, S.W., Evans, J.R., Camilletti, C.R., Bhatt, S., & Brandon, S. (2014). Accusatorial and information-gathering interrogation methods and their effects on true and false confessions: a meta-analytic review. *Journal of Experimental Criminology*, 10(4), 459–486. https://doi.org/10.1007/s11292-014-9207-6

Mendez, J.E., et al. (2021). *Principles on effective interviewing for investigations and information gathering*. Norwegian Centre for Human Rights. Published online May 19, 2021. Retrieved from www.apt.ch/sites/default/files/publications/apt_PoEI_EN_11.pdf

Mihalcea, R., & Strapparava, C. (2009). The lie detector: Explorations in the automatic recognition of deceptive language. Proceedings of the ACL-IJCNLP 2009 conference short papers, 309–312. http://dl.acm.org/citation.cfm?id=1667679.

Miller, G.R., & Stiff, J.B. (1993). *Deceptive communication*. Sage Publications.

Milne, B., & Bull, R. (1999). *Investigative interviewing: Psychology and practice*. Wiley.

Mohamed, F.B., Faro, S.H., Gordon, N.J., Platek, S.M., Ahmad, H., & Williams, J.M. (2006). Brain mapping of deception and truth telling about an ecologically valid situation: Functional MR imaging and polygraph investigation—initial experience. *Radiology*, 238(2), 679–688. https://doi.org/10.1148/radiol.2382050237

Moore, T.E., & Fitzsimmons C.L. (2011). Justice imperiled: False confessions & the Reid Technique. *Criminal Law Quarterly*, 57(4), 509–542.

Myers, B., Latter, R., & Abdollahi-Arena, M.K. (2006). The court of public opinion: Lay perceptions of polygraph testing. *Law and Human Behavior*, 30(4), 509–523. https://doi.org/10.1007/s10979-006-9041-0

Nahari, G., & Vrij, A. (2014). Can I borrow your alibi? The applicability of the verifiability approach to the case of an alibi witness. *Journal of Applied Research in Memory and Cognition*, 3, 89–94. https://doi.org/10.1016/j.jarmac.2014.04.005

Nahari, G., Vrij, A., & Fisher, R.P. (2014). The verifiability approach: Countermeasures facilitate its ability to discriminate between truths and lies. *Applied Cognitive Psychology*, 28(1), 122–128. https://doi.org/10.1002/acp.2974

Nahari, G., Ashkenazi, T., Fisher, R.P., Granhag, P.A., Hershkowitz, I., Masip, J., Meijer, E.H., Nisin, Z., Sarid, N., Taylor, P.J., Verschuere, B., & Vrij, A. (2019). "Language of lies": Urgent issues and prospects in verbal lie detection research. *Legal and Criminological Psychology*, 24(1), 1–23. https://doi.org/10.1111/lcrp.12148

National Research Council. (2003). *The polygraph and lie detection*. Washington, DC: The National Academies Press. https://doi.org/10.17226/10420.

Oberlader, V.A., Naefgen, C., Koppehele-Gossel, J., Quinten, L., Banse, R., & Schmidt, A.F. (2016). Validity of content-based techniques to distinguish true and fabricated statements: A meta-analysis. *Law and Human Behavior*, 40(4), 440–457. https://doi.org/10.1037/lhb0000193

Oleszkiewicz, S., & Watson, S.J. (2021). A meta-analytic review of the timing for disclosing evidence when interviewing suspects. *Applied Cognitive Psychology*, 35(2), 342–359. https://doi.org/10.1002/acp.3767

Parkhouse, T., & Ormerod, T.C. (2018). Unanticipated questions can yield unanticipated outcomes in investigative interviews. *PLoS ONE*, 13(12), e0208751. https://doi.org/10.1371/journal.pone.0208751

Paul Ekman Group (2011). F.A.C.E. training: Interactive training by Dr. Paul Ekman. Retrieved from www.paulekman.com/micro-expressions-training-tools/

Peiris, D.R., Gregor, P., & Alm, N. (2000). The effects of simulating human conversational style in a computer-based interview. *Interacting with Computers*, 12(6), 635–650. https://doi.org/10.1016/S0953-5438(00)00028-X

Pennebaker, J.W., Boyd, R.L., Jordan, K., & Blackburn, K. (2015). *The development and psychometric properties of LIWC2015*. https://repositories.lib.utexas.edu/handle/2152/31333.

Pentland S.J., Burgoon J.K., Twyman N.W. (2015). Face and head movement analysis using automated feature extraction software, in *Proceedings of the 48th Annual Hawaii International Conference on System Sciences* (Kauai).

Pérez-Rosas, V., & Mihalcea, R. (2014). Cross-cultural deception detection. Retrieved from https://aclanthology.org/P14-2072/

Pompedda, F., Zappalà, A., & Santtila, P. (2015). Simulations of child sexual abuse interviews using avatars paired with feedback improves interview quality. *Psychology, Crime & Law*, 21(1), 28–52. https://doi.org/10.1080/1068316X.2014.915323

Pompedda, F., Zhang, Y., Haginoya, S., & Santtila, P. (2022). A mega-analysis of the effects of feedback on the quality of simulated child sexual abuse interviews with avatars. *Journal of Police and Criminal Psychology*, 37(3), 485–498. https://doi.org/10.1007/s11896-022-09509-7

Porter, S., & ten Brinke, L. (2008). Reading between the lies: Identifying concealed and falsified emotions in universal facial expressions. *Psychological Science*, 19(5), 508–514. https://doi.org/10.1111/j.1467-9280.2008.02116.x

Porter, S., ten Brinke, L., & Wallace, B. (2012). Secrets and lies: Involuntary leakage in deceptive facial expressions as a function of emotional intensity. *Journal of Nonverbal Behavior*, 36(1), 23–37. https://doi.org/10.1007/s10919-011-0120-7

Posard, M.N., Johnson, C., Melin, J.L., Ellinger, E., & Reininger H. (2022). *Looking for lies: An exploratory analysis for automated detection of deception*. The RAND Corporation.

Powell, M.B., Brubacher, S.P., & Baugerud, G.A. (2022). An overview of mock interviews as a training tool for interviewers of children. *Child Abuse & Neglect*, 129, 105685. https://doi.org/10.1016/j.chiabu.2022.105685

Russano, M.B., Meissner, C.A., Narchet, F.M., & Kassin, S.M. (2005). Investigating true and false confessions within a novel experimental paradigm. *Psychological Science*, 16(6), 481–486.

R v Béland, 1987 2 SCR 398

Saad, R. (2005). Discovery, development, and current applications of DNA identity testing. *Baylor University Medical Center Proceedings*, 18(2), 130–133. https://doi.org/10.1080/08998280.2005.11928051

Saber, M., Nodeland, B., & Wall, R. (2022). Exonerating DNA evidence in overturned convictions: analysis of data obtained from the national registry of exonerations. *Criminal Justice Policy Review*, *33*(3), 256–272. https://doi.org/10.1177/08874034211033327

Sánchez-Monedero, J., & Dencik, L. (2020). The politics of deceptive borders: "Biomarkers of deceit" and the case of iBorderCtrl. *Information, Communication & Society*, *25*(3), 413–430. https://doi.org/10.1080/1369118x.2020.1792530

Saxe, L., Dougherty, D., & Cross, T. (1985). The validity of polygraph testing: Scientific analysis and public controversy. *The American Psychologist*, *40*(3), 355–366. https://doi.org/10.1037/0003-066X.40.3.355

Segal, A., Pompedda, F., Haginoya, S., Kaniušonytė, G., & Santtila, P. (2022). Avatars with child sexual abuse (vs. no abuse) scenarios elicit different emotional reactions. *Psychology Crime & Law*, 1–21. https://doi.org/10.1080/1068316x.2022.2082422

Smith, T. (2011, August 16). Next in line for the TSA? A thorough "chat-down." Retrieved from www.npr.org/2011/08/16/139643652/next-in-line-for-the-tsa-a-thorough-chat-down

Snook, B., Eastwood, J., Stinson, M., Tedeschini, J., & House, J.C. (2010). Reforming investigative interviewing in Canada. *Canadian Journal of Criminology and Criminal Justice*, *52*(2), 215–229. https://doi.org/10.3138/cjccj.52.2.215

Snook, B., Luther, K., Quinlan, H., & Milne, R. (2012). Let 'em talk: A field study of police questioning practices of suspects and accused persons. *Criminal Justice and Behavior*, *39*(10), 1328–1339. https://doi.org/10.1177/0093854812449216

Snook, B., Eastwood, J., & Barron, W.T. (2014). The next stage in the evolution of interrogations: The PEACE model. *Canadian Criminal Law Review*, *18*(2), 219–239.

Sporer, S.L. (2004). Reality monitoring and detection of deception. In *The detection of deception in forensic contexts* (pp. 64–101). Cambridge University Press. https://doi.org/10.1017/CBO9780511490071.004

Staunton, C., & Hammond, S. (2011). An investigation of the Guilty Knowledge Test polygraph examination. *Journal of Criminal Psychology*, *1*, 1–14. https://doi.org/10.1108/20093829201100001

Steller, M., & Köhnken, G. (2014). Criteria-based content analysis [Data set]. American Psychological Association. https://doi.org/10.1037/t27704-000

Sullivan, E.E. (2001). *The concise book of lying* (1st ed.). Farrar, Straus and Giroux.

Taylor, D., & Dando, C.J. (2018). Eyewitness memory in face-to-face and immersive avatar-to-avatar contexts. *Frontiers in Psychology*, *9*. https://doi.org/10.3389/fpsyg.2018.00507

Triandis, H.C., & Suh, E.M. (2001). Cultural influences on personality. *Annual Review of Psychology*, *53*(1), 133–160. https://doi.org/10.1146/annurev.psych.53.100901.135200

UK Government. (2022). Polygraph testing measures in the Police, Crime, Sentencing and Courts Bill: Equalities impact assessment. Retrieved from www.gov.uk/government/publications/police-crime-sentencing-and-courts-bill-2021-equality-statements/polygraph-testing-measures-in-the-police-crime-sentencing-courts-bill-equalities-impact-assessment

Verschuere, B., Schutte, M., Opzeeland, S., & Kool, I. (2020). The verifiability approach to deception detection: A preregistered direct replication of the information protocol condition of Nahari, Vrij, and Fisher (2014b). *Applied Cognitive Psychology*, 35. https://doi.org/10.1002/acp.3769

Vicianova, M. (2015). Historical techniques of lie detection. *Europe's Journal of Psychology*, 11(3), 522–534. https://doi.org/10.5964/ejop.v11i3.919

Vieth, V., Farrell, R., Johnson, R., Peters, R. (2020). *Conducting and defending a pandemic-era forensic interview*. Zero Abuse Project—National District Attorneys Association.

Vrij, A. (1998). Nonverbal communication and credibility. In A. Memon, A. Vrij & R. Bull (Eds.), *Psychology and law. Truthfulness, accuracy and credibility* (pp. 32–58). McGraw-Hill.

Vrij, A. (2000). *Detecting lies and deceit: The psychology of lying and the implications for professional practice*. John Wiley.

Vrij, A. (2008). *Detecting lies and deceit: Pitfalls and opportunities*. Wiley.

Vrij, A., Akehurst, L., Soukara, S., & Bull, R. (2004). Detecting deceit via analyses of verbal and nonverbal behavior in children and adults. *Human Communication Research*, 30(1), 8–41. https://doi.org/10.1111/j.1468-2958.2004.tb00723.x

Vrij, A., Edward, K., Roberts, K.P., & Bull, R. (2000). Detecting deceit via analysis of verbal and nonverbal behavior. *Journal of Nonverbal Behavior*, 24(4), 239–263. https://doi.org/10.1023/A:1006610329284

Vrij, A., & Fisher, R.P. (2016). Which lie detection tools are ready for use in the criminal justice system? *Journal of Applied Research in Memory and Cognition*, 5(3), 302–307. https://doi.org/10.1016/j.jarmac.2016.06.014

Vrij, A., Fisher, R.P., & Blank, H. (2017). A cognitive approach to lie detection: A meta-analysis. *Legal and Criminological Psychology*, 22(1), 1–21. https://doi.org/10.1111/lcrp.12088

Vrij, A., Fisher, R., Mann, S., & Leal, S. (2006). Detecting deception by manipulating cognitive load. *Trends in Cognitive Sciences*, 10(4), 141–142. https://doi.org/10.1016/j.tics.2006.02.003

Vrij, A., Granhag, P.A., Ashkenazi, T., Ganis, G., Leal, S., & Fisher, R.P. (2022). Verbal lie detection: Its past, present and future. *Brain Sciences*, 12(12), 1644. https://doi.org/10.3390/brainsci12121644

Vrij, A., Hartwig, M., & Granhag, P.A. (2019). Reading lies: Nonverbal communication and deception. *Annual Review of Psychology*, 70(1), 295–317. https://doi.org/10.1146/annurev-psych-010418-103135

Vrij, A., Hope, L., & Fisher, R.P. (2014). Eliciting reliable information in investigative interviews. *Policy Insights from the Behavioral and Brain Sciences*, 1(1), 129–136. https://doi.org/10.1177/2372732214548592

Vrij, A., Leal, S., Granhag, P.A., Mann, S., Fisher, R.P., Hillman, J., & Sperry, K. (2009). Outsmarting the liars: The benefit of asking unanticipated questions. *Law and Human Behavior*, 33, 159–166. https://doi.org/10.1007/s10979-008-9143-y

Vrij, A., Leal, S., Mann, S., & Fisher, R. (2012). Imposing cognitive load to elicit cues to deceit: Inducing the reverse order technique naturally. *Psychology, Crime & Law*, 18(6), 579–594. https://doi.org/10.1080/1068316X.2010.515987

Vrij, A., Mann, S.A., Fisher, R.P., Leal, S., Milne, R., & Bull, R. (2008). Increasing cognitive load to facilitate lie detection: The benefit of recalling an event in reverse order. *Law and Human Behavior*, 32(3), 253–265. https://doi.org/10.1007/s10979-007-9103-y

Vrij, A., Meissner, C.A., Fisher, R.P., Kassin, S.M., Morgan III, C.A., & Kleinman, S.M. (2017). Psychological perspectives on interrogation. *Perspectives on Psychological Science*, 12(6), 927–955. https://doi.org/10.1177/1745691617706515

Waite, J.B. (1931). Report on lawlessness in law enforcement: Comment. *Michigan Law Review*, 30(1), 54–62. https://doi.org/10.2307/1280636

Walczyk, J.J., Roper, K.S., Seemann, E., & Humphrey, A.M. (2003). Cognitive mechanisms underlying lying to questions: response time as a cue to deception. *Applied Cognitive Psychology*, 17(7), 755–774. https://doi.org/10.1002/acp.914

Wang, I., & Ruiz, J. (2021). Examining the use of nonverbal communication in virtual agents. *International Journal of Human-Computer Interaction*, 37(17), 1648–1673. https://doi.org/10.1080/10447318.2021.1898851

Weinberger, S. (2010). Airport security: Intent to deceive? *Nature*, 465(7297), 412–415. https://doi.org/10.1038/465412a

Zloteanu, M., Bull, P., Krumhuber, E.G., & Richardson, D. (2021). Veracity judgement, not accuracy: Reconsidering the role of facial expressions, empathy, and emotion recognition training on deception detection. *Quarterly Journal of Experimental Psychology*, 74(5), 910–927. https://doi.org/10.1177/1747021820978851

Zuckerman, M., DePaulo, B.M., Rosenthal, R. (1981). Verbal and nonverbal communication of deception. *Advances in Experimental Social Psychology*, 14, 1–59. https://doi.org/10.1016/S0065-2601(08)60369-X

2 The Emergence of Police Real-Time Crime Centers

Johnny Nhan

Nestled in dark rooms lit by the glow of dozens of computer monitors and television screens are police officers doing police work in a growing scene around the country. They are proactively monitoring the city for possible crimes occurring and assisting officers on the field. In Winchester County, New York, police identified a stolen rental car and caught a suspect on his way to committing a burglary before any calls by the public were made to the police using a combination of video cameras, automated license plate readers, and a networked database (Eberhart, 2018).

Despite the science fiction images of officers facing a wall of monitors akin to NASA's mission control, this scenario is becoming increasingly common as US law enforcement organizations rapidly invest in real time crime centers (RTCCs; Przeszlowski et al., 2022). RTCCs are centralized operations' centers that synthesize a suite of technologies to enhance police ability to proactively detect and analyze crime in real-time as well as for investigations. As seen in Winchester County, an example of RTCC hardware and software technologies working together includes remote surveillance cameras, automated license plate readers (ALPRs), and gunshot-detection audio devices connected to a network of databases and computer-aided dispatch (CAD). Furthermore, the system can be used to gather data as part of intelligence-led policing that incorporates hot-spot policing and geographic information systems (GIS).

Using culture references, the scenario in New York can elicit two reactions. One can see this as great police work straight out of HBO's crime drama series *The Wire*, where Baltimore Police Officers are rapidly deployed to a drug deal or violent incident at the housing projects known as "The Pit." On the other hand, it is difficult to ignore the images as harbingers of an Orwellian surveillance society found in popular novels and movies, such as *1984*, *The Conversation*, *Enemy of the State*, and *Minority Report*.

The rapid proliferation of RTCCs has many civil rights proponents warning of issues of privacy. In Glendale, Arizona, the RTCC has access to over 1,700 CCTV cameras and has established public-private partnerships to allow access to cameras owned by businesses. Amazon and Google, which produce popular video doorbells Ring and Nest, respectively, allow users to share the footage with police during emergencies without owners' consent or warrants as part of end users' terms-of-service agreements (Crist, 2022). This has drawn the attention of civil rights groups. An Internet watchdog group, Electronic Frontier Foundation (EFF), has launched Atlas of Surveillance, which tracks the proliferation RTCCs. According to the EFF, there were over 80 RTCCs in 29 states in 2020 (Maass, 2020).

This is only the tip of the proverbial iceberg. The London Metropolitan Police, known for their surveillance system that blankets the entire city, is planning on rolling out live facial recognition technology that is linked to aid in identifying individuals on a watchlist. While this technology, and potential pairing with machine learning and artificial intelligence (AI) has many Western civil rights groups concerned, the technology is in widespread deployment in China. Moreover, China has become the world's biggest exporter of facial recognition technology (Knight, 2023).

Police are no strangers to controversies whenever new technologies are implemented. Civil rights and privacy issues also emerged when dashboard cameras were largely adopted in the 1990s and body-worn cameras in the 2010s. However, the endless adoption of technology may be a necessary adaptative mechanism to increase efficiency while limiting legal risk in growing populations that demand more services and accountability from officers.

This paper explores the emergence of RTCCs in the context of the historical adoption of technologies by policing using the nodal governance theoretical framework (see Burris, Drahos, & Shearing, 2005; Shearing & Wood, 2003). This framework posits that security is no longer exclusive to official policing agencies, but a "plural" network of non-state and hybrid security actors that function together by sharing information and resources (Shearing & Wood, 2003). Furthermore, privacy and civil rights issues will be examined, paying particular attention to developing policies, practices, and laws governing the suite of technologies. Lastly, five ($n = 5$) sworn police officers assigned to an RTCC from one large metropolitan city police department located in north Texas were interviewed to give insight into the operations, policies, strengths, and limitations of RTCCs.

A Brief History of Police and Technology

A combination of factors has affected the use of technology in American policing. Among them are increased demands for police services as part of the professionalization movement since the early twentieth century, declining budgets coupled with the rising costs of officers, and new threats and functions, ranging from terrorism and illegal immigration to community-oriented policing. As a response, officers are required to do more with limited manpower and resources. To compensate for this deficit, police have historically turned to technologies, ranging from police cars and two-way radios to computer-aided dispatching systems (CAD) in mobile data terminals (MDTs) in police cars and geographic information systems (GIS) and statistical data analysis (CompStat).

Policing technologies have complemented police professionalism and enhanced their goal of law enforcement. The *reform era* of policing, as defined by Kelling and Moore (1988) in the first half of the twentieth century, was centered around professionalism and efficiency. The movement toward professionalism was intended to ameliorate the image of widespread corruption during the intertwining of politics and the police. Berkeley police chief August Vollmer stressed advancing policing with the use of technology, training, and education. Such technological innovations included motorized patrols for traffic control, police radios, and centralized crime record systems (Vollmer, 1933). His protégé, O. W. Wilson (1953), further advanced policing technologies, investigations, and managerial strategies with computer technology and standards that furthered professionalism and crime control agendas (Fyfe et al., 1997).

The Police Car and Two-Way Radios

Mobilization was a key function of the advancement of policing technologies during the reform era that fundamentally changed policing. Essentially, the vehicle was the perfect complement for police professionalization during the early twentieth century, which had shifted the measures of success from community standards to professional standards based on crime control, such as rapid response and larger coverage area while using fewer personnel resources in the face of budgetary constraints in growing populations and citizen to officer ratios.

Within the same timeframe, police communications were rapidly developing. In the 1920s and 1930s, departments were experimenting with radio communications in cities, such as Detroit. The first forms of police radio communications came in the form of broadcasts to police cars, where officers would use call boxes to return notifications to the station. By the late 1930s and 1940s, two-way radios were introduced and adopted by large departments, which allowed headquarters and patrol officers to communicate freely with each other (Poli, 1942).

However, the widespread use of police patrol cars was not without controversy as it raised privacy concerns and unintentionally exposed biases in policing. The proliferation of the automobile in American society expanded the role of police in enforcing traffic laws. Early courts grappled with the application of the Fourth Amendment to vehicles as police expanded their discretionary powers of search and seizure to traffic laws and not just homes. Consequently, the proliferation of drivers meant that police encountered citizens that they historically did not meet.

Patterns of over-policing of minorities began to emerge and have manifested to this day, such as the case of Sandra Bland, a 28-year-old African American who hanged herself in a jail cell after a traumatic pretextual police stop for not using her turn signal by a Texas Department of Safety Officer forced her to the ground and charged her with assaulting a police officer (Seo, 2019). The case, which drew national attention, resulted in Texas passing Senate Bill 1849, known as the Sandra Bland Act, that addressed a variety of issues including racial profiling, data collection, and police de-escalation.

Mobile Data Terminals, Databases, and the Information Age

Despite the controversies over police cars and two-way radios, their adoption was necessary in their constantly evolving work world. One evolution as society progressed beyond industrialization to one based on technology and networked technologies. Castells (1996) posited that global economic changes ushered in the "information age" that is based on technology, information, and networks. For individuals working in this new economy and social structure, this means that one must be able to gather information, process and synthesize that information, and act on that information to be successful. Castells describes these individuals as "knowledge workers."

Accordingly, modern police officers working as knowledge workers must gather information during encounters with citizens and input the data into networked computer systems in an endless cycle of trying to gain more complete and perfect information. Information is then pulled up and processed by officers during future encounters to manage risk and minimize danger.

Mobile data terminals (MDTs) and CAD when first introduced into police vehicles in the 1980s promised to enhance policing efficiency and effectiveness. For example, officers can quickly and efficiently run license plates and identify stolen vehicles by accessing a database directly without the delays of a dispatcher. More importantly, information technology (IT) in policing allowed officers to "[construct] the identity of individuals in an encounter, constructing an understanding of the event being handled by the officer, and as a resource for structuring the interaction between the citizen and police (Meehan, 1998, p. 227). The officer, acting as a knowledge worker, processes and acts on this information.

MDTs, like other forms of technology introduced into policing, also raised concerns. The use of a closed network meant that citizens could not monitor police activity that was available over the air with police radios which brought up concerns about transparency. Furthermore, information stored within databases can be inaccurate and requires the officer to decipher the truthfulness of the information. Unfortunately, officers have a limited understanding of networked computers and often perceive them as "magic boxes" that retrieve information upon command (Huey, 2002). This phenomenon of "in the screen we trust" is not unique to policing, as even nuclear scientists in Iran unquestionably trusted data displayed, which was corrupted with a computer virus as part of an attack, that led to physically damaging nuclear centrifuges (Goodman, 2015).

Cameras and Policing

As part of the continuum of policing that would ultimately lead to RTCCs are the development of surveillance technologies. Two major developments, dashboard cameras, and body-worn cameras, have impacted policing. Widespread use of police vehicle dashboard cameras was sparked in the 1990s from a combination of technological developments, concerns of racial bias and profiling, and state and federal legal requirements for documentation. In addition, in 2002, the Department of Justice sponsored $21 million in grants and funding to agencies to purchase and research in-car cameras, leading to its ubiquity today. Their study found cameras had a range of benefits, including enhancing officer safety, improving community/media perceptions of officers, and reducing liability (Rosenblatt et al., 2001).

Despite the advantages, the implementation of dashboard cameras was controversial. In the wake of the Chicago Police shooting of Laquan McDonald in 2016, investigators discovered that 80 percent of dashcams did not record audio, citing officer tampering (Lieberman, 2016). The investigation found officers deliberately disabled microphones and video, including destroyed antennas and missing microphones. That same year, St. Louis Police Officers who tased a suspect, disabled their dash camera which disproved the presence of a gun.

In the wake of the death of Michael Brown in Ferguson, Missouri, and the subsequent report by the President's Task Force on 21st Century Policing (2015), body-worn cameras have become commonplace among police officers. These cameras offer the same advantages as police dash cameras but allow for a closer look and dynamic video. For police, body camera footage has been used to counter citizen journalism, stop viral videos from spreading, and even interject a counter-narrative to anti-police sentiments.

For citizens, police bodycams have been described as a powerful tool against stop-and-frisk abuses (Southall, 2020).

Despite its benefits and like dashcams, bodycams have raised privacy concerns and racial disparities with the treatment of minorities (Voigt et al., 2017). Moreover, despite a reduction in citizen complaints of officers, there does not appear to have any impact on police use of force (Ariel, 2017). Furthermore, a study of citizen perceptions of officers who wear body-worn cameras shows that while privacy concerns were lessened by the perceived benefits of the cameras, perceptions of procedural fairness were not improved for non-white and younger respondents (Crow et al., 2022).

Real-Time Crime Centers

RTCCs merge all the stored information and surveillance technologies. Due to its prohibitive costs, full-time and fully staffed RTCCs currently are generally limited to larger police agencies. In Chicago, for example, the control room cost approximately $300,000 to build with analytic and mapping software an additional $1.5 million to set up, and $300,000 annually (Hollywood et al., 2019). Moreover, their uses and policies are still in development at different agencies and nationally, with the National Real Time Crime Center Association, established in 2022. RTCC research is also limited but focused on technologies, processes, and outcomes.

D'Amico's (2006) examination of NYPD's RTCC, which launched in 2005, found three basic elements: (1) data warehouse, (2) data analysis, and (3) data all. The system works by drawing data from various sources stored in the data warehouse, then using analytic software synthesizes relevant police information, such as domestic violence incidents, and displays them on a map. The information is then displayed on a "data wall" consisting of a grid of monitors.

The effectiveness of RTCCs has recently been examined to a limited degree. A 2019 examination of the effectiveness of the Chicago Police Department's RTCC showed a statistically significant drop in major crimes, such as robbery, burglary, homicide, and criminal sexual assaults, since its inception (Hollywood et al., 2019). More generalized research on RTCC effectiveness currently does not exist. A national study revealed difficulties comparing RTCCs and their performance, noting variables such as agency size, differences in personnel configurations, and command structures (Przeszlowski et al., 2022).

Despite its potential in aiding officers in, like the aforementioned technologies, RTCCs have raised privacy concerns. In addition to the concerns of creating an Orwellian police state that can eventually become a panoptic society from the proliferation and eventual ubiquity of cameras, the fusion of RTCC technologies can be unsettling to many. For example,

RTCCs currently can include gunshot detection and automated license plate readers. However, further development can include facial recognition technologies (FRTs) which are currently deployed in countries like China and England (see Purshouse & Cambell, 2019). In addition, machine learning and AI can potentially minimize the role of or even replace the limitations of a few officers monitoring the hundreds and thousands of cameras. When adding the ability to access private companies' surveillance cameras and citizens' doorbell cameras, there is a possibility for abuse.

Methods of Inquiry

These potential hazards of RTCCs have brought up the need for further understanding of the use of such powerful technologies from the officers' and police supervisors' perspectives. The rapid adoption of RTCCs has raised concerns about developing best practices, legal boundaries, and operational guardrails for their use.

This exploratory paper examines these nascent police technologies through qualitative interviews with police officers and supervisors working in a full-time RTCC in a large police department located in a metropolitan area. A series of questions explores the operational uses, benefits, limitations, and issues of privacy, legality, and policy.

Key themes began to emerge from the interviews. Since this is a small sample ($n = 5$) and is limited to one police department, these findings should not be generalized as true for all departments. This is especially true given the wide variation in RTCCs and RTCC technologies. However, the small sample represents a small population of 14 officers, detectives, and supervisors working at the RTCC in this large department.

Findings

RTCCs Help Manage Risks and Minimize Danger

As posited by Castells (1996), knowledge workers, officers working as knowledge workers strive to collect and process information to manage risk and minimize danger. RTCCs serve this function for officers who face potential danger with every citizen interaction. Several officers explicitly mentioned the dangerous aspect of the job. For example, one officer stated:

> If I was on a traffic stop, and I had somebody who was lying about their name, I could call the RTCC. [The RTCC] would give you help you build to identify that person based on the information they're giving you ... You take that [false] information and you look through it because it's usually a thread of truth to be able to figure out who this person was.

Another example given:

> So there's a domestic disturbance. Call that officers are being sent to while they're enroute. We'll review those calls, and we're looking for information on the call details that they gave the 9-1-1 call taker to see if we can determine any information that may allow for a safer outcome, both for the citizen and for the officer ... we're able to see his history if he has warrants or her history or her award status, and we can give that information out to the officer enroute. When they get there, they're not walking into something, but just the bare minimum call details given to the call taker, or they have a little bit more situation awareness which makes it safer for them.

In addition to more background information that helps officers paint a more complete picture of the scene, RTCCs also can serve as an additional pair of eyes. One RTCC supervisor explained:

> We can be looking for stuff that an officer maybe even knows about. We see a large bulge in a pocket from the camera...We can see guns being put in people's pockets and stuff like that. We can alert the offering route that it appears. This person may have a heavy object placed into a pocket. Officers can do a Terry stop[1] first upon arrival.

RTCCs Are "Game Changers" in Increasing Officer Efficiency

As populations have increased and greater demands are placed on officers, departments have looked for ways to increase officer efficiency and productivity. This is especially true with investigations performed by often overwhelmed detectives with large caseloads. While an initial arrest may happen once an officer has a probable cause at the scene, the ensuing investigation can be time-consuming. One officer who called their RTCC a "game changer" for investigations explained:

> [The RTCC is] clearing cases that a detective would have to clear but we're clearing them in real time. So, somebody who committed a burglary, we're able to provide information that can get that suspect stopped today that [would have gone into] a report...So that actor could be out there committing more offenses in the next coming days while that information is getting processed.

---

1 Based on the 1968 case of *Terry v. Ohio*, police officers are allowed to temporarily detain an individual based on a reasonable suspicion that a crime has been committed and perform a pat-down or frisk for concealed weapons. This is different than a search of a person, which can involve examining underneath the clothing and pockets.

Another officer expressed the versatility and robustness of having an RTCC.

> It's changing the game and everybody that starts to try to utilize a real-time Crime Center, whether they're a patrol officer, narcotics officer, or any other specialized unit. There's a way to use our RTCC in the way you do your police work. You have to understand it, know its capabilities, and once you know that then you can morph it to your police work profile.

Privacy and Current Limitations

The widespread surveillance capabilities of RTCCs and their suite of technologies naturally raise privacy concerns. RTCCs rely heavily on CCTVs distributed throughout a city. Several factors related to privacy, have raised concerns: The prevalence of cameras, camera placement, who has access to cameras, and policies in place to safeguard against abuses. Finding the balance between security and privacy is often difficult and takes time.

Currently, despite the growing number of cameras, a "big brother" effect is not a reality, at least yet, due to the human element in monitoring the cameras. This bottleneck may eventually be addressed in the future by machine learning and AI, but currently, RTCCs rely on individuals to monitor, process, and dispatch officers to the scene. When asked if the RTCC can autonomously detect and dispatch officers, one supervisor explained their limitations.

> Yes, so we have 830 cameras that we monitor across the city. So, it's really hard for us to do. You know the vision people always have is we have all these cameras and we're watching, looking for crimes in progress. And we do some of that. We know some of our higher crime areas, some of our cameras, maybe overlooking a convenience store or a game room or something where we know there's crime happening.

The surveillance of high crime areas is by design. The RTCC members interviewed were cognizant of potential abuses of the system and possible civil rights violations. As a result, many agencies have internal policies or practices that limit the placement of cameras and what they can record.

One officer interviewed explained the cameras are only watching places where an officer has a right to observe if he or she was physically there:

> We want to make sure there's something articulable to make an arrest or something like that no different than a patrol officer. I might see a bunch of people there, but I'm not going to go over there and do anything less. I have reasonable suspicion of a crime for detention.

If I don't have that, then I don't need to do it that might continue to moderate as a police officer, so the same thing would happen to the crime center. We see stuff all the time. It looks suspicious. We'll watch it. We'll moderate, but till we see something that makes it reasonable suspicion. We're not going to dispatch.

Another officer echoed this opinion:

We won't put anywhere that a police officer doesn't have the right to be there, so we're not going to focus them into houses. We don't want cameras inside businesses. If you've got a business that's your business.

One officer explained this cognizance of privacy is important to maintaining agency and public support of RTCCs. He fears that if the technology is abused, it can draw scrutiny and potentially be severely restricted or prohibited. In discussing the potential abuse of the cameras, such as invading someone's privacy or using the system in a vindictive way by an individual officer, he underscores the importance of preserving civil rights:

That's one of my personal projects to make sure that my department never violates because it is such a good tool. It only takes one person to ruin that and take away the tool. I know how valuable it is for citizens. So, I never want to become what I swore to protect against constitutionally.

In addition to camera placement, access to cameras is a concern for RTCCs. Limiting access to certain individuals can safeguard against abuses and improper usage.

Police officers have been fired for abuses in technology. For example, police have access to national information networks that they regularly use. Officers routinely search names and license plates for detailed information on individuals, such as during traffic stops. However, numerous officers have abused such access. In Connecticut, an Old Saybrook officer was arrested when he illegally accessed the database to look up a woman's license plate to follow her on Instagram (Rascius, 2022).

One supervisor interviewed stated that limiting access to RTCC cameras can prevent abuses, such as officer stalking and harassment of members of the public:

[Limiting access] takes away the risk that someone may be looking in someone's window or following somebody around, with no reason because it's their boyfriend or for something like that, so we can mitigate risk by limiting who can monitor it.

RTCCs Can Improve Community Policing

Several officers stated that despite concerns about mass surveillance, RTCCs can improve police-community relations. Historically, police have responded to high-crime areas with saturation techniques coupled with aggressive enforcement. These types of enforcement have yielded success in reducing crime, as seen in Dallas in the late 1990s (see Fritsch, Caeti, & Taylor, 1999). However, in recent years, such blanket approaches have drawn public backlash from minority communities and liability for departments violating civil rights. More recently, Dallas Police have used a "focused deterrence" model that targets high-crime individuals instead that commit a disproportionate amount of crime in a small area (Garcia, 2021). Individuals who constitute a disproportionate amount of police interactions and arrests are identified are subject to a range of police activities ranging from intervention programming that may "disrupt" and prevent further crime to more traditional strategies of incapacitation.

RTCCs can aid in targeting individuals and removing them without drawing the attention of a neighborhood. One officer explained:

> Typically, what we would do is go into an area to saturate it, and you're stopping everybody and their mom, and that's going to alienate the community. Tensions will get high, and then, when you do have a person that you have to enforce the law. That is an actual bad guy. You're not going to get the community support.

He adds the new approach which is made more possible using the RTCC.

> You're basically using a scalpel approach now, instead of a fish net. So now you're specifically picking out targets that you know have some criminal activity because you've seen that through the RTCC.

RTCCs Are Still Developing Training and Policies

The rapid growth and improvements in RTCC technologies have outstripped the development of standards, best practices, and rules that govern their operation. Akin to a science fiction movie based in the future, RTCCs can potentially autonomously detect gunshots, identify stolen vehicle license plates, and even individuals through facial recognition technologies by AI and dispatch officers or even drones without human input. As with plots in movies based on Philip K. Dick novels, things often turn dystopian as individuals are misidentified and wrongly treated as computers take over the world. While this vision is extreme and often meant as entertainment, safeguards are being developed to ensure that reality remains fiction.

Officers interviewed expressed that RTCCs are still a nascent suite of technologies that are developing guidelines and best practices. One officer who is on the board of the newly established National Real Time Crime Center Association (NRTCCA) responded to an inquiry on what training is required for individuals working at their RTCC was:

> The NRTCCA doesn't really have standardized training for best practices yet. Everybody is still learning. So, if you're a new officer and you applied to work at RTCC, you're going to come in, you're going to get trained, but it's kind of informal … But as far as formal training goes, it just hasn't been developed yet because everybody's learning.

A supervisor echoed those sentiments:

> It's internal training on how to use the databases and the policies and procedures that we fall under within our department that limit the ability to have gross misconduct. Yeah, so that's what I'm assuming, is it's still in this cloud phase right now, and things the standards are coming are emerging from that. But in the meantime, it's just up to each individual agency to establish their own [policies]. Hopefully, at some point, those best practices will be established by the NRTCCA and then the departments will ensure their internal policies or in line with those or have some reason why they're not.

Discussion and Conclusion

Shortage of officers underscores the need for increased productivity and efficiency from each officer. As seen by the responses, RTCCs show a lot of potential, and their rapid adoption is evident of their effectiveness. This underscores Castell's (1996) assertion that police in the information age relies on officers as knowledge workers. Furthermore, modern police are working in a model that is more collaborative and reliant on a network of security resources and entities.

The nodal governance framework posits that police in the modern age operate in a flattened hierarchy where they no longer exclusively dealt with security but instead, serve as a "node" in a security network (Burris, Drahos, & Shearing, 2005). In this distributed model, police act as one participant in co-producing security with other entities, such as private security and private organizations, as well as federal agencies, that share resources and knowledge. This networked security model can be seen by RTCCs as a police network with private organizations and individuals, tapping into their cameras and eliciting help. Furthermore, national databases are being linked where facial recognition databases and fingerprint matching is possible. This is a far departure from the professional model as envisioned by August Vollmer and O. W. Wilson during professionalization.

As seen throughout this paper, with every new police technology comes concerns for potential abuse and privacy. These concerns are especially apt in today's environment where the public is more aware of AI and machine learning. Recently, chatbot ChatGPT has entered the public lexicon with headlines ranging from it passing the bar exam to writing computer code. However, the AI technology has raised questions of unethical behavior and abuse as a lawyer used ChatGPT to write a legal filing, which referenced case law that did not exist. In higher education, a survey of college students revealed that 30% used the chatbot for schoolwork in the 2022/23 academic year, with nearly half of students using it for English (Kyaw, 2023).

This research (like the RTCCs themselves) is exploratory in nature and meant to shed light on its use and highlight potential issues with the technologies. Obviously, further research is needed as the technologies evolve and policy and legal ramifications emerge.

References

Ariel, B. (2017). Police body cameras in large police departments. *Journal of Criminal Law & Criminology*, 106(4), 729–768.

Burris, S., Drahos, P., & Shearing, C. (2005). Nodal governance. *Australian Journal of Legal Philosophy*, 30, 1–43.

Castells, M. (1996). *The information age: Economy, society and culture vol. 1: The rise of the network society* (2nd ed.). Oxford: Wiley Blackwell.

Crist, R. (2022, July 26). Ring, Google, and the police: What to know about emergency requests for video footage. *CNET*. Retrieved from www.cnet.com/home/security/ring-google-and-the-police-what-to-know-about-emergency-requests-for-video-footage/.

Crow, M.S., Snyder, J.A., Crichlow, V.J., & Smykla, J.O. (2022). Community perceptions of body-worn cameras: The impact of fairness, fear, performance, and privacy. *Criminal Justice & Behavior*, 44(4), 589–610. doi: 10.1177/0093854816688037

D'Amico, J. (2006). Stopping crime in real-time. *Police Chief*, 73(9), 20–24.

Eberhart, C.J. (2018). New police technology is catching suspects thanks to the Real Time Crime Center. *Lohud*. Retrieved from www.lohud.com/story/news/crime/2018/07/23/new-police-technology/746938002/.

Fritsch, E.J. Caeti, T.J., & Taylor, R.W. (1999). Gant suppression through saturation patrol, aggressive curfew, and truancy enforcement: A quasi-experimental test of the Dallas Anti-Gang Initiative. *Crime & Delinquency, 45*(1), 122–139.

Fyfe, J.J., Greene, J.R., Walsh, W.F, Wilson, O.W., & McLaren, R.C. (1997). *Police Administration* (5th ed.). Highstown, NJ: McGraw Hill.

Garcia, E. (2021). Dallas Police Department violent crime reduction plan. Retrieved from www.dallaspolice.net/Shared%20Documents/violent-crime-reduction-plan.pdf.

Goodman, M. (2015). *Future crimes: Inside the digital underground and the battle for our connected world*. New York: Anchor Books.

Hollywood, J.S., McKay, K.N., Woods, D., & Agniel, D. (2019). Real-time crime centers in Chicago. Rand Corporation. Retrieved from https://yidawang.ca/pdf/rand.pdf.

Huey, L. (2002). Policing the abstract: Some observations on policing cyberspace. *Canadian Journal of Criminology, 44*(3), 243–254.

Kelling, G., & Moore, M. (1988). Evolving strategy of policing. *Perspectives on Policing, 4*, 1–15.

Knight, W. (2023, January 24). China is world's biggest facial recognition dealer. *Wired*. Retrieved from www.wired.com/story/china-is-the-worlds-biggest-face-recognition-dealer/.

Kway, A. (2023). Survey: 30% of college S\students used ChatGPT for schoolwork this past academic year. Diverse issues in higher education. Retrieved from www.diverseeducation.com/reports-data/article/15448462/survey-30-of-college-students-used-chatgpt-for-schoolwork-this-past-academic-year.

Lieberman, S. (2016, January 27). Chicago Police have been sabotaging their dash cams. *New York Magazine Intelligencer*. Retrieved from https://nymag.com/intelligencer/2016/01/chicago-police-officers-tampered-with-dash-cams.html.

Maass, D. (2020, November 16). EFF publishes new research on real-time crime centers in the US. *Electronic Frontier Foundation*. Retrieved from www.eff.org/deeplinks/2020/11/eff-publishes-new-research-real-time-crime-centers-us.

Meehan, A.J. (1998). The impact of Mobile Data Terminal (MDT) information technology on communication and recordkeeping in patrol work. *Qualitative Sociology, 21*(3), 225–254.

Poli, J.A. (1942). Development and present trend of police radio communications. *Journal of Criminal Law & Criminology, 33*, 193–197.

President's Task Force on 21st Century Policing. (2015). *Final report of the President's task force on 21st century policing*. Washington, DC: Office of Community Oriented Policing Services.

Przeszlowski, K., Guerette, R.T., & Gutierrez, A. (2022). The centralization and rapid deployment of police agency information technologies: An appraisal of real-time crime centers in the US. *The Police Journal: Theory, Practice and Principles*, online ahead of print. https://doi.org/10.1177/0032258X221107587.

Purshouse, J., & Campbell, L. (2019). Privacy, crime control and police use of automated facial recognition technology. *Criminal Law Review, 3*, 188–204.

Rascius, B. (2022, December 15). Officer working at Walmart runs woman's plates to follow her on Instagram, police say. *Miami Herald*. Retrieved from www.miamiherald.com/news/nation-world/national/article270067367.html#.

Rosenblatt, D.N., Cromartie, E.R., & Firman, J. (2001). The impact of video evidence on modern policing. *International Association of Chiefs of Police/US Department of Justice*. Retrieved from https://bja.ojp.gov/sites/g/files/xyckuh186/files/bwc/pdfs/iacpin-carcamerareport.pdf.

Seo, S.A. (2019, June 3). How cars transformed policing. *Boston Review*. Retrieved from www.bostonreview.net/articles/sarah-seo-how-cars-transformed-policing/.

Shearing, C., & Wood, J. (2003). Nodal governance, democracy, and the new "denizens." *Journal of Law and Society*, 30(3), 400–419.

Southall, A. (2020, November 30). Police body cameras cited as "powerful tool" against stop-and-frisk abuses. *The New York Times*. Retrieved from www.nytimes.com/2020/11/30/nyregion/nypd-body-cameras.html.

Voigt, R., Camp, N.P., Prabhakaran, V., & Eberhardt, J.L. (2017). Language from police body camera footage shows racial disparities in officer respect. *Proceedings from the National Academy of Sciences*, 114(25), 6521–6526. https://doi.org/10.1073/pnas.1702413114.

Vollmer, A. (1933) Police progress in the past twenty-five years. *Journal of the American Institute of Criminal Law and Criminology*, 24, 161–175.

Wilson, O.W. (1953). August Vollmer and the origins of police professionalism. *Journal of Criminal Law and Criminology*, 44(1), 91–103.

3 Facial Recognition Software for Lead Generation and Lineup Construction

Lauren E. Thompson

Automated facial recognition (AFR) is software used to map, digitize, and compare facial templates (Mann & Smith, 2017). The first step in any AFR system is the detection of a face or faces in an image. After a face has been detected, the AFR system then extracts and maps facial features creating an algorithmic template which represents the face within whatever database the information is to be stored (Mann & Smith, 2017; Zhao et al., 2003). The final step involves comparing this facial template to others already stored within a database. AFR is becoming a commonly used technology for various aspects of law enforcement. AFR is mainly used by law enforcement for two purposes: facial verification and facial identification. Facial verification is used to confirm a person's claimed identity (i.e., one-to-one matching; Mann & Smith, 2017). For example, facial verification is commonly used at international border crossings to compare faces with those stored digitally in biometric passports (Mann & Smith, 2017). Facial identification is used to seek the identity of a person in the absence of a claimed identity. It involves comparing a probe image to many facial templates stored in a database. Clearly, using AFR for facial identification is useful for law enforcement's collecting of identification evidence. Most obvious, AFR can be used to identify a suspect (i.e., generate a lead) using images obtained of the perpetrator (e.g., from surveillance footage), and further, but possibly less apparent, AFR also can be used to build lineups for eyewitness identification tasks.

Importantly, the utility of AFR software for collecting identification evidence would be much less so if it were not for the advancements made regarding storage and sharing of identification (ID) photos, as well as widespread implementation of video surveillance (i.e., closed-circuit television, CCTV). Specifically, before advancements in computer storage, mugshots and other photographs only existed as physical copies. In recent years, there has been large technological advancements in the recording of mugshot photographs. Law enforcement agencies can now hold digital copies of millions of photographs in their online mugshot databases.

DOI: 10.4324/9781003323112-4

For example, in the United States, the Federal Bureau of Investigation (FBI) hosts one of the largest photo databases in the country, the Next Generation Identification Interstate Photo System, which contains nearly 25 million state and federal criminal photos (Georgetown Law Center on Privacy & Technology, 2016). Moreover, law enforcement can now share their mugshot photographs between agencies, including agencies across different states.

Not only does law enforcement have access to mugshot photographs, but some agencies also have access to their citizen's driver's license and other ID photo databases. Research from the Centre of Privacy and Technology at Georgetown Law reported that at least 26 American states allow law enforcement to run or request searches of their database of driver's license photos (Georgetown Law Center on Privacy & Technology, 2016). Further, 16 states allow the FBI to search their driver's license and other photo ID databases. Within other countries, such as those in the European Union and Australia, various government organizations have proposed legislation which would allow sharing of mugshot and driver's license photos across borders and between government and police agencies (Directorate-General for Migration and Home Affairs, 2021; Parliament of Australia, n.d.). With access to these large photo databases, law enforcement now has access to millions of photographs of faces which could be used to search for a criminal's identity and build eyewitness identification lineups, among other uses.

Though, to use AFR to search an image database for a criminal's identity, an image of the criminal is first needed. Thanks to the continued and increased use of CCTV, images of criminals and criminal suspects can be identified on surveillance footage. Briefly, CCTV is the use of video cameras to transmit a signal to a specific monitor or set of monitors (as opposed to broadcast television in which the signal is openly transmitted; Kroener, 2014). CCTV cameras are used by different people for various purposes. For example, they can be used by homeowners to monitor their house, by business owners for protection of their property and goods, and, most notably, by governments as a strategy to solve and reduce crime (Kroener, 2014; Piza et al., 2019).

The rise of government use of CCTV can be traced back to Great Britain, where from 1996 to 1998, 75% of the Home Office budget was allocated to CCTV related projects (Armitage, 2002; Piza et al., 2019). Such policy decisions rapidly increased the number of CCTV cameras in England and Whales, from roughly 100 in the early 1990s to over four million less than two decades later (Armitage, 2002; Farrington et al., 2007). Since then, CCTV has surged worldwide. As of 2022, China has the most CCTV cameras with over 200 million cameras installed in the country (Baltrusaitis, 2022). This is followed by the United States with 50 million,

Germany with 5.2 million, and the United Kingdom and Japan each with 5 million CCTV cameras. Various other countries also report having a significant number of CCTV cameras including Vietnam, France, South Korea, the Netherlands, and Australia, who all report over 1 million cameras in use (Baltrusaitis, 2022; Keoghan, 2019).

As a result of the advancements in mugshot and ID photo storage and sharing, and the spreading use of CCTV, AFR software has been able to flourish within law enforcement.

History of Automated Facial Recognition Software

Although AFR systems are fairly new, the concept of a facial matching system has been around since the nineteenth century, with Alphonse Bertillon (Cole, 2001). At the time, there was no scientific way to recognize a person's identity and so Bertillon came up with a solution, which was to create a classification system based on anthropometric measurements. The system, called "Bertillonage," involved taking various measurements of people's body dimensions and facial features. The classification of facial features was based on measurements of a person's head, ears, forehead, eyes, nose, mouth, chin, and neck (Cole, 2001; Evison, 2014). These measurements, along with the body measurements, two photographs, and the noting of "peculiar marks" (i.e., distinct marks such as tattoos or scars), were recorded on a classification card. Once the card was complete, it was brought to a records archive where the card was indexed according to the anthropometric measurements (Cole, 2001). The cards were first indexed by sex, then head length, head breadth, middle finger length, and so on. When trying to identify an unknown criminal's identity, the Bertillon operator would take the newly created classification card into the archive and look for a card with matching anthropometric values.

Based on the system's early success at identifying recidivists, Bertillonage was adopted by law enforcement agencies worldwide. However, in the early years of the twentieth century, various law enforcement personnel started to campaign for the use of dermatoglyphic fingerprinting over Bertillonage. Fingerprinting was quicker, cheaper, and easier to perform than Bertillonage. Although both Bertillonage and fingerprinting were used as criminal identification techniques for the first few decades of the twentieth century, by the beginning of the 1930s, most law enforcement agencies had ceased recording Bertillon measurements (Cole, 2001). However, the introduction of computers brought about the promise of an automated system that could measure and record facial features.

Due to limited computing powers at the time, the first computer facial recognition system was only semi-automated. This system was created in the 1960s by Woodrow Bledsoe and required the operator to manually measure attributes of features (e.g., the distance between relevant facial landmarks). It was not until the early 1990s that a fully automated facial recognition system was developed (Turk & Pentland, 1991; Zhao et al., 2003). In comparison to Bertillonage, which relied fully on human intervention, automated facial recognition systems automatically extract, digitize, and compare the relational and geometric distribution of facial features (Mann & Smith, 2017).

After the notion of a fully automated facial recognition system was realized, interest in developing and exacting AFR systems has grown steadily and significantly. Over the past 30 years, a variety of novel algorithms have been developed, large competitions have taken place, and commercially available systems have been crafted and disseminated (O'Toole & Phillips, 2015; Zhao et al., 2003).

AFR in Law Enforcement

Like fingerprinting, iris, and deoxyribonucleic acid (DNA), facial recognition is a method of biometric identification. Biometric identification can be described as "the recognition of people based on measurement and analysis of their biological characteristics or behavioural data" (Home Office, 2018, p. 5). Biometrics have long played a critical role in national security from crime investigations, to corrections, immigration, border management, to national defense (Goldstein et al., 2008; Home Office, 2018; Meunier et al., 2013). While AFR is a relatively new biometric technology, its use by law enforcement is growing fast and steadily.

Indeed, many law enforcement agencies worldwide either use or are testing AFR technology. In the United States, the Centre of Privacy and Technology at Georgetown Law estimates that 1 in 4 of all American law enforcement agencies have access to AFR technology (Georgetown Law Center on Privacy & Technology, 2016). While some agencies do not have their own facial recognition systems, they can request a search or request access to a partnering organization's AFR system. Many of these partnering programs are expansively networked, such as Pennsylvania's system which is accessible to all 1,020 law enforcement agencies in the state (Legislative Budget and Finance Committee, 2014). Further, the FBI has its own electronic repository of biometric information, Next Generation Identification (NGI). The NGI system includes a facial recognition search where authorized law enforcement can submit a probe image and the system will search against over 30 million photographs (Law Enforcement Resources, n.d.). Notably, other countries do not have comprehensive reports identifying the number of police agencies using AFR technology, however, it is clear that various countries across the world are utilizing AFR in their law enforcement. For example, several Canadian law enforcement agencies including the Ontario Provincial Police, Thunder Bay Police Service, Edmonton Police Service, Calgary Police, Halifax Regional Police, as well as the national police service of Canada (i.e., the Royal Canadian Mounted Police) have been identified as currently using or previously using AFR software (Burke, 2020; Choi, 2022; Canadian Civil Liberties Association, n.d.; Royal Canadian Mounted Police, 2020; Trevithick, 2020). Further, several law enforcement agencies in Europe have been identified as using AFR software (Davies et al., 2018; Goldstein et al., 2008; Kayser-Bril, 2020). For example, police agencies in Italy, Austria, France, and Germany all have implemented AFR software into their investigative policing practices (Kayser-Bril, 2020). As AFR technology continues to make advancements in its reliability and usability, increasingly more law enforcement agencies will want access to this software. Therefore, the number of agencies with access to AFR technology should only increase over time.

AFR for Collecting Identification Evidence

For the purposes of collecting identification evidence, law enforcement can use AFR technology for facial identification; more specifically, for lead generation as well as for building eyewitness identification lineups. Before discussing AFR for lead generation and lineup building, the operation of AFR technology for facial identification will be briefly described.

The process of using AFR technology for facial identification involves various steps. First, it is necessary to have an existing database of facial images. When images are stored for AFR use, they are analyzed so that the facial features associated with each image are extracted and expressed as numerical code. This numerical code, typically referred to as a faceprint, is unique to each person. The next step is for the operator to identify the target face (i.e., the face to compare against the database of facial images). Once the target face has been identified, their facial features are automatically extracted by the software. The software then compares the faceprint of the target face to the faceprints stored within the image database. When two faceprints are compared, the software generates a similarity rating.[1] The similarity rating is a numerical value indicating the likelihood that the faces being compared are of the same person. The higher the similarity rating, the more similar the two faces are. The final step involves the AFR system returning faces (i.e., potential matches) and their associated similarity rating. The software will only return faces that are at or above a pre-specified threshold value. The threshold value indicates the similarity rating

---

1 Similarity rating has also been referred to as a *match score*, *similarity score*, *confidence score*, and *confidence rating*.

needed for a match to occur. Most AFR systems have a default threshold value, however, this value can also be configured by the operator.

AFR for Lead Generation

One way in which law enforcement can use AFR for facial identification is lead generation. Specifically, law enforcement can use an image captured of a criminal to search for a possible identity. The captured image is typically referred to as a probe image. The probe image can come from several different sources including a smartphone, social media post, or security camera footage (Georgetown Law Center on Privacy & Technology, 2016). Thanks to the widespread use of CCTV, it is becoming more common to use CCTV footage with AFR to search for criminals (Purshouse & Campbell, 2022; Georgetown Law Center on Privacy & Technology, 2016).

After law enforcement have secured the probe image (e.g., the image captured on CCTV), this image is uploaded to the AFR system. The operator (i.e., the law enforcement officer) then sets the threshold value for a match (or keeps the default value). Once the threshold value is set, the AFR system compares the facial template extracted from the probe image to the facial templates stored in the image database. The system then returns those faces which are at or above the threshold value. After the list of candidates is returned, law enforcement can decide whether to investigate any of the candidates further. Notably, AFR systems can be integrated with surveillance systems, automating this process even further (Mann & Smith, 2017). Specifically, if a surveillance system is integrated with AFR, law enforcement who detect a criminal on their surveillance footage can immediately initiate a biometric search. In either case, AFR technology is used to search databases for a suspect in a comparable way to other biometric searching, such as searching a DNA database for a sample found at a crime scene. Though, unlike other forms of biometrics such as DNA, fingerprinting, and iris, AFR is less invasive, can operate from a distance, and can be integrated with already operating surveillance systems (Mann & Smith, 2017).

Various examples exist of law enforcement successfully using AFR to aid their investigations (e.g., Parker, 2020). For example, Robert Alexander Kusma was arrested for sexually assaulting a minor with aid of facial recognition software. Police uncovered Kusma's identity by using facial recognition software to match pictures of himself he sent to the victim, to his driver's license photo (*Pennsylvania v. Kusma*). In another case, Devon Robinson was arrested for the murder of three individuals, partly based on the use of facial recognition software used to identify him from surveillance footage obtained from a nearby gas station (*People v. Robinson*).

It may be important to note—and as the previous examples allude to—AFR should not be used in isolation as cause to make an arrest but should serve as a tool to assist law enforcement in their investigation. More specifically, an AFR identification would not be sufficient to make an arrest but instead, could be used as one piece of evidence against a suspect.

AFR for Filler Selection

While AFR can be used to search for possible suspects, it can also be used to build an identification lineup.

Background on Filler Selection

After someone witnesses a crime where they had some sort of view of the criminal, they may be asked to participate in an identification procedure. The most common identification procedure is a lineup, where a suspect and various known innocents are presented to the eyewitness. The "known innocents" are typically referred to as *fillers*. The purpose of including fillers in a lineup presentation is to reduce the chances of the eyewitness making a false identification and to allow for a more precise test of law enforcement's hypothesis that the suspect is indeed the perpetrator (Charman & Wells, 2007; Wixted & Wells, 2017). For these reasons, it is generally agreed upon that fillers should be included in the identification procedure (Wells et al., 2020). Notably, though, research has not clearly identified how best to select fillers or how similar fillers should be to the suspect they surround (Wells et al., 2020). More specifically, there are two primary methods for filler selection: matching the fillers to the description of the perpetrator provided by the eyewitness (i.e., match-to-description), and matching the fillers to the appearance of the suspect (i.e., match-to-suspect; Luus & Wells, 1991). For example, with match-to-description, the eyewitness may report to law enforcement that that the perpetrator was a White male, with dark eyes, and dark hair. To choose fillers, officers would then search their image reservoir and select photos of individuals that match this description. On the other hand, match-to-suspect involves officers using the physical appearance of the suspect and searching their image reservoir to find photos of individuals that look similar to the suspect.

Researchers have noted problems with both filler selection methods. With the match-to-suspect, there are no clear guidelines for how similar the fillers should be to the suspect; how similar is similar enough? As a result of the lack of guidelines, another problem with this strategy is that it has the potential to lead to decreased rates of correct identifications. A police officer attempting to create the fairest lineup (i.e., one where the suspect does not stand out in any way) may select fillers who so closely resemble the suspect that even an eyewitness with a good memory of the perpetrator would have difficulty discriminating the suspect from the fillers (Tunnicliff & Clark, 2000). The final issue with the match-to-suspect strategy is actually contrary to the last in that this strategy may actually lead to an increase in false identifications (Navon, 1992; Tunnicliff & Clark, 2000). Specifically, the issue here is that the suspect and the fillers are placed in the lineup based on different criteria; the suspect is placed in the lineup because they match the description of the culprit provided by the eyewitness, while the fillers are placed in the lineup because they match the suspect's appearance. When the suspect is innocent, that suspect is in the lineup because they are similar to the culprit, while the fillers are in the lineup because they are similar to someone who is *not* the culprit (Tunnicliff & Clark, 2000). Therefore, the suspect is one level removed in terms of similarity to the culprit (the suspect matches the description of the culprit), while the fillers are two levels removed in terms of similarity to the culprit (the fillers match the individual who matches the description). As a result, the innocent suspect may be selected as the culprit as they are the best match to the culprit.

Due to the problems associated with the match-to-suspect strategy, the match-to-description strategy was suggested. The match-to-description strategy addresses many of the drawbacks associated with the match-to-suspect strategy. First, the match-to-description strategy provides an answer to the question of "how similar" the fillers should be to the suspect; the similarity stops where the eyewitness' description of the culprit stops (Luus & Wells, 1991). Second, as the match-to-description strategy has a natural stopping point (the description) it is not likely that the fillers will be *too* similar to the suspect. Finally, the match-to-description strategy should protect against innocent suspects being wrongly identified simply because they are the closest match (i.e., most similar) to the culprit. With the match-to-description strategy, both the suspect and fillers are placed in the lineup because they match the eyewitness' description of the culprit, and therefore, an innocent suspect should be no more likely to be identified than any single filler.

Although the match-to-description appears superior to the match-to-suspect strategy in theory, empirical research comparing the two strategies has not conclusively found this (see Carlson et al., 2019, exp. 2; Wells et al., 1993; cf., Clark et al., 2013; Darling et al., 2008; Lindsay et al., 1994; Tunnicliff & Clark, 2000). Moreover, in actual practice, the match-to-description filler selection method may be insufficient. For one, a description of the culprit is needed to use the match-to-description method, yet, research has found that eyewitnesses typically provide few descriptors, most of which are vague and nondistinctive, and therefore apply to many people (Sporer, 1996). Second, in the most recent comprehensive survey of eyewitness procedures by law enforcement agencies, the Police Executive Research Forum (2013) noted that police departments most commonly select filler photographs by searching through various databases of driver's license and/or mugshot photographs. As mentioned, many law enforcement agencies now have access to very large databases of photographs for which to choose their fillers, in some cases, they may have access to hundreds of thousands to millions of photographs (Georgetown Law Center on Privacy & Technology, 2016). As a result, it may not be realistic to expect law enforcement to search through hundreds of thousands of photographs using only a few descriptors to narrow down the filler pool. Finally, law enforcement's access to AFR software further adds to the undesirability of filler searches based only on descriptors. AFR allows for easy implementation of matching algorithms to search for fillers resembling a suspect. Specifically, with access to large numbers of mugshot and ID photos, law enforcement has numerous options to choose from when selecting fillers for a lineup. As AFR quickly searches for faces that resemble a probe, law enforcement building lineups can submit a photo of the suspect into their AFR system, and similar looking faces will get returned.

Use of AFR for Filler Selection

As AFR software provides a similarity rating for each returned face, operators can find fillers who are at a specific level of similarity to a suspect. As such, a law enforcement officer can upload a photo of a suspect and search some database of images (e.g., database of mugshot images) to locate fillers within a certain range of similarity to that suspect. By manipulating the threshold value to return a match, they can locate fillers of lower and higher absolute similarity. For instance, if an officer is interested in locating fillers who are very high in similarity to a suspect, they could set the threshold value near the high end of the AFR system's similarity range (e.g., set the threshold value to 70 out of a range from 0 to 100). By doing so, only fillers who share a high amount of similarity to the suspect will be returned. On the other hand, if the officer is interested in locating fillers who are low in similarity to a suspect, they could set the threshold value nearing the lowest possible value in the systems similarity range (e.g., set the threshold value to 10); which will return fillers sharing only modest levels of similarity to the suspect.

As such, locating fillers using AFR technology follows the match-to-suspect filler selection strategy. Importantly, I previously discussed three major issues researchers have with the match-to-suspect strategy. First, no optimal level of similarity has been identified (i.e., how similar is similar enough?). Second, because no optimal level of similarity has been identified, fillers may end up being excessively similar to the suspect, which could lead to reductions in culprit identifications. Third, because the suspect and fillers are placed in the lineup based on different criteria—the suspect is placed in the lineup because they fit the eyewitness' description of the culprit while the fillers are placed in the lineup because they resemble the suspect—this may lead to increased false identifications. Though, by choosing fillers based on AFR similarity ratings, the first two issues should no longer exist. Specifically, by using a system that can assess objective similarity, an optimal similarity level can be identified and as such, excessive similarity is no longer an issue. The third issue remains when using AFR to select suspect-matched fillers, however, fillers should not be selected only using AFR, but also in conjunction with the match-to-description method. If a suspect becomes such based on their match to the description of the perpetrator provided by the eyewitness, then the fillers selected should also match that description.

Notably, the research examining and comparing different AFR similarity ranges has only just started (e.g., Thompson, 2023), and as such, there is not currently a similarity range which can be considered optimal. However, as AFR continues to expand into more law enforcement departments, it will become necessary for researchers to provide guidance for filler selection using AFR.

AFR and the Use of Disguises

With police use of AFR for lead generation, one issue that may prove prominent is the use of disguises by criminals. Not surprisingly, facial recognition works best with a high-quality image, where the target person is facing the camera head on, and when the target person is not wearing anything that covers or alters their face. Khan et al. (2022) notes that the accuracy of an AFR system is greatly affected by intentional or unintentional facial disguises. Specifically, the use of accessories such as glasses, hats, scarfs, masks, or imitation beards obscures facial features resulting in inaccurate classification by AFR systems (Khan et al., 2022; Singh et al., 2022). For example, research from the National Institute of Standards and Technology tested the performance of 152 facial recognition algorithms and found that all perform worse when the probe is masked (Ngan et al., 2020). With unmasked probes, the most accurate algorithms failed to identify about 0.3% of persons, with masked probes, this failure rate rose to approximately 5%. Further, while false positive matches were reduced when the probe image was wearing a mask, this effect was modest. Auspiciously, though, the performance of face recognition with face masks at the time of testing was comparable to the state-of-the-art performance of face recognition on unmasked images just three years earlier (Ngan et al., 2020).

Nonetheless, researchers have begun developing AFR systems invariant to disguise variations.

The research to date examining disguised face recognition has resulted in promising algorithms (Singh et al., 2022). For example, in the 2019 Disguised Faces in the Wild competition (Singh et al., 2019), for the category of obfuscation, the most accurate algorithm achieved over 98% true positive rates at 0.1% and 0.01% false positive rates. While encouraging, research on disguised face recognition has tended to focus on high resolution images. When images are used for facial identification in law enforcement contexts, the images are frequently low in resolution as they are often gleaned from surveillance footage. In one recent study, Singh et al. (2022) examined a framework to be used with low resolution disguised faces. They tested this framework on three levels of low-resolution images and found promising results for two of the three levels, however, accuracy dropped significantly when testing the lowest resolution level. The authors noted that more dedicated research is needed to improve accuracy on disguised face recognition with low resolution images. Consequently, until more research is available exploring these effects, law enforcement will need to use caution when using AFR for identification of a disguised face from surveillance footage, or any image with low resolution.

Privacy Issues Related to Police Use of AFR

Although AFR is just one of many biometric surveillance technologies that is in ascendency, it appears to be the one that has most captured the public's interest. Biometric facial data represents the core of individual identity; unlike fingerprints, iris, or DNA, it is a clear marker that allows for quick outward identification by the human eye (Chan, 2021; Office of the Privacy Commissioner of Canada, 2022). As a result, the idea of police agencies using this data for law enforcement purposes has raised privacy, civil liberties, and civil rights concerns among governments, policy makers, academics, and the public.

While the police can use AFR in many ways and for many purposes, the risks to privacy are not the same for all police applications. For instance, a police officer comparing someone who has been arrested against a database of mugshot photos in order to establish their identity, would likely not raise serious privacy concerns. However, if the police officer then compares this person against a database of driver's license photos, privacy concerns may arise. Specifically, a founding principle of privacy law is that information collected for one purpose, should only be used for that purpose, unless informed consent is explicitly obtained (Office of the Privacy Commissioner of Canada, 2019; US Department of Health, Education,

& Welfare, 1973). Therefore, using driver's license photos as a means to search for and identify criminals may infringe on people's right to privacy.

Another high-risk police use of AFR is real-time facial recognition where police apply continuous facial recognition searches on footage from live surveillance. As a fundamental human right, individuals have the freedom to live and develop free from surveillance. In the American constitution, the First Amendment protects people's right to peaceably assemble, to petition the government for a redress of grievances, and to express themselves anonymously, while the Fourth Amendment protects people from unreasonable searches and seizures. Similarly, section 7 of the Canadian Charter of Rights and Freedoms protects the right to life, liberty, and security of the person, while section 8 protects against unreasonable search and seizures. Although some intrusion on these rights can be justified when unique circumstances arise, individuals do not waive their right to privacy simply by participating in the world in ways which expose their face to others or enable their image to be captured on camera (Office of the Privacy Commissioner of Canada, 2022). If people fear their identity is being captured, the use of facial recognition can have a "chilling effect" on freedom of assembly.

While there are various other issues related to the use of facial recognition technology, a full discussion of these issues is beyond the scope of this chapter (for a discussion, see Chan, 2021; Smith & Miller, 2019). However, one other issue regarding law enforcement use of AFR that deserves attention is the bias that facial recognition algorithms can exhibit. Specifically, the National Institute of Standards and Technology tested the performance of 189 facial recognition algorithms and found that most exhibit demographic bias (Grother et al., 2019). They found that the facial recognition algorithms falsely identified Black and Asian individuals 10 to 100 times more often than they did white individuals. Further, false identifications were higher in women than in men, making Black women the most vulnerable to misidentification (Grother et al., 2019). With US law enforcement images specifically, Native Americans were falsely identified more often than any other ethnicity.

Notably, privacy risks need to be weighed against the benefits to law enforcement. As discussed earlier, AFR has been used by police agencies to catch violent criminals and fugitives. AFR also has been used by law enforcement to find missing persons, locate people who may pose a risk of harm to themselves or others, and prevent people who may cause harm from entering a specific area (e.g., a person banned from a sporting arena; Chan, 2021; Miller & Smith, 2021). As these benefits are very much real, it is not likely the position of most that police use of AFR should be banned entirely. Instead, the argument is that governments need to develop and implement laws regulating police use of AFR. These laws need to consider privacy and civil rights issues and clearly define the ways in which police can safely use AFR. They further need to mandate rigorous testing of the facial recognition algorithms to ensure accurate and unbiased results.

Conclusions

AFR is a method of biometric identification which can be used by law enforcement. Compared to other forms of biometric identification, AFR has unique benefits which increases its usability and desirability. Specifically, unlike DNA, iris, and fingerprinting, AFR can operate from a distance, does not require physical contact, can be integrated with existing surveillance, and has systems which are commercially available (Mann & Smith, 2017; Zhao et al., 2003). As a result, AFR has become a popular tool for law enforcement. As discussed in this chapter, AFR can be used by law enforcement to collect identification evidence. AFR can be used to identify a suspect from surveillance or any other image quickly and easily. AFR can also be used to build eyewitness identification lineups by swiftly searching through mass amounts of mugshot photos, narrowing down the pool of potential fillers. As research has yet to identify the optimal method for selecting fillers, AFR provides an opportunity to standardize and improve the way in which fillers are selected.

References

Armitage, R. (2002). To CCTV or not to CCTV? A review of current research into the effectiveness of CCTV systems in reducing crime. *Narco, Crime and Social Policy Section*, 8.

Baltrusaitis, J. (2022, February 15). Top 10 countries and cities by number of CCTV cameras. Retrieved from www.precisesecurity.com/articles/top-10-countries-by-number-of-cctv-cameras

Burke, D. (2020, February 10). Use of facial recognition technology by police growing in Canada, as privacy laws lag. Retrieved from www.cbc.ca/news/canada/nova-scotia/facial-recognition-police-privacy-laws-1.5452749

Canadian Civil Liberties Association. (n.d.). Facial surveillance protecting your privacy rights from AI. Retrieved from https://ccla.org/our-work/privacy/surveillance-technology/facial-recognition/

Carlson, C.A., Jones, A.R., Whittington, J.E., Lockamyeir, R.F., Carlson, M.A., & Wooten, A.R. (2019). Lineup fairness: Propitious heterogeneity and the diagnostic feature-detection hypothesis. *Cognitive Research: Principles and Implications*, 4(1), 1–16. https://doi.org/10.1186/s41235-019-0172-5

Chan, G.K.Y. (2021). Towards a calibrated trust-based approach to the use of facial recognition technology. *International Journal of Law and Information Technology*, 29(4), 305–331. https://doi.org/10.1093/ijlit/eaab011

Charman, S.D., & Wells, G.L. (2007). Applied lineup theory. In R.C.L. Lindsay, D.F. Ross, M.P. Toglia, & D. Read (Eds.), *The handbook of eyewitness psychology, Vol 2. Memory for people.* (pp. 219–254). Lawrence Erlbaum Associates Publishers.

Choi, T. (2022, July 7). BriefCam video search with limited facial recognition licensed by Canadian police force. Retrieved from www.biometricupdate.com/202206/briefcam-video-search-with-limited-facial-recognition-licensed-by-canadian-police-force

Clark, S.E., Rush, R.A., & Moreland, M.B. (2013). Constructing the lineup: Law, reform, theory, and data. In B. L. Cutler (Ed.), *Reform of eyewitness identification procedures* (pp. 87–112). American Psychological Association.

Cole, S. (2001). *Suspect identities: A history of fingerprinting and criminal identification.* Harvard University Press.

Darling, S., Valentine, T., & Memon, A. (2008). Selection of lineup foils in operational contexts. *Applied Cognitive Psychology, 22*(2), 159–169. https://doi.org/10.1002/acp.1366

Davies, B., Innes, M., & Dawson, A. (2018). An evaluation of South Wales police's use of automated facial recognition. Retrieved from www.statewatch.org/media/documents/news/2018/nov/uk-south-wales-police-facial-recognition-cardiff-uni-eval-11-18.pdf

Directorate-General for Migration and Home Affairs. (2021). *Boosting police cooperation across borders for enhanced security.* European Commission, Migration and Home Affairs. https://home-affairs.ec.europa.eu/news/boosting-police-cooperation-across-borders-enhanced-security-2021-12-08_en

Evison, M.P. (2014). Forensic facial analysis. In G. Bruinsma, & D. Weisburd (Eds.), *Encyclopedia of Criminology and Criminal Justice* (pp. 1713–1739). Springer. https://doi.org/10.1007/978-1-4614-5690-2_170

Farrington, D.P., Gill, M., Waples, S.J., & Argomaniz, J. (2007). The effects of closed-circuit television on crime: Meta-analysis of an English national quasi-experimental multi-site evaluation. *Journal of Experimental Criminology, 3*(1), 21–38. https://doi.org/10.1007/s11292-007-9024-2

Georgetown Law Center on Privacy & Technology. (2016). The Perpetual Lineup. Retrieved from www.perpetuallineup.org.

Goldstein, J., Angeletti, R., Holzbach, M., Konrad, D., & Snijder, M. (2008). *Large-scale biometrics deployment in Europe: Identifying challenges and threats.* European Commission. https://publications.jrc.ec.europa.eu/repository/bitstream/JRC48622/jrc48622.pdf

Grother, P., Ngan, M., & Hanaoka, K. (2019). *Face Recognition Vendor Test (FRVT) part 3: Demographic effects.* National Institute of Standards and Technology, US Department of Commerce. https://nvlpubs.nist.gov/nistpubs/ir/2019/nist.ir.8280.pdf

Home Office. (2018). *Home office biometrics strategy.* https://assets.publishing.service.gov.uk/government/uploads/system/uploads/attachment_data/file/720850/Home_Office_Biometrics_Strategy_-_2018-06-28.pdf

Kayser-Bril, N. (2020, June 18). *At least 11 police forces use face recognition in the EU, AlgorithmWatch reveals.* AlgorithmWatch. https://algorithmwatch.org/en/story/face-recognition-police-europe/

Keoghan, S. (2019, September 11). Sydney in the top 15 cities for surveillance levels. *The Sydney Morning Herald.* Retrieved from www.smh.com.au/national/

nsw/sydney-in-the-top-15-cities-for-surveillance-levels-20190820-p52irf. html#:~:text=The%20number%20of%20CCTV%20cameras,Liverpool%20 and%20Camden%20by%201000.

Khan, M.J., Khan, M.J., Siddiqui, A.M., & Khurshid, K. (2022). An automated and efficient convolutional architecture for disguise-invariant face recognition using noise-based data augmentation and deep transfer learning. *The Visual Computer, 38*(2), 509–523. https://doi.org/10.1007/s00371-020-02031-z

Kroener, I. (2014). *CCTV: A technology under the radar?* Routledge. https://doi.org/10.4324/9781315571089

Law Enforcement Resources. (n.d.). *Next Generation Identification (NGI)*. https://le.fbi.gov/science-and-lab-resources/biometrics-and-fingerprints/biometrics/next-generation-identification-ngi

Legislative Budget and Finance Committee. (2014). *Police consolidation in Pennsylvania*. http://lbfc.legis.state.pa.us/Resources/Documents/Reports/497.pdf

Lindsay, R.C.L., Martin, R., & Webber, L. (1994). Default values in eyewitness descriptions: A problem for the match-to-description lineup foil selection strategy. *Law and Human Behavior, 18*(5), 527–541. https://doi.org/10.1007/BF01499172

Luus, C.A.E., & Wells, G.L. (1991). Eyewitness identification and the selection of distracters for lineups. *Law and Human Behavior, 15*(1), 43–57. https://doi.org/10.1007/BF01044829

Mann, M., & Smith, M. (2017). Automated facial recognition technology: Recent developments and approaches to oversight. *University of New South Wales Law Journal, 40*(1), 121–145.

Meunier, P., Xiao, Q., & Vo, T. (2013). *Biometrics for national security: The case for a whole of government approach*. Defence R&D Canada—Centre for Security Science. https://cradpdf.drdc-rddc.gc.ca/PDFS/unc124/p537494_A1b.pdf

Miller, S., & Smith, M. (2021). Ethics, public health and technology responses to COVID-19. *Bioethics, 35*(4), 366–371. https://doi.org/10.1111/bioe.12856

Navon, D. (1992). Selection of lineup foils by similarity to the suspect is likely to misfire. *Law and Human Behavior, 16*(5), 575–593. https://doi.org/10.1007/BF01044624

Ngan, M., Grother, P., & Hanaoka, K. (2020). *Ongoing Face Recognition Vendor Test (FRVT) Part 6B: Face recognition accuracy with face masks using post-COVID-19 algorithms*. National Institute of Standards and Technology, US Department of Commerce. https://pages.nist.gov/frvt/reports/facemask/frvt_facemask_report_6b.pdf

Office of the Privacy Commissioner of Canada. (2019, August). The Privacy Act in brief. Retrieved from www.priv.gc.ca/en/privacy-topics/privacy-laws-in-canada/the-privacy-act/pa_brief/

Office of the Privacy Commissioner of Canada. (2022, May). Privacy guidance on facial recognition for police agencies. Retrieved from www.priv.gc.ca/en/privacy-topics/surveillance/police-and-public-safety/gd_fr_202205/#toc3-2-1

O'Toole, A., & Phillips, P.J. (2015). Evaluating automatic face recognition systems with human benchmarks. In T. Valentine & J.P. Davis (Eds.). *Forensic facial identification: Theory and practice of identification from eyewitnesses, composites and CCTV* (pp. 263–283). Wiley Blackwell.

Parker, J. (2020, July 16). Facial recognition success stories showcase positive use cases of the technology. Retrieved from www.securityindustry.org/2020/07/16/facial-recognition-success-stories-showcase-positive-use-cases-of-the-technology/

Parliament of Australia. (n.d.). Identity-matching Services Bill 2019. Retrieved from www.aph.gov.au/Parliamentary_Business/Bills_Legislation/Bills_Search_Results/Result?bId=r6387

Pennsylvania v. Kusma, 1:20-cr-00046 (M.D. Pennsylvania, 2020). Retrieved from www.pacermonitor.com/public/case/32573363/USA_v_Kusma

People v. Robinson, LEXIS 6461, 2022 WL 15525821 (Mich. Ct. App. 2022).

Piza, E.L., Welsh, B.C., Farrington, D.P., & Thomas, A.L. (2019). CCTV surveillance for crime prevention: A 40-year systematic review with meta-analysis. *Criminology & Public Policy*, 18(1), 135–159. https://doi.org/10.1111/1745-9133.12419

Police Executive Research Forum. (2013). *A national survey of eyewitness identification procedures in law enforcement agencies* (Document No. 242617). Retrieved from www.ncjrs.gov/pdffiles1/nij/grants/242617.pdf

Purshouse, J., & Campbell, L. (2022). Automated facial recognition and policing: A bridge too far? *Legal Studies*, 42(2), 209–227. https://doi.org/10.1017/lst.2021.22

Royal Canadian Mounted Police. (2020, February 27). RCMP use of facial recognition technology. Retrieved from www.rcmp-grc.gc.ca/en/news/2020/rcmp-use-facial-recognition-technology

Singh, M., Chawla, M., Singh, R., Vatsa, M., & Chellappa, R. (2019, October 27–28). *Disguised faces in the wild 2019* [Paper presentation, 542–550]. 2019 IEEE/CVF International Conference on Computer Vision Workshop (ICCVW), Seoul, South Korea. https://doi.org/10.1109/ICCVW.2019.00067

Singh, M., Nagpal, S., Singh, R., & Vatsa, M. (2022). Disguise resilient face verification. *IEEE Transactions on Circuits and Systems for Video Technology*, 32(6), 3895–3905. https://doi.org/10.1109/TCSVT.2021.3120772

Smith, M., & Miller, S.R.M. (2021). The ethical application of biometric facial recognition technology. *AI & Society*, 37(1), 167–175. https://doi.org/10.1007/s00146-021-01199-9

Sporer, S.L. (1996). Psychological aspects of person descriptions. In S.L. Sporer, R.S. Malpass, & G. Koehnken (Eds.), *Psychological issues in eyewitness identification* (p. 53–86). Lawrence Erlbaum Associates Publisher.

Thompson, L.E. (2023). Using automated facial recognition to select fillers for eyewitness identification lineups [Unpublished doctoral dissertation]. Carleton University.

Trevithick, M. (2020). London police officers may have accessed controversial facial recognition technology, force says. *Global News*. https://globalnews.ca/news/6630355/london-police-clearview-ai-facial-recognition/

Tunnicliff, J.L., & Clark, S.E. (2000). Selecting foils for identification lineups: Matching suspects or descriptions? *Law and Human Behavior*, 24(2), 231–258. https://doi.org/10.1023/A:1005463020252

Turk, M., & Pentland, A. (1991). Eigenfaces for recognition. *Journal of Cognitive Neuroscience*, 3(1), 71–86. https://doi.org/10.1162/jocn.1991.3.1.71

US Department of Health, Education, & Welfare. (1973, July). Records, computers, and the rights of citizens (Publication No. (OS)73-94). Retrieved from www.justice.gov/opcl/docs/rec-com-rights.pdf

Wells, G.L., Rydell, S.M., & Seelau, E.P. (1993). The selection of distractors for eyewitness lineups. *Journal of Applied Psychology*, 78(5), 835–844. https://doi.org/10.1037/0021-9010.78.5.835

Wells, G.L., Kovera, M.B., Douglass, A.B., Brewer, N., Meissner, C.A., & Wixted, J.T. (2020). Policy and procedure recommendations for the collection and preservation of eyewitness identification evidence. *Law and Human Behavior*, 44(1), 3–36. https://doi.org/10.1037/lhb0000359

Wixted, J.T., & Wells, G.L. (2017). The relationship between eyewitness confidence and identification accuracy: A new synthesis. *Psychological Science in the Public Interest*, 18(1), 10–65. https://doi.org/10.1177/1529100616686966

Zhao, W., Chellappa, R., Phillips, P., & Rosenfeld, A. (2003). Face recognition: A literature survey. *ACM Computing Surveys*, 35(4), 399–458. https://doi.org/10.1145/954339.954342

4 Advances and Future Prospects in Evolving Face Matching Technologies for Crime Prevention and Investigation

Tia C. Bennett, Harriet M. J. Smith, and Heather D. Flowe

Surveillance systems like closed-circuit television (CCTV) are globally recognized as an essential tool for security and law enforcement. CCTV has been implemented in numerous contexts, from public streets to private homes. Cities in China, India, and Russia, alongside Seoul, Singapore, London, Dhaka, New York, and Los Angeles, are among those best known for the widespread deployment of CCTV (Comparitech, 2023). The images captured by CCTV can be compared for identification against police databases of individuals known to the police, which is an example of forensic face matching. The case for CCTV and forensic face matching technology often rests on public concerns for safety, with public attitudes towards CCTV and CCTV public installation being typically positive (Gill et al., 2007; Spriggs et al., 2005).

A prime example of public safety concerns driving the use of forensic face matching technology is the murder case of James Bulger, a toddler who was abducted from a Liverpool shopping center by two ten-year-old boys in February 1993 (Halliday, 2023). The police secured CCTV footage showing the toddler being led away from his mother by the boys, which led to their arrest. The footage was widely broadcast in the news media and led to national outrage and support for surveillance systems based on their expected public protection benefits (Police Foundation, 2014). After this tragic incident, the UK widely adopted public CCTV systems and channeled substantial funding towards their use in nationwide crime prevention initiatives (Armitage, 2002).

The global implementation of CCTV is not only a testament to the growing recognition of its potential utility in maintaining public safety, but also an illustration of societal willingness to embrace surveillance and forensic face matching technologies as a critical measure in crime prevention and investigation. Well over 4 million CCTV cameras are in use in the UK (BBC News, 2015), and there are at least 70 million security cameras in use in the US (Ivanova, 2019). Several cities in China, including

DOI: 10.4324/9781003323112-5

Beijing and Taiyuan, are ranked the highest per capita in security camera use globally (Keegan, 2020). The rapid increase in popularity for home security cameras (Bridges, 2021; Molla, 2020) further suggests that the public perception of surveillance is generally positive since people are willing to purchase their own personal systems at considerable expense. In the UK, prices start at around £1,000 for a basic four-camera wired system (Checkatrade, 2023), while in the US, similar systems cost between $500–1,600 (Homeguide, 2023). Furthermore, CCTV has permeated our homes more recently in the form of smart doorbells. These devices have made it possible for homeowners to closely monitor their premises, and potentially provide an effective deterrent to potential intruders. Wright and colleagues (2021) investigated users' attitudes towards smart home technology and found that, on average, users reported that they felt positively inclined towards video doorbells. Collectively, it appears that CCTV and other security systems, alongside the use of face matching technology, are generally perceived as beneficial tools in our society.

This chapter presents an overview of the role of surveillance and forensic face matching technology in crime prevention and investigation, with a particular focus on the human and machine elements in the operation of these systems. The chapter will include an overview of psychological theories about the capacity of humans to utilize face matching effectively in criminal contexts, as well as discussions about new and anticipated future developments in automated face recognition systems.

CCTV and Crime Prevention

The use of CCTV for face recognition is an example of situational crime prevention, which is based on rational choice theory (Clarke, 1997). According to this perspective, criminal acts are the result of conscious decisions on the part of would-be criminal offenders who consider the perceived risks and rewards of committing a crime. In this sense, the installation of CCTV systems aims to affect an offender's decision-making process and discourage them from engaging in criminal activities. By intensifying formal surveillance in targeted areas via CCTV, potential offenders are being alerted that engaging in criminal activities within these areas significantly heightens their chances of being apprehended and arrested. Therefore, the use of CCTV should theoretically reduce opportunities for criminal acts.

Although primarily deployed for crime prevention, the use of CCTV surveillance can also facilitate crime reduction through other mechanisms, such as by increasing offender apprehension, raising public awareness about crime, and improving emergency responses (Piza et al., 2019). CCTV can also lead to an increase in reported crime. It can detect previously unreported offenses, or inadvertently make citizens more vulnerable to criminal victimization by creating a false sense of security, causing the public to lower their guard against crime.

Numerous studies have been conducted to ascertain whether CCTV can prevent crime. A recent metanalysis of this literature (n = 80 studies) from nine countries found that CCTV has a noteworthy, albeit modest, impact on reducing crime, especially in the domains of vehicle and property crime, but also drug crime, and its effectiveness is enhanced when the systems are actively rather than passively monitored (Piza et al., 2019). Piza et al. (2019) conducted pooled analyses across 76 studies, revealing overall that crime decreased by around 13% in areas with CCTV compared to areas with no CCTV.

Beyond acting as a crime prevention tool, the footage from CCTV surveillance is also routinely used as an investigation tool. CCTV footage can provide the police with photographic evidence of the perpetrator and crime. Therefore, such evidence is used in criminal investigations.

For example:

- In the April 2013 Boston Marathon bombings case involving two brothers (Tamerlan and Dzhokhar Tsarnaev), the crucial role of CCTV and surveillance tools in public safety and criminal investigation was brought to the fore. The two suspects, initially identified as "Black Hat" and "White Hat" from grainy footage, were spotted amongst the marathon spectators before and after they allegedly planted the bombs that killed three people and injured over 200. The images led to their swift identification and subsequent capture (Klausen, 2021).
- In June 2020, in Detroit, Michigan, Robert Julian-Borchak Williams was erroneously arrested due to a misidentification by facial recognition technology. The system incorrectly matched Williams, who is a Black man, with a CCTV recording of another individual involved in a theft. This case highlights the persisting issue of racial bias within facial recognition technology, particularly concerning the Black and East Asian communities (Hill, 2020).
- In March 2021, in London, UK, Sarah Everard, a 33-year-old woman, was kidnapped by off-duty police officer Wayne Couzens, who raped and murdered her. By analyzing thousands of hours of CCTV footage analysis obtained from a range of sources, from home to car dashboard systems, detectives reconstructed Everard's final moments and traced Couzens's movements. Key evidence that led to the capture and conviction of Couzens emerged from a bus's CCTV, which linked Everard to a car hired by Couzens (Coles & Hayes, 2021).

As the foregoing examples illustrate, CCTV footage can play a key role in apprehending criminal suspects. For example, two thirds of crimes reported to the British Transport Police are followed up for further investigation, and this is largely due to the presence of CCTV evidence available with around 150,000 CCTV cameras across the rail network (HMICFRS, 2022). However, it is important to keep in mind that the identification of criminal suspects from CCTV footage can be erroneous, as the Williams case cited above illustrates.

In the next section, we provide an overview the different approaches that are used in the analysis of CCTV footage to apprehend criminal suspects and discuss some of the advantages and limitations of using this technology for face recognition.

Recognizing Perpetrators in CCTV Footage

There are multiple ways in which perpetrators are recognized using CCTV footage. Firstly, CCTV images may be released to the public with an appeal for individuals to contact the authorities if they recognize the individual captured on CCTV. During the 2011 London Riots, for example, the Metropolitan Police searched through approximately 200,000 hours of CCTV footage to identify suspects, and these suspect images were published (BBC News, 2011). Many suspects from these CCTV images were identified using face matching techniques like those discussed later in the chapter (Venkataramanan, 2015).

In releasing CCTV evidence to the public, the police are hoping that a family member, friend, colleague, or acquaintance of the perpetrator can identify and report them to the authorities (Bobak, Hancock, et al., 2016). The task of matching an image to a "known" individual is called *one-to-one familiar face matching* in research parlance. It is well-established that people are typically good at familiar face matching. People can match different images of the same person with a high degree of accuracy if they are familiar with the face, even if the quality of the to-be-matched image is degraded, or if portions of the face are occluded by eyeglasses or another type of accessory (Bruce et al., 2001; Burton, 2013; Burton et al., 1999; Young & Burton, 2017).

Police officers also use forensic face matching to compare a CCTV image to custody mugshot images in an attempt to identify suspects. Crucially, while CCTV images tend to be low quality with faces captured from above (i.e., non-frontal viewing angles) and under poor lighting conditions (Burton et al., 1999; Mileva & Burton, 2019), mugshots are of much higher quality. Greater differences between to-be-compared images are associated with significant reductions in face matching accuracy (e.g., Estudillo & Bindemann, 2014; Megreya et al., 2013; Noyes & Jenkins, 2017).

The process of matching a CCTV image with a custody image for an unknown perpetrator is an example of one-to-one unfamiliar face matching.

Unlike familiar face matching, people are not as accurate when matching two images that depict the same unfamiliar person, even with good image quality. Furthermore, errors, which are typically around 20%, are exacerbated when the image quality is poor due to quality, lighting, or viewpoint (Bruce et al., 1999, 2001; Henderson et al., 2001; Johnston & Edmonds, 2009) or in circumstances where the person who is deciding whether the faces match is of a different race than the persons portrayed in the to-be-matched images (Phillips et al., 2011).

Forensic face matching using CCTV evidence is also carried out by jurors in court. That is, once a suspect has been charged, a court jury may be asked to decide whether the suspect on trial matches the individual shown in the CCTV footage. In this instance, it is recommended that a photograph taken close to the time of the incident should also be available for the jury to make a comparison (Attorney General's Reference [No. 2 of 2002], 2003).

Finally, CCTV systems may be enhanced by machine algorithms that offer sophisticated automated surveillance and forensic face matching capabilities (see below). In the context of forensic face matching, an algorithm refers to a complex computational process, or set of rules, used by a machine to detect and recognize entities like people, vehicles, or specific items, such as weapons, within video frames (see Noyes & Hill, 2021). Motion detection algorithms focus on dynamic parts of the footage, alerting operators to unusual activities. Facial recognition adds another layer of security by verifying identities or tracking individuals across different camera views. More advanced behavior analysis can discern suspicious or erratic activities. License plate recognition allows for vehicle tracking and automatic enforcement of parking regulations.

In the sections that follow, our focus is primarily on the psychology behind human face matching performance. We will provide an overview of some of the key studies on this topic to explore how our cognitive and perceptual processes affect our ability to match faces. This exploration will also extend to a review of the innovative systems that are being developed to enhance forensic face matching capability.

Challenges of Establishing Identity

The use of CCTV images as evidence requires accurate matching decisions. However, there are fundamental challenges associated with this process that extend beyond poor image quality (Bruce & Young, 2012), as discussed next.

Our ability as humans to verify the identity of unfamiliar people from photographs can be error prone. In a ground-breaking study, Bruce et al. (1999) showed that, even when image quality is high, and viewpoint and expression of the to-be-matched images are the same, the error rate was 30% in a face matching task that required participants to decide whether a person shown in a video-image was present in an array of 10 face images. This type of task is known as a one-to-many matching task. Other researchers report similar levels of accuracy for one-to-many matching of high-quality images (Davis & Valentine, 2009; Henderson et al., 2001). Errors increase in line with greater discrepancies between the comparison image and the images in an array in terms of facial expression (Bruce et al., 1999), image quality (Henderson et al., 2001), or time of image capture (Davis & Valentine, 2009).

Underpinning human errors in face matching is the unpredictable nature of within-person and between-person variability and the difficulty of deciding to which category to attribute image differences (Fysh & Bindemann, 2017). The same person can look very different across different facial expressions, lighting conditions, and poses, and variations across images of the same person are compounded by ageing. Further, the extent to which people's appearance differs across images varies. That is, within-person variability is idiosyncratic and difficult to predict (Bindemann & Burton, 2021; Burton et al., 2016; Jenkins et al., 2011). While it is obvious to say that faces are unique and differ across people (between-person variability), individuals can exhibit coincidental similarity in facial appearance, which complicates the matching decision even more.

Context effects are likely to further cloud judgments and have been observed in a range of forensic settings. For example, if fingerprint analysts are misleadingly told that it is unlikely that two fingerprints were of the same person, they unsuspectingly provide contradictory "no match" judgements when previous positive identifications had been made without such contextual information (Dror et al., 2006). Similar effects occur in face matching. Studies have manipulated mismatch prevalence, finding that less frequent mismatches influence bias in favor of participants responding that the faces they are being shown are of the same person (Papesh & Goldinger, 2014; Stephens et al., 2017; Weatherford et al., 2020).

Of course, this is most obviously relevant when face matching is conducted at border control or when police are checking personal documents such as photo ID. However, context effects and bias should not be disregarded when considering CCTV identifications. Expectations about the likelihood of matches are very likely to influence responses in a similar way and further research should be conducted to explore the effect on performance, particularly when an image needs to be matched to another image in an array.

Since Bruce et al.'s (1999) surprising findings, scores of face matching studies have been conducted. Much of the more recent research has focused on one-to-one tasks, where two images are presented to participants, and they must decide whether the images feature the same person or different people. For example, the mismatch prevalence literature has exclusively used a one-to-one methodology. This approach allows for higher levels of control and a more in-depth consideration of the cognitive processes informing matching decisions.

The one-to-one task has clear parallels in applied settings, such as identity verification/authentication in security contexts (e.g., passport control, issuing of passports) and controlling access to age-restricted goods and services. The one-to-many matching task is also relevant to the use of CCTV images as evidence, particularly (as we explain below) when comparing human and machine performance in face identification or recognition (O'Toole et al., 2007; Phillips et al., 2018) and exploring how best to combine machine and human judgements to reach a final decision about a person's identity.

Individual Differences

Face perception and recognition performance varies widely across individuals (Tardif et al., 2019; for reviews see Bate et al., 2021; Noyes et al., 2018), with "super-recognizers" (Russell et al., 2009), see Chapter 11, demonstrating extremely high levels of accuracy in face recognition and consistently outperforming typical recognizers on memory and perception tests using familiar, learned, and unfamiliar faces (Russell et al., 2012).

Some police forces already deploy super-recognizers to identification-critical roles in an attempt to mitigate the danger associated with inherently error-prone human performance (Davis et al., 2016; Robertson et al., 2016). The potential value of this approach in the context of CCTV identifications is evident when considering the effect on practice and case outcomes.

For example, 20 individuals in the London Metropolitan Police were found to outperform typical recognizers on a range of face identification tests. Davis et al. (2016) and Robertson et al. (2016) were reported to have made over 600 positive identifications of London rioters in 2011 (Manzoor, 2016) by matching CCTV images to mugshots. Over two-thirds of the suspects identified were convicted once additional evidence had been secured. Following this, a full-time New Scotland Yard Super-Recognition Unit was established in May 2015 with the media reporting MET statistics that suggest associated increases in identification rates, prosecutions, and convictions (Davis, 2020; Keefe, 2016).

However, correctly classifying individuals as super-recognizers suitable for deployment is currently challenging. At present, there is a lack of evidence that lab results translate well to real-world applied settings (see Ramon et al., 2019) and an absence of standardized face matching tests that have been rigorously validated with clear statistical cut-offs for distinguishing typical from super-recognizers (Bate et al., 2021; Young & Noyes, 2019). Ideally, such tests would be informed by knowledge about whether typical and super-recognizers differ from each other in a quantitative or qualitative way, but the limited existing literature on this topic provides mixed evidence (Bate et al., 2021; Noyes et al., 2018). Nevertheless, the existence of high-performing face recognizers is not in doubt, and nor is the potential impact super-recognizers can have on policing and conviction rates. Further research addressing the issues outlined above will have important implications for personnel selection and practice.

Improvements through Training?

The current literature suggests that the scope for improving face identification through training is limited. Perhaps surprisingly, experience appears to have little or no bearing on face matching accuracy. Indeed, White et al. (2014) showed that face matching error rates are stable across passport issuing officers and the general population. While some officers performed better than others, this was accounted for by individual differences rather than length of service or training.

Evaluations of a range of professional facial image comparison training courses designed for police forces in the US, Australia, UK, and Netherlands reveal no indication of improvements in practice-relevant tasks (Towler et al., 2019). However, it appears that some types of training do have the potential to deliver improvements. Informed by studies suggesting that accurate unfamiliar face matching relies less on holistic processing than familiar face matching (Ramon, 2015) or face memory (Longmore et al., 2008), Towler et al. (2017) encouraged a group of participants to use feature-comparison strategies, and another group to attend to holistic features such as judgements of personality traits. Improvements in accuracy were greatest for the group using feature-based comparison. Featural comparison is consistent with image comparison strategies used by high-performing professional facial examiners, who undertake rigorous morphological analysis (see Moreton et al., 2021).

Unlike facial reviewers (i.e., those conducting rapid face-matching decisions in professional settings), facial examiners do outperform control groups (see meta-analysis by White et al., 2021). However, some features are more important than others; facial examiners' similarity ratings of ear and facial marks are most predictive of accurate "same" or "different" decisions (Towler et al., 2017). This further underlines the different routes to accurate face memory and matching, with memory studies suggesting that eyes are most diagnostic of identity (Vinette et al., 2004). Towler et al. (2021) showed that it is possible to improve face matching performance of novices by using an expert knowledge elicitation technique and training them to focus on ear and facial marks in a similar way to facial examiners.

Based on these findings, it might be tempting to hypothesize that super-recognizers employ feature-based comparison strategies, which accounts for their better face identification performance. However, this hypothesis is not supported by the literature. On the contrary, some studies have observed super-recognizers exhibiting a heightened inversion effect (Russell et al., 2009), and greater reliance on holistic processing than typical recognizers (Bobak, Bennetts et al., 2016). Belanova et al. (2019) tested some super-recognizers exhibiting enhanced holistic processing while others exhibited the opposite pattern of performance.

It is important to note that variation in performance associated with training pale in comparison to variation in performance across individuals. Observed improvements in accuracy following successful training do not exceed 10% (Towler et al., 2017, 2021). In contrast, White et al. (2014) reported wide ranging performance variation across passport issuing officers, with some performing below 70% accuracy and others at 100% accuracy. This range is consistent with other studies, and performance tends to be stable across repeated sessions of testing (e.g., Burton et al., 2010). This means that while some small improvements in face matching performance may be possible through training, typical recognizers cannot attain super-recognizer levels of accuracy. In the first instance, personnel selection is the most effective way of reducing face matching errors in practice. That said, once the best-performing individuals have been selected, it may be possible to train super-recognizers in order to fully optimize human performance. We explore this possibility below (see section on interactivity).

Interactive Procedures

There are various ways of reducing unfamiliar face matching errors to improve identification from CCTV. We have considered ways of harnessing individual differences, algorithms, and training. The optimal solution is likely to involve using technology in a way that facilitates improvements to several approaches that can be combined. One such innovation is interactive face matching. The interactive system has been shown to improve lineup performance (Colloff et al., 2021, 2022; see also Chapter 3, this volume) and has also shown great promise in improving face matching (Smith et al., 2021). It enables the user to interact with a facial image, fluidly maneuvering it to different viewpoints on a fixed axis to support comparisons. The procedure would be easy to implement in practice: Interactive faces can be rendered from videos of faces moving from side to side, like those of suspects recorded in England and Wales (Home Office, 2017). Police forces already have access to growing databases of such videos.

Smith et al. (2021) show that the interactive procedure improves accuracy for typical as well as face super-recognizers, who possess exceptional face identification skills, see Chapter 11. We are not aware of any other innovation that boosts super-recognizers' performance. Although the procedure has only been tested so far using a one-to-one methodology, results from lineup studies (Colloff et al., 2021, 2022) where there are multiple faces to choose from suggest that it would also benefit users attempting to match a comparison image to a single image in an array. In this way, the interactive procedure could be integrated into an identification process involving candidate lists generated by algorithms.

The interactive procedure is a theoretically driven innovation. First, it is designed to allow the user to overcome the problem of viewpoint dependence. Matching performance suffers when the viewpoints of the face images to be compared differ, but if a face is unfamiliar, the viewer has no knowledge about how appearance might vary across viewpoints. The interactive system allows the user to match images for viewpoint, thereby reducing within-person variability (i.e., the extent to which images of the same person look different), and thus overcoming a source of error in face processing (Jenkins et al., 2011). Second, it should confer some of the benefits of familiar face processing by facilitating the building of a 3D view-independent representation through fluid movement (Pike et al., 1997).

Despite theory informing the interactive design, little is known about the behavior and relative contribution of cognitive mechanisms which account for its performance advantage. We plan to thoroughly test the system to provide a full understanding of its potential applications and limitations. As part of this program of research, we will explore the feasibility of using training to optimize the use of the interactive system. Once we have identified characteristics of accurate performance, we will use prompts to encourage this behavior, implementing manipulation checks and measuring performance pre- and post-training (Towler et al., 2019) in line with an expert knowledge elicitation approach (Biederman & Shiffrar, 1987; Williams et al., 2002).

Automated Face Recognition

Automated face recognition systems, such as Automated Border Control electronic gates (E-gates) at border control points, are critical in security and policing, and support identity verification processes in numerous contexts. These systems compare live images of individuals with their respective passport photos and against a watchlist database (i.e., individuals who are suspected of crimes by law enforcement or court-involved). These systems match biometric patterns to determine the likelihood that two images are of the same person. Another example of this technology in forensic settings include its use to examine whether individuals captured next to President Vladimir Putin in publicity photos circulated by the Russian government are not military personnel or public sector workers in support of Putin, as they are claimed to be, but rather actors posing in these roles (Smith, 2022).

These systems have grown increasingly prevalent—owing to major advances in the technology of algorithms—and promise faster and more accurate forensic face matching decisions when compared to human performance alone. Moreover, whereas machines do not fatigue, human operators do when they analyze images over extended periods of time, which in turn decreases the accuracy of performance (Fysh & Bindemann, 2017). Therefore, it is simply not feasible to rely solely on humans to make matching decisions, especially considering that the police nowadays have large volumes of digital information to sift through, owing to the proliferation of CCTV systems, camera phones, and social media.

Face matching algorithms typically involve multiple stages of processing, including face detection, feature extraction, and finally, the comparison or matching process. Algorithms analyze a captured image or video to locate human faces, then extract distinct characteristics from the face, such as the distance between the eyes or the shape of the chin, to create a unique "faceprint." This faceprint is then compared against a database of known faces or faceprints. Algorithms are fundamental to artificial intelligence (AI) or machines that either learn from data how or use logic or statistical approaches to perform tasks that normally would require human intelligence.

Most algorithms produce a similarity score to measure how likely images from the database represent the same individual. System designers establish a criterion score, or a similarity threshold value, above which two faces are deemed to be a match or otherwise a nonmatch. The criterion score is established based on operational need. For example, consider an E-gate scenario wherein an international traveler is using a stolen passport. If the danger of mistakenly allowing the person to pass through the gate (i.e., concluding that a passport face image matches the face of the passport holder) is higher than mistakenly concluding that images are not of the same person, then a stricter criterion should be used. As algorithm results can be in error, human operators view the images deemed to be high in similarity to determine whether there has been a match. Algorithms use statistical analysis and machine learning to increase their accuracy over time, making them a powerful tool for identifying individuals in a vast array of images or video data within seconds. However, the identification task becomes increasing difficult for human operators of these systems when high similarity matches are returned (White et al., 2015).

Early databases contained face images captured in frontal pose (Phillips et al., 2000), whereas today's databases include faces captured under varied illumination conditions and in 3D (Phillips et al., 2005), as well as images of faces captured "in the wild" (i.e., under naturalistic conditions; Huang et al., 2008). In the UK, comprehensive digital facial databases have been established, which may be used for face identification or verification purposes. Police forces routinely capture photographs of individuals charged with offenses. Images of innocent individuals have been retained by some police forces, despite this practice being deemed unlawful. These facial images are not only held by local forces but are also searchable on the Police National Database. Furthermore, databases containing passport and driver's license images are accessible to government departments and police forces upon request. Compared to the United States, the UK police have access to proportionally fewer facial images. According to a report from Georgetown Law's Center on Privacy and Technology (Garvie et al., 2016), approximately 117 million adults or almost half of all Americans are included in databases that can be scanned by the police. These databases often contain images from non-criminal sources such as passports, visa applications, and driving licenses. In some US cities, police departments are known to compare suspect images with those obtained by Clearview AI, a controversial company that scrapes images from social media platforms without users' permission.

One of the most intriguing aspects of face detection technology is its integration into "smart" CCTV systems for live facial recognition. This allows for the discreet operation of facial recognition algorithms within existing CCTV networks, without requiring the consent of those being monitored. These covert surveillance systems are employed in supermarkets, casinos, large events like music festivals, and in airports to detect individuals who are on watchlists, or to make predictions about where crime is likely to occur, known as predictive policing. Proponents argue that this is a "game-changing" approach to crime-fighting, providing a focused method to identify suspects; however, the use of live facial recognition has sparked significant controversy.

Considerable human rights and rule of law concerns have been raised about these systems (House of Lords, 2022). Advances in this technology are expected and may improve the accuracy of live facial recognition systems over time. Nevertheless, live facial recognition systems can be considered as a form of mass surveillance and create the potential for false matches and wrongful accusations and the ability of the government to track the movements of people. Algorithms play a critical role in the accuracy of systems, but they are not errorfree, and often how these systems work is considered proprietary, and therefore, not disclosed and subjected to independent ethics oversight, or independent testing to verify claims that companies make about accuracy (House of Lords, 2022). Further, race, sex, and age biases have been known to affect the performance of systems (as well as humans, see Flowe, 2012; Ward et al., 2012).

Biases also can influence the surveillance process. Norris and Armstrong (1999) found during an observational study of CCTV control room operators that 90% of targets were male, young and from ethnic minorities, with the homeless, vagrants and alcoholics a secondary target. Similar potentially discriminatory targeting has been found in Oslo and Copenhagen (Sætnan et al., 2004). Nevertheless, recent UK local authority guidelines have specifically highlighted the negative connotations and in a later examination of three London control rooms in 2002, almost 50% of targets were believed to be over 30-years of age and there was no evidence of monitoring based on ethnicity (McCahill & Norris, 2003).

In response to the growing controversy surrounding live facial recognition, particularly biometric systems that can place people under police suspicion, the UK College of Policing issued national guidance for police forces in 2022 (College of Policing, 2022). The guidance emphasizes the targeted and intelligence-based use of these systems within specific timeframes. Databases used for live facial recognition must meet certain criteria of proportionality and necessity, and the public should be informed about when and where live facial recognition is being deployed. However, the UK's response to live facial recognition-related concerns has been relatively limited compared to some US cities, where moratoriums have been placed on facial recognition technology owing to concerns about civil rights, civil liberties, and racial injustice (see House of Lords, 2022).

Human versus Machine Performance

Studies comparing human and computer face recognition ability have been conducted. For instance, in a test of early systems, Burton et al. (2001) directly compared a principal components analysis (PCA) based systems with the performance of humans participating in the Bruce et al. (1999) face matching studies. With PCA, systems are trained without any feedback with respect to face identity. In that experiment, a high-quality close-up full-face video still was simultaneously presented alongside target present arrays of 10 high quality photographs. Whereas humans failed to correctly identify 24% of targets from the series of 20 arrays, the error rate with the most successful PCA technique was only 6%. In a second study, pose was changed (three-quarters) in the video still. In this condition, humans made slightly more errors than in the first unchanged-pose study (29%). However, using the best PCA-based system, the error rate was far higher (40%), suggesting these systems are most effective when photographic viewpoint is matched.

Tests of later and more advanced algorithms demonstrate significantly improved machine performance, particularly when different algorithms are combined through fusion, which is based on the notion that the "wisdom of the crowds" leads to enhanced performance (see Noyes & Hill, 2021 for an overview of this research).

Human Matching Compared to Machine Performance

While there is no simple solution to the problem of error-prone face matching by humans, involving automatic face recognition systems and algorithms in the identification process presents a highly promising approach. Consider a situation where the police need to identify a person captured by CCTV. An algorithm can be used to compare this image against mugshots in a database, quickly returning a pre-determined number of the most-similar looking individuals. A police officer would then review this "candidate list" and decide whether the person in question appeared or not. Recent advances in computer science have led to the use of deep convolutional neural networks, which can be trained on varied image sets and so can tolerate a range of image scenarios including pose (Zhang et al., 2016) and illumination variation (Phillips et al., 2018).

In lab-based tests, algorithms match the performance of some of the best humans (Phillips et al., 2018), while results obtained in practice reveal more limited tolerance of machines for lower-quality images and faces partially occluded by clothing or accessories as well as discrepancies between human and machine decisions on "true matches" (Davies et al., 2018). Nevertheless, algorithms are vastly superior to humans in terms of the number of images they can search, and the speed at which they can compile candidate lists (see Noyes & Hill, 2021). As such they are a valuable tool in assisting human decision-making during investigations (Davies et al., 2018).

At the current time, the most accurate possible results in frontal image matching are obtained by combining decisions from the best-performing algorithms with the best-performing humans (Phillips et al., 2018). This approach may of course need to be revised in light of future advances (see Noyes & Hill, 2021).

Conclusion

This chapter provided an overview of forensic face matching and potential future advances in the domain of face matching technology. As we face the future, forensic face matching will become increasingly common. By 2024, it is estimated that facial recognition capabilities will be present in more than 1.3 billion devices (Juniper Research, 2020). Consequently, the use of automated face recognition systems will become increasingly prevalent in security and law enforcement. At the same time, human intelligence in implementing these systems to ensure civil liberties are safeguarded will be more important than ever before to ensure that these systems facilitate rather than impede human flourishing.

References

Armitage, R. (2002). To CCTV or not to CCTV? A review of current research into the effectiveness of CCTV systems in reducing crime. Retrieved from http://eprints.hud.ac.uk/id/eprint/2542/

Attorney General's Reference [No.2 of 2002] (2003). 1 Cr. App. R. 321, England.

Bate, S., Portch, E., Mestry, N. (2021). When two fields collide: Identifying "super-recognisers" for neuropsychological and forensic face recognition research. *Quarterly Journal of Experimental Psychology*, 74(12), 2154–2164. https://doi.org/10.1177/17470218211027695

BBC News (2011, December 14). London riots: Most wanted suspect CCTV images released. Retrieved from www.bbc.co.uk/news/uk-england-london-16171972

BBC News (2015, January 26). CCTV: Too many cameras useless, warns surveillance watchdog Tony Porter. Retrieved from www.bbc.co.uk/news/uk-30978995

Belanova, E., Davis, J.P. & Thompson, T. (2021). The part-whole effect in super-recognisers and typical-range-ability controls. *Vision Research*, 187, 75–84. https://doi.org/10.1016/j.visres.2021.06.004

Biederman, I. & Shiffrar, M.M. (1987). Sexing day-old chicks: A case study and expert systems analysis of a difficult perceptual-learning task. *Journal of Experimental Psychology: Learning, Memory, and Cognition*, 13(4), 640–645. https://doi.org/10.1037/0278-7393.13.4.640

Bindemann, M., & Burton, A.M. (2021). Steps towards a cognitive theory of unfamiliar face matching. In M. Bindemann (Ed.), *Forensic face matching: Research and practice* (pp. 38–61). Oxford University Press. https://doi.org/10.1093/oso/9780198837749.003.0003

Bobak, A.K., Bennetts, R.J., Parris, B.A., Jansari, A. & Bate, S. (2016). An in-depth cognitive examination of individuals with superior face recognition skills. *Cortex*, 82, 48–62. https://doi.org/10.1016/j.cortex.2016.05.003

Bobak, A.K., Hancock, P.J.B & Bate, S. (2016). Super-recognisers in action: Evidence from face-matching and face memory tasks. *Applied Cognitive Psychology*, 30(1), 81–91. https://doi.org/10.1002/acp.3170

Bridges, L. (2021, May 18). Amazon's Ring is the largest civilian surveillance network the US has ever seen. *The Guardian*. Retrieved from www.theguardian.com/commentisfree/2021/may/18/amazon-ring-largest-civilian-surveillance-network-us

Bruce, V., Henderson, Z., Greenwood, K., Hancock, P.J.B., Burton, A.M., & Miller, P. (1999). Verification of face identities from images captured on video. *Journal of Experimental Psychology: Applied*, 5(4), 339–360. https://doi.org/10.1037/1076-898X.5.4.339

Bruce, V., Henderson, Z., Newman, C. & Burton, A.M. (2001). Matching identities of familiar and unfamiliar faces caught on CCTV images. *Journal of Experimental Psychology: Applied*, 7(3), 207–218. https://doi.org/10.1037/1076-898X.7.3.207

Bruce, V., & Young, A. (2012). *Face Perception*. Psychology Press.
Burton, A.M. (2013). Why has research in face recognition progressed so slowly? The importance of variability. *The Quarterly Journal of Experimental Psychology*, 66(8), 1467–1485. http://doi.org/10.1080/17470218.2013.800125
Burton, A.M., Kramer, R.S.S., Ritchie, K.L., & Jenkins, R. (2016). Identity from variation: Representations of faces derived from multiple instances. *Cognitive Science*, 40(1), 202–223. https://doi.org/10.1111/cogs.12231
Burton, A.M., Miller, P., Bruce, V., Hancock, P.J.B. & Henderson, Z. (2001). Human and automatic face recognition: a comparison across image formats. *Vision Research*, 41(24), 3185–3195. https://doi.org/10.1016/S0042-6989(01)00186-9
Burton, A.M., White, D. & McNeill, A. (2010). The Glasgow Face Matching Test. *Behavior Research Methods*, 42, 286–291. https://doi.org/10.3758/BRM.42.1.286
Burton, A.M., Wilson, S., Cowan, M. & Bruce, V. (1999). Face recognition in poor quality video: Evidence from security surveillance. *Psychological Science*, 10(3), 243–248. https://doi.org/10.1111/1467-9280.00144
Checkatrade (2023, May 29). How much does home CCTV installation cost? Retrieved from www.checkatrade.com/blog/cost-guides/cctv-installation-cost/
Clarke, R.V. (1997). Introduction. In R.V. Clarke (Ed.), *Situational crime prevention: Successful case studies* (2nd ed.) (pp. 1–42). Harrow and Heston.
Coles, A. & Hayes, A. (2021, September 29). Sarah Everard: Images show victim with her killer Wayne Couzens moments before he abducted her, court hears. https://news.sky.com/story/sarah-everard-images-show-victim-with-her-killer-wayne-couzens-moments-before-he-abducted-her-court-told-12421032.
College of Policing (2022). Live facial recognition. Retrieved from www.college.police.uk/app/live-facial-recognition?s=
Colloff, M.F., Flowe, H.D., Smith, H.M.J., Seale-Carlisle, T.M., Meissner, C.A., Rockey, J.C., Pande, B., Kujur, P., Parveen, N., Chandel, P., Singh, M.M., Pradhan, S., & Parganiha, A. (2022). Active exploration of faces in police lineups increases discrimination accuracy. *American Psychologist*, 77(2), 196–220. https://doi.org/10.1037/amp0000832
Colloff, M.F., Seale-Carlisle, T.M., Karoğlu, N., Rockey, J.C., Smith, H.M.J., Smith, L., Maltby, J., Yaremenko, S. & Flowe, H.D. (2021). Perpetrator pose reinstatement during a lineup test increases discrimination accuracy. *Scientific Reports*, 11(1). https://doi.org/10.1038/s41598-021-92509-0
Comparitech (2023, May 23). Surveillance camera statistics: which cities have the most CCTV cameras? Retrieved from www.comparitech.com/vpn-privacy/the-worlds-most-surveilled-cities/
Davies, B., Innes, M., & Dawson, A. (2018). An evaluation of South Wales police's use of automated facial recognition. Retrieved from www.statewatch.org/news/2018/nov/uk-south-wales-police-facial-recognition-cardiff-uni-eval-11-18.pdf
Davis, J.P. (2020). CCTV and the super-recognisers. In C. Stott, B. Bradford, M. Radburn, & L. Savigar-Shaw (Eds.) *Making an impact on policing and crime: Psychological research, policy and practice* (pp. 34–67). Routledge.
Davis, J.P., Lander, K., Evans, R. & Jansari, A. (2016). Investigating predictors of superior face recognition ability in police super-recognisers. *Applied Cognitive Psychology*, 30(6), 827–840. https://doi.org/10.1002/acp.3260

Davis, J.P. & Valentine, T. (2009). CCTV on trial: Matching video images with the defendant in the dock. *Applied Cognitive Psychology*, 23(4), 482–505. https://doi.org/10.1002/acp.1490

Dror, I.E., Charlton, D., & Péron, A.E. (2006). Contextual information renders experts vulnerable to making erroneous identifications. *Forensic Science International*, 156(1), 74–78. https://doi.org/10.1016/j.forsciint.2005.10.017

Estudillo, A.J. & Bindemann, M. (2014). Generalization across view in face memory and face matching. *i-Perception*, 5(7), 589–601. https://doi.org/10.1068/i0669

Flowe, H.D. (2012). Do characteristics of faces that convey trustworthiness and dominance underlie perceptions of criminality? *PLoS ONE*, 7(6), e37253. https://doi.org/10.1371/journal.pone.0037253

Fysh, M.C. & Bindemann, M. (2017). Effects of time pressure and time passage on face matching accuracy. *Royal Society Open Science*, 4(6). https://doi.org/10.1098/rsos.170249

Garvie, C., Bedoya, A. & Frankle, J. (2016). The perpetual lineup. *Georgetown Law Center on Privacy & Technology*. Retrieved from www.perpetuallineup.org.

Gill, M., Bryan, J., & Allen, J. (2007). Public perceptions of CCTV in residential areas: "It is not as good as we thought it would be". *International Criminal Justice Review*, 17(4), 304–324. https://doi.org/10.1177/1057567707311584

Halliday, J. (2023, February 10). "The wounds don't ever heal": 30 years after James Bulger's murder, Bootle cannot forget. *The Guardian*. Retrieved from www.theguardian.com/uk-news/2023/feb/10/30-years-after-james-bulger-murder-strand-bootle-youth-justice

Henderson, Z., Bruce, V., & Burton, A.M. (2001). Matching the faces of robbers captured on video. *Applied Cognitive Psychology*, 15(4), 445–464. https://doi.org/10.1002/acp.718

Hill, K. (2020, June 24). Wrongly accused by an algorithm. *New York Times*. Retrieved from www.nytimes.com/2020/06/24/technology/facial-recognition-arrest.html.

HMICFRS. (2022). An inspection of the service provided to victims of crime by British Transport Police. Retrieved from www.justiceinspectorates.gov.uk/hmicfrs/publication-html/inspection-of-the-service-provided-to-victims-of-crime-by-british-transport-police/

Home Office (2017). Police and Criminal Evidence Act 1984 (PACE) Code D. Retrieved from www.gov.uk/government/publications/pace-code-d-2017

Homeguide (2023, April 5). Security camera installation cost. *Homeguide*. https://homeguide.com/costs/security-camera-installation-cost

House of Lords (2022). Technology rules? The advent of new technologies in the justice system. https://publications.parliament.uk/pa/ld5802/ldselect/ldjusthom/180/180.pdf

Huang, G.B., Ramesh, M., Berg, T., & Learned-Miller, E. (2008). Labeled faces in the wild: A database for studying face recognition in unconstrained environments. Workshop on Faces in "Real-Life" Images: Detection, Alignment, and Recognition. http://vis-www.cs.umass.edu/lfw/lfw.pdf

Ivanova, I. (2019, December 10). Video surveillance in U.S. described as on par with China. *CBS News*. Retrieved from www.cbsnews.com/news/the-u-s-uses-surveillance-cameras-just-as-much-as-china/

Jenkins, R., White, D., Van Monford, X., Burton, A.M. (2011). Variability in photos of the same face. *Cognition*, *121*(3), 313–323. https://doi.org/10.1016/j.cognition.2011.08.001

Johnston, R.A. & Edmonds, A.J. (2009). Familiar and unfamiliar face recognition: A review. *Memory*, *17*(5), 481–607. https://doi.org/10.1080/09658210902976969

Juniper Research (2020, 7 January 7). Facial recognition hardware to feature on over 800M mobiles by 2024, but software will win out. Retrieved from www.juniperresearch.com/press/facial-recognition-hardware-to-feature-on-over-800

Keefe, P.R. (2016, August 15). The detectives who never forget a face. *New Yorker*. Retrieved from www.newyorker.com/magazine/2016/08/22/londons-super-recognizer-police-force

Keegan, M. (2020, August 14). The most surveilled cities in the world. Retrieved from www.usnews.com/news/cities/articles/2020-08-14/the-top-10-most-surveilled-cities-in-the-world

Klausen, J. (2021). The Boston Marathon Bombers. In J. Klausen (Ed.) *Western Jihadism: A thirty year history* (pp. 121–140). Oxford University Press. https://doi.org/10.1093/oso/9780198870791.003.0010

Longmore, C.A., Liu, C.H. & Young, A.W. (2008). Learning faces from photographs. *Journal of Experimental Psychology: Human Perception and Performance*, *34*(1), 77–100. https://doi.org/10.1037/0096-1523.34.1.77

Manzoor, S. (2016, November 5). You look familiar: On patrol with the Met's super-recognisers. *The Guardian*. Retrieved from www.theguardian.com/uk-news/2016/nov/05/metropolitan-police-super-recognisers

McCahill, M., & Norris, C. (2003, June). *Estimating the extent, sophistication and legality of CCTV in London*. [Paper presentation]. Is CCTV Working? Conference 2003, Leicester, UK.

Megreya, A.M., Sandford, A. & Burton, A.M. (2013). Matching face images taken on the same day or months apart: The limitations of photo ID. *Applied Cognitive Psychology*, *27*(6), 700–706. https://doi.org/10.1002/acp.2965

Mileva, M. & Burton, A.M. (2019). Face search in CCTV surveillance. *Cognitive Research: Principles and Implications*, *4*(1), Article 37. https://doi.org/10.1186/s41235-019-0193-0

Molla, R. (2020, January 21). Amazon Ring sales nearly tripled in December despite hacks. *Vox*. Retrieved from www.vox.com/recode/2020/1/21/21070402/amazon-ring-sales-jumpshot-data

Moreton, R., Havard, C., Strathie, A. & Pike, G. (2021). An international survey of applied face-matching training courses. *Forensic Science International*, *327*, 110947. https://doi.org/10.1016/j.forsciint.2021.110947

Norris, C. & Armstrong, G. (1999). CCTV and the social structuring of surveillance. *Crime Prevention Studies*, *10*, 157–178.

Noyes, E., & Hill, M.Q. (2021). Automatic Recognition Systems and Human Computer Interaction in Face Matching. In M. Bindemann (Ed.), *Forensic face matching: Research and practice* (pp. 193–215). Oxford University Press. https://doi.org/10.1093/oso/9780198837749.003.0009.

Noyes, E., Hill, M.Q. & O'Toole, A.J. (2018). Face recognition ability does not predict person identification performance: using individual data in the interpretation of group results. *Cognitive Research: Principles and Implications*, *3*, Article 23. https://doi.org/10.1186/s41235-018-0117-4

Noyes, E. & Jenkins, R. (2017). Camera-to-subject distance affects face configuration and perceived identity. *Cognition*, *165*, 97–104. https://doi.org/10.1016/j.cognition.2017.05.012

O'Toole, A.J., Phillips, P.J., Jiang, F., Ayyad, J., Pénard, N., & Abdi, H. (2007). Face recognition algorithms surpass humans matching faces over changes in illumination. *IEEE Transactions on Pattern Analysis and Machine Intelligence*, *29*(9), 1642–1646. https://doi.org/10.1109/TPAMI.2007.1107.

Papesh, M.H., Goldinger, S.D. (2014). Infrequent identity mismatches are frequently undetected. *Attention, Perception, & Psychophysics*, *76*(5), 1335–1349. https://doi.org/10.3758/s13414-014-0630-6

Phillips, P.J., Flynn, P.J., Scruggs, T., Bowyer, K.W., Chang, J., Hoffman, K., et al. (2005). Overview of the face recognition grand challenge. *IEEE Computer Society Conference on Computer Vision and Pattern Recognition*, 947–954. https://doi.org/10.1109/CVPR.2005.268

Phillips, P.J., Jiang, F., Narvekar, A., Ayyad, J., & O'Toole, A.J. (2011). An other-race effect for face recognition algorithms. *ACM Transactions on Applied Perception (TAP)*, *8*(2), 1–11. https://doi.org/10.1145/1870076.1870082

Phillips, P.J., Moon, H., Rizvi, S.A., & Rauss, P.J. (2000). The FERET evaluation methodology for face-recognition algorithms. *IEEE Transactions on Pattern Analysis and Machine Intelligence*, *22*(10), 1090–1104. https://doi.org/10.1109/34.879790

Phillips, P.J., Yates, A.N., Hu, Y., Hahn, C.A., Noyes, E., Jackson, K., Cavazos, J.G., Jeckeln, G., Ranjan, R., Sankaranarayanan, S., Chen, J., Castillo, C.D., Chellappa, R., White, D. & O'Toole, A.J. (2018). Face recognition accuracy of forensic examiners, superrecognizers, and face recognition algorithms. *Proceedings of the National Academy of Sciences*, *115*(24), 6171–6176. https://doi.org/10.1073/pnas.1721355115

Pike, G.E., Kemp, R.I., Towell, N.A. & Phillips, K.C. (1997). Recognizing moving faces: The relative contribution of motion and perspective view information. *Visual Cognition*, *4*(4), 409–438. https://doi.org/10.1080/713756769

Piza, E.L., Welsh, B.C., Farrington, D.P., & Thomas, A.L. (2019). CCTV surveillance for crime prevention: a 40-year systematic review with meta-analysis. *Criminology & Public Policy*, *18*(1), 135–159. https://doi.org/10.1111/1745-9133.12419

Police Foundation (2014). The briefing: CCTV. Retrieved from www.police-foundation.org.uk/wp-content/uploads/2017/08/cctv.pdf

Ramon, M. (2015). Perception of global facial geometry is modulated through experience. *PeerJ*, *3*, e850. https://doi.org/10.7717/peerj.850

Ramon, M., Bobak, A.K. & White, D. (2019). Towards a "manifesto" for super-recognizer research. *British Journal of Psychology*, *110*(3), 495–498. https://doi.org/10.1111/bjop.12411

Robertson, D.J., Noyes, E., Dowsett, A.J., Jenkins, R., & Burton, A.M. (2016). Face recognition by metropolitan police super-recognisers. *PLoS ONE*, *11*(2), Article e0150036. https://doi.org/10.1371/journal.pone.0150036

Russell, R., Chatterjee, G., & Nakayama, K. (2012). Developmental prosopagnosia and super-recognition: No special role for surface reflectance processing. *Neuropsychologia*, *50*(2), 334–340. https://doi.org/10.1016/j.neuropsychologia.2011.12.004

Russell, R., Duchaine, B., & Nakayama K. (2009). Super-recognizers: People with extraordinary face recognition ability. *Psychonomic Bulletin & Review*, *16*(2), 252–257. https://doi.org/10.3758/PBR.16.2.252

Sætnan, A.R., Lomell, H.M. & Wiecek, C. (2004). Controlling CCTV in public spaces: Is privacy the (only) issue? Reflections on Norwegian and Danish observations. *Surveillance & Society*, *2*(2/3), 396–414. https://doi.org/10.24908/ss.v2i2/3.3385

Smith, H.M.J., Andrews, S., Baguley, T., Colloff, M.F., Davis, J.P., White, D., Rockey, J.C., & Flowe, H.D. (2021). Performance of typical and superior face recognisers on a novel interactive face matching procedure. *British Journal of Psychology*, *112*(4), 964–991. https://doi.org/10.1111/bjop.12499

Smith, O. (2022, January 7). Facial recognition deployed to test whether Putin's supporters are paid Kremlin stooges. Retrieved from www.express.co.uk/news/world/1718204/Vladimir-Putin-supporters-stooges-actors-New-Year-s-Eve-address-BBC-facial-recognition

Spriggs, A., Argomaniz, J., Gill, M., & Bryan, J. (2005). Public attitudes towards CCTV: Results from the pre-intervention public attitude survey carried out in areas implementing CCTV. *Home Office Online Report*. https://library.college.police.uk/docs/hordsolr/rdsolr1005.pdf

Stephens, R.G., Semmler, C., & Sauer, J.D. (2017). The effect of the proportion of mismatching trials and task orientation on the confidence–accuracy relationship in unfamiliar face matching. *Journal of Experimental Psychology: Applied*, *23*(3), 336–353. https://doi.org/10.1037/xap0000130

Tardif, J., Duchesne, X.M., Cohan, S., Royer, J., Blais, C., Fiset, D., Duchaine, B. & Gosselin, F. (2019). Use of face information varies systematically from developmental prosopagnosics to super-recognizers. *Psychological Science*, *30*(2), https://doi.org/10.1177/0956797618811338

Towler, A., Kemp, R.I., Burton, A.M., Dunn, J.D., Wayne, T., Moreton, R. & White, D. (2019). Do professional facial image comparison training courses work? *PLoS One*, *14*(2), e0211037. https://doi.org/10.1371/journal.pone.0211037

Towler, A., Keshwa, M., Ton, B., Kemp, R.I. & White, D. (2021). Diagnostic feature training improves face matching accuracy. *Journal of Experimental Psychology: Learning, Memory, and Cognition*, *47*(8), 1288–1298. https://doi.org/10.1037/xlm0000972

Towler, A., White, D., & Kemp, R.I. (2017). Evaluating the feature comparison strategy for forensic face identification. *Journal of Experimental Psychology: Applied*, *23*(1), 47–57. https://doi.org/10.1037/xap0000108

Venkataramanan, M. (2015). The superpower police now use to tackle crime. *BBC News*. Retrieved from www.bbc.com/future/article/20150611-the-superpower-police-now-use-to-tackle-crime

Vinette, C., Gosselin, F. & Schyns, P.G. (2004). Spatio-temporal dynamics of face recognition in a flash: it's in the eyes. *Cognitive Science, 28*(2), 289–301. https://doi.org/10.1207/s15516709cog2802_8

Ward, C., Flowe, H.D., & Humphries, J.E. (2012). The effects of masculinity and suspect gender on perceptions of guilt. *Applied Cognitive Psychology, 26*(3), 482–488. https://doi.org/10.1002/acp.2823

Weatherford, D.R., Erickson, W.B., Thomas, J., Walker, M.E. & Schein, B. (2020). You shall not pass: how facial variability and feedback affect the detection of low-prevalence fake IDs. *Cognitive Research: Principles and Implications, 5*(1), article 3. https://doi.org/10.1186/s41235-019-0204-1

White, D., Dunn, J.D., Schmid, A.C., & Kemp, R.I. (2015). Error rates in users of automatic face recognition software. *PLoS One, 10*(10), e0139827. https://doi.org/10.1371%2Fjournal.pone.0139827

White, D., Kemp, R.I., Jenkins, R., Matheson, M., & Burton, A.M. (2014). Passport officers' errors in face matching. *PLoS One, 9*(8), e103510. https://doi.org/10.1371%2Fjournal.pone.0103510

White, D., Towler, A., & Kemp, R.I. (2021). Understanding professional expertise in unfamiliar face matching. In M. Bindemann (Ed.), *Forensic face matching: Research and practice* (pp. 62–88). https://doi.org/10.1093/oso/9780198837749.003.0004

Williams, A.M., Ward, P., Knowles, J.M., & Smeeton, N.J. (2002). Anticipation skill in a real-world task: Measurement, training, and transfer in tennis. *Journal of Experimental Psychology: Applied, 8*(4), 259–270. https://doi.org/10.1037/1076-898X.8.4.259

Wright, D., Shank, D.B., & Yarbrough, T. (2021). Outcomes of training in smart home technology adoption: A living laboratory study. *Communication Design Quarterly, 9*(3), 14–26. https://doi.org/10.1145/3468859.3468861

Young, A.W. & Burton, A.M. (2017). Recognizing faces. *Current Directions in Psychological Science, 26*(3), 212–217. https://doi.org/10.1177/0963721416688114

Young, A.W. & Noyes, E. (2019). We need to talk about super-recognizers: Invited commentary on Ramon, M., Bobak, A.K., & White, D. Super-recognizers: From the lab to the world and back again. British Journal of Psychology. *British Journal of Psychology, 110*(3), 492–494. https://doi.org/10.1111/bjop.12395

Zhang, T., Zheng, W., Cui, Z., Zong, Y., Yan, J. & Yan, K. (2016). A deep neural network-driven feature learning method for multi-view facial expression recognition. *IEEE Transactions on Multimedia, 18*(12), 2528–2536. http://dx.doi.org/10.1109/TMM.2016.2598092

5 Insanity Evaluations in the Age of Neuroimaging

Michael J. Vitacco and Savanna Coleman

The insanity defense remains one of the most contentious areas of mental health law. Rooted in Aristotelian ethics, it has long been contented that there are certain circumstances that make an individual who committed an illegal act not responsible for their criminal behavior. Understanding the complex relationship between behavior and mental states has always been a goal of forensic evaluators. Over the last decade, neuroimaging increasingly has been used as part of a comprehensive evaluation for insanity cases. However, the use of neuroimaging may not be as helpful as some claim, and it has more than its share of limitations. This chapter will provide a brief history of the insanity defense, discuss limitations of insanity evaluations, outline neuroimaging findings within the context of insanity evaluations, and provide a review of imaging strengths and limitations that are relevant for insanity evaluations.

Brief History of the Insanity Defense

Consider this from *Nicomachean Ethics*, people who have "ignorance of the circumstances of the act and of the things affected by it, in this case the act is pitied and forgiven, because he who acts in ignorance of any of these circumstances is an involuntary agent" (Aristotle, 1934, 1110b–1111a). Plato wrote of similar circumstances where he discussed a pathway for relief for individuals who engaged in illegal acts when "In a state of madness or when affected by disease ... And if this be made evident to the judges elected to try the cause, on the appeal of the criminal or his advocate, and he be judged to have been in this state when he committed the offence, he shall simply pay for the hurt which he may have done to another" (Plato, 2013, Book IX). In this statement, Plato acknowledged that although there may be a monetary penalty for committing a crime, individuals who acted in a state of "madness" should otherwise be excused for their behavior. There have been other variants of earlier versions of the insanity defense, most notably the Wild Beast Test, which allowed people who had the reasoning of "no more than a wild beast or a brute, or an infant" to be found not responsible for their criminal behavior (see Maeder, 1985).

Modern insanity law is predicated on the case of Daniel M'Naghten. The *M'Naghten* test, was developed in reaction to his acquittal in 1843 for the murder of Edward Drummond, whom M'Naghten allegedly mistook for the prime minister of England (Cornell Law School, 2022). After a very unpopular verdict, the House of Lords created a panel of judges and lawyers to create a new law for insanity. Based on the panel's recommendation, what has come to be known as the *M'Naghten* standard came to fruition. This insanity standard was as follows:

> to establish a defence on the ground of insanity, it must be clearly proved that, at the time of the committing of the act, the party accused was labouring under such a defect of reason, from disease of the mind, as not to know the nature and quality of the act he was doing; or if he did know it, that he did not know he was doing what was wrong.
>
> (*Rex v. M'Naghten*, 1843)

In the United States, 46 states and the Federal government have adopted some form of the *M'Naghten* test, where the inability to differentiate right from wrong resulting from a mental disease or defect forms the crux for a successful insanity defense. Some states have added a second, volitional prong, that a person is not criminally responsible if because of mental disease or defect, they lack sufficient capacity "to conform his [her] conduct to the requirements of the law" (Model Penal Code § 4.01(1)). It should be noted that four states (Idaho, Kansas, Montana, and Utah) do not have a formal insanity defense. Yet, the insanity defense is not frequently used, with estimates of approximately one time in every 1,000 felony cases. When employed, it is estimated that the defense is successful approximately 25% of the time (Packer, 2009).

Beyond its contentiousness, conducting insanity evaluations is frequently complicated and nuanced. These evaluations require the clinician to retrospectively reconstruct an individual's mental state to determine if there was a presence of a mental disease or defect that interfered with the individual's abilities to understand and appreciate their behavior or control their behavior to the requirements of the law. Packer (2009) described best practices when conducting insanity examinations, which included clinical interviewing of the individual's history, review of official documents (e.g., police reports), evaluating toxicology screens, and psychological testing if the evaluator deems it necessary. Within the last 10 years, neuroimaging has been increasingly used in evaluations of insanity, and it is becoming more likely that clinicians will be asked about or exposed to neuroscientific explanations for an individual's behavior (Vitacco et al., 2020). The most frequently used imaging tests in insanity evaluations are magnetic resonance imaging (MRI) and functional MRI (fMRI; Aono et al., 2019).

Neuroscience in Court is Not New, and it is Increasing

Since there have been claims linking the brain with behavior, scientists and lawyers have not been shy about using this type of evidence to convince the trier of fact of a particular position (Gaudet & Marchant, 2016). Attempts at admitting evidence regarding brain function and structure has been tried long before the development of even basic imaging. Consider the idea of phrenology, which involved measurements on the skull, which were then purportedly linked to personality traits and behavior (Weiss, 2007). Now debunked as pseudoscience, it should not be surprising that phrenology was attempted to be introduced in court to excuse behavior. The attempted use of phrenology in court is highlighted by the case of Major Mitchell, a nine-year-old boy who assaulted a classmate over several hours in Durham, Maine in 1834 (see Weiss, 2007). His lawyer, convinced of the strength of this type of evidence, worked diligently to get measurements of the boy's skull introduced to excuse the child's behavior. Ultimately, the judge denied the admissibility of the evidence because phrenology was based on "mere theories" and told the jury to focus on whether the boy understood right from wrong. Ultimately, the child was found guilty and sentenced to eight years of hard labor. Although this was the first time these types of brain-based behavior links were attempted to be introduced in court, it certainly would not be the last.

Consider how neuroscience has been used in some high-profile cases. The first is John Hinckley, Jr., who was administered a CAT scan as part of his evaluation (Kiernan, 1982). Mr. Hinckley was arrested and ultimately found not guilty by reason of insanity for the attempted assassination of then-president Ronald Reagan outside a Washington D.C. hotel on March 30, 1981. As noted in the New York Times, the headline from June 2, 1982 read, "CAT scans said to show shrunken Hinckley brain." To the defense, the CAT scan results were evidence of abnormality, organic brain disease, and permanent neurological damage. The prosecution expert had a dramatically different take, indicating the scan results were "normal" and "no more sign of mental illness than premature balding would be" (*United States v. Hinckley*, 1981).

Also, the case of Charles Whitman had neuroscientific implications. On August 1, 1966, Charles Whitman climbed a clock tower on the campus of the University of Texas and killed 14 people and injured many more (Mclellan, 2001). Earlier in the day, he murdered both his wife and his mother. After Whitman was killed by police gunfire during the incident, many questions were asked about his reasons for committing such an act. An autopsy revealed that a small tumor was pressing on Whitman's amygdala. Whether the tumor was a contributory factor remains unanswered, but speculation continues (Bogerts, 2021; Lavergne, 1997).

The case of Herbert Weinstein has drawn critical attention and became the impetus for a book titled, *The Brain Defense* (Davis, 2017). Weinstein, who was 65 years old at the time of his arrest, reportedly strangled his wife and threw her body off a balcony in their Manhattan home, ostensibly to make her death appear to be a suicide. After his arrest, Weinstein underwent neurological testing and brain imaging, including receiving an MRI where an arachnoid cyst was discovered. It was subsequently argued that he was less culpable for the murder because of this cyst. Partially based on the MRI finding, Weinstein was offered a plea deal and accepted a lesser charge of manslaughter. It was later acknowledged that the prosecutors feared the imaging data would lead to a not guilty verdict, prompting them to make a favorable plea offer. Similar to Whitman, the ultimate impact of the cyst on Weinstein's behavior remains debatable. What is not debatable is the impact this case had on the consideration of neuroimaging in future criminal cases (Rosen, 2007).

Neurolaw is broadly defined as a field of interdisciplinary study that explores the effects of discoveries in neuroscience on legal rules and standards (Petoft, 2015). Neurolaw considers perspectives from multiple fields including neuroscience, psychology, psychiatry, and criminology (Petoft & Abbasi, 2020). Neurolaw centers have been created at academic centers around the world, most notably at Vanderbilt University, Harvard University, and Stanford University, to name but a few. It should not be surprising that similar to increasing use, scholarship devoted to the brain and behavior has evidenced a dramatic increase over the last several years (Shen, 2016). As expected based on its increased attention, the use of neuroscience in courtrooms is also increasing. Greely and Farahany (2018) reviewed cases from 2005 to 2015, finding ever increasing use of neuroscience in criminal cases. There were notable increases in both homicide and non-homicide cases that involved neuroscience, including neuroimaging. Once primarily reserved for mitigation in death penalty cases, the use of neuroscience has greatly expanded and is now seen in competency to proceed, juvenile transfer cases, and insanity evaluations (Aono et al., 2019).

Unreliability of Insanity Defense Evaluations

Specific to the insanity defense, there have been major problems with reliability that have emerged in the scientific literature (Gowensmith et al.,

2012, 2013; Phillips et al., 1988). In situations where more than one evaluator has conducted an insanity evaluation, the results can be contradictory. A study of 66 cases in Alaska from the years 1977 to 1981 found agreement between the evaluators in 76% of the insanity cases (24% disagreement; Phillips et al., 1988). Another study reviewed 483 legal sanity evaluations that addressed 165 cases dated between 2007 and 2008 with notably lower rates of agreement than previous research (Gowensmith et al., 2013). Evaluators unanimously agreed in only 55% of cases and tended to disagree more when the defendant was under the influence of substances at the time of the offense. These results reflect poorer agreement in sanity evaluations when compared with other types of criminal forensic evaluations (Gowensmith et al., 2012). Taken in their totality, these studies have pointed to significant issues with reliability in insanity evaluations. These issues can directly and indirectly undermine the credibility of forensic examiners and undermine the confidence jurors have that they are receiving unbiased information when they are listening to an examiner's testimony in insanity evaluations (McAuliff & Arter, 2016).

Can Imaging Improve the Objectiveness of Insanity Evaluations?

An option to decrease bias in insanity evaluations is by using neuroimaging. It is uncertain how often neuroimaging is used in insanity evaluations. However, it has been argued that using imaging is more objective and can provide critical insight into criminal responsibility (Scarpazza et al., 2018). The increase of neuroimaging in court is undeniable, and it has been suggested that structural neuroimaging is "extremely relevant in psychiatric assessments of criminal responsibility" (Scarpazza et al., 2018, p. 1). In showing how this works, we discuss several case examples.

Case Examples

Specific case examples where neuroimaging was relevant to the legal concept of criminal responsibility are not readily available, but some do exist. Consider the case of acquired pedophilia where the onset of inappropriate sexual behaviors toward children was associated with a finding of an orbitofrontal tumor on the right side of the brain. The defendant was found guilty, and it was only after being sentenced to rehabilitation did the presence of the tumor become evident (Burns & Swerdlow, 2003). Scarpazza and colleagues (2018) discussed two cases where imaging detected large meningiomas in the right side of the frontoparietal lobes and how these benign tumors were linked to the defendants' sexual behaviors. These cases illustrate potential utility of imaging to the question of criminal responsibility.

In the case of Stephen Stanko, who was accused of murder and rape in 2005, a psychiatrist testified that Mr. Stanko had frontal lobe damage, causing him to have a personality disorder with "little regard for others" (i.e., psychopathy). Mr. Stanko was found guilty and is currently on death row in South Carolina (Gelman & Robichaux, 2007).

Similarly, in Lisa Montgomery's case, a psychiatrist hired by the defense was prepared to testify that results from an MRI demonstrated structural abnormalities that could lead to diminished responsibility for murder and kidnapping charges (Biddle & Chamberlain, 2013). The trial court refused to allow the testimony as it was "not based on scientifically reliable principles" (*United States v. Montgomery*, 2011). In her capital trial, Ms. Montgomery was found guilty of the murder of Bobbie Jo Stinnett and kidnapping after she removed an eight-month preborn baby from Ms. Stinnett's womb. Ms. Montgomery was executed in 2021.

Scientists and clinicians who support the use of neuroimaging in insanity evaluations have suggested that multidisciplinary and multimodal evaluations are superior and, as noted earlier, that the use of imaging allows for a more objective approach to insanity evaluations. Buttressed by the previous findings of low reliability for insanity evaluations, proponents of view imaging as a step forward over traditional insanity evaluations that are more likely to heavily rely on clinical interviewing and legal records (Scarpazza et al., 2021). As noted, many traditional interviews rely on the defendant's self-report, where the obtained data can be impacted by memory loss, mental illness, and response styles (e.g., malingering). Clearly, neuroimaging results are not impacted by response style as a defendant is unable to "fake" results on an imaging scan.

Trial courts have not been quick to embrace neuroimaging explanations in insanity defense trials. However, advocates of using imaging and neuroscientific techniques have suggested that imaging can be useful for assisting in diagnosing mental illness, evaluating the ability to know the nature and quality of the act, and intention (Egbenya & Adjorlolo, 2021). These authors stated, "However, neuroscientific assessments may add more objective information to bolster and add validity of clinical opinions that are based largely on psychosocial data" (p. 6).

Neuroimaging and Juries

With the increased focus on neuroscientific explanations to explain and excuse criminal behavior, there have been concerns that the admission of neuroimaging will compromise jury objectivity. Snyder (2016) authored a review of neuroimaging use in court and proposed ways to decrease potential juror bias when presented with imaging results (see also Diamond, 2006). Getting jurors to understand complicated information, like the data generated from neuroimaging, is important. Diamond (2006) found that jurors believe experts have appropriate knowledge but will be biased toward the side that retains them. Snyder (2016) encouraged clinicians explaining neuroimaging to make useful comparisons with less culpable groups (e.g., children) so the jury can better understand the information presented to them. Data on the persuasiveness of neuroscientific explanations on jury decision-making are mixed.

In a study showing differences when neuroimages were presented and when they were not, Saks and colleagues (2014) found that jurors were less likely to vote for the death penalty in a simulation when presented with neuroimages when the defendant was diagnosed with schizophrenia. In this instance, imaging was persuasive, but only with individuals diagnosed as psychotic. Similar results were found by Greene and Cahill (2012), who found neuroscientific findings presented to jurors were associated with decreased death sentences. A noteworthy finding was that the neuro-findings were strongest with mock defendants who were opined to be a high risk for committing future violence, showing that the usefulness for imaging results may be found in mitigation.

To date, the largest study of this kind was conducted by Schweitzer and colleagues (2011) using 1,476 jury-eligible individuals. In four separate experiments relying on meta-analytic techniques, Schweitzer et al. (2011) considered how viewing imaging results would potentially impact jurors' decision-making in several contexts. The authors wrote, "The essential results were that neuroimages had no especially potent or consistent impact on verdicts or sentences. But, importantly, the presence or nature of the neuroimages had no impact on mock jurors' perception of the defendant's responsibility" (p. 387). These results were consistent with findings from Marshall et al. (2017) that found brain imaging did not influence juror findings on psychopathic traits and ultimate guilt or innocence. However, the neuroscientific findings led jurors to believe the person is more amendable to treatment and ultimately less dangerous. Gurley and Marcus (2008) relied on university students in a 2 (psychosis v. psychopathy) × 2 (images v. no images) design in a simulation of criminal responsibility. As expected, individuals with psychotic disorders were most likely to be found not responsible for their behavior. A critical finding was that mock jurors exposed to testimony and neuroimages were the most likely to find for insanity in the mock case.

The Insanity Defense and Clinical Diagnoses: Findings from Neuroimaging

One potential use of neuroimaging is for assisting with diagnostics. There is no doubt that mental illnesses are brain-involved (Insel & Cuthbert,

2015). As this section of the chapter will describe, even using neuroimaging for diagnostic purposes in the courtroom is not without controversy. This section deals with the scientific evidence and controversies that come with the use of neuroimaging for assisting with diagnosis. Mental health disorders are brain-based disorders that are frequently, but not always, associated with anatomical and functional brain abnormalities. To that end, MRI, fMRI, and PET scans have generated significant research and notable findings across several diagnoses and diagnostic categories, which we will discuss shortly. In the writing of this chapter, we conducted a search for the previous five years and found wide-ranging imaging results for, but not limited to, the following disorders: schizophrenia, schizoaffective disorder, bipolar disorder, major depression, anxiety disorders, borderline personality disorder, and antisocial personality disorder (psychopathy). The findings associated with these studies provide critical insights regarding the neuropathways of mental health disorders.[1]

Consider schizophrenia as a primary example. Schizophrenia and its symptoms have been associated with enlarged lateral ventricles, loss of frontal lobe matter, manifestations in the corpus callosum, white matter distortions, grey matter disturbance in the temporal gyri, and decreased cortical surface area, to name a few (Asmal et al., 2019; Cobia et al., 2021; Gur & Gur, 2010; Kelly et al., 2018; Kuo et al., 2022; Zhuo et al., 2021). Bipolar disorder and major depression are mood disorders with significant imaging research. Bipolar disorder and major depression have been associated with brain issues in the prefrontal and anterior cingulate cortices, white matter dysfunction, and irregularities in the subcortical limbic structures (Clark & Sahakian, 2008; Tang et al., 2022; Tassone, 2022; Wang, 2019; Yan, 2022). These are but a few examples from a plethora of studies demonstrating brain abnormalities associated with major mental disorders that could be used to justify an insanity defense.

Imaging has also found evidence for brain involvement for personality disorders. Personality disorders are defined by the American Psychiatric Association (2022) as "an enduring pattern of inner experience and behavior that deviates markedly from the norms and expectations of an individual's culture, is pervasive and inflexible, has an onset in adolescence or early childhood, is stable over time, and leads to distress or impairment" (p. 733). In forensic and correctional settings, two of the most seen personality disorders are antisocial (including psychopathy) and borderline personality disorders. These disorders also have been significantly studied with neuroimaging techniques. For example, psychopathy has been associated with decreased grey matter volume, increased striatal volume, and

---

1 Interested parties can contact mvitacco@augusta.edu for a table of these findings.

limbic system dysfunction (Choy et al., 2022; da Cunha-Bang et al., 2017; Johanson et al., 2020; Miglin et al., 2021). Borderline personality disorder has findings of less activation in the left anterior parietal lobule, implications in the bilateral frontal lobes, decreased grey matter, and altered glucose metabolism (Amad & Radua, 2017; Bøen et al., 2018; Massó Rodriguez, 2021; Pan et al., 2022). Personality disorders do not typically qualify for the insanity defense; however, given their brain-based connections, some clinicians have argued that these brain implications should make the courts consider them for insanity.

However, the mere association between a brain-based finding and clinical symptom is insufficient to denote validity. This is especially relevant when it deals with admissibility in court to excuse criminal behavior. To underscore this point, First et al. (2012) reviewed the state of the science of the utility of neuroimaging and clinical work, ultimately recommending against using these data for diagnostics. In contrast, Henderson and colleagues (2020) focused on positives of neuroimaging by noting, "functional neuroimaging can offer clues and information about psychiatric disorders and their comorbid conditions" (p. 7) and that incremental steps are being taken to improve diagnostics through neuroimaging. The question for courts remains on neuroimaging and its admissibility. The question for clinicians concerns the benefits of imaging on incremental validity and the development of a better, well-defined product (i.e., accurate psycholegal opinion). The debate on the utility of neuroimaging for insanity will continue. Likewise, the use and admission of imaging into the court for diagnostic purposes will march forward undeterred by significant controversies and limitations.

Imaging and Diagnoses Where Neuroimaging Falls Short in Insanity Evaluations

This chapter has discussed the role neuroimaging has in various aspects of psychology and psychiatry. This section is going to consist of the issues that limit the use of neuroimaging technology in insanity evaluations. Unfortunately, these issues have not been adequately addressed by researchers and clinicians who continue to advocate for the use of imaging in retrospective evaluations of responsibility. As we discuss these limitations, we want to orient the reader that, although neuroimaging has evidenced usefulness in demonstrating the presence of a mental illness, one must be mindful of relevant legal criteria. Even the presence of a clinical finding does not mean the individual lacks criminal responsibility. The "Cautionary Statement for Forensic Use of DSM-5" correctly points out that in most cases the presence of a mental disorder does not answer the psycholegal question (American Psychiatric Association, 2022).

Although there have been claims that neuroimaging provides more objectivity to insanity evaluations (Scarpazza et al., 2018), the reading and interpretation of neuroimaging findings are subject to the same biases as other psychological factors. Consider the Hinckley case where opposing experts had strongly divergent views on the results of the same brain scan (*United States v. Hinckley*, 1981). Busby and Courtier (2017) explored biases in reading imaging and the negative impact on radiology results. The notion that neuroimaging is not subject to clinical biases has not been established, and interpretations of imaging likely suffers from the same cognitive biases that have impacted forensic evaluations.

Insanity evaluations, by definition, require an individual to retrospectively reconstruct an individual's mental state around the time and at the time of the alleged criminal offense. These evaluations frequently occur days, months, or even years after the alleged offense. The reconstruction of one's mental state is not an easy task, and traditional methods have relied on interviewing the defendant, interviewing witnesses (and sometimes victims), relying on discovery information, and considering body cam and other relevant video evidence. Scans may be able to detect the presence of long-term brain abnormalities but certainly are unable to ascertain the mental condition an individual was experiencing at the time of the offense. The retrospective nature of insanity evaluations fails to account for brain malleability (Erickson, 2010). It is now understood that the brain is dynamic, and can change based on circumstances and environment (Erickson, 2010). Brain plasticity is a barrier to neuroimaging accurately depicting the functionality of the brain in the days, weeks, and months after an alleged offense (Poldrack, 2020).

Proponents of neuroimaging in insanity defense evaluations also have a fundamental problem of providing empirical support for the utility of imaging in forensic insanity examinations. In theoretical articles, proponents of neuroimaging have suggested its use creates more objectivity in insanity evaluations and allows evaluations to generate a more multidisciplinary perspective with enhanced accuracy (Scarpazza et al., 2018). The data supporting these statements are lacking. Considering these statements, we urge clinicians and researchers interested in this field to search for empirical support for using imaging for insanity cases.

We were unable to find data showing that neuroimaging provides incremental validity compared with traditional methods of evaluating insanity. There is an absence of research that demonstrates that imaging provided more accurate outcomes for the trier of fact. In fact, it appears that results from neuroimaging are susceptible to the same cognitive biases as the traditional methods of forensic evaluations. Without stringent guidelines, neuroimaging introduces another source of error, without improving tried and true techniques. However, even using appropriate guidelines, the field is lacking normative data. There are no large-scale studies to make appropriate comparisons between individuals found insane and those adjudicated responsible.

A final issue that warrants discussion is the lack of specificity and sensitivity with neuroimaging with respects to insanity evaluations. Simply put, there are two issues that one must consider. First, the presence of abnormal findings does not always correlate or predict the presence of a mental disorder or mental health symptoms. More to the point, even if scans show the presence of structural abnormality or functional impairment, those do not necessarily translate to behavior. Likewise, lack of findings does not mean an absence of mental illness or lack of behavioral control. Neuroscience, like a lot of research, is plagued by publication bias, as null findings are frequently not published (Jennings & Van Horn, 2012), which could lead to overconfidence in the meaning of imaging results based on a skewed literature, which decreases the strength and generalizability of meta-analytic studies.

Neurohype and Pseudoscience

In a review of the way neuroscientific findings have been employed, Satel and Lilienfeld (2013) discussed growing misuse of neuroscience in industry and clinical work. This leads to a problem dubbed "neurohype," which has been defined as "a broad class of neuroscientific claims that greatly outstrip available evidence" (Lilienfeld et al., 2018; p. 241). Lilienfeld and colleagues underscored that the use of unsubstantiated findings is a cardinal sign of pseudoscience (2018). Unfortunately, neurohype is alive and well in forensic psychiatry and psychology. For example, imaging results are often viewed as a panacea to many psycholegal questions, like competency to proceed to trial (Perlin & Lynch, 2018; Philipsborn & Hamilton, 2021). Perlin and Lynch (2018) note that using neuroimaging is useful with competency to proceed to trial evaluations. Such claims have not been backed up by empirically-based research and are especially dubious since competency to proceed to trial (and other legal competencies) is based on legal knowledge, rational decision-making, and ability to provide attorney consultation (see *Dusky v. United States*, 1960).

Satel and Lilienfeld (2013) underscore the idea that just because behavior is evident in the brain and causation is assumed is insufficient for a finding of insanity/non-responsibility. The problem remains that researchers and clinicians attempt to use imaging to understand complicated, multifaceted human behavior. Neurofallacies rely on face-valid brain-based explanations to make complex behavior parsimonious, even though the evidence is lacking or incomplete. Bernard (2020) discussed two primary types of fallacies that occur in neuroscience: affirming the consequent and denying the antecedent. Brain imaging techniques to support an insanity defense has relied on both these fallacies. Reductionistic techniques, like brain imaging, have tremendous allure and carry the imprimatur of reliability; however, these techniques are dubious in understanding complex, multidetermined behavior.

Conclusion

Neuroimaging has developed to the point where it has provided great knowledge to the scientific and medical communities. In many cases, neuroimaging has provided life-saving technology to evaluate various tumors with unparalleled findings never before available to the medical community. We believe this endorsement of imaging is without controversy, and we predict imaging techniques will continue to evidence significant advancement in the decades to come. Yet, we wrote about the use of imaging as it relates to the insanity defense. To that end, it is our contention that imaging is not near ready to provide adequate information to these complicated cases. Baskin and colleagues (2007) wrote, "With respect to understanding the brain and certain behaviors, the state of scientific knowledge is nascent, but promising. The more complex and specific the behavior examined, the more speculative the connection" (p. 239). Even though this statement is over 20 years old, the underlying premise remains true today. It is important that we acknowledge that neuroimaging provides little to understanding multidetermined complex behavior, and this is especially true for insanity cases.

References

Amad, A., & Radua, J. (2017). Resting-state meta-analysis in borderline personality disorder: Is the fronto-limbic hypothesis still valid? *Journal of Affective Disorders*, *212*, 7–9. https://doi.org/10.1016/j.jad.2017.01.018

American Psychiatric Association. (2022). *Diagnostic and statistical manual of mental disorders: DSM-5* (5th ed.) Text Revision. American Psychiatric Publishing, Inc. https://doi.org/10.1176/appi.books.9780890425596

Aono, D., Yaffe, G., & Kober, H. (2019). Neuroscientific evidence in the courtroom: A review. *Cognitive Research: Principles and Implications*, *4*(1). https://doi.org/10.1186/s41235-019-0179-y

Aristotle. (1934). *Nicomachean ethics* (H. Rackham, Trans.). Harvard University Press and William Heinemann, Limited. http://data.perseus.org/citations/urn:cts:greekLit:tlg0086.tlg010.perseus-eng1:1110b (Original work published 350 BCE)

Asmal, L., Kilian, S., du Plessis, S., Scheffler, F., Chiliza, B., Fouche, J.-P., Seedat, S., Dazzan, P., & Emsley, R. (2019). Childhood trauma associated white matter abnormalities in first-episode schizophrenia. *Schizophrenia Bulletin*, *45*(2), 369–376. https://doi.org/10.1093/schbul/sby062

Baskin, J.H., Edersheim, J.G., & Price, B.H. (2007). Is a picture worth a thousand words? Neuroimaging in the courtroom. *American Journal of Law & Medicine*, 33(2–3), 239–269. https://doi.org/10.1177/009885880703300205

Bernard, C. (2020). On fallacies in neuroscience. *eNeuro*, 7(6). https://doi.org/10.1523/eneuro.0491-20.2020

Biddle, J., & Chamberlain, J. (2013). Admission of brain imaging in criminal proceedings. *Journal of the American Academy of Psychiatry and the Law*, 41(4), 597–599. https://jaapl.org/content/41/4/597

Bogerts, B. (2021). *Where does violence come from? A multidimensional approach to its causes and manifestations.* Springer. https://doi.org/10.1007/978-3-030-81792-3

Bøen, E., Hjørnevik, T., Hummelen, B., Elvsåshagen, T., Moberget, T., Holtedahl, J.E., Babovic, A., Hol, P.K., Karterud, S., & Malt, U.F. (2018). Patterns of altered regional brain glucose metabolism in borderline personality disorder and bipolar II disorder. *Acta Psychiatrica Scandinavica*. https://doi.org/10.1111/acps.12997

Burns, J.M., & Swerdlow, R.H. (2003). Right orbitofrontal tumor with pedophilia symptom and constructional apraxia sign. *Archives of Neurology*, 60(3), 437–440.

Busby, L.P., Courtier, J.L., & Glastonbury, C.M. (2017). Bias in radiology: The how and why of misses and misinterpretations. *RadioGraphics*, 38(1), 236–247. https://doi.org/10.1148/rg.2018170107

Choy, O., Raine, A., & Schug, R. (2022). Larger striatal volume is associated with increased adult psychopathy. *Journal of Psychiatric Research*, 149, 185–193. https://doi.org/10.1016/j.jpsychires.2022.03.006

Clark, L., & Sahakian, B.J. (2008). Cognitive neuroscience and brain imaging in bipolar disorder. *Dialogues in Clinical Neuroscience*, 10(2), 153–163. https://doi.org/10.31887/DCNS.2008.10.2/lclark

Cobia, D., Rich, C., Smith, M.J., Mamah, D., Csernansky, J.G., & Wang, L. (2021). Basal ganglia shape features differentiate schizoaffective disorder from schizophrenia. *Psychiatry Research: Neuroimaging*, 317, 111352. https://doi.org/10.1016/j.pscychresns.2021.111352

Cornell Law School. (2022, June). M'Naghten rule. Retrieved from www.law.cornell.edu/wex/m%27naghten_rule (accessed January 14, 2023).

da Cunha-Bang, S., Hjordt, L.V., Perfalk, E., Beliveau, V., Bock, C., Lehel, S., Thomsen, C., Sestoft, D., Svarer, C., & Knudsen, G.M. (2017). Serotonin 1B receptor binding is associated with trait anger and level of psychopathy in violent offenders. *Biological Psychiatry*, 82(4), 267–274. https://doi.org/10.1016/j.biopsych.2016.02.030

Davis, K. (2017). *The brain defense: Murder in Manhattan and the dawn of neuroscience in America's courtrooms*. Penguin.

Diamond, Shari S. (2006), Between fantasy and nightmare: A portrait of the jury. *Buffalo Law Review*, 54, 717–63.

Dusky v. United States, 362 U.S. 402 (1960)

Egbenya, D.L. & Adjorlolo, S. (2021). Advancement of neuroscience and the assessment of mental state at the time of offense. *Forensic Science International: Mind and Law*, 2(100046-). https://doi.org/10.1016/j.fsiml.2021.100046

Erickson, S.K. (2010). Blaming the brain. *Minnesota Journal of Law and Science Technology*, 11, 27–76.

First, M., Carter, C.S., Castellanos, F.X., Dickstein, D.P., Drevets, W.C., Kim, K.L., Pescosolido, M.F., Rausch, S., Seymour, K.E., & Zubieta, J. (2012). Consensus report of the APA work group on neuroimaging markers of psychiatric disorders. Resource document.

Gaudet, L.M., & Marchant, G.E. (2016) Under the radar: Neuroimaging evidence in the criminal courtroom. *Drake Law Review*. https://ssrn.com/abstract=2838996

Gelman, J., & Robichaux, M.N. (2007, August 31). Murder on his mind. Retrieved from www.cbsnews.com/news/murder-on-his-mind-11-01-2007/

Gowensmith, WN, Murrie, DC, & Boccaccini, MT. (2012). Field reliability of competency to stand trial evaluations: How often do evaluators agree, and what do judges decide when evaluators disagree? *Law and Human Behavior*, 36, 130–139.

Gowensmith, W.N., Murrie, D.C., & Boccaccini, M.T. (2013). How reliable are forensic evaluations of legal sanity? *Law and Human Behavior*, 37, 98–106.

Greely, H.T., & Farahany, N.A. (2018). Neuroscience and the criminal justice system. Annual Review of Criminology, 2(1), 451–471. https://doi.org/10.1146/annurev-criminol-011518-024433

Greene, E., & Cahill, B.S. (2012). Effects of neuroimaging evidence on mock juror decision making. *Behavioral Sciences & the Law*, 30(3), 280–296. https://doi.org/10.1002/bsl.1993

defenses. *Behavioral Sciences & the Law*, 26(1), 85–97.

Gur, R.E., & Gur, R.C. (2010). Functional magnetic resonance imaging in schizophrenia. *Dialogues in Clinical Neuroscience*, 12(3), 333–343. https://doi.org/10.31887/DCNS.2010.12.3/rgur

Gurley, J.R., & Marcus, D.K. (2008). The effects of neuroimaging and brain injury on insanity

Henderson, T.A., van Lierop, M.J., McLean, M., Uszler, J.M., Thornton, J.F., Siow, Y.-H., Pavel, D.G., Cardaci, J., & Cohen, P. (2020). Functional neuroimaging in psychiatry—aiding in diagnosis and guiding treatment. What the American Psychiatric Association does not know. *Frontiers in Psychiatry*, 11. https://doi.org/10.3389/fpsyt.2020.00276

Insel, T.R., & Cuthbert, B.N. (2015). Brain disorders? Precisely: Precision medicine comes to psychiatry. *Science*, 348(6234), 499–500. https://doi.org/10.1126/science.aab2358

Jennings, R.G., & Van Horn, J.D. (2012). Publication bias in neuroimaging research: Implications for meta-analyses. *Neuroinformatics*, 10(1), 67–80. https://doi.org/10.1007/s12021-011-9125-y

Johanson, M., Vaurio, O., Tiihonen, J., & Lähteenvuo, M. (2020). A systematic literature review of neuroimaging of Psychopathic traits. *Frontiers in Psychiatry*, 10. https://doi.org/10.3389/fpsyt.2019.01027

Kelly, S., Jahanshad, N., Zalesky, A., Kochunov, P., Agartz, I., Alloza, C., Andreassen, O.A., Arango, C., Banaj, N., Bouix, S., Bousman, C.A., Brouwer, R.M., Bruggemann, J., Bustillo, J., Cahn, W., Calhoun, V., Cannon, D., Carr, V., Catts, S., ... Donohoe, G. (2018). Widespread white matter microstructural differences in schizophrenia across 4322 individuals: Results from the Enigma schizophrenia DTI Working Group. *Molecular Psychiatry*, 23(5), 1261–1269. https://doi.org/10.1038/mp.2017.170

Kiernan, L.A. (1982, June 2). Hinckley judge reverses himself, admits pictures of defendant's brain. *The Washington Post*. Retrieved from www.washingtonpost.com/archive/politics/1982/06/02/hinckley-judge-reverses-himself-admits-pictures-of-defendants-brain/3bec96a2-ceab-4ac9-a73e-5aff2febb3b5/

Kuo, S.S., Roalf, D.R., Prasad, K.M., Musket, C.W., Rupert, P.E., Wood, J., Gur, R.C., Almasy, L., Gur, R.E., Nimgaonkar, V.L., & Pogue-Geile, M.F. (2022). Age-dependent effects of schizophrenia genetic risk on cortical thickness and cortical surface area: Evaluating evidence for neurodevelopmental and neurodegenerative models of schizophrenia. *Journal of Psychopathology and Clinical Science*, 131(6), 674–688. https://doi.org/10.1037/abn0000765.supp (Supplemental)

Lavergne, G.M. (1997). *A sniper in the tower: The Charles Whitman murders*. University of North Texas Press.

Lilienfeld, S.O., Aslinger, E., Marshall, J., & Satel, S. Neurohype: A field guide to exaggerated brain-based claims. (2018). In LSM. Johnson & KS. Rommelfanger (Eds.), *The Routledge handbook of Neuroethics*. Routledge/Taylor & Francis Group; 241–261.

Maeder, T. (1985). *Crime and madness: The origins and evolution of the insanity defense*. Harper & Row.

Marshall, J., Lilienfeld, S.O., Mayberg, H., & Clark, S.E. (2017). The role of neurological and psychological explanations in legal judgments of psychopathic wrongdoers. *Journal of Forensic Psychiatry & Psychology*, 28(3), 412–436. https://doi.org/10.1080/14789949.2017.1291706

Massó Rodriguez, A., Hogg, B., Gardoki-Souto, I., Valiente-Gómez, A., Trabsa, A., Mosquera, D., García-Estela, A., Colom, F., Pérez, V., Padberg, F., Moreno-Alcázar, A., & Amann, B.L. (2021). Clinical features, neuropsychology and neuroimaging in bipolar and borderline personality disorder: A systematic review of cross-diagnostic studies. *Frontiers in Psychiatry*, 12. https://doi.org/10.3389/fpsyt.2021.681876

McAuliff, B.D., & Arter, J.L. (2016). Adversarial allegiance: The devil is in the evidence details, not just on the witness stand. *Law and Human Behavior*. https://doi.org/10.1037/lhb0000198

Mclellan, D. (2001, November 16) David H. Gunby, 58; hurt in '66 Texas shooting rampage. *Los Angeles Times*. Retrieved from *www.latimes.com/archives/la-xpm-2001-nov-16-me-4897-story.html* (accessed January 11, 2023).

Miglin, R., Rodriguez, S., Bounoua, N., & Sadeh, N. (2021). A multidimensional examination of psychopathy traits and gray matter volume in adults. *Social Cognitive and Affective Neuroscience*, 17(7), 662–672. https://doi.org/10.1093/scan/nsab131

Model Penal Code, § 4.01 (P.O.D. 1962).

Packer, I.K. (2009). *Evaluation of criminal responsibility*. Oxford University Press.

Pan, N., Wang, S., Qin, K., Li, L., Chen, Y., Zhang, X., Lai, H., Suo, X., Long, Y., Yu, Y., Ji, S., Radua, J., Sweeney, J.A., & Gong, Q. (2022). Common and distinct neural patterns of attention-deficit/hyperactivity disorder and borderline personality disorder: A multimodal functional and structural meta-analysis. *Biological Psychiatry: Cognitive Neuroscience and Neuroimaging*. https://doi.org/10.1016/j.bpsc.2022.06.003

Perlin, M.L., & Lynch, A.J. (2018). "My brain is so wired": Neuroimaging's role in competency cases involving persons with mental disabilities. *Boston University Public Interest Law Journal*, 27(1), 73–98.

Petoft A. (2015). Neurolaw: A brief introduction. *Iranian Journal of Neurology*, 14(1), 53–58.

Petoft, A., & Abbasi, M. (2020). Current limits of neurolaw: A brief overview. *Médecine et Droit*, 2020(161), 29–34. https://doi.org/10.1016/j.meddro.2019.11.002

Philipsborn, J.T., & Hamilton, M. (2021). Competence to stand trial ingredients: The role of neuroscience. *University of St. Thomas Journal of Law and Public Policy*, 259–295.

Phillips M.R., Wolf, A.S., & Coons, D.J. (1988). Psychiatry and the criminal justice system: Testing the myths. *American Journal of Psychiatry*, 145, 605–610. https://doi.org/10.1176/ajp.145.5.605

Plato. (2013). *Laws* (B. Jowett, Trans.). Project Gutenberg. Retrieved from www.gutenberg.org/files/1750/1750-h/1750-h.htm (Original work published 360 BCE)

Poldrack, R.A. (2020). *The new mind readers: What neuroimaging can and cannot reveal about our thoughts*. Princeton University Press.

R v. M'Naghten, 8 E.R. 718; (1843).

Rosen, J. (2007, March 11). The brain on the stand. The New York Times. Retrieved from www.nytimes.com/2007/03/11/magazine/11Neurolaw.t.html (accessed December 21, 2022).

Saks, M.J., Schweitzer, N.J., Aharoni, E., & Kiehl, K.A. (2014). The impact of neuroimages in the sentencing phase of capital trials. *Journal of Empirical Legal Studies*, 11(1), 105–131. https://doi.org/10.1111/jels.12036

Satel, S., & Lilienfeld, S.O. (2013). *Brainwashed: The seductive appeal of mindless neuroscience*. Basic Civitas Books.

Scarpazza, C., Ferracuti, S., Miolla, A., & Sartori, G. (2018). The charm of structural neuroimaging in insanity evaluations: Guidelines to avoid misinterpretation of the findings. *Translational Psychiatry*, 8(1). https://doi.org/10.1038/s41398-018-0274-8

Scarpazza, C., Zampieri, I., Miolla, A., Melis, G., Pietrini, P., & Sartori, G. (2021). A multidisciplinary approach to insanity assessment as a way to reduce cognitive biases. *Forensic Science International*, 319, 110652. https://doi.org/10.1016/j.forsciint.2020.110652

Schweitzer, N.J., Saks, M.J., Murphy, E.R., Roskies, A.L., Sinnott-Armstrong, W., & Gaudet, L.M. (2011). Neuroimages as evidence in a mens rea defense: No impact. *Psychology, Public Policy, and Law*, 17(3), 357–393. https://doi.org/10.1037/a0023581

Shen, F.X. (2016). Neurolegislation: How U.S. legislators are using brain science. *Harvard Journal of Law & Technology*, 29(2), 495–526.

Snyder, A.A. (2016). Neuroimaging and jury decision making: In defense of the defense? Retrieved from https://ideaexchange.uakron.edu/honors_research_projects/421

Tang, Q., Cui, Q., Chen, Y., Deng, J., Sheng, W., Yang, Y., Lu, F., Zeng, Y., Jiang, K., & Chen, H. (2022). Shared and distinct changes in local dynamic functional connectivity patterns in major depressive and Bipolar Depressive

Disorders. *Journal of Affective Disorders*, *298*, 43–50. https://doi.org/10.1016/j.jad.2021.10.109

Tassone, V.K., Demchenko, I., Salvo, J., Mahmood, R., Di Passa, A.-M., Kuburi, S., Rueda, A., & Bhat, V. (2022). Contrasting the amygdala activity and functional connectivity profile between antidepressant-free participants with major depressive disorder and healthy controls: A systematic review of comparative fMRI studies. *Psychiatry Research: Neuroimaging*, *325*, 111517. https://doi.org/10.1016/j.pscychresns.2022.111517

Taylor Jr., S. (1982, June 2). CAT scans said to show shrunken Hinckley brain. *The New York Times*. Retrieved from www.nytimes.com/1982/06/02/us/cat-scans-said-to-show-shrunken-hinckley-brain.html

United States v. Hinckley, 525 F. Supp. 1342 (1981).

United States v. Montgomery, 635 F.3d 1074 (2011).

Vitacco, M.J., Gottfried, E., Lilienfeld, S.O., & Batastini, A. (2020). The limited relevance of neuroimaging in insanity evaluations. *Neuroethics*, *13*(3), 249–260. https://doi.org/10.1007/s12152-019-09421-8

Wang, X., Luo, Q., Tian, F., Cheng, B., Qiu, L., Wang, S., He, M., Wang, H., Duan, M., & Jia, Z. (2019). Brain grey-matter volume alteration in adult patients with bipolar disorder under different conditions: a voxel-based meta-analysis. *Journal of Psychiatry & Neuroscience: JPN*, *44*(2), 89–101. https://doi.org/10.1503/jpn.180002

Weiss K.J. (2007). Isaac Ray at 200: Phrenology and expert testimony. *The Journal of the American Academy of Psychiatry and the Law*, *35*(3), 339–345.

Yan, W., Zhao, M., Fu, Z., Pearlson, G.D., Sui, J., & Calhoun, V.D. (2022). Mapping relationships among schizophrenia, bipolar and schizoaffective disorders: A deep classification and clustering framework using fMRI time series. *Schizophrenia Research*, *245*, 141–150. https://doi.org/10.1016/j.schres.2021.02.007

Zhuo, C., Ji, F., Lin, X., Tian, H., Wang, L., Xu, Y., Wang, W., Zhong, B., & Lin, X. (2021). Common and distinct brain functional alterations in pharmacotherapy treatment-naïve female borderline personality disorder patients with and without auditory verbal hallucinations: A pilot study. *European Archives of Psychiatry and Clinical Neuroscience*, *271*, 1149–1157. https://doi.org/10.1007/s00406-020-01102-5

6 A Decade of Evolution in the Forensic Investigative Field

A South African Overview

Bernadine Carol Benson, Juanida Suzette Horne, and Gideon Jones

Introduction

South Africa, located at the southern tip of the African continent, covers an area of 1,219,089 km² and is the only country in the world with three capital cities: Pretoria as the administrative capital, Cape Town as the legislative capital, and Bloemfontein as the judicial capital. This multicultural, multi-racial, and multilingual country has a past marked by inequality, racial discrimination, and violence. In April 1994, South Africa held its first open and multi-racial election, putting an end to the reign of a segregated and authoritative government.

As a constitutional democracy, South Africa adheres to the rule of law, with law enforcement being the responsibility of the South African Police Service (SAPS), mandated to ensure the safety and security of citizens, visitors, and property. Despite the presence of dedicated and experienced investigators in the SAPS, the quality and standard of law enforcement in South Africa have been steadily declining over the past decades, particularly in terms of investigative capacity. To address this apparent investigative deficit, civil society groups and institutions outside of government have taken on a more active role in investigating and prosecuting alleged perpetrators, often with the support of or even as a coordinated effort with the SAPS.

This chapter explores the investigative context in South Africa external to the SAPS, focusing on the most prominent sections of legislation that frame this context. Drawing on an extensive literature review and empirical data, the chapter examines how investigators, particularly those from within the private investigation setting, are harnessing the capabilities of voice biometrics and artificial intelligence (AI) in their investigations. Specifically, the research focuses on voice-related investigative tools, including polygraphs, Computer Voice Stress Analysis (CVSA), Layered Voice Analysis (LVA), and forensic voice comparisons, and their evidential value, to support or refute eye-witness testimony.

DOI: 10.4324/9781003323112-7

The South African Investigative and Legislative Landscape

In South Africa, the issue of crime and its effective management is no longer solely the responsibility of the South African Police Service (SAPS). The past two decades have seen several companies, organizations, and institutions establish their own in-house capacity to address crime when it affects them (Holtz, 2022; South African Insurance Association, 2022) and crime victims hiring private investigators when the SAPS fail them (Minnaar, 2004, p. 14). The dissatisfaction with the SAPS is evident in recent research, conducted by Statistics South Africa, which found that only 17.5% of respondents believed that the SAPS could protect them from crime (Staff Writer, 2022a). Similarly, other independent research and reports indicate comparable dissatisfaction with the SAPS in various communities (Dlamini, 2020; Faull, 2010; SAPS, 2023).

Reports from popular media and major news outlets continue to expose criminal activities within and outside government sectors (News24, 2021; SA Government, 2022; Staff Writer, 2022b; Timeslive, 2022). For instance, the recent allegations of widespread corruption and collusion within Eskom made by the former CEO, Mr. de Ruyter, have been the subject of investigations by law enforcement agencies and private investigative firms (Bloom, 2023; Grootes, 2023; O'Regan, 2022). At the time of the writing of this chapter, questions about the veracity of these allegations remain largely unverified.

It has also become commonplace in South Africa that criminal activities by prominent individuals are uncovered by whistle-blowers or investigative journalists, rather than law enforcement agencies (Bloom, 2023; Harper, 2022; Roper, 2013). Whistle-blowers, specifically, often bear significant personal costs to themselves and their families (Clark, 2021; Nather, 2019; Wright, 2022). In many instances, these whistleblowers offered stark eyewitness accounts of blatant malfeasance perpetrated by key individuals. Some of them pay the ultimate price (Farmer & Thornycroft, 2022).

Legislative Parameters of Investigations

The criminal justice process in South Africa, within which the SAPS remains a key role player, is initiated by a victim reporting a crime or the police being called to a crime scene (Lötter, 2014, p. 14). Once a criminal case has been registered at the local police station a detective is assigned to resolve the matter. This may lead to various outcomes ranging from an investigation where no suspect is identified or found, and the case is closed; to one where a suspect is identified, arrested, and prosecuted. The criminal justice process operates within a complex and intricate system with numerous government-based stakeholders or participants (Swanepoel, 2014, p. 104).

A Decade of Evolution in the Forensic Investigative Field 113

For the criminal justice process to be fair and equitable, all the participants must be provided with clear parameters within which to operate. Such parameters are enshrined in legislation, including the Constitution of the Republic of South Africa, 1996, which includes the Bill of Rights, substantive and adjectival law, and criminal law, which outlines which acts or conduct within society constitute an offense and are punishable by law (Swanepoel, 2014, p. 116). The rules and principles of criminal procedure enforce the substantive law and the sanctions of the criminal law. To perform their duties effectively, police officials, including detectives/investigators, are expected to be knowledgeable about criminal law, criminal procedure, and evidence (Lötter, 2014, p. 3).

While one of the legislated duties of the South African Police Service (SAPS) is to investigate crime, other role players have entered the space for various additional reasons. These role players include members of metropolitan police services, members of the South African National Defence Force (SANDF), Environmental Management Inspectors (EMIs), and investigators attached to the Independent Police Investigative Directorate (IPID) (van Rooyen, 2018, p. 3), to name a few. In this chapter, investigators from these entities are referred to as "law enforcement officers" as they are appointed under different pieces of legislation and are authorized to carry out specific types of investigations only. Corporate, forensic, or private investigators are usually referred to as investigators, but they are not law enforcement officers and therefore have no special "investigative powers," like their law enforcement counterparts.

Yet, regardless of their designation or affiliation, all individuals conducting investigations in South Africa must adhere to the parameters set out in the Constitution. The specific court or tribunal for which a case (criminal or civil) is being prepared, may prescribe additional rules.

The following discussion focuses on the most prominent role players and stakeholders in the investigative landscape, external to government agencies. This includes the Private Security Regulating Authority (PSiRA), the Association of Certified Fraud Examiners (ACFE) and the Institute of Commercial Forensic Practitioners (ICFP). The authors note that while there are a substantive number of other role players and stakeholders that occupy this space, through research conducted, the ACFE and the ICFP have taken the initiative in focusing on, and directing of, the private investigative environment.

PsiRA

The Private Security Regulation Act, Act 56 of 2001 (PsiRA), regulates South Africa's security industry (Netshivhuyu, 2018, p. 2). Under this act, all private investigators must be registered with PsiRA as a security service provider. The legislation provides a definition of private investigators, which includes individuals who investigate in a private capacity and for the benefit of another person (Netshivhuyu, 2018, p. 19). Auditors, advocates, accountants, and internal investigators who perform investigations as part of their *standard duties* for their employing company or organization are excluded from this definition. Private investigators hired on a case-by-case basis by any of these entities must be registered under the PsiRA legislation.

ACFE and ICFP

The Association of Certified Fraud Examiners (ACFE) and the Institute of Commercial Forensic Practitioners (ICFP) are the two primary professional organizations in South Africa, setting the standards for professional forensic investigation. They are not companies who hire investigators, but rather professional bodies whose purpose it is to give credibility to the profession of forensic investigations external to law enforcement.

Both the ACFE and ICFP have taken significant steps in establishing and regulating forensic investigative standards in South Africa, in its quest for professionalization. These include the Forensic Standards for Polygraph Examiners, Layered Voice Analysis (LVA), and Voice Stress Detection Standard (see www.acfesa.co.za), Reporting Standards, Attribute Standards, and Information Gathering Standards respectively (ICFP, 2022a, 2022b, 2022c). While these standards are not contained in legislation, they represent an essential component of the professionalization of the commercial forensic industry and the private investigation occupation in general. These standards are aligned with the evidential standards set by South African legislation. Investigators, both internal and external to government agencies, who become either *Certified Fraud Examiners (CFE)* or *Forensic Practitioners (FP)* are often viewed as having a higher level of skill and professionalism, than their counterparts without such a certification.

Evidence and the Rules of Evidence

The pursuit of truth is the quintessential objective of any investigation; it is characterized as a systematic search for the truth (Benson, Jones & Horne, 2015, p. 19). Investigations must be conducted in compliance with established procedures and protocols, legal frameworks, and scientific principles. The investigator's role entails collecting relevant information and evidence of a crime, irregularity, or transgression.

To be admissible in a court of law, evidence must adhere to strict legal requirements stipulated in the Criminal Procedure Act 51 of 1977.

Evidence and information can be gathered using various methods, such as physical evidence collection, crime scene investigations, and interviews or interrogations.

The Skilled Investigator

Because investigators engage with people from all levels of society, the ability to communicate effectively is a skill that they need to possess but also that they need to keep developing (Benson et al., 2015, p. 27). In most societies, there are investigators who stand out from the crowd and often attract media attention, for various reasons. The concept of the master detective or super sleuth has always been a fascinating topic; Sherlock Holmes is a good example. Unfortunately, that is not the reality, as most investigations require teamwork. Our modern-day human and investigation environment is highly complex and constantly requires new and updated skills from investigators.

Modern-day investigations are often conducted in a project approach, where the abilities and skills of various professionals are used together to achieve a successful outcome. While that is the case, the basic principles of investigation have not changed. An investigator still must interact with people—victims, witnesses and suspects. Furthermore, an investigator must record and present their efforts to a court where every detail and aspect of an investigation is scrutinized. People perpetrate all crimes, irregularities, and indiscretions. While technological advancements have facilitated the commission of crimes, human involvement remains the crux of the matter. High-performing investigators "have highly developed interpersonal and communication skills" (Saldivar 2017, p. 6). This implies that they are good listeners too.

An investigator must be able to detect when the person that they are talking to is being deceitful or outright lying to them. It is critical to the success of any investigation to detect when a suspect, witness or victim is lying. There have been various examples in online media reports where witnesses and sometimes victims are caught out for lying (Lee-Jacobs, 2021; Regchand, 2020). Unfortunately, no human being has even proven to be a faultless "lie-detector," despite some claiming to be the first "human lie-detector" (Myburgh, 2022). Therefore, experienced investigators employ alternative strategies to detect deception. Some of them involve the use of tried and trusted strategies, while others may involve the use of artificial intelligence (AI) enhanced technologies.

In the context of an investigation, the primary objective of an interview is to obtain information. The interview process involves determining the value of specific pieces of information and the interview's overall value. Ultimately the investigator will attempt to determine whether the person being interviewed, was truthful or deceptive. There are several historical tales about methods used to determine this. The Chinese were of the view that people who were lying had a dry mouth. They would give such a person rice powder to chew and spit out: allegedly this assisted them to determine innocence or guilt. Similarly, the Bedouin tribe of Arabia, required the two conflicting parties to lick hot coals: the one whose tongue blistered was believed to be the liar (Lockett, 2010, p. 3). Fortunately, these methods have evolved into more sophisticated truth verification techniques.

In Indigenous African culture, the characteristic of honesty is highly regarded, and there are many proverbs in their folklore that illustrate the importance and value of being truthful (Okelo, 2022). Their proverbs are applicable to both personal life as well as to the professional life. One such proverb: "The path of a liar is very short" highlights that the person who lies is often caught out very quickly, and then there are severe consequences to deal with (Okelo, 2022).

Despite traditional values steeped in rich culture and well-intended codes of conduct, people lie a great deal of the time. And uncovering the truth is often the unenviable task of the corporate/forensic investigator. Technological and forensic advancements have become a standard part of such investigations. Forensic experts use traditional methods to collect fingerprints, blood, and DNA samples for analysis and individualization. However, other techniques for truth verification are necessary when the evidence lies within the human context. One such method is the use of the polygraph to detect deception. This method will be discussed further below.

In an investigative context, the principle of "he who alleges must prove" is called the burden of proof. This means that the person/organization who makes an allegation about something, will be required by the tribunal hearing the allegation/charge, to provide evidence in proof of such an allegation. Thus, if company A (or the SAPS) allege that person B stole money, the burden of proof rests with them to provide evidence in support of the allegation. Evidence is weighed differently in criminal and civil hearings. In a criminal trial, the standard of proof is "beyond a reasonable doubt" (Joubert, 2013, p. 34). Thus, evidence needs to be provided which proves the allegation "beyond reasonable doubt." Similarly, in investigations into irregularities or indiscretions that do not constitute a crime, the standard of proof is to establish on a "balance of probabilities" (Joubert, 2013, p. 34).

Investigative tools such as eyewitness testimony, body language and statement analysis are often used to determine the credibility of witnesses and suspects in legal proceedings. However, the effectiveness of these tools depends on the knowledge, skills, and experience of the investigator using them.

Eyewitness testimony consists of two separate elements, the credibility of the witness and the accuracy of the evidence, and it is important to obtain a detailed narrative from witnesses and suspects as soon as possible after an incident to be investigated. Investigators should never dictate or alter a witness or suspect's narrative and should focus on obtaining information surrounding the incident to catch deceptive interviewees in their own web of lies. This narrative establishes or destroys the credibility of a witness or suspect.

The investigation tools used by some investigators to detect deception are not readily admitted as evidence in a court of law. Still, presiding judges and magistrates often make decisions about the truthfulness or deception of witnesses and accused based on them.

4IR

The Fourth Industrial Revolution (4IR), also known as Industry 4.0, was coined by Klaus Schwab and is now widely used in business and political institutions (Peckham, 2021, p. 30). According to Schwab (2016), the advancement of the 3IR, is more into the use of electronics and information technology for production (Schwab, 2016, 2017). The way technology is evolving may have some implications for human life and the scale, scope, and complexity of the 4IR will be vastly different from anything humans have previously encountered. The 4IR holds great promise but also great risk, as organizations may be unable to adapt, and governments may be unable to employ and regulate new technologies (Schwab, 2016). The 4IR is made up of three spheres: physical, digital, and biological, which merge as a result of the new technologies in the 4IR. The union of these three spheres has impacted all disciplines, economies, and industries (Caluza, 2022, p. 6). Failure to capitalize on the benefits of these technologies will result in inequality and social fragmentation (Schwab, 2016).

A confluence of technologies, including artificial intelligence (AI), sensors, and communications infrastructure such as 5G, has resulted in a new way of doing things (Peckham, 2021:31). Many people now consider data, which is essential for training AI algorithms, to be the "new oil" and the backbone of the digital economy (Peckham, 2021, p. 32). The 4IR has enormous potential for the South African Police Service (SAPS) to transform and realign public service delivery processes. Rapid advances in technologies such as AI, Robotics, the Internet of Things (IoT), Data Analytics, Nanotechnology, and Biotechnology, to name a few, underpin it (Grace, Jacob, Olutola, & Morero, 2022, p. 447).

Artificial Intelligence

Alan Turing's seminal work on Computing Machinery and Intelligence in the 1950s inspired the concept of AI (Caluza, 2022, p. 6). In July 1956, Dartmouth College's Summer Research Project, hosted by John McCarthy and Marvin Minsky, introduced AI (also known as machine intelligence at the time) as a research discipline. Marvin Minsky and John McCarthy defined AI as any task performed by a machine that was previously thought to require human intelligence. AI can be defined in two ways: as a science aimed at discovering the essence of intelligence and developing intelligent machines, or as a science aimed at discovering methods for solving complex problems that require the application of some intelligence (e.g., making correct decisions based on large amounts of data) (Dilek, Çakır, & Aydn, 2015, p. 22).

AI is regarded as the mechanism that allows machines to learn, allowing them to adapt to their surroundings and complete tasks without human intervention (Caluza, 2022, p. 6; Jadhav, Sankhla, & Kumar, 2020, p. 2065). Machine learning is often considered a subset of AI. It is the science of continuously learning and improving computer algorithms. It enables the software to predict outcomes accurately without training (Chowdhury, 2021).

These machines or computer programs have been greatly improved to perform human-like tasks such as visual perception, speech recognition, cognitive thinking, decision making, learning from experiences, and solving complex problems at a faster and lower error rate than humans (Jadhav, Sankhla, & Kumar, 2020, p. 2065). AI and machine learning rapidly transform the security landscape, forcing the industry to reconsider its traditional methods. This technology appears to have caused security professionals to rethink how they will build their teams, structure engagements, and define their value (Caluza, 2022, p. 6).

In addition, AI is a rapidly developing field that is also being used to advance forensic science and the justice system. In today's forensic science and criminal investigation world, experts face numerous challenges due to massive amounts of data, tiny pieces of evidence in a chaotic and complex environment, traditional laboratory structures, and sometimes insufficient knowledge, which can lead to investigation failure or miscarriage of justice. AI may be considered a weapon to combat these challenges.

AI-based algorithms can detect risk in massive amounts of data and are used for detection, prevention, and even prediction of future crime or criminal behavior (Jadhav, Sankhla, & Kumar, 2020, p. 2064). In the future, AI and investigative analytics will continue to play an essential role in assisting police departments in keeping their communities safe (Mahalik, 2020).

AI has the potential to become an indelible part of our criminal justice ecosystem, assisting investigators and allowing criminal justice professionals to do their jobs more effectively (Rigano, 2019, p. 17). In the forensic field, artificial intelligence and machine learning are extremely important. With these two technologies, investigators can automate their procedures, allowing them to quickly identify information and insights while saving time (Chowdhury, 2021). However, the use of AI-based tools may raise privacy and racial bias concerns: it is therefore vital that law enforcement agencies adhere to all relevant legal and ethical guidelines when utilizing these tools. A recent Twitter post highlighted this when AI was asked what it thought professors from various departments such as Philosophy, Political Science, Biology, Economics, Education and Ethnic studies look like. The racial and gender biases was evident (Growcoot, 2023).

Many court cases are decided by expert forensic opinion. The expert examiner's opinion frequently concerns individualization, which occurs when an object taken from a crime scene (fingerprint, handwriting, bite marks, hair sample, etc.) is visually compared with an exemplar taken from a suspect or a database. If the evidence is usable, the expert determines whether the comparison is a match, an exclusion, or inconclusive. Individualization judgment is so strong that courts may convict defendants solely based on the expert's opinion (Jadhav, Sankhla & Kumar, 2020, p. 2065). Unfortunately, AI technology has not yet developed to the extent that it can produce individualization evidence (similar to DNA or fingerprint evidence), which has been accepted in a court of law, in South Africa. It seems that the investigator will need to tackle this aspect on their own.

Biometrics and Voice Biometrics

The term biometrics or biometry, also called a biometric characteristic or a biometric trait, (Allan, 2002b: Prabhakar et al., 2003) can be seen as a scientific discipline—a "life measurement" and comes from the Greek words *bios* meaning life and *metron* or *metrikos* meaning measure. Biometrics can be defined as measurable physiological and/or behavioral characteristics that can be utilized to verify the identity of an individual, and include fingerprint verification, hand geometry, retinal scanning, iris scanning, face recognition and signature verification. Hence, technological systems that are capable of life measurement: aptly called biometric systems.

No human is exempt from having had their biometrics (in one form or another) captured or collected at one time or another. And for the most part, we provided the requested data or sample voluntarily. Whether it was to open a bank account and a fingerprint forms part of the biometric registration process or to unlock your cellphone using the pre-programmed facial recognition technology contained in the cellphone software: we readily engage and present or offer our biometrical data without a second thought. Biometrics in one form or another is an undeniable part of our daily existence.

Biometric recognition is a rapidly evolving field of science, it is convenient and dependable, and a myriad of biometric systems have been in use for several decades already. They have been used to process travelers at international borders, authenticate account holders, and to identify suspects involved in criminal activities (Ross & Jain, 2007, p. 11). Whether for business or pleasure, the use of biometrics in some form or another, is not negotiable.

While physical access controls, such as gates and high walls, are simple to bypass, using biometrics as part of a security system has added an additional layer of security. Biometrics includes the following advantages: convenience, increased security, accuracy, non-imitative, non-sharable, cannot be lost, reduced paperwork and easy to access. Because of these benefits, biometric systems are more secure and accurate (Singh, Agrawal, & Khan, 2018, p. 2). This practice is gaining prominence and will continue to do so, as a foundational requirement for effective cyber-security.

Biometric systems utilize a variety of bodily features (fingerprints, iris matching, facial recognition, or even gait recognition) for either identification or verification purposes. On the one hand, verification happens when a system verifies that an individual is who they claim to be. The biometric sample submitted by an individual is compared to the sample that is on record for this individual: there will either be a match (verification of the person) or not (perhaps an imposter). This is referred to as 1:1 (one-to-one) search or matching (Woodward, Webb, Newton, Bradley, Rubenson, Larson, Lilly, Smythe, Houghton, Pincus, Schachter & Steinberg, 2001, p. 10). Identification biometrics, on the other hand, are employed to identify an individual; this is referred to as 1:N (one-to-many matching) (Woodward et al., 2001, p. 10). Obviously, a match can only be made if the database contains a sample of that individual.

Biometrics is widely considered to be one of the most effective tools for ensuring security and detecting cybercrime. Biometric-based technologies are most commonly used in security, monitoring, and fraud prevention, where one person can positively be identified and differentiated from another person.

Human voices are as unique to an individual as fingerprints (Phonexia 2023b). Using technology, it is possible to identify and authenticate a specific human voice, under the correct circumstances. Developers of voice biometrics referred to this as a "reference voiceprint" (Markowitz, 2000, p. 67; Phonexia, 2023b). In an investigative context, it may be as simple as comparing the "reference voiceprint—as sample A" with another recording (sample B) to determine whether they are the same person: without being about to accurately identify the Person, in either of the samples. Other systems are used to determine if Sample A (unknown voice) is that of Sample B (known voice).

Voice biometrics, like human listeners, use characteristics of a person's voice to identify or match the speaker. Systems that perform this function have been used in real-world security applications for more than a decade. The most significant distinction between voice biometrics systems and other speech-processing technologies, such as speech recognition, is that voice biometrics technologies do not understand what a person is saying and must rely on speech recognition to do so. Furthermore, the speaker independence trend that characterizes speech recognition cannot exist in voice biometrics. By definition, voice biometrics is always associated with a specific speaker (Markowitz 2000, p. 66). There are presently a variety of methods using voice as foundation from which to draw inferences. The tool that the investigator will select will be determined by the question the investigator is seeking to answer.

If the question is related to whether a person is telling the truth or not, then technology such as CVSA or psychological stress evaluator (PSE) may be harnessed (Kirchhübel, 2013, p. 20). From these technologies, the layered voice analysis (LVA) is possibly the most well-known approach used by modern day investigators: for criminal and other investigations. Thus, if the testimony of a witness needs verification on specific elements, then an LVA may be utilized for that purpose.

While if the investigator is asking whether the voice in the recording labelled as sample "A" is the same or different from the voice in the recording labelled as sample "B," then a Forensic Voice Comparison may be used. Each of these will be discussed below, and their evidential value in criminal and civil tribunals will be considered. While the use of the voice as biometric is fundamental to these investigative techniques, in a polygraph exam, the actual voice of the individual is less significant than the physiological responses of the human subject to questions asked. A brief discussion of this method is offered below.

Polygraph

Humankind has always searched for a reliable way, technique, or instrument to distinguish between truth and lies. In 1921, John Larson invented the first polygraph (Marcolla, de Santiago, & Dazzi, 2020, p. 742). A polygraph assumes that telling a lie causes stress, which can be read. A polygraph instrument is a piece of equipment that measures physiological changes in a person when asked specific questions, indicating possible deception. It detects physiological disturbances in the target person's body.

A polygraph should not be considered as a "lie-detector" because it is not. "A polygraph ... is a probabilistic test that involves the recording of physiological responses to stimuli and uses statistical decision theory to quantify the margin of error or level of statistical significance—or alternatively the odds or confidence level—associated with the test result" (Nelson, 2015, p. 49). A polygraph does not measure lies (Nelson, 2015,

p. 50) since the results are presented as probabilistic phrases. These are then interpreted by a human based on set standards or principles. The continued reference to this tool as a "lie detector" for reasons such as "ease of reference" is irresponsible and lazy. It perpetuates the misconception of what the tool was designed for and therefore a misalignment of the ultimate expectation: thus the meaning of the interpreted results.

The popularity of the polygraph as a tool to detect deception has only increased over time. The polygraph as a reliable tool has also been the object of extensive scientific research (Nelson, 2015). In South Africa, polygraph results are not yet accepted as reliable evidence in criminal courts, but they are admissible in civil cases under specific circumstances. The South African Labour Court held in *Truworths Ltd v CCMA and others* (2009) 30 ILJ (LC), that polygraph tests are admissible when clear evidence of the polygraphist's qualifications and adherence to acceptable standards is presented. The probative value of a polygraph test on its own is insufficient to find an individual guilty, and a test result is one of several factors that may be considered. In *Nyathi v Special Investigating Unit* (2011) JOL 27537 (LC), the court held that an employee's refusal to undergo a polygraph test regarding alleged misconduct was a material breach of the employment contract.

The available information shows that polygraph test results can be accepted as evidence in the Labour Court and disciplinary hearings only: pending specific requirements. Polygraph test results, on their own, cannot be used as a basis to determine guilt, but they can be used in support of other evidence.

Polygraphs are ineffective on video and audio resources because they require the presence of the subject (Marcolla et al., 2020, p. 742). To address these issues, some polygraph software versions that use voice stress analyzers have been proposed: but then it would no longer be a polygraph examination in the true sense of the word—but rather a form of stress test on a voice. This will be discussed further below. A polygraph examination can sometimes be viewed as intrusive, as it requires the physical presence of the person to be polygraphed.

The ACFE has published forensic standards for polygraph examiners (Griesel & Sappa, 2018). The ACFE standards are intended to set minimum guidelines for specific forensic disciplines. In their training materials, they underscore the adherence to professional standards and the importance of adhering to evidential procedures (Griesel & Sappa, 2018, p. 5).

Computer Voice Stress Analysis

Our bodies react to stress and stressful situations in a variety of ways; hands shake, eyes twitch, and voices change. Based on the analogy that when humans are deceptive, their bodies will emit micro-signals and other biological signs, scientists have tried to study and monitor these signals and signs to develop "lie-detection" methods. For several decades, researchers have been testing and evaluating the accuracy of voice stress analyzers (also called psychological stress evaluators, PSE) to detect deception and/or to identify lies in human communication (Bhatt & Brandon, 2008; Harnsberger, Hollien, Martin, & Hollien, 2009; Horvath, 1982; Podlesny & Raskin, 1977; Van Puyvelde, Neyt, McGlone, & Pattyn, 2018). The literature shows that voice stress analyzers remain ineffective to accurately detect deception beyond a 50:50 chance (Bhatt & Brandon, 2008; Harnsberger, Hollien, Martin, & Hollien, 2009; Horvath, 1982; Podlesny & Raskin, 1977; Van Puyvelde, Neyt, McGlone, & Nathalie Pattyn, 2018), despite what the designers claim.

Voice stress analysis is a method, where microtremor detection is ostensibly used to identify deception or blatant lies (Kirchhübel, Howard, & Stedmon, 2011, p. 89). This nexus (between microtremors and deception) has been debunked by Eriksson and Laserda (2007, pp. 173–174), who argue that nowhere in his research did Lippold suggest that the discovery (microtremors) can be used in applications designed to detect lies or deception.

In investigative and security settings, voice stress analysis software, designed to detect disturbances in a subject's voice pattern, is then used to determine truthfulness and deception. This software interprets the voice disruptions and returns the outcome (Marcolla, de Santiago & Dazzi, 2020, p. 742). There are various software programs designed for this purpose.

The South African chapter of the ACFE has drafted forensic standards for the use of Voice Stress Detection (VSD) but do highlight that the VSD is an investigative tool (Potgieter, Coetzee, Swart, de Jager, & Ferreira, 2019, p. 7).

Layered Voice Analysis

The Layered Voice Analysis (LVA) is a type of voice stress analyzer. The investigator uses software to detect and analyze unconscious emotional cues, which could be useful for screening potential deviant behavior, criminal investigation, and comprehending layers of emotional cues and cognitive processes. LVA detects the speaker's current mental state to detect the speaker's internal reaction to the lie (Srivastava, Hussain & Gupta, 2022). An LVA can be conducted over the phone, and such an analysis can also be done on a voice recording (Townsend, van Rooyen, Ferreira, & de Jager, 2019, p. 8).

The legitimacy of the LVA remains questionable within the criminal justice arena (Harnsberger, Hollien, Martin & Hollien, 2009:642), although it is open for consideration during disciplinary hearings, provided specific requirements are met (Townsend et al., 2019, p. 9). This is very similar to the requirement for the permissibility of polygraph results at such hearings.

In addition to the microtremors argument put forth by proponents of CVSA to detect deception, there are also arguments that the LVA employs sophisticated "algorithms that extract more than 120 emotional parameters from each voice segment" (Erikson & Lacerda 2007, p. 179). The mathematical reliability of this statement has been questioned by the preceding authors, since there is no research documented which proves the assertion. The use of scientific sounding terminology should surely be backed-up by verifiable evidence, or at least access to the published research results on a reputable platform. Erikson and Lacerda (2007, p. 189) put forth the argument that the "bogus pipeline effect" may be what is contributing to the apparent "success" of CVSA.

In 1971, Jones and Sigall (1971) published research illustrating the impact of the "bogus-pipeline effect." This effect occurs when a subject believes that the researcher/interviewer has a "pipeline" to the truth: they have a way (the use of an LVA or CVSA technology) to tell whether the subject is telling the truth or not. It illustrates that if a subject believes that their answers can be tested for accuracy, they will be more inclined to be truthful (Damphousse, Pointon, Upchurch, & Moore, 2007, p. 82; Jones & Sigall, 1971, p. 349).

Voice Comparison

Similar to fingerprint individuality, the voice of each individual is unique to that person (Phonexia, 2023b). Voice biometrics, as technological tool, have been evolving within the investigative space as well as the cyber context for a couple of decades already. Banks, retailers and other online trading sites have used this technology to enable the voice authentication of clients, making the use of passwords obsolete. In addition, it has been used as an additional security layer, and to assist in the timeous identification of subscription fraud (Phonexia, 2023b). In the law enforcement and forensic contexts, the use of voice biometric technology has been helpful to identify individual speakers, to search through large data sets for the voice of an individual speaker, to undertake automatic forensic voice comparisons and the analysis of voice evidence for use in criminal courts (Phonexia, 2023b).

Researchers in speech processing prefer the term "speaker recognition." Outside of the speech-processing industry, it is frequently confused with "speech recognition," which refers to speech-processing technology that recognizes what a person is saying. As a result of this misunderstanding, some people use speech-recognition tools for security purposes that exceed speech-recognition technology's capabilities. As a result, the password or passcode's security is jeopardized. Another perplexing term is "voice recognition," which is frequently used to refer to speech recognition but implies some level of speaker identification.

Forensic voice comparison (FVC), also known as "forensic speaker identification, forensic speaker recognition, and forensic speaker identification" (Morrison & Enzinger 2018, p. 560), is an investigative tool used to compare two or more audio recordings to determine if they are or are not the voice of the same person. This evidence is often required to assist a court in reaching a just finding (Kirchhübel, Brown, & Foulkes, 2023, p. 251). The two primary techniques used for voice comparison analysis are the auditory-phonetic and acoustic (AuPhA) analysis (which is done by an expert) and the utilization of an "automatic speaker recognition system" (supplemented by human analysis). In the United Kingdom, the courts only accept voice comparison analysis when done with the AuPhA approach (Kirchhübel et al, 2023, p. 251). Morrison and Enzinger refer to four different approaches, namely auditory, spectrographic, acoustic-phonetic and automatic (Morrison & Enzinger, 2018, p. 601). Practitioners rarely use only one approach but opt for a combination of approaches. Research undertaken by Gold and French (2011) and Morrison, Sahito, Jardine, Djokic, Clavet, Berghs, and Goemans Dorny (2017) shows that the most popular method in use by practitioners is the AuPhA analysis.

In a South African investigative context, the use of forensic voice comparison (FVC) software, as a tool in any form of investigation, is still in its infancy. It was used during the 2022 trial of Mr Bruce Nimmerhoudt, who was accused of inciting violence during the 2021 civil unrest in parts of South Africa. The State alleged that "he circulated a WhatsApp voice note, inciting public violence and calling on people to block national highways" (Pijoos, 2022). A voice comparison expert testified at his trial but could not satisfy the court that the technology used to compare the voices was scientific and reliable.

While several companies have been using forensic voice comparison technology as part of an investigative process, it has yet to prove itself in a court of law, or any other formal tribunal for that matter, in South Africa. It is however, being used by insurance companies when claims are "red flagged" by the consultant (Danckwerts, Naran, & Swana, 2020, p. 53; RixForensica, 2023).

Methodological Framework

The data for this chapter is based on empirical data gathered as part of a larger study titled "An Exploration of the Transformation of Forensic Investigations in the South African Criminal Justice Context." The study is being conducted with ethical clearance from the College of Law Ethics

Committee, ERC Reference P17: 2022. The authors noted in this paper are the three researchers conducting the study.

The overarching research question that guided the research is "To what extent have forensic investigators in South Africa kept abreast of developments in the evolving discipline on investigative practice." Following a purely qualitative approach, data were gathered through in-depth, semi-structured interviews (both online and in person) from forensic investigators (all investigators external to law enforcement) using a combination of key informant sampling and snowball sampling for selection. Inclusion criteria for possible selection is "forensic investigators currently employed by organizations, institutions or companies (external to the SAPS) who have investigative experience of 15 years or more."

Since ethical clearance was obtained for this research (as mentioned above) the participants may not be identified, but it is possible to provide an overview of these individuals. There were in total seven participants selected for interviews: six male and one female (numbered P1 to P7 in reporting the findings below). This is not indicative of the gender distribution in this space but rather attributed to time available to the researchers and those approached for interviews. Of the seven participants, six have a CFE certification, three have significant experience (26 years collectively) in the insurance industry, four have a law enforcement background, and five are either in middle management or senior management positions (still operational) at their places of employment. In total, the seven research participants have a total of 182 years investigative experience in a range of disciplines. Thus what the sample may lack in numbers, it makes up for by its sheer depth.

Interviews were conducted until data saturation was reached in the primary themes of the study. Data were extrapolated from the sub-question: To what extent has witness testimony been affected using AI in preparation for the litigation (court) process?

The three researchers were present when the first interview (in person) was done. Each researcher transcribed a portion of the three-hour interview, after which the transcriptions were joined into one document. The three researchers did initial coding. The data were analyzed using Creswell's Data Analysis Spiral. From the data analysis, codes, categories, and finally themes were identified. Thereafter, using a combination of snowball sampling and key informant sampling, six additional participants were identified. Each researcher volunteered for two interviews, which were then done solo. Each researcher was responsible for the transcriptions and coding of these interviews.

The trustworthiness of the research is measured against the criteria of dependability, confirmability, transferability, and credibility. Dependability and credibility are interdependent. The researchers used several strategies to address these two criteria. The interviews and the subsequent analysis and interpretation of the data are being documented in a "research journal" to ensure that there is an audit trail. Any research text produced will include "in vivo" quotes from the participants. The extent to which the data are transferable to other contexts will depend on the reader's consideration. To enable the reader to make an informed decision, the researchers have tried to clarify the research process followed in as much detail as the page limitations permitted. All three researchers intentionally bracketed their own ideas, experiences, and notions. In addition, the researchers used member checks to confirm the validity of the data gathered and the analysis thereof.

In the following section, the researchers discuss the primary themes that emerged from the data and their relevance in the field of forensic investigation.

Discussion and Recommendations

Developments in the Investigative Field: Role Players and Service Providers

The private security industry has grown exponentially over the past two decades (Kole, 2015; Minnaar, 2004; PMG, 2023). The number of registered and active security officers exceed the number of police officials in the SAPS. This implies that the constitutionally mandated law enforcement agency (SAPS) has fewer members with which to "prevent, investigate and combat crime; maintain public order; protect and secure the inhabitants of South Africa and their property; and uphold and enforce the law" (PMG, 2023), than is at the disposal of the registered security companies in South Arica. The escalation in the number of registered security officers and security companies over the past decade may indicate society's loss of confidence in the SAPS. One of the participants expressed that "the capacity of the police … is stretched beyond its limits" (P6, December 5, 2022).

A search on Google, using "private investigation companies in South Africa" produced close to 50 million hits. Some advertise the "Top 10 investigators" (Kinuthia, 2023) or "The best 10 forensic investigators in South Africa" (Infoserve, 2023). It is improbable that these "rankings" are because of anything other than a marketing algorithm designed to flag these businesses when specific search terms are used. Many more options can be found in addition to these mentioned.

On closer inspection one finds that not all offering their services are registered with PSiRA, as required by law (Netshivhuyu 2018, p. 4). In addition to a PsiRA registration, a person wanting to become a private investigator must be 18 years or older, a South African citizen without a criminal record. They will have to complete a PI licensing program, approved by the South African government, and not be a member of the SAPS or other national security agency (PsiRA 2023). The participants in this research are well versed in these legislative requirements and commented that "Forensic investigators, auditors and other similar occupational groups such as those who are employed primarily to conduct investigations, are exempt from being registered (P6, December 5, 2022). Another participant furthermore emphasized that "business has got a huge role to play because the majority of the cases that gets reported is reported by business" (P6, December 5, 2022).

A recent study conducted by PSiRA highlights that there are still many challenges in relation to the registration of private investigator, and many rogue investigators are still flouting the rules, with apparent impunity (Netshivhuyu 2018, p. 13). In this regard one of the participants accentuated that "a lot of companies actually … called themselves a forensic audit department … misleading the public out there—they were not auditing … Remember, you can go in you can really do random audits, that doesn't make you an auditor" (P6, December 5, 2022).

There are numerous investigative organizations or companies that offer an array of investigative services, some of which are very specialized. Among these companies are the so called "big 4" (Part 6, 2022; Netshivhuyu 2018, p. 19) auditing firms in South Africa: PricewaterhouseCoopers (PWC), Deloitte, KPMG and Ernest & Young. A large number of them have employed ex-police detectives. In addition, most insurance companies utilize their own investigative capacities to investigate potential fraudulent claims.

Other than the PsiRA legislation, no specific piece of legislation regulates who and how investigations are to be conducted, external to the SAPS. The Association of Certified Fraud Examiners (ACFE) and the Institute of Commercial Forensic Practitioners (ICFP) are possibly the two best known and respected bodies in the South African investigation space. They indicate on their websites that they are regulatory in nature. One of the participants expanded by stating "the police and us [ACFE] are working together and looking at other ways to get members involved and provide services to the police" (P6, December 5, 2022).

On Sunday evening, January 29, 2023, the television program *Crime Watch* featured interviews with several role players in the private security industry. The focus of the program was on the increase in demand for "lie detection" tests in the industry (Crime Watch, 2023). The presenter interviewed several role players who specialize in the use of voice analysis to detect deception (amongst other things).

Unfortunately, the claims made in popular media and on other platforms by a variety of service providers, promising the accurate identification of deception, and "lie-detection" may result in honest people being branded as dishonest and dishonest people being identified as truthful. It was remarked by a participant that "professionals in the field of truth verification know there is no such thing as a real Lie Detector—as lying is not associated with a single specific mental state" (P2, January 30, 2023).

The investigative field, external to the SAPS has undergone a metamorphosis of sorts, over the past two decades. Role players and stakeholders from within civil society have taken it upon themselves to situate investigative capacity into the spaces vacated as large numbers of experienced and skilled police officials left the ranks of the SAPS.

Impact of Research in this Field

The researchers conducted an extensive search for available online sources that featured vital terms such as artificial intelligence (AI), AI and the South African legal system, 4IR and its impact on investigations, the South African investigative context (police, parastatal, corporate and private), identification and individualization techniques in investigations, biometrics, LVA, CVSA, voice comparisons/forensic voice comparisons, polygraphs, the burden of proof within the South African legal system, communication, effective interview in an investigative context and the impact of the COVID pandemic on investigations. The results led the researchers to believe that there existed a gap in legitimate and authentically South African research that addressed their research topic.

While there is an extensive body of literature on the topics of biometrics, LVA, CVSA, polygraphs, and their use in criminal and civil investigations at an international level (Erikson & Lacerda, 2007; Kirchhübel, Brown & Foulkes 2023; Morrison, 2009; Morrison & Enzinger, 2019; Palmatier 2016; Van Puyvelde, Neyt, McGlone & Pattyn 2018) the same cannot be said about the South African context specifically.

Numerous academic and other reliable sources did partially address aspects of this paper: but nothing came close to what the authors purposed to do. Sources that were accessed include but are not limited to Breedt and Olivier (2004), Chigada (2020), Graham (2020), Griesel & Sappa (2018), Kole (2015), Lamb (2021), Madihlaba (2021), Martin (2001), Minnaar (2004), Netshivuyu (2018), Newham (2021b), Opperman (2014), Potgieter, Coetzee, Swart, de Jager & Ferreira (2019), Sudheim (2015), Swales (2017), and Townsend, van Rooyen, Ferreira, and de Jager (2019).

It is evident that while there has been a concerted focus on research in "Partnership Policing" initiatives in South Africa, very little published research could be found that has focussed on the judicial value of polygraphs, LVA, other CVSA and the use of forensic voice comparison (voice recognition technology) in an investigative context.

The Use of LVA, CVSA and Forensic Voice Comparison Technology as Investigative Tools to Detect Deception

The research participants are all familiar with the concept of LVA and CVSA. Some have been using a version of the LVA for several years already. One of the participants expressed their viewpoint in this regard:

> during this time of investigation, it came to my knowledge that there was new technology in the world being used … about 2002 … it was developed by the Mossad, Israel for interviews at their airports … on a voice algorithm. And it was developed in such a way that it will give you an indication where the interviewer or the person being interviewed is not sharing about the facts that he conveyed to you, or whether he actually blatantly tell [told] you a lie.
> (P7, January 27, 2023)

Furthermore, one of the participants expanded upon the use of LVA, CVSA, and forensic voice comparison technology as an investigative tool to detect deception and emphasized "the LVA is a forensic tool used to determine if a person being interviewed is untruthful or nervous about a specific aspect that he is being questioned about … The system is mostly used in the insurance industry" (P1, January 28, 2023). In addition, another participant offered:

> This data can be further processed by statistical learning algorithms to predict the probability of deceptive or fraudulent intention in a sentence or for any other psychological analysis. While the basic technology used in LVA is protected by 2 different patents, most of its internal processes are … secret know-how.
> (P3, January 30, 2023)

But not all of the participants make use of the LVA or voice stress analyzer technology. Instead, voice comparison technology is used in their investigative context. In this regard one of the participants conveyed:

> we do not have a device or layered voice analysis that we are checking in the background whether this person is talking the truth or not … I will go and listen to the two calls … I analyze it, I run it through … software that we have and then the software will then indicate whether there's a similarity between the two voices …
> (P4, January 20, 2023)

The findings are insightful when comparing the research published on LVA/CVSA technology with the research that focusses on voice comparison technology. The literature gathered for this study highlights that much of the results from the "scientific" tests conducted on LVA/CVSA technology, are guesstimates (Bhatt & Brandon, 2008; Erikkson & Lacerda, 2007; Kirchhübel, 2013) at best. Research focussing on voice comparison technology appears to be more promising in delivering on claims of "voice identification" and "voice verification" (Lindh 2017; Morrison & Enzinger 2018). The former is however "more complex" to do than the latter.

In addition, this methodology (LVA) is significantly impacted by the experience and skill of the person who conducts the interview and the person who analyzes the result. The experience of the interviewer was highlighted by P7 (January 27, 2023), who indicated that "I definitely know it is a shortcut and it is a good indicator, but you have to have a proper skilled interviewer and a proper skilled operator on the editing of the machine …" In this regard P7 added that "The conversation must be properly recorded so it can be properly analyzed. Then the person who conducts the interview must be experienced and skilled … And then the person who interprets the results must also be skilled … Otherwise, I'm gonna give you the wrong information."

Impact of Practice on Policy or Legislation

This research, though limited in terms of the number of participants, has illustrated to what extent the investigative practice has been influenced over the past decade by technology. As mentioned above, while the number of participants interviewed for this study may seem limited, their collective experience in the South African investigative context spans approximately 182 years.

There are NO laws directly applicable to these technologies in SA. The ACFE and the ICFP have drafted standards, informed by practice, for use by their members, but this has yet to translate into legislation.

Mindful of this, from a legislative standpoint, there are several laws that frame the rights of people in an employment setting. These are among others:

- The Constitution of the Republic of SA—specifically the Bills of Rights.
- The Labour Relations Act—Act 66 of 1995.
- The Basic Conditions for Employment Act, Act 75 of 1997.
- Employment Equity Act, Act 55 of 1998.

There have been several decided court cases (*Truworths Ltd v CCMA and others* (2009) 30 ILJ (LC) and *Nyathi v Special Investigating Unit* (2011) JOL 27537 (LC)); these have been in a Labour court setting, and against very specific and stringent evidentiary parameters. The impact of practice on policy and legislation was addressed by P1 (January 28, 2023), who commented:

> the Labour Relations Act (LRA) makes provision for the LVA, similar to the polygraph examination to be used in disciplinary enquiries, CCM and bargaining council, and Labour Court as long as it is supported with corroborating evidence. It is not accepted in criminal court as it is not 100% accurate and no act makes provision for it to be used in the criminal justice system.

In addition, it was underscored that "The examiner has to sit and testify as an expert witness. They need to be open for cross examination. The commissioner is testing for reliability and ... the commissioner will have to decide how much weight does this all have" (P5, January 31, 2023).

Admissibility of Forensic Voice Comparison and LVA as Evidence

Presently the rules of evidence as per the Criminal Procedure Act (act 51 of 1977) have to a large extent set the requirements for the admissibility of evidence in criminal courts. Thus, any evidence being offered must meet these requirements: failure will result in the rejection of the evidence.

Drawing on the perspectives of the participants in this study, LVA is utilized as an investigative tool. The admissibility of LVA in applicable scenarios, such as CCMA and civil matters, is based on similar principles to the Polygraph. Its use in a labor court setting is gaining some prominence. Expanding on the admissibility of forensic voice comparison and Layered Voice Analysis (LVA) as evidence P2 (January 30, 2023) explained that "LVA is not admissible in criminal but in the labor issues ... Voice biometrics can be used and is accepted in criminal court as well, as long as it can be tested, validated and should any other expert use the same tool they would come to a similar conclusion."

Forensic voice comparison (voice biometrics) on the other hand may be offered as evidence in a criminal court, but with very specific parameters. The researchers could not find any court case where voice comparison technology was accepted as evidence during trial. This is probably since its current use is within an insurance context, as part of a bundle of evidence and "so in 80% of these cases, ... after analyzing the data given by algorithm ... you're finding was there was impersonation ... the company refuses to pay out and you close the file" (P4, January 20, 2023). There is thus no criminal charge to be validated in a criminal court.

Forensic Voice Comparison (Voice Biometrics) and LVA as Tools for Investigators: Advantages and Applications

Participants in the study indicated that the LVA can be a useful tool for investigators (P2, January 30, 2023; P4, January 20, 2023). It can help identify a suspect's involvement or eliminate them from suspicion. The insight into the subject's mental state can be valuable in focusing the investigation, such as when a particular topic triggers fear or unwillingness to discuss it. Deceptive parts of the interview can highlight areas that require further investigation (P7, January 27, 2023).

The LVA can also help eliminate honest subjects from many potential suspects. After testing, a Certified Fraud Examiner (CFE) can verify the outcome by reviewing all the analysis layers presented by the test, eliminating many possible inconsistencies during a verbal interview. Once deceptions are identified, the CFE can focus the investigation on specific areas of interest in preparation for a final face-to-face interview. One of the participants expressed that "you must remember that LVA is a good indicator. It's a tool. It's not something I would use in court ... there will always be an investigator you have to verify the facts."

The Impact of Technology on the Future of Investigations: A Look Ahead

Expanding upon the perspectives highlighted by the participants in this study, access to and knowledge of technology is increasingly important and widely being used in investigations. The COVID-19 pandemic highlighted these aspects, when South Africans were placed under rigid movement restrictions between 2020 and much of 2022, and work-life activities had to be taken online.

Technology aided tools are increasingly being used to minimize complexity and assist in coming to data conclusions, which are then tested through other investigation techniques. It has also been noted that while evidence produced by these AI-enhanced voice-related tools are accepted in disciplinary inquiries and labor proceedings, this must be as a collective with additional evidence. As such, the research highlighted that human interaction, intuition, and other non-technical skills, remain crucial in investigations.

Conclusion

As a constitutional democracy, South Africa has legislated the rights of citizens. The right to safety and security are amongst them. Regrettably, these rights are far from being protected by those empowered to do so. It is evident from the preceding discussions that policing and investigation as praxis have evolved considerably over the past few decades in

South Africa. This evolution has only sometimes been to the benefit of society and crime seems to continue unabated.

In this context, private institutions and other civil society groups have taken it upon themselves to take a "proverbial stand" and address crime. Whistleblowers have often paid the ultimate price for "speaking truth to power," and their sacrifices seem wasted when viewed through the lack of prosecution lens.

The investigative capacity, external to the SAPS, has grown significantly during this same period of law enforcement decline. The use of AI in the fields of deception detection and voice comparisons has also seen significant changes. Various investigative organizations are making use of polygraphs, CVSA and LVA to detect deception: with varying degrees of success. The research also highlighted the existence of the "Bogus Pipeline effect" and posited that it may be more responsible for the "successes" of these technologies than the technologies themselves. However, since this research did not focus on the "Bogus Pipeline Effect," this is but speculation on the part of the researchers.

Alternative approaches using forensic voice comparison (FVC) technology are also being utilized within the investigative context in South Africa, but to a lesser degree than CVSA and LVA. These technologies (CVSA, LVA, and FVC) have been utilized by the participants, during both suspect and witness interviews: all in the interest of detecting deception or verifying facts. Those using them, swear by them.

While the ACFE and the ICFP are harnessing the AI enhanced tools at their disposal, the results are clear. While some of these tools have proven themselves over time, through valid scientific research, others have not. AI enhanced investigative tools are just that; investigative tools to assist the investigator in the search for the truth. They cannot, at this time, replace the human being. It would seem that Sherlock Holmes is safe from the machines … for now.

References

ACJR Factsheet. 2021. Failing to discipline in SAPS: Fostering a culture of impunity. Factsheet 9. Retrieved from https://acjr.org.za/resource-centre/fact-sheet-9-failing-to-discipline-v-3.pdf (accessed on January 26, 2023).

Bester, P.C. 2017. South Africa: The current state of the rule of law and key challenges in strengthening the rule of law. Unpublished manuscript, Wits School of Governance, University of Witwatersrand, Johannesburg.

Bhatt, S. & Brandon, S.E. 2008. Review of voice stress based technologies for the detection of deception. Retrieved from https://missouripolygraph.com/downloads/cvsa-review.pdf (accessed on January 30, 2023).

Bloom, K. 2023. Eskom Intelligence Files, Part One: Introducing the four crime cartels that have brought Eskom and South Africa to their knees. Retrieved from www.dailymaverick.co.za/article/2023-02-27-introducing-the-four-crime-cartels-that-have-brought-eskom-and-south-africa-to-their-knees/ (accessed on February 27, 2023).

Booysen, S. 2013. Twenty years of South African democracy: Citizen views of human rights, governance and the political system. Retrieved from https://freedomhouse.org/sites/default/files/Twenty%20Years%20of%20South%20African%20Democracy.pdf (accessed on January 26, 2023).

Breedt, M. & Olivier, M.S. 2004. Using a central data repository for biometric authentication in passport systems. Retrieved from www.researchgate.net/publication/237211517_USING_A_CENTRAL_DATA_REPOSITORY_FOR_BIOMETRIC_AUTHENTICATION_IN_PASSPORT_SYSTEMS_1 (accessed on March 1, 2023).

Burger, J. 2011. To protect and serve: Restoring public confidence in the SAPS. *SA Crime Quarterly*, 36(June): 13–22. doi.org/10.17159/2413-3108/2011/v0i36a863

Chigada, J.M. 2020. A qualitative analysis of the feasibility of deploying biometric authentication systems to augment security protocols of bank card transactions. *South African Journal of Information Management*, 22(1), 1–9. https://doi.org/10.4102/

Crime Watch. 2023. *eNCA DSTV 403*, 29 January 2023.

Čut, M 2022. Digital natives and digital immigrants—How are they different. Retrieved from https://medium.com/digital-reflections/digital-natives-and-digital-immigrants-how-are-they-different-e849b0a8a1d3 (accessed on September 29, 2022).

Damphousse, K.R., Pointon, L., Upchurch, D. & Moore, R.K. 2007. Assessing the validity of voice stress analysis tools in a jail setting. Retrieved from www.ojp.gov/library/publications/assessing-validity-voice-stress-analysis-tools-jail-setting (accessed on June 6, 2023).

Danckwerts, M., Naran, K. & Swana, A. 2020. *Resilience: The South African Insurance Industry Survey 2020*. Pretoria: KPMG.

Dlamini, S. 2020. Citizen's satisfaction with the South African Police Services and community police forums in Durban, South Africa. *International Journal of Social Sciences and Humanities Studies*, 12(2), 593–606.

Farmer, B. & Thornycroft, P. 2022 Mystery of murdered whistleblower who uncovered hospital corruption. Retrieved from www.telegraph.co.uk/global-health/terror-and-security/mystery-murdered-whistleblower-babita-deokaran-who-uncovered/ (accessed on April 4, 2023).

Faull, A. 2010. Missing the target: when measuring performance undermines police effectiveness. *SA Crime Quarterly*, 31, 19–25.

Graham, V. 2020. South Africa's democracy: The quality of political participation over 25 years. *Journal of African Elections*, 19(1), 28–51. doi: 10.20940/JAE/2020/v19i1a2

Griesel, A. & Sappa. 2018. *ACFE Forensic Standards for polygraph examiners*. Pretoria: ACFE South African Chapter.

Grootes, S. 2023. André de Ruyter, ANC and the end of Eskom as we know it. Retrieved from www.msn.com/en-za/news/other/andr%C3%A9-de-ruyter-anc-and-the-end-of-eskom-as-we-know-it/ar-AA17WPqJ?ocid=entnewsntp&cvid=710b821edeba4d20b8601ece49af5d01&ei=12 (accessed on February 27, 2023).

Growcoot, M. 2023. AI reveals its biases by generating what it thinks professors look like. 13 May. Retrieved from https://petapixel.com/2023/05/04/ai-reveals-its-biases-by-generating-what-it-thinks-professors-look-like/ (accessed on May 13 2023).

Harnsberger, J.D., Hollien, H., Martin, C.A. & Hollien, K.A. 2009. Stress and deception in speech: evaluating layered Voice Analysis. *Journal of Forensic Science*, 54(3), 642–650.

Holtz, B. 2022. Werksman Attorneys: Business crimes and investigations. Retrieved from www.werksmans.com/practices/business-crimes-investigations/ (accessed on September 27, 2022).

ICFP. [Sa]. About the ICFP. Retrieved from www.icfp.co.za/about-the-icfp/ (accessed on January 30, 2023).

ICFP. 2022a. Attribute standards. Retrieved from www.icfp.co.za/wp-content/uploads/2022/08/ICFP-Attribute-Standards.pdf (accessed on January 30, 2023).

ICFP. 2022b. Information gathering standards. Retrieved from www.icfp.co.za/wp-content/uploads/2022/08/ICFP-Information-Gathering-Standards.pdf (accessed on January 30, 2023).

ICFP. 2022c. Reporting standards. Retrieved from www.icfp.co.za/wp-content/uploads/2022/08/ICFP-Reporting-Standards.pdf (accessed on January 30, 2023).

Infoserve. 2023. The 10 Best Forensic Investigators in South Africa. Retrieved from www.infoisinfo.co.za/search/forensic-investigator (accessed on May 30, 2023).

Joubert, C. 2013. *Applied law for police officials*. 4th edition. Claremont: Juta.

Karels, M. 2014. Introduction to constitutional law (Pp. 17–37). In J. P. Swanepoel, S. Lötter & M. Karels (Eds.). *Policing and the law: A practical guide*. Durban: Lexis Nexis.

Kinuthia, P. 2023. Home Facts and lifehacks Top 10 TOP 10 Private detective in Johannesburg (2023): Top 10 best investigators. Retrieved from https://briefly.co.za/facts-lifehacks/top/153999-private-detective-johannesburg-2023-top-10-investigators/ (accessed on May 30, 2023).

Kirchhübel, C., Howard, D.M. & Stedmon, A.W. 2011. Acoustic Correlates of Speech when Under Stress: Research, Methods and Future Directions. *International Journal of Speech Language and the Law*, 18(1), 75–98. doi:10.1558/ijsll.v18i1.75.

Kirchhübel, C., Brown, G. & Foulkes, P. 2023. What does method validation look like for forensic voice comparison by a human expert? *Science & Justice*, 63, 251–257.

Kole, J.O. 2015. Partnership policing between the South African Police Service and the private security industry in reducing crime in South Africa. Unpublished PhD thesis. Pretoria: University of South Africa.

Korzeniowski, P. 2022. Voice biometrics are not 100 percent foolproof, but steadily improving. Retrieved from www.destinationcrm.com/Articles/Editorial/Magazine-Features/Voice-Biometrics-Are-Not-100-Percent-Foolproof-but-Steadily-Improving-152171.aspx#:~:text=It%20relies%20on%20two%20levels,identify%20who%20the%20caller%20is (accessed on February 3, 2023).

Lamb, G. 2021. Safeguarding the Republic? The South African Police Service, Legitimacy and the tribulations of policing a violent democracy. *Journal of Asian and African Studies*, 56(1), 92–108. DOI: 10.1177/0021909620946853

Lee-Jacobs, S. 2021. Lying under oath makes you guilty of a crime. Retrieved from www.news24.com/news24/community-newspaper/peoples-post/lying-under-oath-makes-you-guilty-of-a-crime-20211025-2 (accessed on May 15, 2021).

Lindh, J. 2017. Forensic comparison of voices, speech and speakers: tools and methods in forensic phonetics. Unpublished PhD in the Department of Philosophy, Linguistics and the Theory of Science, University of Gothenburg.

Lockett, K.L. 2010. Liar! Liar! Deception detection in 2035. Retrieved from https://apps.dtic.mil/sti/pdfs/AD1019260.pdf (accessed on May 15, 2023).

Marcolla, F., de Santiago, R. & Dazzi, R. 2020. Novel Lie Speech Classification by using Voice Stress (pp. 742–749). Proceedings of the 12th International Conference on Agents and Artificial Intelligence (ICAART 2020). doi:10.5220/0009038707420749.

Martin, R.C. 2001. The application of the polygraph in the criminal justice system. Unpublished Masters dissertation. Pretoria: University of South Africa.

Minnaar, A. 2004. Crime prevention, partnership policing and the growth of private security: The South African experience. (Pp. 1–25). In G, Mesko, M Pagon & B Dobovsek. *Policing in Central and Eastern Europe: Dilemmas of contemporary criminal justice*. Slovenia: University of Maribor.

Morrison, G.S. 2009. The place of forensic voice comparison in the ongoing paradigm shift. *The 2nd International Conference on Evidence Law and Forensic Science Conference Thesis*, 1, 20–34.

Morrison, G.S. & Enzinger, E. 2019. Introduction to forensic voice comparison. (Pp. 599–634). In W.F. Katz & P.F. Assmann (Eds.) *The Routledge handbook of phonetics*. Abingdon, UK: Taylor & Francis. doi.org/10.4324/9780429056253-22.

Morrison, G.S., Sahito, F.H., Jardine, G., Djokic, D., Clavet, S., Berghs, S. & Goemans Dorny, C. 2017. INTERPOL survey of the use of speaker identification by law enforcement agencies. *Forensic Science International*, 263, 92–100. Retrieved from http://dx.doi.org/10.1016/j.forsciint.2016.03.044

Myburgh, J. 2022. Don't fib to Lizette Volkwyn—she's a highly trained human lie-detector and she'll catch you out almost every time. Retrieved from www.news24.com/you/news/local/dont-try-to-fib-to-lizette-volkwyn-shes-a-highly-trained-human-lie-detector-and-shell-catch-you-out-almost-every-time-20230110 (accessed on April 4, 2023).

NATGEO. 2014. National Geographic Kids. Retrieved from https://kids.nationalgeographic.com/geography/countries/article/south-africa (accessed on January 26, 2023).

Netshivhuyu, D. 2018. PSiRA: The Private eye under the microscope. Retrieved from www.psira.co.za/dmdocuments/research/Private_investigations_web.pdf (accessed on January 26, 2023).

Newham, G. 2021a. Briefing note: South African Police Service resourcing and performance 2012 to 2020. Retrieved from https://issafrica.s3.amazonaws.com/site/uploads/SAPS-resourcing-and-performance-2012-2020.pdf (accessed on February 2, 2023).

Newham, G. 2021b. SA police failures demand urgent reform before it's too late. Retrieved from https://issafrica.org/iss-today/sa-police-failures-demand-urgent-reform-before-its-too-late (accessed on January 26, 2023).

News24. 2021. 7 investigative stories that rocked SA. Retrieved from www.news24.com/news24/opinions/reader_hub/7-investigative-stories-that-rocked-sa-20210511 (accessed on September 28, 2022).

Okelo, S.J. 2022. Changing the narrative about Africa: African proverbs on honesty. Retrieved from https://simonjavanokelo.com/2022/07/12/african-proverb-that-speaks-to-the-importance-of-honesty/ (accessed on July 11, 2023).

Opperman, C.A. 2014. Peer-to-peer verification using NFC-enabled smartphones. Unpublished Masters dissertation: computer engineering. Pretoria: University of Pretoria.

O'Reagan, V. 2022. Auditor-General's accuser Mlungisi Mabaso axed for misconduct and dishonesty. Retrieved from www.msn.com/en-za/news/other/auditor-general-s-accuser-mlungisi-mabaso-axed-for-misconduct-and-dishonesty/ar-AA12pnR2?ocid=msedgntp&cvid=94470d5f9b044897a854fe83dd9f40a8 (accessed on September 30, 2022).

Palmatier, J. 2000. The validity and comparative accuracy of voice stress analysis as measured by the CVSA: a field study conducted in a Psychophysiological context. Unpublished manuscript, Michigan Department of State Police.

Phonexia. 2023a. Forensic voice comparison: the essential guide. Retrieved from www.phonexia.com/knowledge-base/forensic-voice-comparison-essential-guide/ (accessed on May 15, 2023).

Phonexia. 2023b. Voice biometrics: essential guide. Retrieved from www.phonexia.com/knowledge-base/voice-biometrics-essential-guide/ (accessed on May 15, 2023).

Pijoos, I. 2022. PA leader Bruce Nimmerhoudt discharged, acquitted of inciting public violence during July unrest. Retrieved from www.news24.com/news24/southafrica/news/pa-leader-bruce-nimmerhoudt-discharged-acquitted-of-inciting-public-violence-during-july-unrest-20220923 (accessed on January 30, 2023).

PMG. 2023. *Parliamentary working group: ATC230517: Report of the Portfolio Committee on Police on the 2023/24 Budget, Annual Performance Plan and 2020-2025 Strategic Plan of the Private Security Industry Regulatory Authority (PSIRA), dated 17 May 2023*. Retrieved from https://pmg.org.za/tabled-committee-report/5350/ (accessed on June 2, 2023).

Potgieter, J., Coetzee, C., Swart, K., de Jager, J. & Ferreira, D. 2019. *ACFE Forensic Standard: Voice Stress Detection (VSD)*. Pretoria: ACFE South African Chapter.

PSiRA. 2023. Private Security Industry Regulatory Authority. Retrieved from www.psira.co.za/ (accessed on January 30, 2023).

Regchand, S. 2020. Lying to cops? Think again. Retrieved from www.citizen.co.za/witness/news/lying-to-cops-think-again-20200217-2/ (accessed on May 15, 2023).

RixForensica. 2023. Forensic investigations, detection & prevention of fraud. Retrieved from https://rixforensica.co.za/index.html#features18-2 (accessed on June 6, 2023).

Ross, A. & Jain, A.K. 2007. Human recognition using biometrics: an overview. *Annals of Telecommunication*, 62(1/2):11–35.

SAPS. 2023. Annual performance plan: 2022/2023. Retrieved from www.saps.gov.za/about/stratframework/strategic_plan/2022_2023/annual_performance_plan_2022_2023.pdf (accessed on February 27, 2023).

Singh, D., Smit, J. & Kempen. A. 2022. Commentary: Policing in the 4th Industrial Revolution (4IR): Balancing the benefits and bias. *Just Africa*, 1, 53–62.

South African Government. 2023. Let's grow South Africa together. Retrieved from www.gov.za/about-sa/geography-and-climate (accessed on January 26, 2023).

South African Insurance Association. 2022. South African Insurance Crime Bureau. Retrieved from www.saia.co.za/index.php?id=354 (accessed on September 27, 2022).

Staff Writer. 2022a. Businesstech: What the official crime stats don't tell you about hijacking in South Africa. https://businesstech.co.za/news/government/620979/what-the-official-crime-stats-dont-tell-you-about-hijacking-in-south-africa/ (accessed on September 27, 2022).

Staff Writer. 2022b. Businesstech: Government launches investigation into South Africa's biggest university. Retrieved from https://businesstech.co.za/news/government/625396/government-launches-investigation-into-south-africas-biggest-university/ (accessed on September 28, 2022).

Swales, L. 2018. An analysis of the regulatory environment governing hearsay electronic evidence in South Africa: suggestions for reform—Part One. *PER*, 21, 1–30. doi.org/10.17159/1727-3781/2018/v21i0a2916

Townsend, L., van Rooyen, H., Ferreira, D. & de Jager, J. 2019. *ACFE Forensic Standard: Layered Voice Analysis*. Pretoria: ACFE South African Chapter.

Timeslive. 2022. Four articles to read about investigations by the Hawks. Retrieved from www.timeslive.co.za/news/south-africa/2022-08-24-four-articles-to-read-about-investigations-by-the-hawks/ (accessed on September 28, 2022).

Sudheim, A. 2015. Public crime, private justice: the tale of how one of South Africa's top private investigators gets impressive results and what lessons the men and women of the public police force and the SAPS as an institution might learn from this. Unpublished Minor MA Dissertation in Media, Theory and Practice, University of Cape Town. Cape Town.

Van Puyvelde, M., Neyt, X., McGlone, F. & Pattyn, N. 2018. Voice Stress Analysis: A New Framework for Voice and Effort in Human Performance. *Frontiers in Psychology*, 9(1994), 1–25. doi: 10.3389/fpsyg.2018.01994

Van Rooyen, M. 2018. *Evidential aspects of law enforcement*. Cape Town: Juta.

Woodward, J.D., Webb, K.W., Newton, E.M., Bradley, M., Rubenson, D., Larson, K., Lilly, J., Smythe, K., Houghton, B., Pincus, H.A., Schachter, J.M., & Steinberg, P. 2001. A primer on biometric technology. (Pp. 9–20). Army Biometric Applications: Identifying and Addressing Sociocultural Concerns. RAND Corporation. Retrieved from www.jstor.org/stable/10.7249/mr1237a.10 (accessed on June 4, 2023).

Wright, J. 2022. Whistleblowers in South Africa have some protection but gaps need fixing. Retrieved from https://theconversation.com/whistleblowers-in-south-africa-have-some-protection-but-gaps-need-fixing-183992 (accessed on February 2, 2023).

Part II

Collecting and Evaluating Eyewitness Evidence from Lay Witnesses, Police Body Cameras, and Super-recognizers

7 Who Are You Looking at?
Using Eye Tracking to Understand Eyewitness Decision Making

Jamal K. Mansour and Jonathan P. Vallano

In essence, eye trackers do exactly what it says on the tin: they *track* people's *eyes*. Doing so provides information about what people are attending to, which in turn reflects or influences the cognitive processes they engage in (e.g., encoding, decision making, etc.) and their capacity for and approach to later cognitive processing (e.g., retrieval). Despite these benefits, eyewitness identification researchers have not yet made significant use of this technology. However, eye trackers are increasingly being used in forensic psychology (Cantoni et al., 2018) and psychology more generally (Carter & Luke, 2020). Within investigative psychology, deception detection (see Gamer & Pertzov, 2018) and eyewitness identification—this chapter's focus—have been explored using eye tracking. In this chapter, we will briefly discuss the nature of eye trackers, review the extant research using eye tracking to study eyewitness identification—including cooperative and uncooperative eyewitnesses—and suggest directions for future research. Finally, we will summarize best practices for eyewitness researchers considering using eye tracking.

What Do Eye Trackers Measure?

Researchers use a variety of eye tracking metrics to learn about basic cognitive processes (e.g., attention, perception) as well as higher level cognitive processes (e.g., memory, decision making; Duchowski, 2017). To do this, they consider fixations (focusing on a specific location for a certain duration), pupil dilation (the size of the pupil), saccades (i.e., the movement of the focus of the eyes from one location to the next), smooth pursuit eye movements (i.e., how we follow a moving object), and vergence (the movement of each eye in a different direction to control where a gazed-at item falls on the retina). Fixating a location is a measure of attention because it involves directing the fovea—the area of the eye able to perceive with the greatest precision—to a target location. For example, people typically scan faces in a triangular pattern, focusing primarily on eyes (Janik et al., 1978;

Yarbus, 1967) while face recognition occurs within two fixations (Hsaio & Cottrell, 2008).

Eyewitness identification researchers have sought to learn about eyewitness memory and identification by assessing the number of fixations/dwell time (the number of times a location was viewed), duration of fixations (for how long a location was viewed), first fixations (where people looked first), and returns (how often people looked at a location and then later came back to that location). Often these measures are converted into proportions which reflect the relative value of these measures for a particular location—an area of interest (AOI) or region of interest (ROI)—compared to other locations. Eyewitness researchers have also considered scan paths—sequences of fixations from one location to another—and the number of AOIs visited. More recently, eyewitness researchers have begun measuring degree of pupil dilation as an indicator of cognitive load, affective processing, memory strength, and (covert) recognition. Rahal and Fiedler (2019) provide an accessible review of these and other measures.

We now review how eye tracking has been used to study eyewitness identification. We separate this discussion into research on cooperative eyewitnesses—those making an honest attempt to assist the police in their investigation by deciding whether the culprit is in a lineup they are shown—and uncooperative eyewitnesses—those who attempt to mislead the police about the identity of the culprit by not selecting the suspect. Both types of eyewitnesses contribute to wrongful convictions. Indeed, out of 873 exonerations in the United States between 1989 and 2012, 43% involved honestly mistaken eyewitness identifications while 38% involved deliberate misidentifications or fabricated crimes (Gross & Shaffer, 2012). Thus, the oft-cited approximately 75% of wrongful convictions involving eyewitness identification errors reflects the actions of both cooperative and uncooperative (i.e., deceptive) eyewitnesses. Eye tracking provides unique insights into both types of eyewitnesses.

Cooperative Eyewitnesses

Police investigations often rely on the memory of cooperative eyewitnesses. Eye trackers can be used to learn about how eyewitnesses process information during and after the crime—at encoding and retrieval, respectively—because they provide information about how people allocate attentional resources and therefore provide data relevant to memory accuracy.

Gaze During Encoding

Researchers have measured gaze behavior to study the relationship between attention and memory. Attard and Bindemann (2014) found that participants who later made a correct identification viewed the culprit during a mock crime for longer than those who identified a filler or incorrectly rejected the lineup. Additionally, participants who incorrectly rejected the lineup spent more time looking at the culprit than those who identified a filler. Although eyewitnesses are unlikely to be wearing an eye tracker during a crime, these gaze findings are relevant for theory because they demonstrate the relationship between memory quality and eyewitness performance.

Gaze behavior can improve our understanding of how certain variables—such as estimator variable (i.e., factors outside the criminal justice system's control; Wells, 1978)—affect eyewitness accuracy and inform theory. Harvey, Kneller, and Campbell (2013) provide a great illustration. Per alcohol myopia theory (Steele & Josephs, 1990), they expected intoxicated and sober participants would gaze similarly at central parts of a scene—such as the culprit of the crime's face, but that intoxicated participants would gaze less at peripheral parts—such as items in the room where the crime occurred. Contrary to their hypothesis, they found that sober and intoxicated participants fixated as often and for similar amounts of time on peripheral features of a mock crime, though as expected, they gazed similarly at central features. Thus, eye tracking provided insights about the impact of alcohol on eyewitness behaviors which are relevant to alcohol myopia theory.

Cognitive Load and Eyewitness Memory

Memory quality can be reduced by stimuli which distract eyewitnesses from encoding key information. The higher the cognitive load—or the degree to which distractions consume an eyewitness's cognitive resources—the more difficult it should be to encode key information (e.g., Camos & Portrat, 2015). Greene, Murphy, and Januszewski (2017) used eye tracking to examine whether perceptual load (a type of cognitive load; i.e., how busy a scene is) affected study of a central character (a thief) and a peripheral character (an actor who witnessed the crime through a window). Participants gazed more at the thief (body and face combined) when load was high but gazed more at the thief's face when load was low. Furthermore, despite these differences in gaze behavior, identifications of both actors (from target-present lineups) were unaffected. Based on the participants' gaze behavior, the authors concluded that a reduction in identification accuracy in a prior study was due to the attentional failure rather than a difference in search strategy when load is high versus low (consistent with load theory; Lavie, 1995).

Greene et al.'s (2017) findings are consistent with the interpretation that eyewitness memory is better for central (vs. peripheral) actors because of differential allocation of attention to those actors, concurrently influenced by scene complexity. Practically, eye tracking may be useful for pilot testing mock-crime videos: researchers could show participants various mock-crime videos and measure their gaze on the targets to determine which videos produce better/worse memory for the targets.

Cross-Race Effects

Face recognition researchers have studied how gaze at encoding relates to the cross-race effect—that is, the tendency for people to make more correct identifications and fewer false identifications of people who are of the same versus another race (Lee & Penrod, 2022; Meissner & Brigham, 2001; Singh et al., 2022). Often gaze at encoding and retrieval are combined for analysis (e.g., Hills & Pake, 2013). Also, sometimes the same images are used at study and test, meaning that these studies may measure image rather than face recognition (Read, Vokey, & Hammersley, 1990). Nonetheless, this research has been informative for understanding how the cross-race effect is influenced by other variables and for refining theory.

Theories of the cross-race effect have proposed that (1) people look at other-race faces differently (socio-cognitive accounts) or (2) the perceptual processes of people of various races differ (perceptual expertise accounts), though hybrid models have emerged (e.g., Young et al., 2012). Socio-cognitive accounts predict different gaze behaviors when viewing own- versus other-race faces because people are more motivated to individuate own- than other-race faces and thus will use better strategies. In contrast, perceptual expertise accounts predict people will gaze in the same way at own- and other-race faces because they have learned a specific pattern was effective with own-race faces—but it may be less effective with other-race faces.

Consistent with socio-cognitive accounts, people gaze at diagnostic features when learning a face, with better ability to do so with own-race faces. For example, Goldinger, He, and Papesh (2009) found that White and Asian participants fixated more on own-race faces' eyes and hair and other-race faces' noses and mouths. Fu and colleagues (2012) found that Chinese participants fixated most on the noses and mouths of Asian (Chinese) faces and the eyes of White faces. Other research also suggests a bias to look at upper facial features for own- versus other-race faces (McDonnell et al., 2014; Wu, Laeng, & Magnussen, 2012).

Importantly, gaze at encoding is at least partially predictive of recognition accuracy (McDonnell et al., 2014). In Experiment 1, McDonnell and colleagues' White participants gazed more and fixated faster on the hair of own-race faces and gazed more and fixated faster on the mouth of other-race faces. Importantly, gazing longer at the hair of own-race faces was associated with more hits, gazing longer at the hair of other-race faces with decreased hits, and faster first fixations to the mouth of other-race faces with increased hits.

Given the third finding, in Experiment 2, McDonnell et al. (2014) instructed some White participants to attend to the mouth (cf. hair or eyes) of other-race faces. Participants who received these instructions did gaze more at the mouth of other-race faces, and in general, increased gaze on other-race faces improved differentiation between seen-before and new faces (i.e., discriminability), but surprisingly, gazing more at the mouth of other-race faces was not associated with higher accuracy. They also found that faster first fixations to the eyes of a same-race (but not other-race) face increased hits. Recently, Wittwer et al. (2019) similarly failed to find that training participants to focus on specific features mitigates the cross-race effect, even though participants did alter their gaze behavior in line with their training. These two results are surprising because forcing a participant's first fixation to land on the most diagnostic part of the face has been shown to mitigate the cross-race effect (Hills, Cooper, & Pake, 2013; Hills & Lewis, 2006).

Also consistent with socio-cognitive accounts, encoding other-race faces seems to be more cognitively demanding: Other-race (versus own-race) faces elicit more pupil dilation and active scanning (i.e., fewer saccades, fewer fixations, longer fixations; Goldinger et al., 2009; Wu et al., 2012). Thus, the cross-race effect may occur because people do not increase their effort when encoding other-race compared to own-race faces. Consistent with this proposition, Goldinger et al. found that when they split participants into those who performed well and poorly on cross-race recognition, the poor performers' visual efforts to encode other-race faces were similar to same-race faces only for the first few trials, decreasing substantially on later trials. Conversely, good performers were consistent in how they studied own- and other-race faces across trials. The difference in effort was also reflected in participants' pupil dilation (greater pupil dilation is associated with greater effort). Simply put, effort predicted the strength of the cross-race effect.

Other research is consistent with perceptual expertise theories. Differences in gaze have been found for White and African American participants (Ellis, Deregowski, & Shepherd, 1975; Hills et al., 2013; Hills & Pake, 2013) and for White and Asian participants (Blais et al., 2008; Kelly, Miellet, & Caldara, 2010) which cannot be accounted for by the race of the viewed face. For example, Blais and colleagues found that Western Caucasians focused on eyes while East Asians focused on noses and mouths. However, Goldinger et al. (2009) suggested their results could be accounted for by differences in stimuli placement (center vs. one of four quadrants) or the use of different facial expressions (neutral vs. four expressions including neutral). Hills and Pake (2013) also found support for perceptual expertise accounts but could not differentiate between competing mechanisms—that people do more holistic/configural processing with own-race faces and more featural processing with other-race faces

(Hancock & Rhodes, 2008) versus that people have a more diagnostic face-space for own- compared to other-race faces (Valentine, 1991).

The empirical evidence from eye tracking research supports both socio-cognitive and perceptual expertise accounts; therefore, a hybrid account is likely necessary. Consistent with this notion and, importantly, within a single study, Burgund (2021) found that gazing at eyes predicted recognition for both own- and other-race faces, consistent with socio-cognitive accounts, but also that gazing at the nose/mouth area improved recognition of Black faces, regardless of participant race, consistent with perceptual expertise accounts. Stelter, Rommel, and Degner (2021) also considered a hybrid account. They showed White German participants White, Middle Eastern, East Asian, and Black faces which represented increasingly distal racial groups. Increased distance was associated with differences in gaze behavior consistent with socio-cognitive accounts, but gaze did not predict recognition accuracy, therefore the support was only partial. Considering specific socio-cognitive accounts, their results were inconsistent with holistic processing (Hancock & Rhodes, 2008) as well as active scanning (i.e., that we make a greater effort to study own- versus other-race faces) as mechanisms. But their findings were also inconsistent with perceptual expertise accounts: gazing more at diagnostic features (i.e., the nose and mouth of Asian and Black faces and the eyes of White faces) was not associated with higher recognition accuracy. Thus, there is still considerable work to be done on the cross-race effect.

Weapon Focus

The weapon focus effect—the phenomenon whereby the presence (versus absence) of a weapon harms eyewitness memory accuracy—has also been studied using eye tracking. Loftus and Mackworth (1978) established that gaze is drawn to semantic inconsistencies—and weapons are unusual in our everyday life. Loftus, Loftus, and Messo (1987) established that the presence of a weapon impacts eyewitness memory through attention. They tracked participants' gaze while they watched a slide show depicting a restaurant patron (the target) handing a cashier a cheque or a gun. Participants fixated more often and for longer on the gun than the cheque and participants who saw the gun tended to identify a filler (vs. the target) from a target-present lineup. Loftus and colleagues concluded that participants allocated more attention to the gun and therefore attended less well to the target, resulting in a poorer memory for the target.

Conclusions about Encoding

Eye tracking provides valuable information about attention and memory. Tracking gaze during encoding provides insights into how estimator variables (Wells, 1978) such as intoxication, cross-race culprits, and weapon presence affect eyewitness memory as well as relevant theories. To date, few variables related to memory at encoding have been examined, but future researchers could fruitfully utilize eye tracking to address the main effect problem. That is, eyewitness research tends to require large sample sizes and as a result, research on both gaze behavior and estimator variables has typically studied main effects. Measuring gaze in pilot studies could ensure manipulations are effective. Once effective manipulations are established, it would become easier to produce mock crime videos that vary multiple estimator variables and to examine interactions. This approach could then be used to study topics like exposure duration (at what point does an eyewitness habituate to the culprit and start focusing elsewhere), stress (at what level does ability to focus on the culprit change), distance (is more time spent studying the culprit if they are further away but to a lesser effect? Is there a trade-off?), disguise (does the eyewitness gaze less or at different things), and distinctive features (to what extent do eyewitnesses gaze more at the feature than the rest of the culprit's face).

Gaze During Retrieval

Unlike encoding conditions which involve estimator variables, retrieval conditions also involve system variables—variables controllable by the legal system (Wells, 1978)—which is probably why more eye tracking research has studied retrieval processes. At retrieval, eye movements can serve as an index of face recognition. For example, Althoff & Cohen (1999) found that people fixate less often but for longer on familiar (cf. unfamiliar) faces. Ryan, Hannula, and Cohen (2007) demonstrated this eye-movement-based memory effect (EMME) in simultaneous arrays of three or more faces. In their first two experiments, participants studied 24 face images presented sequentially for five seconds each. Later, participants viewed arrays of three (or two) faces which contained either one of the 24 previously studied faces and two (one) new faces (target-present) or three (two) new faces (target-absent). Consistent with the eyewitness identification literature (e.g., Dunning & Perretta, 2002), correct identifications were faster than false identifications. More importantly, fixation durations on previously studied faces were longer than on new faces.

Lineup Performance

While Loftus and colleagues (1987) used eye tracking to measure memory quality as a predictor of lineup performance, it was not until over 20 years later that researchers used eye tracking to directly examine lineup decisions. The first published study (Mansour et al., 2009) manipulated whether participants viewed target-present or target-absent lineups and considered whether gaze to lineup members differentiated accurate from inaccurate lineup decisions. Correct and incorrect identifications were differentiated by only one measure: second-order comparisons to the identified individual (wherein one looks at a face, then two other faces, and then returns to the first face; first order comparisons involve looking a one face, then another, and returning to the first). Those who correctly identified the culprit made fewer second-order comparisons than those who incorrectly identified another lineup member. Participants who correctly rejected a lineup made fewer fixations and comparisons (first- and second-order) with the face they most often fixated relative to the target by those who incorrectly rejected the target. Gaze also differentiated identifications and rejections, whereby identifiers gazed for less time but made similar numbers of fixations and comparisons between faces. Importantly, these differences were small—approximately one fixation or comparison—leading them to conclude that eye tracking is not a viable tool for police. But much like the use of eye tracking with the weapon focus effect, its value for understanding *how* lineup decisions are made may better inform theory than practice. For example, Mansour and colleagues found that participants' self-reports of their decision process matched poorly with what their gaze behavior suggested. That is, while 63% of the sample reported they had made an absolute judgment (i.e., compared faces to their memory), their gaze behavior was more indicative of a relative judgment (comparing between faces; Wells, 1984).

Also interested in lineup performance, Flowe and Cottrell (2011) examined whether gaze while viewing a lineup indexes memory quality. Using composite images, they considered the number of fixations to faces as well as the average duration of first and return fixations, and the duration of all fixations. Like Mansour et al. (2009), they found that returning to a face predicted identification accuracy. However, they also found that the length of time participants spent fixating on a face for the first time was positively correlated with the likelihood that participants would identify that face, though not their identification accuracy. Interestingly, their results suggested that gaze behavior does not index memory quality but rather perceived familiarity.

Like Mansour et al. (2009), Flowe (2011) found that identified faces were gazed at more than non-identified faces. However, Flowe focused her efforts on how eye tracking can help us better understand identification decision making. In two experiments, she examined the total time spent on composite faces and their features when participants viewed simultaneous versus sequential lineups (Experiment 1) or showups (Experiment 2). There were significant differences in these gaze behaviors even though she found no differences in performance across identification procedures. Participants spent more time evaluating the suspect's face in sequential lineups than simultaneous lineups and similar time in showups. These results suggest that the amount of attention to a suspect may be influenced by opportunities to consider other options (fillers). When eyewitnesses are not fixating on a face they are considering identifying, they may be considering it in relation to the other faces in the lineup.

Pupil size has recently been explored as a predictor of lineup decisions. Elphick, Pike, and Hole (2020) measured pupil size while participants viewed a target-present or target-absent sequential video lineup—similar to those conducted in the UK—in three studies, including a field study where they used only target-present lineups. They found that pupil sizes were larger when participants viewed the target in a target-present lineup compared to when they viewed the fillers, and that accuracy for target-present lineups was predicted by pupil size when viewing the target. However, they found no effects of pupil size when viewing target-absent lineups and did not analyze whether pupil size predicted the accuracy of identification decisions across target-present and -absent lineups. Nonetheless, their research suggests that pupil size may be a useful index of eyewitness memory.

Cross-Race Effect

Despite many researchers using eye tracking to understand how own- and other-race faces are encoded, few have considered its relation to gaze at retrieval. This may be because similar gaze patterns are often found for encoding and recognition (e.g., Burgund, 2021; Stelter et al., 2021) and so they are often combined. Using a face recognition paradigm and looking exclusively at gaze during retrieval, Blais et al. (2008) found, regardless of face race, more fixations to eyes and mouths by White participants and more fixations to the nose by Asian participants—a pattern consistent across recognition, encoding, and a face race categorization task. Wu et al. (2012) found gaze but not pupillary response differences during recognition of own- and other-race faces by White participants. Participants fixated on the eyes longer and the nose shorter for White versus Asian faces, though this varied with response type (hit, false alarm, correct rejection, or miss; see their fig. 6c). Finally, Josephson and Homes (2010) showed 20 participants a mock-crime video of a White or Black target and then a target-present lineup. Own-race and other-race decisions resulted in similar gaze to the lineup overall, but differences in gaze on the target occurred. White participants looked at the target less often and for less time than Black participants. They also analyzed scan path complexity, defined as the sequential movements made from face to face when viewing the lineup. White participants identifying a White target engaged in the shortest scan paths (i.e., fewest fixations within a sequence) while cross-race identifications resulted in the longest scan paths.

Lineup Decision Processes

While differentiating accurate and inaccurate eyewitnesses directly with eye tracking has been somewhat successful, another way eye tracking could benefit theory and practice is to examine the strategies eyewitnesses use and how these relate to lineup performance. Looking across lineup responses, Flowe and Cottrell (2011) reported a tendency for participants to engage in a scan path such that they looked from the upper left across to the upper right then down to the lower right and back across to the lower left (i.e., a circular pattern).

Self-reports indicate that accurate eyewitnesses are more likely (cf. inaccurate eyewitnesses) to report that the "face just popped out at me" (Dunning & Stern, 1994) or to give similar responses indicating an automatic recognition experience (Kneller, Memon, & Stevenage, 2001; Lampinen et al., 2020; Sauerland & Sporer, 2007). Megreya and colleagues (2012) examined whether eye tracking could provide direct behavioral evidence of the pop-out effect but, surprisingly, they found no evidence for it. When a first fixation on the lineup was to the target, participants were no more accurate than when their first fixation landed elsewhere. If anything, less accurate participants showed a stronger tendency to select the first person they fixated on. On average, participants made a first fixation to the target and then selected the target just 18.4% (SD = 5.8) of the time—slightly below chance (20%). In fact, only one of the 20 participants was drawn to the target for their first fixation at greater than chance frequency (therefore, this result itself may be due to chance). The pop-out that participants report occurring may reflect retrospective judgments about their decision process, rather than the decision process itself.

De Sola, Perez-Mata, and Diges (2021) varied whether participants were instructed to make relative (compare between lineup members) or absolute judgments (compare to memory; Wells, 1984) and tracked their gaze while they viewed a simultaneous target-present or target-absent lineup. Participants followed the instructions such that fewer fixations were made in the absolute compared to relative condition for both target-present (marginal) and target-absent lineups. Interestingly, participants made more correct identifications in the relative condition, as expected, but there was no difference in correct rejections—the primary reason to encourage absolute judgments. The authors did not measure comparisons between the suspect and other lineup members, so it is unclear how the instructions influenced decision making. Perhaps in the absolute condition, participants forwent a checking procedure or perhaps comparisons were made in all conditions but participants focused only on the most similar face in the absolute condition. Regardless, the impact of lineup instructions on gaze should be examined further.

Paterson et al. (2017) used eye tracking to consider whether training eyewitnesses to study internal features improves identification accuracy because relying on internal (cf. external) features improves face recognition. Eye tracking confirmed participants followed their training and preferentially focused on specific features during their lineup decision. Participants trained to study internal features only made significantly more correct identifications post- versus pre-training, while those trained to study external features only made significantly fewer correct identifications, with those trained to study both showing no change in performance. A second study replicated the utility of training with internal features but found that the advantage did not extend to faces with altered features (e.g., a hairstyle change). Unfortunately, they did not examine whether eye movements directly predicted performance. Recently, Wittwer et al. (2019) trained White participants to preferentially study the lower half of Black faces to reduce the cross-race effect, but this instead increased the effect (using a face recognition paradigm).

Finally, Flowe (2011) considered whether eye tracking could be used to understand differences in decision making when participants view simultaneous and sequential lineups. She found that participants who viewed sequential lineups gazed more at external features during the lineup decision than those who viewed simultaneous lineups or showups (both gazed more at internal features). Although this difference did not predict performance, Flowe's use of composite images rather than photographs may have mitigated the size of the effect (her stimuli had minimal external features for consideration), therefore future research should further explore this question.

Lineup Fairness and Construction

Another area where eye tracking may be informative is assessments of lineup fairness. Existing measures of lineup fairness show some validity (e.g., Lee, Mansour, & Penrod, 2022; Mansour et al., 2017) but require showing people who have not witnessed the crime (i.e., mock witnesses) the lineup and asking them who they think is the suspect. This is problematic because eyewitnesses (should) rely primarily on their memory while mock witnesses rely primarily on the lineup itself to make a decision. Tiemens et al. (unpublished manuscript) illustrated the potential utility of eye tracking in response to a legal argument that a specific police lineup was biased. Robert Tiemens testified in court that the suspect stood out in the lineup. Presumably in preparation for his testimony, he had seven people who had not witnessed the crime view the lineup while their gaze was tracked and asked them who they thought was the suspect. On the judge's request, he repeated the procedure with another 22 participants. These mock witnesses not only selected the suspect most often, but also focused more quickly and for longer on the suspect than the fillers. Thus, gaze may index the extent to which a suspect stands out in a lineup.

Megreya et al. (2012; Experiment 2) also used eye tracking to examine an issue related to lineup fairness. They considered whether there are position effects in simultaneous 5-person lineups (all faces in one row), which they predicted may occur because people have a left visual field processing bias. The paradigm was more removed from reality than the typical eyewitness identification study, however, because the target's face was displayed above the lineup during the lineup decision. The target's position did not influence target-present lineup performance. However, participants showed a preference for selecting faces from the left side of the target-absent lineup compared to the middle or right. Thus, the left visual field processing bias was evident for target-absent but not target-present lineups. First fixations on the lineup tended to be on the two leftmost lineup members or the middle lineup members, providing behavioral evidence for the left visual field processing bias. This contrasts with Palmer, Sauer, and Holt (2017) who found edge aversion (i.e., a preference to identify lineup members from the center of a lineup) for eight-person (2 × 4) simultaneous lineups using only behavioral responses. An implication of the left visual field processing bias is that it can explain why Megreya et al. (2012) failed to detect a pop-out effect with their lineups. The left visual field processing bias suggests that people may engage in an orienting stage when presented with a lineup. A pop-out may occur immediately following this orienting stage, meaning a pop-out is undetectable until the orienting stage is complete.

Conclusions about Retrieval

The little work that has used gaze to study retrieval in an eyewitness context indicates that there are small but reliable differences between accurate and inaccurate eyewitnesses and that the role of instructions (e.g., De Sola et al., 2021) and task (e.g., Flowe, 2011) play a key role, as is true with eye tracking research in general (Holmqvist et al., 2022). Yet it is noteworthy that, except for research on the cross-race effect, none of the effects we reported have been replicated. While eye tracking research on the cross-race effect has been more extensive, it has primarily used face recognition paradigms. Therefore, more research with lineups is needed. We also discussed an area where eye tracking has been used in court but for which there is no published eye tracking research: lineup fairness and lineup construction.

Given that eye tracking indexes attention, eye tracking holds considerable promise as an objective measure of lineup fairness that does not require a separate study after an eyewitness has made their decision. Given the drop in cost of eye trackers, it may soon be possible for police departments to collect gaze information while viewing lineups for multiple reasons. One reason is to confirm the fairness of their lineup but the other, as we will discuss below, is to index familiarity when an eyewitness is uncooperative.

Uncooperative Eyewitnesses

To this point, we have discussed the use of eye tracking in relation to cooperative eyewitnesses—those motivated to assist the police. However, sometimes eyewitnesses are uncooperative—because they wish to protect the culprit or are themselves the culprit. Next, we review research that has used eye tracking to assess attempts to conceal recognition of faces.

Detection

In an effort to detect uncooperative witnesses, Schwedes and Wentura (2012) reasoned that gaze would be effective for measuring concealed recognition because eye movements reflect memory (Hannula et al., 2010). Recall that people fixate familiar faces less often and for longer than unfamiliar faces such that memory strength is indexed by gaze (i.e., the EMME; Ryan et al., 2007). Schwedes and Wentura modified Ryan and colleagues' paradigm (see the Gaze During Retrieval section) to examine concealed recognition. Participants studied 12 faces three times, with each face presented one at a time in the center of the screen. Simultaneously, the upper left of the screen contained faces to be considered friends and the upper right contained faces to be considered foes. During the test phase, the researchers presented six faces in a circle and instructed participants to respond differently based on whether they recognized no one (neutral condition) or the target. If the target was a foe, they were to select that face but if the target was a friend, they were to conceal this and select another face. Fixations to the target were significantly shorter when the target was a friend versus a foe. Furthermore, fixation durations to the target were longer when the target was a friend versus a neutral person. Finally, the authors considered whether the gaze could differentiate liars and truth tellers and found that using total fixation duration, 8.1% of participants would have been falsely accused of concealing knowledge while 64.9% of guilty participants would have been correctly accused. Thus, this study established the potential utility of eye tracking for detecting deceptive lineup identifications.

Millen et al. (2017) built on Schwedes and Wentura (2012) by examining recognition of personally known faces (members of the participant's tutorial group) and famous faces compared to newly familiar faces (faces seen once before). They also considered whether the EMME persists under cognitive load, because deception is more difficult under cognitive load (Blandón-Gitlin et al., 2014). They established the EMME for the familiar faces and showed that the effect became stronger as familiarity increased, regardless of the decision maker's intention (truth or concealment). They found fewer fixations, fewer areas of interest (AOIs) visited, and fewer multiple fixations to AOIs for famous faces (cf. unfamiliar) as well as fewer fixations, fewer AOIs visited, fewer multiple fixations to AOIs, and a smaller proportion of fixations to the inner features of the face for personally familiar faces (cf. unfamiliar). When participants made truthful recognition responses versus rejected unfamiliar faces, their gaze behavior also consistently indexed recognition. However, when participants attempted to conceal recognition of a newly learned face versus honestly rejecting an unfamiliar face, they made only marginally fewer fixations. Thus, gaze was less effective for indexing concealed recognition for newly familiar faces—which would correspond with a criminal seen briefly.

Millen, Hope, and Hillstrom, 2020 (Experiment 1) also found that gaze behavior reveals concealed recognition of personally familiar faces. Gaze while viewing a face in a lineup indexed recognition regardless of the participant's behavioral response. Specifically, participants responded faster, fixated less, fixated fewer parts of the face, returned to the face less, spent less time fixating the inner part of the face, and made longer fixations when the face was personally familiar (cf. unfamiliar). Yet, like Millen et al. (2017), gaze was ineffective for predicting recognition of newly familiar faces, indicating that gaze may not be useful when an eyewitness recognizes a culprit seen only once before but has been threatened or intimidated. Nonetheless, gaze is clearly effective for detecting concealed recognition of a more familiar person.

Countermeasures

A concern for deception detection is whether countermeasures can be used to avoid detection. Millen and Hancock (2019) wondered whether instructing participants to engage in countermeasures could mitigate the EMME. Like the polygraph, if gaze behavior can be modified to conceal recognition, its effectiveness depends on awareness by the individual tested. Given the automatic nature of attention and eye movements, Millen and Hancock predicted that participants would be unable to exert sufficient control to conceal recognition. They instructed two groups to conceal their recognition: One group received no further instructions while the other was instructed to look at all faces in the same way and to use a specific sequence of eye movements. The first group showed the EMME and for the second, concealed recognition was reliably detectable by longer fixation durations, and evident from the participant's first fixation. Thus, the countermeasure was ineffective. In contrast, Nahari et al. (2019) found that asking participants to look at all faces equally mitigated the EMME and therefore concealed familiarity.

In another study on countermeasures, Zuo, Gedeon, and Qin (2019) manipulated familiarity by showing participants images of university lecturers from their own or a different university. They instructed participants to respond truthfully or to conceal recognition and captured gaze during the recognition decision. They then used machine learning to produce an algorithm for classifying participants' responses as lies or truths based on their gaze behavior. They generated four average eye movement patterns from the algorithm, one each associated with telling the truth about a familiar face, lying about a familiar face, telling the truth about an unfamiliar face, and lying about an unfamiliar face. The resultant patterns classified participants best when they lied about a familiar face (86%), similarly if they told the truth about a familiar face or lied about an unfamiliar face (81%), and performed worst when participants told the truth about an unfamiliar face (71%). Thus, machine learning algorithms may enhance deception detection particularly for newly familiar faces, where directly measuring gaze behavior has been ineffective (Millen et al., 2017, 2020).

Conclusions

Gaze behavior reliably indexes memory for faces—and therefore can reveal when an individual is trying to conceal their familiarity. A limitation, though, is that this approach has been unreliable for differentiating deceptive responses to newly learned faces. Only when familiarity is high—because an individual is personally familiar or famous—has gaze effectively differentiated concealed recognition from an honest lack of recognition. This is important because witness intimidation is one reason an eyewitness would fail to identify a guilty suspect from a lineup. Nonetheless, it may be more common to deceive police about recognizing an accomplice who is a friend or family member—and this is detectable from gaze behavior. Encouragingly, machine learning algorithms may enhance detection of concealed recognition of newly familiar faces. Given the effective role of cognitive load on deception detection, future research could explore whether requiring eyewitnesses to engage in a secondary task while viewing a lineup improves the ability of gaze to differentiate newly familiar faces that are recognized honestly versus deceptively. Indeed, cognitive load in real-world cases may already be sufficiently high for the approach to be effective.

Future Directions

Gaze behavior has promise for enhancing our understanding of eyewitness identification. This approach may be particularly useful for expanding theories of eyewitness memory because of the nuanced nature of the data. Eye trackers do require a sizable time and monetary commitment, but researchers should take advantage of the lowering costs and increasingly user-friendly software. Throughout this chapter we have noted potential ways to build on existing research. In this section we highlight additional promising areas for future research.

At the encoding stage, eye tracking can help confirm whether crime-relevant stimuli similarly capture attention. For example, multiple theories predict the attentional effect caused by weapons: that they capture attention because they are threatening, central to the event, and/or unusual (see Kocab & Sporer, 2016). Eye tracking could help differentiate between these accounts through comparisons of gaze on objects that reflect different levels of perceived threat and unusualness. First fixations and pupil dilation could be used to examine the degree of experienced threat versus attention.

Gaze behavior can also facilitate understanding of lineup decision making. Scan paths and transitions between lineup members may help clarify the strategies eyewitnesses use given different lineup instructions or procedures. Relatedly, eye tracking using an eyewitness paradigm could be used to study the occurrence of pop-out from lineups—which is relevant to the study of lineup fairness, to techniques for managing distinctive characteristics, and for understanding when recognition occurs. For example, eye tracking could be used in pilot tests to determine how quickly participants notice a feature, which could guide the creation of mock-crime videos. Alternatively, eye tracking could be used to check whether a suspect stands out in intentionally biased and/or fair lineups.

Eye tracking may also provide insights into how legal practitioners and/or jurors engage with eyewitness evidence. For example, tracking participants' gaze while they read trial vignettes could inform our understanding of the factors jurors attend to and point towards interactions amongst variables. Similarly, eye tracking could be used to examine how jurors evaluate in-court eyewitness testimony (e.g., what aspects of eyewitnesses jurors attended to) or what jurors attend to when reviewing a recorded investigative interview or interrogation. No doubt there are other avenues where eye tracking could provide insights and we hope our discussion has drawn some of these to mind. We now turn to more practical considerations.

Best Practices for Eye Tracking Research on Eyewitness Identification

The use of eye tracking to study eyewitness memory is growing but still in its infancy. To facilitate high quality research, we now review best practices and special considerations. We recommend Carter and Luke (2020), Orquin and Holmqvist (2018, 2019), Beesley, Pearson, and Le Pelley (2019), and Rahal and Fiedler (2019) for getting started. Furthermore, although likely too technical for a beginner, Holmqvist et al. (2022) provide minimal reporting guidelines as well as comprehensively review different eye trackers, eye tracking measures, metrics for evaluating eye tracking data, and approaches for processing eye tracking data. Much of our advice derives from their excellent review.

Selecting an Eye Tracker

Resolution and Cost

The selection of an eye tracker must balance cost with the ability to answer the researcher's questions. Hardware is an important consideration when measurement precision (reliability) is critical while the participant, calibration, and the geometry of the eye tracker's set up in relation to the participant are more critical when accuracy (validity) is paramount. The gaze behaviors detected by the eye tracker should be fine-grained enough to reflect the cognitive processes of interest. Broadly, the lower the sampling frequency (i.e., the number of times per second data is collected; Hz), the less likely this is. Eyewitness researchers are likely to be interested in how often/how long people gaze at a target in a scene (or lineup), therefore a relatively low sampling frequency may be acceptable (60–150 Hz). Low sampling frequencies more negatively impact measurements of saccades than measures such as fixation duration (Holmqvist et al., 2022). It is helpful to review published tests of the validity of gaze capture for specific eye trackers under typical or non-ideal circumstances (e.g., Spitzer & Mueller, 2022; see table 2 in Holmqvist et al., 2022 for a list of studies) as well as manufacturers' reports which test under ideal circumstances.

Eyewitness researchers have most often used SR Research's EyeLink II (usually an EyeLink 1000 at 250 Hz; www.sr-research.com) or a Tobii eye tracker (www.tobii.com). Tobii's systems feature easy-to-use experimental design and data analysis software. Similar eye trackers are available from GazePoint (www.gazept.com), SmartEye (https://smarteye.se), and EyeLogic (www.eyelogicsolutions.com). For many of these, open-source (e.g., PsychoPy; www.psychopy.org) and purchasable (e.g., iMotions; https://imotions.com, E-Prime; https://pstnet.com) software exist. Often the software can integrate equipment such as EEG and BioPac. There is even open-access software for using webcams as low-resolution eye trackers (e.g., Semmelmann & Weigelt, 2018; Werchan, Thomason, & Brito, 2022).

Eye trackers can be expensive—and greater precision generally means greater cost. Tobii's machines (50–250 Hz) are more affordable than SR Research's, which are often used by perception researchers (250–2000 Hz) because of their high precision. Pupillometry (i.e., measuring pupil dilation) requires a sampling frequency of 120 Hz or greater, although this can be feasible with a 60 Hz machine that combines the samples from both eyes. Some eye trackers, particularly mobile eye trackers, record gaze from both eyes and combine the signals which can reduce or improve accuracy (see Hooge et al., 2019). Another factor that influences cost is whether the eye tracker is stationary or mobile. Mobile eye trackers tend to be both lower resolution and more expensive. For lab-based research that involves showing a mock-crime video and lineup on a computer, a stationary eye tracker will suffice. To our knowledge, no eyewitness research has used mobile eye tracking, though this approach could be used to enhance the ecological validity of gaze data while witnessing a crime.

Data Quality

Another concern when choosing an eye tracker is the data's temporal precision. Latency is the time between when an eye event occurs and when it is detected. This is particularly important when eye tracking occurs with other devices (e.g., BioPac), is gaze-contingent (i.e., only the fixated location is clearly displayed), and/or synchronization between stimulus onset and eye movement is important (e.g., perceptual research). A static latency is straightforward to account for; variable latency is harder to detect, measure, and accommodate which reduces validity (Holmqvist et al., 2022 lists eye trackers with unstable sampling frequencies).

Spatial precision also affects the validity of gaze data. If the eye tracker is ineffective at detecting *where* a participant looks, then those measurements will be uninformative. Interested readers should refer to table 2 of Holmqvist et al. (2022) and Niehorster et al. (2020) for more information. Filters can increase precision by compensating for noise caused by outside stimuli like sensors, fans, and lights. Different eye trackers use different filters and each affects gaze measures differently (see Špakov, 2012). Thus, publications should describe any filters used.

Data loss—not detecting what a person is looking at—varies by eye tracker and is influenced by participant characteristics, operator skill, and head movements (i.e., large head movements increase data loss). Event detection (i.e., detection of fixations, saccades, etc.) is affected by data loss such that events during the data loss are terminated, therefore, the more data loss that occurs, the less valid the data is (Holmqvist, Nyström, & Mulvey, 2012). Some eye tracking software uses algorithms to merge gaze data (e.g., Pupil Capture) while others allow users to interpolate synthetic data into the time/space of the loss (e.g., Tobii Pro Lab).

The algorithm used for event detection influences the data obtained and depends on the frame of reference (i.e., whether the eye tracker is screen-mounted or head-mounted) and the noise level in the eye tracking system. Greater noise reduces precision, but the degree of change depends on the algorithm and the parameters entered into the algorithm—including sampling rate (Holmqvist, 2016). Holmqvist concluded that velocity-based algorithms (I-VT) outperform dispersion-based algorithms (I-DT). Another consideration is how different algorithms operationalize measures like fixations and fixation durations: Two researchers using an identical method, but a different eye tracker, could find different results. A related consideration is how dynamic AOIs (e.g., an AOI for a gun during a mock-crime video) change between video key frames. Changing the parameters of an algorithm and the use of a different algorithm can influence whether a hypothesis is supported or not, particularly with between-subjects designs (Holmqvist et al., 2022).

To conclude, temporal latency, spatial precision, filters, data loss, and the algorithms used vary across eye trackers and influence the validity and reliability of the collected gaze data. Researchers should be aware of these influences and report this relevant information.

Environment for Data Collection

Physical environment matters. Lighting levels should be consistent, particularly between calibration and testing (Holmqvist et al., 2022). Accuracy is better if pupil size is smaller. However, direct sunlight reduces data quality, therefore, windows near an eye tracker should be avoided. A sufficiently lit room with stable illumination is preferable. Lighting is particularly important for pupillometry because changes can cause pupil-size artefacts (i.e., changes in the size of the pupil due to light rather than cognitive processing)—with lighting changes accounting for 1–5 degrees of inaccuracy.

Vibrations can increase variability in gaze signals. Therefore, researchers should avoid placing an eye tracker in a room near an elevator shaft, powerful air conditioner, etc. Even the vibrations from someone walking on hard floors can impact sensitive eye trackers. Eye trackers are often housed in soundproof booths to mitigate these confounds.

Researchers should also minimize the presence of others (Holmqvist et al., 2022). First, doing so avoids social appropriateness concerns: participants may avoid looking where they would normally look if watched.

Second, other people can be distracting. Third, mismeasurements can occur if the eye tracker detects the eyes of the other person. This is particularly problematic for research involving a parent and child together.

Regarding the participant themselves, it is important they are seated within the recommended distance from screen—which varies across eye trackers. Being outside the recommended distance increases data loss and inaccuracy. Restricting head movements can significantly improve accuracy so researchers should consider pilot testing how accurately gaze is captured for their measure of interest with and without restrictors. Restrictors include chinrests, forehead rests, and bite bars/boards. To date, eyewitness researchers have used a chinrest only or nothing. Generally, but particularly with children, a chin rest reduces movement.

Calibration and Drift Correction

Calibration involves determining the difference between where an eye tracker recorded a participant as looking and where they actually looked. Typically, participants direct their eyes to dots that appear sequentially on different areas of a computer monitor. Calibration allows the eye tracker to adjust the reported gaze locations to accurately reflect what participants are looking at.

A nine-point calibration is most common and may provide better calibration than five or two points (Akkil et al., 2014). People tend to have a dominant eye and calibration of each eye separately may be preferable because averaging them can give erroneous disparity measures. Recording from the dominant eye leads to better accuracy (about 0.2 degrees; Holmqvist et al., 2022). Holmqvist et al. also recommend validating after calibration to confirm accuracy.

The accuracy of gaze monitoring decreases over time due to small body adjustments, head-mount slippage, changes in pupil size, and/or changes in hardware or software setup—this is known as drift. Thus, calibrating just before participants view key stimuli is best practice. For example, researchers studying how eyewitnesses view lineups should calibrate directly before showing the lineup. Some systems allow drift corrections via single-trial fixations on a target, which can occur between trials (e.g., EyeLinks utilize these as they are particularly prone to drift). Other systems (e.g., Tobii, GazePoint) claim drift corrections are unnecessary (e.g., the GazePoint HD3 uses a fixation detection algorithm to account for drift such that the average of the fixation gaze data shifts slightly to follow the drift).

Who is being calibrated matters. Calibration is more difficult with animals, children, and people with eye conditions (e.g., age-related macular degeneration, nystagmus). One option is to use the calibration of another person. According to Holmqvist et al. (2022), this increases error by 4–8 degrees but does not change the accuracy of gaze detection depending on the space (i.e., non-linearities) and so allows for valid gaze recording. For some eye conditions, such as nystagmus, some eye trackers provide calibration routines specific to these conditions.

To summarize, calibration is critical for obtaining valid gaze data as it ensures that the eye tracker correctly records what the participant is looking at. Eyewitness researchers should be aware of factors that reduce calibration quality and take steps to minimize and report their influence.

Experimental Design and Stimuli Considerations

Considering typical human behavior facilitates practices that maximize data quality. These include discarding the first and last fixations when looking at fixation duration (Nuthmann, 2013), appreciating that there are differences in how people view short versus long-lasting trials, and appreciating that gaze behaviors differ when tasks are switched from trial to trial (Holmqvist et al., 2022). Moreover, question/instruction wording can influence how people view a screen. For researchers examining gaze on lineups, it may be particularly important to counterbalance lineup member order because people tend to fixate at the middle and top left of an array (Orquin & Loose, 2013). Another consideration is that, particularly for pupillometry, gaze is more accurately measured when the target is in the center of the screen compared to the corner of the screen. The pupil foreshortening artefact is a further concern in pupillometry: the pupil appears more oval when gaze moves away from the eye-tracker camera axis. Researchers should consider using compensation algorithms if their task involves visual search. Pupillary response is also affected by the use of color images so black and white stimuli may be more appropriate, if feasible (Porter & Troscianko, 2003, as cited in Holmqvist et al., 2022).

Data Collection Considerations

Training and practice are important. Experienced operators can often calibrate participants that less experienced operators cannot. There is about a 0.2-degree experience-based advantage to accuracy indicating that experienced operators may also obtain better calibrations (Hessels & Hooge, 2019; Nyström et al., 2013).

Also important is the nature of the participants. Strong age effects have been found, though gender effects appear negligible (e.g., Coors et al., 2021). Research indicates that attrition is lower for adults (Holmqvist et al., 2022). It is more difficult to collect gaze data from children and the elderly. Challenges may include a poorer attention span, which causes lower precision and greater data loss, as well as greater difficulty calibrating and/or more data loss due to glasses, droopy eyelids, and other advanced age eye problems. Further, ethnicity differences exist with East Asian participants being particularly difficult to collect gaze data from, due to the shape of their eyes.

In addition, the nature of a participant's face matters. Glasses, contact lenses, and makeup (mascara, thick black eyeliner) make calibration more difficult. Glasses with reflective coatings are particularly problematic. Large droopy eye lashes, even without makeup, can interfere with pupil detection as do blue eyes because the infrared light used to record gaze means a blue (compared to a brown) iris is dark and therefore confusable with a pupil. Darker hair, eyes, and skin are associated with better accuracy as are larger eyes.

Cognitive factors also play a role. Mental fatigue (e.g., due to sleep deprivation) and cognitive load impact gaze. This may be particularly important when testing estimator variables where the researcher uses gaze as a proxy for memory quality. Task expertise also affects gaze behavior, which may have implications for comparing gaze when viewing familiar and unfamiliar faces. Finally, pathology, personality, medications, and other drugs affect gaze (Holmqvist et al., 2022; Nyström, Hooge, & Holmqvist, 2013).

In summary, researchers should carefully train research assistants as well as consider factors that reduce accuracy as outlined here and in previous section as well as by Orquin and Holmqvist (2019, table 4.2): lighting, ambient vibrations, the presence of others, participant position, type of calibration, which eye is recorded form, glasses, contacts, eye color, makeup, whether stimuli are in corners, as well as individual differences in age, cognitive processing, and task expertise.

Gaze Data Processing

The software used to pre-process gaze data (in the box) is often not reported, though this affects validity (Orquin & Holmqvist, 2018). Pre-registering one's data pre-processing steps and providing open analysis scripts can facilitate replication. To this end, Fiedler et al. (2019) provide reporting guidelines for pre-registration. Kret and Sjak-Shie (2019) provide advice for pre-processing pupil dilation data.

Researchers should be conscientious of the size of AOIs they are using and the precision of the eye tracker because it is possible for a participant to be gazing at a target but for their gaze to be outside the AOI and vice versa. It is recommended that researchers make AOIs larger than the target because gaze capture tends not to be 100%, but only if neighboring objects are relatively far from the target. Thus, eyewitness identification researchers should aim to create stimuli with good separation between objects of interest.

According to Holmqvist et al. (2022), there are "complex, non-linear interactions between data quality measures and AOI properties" (p. 393). When a viewed image is sparsely detailed, AOIs should be as large as possible. Higher-order measures derived from AOIs, such as scan paths, have many settings that can be varied and the size of the AOI will impact these, along with data loss, precision, and accuracy, in a way that propagates from the detection of a gaze event through to the calculation of the higher-order measure (Holqvist et al., 2022).

Reporting

Wu et al. (2012) and Stelter et al. (2021) are examples of clear reporting of eye tracking hardware, software, measures, and procedures. We also refer readers to Holmqvist et al. (2022). Notably, their tables 7, 8, and 12 provide minimal reporting guidelines relevant to the types of designs eyewitness researchers use.

Conclusions

In conclusion, eye tracking is a useful tool for measuring attention and memory but has been used infrequently by eyewitness researchers. Extant work has focused on how gaze at encoding influences the cross-race effect (primarily using face recognition paradigms; it does!), whether gaze predicts lineup decisions (it does!), and whether gaze can help us detect deceptive eyewitnesses (it can!). However, eye tracking may also be particularly effective for testing the impact of estimator variables (Wells, 1978) as well as for developing or augmenting theories about how eyewitnesses make lineup decisions, particularly when used in conjunction with other measures. Despite the promise of this technique, it is a particularly technical area and more consistency is needed in its conduct and reporting to ensure that researchers do not draw different conclusions due to opaque or unreported methodological differences that reflect artifacts of the measurement approach. To that end, we have tried to provide readers with a pragmatic summary of current best practices and direct them to sources that will facilitate good practice. We hope other eyewitness researchers share our excitement about the possibilities this technology has for the study of eyewitness memory, identification accuracy, and legal decision-making.

References

Akkil, D., Isokoski, P., Kangas, J., Rantala, J., & Raisamo, R. (2014). TraQuMe: a tool for measuring the gaze tracking quality. In *Proceedings of the Symposium on Eye Tracking Research and Applications, USA*, 327–330. https://doi.org/10.1145/2578153.2578192

Althoff, R.R., & Cohen, N.J. (1999). Eye-movement-based memory effect: a reprocessing effect in face perception. *Journal of Experimental Psychology: Learning, Memory, and Cognition, 25*(4), 997–1010. https://doi.org/10.1037/0278-7393.25.4.997

Attard, J., & Bindemann, M. (2014). Establishing the duration of crimes: An individual differences and eye-tracking investigation into time estimation. *Applied Cognitive Psychology, 28*(2), 215–225. https://doi.org/10.1002/acp.2986

Beesley, T., Pearson, D., & Le Pelley, M. (2019). Eye tracking as a tool for examining cognitive processes. In G. Foster (Ed.), *Biophysical measurement in experimental social science research: Theory and practice* (pp. 1–30). Academic Press. https://doi.org/10.1016/B978-0-12-813092-6.00002-2

Blais, C., Jack, R.E., Scheepers, C., Fiset, D., & Caldara, R. (2008). Culture shapes how we look at faces. *PloS one, 3*(8), e3022. https://doi.org/10.1371/journal.pone.0003022

Blandón-Gitlin, I., Fenn, E., Masip, J., & Yoo, A.H. (2014). Cognitive-load approaches to detect deception: Searching for cognitive mechanisms. *Trends in Cognitive Sciences, 18*(9), 441–444. https://doi.org/10.1016/j.tics.2014.05.004

Burgund, E.D. (2021). Looking at the own-race bias: Eye-tracking investigations of memory for different race faces. *Visual Cognition, 29*(1), 51–62. https://doi.org/10.1080/13506285.2020.1858216

Camos, V., & Portrat, S. (2015). The impact of cognitive load on delayed recall. *Psychonomic Bulletin & Review, 22*(4), 1029–1034. https://doi.org/10.3758/s13423-014-0772-5

Cantoni, V., Musci, M., Nugrahaningsih, N., & Porta, M. (2018). Gaze-based biometrics: An introduction to forensic applications. *Pattern Recognition Letters, 113*(1), 54–57. https://doi.org/10.1016/j.patrec.2016.12.006

Carter, B.T., & Luke, S.G. (2020). Best practices in eye tracking research. *International Journal of Psychophysiology, 155*, 49–62. https://doi.org/10.1016/j.ijpsycho.2020.05.010

Coors, A., Merten, N., Ward, D.D., Schmid, M., Breteler, M.M.B., & Ettinger, U. (2021). Strong age but weak sex effects in eye movement performance in the general adult population: Evidence from the Rhineland study. *Vision Research, 178*, 124–133. https://doi.org/10.1016/j.visres.2020.10.004

De Sola, I.S., Pérez-Mata, N., & Diges, M. (2021). The effect of the instructions on face recognition: accuracy and eye movements. *Psychological Applications and Trends 2021, Portugal*, 462–464. https://doi.org/10.36315/2021inpact104

Duchowski, A.T. (2017). *Eye tracking methodology: Theory and practice*. Springer.

Dunning, D., & Perretta, S. (2002). Automaticity and eyewitness accuracy: A 10- to 12-second rule for distinguishing accurate from inaccurate positive identifications. *Journal of Applied Psychology, 87*(5), 951–962. https://doi.org/10.1037/0021-9010.87.5.951

Dunning, D., & Stern, L.B. (1994). Distinguishing accurate from inaccurate eyewitness identifications via inquiries about decision processes. *Journal of Personality and Social Psychology*, 67(5), 818–835. https://doi.org/10.1037/0022-3514.67.5.818

Ellis, H.D., Deregowski, J.B., & Shepherd, J.W. (1975). Descriptions of white and black faces by white and black subjects (1). *International Journal of Psychology*, 10(2), 119–123. https://doi.org/10.1080/00207597508247325

Elphick, C.E., Pike, G.E., & Hole, G.J. (2020). You can believe your eyes: Measuring implicit recognition in a lineup with pupillometry. *Psychology, Crime & Law*, 26(1), 67–92. https://doi.org/10.1080/1068316X.2019.1634196

Fiedler, S., Schulte-Mecklenbeck, M., Reenkewitz, F., & Orquin, J.L. (2019). A primer on eye-tracking methodology for behavioral science. In J.L. Orquin, & K. Holmqvist (Eds.), *Increasing reproducibility of eye-tracking studies: The Eye-Guidelines* (pp. 65–75). Routledge.

Flowe, H. (2011). An exploration of visual behaviour in eyewitness identification tests. *Applied Cognitive Psychology*, 25(2), 244–254. https://doi.org/10.1002/acp.1670

Flowe, H., & Cottrell, G.W. (2011). An examination of simultaneous lineup identification decision processes using eye tracking. *Applied Cognitive Psychology*, 25(3), 443–451. https://doi.org/10.1002/acp.1711

Fu, G., Hu, C.S., Wang, Q., Quinn, P.C., & Lee, K. (2012). Adults scan own- and other-race faces differently. *PloS one*, 7(6), e37688. https://doi.org/10.1371/journal.pone.0037688

Gamer, M., & Pertzov, Y. (2018). Detecting concealed knowledge from ocular responses. In J.P. Rosenfeld (Ed.), *Detecting concealed information and deception* (pp. 169–186). Academic Press. https://doi.org/10.1016/B978-0-12-812729-2.00008-2

Goldinger, S.D., He, Y., & Papesh, M.H. (2009). Deficits in cross-race face learning: insights from eye movements and pupillometry. *Journal of Experimental Psychology: Learning, Memory, and Cognition*, 35(5), 1105–1122. https://doi.org/10.1037%2Fa0016548

Greene, C.M., Murphy, G., & Januszewski, J. (2017). Under high perceptual load, observers look but do not see. *Applied Cognitive Psychology*, 31(4), 431–437. https://doi.org/10.1002/acp.3335

Gross, S.R., & Shaffer, M. (2012). *Exonerations in the United States, 1989–2012: Report by the national registry of exonerations*. Retrieved from https://repository.law.umich.edu/other/92

Hancock, K.J., & Rhodes, G. (2008). Contact, configural coding and the other-race effect in face recognition. *British Journal of Psychology*, 99(1), 45–56. https://doi.org/10.1348/000712607X199981

Hannula, D.E., Althoff, R.R., Warren, D.E., Riggs, L., Cohen, N.J., & Ryan, J.D. (2010). Worth a glance: Using eye movements to investigate the cognitive neuroscience of memory. *Frontiers in Human Neuroscience*, 4, 166. https://doi.org/10.3389/fnhum.2010.00166

Harvey, A.J., Kneller, W., & Campbell, A.C. (2013). The effects of alcohol intoxication on attention and memory for visual scenes. *Memory*, 21(8), 969–980. https://doi.org/10.1080/09658211.2013.770033

Hessels, R.S., & Hooge, I.T.C. (2019). Eye tracking in developmental cognitive neuroscience—The good, the bad and the ugly. *Developmental Cognitive Neuroscience, 40*, 100710. https://doi.org/10.1016/j.dcn.2019.100710

Hills, P.J., Cooper, R.E., & Pake, J.M. (2013). Removing the own-race bias in face recognition by attentional shift using fixation crosses to diagnostic features: An eye-tracking study. *Visual Cognition, 21*(7), 876–898. https://doi.org/10.1016/j.actpsy.2012.11.013

Hills, P.J., & Lewis, M.B. (2006). Reducing the own-race bias in face recognition by shifting attention. *The Quarterly Journal of Experimental Psychology, 59*(6), 996–1002. https://doi.org/10.1080/17470210600654750

Hills, P.J., & Pake, J.M. (2013). Eye-tracking the own-race bias in face recognition: Revealing the perceptual and socio-cognitive mechanisms. *Cognition, 129*(3), 586–597. https://doi.org/10.1016/j.cognition.2013.08.012

Holmqvist, K. (2016). Optimal settings for commercial event detection algorithms based on the level of noise. (Accepted for publication in *Behavior Research Methods*, 1–21; not published for legal reasons) https://doi.org/10.13140/RG.2.2.26871.55200

Holmqvist, K., Nyström, M., & Mulvey, F. (2012). Eye tracker data quality: What it is and how to measure it. In *Proceedings of the Symposium on Eye Tracking Research and Applications, USA*, 45–52. https://doi.org/10.1145/2168556.2168563

Holmqvist, K., Örbom, S.L., Hooge, I.T., Niehorster, D.C., Alexander, R.G., Andersson, R., Andersson, R., Benjamins, J.S., Blignaut, P., Brouwer, A-M., Chuang, L.L., Dalrymple, K.A., Drieghe, D., Dunn, M.J., Ettinger, U., Fielder, S., Foulsham, T., van der Deest, J.N., Hansen, D.W., ... & Hessels, R.S. (2022, advance online publication). Eye tracking: empirical foundations for a minimal reporting guideline. *Behavior Research Methods*. https://doi.org/10.3758/s13428-021-01762-8

Hooge, I.T.C., Holleman, G.A., Haukes, N.C., & Hessels, R. S. (2019). Gaze tracking accuracy in humans: One eye is sometimes better than two. *Behavior Research Methods, 51*(6), 2712–2721. https://doi.org/10.3758/s13428-018-1135-3

Hsiao, J.H.W., & Cottrell, G. (2008). Two fixations suffice in face recognition. *Psychological Science, 19*(10), 998–1006. https://doi.org/10.1111/j.1467-9280.2008.02191.x

Janik, S.W., Wellens, A.R., Goldberg, M.L., & Dell'Osso, L.F. (1978). Eyes as the center of focus in the visual examination of human faces. *Perceptual and Motor Skills, 47*(3), 857–858. https://doi.org/10.2466/pms.1978.47.3.857

Josephson, S., & Holmes, M.E. (2010). Have you seen any of these men? Looking at whether eyewitnesses use scanpaths to recognize suspects in photo lineups. In *Proceedings of the 2010 Symposium on Eye-Tracking Research & Applications*, 49–52. https://doi.org/10.1145/1743666.1743677

Kelly, D.J., Miellet, S., & Caldara, R. (2010). Culture shapes eye movements for visually homogeneous objects. *Frontiers in Psychology, 1*, 6. https://doi.org/10.3389/fpsyg.2010.00006

Kneller, W., Memon, A., & Stevenage, S. (2001). Simultaneous and sequential lineups: Decision processes of accurate and inaccurate eyewitnesses. *Applied Cognitive Psychology, 15*(6), 659–671. https://doi.org/10.1002/acp.739

Kocab, K., & Sporer, S.L. (2016). The weapon focus effect for person identifications and descriptions: A meta-analysis. In M.K. Miller, & B.H. Bornstein (Eds.), *Advances in psychology and law*, vol. 1 (pp. 71–117). Springer.

Kret, M.E., & Sjak-Shie, E.E. (2019). Preprocessing pupil size data: Guidelines and code. *Behavior Research Methods*, 51(3), 1336–1342. https://doi.org/10.3758/s13428-018-1075-y

Lampinen, J.M., Race, B., Wolf, A.P., Phillips, P., Moriarty, N., & Smith, A.M. (2020). Comparing detailed and less detailed pre-lineup instructions. *Applied Cognitive Psychology*, 34(2), 409–424. https://doi.org/10.1002/acp.3627

Lavie, N. (1995). Perceptual load as a necessary condition for selective attention. *Journal of Experimental Psychology: Human Perception and Performance*, 21(3), 451–468. https://doi.org/10.1037/0096-1523.21.3.451

Lee, J., Mansour, J.K., & Penrod, S.D. (2022). Validity of mock-witness measures for assessing lineup fairness. *Psychology, Crime & Law*, 28(3), 215–245. https://doi.org/10.1080/1068316X.2021.1905811

Lee, J., & Penrod, S.D. (2022). Three-level meta-analysis of the other-race bias in facial identification. *Applied Cognitive Psychology*, 36(5), 1106–1130. https://doi.org/10.1002/acp.3997

Loftus, E.F., Loftus, G.R., & Messo, J. (1987). Some facts about "weapon focus." *Law and Human Behavior*, 11(1), 55–62. https://doi.org/10.1007/BF01044839

Loftus, G.R., & Mackworth, N.H. (1978). Cognitive determinants of fixation location during picture viewing. *Journal of Experimental Psychology: Human Perception and Performance*, 4(4), 565–572. https://doi.org/10.1037/0096-1523.4.4.565

Mansour, J.K., Beaudry, J.L., Kalmet, N., Bertrand, M.I., & Lindsay, R.C.L. (2017). Evaluating lineup fairness: Variations across methods and measures. *Law and Human Behavior*, 41(1), 103–115. https://doi.org/10.1037/lhb0000203

Mansour, J.K., Lindsay, R.C.L., Brewer, N., & Munhall, K.G. (2009). Characterizing visual behaviour in a lineup task. *Applied Cognitive Psychology*, 23(7), 1012–1026. https://doi.org/10.1002/acp.1570

McDonnell, G.P., Bornstein, B.H., Laub, C.E., Mills, M., & Dodd, M.D. (2014). Perceptual processes in the cross-race effect: Evidence from eyetracking. *Basic and Applied Social Psychology*, 36(6), 478–493. https://doi.org/10.1080/01973533.2014.958227

Megreya, A.M., Bindemann, M., Havard, C., & Burton, A.M. (2012). Identity-lineup location influences target selection: Evidence from eye movements. *Journal of Police and Criminal Psychology*, 27(2), 167–178. https://doi.org/10.1007/s11896-011-9098-7

Meissner, C.A., & Brigham, J.C. (2001). Thirty years of investigating the own-race bias in memory for faces: A meta-analytic review. *Psychology, Public Policy, and Law*, 7(1), 3–35. https://doi.org/10.1037/1076-8971.7.1.3

Millen, A.E., & Hancock, P.J. (2019). Eye see through you! Eye tracking unmasks concealed face recognition despite countermeasures. *Cognitive Research: Principles and Implications*, 4(1), 1–14. https://doi.org/10.1186/s41235-019-0169-0

Millen, A.E., Hope, L., & Hillstrom, A.P. (2020). Eye spy a liar: assessing the utility of eye fixations and confidence judgments for detecting concealed recognition of faces, scenes and objects. *Cognitive Research: Principles and Implications*, 5(1), 1–18. https://doi.org/10.1186/s41235-020-00227-4

Millen, A.E., Hope, L., Hillstrom, A.P., & Vrij, A. (2017). Tracking the truth: the effect of face familiarity on eye fixations during deception. *Quarterly Journal of Experimental Psychology*, 70(5), 930–943. https://doi.org/10.1080/17470218.2016.1172093

Nahari, T., Lancry-Dayan, O., Ben-Shakhar, G., & Pertzov, Y. (2019). Detecting concealed familiarity using eye movements: the role of task demands. *Cognitive Research: Principles and Implications*, 4(1), 1–16. https://doi.org/10.1186/s41235-019-0162-7

Niehorster, D.C., Zemblys, R., Beelders, T., & Holmqvist, K. (2020). Characterizing gaze position signals and synthesizing noise during fixations in eye-tracking data. *Behavior Research Methods*, 52(6), 2515–2534. https://doi.org/10.3758/s13428-020-01400-9

Nuthmann, A. (2013). On the visual span during object search in real-world scenes. *Visual Cognition*, 21(7), 803–837. https://doi.org/10.1080/13506285.2013.832449

Nyström, M., Andersson, R., Holmqvist, K., & van de Weijer, J. (2013). The influence of calibration method and eye physiology on eyetracking data quality. *Behavior Research Methods*, 45(1), 272–288. https://doi.org/10.3758/s13428-012-0247-4

Nyström, M., Hooge, I.T.C., & Holmqvist, K. (2013). Post-saccadic oscillations in eye movement data recorded with pupil-based eye trackers reflect motion of the pupil inside the iris. *Vision Research*, 92, 59–66. https://doi.org/10.1016/j.visres.2013.09.009

Orquin, J.L., & Holmqvist, K. (2018). Threats to the validity of eye-movement research in psychology. *Behavior Research Methods*, 50(4), 1645–1656. https://doi.org/10.3758/s13428-017-0998-z

Orquin, J.L., & Holmqvist, K. (2019). A primer on eye-tracking methodology for behavioral science. In J.L. Orquin, & K. Holmqvist (Eds.), *A handbook of process tracing methods* (pp. 53–64). Routledge.

Orquin, J.L., & Loose, S.M. (2013). Attention and choice: A review on eye movements in decision making. *Acta Psychologica*, 144(1), 190–206. https://doi.org/10.1016/j.actpsy.2013.06.003

Palmer, M.A., Sauer, J.D., & Holt, G.A. (2017). Undermining position effects in choices from arrays, with implications for police lineups. *Journal of Experimental Psychology: Applied*, 23(1), 71–84. https://doi.org/10.1037/xap0000109

Paterson, H.M., Luppino, D., Calderwood, C., MacDougall, H.G., Taubert, J., & Kemp, R.I. (2017). Can training improve eyewitness identification? The effect of internal feature focus on memory for faces. *Psychology, Crime & Law*, 23(10), 927–945. https://doi.org/10.1080/1068316X.2017.1346099

Rahal, R.M., & Fiedler, S. (2019). Understanding cognitive and affective mechanisms in social psychology through eye-tracking. *Journal of Experimental Social Psychology*, 85, 103842. https://doi.org/10.1016/j.jesp.2019.103842

Read, J.D., Vokey, J.R., & Hammersley, R. (1990). Changing photos of faces: Effects of exposure duration and photo similarity on recognition and the accuracy-confidence relationship. *Journal of Experimental Psychology: Learning, Memory, and Cognition*, 16(5), 870–882. https://doi.org/10.1037/0278-7393.16.5.870

Ryan, J.D., Hannula, D.E., & Cohen, N.J. (2007). The obligatory effects of memory on eye movements. *Memory*, *15*(5), 508–525. https://doi.org/10.1080/09658210701391022

Sauerland, M., & Sporer, S.L. (2007). Post-decision confidence, decision time, and self-reported decision processes as postdictors of identification accuracy. *Psychology, Crime & Law*, *13*(6), 611–625. https://doi.org/10.1080/10683160701264561

Schwedes, C., & Wentura, D. (2012). The revealing glance: Eye gaze behavior to concealed information. *Memory & Cognition*, *40*(4), 642–651. https://doi.org/10.3758/s13421-011-0173-1

Semmelmann, K., & Weigelt, S. (2018). Online webcam-based eye tracking in cognitive science: A first look. *Behavior Research Methods*, *50*(2), 451–465. https://doi.org/10.3758/s13428-017-0913-7

Singh, B., Mellinger, C., Earls, H.A., Tran, J., Bardsley, B., & Correll, J. (2022). Does cross-race contact improve cross-race face perception? A meta-analysis of the cross-race deficit and contact. *Personality and Social Psychology Bulletin*, *48*(6), 865–887. https://doi.org/10.1177/01461672211024463

Špakov, O. (2012). Comparison of eye movement filters used in HCI. In *Proceedings of the Symposium on Eye Tracking Research and Applications, USA*, 281–284. https://doi.org/10.1145/2168556.2168616

Spitzer, L., & Mueller, S. (2022). Using a test battery to compare three remote, video-based eye-trackers. Proceedings of the *Symposium on Eye Tracking Research and Applications, USA*, 28, 1–7. https://doi.org/10.1145/3517031.3529644

Steele, C.M., & Josephs, R.A. (1990). Alcohol myopia: Its prized and dangerous effects. *American Psychologist*, *45*(8), 921–933. https://doi.org/10.1037/0003-066X.45.8.921

Stelter, M., Rommel, M., & Degner, J. (2021). (Eye-) Tracking the other-race effect: Comparison of eye movements during encoding and recognition of ingroup faces with proximal and distant outgroup faces. *Social Cognition*, *39*(3), 366–395. https://doi.org/10.1521/soco.2021.39.3.366

Tiemens, R.K., Josephson, S., Utzinger, T., & Hendricks, R. (unpublished manuscript). *Have you seen this man? An eye-tracking study of the photo array used in State v. Rettenberger*.

Valentine, T. (1991). A unified account of the effects of distinctiveness, inversion, and race in face recognition. *The Quarterly Journal of Experimental Psychology*, *43*(2), 161–204. https://doi.org/10.1080/14640749108400966

Wells, G.L. (1978). Applied eyewitness-testimony research: System variables and estimator variables. *Journal of Personality and Social Psychology*, *36*(12), 1546–1557. https://doi.org/10.1037/0022-3514.36.12.1546

Wells, G.L. (1984). The psychology of lineup identifications. *Journal of Applied Social Psychology*, *14*(2), 89–103. https://doi.org/10.1111/j.1559-1816.1984.tb02223.x

Werchan, D.M., Thomason, M.E., & Brito, N.H. (2022). OWLET: An automated, open-source method for infant gaze tracking using smartphone and webcam recordings. *Behavior Research Methods*. https://doi.org/10.3758/s13428-022-01962-w

Wittwer, T., Tredoux, C.G., Py, J., & Paubel, P.V. (2019). Training participants to focus on critical facial features does not decrease own-group bias. *Frontiers in Psychology*, *10*, 2081. https://doi.org/10.3389/fpsyg.2019.02081

Wu, E.X.W., Laeng, B., & Magnussen, S. (2012). Through the eyes of the own-race bias: Eye-tracking and pupillometry during face recognition. *Social Neuroscience*, 7(2), 202–216. https://doi.org/10.1080/17470919.2011.596946

Yarbus, A.L. (1967). Eye movements during perception of complex objects. In *Eye movements and vision* (pp. 171–211). Springer. https://doi.org/10.1007/978-1-4899-5379-7_8

Young, S.G., Hugenberg, K., Bernstein, M.J., & Sacco, D.F. (2012). Perception and motivation in face recognition: A critical review of theories of the cross-race effect. *Personality and Social Psychology Review*, 16(2), 116–142. https://doi.org/10.1177/1088868311418987

Zuo, J., Gedeon, T., & Qin, Z. (2019, July). Your eyes say you're lying: An eye movement pattern analysis for face familiarity and deceptive cognition. In *2019 International Joint Conference on Neural Networks, Hungary*, 1–8. https://doi.org/10.1109/IJCNN.2019.8851789

8 Understanding Eyewitness Testimony with Virtual Reality

Markus Bindemann and Matthew C. Fysh

Introduction

Around the world, police and legal systems rely heavily on eyewitnesses in the investigation, prosecution and defense of criminal events. Eyewitnesses are often required to provide first-hand accounts of the circumstances surrounding a crime, may be asked to attempt to identify a perpetrator, and their evidence can be persuasive for jurors in reaching decisions about a suspect's guilt. Progress in the theoretical understanding of eyewitness accuracy has been driven largely by researchers in psychology (Wells et al., 2006). For many decades now, the discipline has been critical in conducting scientific experiments into eyewitness identification and memory. This has served to inform the application of eyewitness testimony in the criminal justice system through dialogue between psychologists and practitioners.

Over this time, two approaches to research have become dominant in psychology to study eyewitness accuracy. One approach has been to study eyewitness accuracy in the laboratory by presenting visual material on a computer screen under highly controlled conditions. For example, in studies on the accuracy with which eyewitnesses can identify the perpetrator of a crime, participants may be presented with a target face that is cropped of extraneous background and shown on an otherwise blank display. This is then followed by a lineup of faces from which the target has to be identified. Many variations of this paradigm exist, which involve replacing the initial exposure to a target photo with a video, varying the number of targets or by presenting different lineup types, or manipulating the duration between exposure to the target and the identification phase of the experiment (e.g., Bindemann et al., 2012; Bruce et al., 1999; Clifford & Hollin, 1981; Megreya & Burton, 2006; Meissner et al., 2005).

This experimental approach has some clear advantages. It allows for the tight control of variables to isolate processes of specific interest, for instance. It also enables researchers to test the same participants over many trials to obtain a more reliable estimate of performance, and the resulting data can be analyzed with powerful parametric statistics. Consequently, laboratory studies are often considered to have high *internal validity*, whereby replicable experiments can provide clear insight into cause-and-effect relationships among variables, and therefore speak more strongly to the true nature of the phenomenon under investigation. The downside is that such highly controlled experimentation provides a piece-meal approach to study eyewitness identification, in which individual variables are the focus of investigation. With this approach, the complexity, dynamics, and real-world context within which an event occurs are not considered essential for understanding the process. This imposes limits on the generalizability of research with regards to the extent to which laboratory findings speak to real-world cognition. The potential consequences of this approach can be profound. If the experimental paradigms to study eyewitness accuracy fail to incorporate important aspects of the real-world then this can lead to the development of theories that fail to adequately explain real-world cognition.

An alternative approach to highly controlled laboratory experiments are field studies in which an experiment is set up outside of the laboratory, for example, by using confederates that act as the perpetrators of crime in a real-world setting. By observing participants in settings outside of the laboratory, it becomes possible to study behavior under more natural conditions. This can provide greater *external validity*, by enabling researchers to draw conclusions about real-world behavior and cognition with greater confidence. However, while these field studies acknowledge the importance of context by providing better opportunities to understand behavior in natural and social environments, these studies also relinquish systematic control over many of the variables that are at play. This can include fundamental information that is *known* to be important for eyewitness accuracy and face identification, such as the visibility of the target in terms of factors such as exposure time (see, e.g., Bornstein et al., 2012), face view (e.g., Longmore et al., 2008), and the ambient viewing conditions (e.g., Jenkins et al., 2011), as well as unknown factors that might be at play. Field studies are also logistically challenging and may be impossible to set up in some contexts altogether, such as security-sensitive operational environments or crime scenes. In addition, this approach to research often renders psychological experiments into single-trial "one-shot" studies. This puts limits on replication and can place reliance on less powerful non-parametric methods for data analysis, which reduces the probability of demonstrating links between variables that are truly associated. Field studies can also pose ethical dilemmas in eyewitness research - for example, whether it is acceptable to draw unsuspecting passers-by as participants into psychological experiments without their prior consent, and if so, what kind of scenarios can be studied in this way.

The dichotomy between laboratory and field studies has important consequences for the study of eyewitness accuracy. On one hand, laboratory studies may not sufficiently capture the real-world phenomena that are the subject of study. On the other, field studies may not allow to establish cause-and-effect with precision. Therefore, to maximize knowledge gain and theory development, experimental control in eyewitness research must be balanced against the real-world behavior that one is seeking to address. This balance can be difficult to achieve with the current methods. For example, some studies have attempted to address this discrepancy between the laboratory and the real world by employing videos of faces to provide more "realistic" stimuli (Hermens & Walker, 2012; Keemink et al., 2021; Lander et al., 2001; O'Toole et al., 2011) or by recruiting live confederates to act as stimuli (Kemp et al., 1997; Megreya & Burton, 2008; Ritchie et al., 2020; White et al., 2014), but such approaches come with their own limitations. While pre-recorded videos display dynamic faces, these representations are seldom interactive. For live confederates, on the other hand, it is challenging to behave consistently across participants, as may be necessary to preserve specific experimental manipulations. There is also, of course, a practical limit to the number of live confederates one can employ for a given study. Consequently, field studies often consist of scenarios that involve only a small number of people. Gang crimes, for example, are difficult to implement and control with the existing research approaches, despite their prevalence in real-world settings (see, e.g., Curry et al., 1994).

This dichotomy between laboratory research and field studies in eyewitness research in psychology raises a key question for researchers and practitioners: How is it possible to conduct behaviorally relevant eyewitness research under conditions that also provide the necessary experimental control to isolate variables of interest? In this chapter, we introduce virtual reality (VR) as a technology that has great potential to bridge the paradigmatic gap between the laboratory and field settings. VR enables researchers to immerse participants, via a head-mounted display, in interactive three-dimensional environments that are complex and increasingly realistic, but which also preserve the controlled nature of laboratory experiments and enable sophisticated scientific measurement of human behavior. This technology has undergone rapid development in recent years and a great number of solutions now exist to provide detailed real-world scenarios containing visual objects and person characters that can be adapted for psychological experiments. A key proponent for the development of VR technology has been the video gaming industry, with some of the most popular VR titles that are currently available focusing heavily on player-perpetrated crime and violence (e.g., *Superhot*, *Fallout*, *Half-Life: Alyx*). Based on the capacity of VR to host environments within which criminal and violent encounters can occur, the world of VR also appears to be well-placed for research into eyewitness accuracy. Here, we argue that the adaptation of such VR technology has the potential to transform the study of eyewitness accuracy. We describe the current feasibility of VR for implementing eyewitness research and review studies that have started to transition to this technology.

Virtual Reality

VR is a computer-generated simulation that can provide detailed three-dimensional (3D) models of real-world and imaginary environments. These environments can be filled with 3D objects and digital humans, which participants can interact with in ways that can seem surprisingly real. The application of VR technology to psychological experiments enables researchers to immerse participants in "real-world" environments that are increasingly complex and realistic, but which also preserve the controlled nature of laboratory experiments. This provides a means of studying behavior in scenarios that are impossible to simulate effectively in the laboratory, but which are also difficult to access or control in the field.

In VR experiments, this can be combined with sophisticated measurement, such as the accuracy and speed of responses via handheld controllers, spatial coordinates as participants navigate through a virtual space, and eye-tracking capability to determine what is looked at and when. Over the last decade, the cost of VR hardware and software has also reduced dramatically, while access to digital 3D models of virtual environments, objects and humans (often called avatars) has become easier and more affordable. This technology continues to develop at pace, offering possibilities such as hand gesture recognition to interact more naturally with objects and environments, haptic gloves that provide "true contact" feedback sensations from the touch of virtual objects, and omni-directional treadmill technology to facilitate horizontal movement in any direction.

Virtual Objects and Environments

In recent years, VR has been utilized increasingly for psychological research (e.g., Loomis et al., 1999; McCall & Blascovich, 2009; Wilson & Soranzo, 2015; for review see, e.g., Pan & Hamilton, 2018). However, the adaptation of VR for eyewitness research depends on the feasibility with which convincing virtual environments, scenarios and digital humans for eyewitness can be constructed. Online distributors (see www.turbosquid.com) now provide a multitude of objects and environments that are suitable for different aspects of eyewitness research or that can be adapted and modified for this purpose. For example, it is possible to purchase 3D models of crime scenes, police stations with prison cells and interrogation rooms, morgues and pathology laboratories, and courtrooms to study different aspects of eyewitness scenarios and criminal investigations. It is also possible to purchase ready-made environments of everyday places where crimes might occur, such as city parks and building landscapes, underground and outdoor car parks, playgrounds, and shopping malls, while lighting sources can be adapted in VR to simulate these settings at different day and night times. These environments can be equipped with an astonishingly large range of virtual objects to enhance the detail, functionality, and realism of environments. On the theme of crime and eyewitness testimony, for example, models of police cars, motorcycles and helicopters exist, and a diverse range of weaponry is available. This is further complemented by the availability of crime-related paraphernalia, such as crime scene tape and police barriers, body bags and corpses, police cones, cartridge cases, chalk lines, and forensic evidence signs and packages.

The range of possible virtual environments and objects allow for the creation of a much broader range of eyewitness scenarios in VR than has been possible to study previously with laboratory and field studies (Kane et al., 2012). It also allows for the study of scenarios that might be more emotive, frightening, or violent than field studies can ethically and practically provide. This also allows researchers to examine whether scenarios that mimic real-life incidents more closely evoke different eyewitness responses. Although the application of VR to eyewitness identification is still limited, evidence is beginning to emerge that suggests this to be the case. In one recent study, participants viewed a threatening eyewitness scenario, comprising of an armed store robbery, or a non-threatening scenario, in which a target person donated money in the same setting (Nyman et al., 2020). This was experienced either as a 2D video recording or as a 3D video recording in 360-degree VR. Target identifications were considerably lower in VR (66%) than in 2D videos (91%). Moreover, eyewitness identification accuracy was higher with the threatening (85%) than the non-threatening scenario (40%), but only in VR. This demonstrates that the mode of presentation, in the extent to which this mimics real-life, can exert strong effects on behavior that change the inferences that can be made about eyewitness accuracy. One effect, for example, that has been linked to eyewitness accuracy is the weapon focus effect, whereby the presence of a weapon *impairs* eyewitness memory (Erickson et al., 2014; Fawcett et al., 2013). One potential implication of these preliminary findings with VR is that laboratory studies may not correspond with the real-life effects of this variable.

If VR environments allow for the study of eyewitness scenarios that are anchored more strongly to the places or settings in which such incidents may occur in real life, then this can give psychological paradigms additional plausibility. The importance of getting these elements right - the place (or setting) of an eyewitness scenario and the plausibility of the event - is often considered insufficiently in eyewitness research. In the VR domain, some parallels exist that are therefore interesting to consider. For example, the concepts of *place illusion* and *plausibility illusion* are considered important for providing convincing immersive experiences that enhance the realism of virtual experiences. Place illusion refers to the compelling experience of being in a real place, despite the participants' actual knowledge that they are not there, as they are only experiencing the place through immersion in virtual reality (Slater, 2009). This experience arises from compelling visual and auditory sensory input, and is therefore linked to the real-life qualities of the VR environment and the display technology. The concept of plausibility, on the other hand, refers to the quality of real-time interaction with a VR environment, and is influenced by the interactivity and animation of virtual environments, objects and characters (Slater, 2009). For example, this illusion has been linked to sensorimotor contingency (see O'Regan & Noë, 2001), whereby changes in sensorimotor input as participants move through virtual environments corresponds to the movement and associated changes that one would experience in reality (Pan et al., 2012). Essentially, the place illusion speaks to the visual and auditory credibility of a virtual environment, whereas the plausibility illusion speaks to the interactive credibility of such settings. It is entirely possible for the requirements of these illusions to be separately fulfilled. For example, with sufficient graphics and auditory cues, the realism of a virtual environment can be remarkably compelling. However, if objects in such an environment cannot be manipulated by the user in a manner that feels real, then the plausibility illusion is shattered. The opposite is also true—an environment can be highly interactive and subsequently immersive, resulting in a strong feeling of plausibility, without meeting the necessary visual and auditory criteria to seem real.

Concerns about plausibility, in the sense of sensorimotor contingency, may not apply to laboratory and field studies in the eyewitness domain, but plausibility may be important here in a different sense. For example, laboratory and field studies are often set in places or implemented in a fashion that lacks the plausibility that one is experiencing a *real* crime scenario. It is an open question whether this affects what we can learn from these studies, but phenomena such as the weapons effect (e.g., Steblay, 1992) and context-dependent memory (e.g., Smith & Vela, 1992) demonstrate the importance of context and credibility for understanding eyewitness accuracy. In this sense, concepts of place and plausibility in the VR domain can serve to highlight how eyewitness accuracy is often studied under conditions that may not meet related real-life criteria.

The VR domain also points to solutions for addressing these shortcomings, not only through the implementation of eyewitness paradigms in VR, but through the adaptation of measures of place and plausibility that already exist in the VR domain. Here, place presence and plausibility are measured through questionnaires to reflect the fact that these illusions are ultimately subjective experiences (see Usoh et al., 2000; Witmer & Singer, 1998). Thus, participants may be asked questions such as "To what extent did you have a sense that you were in the same place as person X?" to determine the extent to which a VR paradigm can capture a crime scene and give participants the sense that they are a part of it.

Crucially, if the application of VR succeeds in enabling eyewitness scenarios of greater plausibility, then concerns about participant safety might also increase. An advantage of VR is that any scenario can be administered under much more controlled and predictable, and therefore safer conditions, than field studies can provide. VR also provides a safe way to interrupt an experiment, for example, should an eyewitness experience in VR become overwhelming or disconcerting. In VR, the observer and their exact perceptual experience can be monitored in real time, and if need be, immersion in a scenario can be broken immediately at any point by the simple removal of the VR headset or termination of the experiment program.

Virtual People

A key aspect of the application of VR to the study of eyewitness accuracy is the person content that can be presented in these environments. Similar to 3D objects and environments, a wide range of ready-made 3D models of people are available for purchase. This includes avatars of men, women and children, of different ages, body shapes and ethnicities. These can be acquired readily dressed as particular personnel (e.g., police) or as civilians. The visual realism of these avatars can vary considerably. Some basic avatars resemble cartoon or anime characters. At the other end of the realism spectrum are highly detailed avatars that can include even fine structural detail, such as strands of hair, and textural detail, such as freckles, moles, veins, and skin pores. These avatars can be rigged with a virtual skeleton and animated to display a wide range of body movement. Hundreds of pre-existing generic movement sequences and behaviors can be downloaded onto avatars with specialist software, such as walking, running, or fighting animations. Avatars can also be rigged for facial movement, such as different emotional expressions, eye gaze, speech and tongue movement.

However, although high-realism avatars are available for purchase, there is no established standard to define or implement the level of realism that is achieved. Instead, this a judgement for the content creator and end user. This presents a potential problem for the application of virtual reality in psychology. For some types of research, a level of realism that falls short of real-world standards may be sufficient to address a question at hand, provided that key aspects are captured in VR. For example, even environments of relatively low visual realism can induce realistic emotions associated with particular situations (Kane et al., 2012), such as feelings of fear induced by virtual heights in fictional environments (e.g., virtual climbing games). In other cases, such as human social interaction, the behavior of participants in psychological experiments is likely to depend on the realism of a person avatar. The study of perspective-taking shows, for example, that the perceived correspondence between avatar and participant can affect the participant's interpretation of what the avatar can see (Ferguson et al., 2018; Nielsen et al., 2015). Thus, how we adopt avatars' perspectives depends on the humanness of avatars, and this is likely to hold for other psychological processes too. Perhaps most importantly for eyewitness identification, avatars' faces must resemble real people.

Avatars of Real People

An important disconnect exists between commercial virtual avatars and the requirements of eyewitness research. Although commercial avatars may *appear* realistic, these are typically based on people who are unfamiliar to the end user. Consequently, when it is not known which person an avatar is based on, it is difficult to establish whether that person is represented accurately. This is paradoxical in the sense that some avatars may appear detailed and highly realistic, but actually bear a poor resemblance to the person upon whom they are based. Indeed, highly sophisticated character creator engines now exist that enable people to create virtual humans of great realism (e.g., *Unreal Character Creator*). As such, many of the avatars that populate digital marketplaces today may not be based on real people at all, putting potential limits not only on whether these avatars accurately resemble a specific individual but whether they capture the psychologically important aspects of a *human*.

For the application of VR to the study of eyewitness accuracy, the requirements are different. Here, avatars should be photo-realistic and veridical representations of real people, that can be recognized as accurately and via the same visual information and cognitive processes as the person upon whom they are based. If avatars of multiple persons are used in an experiment, it also seems sensible to apply the same construction method to all, so that variation in construction cannot induce additional noise into an experiment. This may be particularly important for eyewitness experiments that are likely to involve more than one person, such as a victim and a perpetrator, or a lineup with a suspect and several foils. Indeed, evidence already exists in the eyewitness domain to show that *irrelevant* variation between persons in the construction of a lineup can influence identification decisions, such as subtle changes in the color of the background against which a person is depicted (Havard et al., 2019). This points to

Understanding Eyewitness Testimony with Virtual Reality 181

the importance of standardizing avatar construction methods to produce avatars of real people for psychological experiments.

Such methods now exist. Figure 8.1 outlines the workflow of a method that is available for scientists in this domain. Here, a 3D scan of the face of a real person was captured with a small, handheld 3D scanner. For a

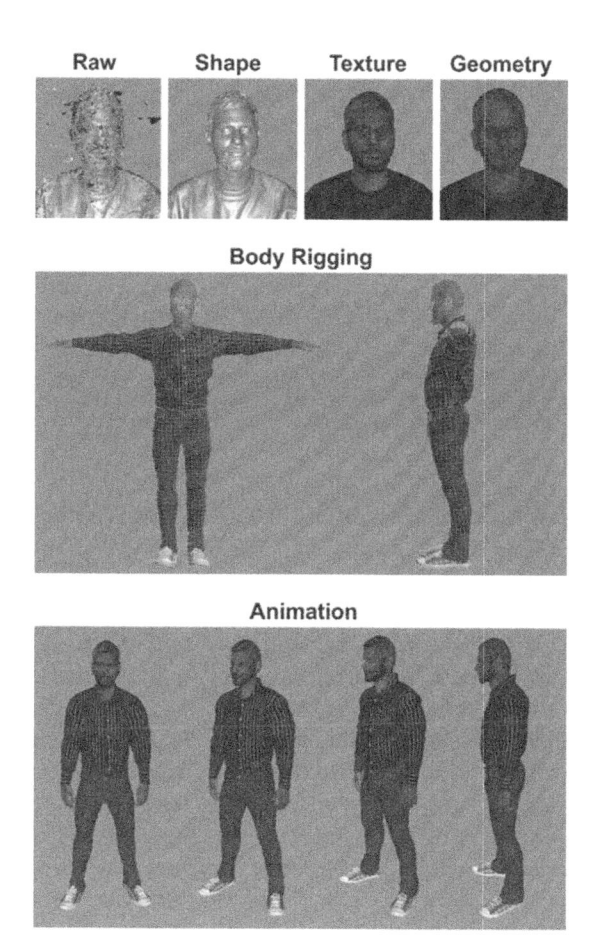

Figure 8.1 An illustration of the avatar construction process. The upper four images depict the processing sequence of 3D headscans. The middle panel represents the process of attaching the head scan to an avatar body that was created separately. The final panel illustrates the fully animated VR-ready avatar.

Source: Reproduced from Fysh, M. C., Trifonova, I. V., Allen, J., McCall, C., Burton, A. M., & Bindemann, M. (2022). Avatars with faces of real people: A construction method for scientific experiments in virtual reality. *Behavior Research Methods, 54*, 1461–1475, Figure 1. https://doi.org/10.3758/s13428-021-01676-5

Figure 8.2 Examples of avatars produced from 3D face scans of real people.

Source: Adapted from Fysh, M. C., Trifonova, I. V., Allen, J., McCall, C., Burton, A. M., & Bindemann, M. (2022). Avatars with faces of real people: A construction method for scientific experiments in virtual reality. *Behavior Research Methods*, 54, 1461–1475, Figure 2. https://doi.org/10.3758/s13428-021-01676-5

practiced operator, the acquisition of such a face scan can be completed in a few minutes. The scan is processed with specialist software to create a "wireframe" mesh that represents the model's head geometry. It is then wrapped in the model's texture—essentially a photo-image map of the facial tapestry of skin, hair and features. It is also possible to scan a model in full or to attach the model's head to a pre-existing avatar body. This can then be imported into body-editing software, to be dressed and adapted in terms of height and weight. At this point the avatar represents a visually complete but static and immobile 3D object. To create movement, it can now be equipped with a skeleton and a broad range of movement animations using motion rigging software. These animations can range from sitting, standing, turning, and walking to sophisticated action sequences.[1] An illustration of these avatars can be viewed in Figure 8.2. An unlimited variety of such characters can be produced in this way. A practiced operator can create such avatars in less than 2 hours, though further time may be necessary depending on factors such as the specific visual characteristics of the model or the desired complexity of the avatar in terms of visual detail and facial animation.

---

1 A time-lapse video of this construction process can be viewed at www.kent.ac.uk/school-of-psychology/vr-avatars/.

Several studies were conducted to examine the psychological properties of avatars that are produced with this method, to determine correspondence with the visual characteristics of the faces of real people. The first of these studies focused on examining whether avatars could be identified by persons who were familiar with their real-life counterparts (face recognition test). For this purpose, avatars entered a virtual room and walked up to the participants, who then attempted to name them. This was compared with naming rates for digital photographs of the same persons. In this recognition test, observers recognized a high proportion of avatar faces (88%) and this was comparable to the naming rates for the digital photographs (92%).

In a second study, upon entering the virtual room, avatars were shown next to a photograph of a face. This face-matching task eliminates the demand to recognize the avatar from memory and can therefore be performed by observers who are unfamiliar with these identities. Avatars were successfully matched to photographs with over 90% accuracy, demonstrating that even observers who are unfamiliar with these identities can detect their correspondence. This is an important finding for eyewitness research, as crimes often involve perpetrators unknown to the witness, and this lack of familiarity is a key source of identification errors (see, e.g., Memon et al., 2011; Megreya & Burton, 2006, 2008). These findings show that these avatars are suitable for such research.

A third study compared the similarity space of avatars and photographs of real faces using principal components analysis (PCA), to establish whether people who look similar (or different) to each other in their photos also look similar (or different) in their avatars. By quantifying the similarity in this way, it is possible to examine whether the overall set of relations between faces is preserved as we move from photos into VR. In typical use, PCA takes a large number of face images and derives a relatively small number of dimensions, within which any face can be described. This is a popular technique for representing the "space" spanned by a set of faces and is used both for automatic recognition purposes and for understanding human face perception (Burton et al., 2016; Kirby & Sirovich, 1990; Phillips et al., 2000; Turk & Pentland, 1991). In the analysis of avatar faces and face photos, the similarity of 120 faces within these two categories were computed. The pairwise distances between all individuals in the stimulus set were then computed to create a "photo-space" and an "avatar-space." The output of this analysis is visualized in Figure 8.3, which provides a color-coded format to show whether faces are more or less similar to each other according to how close they lie in space. This shows strong correspondence between photo- and avatar-space.

This analysis adds a particularly useful source of evidence over the tests of face recognition and face matching that rely on human observers, who

184　*Markus Bindemann & Matthew C. Fysh*

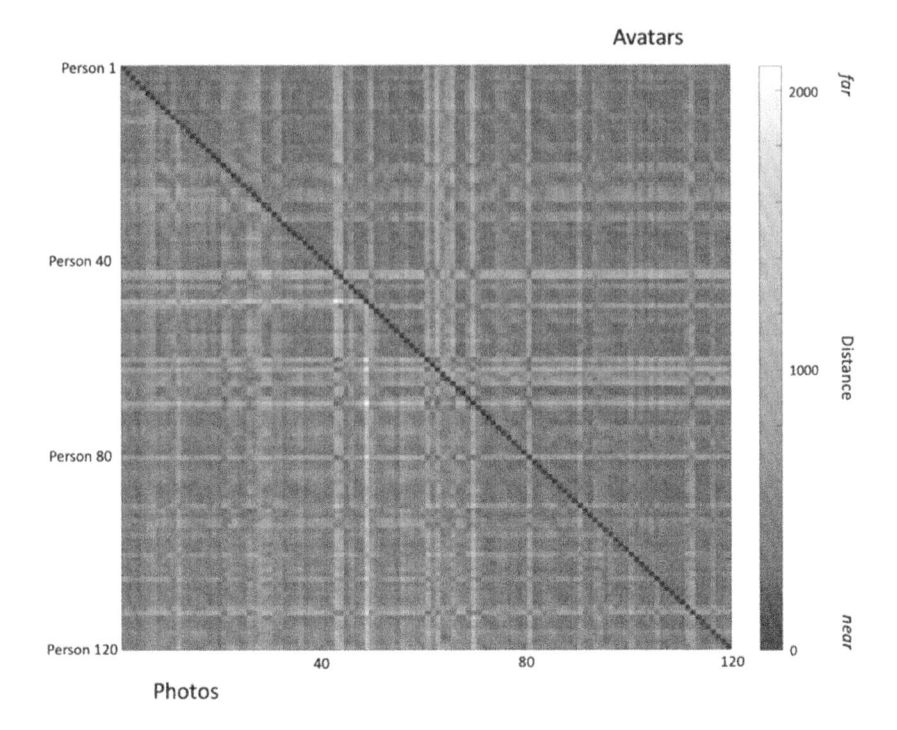

Figure 8.3 Similarity matrices for photos (lower left triangle) and avatars (upper right triangle). Persons 1 through 120 are depicted along the x-axis, from left to right. For the y-axis, Persons 1 through 120 are depicted from top to bottom. Units denote Euclidean distance in PCA-space.

Source: Reproduced from Fysh, M. C., Trifonova, I. V., Allen, J., McCall, C., Burton, A. M., & Bindemann, M. (2022). Avatars with faces of real people: A construction method for scientific experiments in virtual reality. *Behavior Research Methods*, *54*, 1461–1475, Figure 7. https://doi.org/10.3758/s13428-021-01676-5

can sometimes solve these tasks even when stimuli comprise severely degraded, poor-quality images (see, e.g., Bindemann et al., 2013; Bruce et al., 1999, 2001; Jenkins & Kerr, 2013). Therefore, the human data provides only some evidence for a good correspondence between face photographs and avatars, as any loss of information caused by a move to VR might be compensated for by the flexibility of the cognitive system. The image analysis, on the other hand, is based entirely on the physical, pixel-by-pixel properties of the stimuli and therefore adds a further strand of direct evidence for high correspondence between avatars and face photographs.

These studies provide converging support that this method can produce avatars that preserve the identity information of their real-life counterparts. This demonstrates that it is now possible to produce avatars of real

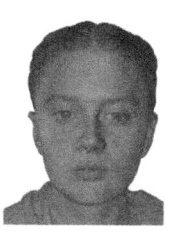

Figure 8.4 Avatar faces created from 3D scans of real people.

people for psychological experiments with relatively little effort. This is a timely development for eyewitness researchers seeking to investigate human behavior in VR. For VR to successfully bridge the gap between laboratory and field studies in the eyewitness domain, the adaptation of this method requires avatars that capture the appearance of, and similarities and differences between, real people. By creating avatars that are based on actual people and which bear a close correspondence to their real-life counterparts, progress is made towards resolving this barrier between the physical and virtual world. The reader can judge the current state-of-the-art for themselves. Figure 8.4 depicts examples of avatar faces created from 3D scans of real people.

Affective Realism

As the continuing development of virtual characters and avatars makes high realism more achievable, the question arises of whether realistic avatars also elicit emotions in viewers in the same way that real people do. In humans, visual identification of a person is typically accompanied by an autonomic *affective* response—a "feeling" that someone is who we think they are. This affective response can be indexed with physiological measures of arousal, such as skin conductance and pupil dilation. This physiological response is an integral part of a working person identification system (Schweinberger & Burton, 2003; Ellis & Lewis, 2001), and the importance of this affective response becomes apparent when it is absent. In Capgras syndrome, which occurs in conditions such as schizophrenia or dementia, visual identification remains intact but the affective response is impaired. As a consequence, patients who suffer with Capgras syndrome visually recognize familiar people, but believe that they have been replaced by aliens or impostors because they do not evoke appropriate feelings of familiarity (Hirstein & Ramachandran, 1997; Ellis, Lewis, Moselhy, & Young, 2000; Ellis & Young, 1990; Ellis, Young, Quayle, & Depauw, 1997).

This issue not only points to the importance for understanding what makes the avatar of a specific familiar person feel real, but also the point at which *any* avatar starts to feel real. In the computing domain, this problem is exemplified by the *Uncanny Valley* phenomenon (Mori, 1970), which refers to the relationship between the resemblance of non-human agents (e.g., robots) to human beings, and the emotional response elicit by this resemblance. At the heart of this phenomenon lies the idea that increasing similarity to humans is appealing but only up to a critical point, at which close resemblance by a non-human agent might suddenly become unsettling. This phenomenon has occupied scientists for many years but the extent of this issue remains unresolved (Pan & Hamilton, 2018; de Borst & de Gelder, 2015).

Such phenomena highlight that research into avatars must not only focus on how to make avatars look real, but also understand how to make them *feel* real. In the VR domain, a concept that speaks to this is that of social presence (or co-presence), which refers to the subjective experience that a character is alive and present in a virtual environment with an immersed observer (see, e.g., Casanueva & Blake, 2001; Garau et al., 2003; for a review see Oh et al., 2018). For example, feelings of social presence can be elicited when avatars engage in social interactions that indicate awareness of the viewer's presence, such as eye contact (Bailenson et al., 2003; Bente et al., 2008), head nodding (von der Pütten et al., 2010), or blushing (Pan et al., 2008).

A related concept in psychology is that of agency, which refers to the ability of "something" to act with autonomy (see, e.g., Moore, 2016). Agents can monitor their environment and act with intent and purpose, by changing the environment or interacting with objects and people within it, to achieve an intended goal. In VR, the perception of agency is typically studied by introducing avatars under the pretext that these are controlled by an actual human, a computer program or artificial intelligence. In these scenarios, participants often attribute greater agency to avatars when they believe that they are interacting with a real person, despite avatar behavior being consistent across conditions (see, e.g., Appel et al., 2012; Lim & Reeves, 2010).

One of the tests that has been proposed to establish whether a virtual character is of realistic human appearance, and exhibits human nonverbal behavior and intelligence, is a VR version of the Turing test (Pan & Hamilton, 2018). As technologies often imitate life, Alan Turing proposed an influential test to distinguish artificial creations and imitations from the real thing (Turing, 1950). According to Turing, an imitation was successful if an observer cannot distinguish a human from a human imitation in a direct comparison. It is easy to conceive a range of Turing tests to examine the realism, social presence and agency of avatars. For instance, participants might be asked to determine which one of two images depicts a virtual character or a real person, based purely on visual appearance. In other versions of such a test, participants might interact with humans/avatars via video link and have to determine which is which, or be immersed in virtual environments with several avatars and asked to determine which are controlled by another human and which are controlled by a computer.

Whether it is necessary to pursue such Turing-test levels of realism for eyewitness research with VR is an open question, but we make two observations here. First, as real-world eyewitness scenarios are often emotionally-charged and capable of eliciting feelings such as anxiety, anger or fear in the observers, it is possible that the affective properties that imbue avatars with realism, social presence and agency are also particularly important to create relevant eyewitness experiments. Second, as awareness of VR grows, not only among scientists but the participants of research, expectations of realism might also grow. In the VR literature, it has been suggested that effects of avatar agency on social presence might be waning over time as users form higher expectations of visual and behavioral avatar realism (see Oh et al., 2018). If eyewitness research moves to adapt VR more widely, meeting expectations of avatar realism may therefore be crucial to the continued success of this work.

Example I: Person Identification at a Virtual Airport

Although the application of VR to eyewitness research is still gathering pace, many examples now exist to demonstrate the applicability and potential of this technology. We review three examples here. The first of these comes from the study of unfamiliar face matching, in which participants have to compare two faces to decide whether these depict the same person or two different people. Some key parallels exist between the study of face matching and eyewitness accuracy. Both tasks typically require the identification of people who are unknown to the observer and identification is based primarily on the face. Both tasks are also known to be prone to identification errors, yet are conducted routinely in real-world settings. Face matching, for example, can be performed for the purpose of identity verification during the purchase of age-restricted goods or for access to restricted areas, or by facial examiners in the police to identify perpetrators from crime footage. However, one of its most widespread and important applications is for the identification of travelers at airports and borders. Most research in this domain has focused on laboratory tasks in which pairs of disembodied face photographs are presented in isolation on a blank background (for reviews, see Fysh & Bindemann, 2017; Fysh, 2021). Only limited field research exists due to the security sensitive nature of airport and border control settings, though some studies have implemented simplistic field paradigms in non-security settings (e.g., White et al., 2014).

We have recently developed a virtual reality airport to study face identification at passport control *in situ* (Tummon et al., 2019) and combined this technology with the standardized construction of a set of 120 avatars with photo-realistic faces of real people for psychological experimentation (Fysh et al., 2022), which are used to populate the airport with travelers. This virtual world paradigm is illustrated in Figure 8.5. In this paradigm, participants take on the role of a passport control officer at an airport. Using a VR headset, they are immersed in a passport control booth while a queue of travelers builds up. On each trial, the avatar at the front of the queue would then approach the participant situated in the passport control booth. The participant's task is to compare the avatar with a digital photograph in a photo-ID card, which would display either the same person or a different identity. The subsequent classification of each avatar would then trigger it to exit the participant's field of view, either by walking in one direction or the other, depending on whether a "match" or "mismatch" response was submitted.

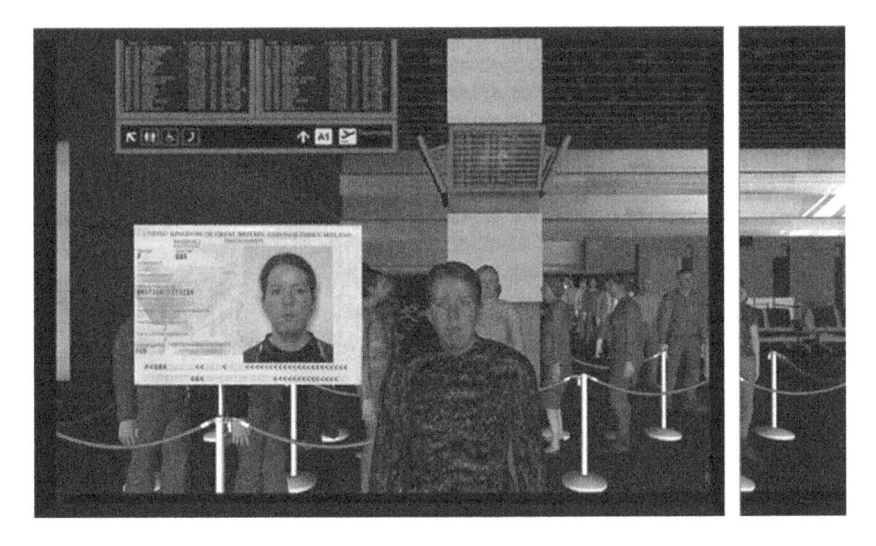

Figure 8.5 An illustration of the airport environment from the perspective of a participant performing the identification task.

Source: Adapted from Bindemann, M., Fysh, M. C., Trifonova, I. V., Allen, J., McCall, C., & Burton, A. M. (2022). Face identification in the laboratory and in virtual worlds. *Journal of Applied Research in Memory and Cognition, 11*(1), 120–134, Figure 4. https://doi.org/10.1016/j.jarmac.2021.07.010

To compare identification of avatars in the virtual airport environment with the type of experimental paradigm that are used to study face matching in the laboratory, performance in the airport was compared with the Glasgow Face Matching Test (GFMT; Burton et al., 2010) and the Kent Face Matching Test (KFMT; Fysh & Bindemann, 2018). In these tests, observers compare pairs of cropped faces to determine whether these depict the same person or two different people. The GFMT is constructed to provide an optimized test that measures best-possible performance, by comparing face images that were only taken a few minutes apart and under similar exposure conditions. The KFMT compares pairs of photos that were taken several months apart and under different capture conditions, and which are therefore more difficult to match.

Two insights emerge by comparing person identification in the virtual airport with the established laboratory tests of face matching. The first insight is that the matching performance of participants correlates consistently between these tests. Thus, individuals who performed well with the face-matching tests were also more likely to accurately match people in the airport. This demonstrates the correspondence between these laboratory paradigms and avatar identification, and extends these to a scenario where avatar identifications are made in the context of passport control at a VR airport. This indicates that VR can be used to conduct behaviorally relevant research on face identification in more complex settings than traditional laboratory experiments allow, whilst maintaining correspondence between tasks.

Despite these similarities, identification performance in the airport was also distinctly different from the laboratory face-matching tests. For the face-matching tests, performance for pairs of the same person (identity matches) was comparable to pairings that combined images of different people (identity non-matches). In contrast, a response bias emerged in the airport, whereby observers were more likely to classify photos of different people as the same person. Crucially, this bias was not observed in another experiment in which the avatars were presented as face photographs without the airport. Thus, the airport *context* appeared to change the demands of the identification task. These findings converge with other research which indicates that contextual manipulations that mimic specific aspects of applied settings produce similar response biases in person identification. The practice of embedding photographs in photo-identity documents, for example, also biases face identification by impairing the classification of mismatches (Feng & Burton, 2019; McCaffery & Burton, 2016). Furthermore, a study of passport officers making photo-ID checks on live participants also showed a bias towards accepting more "fraudulent" ID (i.e., mismatch trials: White et al., 2014).

This convergence between studies provides an important demonstration of the behavioral relevance of VR to the study of perception, such as eyewitness identification. The simplified laboratory paradigms that are prevalent in the study of human cognition provide a limited context for understanding behavior in the social and environmental contexts within which it occurs. It is becoming increasingly clear that these contextual factors cannot be regarded as simple "add-ons" to understanding the process of face perception, but represent an important component in the processes of perception (Cole et al., 2016; Hayward et al., 2017; Ramon et al., 2019; Skarratt et al., 2012). Through VR, it is possible to link the study of controlled laboratory processes and the complex contexts in which these processes typically occur.

Another strength of this application of VR is that it allows for an examination of variables that are difficult to investigate in laboratory and field studies. Nonverbal behavior such as body language, for example, can have substantial impact on interpersonal interaction and person judgements (e.g., Burgoon et al., 2011; Knapp et al., 2013). In passport control settings, a heuristic technique utilizing body language may be pivotal, for example, by seeking out those who appear to be behaving unusually. However, while substantial effort has been invested in programs that train staff to look for such nonverbal cues in aviation settings, such as the Screening of Passengers by Observation Techniques program in the United States (see United States Government Accountability Office, 2010), it is debated whether this has enhanced security (United States Government Accountability Office, 2013). With VR, body language can be controlled systematically, to provide exact experimental manipulations that are consistent across participants. For example, it is possible to equip avatars with specific motion animations or to change the speed or intensity of specific animations.

We have also begun to explore this in the VR airport by manipulating the activity level of a subset of avatars while these wait in a passport control queue, to produce body language that ranges from a calm resting state to lively and hyper (Tummon et al., 2020). When observers were asked to look out for unusual body language to support identification decisions, differences in body language between passengers enhanced the detection of identity mismatches. This effect was driven by increased activity levels rather than body language that simply differed from the behavior of the majority of passengers. Thus, a passenger exhibiting "hyper" body language in a "lively" crowd was more likely to be classified as an identity mismatch than someone exhibiting a calm resting state. Experiments such as these demonstrate the unique characteristics of VR to complement the laboratory and field-based approaches, by providing more complex environments to examine face perception while also retaining experimental control.

Example II: Intergroup Violence

The second example of VR application is drawn from the domain of social psychology and focuses on ingroup-outgroup scenarios and intergroup contact. Here, VR has been applied to study intergroup conflict phenomena such as prejudice (e.g., Banakou et al., 2016; Breves, 2020; Dotsch & Wigboldus, 2008; Groom et al., 2009; Peck et al., 2013). Such instances are of clear relevance to the study of eyewitness testimony, where differences between groups have been studied too. VR is a particularly useful methodology to study some aspects of these phenomena because intergroup conflict outside of the laboratory is often confrontational and violent, and is therefore difficult to study experimentally for ethical and practical reasons. VR allows for the study of such scenarios in experimental settings whilst also enabling a level of systematic control over variables that can be difficult to achieve with other approaches. This includes the simulation of direct intergroup encounters with groups of people who are programmed to behave consistently across participants, and the simulation of such contact both from minority and majority perspectives.

One example of such work comes from the study of bystander interventions in violent attacks. An interesting question here concerns whether bystanders are more likely to intervene in an attack when they share a social identity with a victim. To investigate this, a virtual pub scenario was created in which supporters of a real football club witness a confrontation (Slater et al., 2013). In this confrontation, the perpetrator sits at the bar of a pub when the victim enters and then gets up to start an argument. During this argument, the perpetrator is verbally aggressive at first and then becomes physically aggressive too. Participants are immersed in this virtual environment and observe the perpetrator-victim interaction. To manipulate group membership, the victim is either wearing the same shirt as the real-life club that the participants support, and therefore identifies as a fan of the same team (ingroup), or is a general football fan (outgroup). The measure of interest was whether this affects the likelihood that participants intervene in the observed confrontation. In this scenario, participants made a greater number of interventions, which comprised of verbal utterances or physical moves towards the two virtual characters, during the violent argument in the ingroup condition. Moreover, the victim's behavior also influenced participants in the ingroup condition. The more the victim was looking to the participants for help, the more interventions were made.

192 *Markus Bindemann & Matthew C. Fysh*

Another study extended these findings by investigating whether group affiliation of additional bystanders also influences intervention behavior (Rovira et al., 2021). This study replicated the pub scenario but included three virtual bystanders who were also present during the altercation (see Figure 8.6). These bystanders could belong to the same or a different group as the victim and the participants. In this context, participants were more likely to intervene when the bystanders were *outgroup* members. Thus, the

Figure 8.6 The scenario (a) the in-group bystanders sitting around a table, (b) the out-group bystanders sitting around a table, (c) the perpetrator (in blue) picks an argument with the victim, and (d) a photograph of the scenario showing a participant, a bystander, and the perpetrator being aggressive against the victim.

Source: Reproduced from Rovira, A., Southern, R., Swapp, D., Campbell, C., Zhang, J. J., Levine, M., & Slater, M. (2021). Bystander affiliation influences intervention behavior: A Virtual Reality study. *SAGE Open, 11*(3), Figure 1. https://doi.org/10.1177/21582440211040076

presence of in-group bystanders can reduce helping of in-group victims, compared to the helping of in-group victims in the presence of out-group bystanders. This suggests a diffusion of responsibility effect in the presence of other in-group members who might also be expected to help.

Although this research is cast from a social psychology perspective, there are parallels here to highlight the relevance of this VR application to the study of eyewitness accuracy. While social identity and intergroup conflict has been studied extensively in social psychology, it is also a topic of great interest in the eyewitness domain. The other-race effect or own ethnicity effect, for example, refers to the phenomenon that observers are less likely to recognize outgroup than ingroup faces, and the importance of this has been studied extensively in the eyewitness domain (for reviews, see Meissner & Brigham, 2001; Shapiro & Penrod, 1986). Similarly, eyewitness research has examined the bystander effect, for example, to determine whether victims or bystanders are more accurate in making perpetrator identifications (Hosch & Cooper, 1982; Hosch et al., 1984; Kassin, 1984), or to study the phenomenon of unconscious transference, whereby eyewitnesses make mistakenly identify bystanders as the perpetrators of crime (Loftus, 1976; Ross et al., 1994; Davis & Loftus, 2007). The violence in these intergroup scenarios also overlaps with research questions in the eyewitness domain. Violence in videotaped reenactments of crime can lead to reduced identification accuracy (Clifford & Hollin, 1981; Clifford & Scott, 1978), as can the presence of weapons or the stress induced by a crime (for reviews, see Deffenbacher et al., 2004; Steblay, 1992). The intergroup conflict literature in social psychology demonstrates how these diverse topics can be integrated also in the eyewitness domain to observe behavior in complex but controlled social settings.

Example III: Crime Scene Visits and Jury Decision-Making

The third example of how VR can enhance the study of eyewitness testimony comes from the use of this technology as a means of revisiting crime scenes. Crime scenes are an important form of evidence for reconstructing in an investigation how a crime may have unfolded. They can also provide context for eliciting eyewitness memory and support jury decision-making. However, the reconstruction of crime scenes is a challenging endeavor that often requires the recording of photos and videos, diagrams and sketches, and detailed written notes (Houck et al., 2017; Gardner, 2011). Even so, these methods provide an incomplete representation that requires a level of effortful interpretation and motivation by the viewer to do so. Spatial distances and relationships between objects in scenes, for example, may be difficult to capture. This makes it challenging to understand complex environments and information that may be critical in criminal investigations and proceedings, such as the visibility of a victim or a perpetrator from the third-person perspective of an eyewitness.

As an understanding of what can be seen from different vantage points of a crime scene can help piece together of what may have occurred during an investigation, a recent project examined the potential of using VR in a court of law in aiding such decision-making (Reichherzer et al., 2018). In this study, participants were provided with a narrative of a burglary crime, which included information on the spatial location of stolen items. They then viewed the burglary scene as photographs, through a physical real-life visit, or as a 3D virtual reconstruction of the crime scene in immersive VR. When memory for the spatial locations of evidence and the crime narrative was subsequently measured, this was similar in VR to real-life crime scene visits and appeared to be more reliable than from the viewing of photographs.

Such virtual reconstructions of crime scenes can also help juror's judgement of weather a crime has taken place, for example, in the context of contrasting information provided by defense and prosecution. A recent project examined the potential of using VR in a court of law in aiding such decision-making (Reichherzer et al., 2021). In this study, participants were introduced to a potential hit-and-run scenario, in which a person was struck by a car. A virtual reconstruction of this crime scene included a damaged car, a victim lying on the floor, and other evidence items strewn across the street (see Figure 8.7). Participants were then able to explore the crime scene with a headset in interactive VR or by viewing 2D images on a computer screen.

In a scenario like this a key question for jurors to assess may be whether the driver was able to see the victim at the point of impact, and was

Figure 8.7 Virtual reconstruction of a real-world crime scene with added evidence items, car and victim.

Source: Adapted from Reichherzer, C., Cunningham, A., Coleman, T., Cao, R., McManus, K., Sheppard, D., Kohler, M., Billinghurst, M., Thomas, B. H. (2021). Bringing the jury to the scene of the crime: Memory and decision-making in a simulated crime scene. *CHI '21: Proceedings of the 2021 CHI Conference on Human Factors in Computing Systems, 709*, 1–12, Figure 1.

therefore guilty of dangerous driving. Participants explored the crime scene thoroughly in VR and commented that it heightened their spatial awareness between key items and views of the scene. This subjective feedback was also reflected in better spatial recall for items from the crime scene and lower mental effort required to interpret space. Most importantly perhaps, the medium of presentation was also reflected in the juror decisions that participants made. In the 2D image viewing conditions, about half of the participants (53%) decided that the accident was caused by "driving without due care," whereas the majority of participants (87%) in the VR condition reached a more severe verdict of "death by dangerous driving." Thus, immersive VR alters how events are perceived and increases convergence between observers, so that jurors are more likely to reach the same conclusion (Reichherzer et al., 2021).

These studies demonstrate the potential of VR for studying a range of cognitive processes related to eyewitness testimony, such as spatial memory, cognitive load, perspective taking, and juror decision making. By combining this VR technology with eye-tracking, it can also be used to understand how eyewitnesses, investigators or jurors are likely to look at crime scenes and whether the important aspects of a crime scene have been evaluated. This can feed into understanding of further processes, for example, pertaining to the aspects of scenes that are visually salient and may be easily missed or to identify where further processing of a crime scene may be necessary. Here are other advantages to the application of 3D scanning and VR for capturing crime scenes too. This technology can provide a suitable compromise for scene viewing in cases where visitation of the real-world scene is not possible. Similarly, the technology can be used to preserve a crime scene that will otherwise be disturbed naturally (e.g., by weather) or that must be restored for other users (e.g., a road in car accidents). This can also allow for "revisits" of a crime scene many years later, to review items whose importance may be initially missed. In addition, VR also offers the opposite opportunity, of eliminating items from a crime scene before it is viewed. This offers investigators and courts the chance to remove objects that they believe could bias jurors, and provides scientists with the opportunity to study these processes. Ultimately, these developments should lead to a better scientific understanding and more robust theorizing, to impact positively on the accuracy of eyewitness evaluations, criminal investigations, and judicial proceedings in applied settings.

Summary and Conclusions

Two approaches have become dominant in psychology, laboratory and field studies, each with its own strengths and limitations. The adaptation of VR technology as a research methodology has the potential to bridge these approaches, by preserving their strengths and reducing their weakness. Similar to field studies VR can provide experiments that are situated in rich, complex, interactive 3D environments, but that also preserve the experimental control and sophisticated measurement of laboratory-based approaches.

This technology has undergone rapid development in recent years and a great number of off-the-shelf solutions now exist to provide detailed virtual environments, 3D objects and person characters that can be adapted for psychological experiments. Many of these options were developed for the gaming industry, and as much of gaming involves crime, aggression and violence, the world of VR is already well prepared for research into eyewitness accuracy. However, to conduct experiments in VR also requires some new skill sets from researchers. Therefore, the adaptation of this technology depends on the feasibility with which environments, objects and digital characters can be constructed, and how these processes can be facilitated for researchers. Such developments are now emerging, such as empirically validated methods to construct avatars for psychological research (e.g., Fysh et al., 2022). Further development of these digital characters is crucial to maximize VR's potential for eyewitness research, for example, to produce avatars that are seemingly autonomous and elicit the same affective responses in observers that real people do.

A growing number of examples now exist to demonstrate the potential and applicability of this method to the eyewitness domain, and three of these were reviewed here. The first of these examples shows that VR research can be used to study forensic person identification in security settings that are difficult to access in real life, such as airports and borders. The second example demonstrates how VR can be used to study concepts relevant to the eyewitness domain, such as violent encounters, intergroup conflict and bystander effects in meaningful environments such as bars. In contrast to the corresponding real-world settings, VR allows for this research to be conducted under systematic control that is difficult to achieve with other methods, whilst also providing a more predictable and ethically sound setting for this research. Finally, we reviewed how VR can be used to map and preserve crime scenes in 3D. This visualization can be used to help observers understand a crime scene better, with less effort and in a more natural manner (e.g., by physically walking around). Thus, VR can facilitate observers' comprehension of complex information and help gather additional information. In turn, this provides additional tools for researchers to understand how crime scenes are parsed and processed by observers. These developments can be applied to help improve jurors' understanding and judgement of whether a crime has taken place. It can also preserve crime scenes and make these accessible many years later, facilitating the storage of evidence and the re-evaluation of crimes when new information comes to light.

These research examples are unified by a key quality of VR—that it allows for the presentation and systematic study of eyewitness and crime-relevant information in contexts that mimic the nature of the setting in which this task is actually performed. This characteristic speaks to a simple truth that is often overlooked in the design of psychological experiments: how we study a cognitive process not only determines but also limits what we can learn about it. While laboratory research and field studies have long been key to understanding eyewitness accuracy in all its diversity and richness, VR can bridge these methods to unlock exciting new avenues for knowledge gain.

We are now entering an epoch where it will become increasingly evident how VR research will *impact on the legal systems*. At this point, more investigations into the correspondence between VR and the real-world phenomena surrounding crime and eyewitness testimony are needed, so that we can have greater confidence in the strength of the inferences that can be made from this method about the real-world problem that we seek to study. Achieving closer correspondence under conditions of controlled experimentation should lead to better research of more interactive behaviors, in more complex environments, with more people, and in more extreme scenarios. In turn, this should facilitate more robust theorizing, whilst also providing new practical tools for visualizing and preserving crime scenes, for supporting criminal investigations and jury decision-making, and for bringing juries to crime scenes. In an age where virtual reality is becoming ubiquitous in many areas of life, from recreational activities such as gaming, to cinema, architecture, medical training or clinical interventions, the time has come to adapt this methodology much more widely into eyewitness research, too.

References

Appel, J., von der Pütten, A., Krämer, N.C., & Gratch, J. (2012). Does humanity matter? Analyzing the importance of social cues and perceived agency of a computer system for the emergence of social reactions during human-computer interaction. *Advances in Human-Computer Interaction, 13*, 324694. https://doi.org/10.1155/2012/324694

Bailenson, J.N., Blascovich, J., Beall, A.C., & Loomis, J.M. (2003). Interpersonal distance in immersive virtual environments. *Personality and Social Psychology Bulletin, 29*(7), 819–833. https://doi.org/10.1177/0146167203029007002

Banakou, D., Hanumanthu, P.D., & Slater, M. (2016). Virtual embodiment of white people in a black virtual body leads to a sustained reduction in their implicit racial bias. *Frontiers in Human Neuroscience, 10*, 601. https://doi.org/10.3389/fnhum.2016.00601

Bente, G., Rüggenberg, S., Krämer, N.C., & Eschenburg, F. (2008). Avatar-mediated networking: Increasing social presence and interpersonal trust in net-based collaborations. *Human Communication Research*, *34*(2), 287–318. https://doi.org/10.1111/j.1468-2958.2008.00322.x

Bindemann, M., Attard, J., Leach, A., & Johnston, R.A. (2013). The effect of image pixelation on unfamiliar-face matching. *Applied Cognitive Psychology*, *27*(6), 707–717. https://doi.org/10.1002/acp.2970

Bindemann, M., Fysh, M.C., Trifonova, I.V., Allen, J., McCall, C., & Burton, A.M. (2022). Face identification in the laboratory and in virtual worlds. *Journal of Applied Research in Memory and Cognition*, *11*(1), 120–134. https://doi.org/10.1016/j.jarmac.2021.07.010

Bindemann, M., Sandford, A., Gillatt, K., Avetisyan, M., Megreya, A.M. (2012). Recognising faces seen alone or with others: Why are two heads worse than one? *Perception*, *41*(4), 415–35. https://doi.org/10.1068/p6922

Bornstein, B.H., Deffenbacher, K.A., Penrod, S.D., & McGorty, E.K. (2012). Effects of exposure time and cognitive operations on facial identification accuracy: A meta-analysis of two variables associated with initial memory strength. *Psychology, Crime & Law*, *18*(5), 473–490. https://doi.org/10.1080/1068316X.2010.508458

Breves, P. (2020). Bringing people closer: The prosocial effects of immersive media on users' attitudes and behavior. *Nonprofit and Voluntary Sector Quarterly*, *49*(5), 1015–1034. https://doi.org/10.1177/0899764020903101

Bruce, V., Henderson, Z., Greenwood, K., Hancock, P.J.B., Burton, A.M., & Miller, P. (1999). Verification of face identities from images captured on video. *Journal of Experimental Psychology: Applied*, *5*(4), 339–360. https://doi.org/10.1037/1076-898X.5.4.339

Bruce, V., Henderson, Z., Newman, C., & Burton, A.M. (2001). Matching identities of familiar and unfamiliar faces caught on CCTV images. *Journal of Experimental Psychology: Applied*, *7*(3), 207–218. https://doi.org/10.1037/1076-898X.7.3.207

Burgoon, J.K., Guerrero, L.K., & Manusov, V. (2011) Nonverbal signals. In M.L. Knapp & J.A. Daly (Eds.), *The SAGE handbook of interpersonal communication* (4th ed., pp. 239–281). SAGE Publications Inc.

Burton, A.M., Kramer, R.S.S., Ritchie, K.L., & Jenkins, R. (2016). Identity from variation: Representations of faces derived from multiple instances. *Cognitive Science*, *40*(1), 202–223. https://doi.org/10.1111/cogs.12231

Burton, A.M., White, D., & McNeill, A. (2010). The Glasgow Face Matching Test. *Behavior Research Methods*, *42*(1), 286–291. https://doi.org/10.3758/BRM.42.1.286

Casanueva, J.S., & Blake, E.H. (2001). The effects of avatars on co-presence in a collaborative virtual environment. *Annual Conference of the South African Institute of Computer Scientists and Information Technologists* (SAICSIT2001) (Pretoria).

Clifford, B.R., & Hollin, C.R. (1981). Effects of the type of incident and the number of perpetrators on eyewitness memory. *Journal of Applied Psychology*, *66*(3), 364–370. https://doi.org/10.1037/0021-9010.66.3.364

Clifford, B.R., & Scott, J. (1978). Individual and situational factors in eyewitness testimony. *Journal of Applied Psychology, 63*(3), 352–359. https://doi.org/10.1037/0021-9010.63.3.352

Cole, G.G., Skarratt, P.A., & Kuhn, G. (2016). Real person interaction in visual attention research. *European Psychologist, 21*, 141–149. https://doi.org/10.1027/1016-9040/a000243

Curry, G.D., Ball, R.A., & Fox, R.J. (1994). Gang crime and law enforcement record-keeping, research in brief. *National Institute of Justice*, 148345. https://nij.ojp.gov/library/publications/gang-crime-and-law-enforcement-recordkeeping-research-brief

Davis, D., & Loftus, E.F. (2007). Internal and external sources of misinformation in adult witness memory. In M.P. Toglia, J.D. Read, D.F. Ross, & R.C.L. Lindsay (Eds.), *The handbook of eyewitness psychology*, Vol. 1. Memory for events (pp. 195–237). Lawrence Erlbaum Associates Publishers.

de Borst, A.W., & de Gelder, B. (2015). Is it the real deal? Perception of virtual characters versus humans: An affective cognitive neuroscience perspective. *Frontiers in Psychology, 6*, 1–12. https://doi.org/10.3389/fpsyg.2015.00576

Deffenbacher, K.A., Bornstein, B.H., Penrod, S.D., & McGorty, E.K. (2004). A meta-analytic review of the effects of high stress on eyewitness memory. *Law and Human Behavior, 28*(6), 687–706. https://doi.org/10.1007/s10979-004-0565-x

Dotsch, R., & Wigboldus, D.H.J. (2008). Virtual prejudice. *Journal of Experimental Social Psychology, 44*(4), 1194–1198. https://doi.org/10.1016/j.jesp.2008.03.003

Ellis, H.D., & Lewis, M.B. (2001). Capgras delusion: A window on face recognition. *Trends in Cognitive Sciences, 5*(4), 149–156. https://doi.org/10.1016/s1364-6613(00)01620-x

Ellis, H.D., Lewis, M.B., Moselhy, H.F., & Young, A.W. (2000). Automatic without autonomic responses to familiar faces: Differential components of covert face recognition in a case of Capgras delusion. *Cognitive Neuropsychiatry, 5*(4), 255–269. https://doi.org/10.1080/13546800050199711

Ellis, H.D. Young, A.W., Quayle, A.H., & Depauw, K.W. (1997). Reduced autonomic responses to faces in Capgras delusion. *Proceedings of the Royal Society of London B: Biological Science, 264*(1384), 1085–1092. https://doi.org/10.1098/rspb.1997.0150

Ellis, H.D., & Young, A.W. (1990). Accounting for delusional misidentifications. *British Journal of Psychiatry, 157*, 239–248. https://doi.org/10.1192/bjp.157.2.239

Erickson, W.B., Lampinen, J.M., & Leding, J.K. (2014). The weapon focus effect in target-present and target-absent line-ups: The roles of threat, novelty, and timing. *Applied Cognitive Psychology, 28*(3), 349–359. https://doi.org/10.1002/acp.3005

Fawcett, J.M., Russell, E.J., Peace, K.A., & Christie, J. (2013). Of guns and geese: A meta-analytic review of the "weapon focus" literature. *Psychology, Crime & Law, 19*(1), 35–66. https://doi.org/10.1080/1068316X.2011.599325

Feng, X., & Burton, A.M. (2019). Identity documents bias face matching. *Perception, 48*(12), 1163–1174. https://doi.org/10.1177/0301006619877821

Ferguson, H.J., Brunsdon, V.E.A., & Bradford, E.E.F. (2018). Age of avatar modulates the altercentric bias in a visual perspective-taking task: ERP and behavioral evidence. *Cognitive, Affective and Behavioral Neuroscience, 18*(6), 1298–1319. https://doi.org/10.3758/s13415-018-0641-1

Fysh, M.C. (2021). Factors limiting face matching at passport control and in police investigations. In M. Bindemann (Ed.), *Forensic face matching: Research and practice* (pp. 255–261). Oxford University Press. https://doi.org/10.1093/oso/9780198837749.003.0011

Fysh, M.C., & Bindemann, M. (2017). Forensic face matching: A review. In M. Bindemann & A.M. Megreya (Eds.), *Face processing: Systems, Disorders and Cultural Differences* (pp. 1–20). Nova: Science Publishers.

Fysh, M.C., & Bindemann, M. (2018). The Kent Face Matching Test. *British Journal of Psychology, 109*(2), 219–231. https://doi.org/10.1111/bjop.12260

Fysh, M.C., Trifonova, I.V., Allen, J., McCall, C., Burton, A.M., & Bindemann, M. (2022). Avatars with faces of real people: A construction method for scientific experiments in virtual reality. *Behavior Research Methods, 54*, 1461–1475. https://doi.org/10.3758/s13428-021-01676-5

Garau, M., Slater, M., Vinayagamoorthy, V., Brogni, A., Steed, A., & Sasse, M.A. (2003). The impact of avatar realism and eye gaze control on perceived quality of communication in a shared immersive virtual environment. *Proceedings of the SIGCHI Conference on Human Factors in Computing Systems* (New York, NY: ACM).

Gardner, R.M. (2011). *Practical crime scene processing and investigation.* CRC Press.

Groom, V., Bailenson, J.N., & Nass, C. (2009). The influence of racial embodiment on racial bias in immersive virtual environments. *Social Influence, 4*(3), 231–248. https://doi.org/10.1080/15534510802643750

Havard, C., Richter, S., & Thurkettle, M. (2019). Effects of changes in background color on the identification of own- and other-race faces. *I-Perception, 10*(2). https://doi.org/10.1177/2041669519843539

Hayward, D.A., Voorhies, W., Morris, J.L., Capozzi, F., & Ristic, J. (2017). Staring reality in the face: A comparison of social attention across laboratory and real-world measures suggests little common ground. *Canadian Journal of Experimental Psychology/Revue Canadienne de Psychologie Expérimentale, 71*(3), 212–225. https://doi.org/10.1037/cep0000117

Hermens, F., & Walker, R. (2012). Do you look where I look? Attention shifts and response preparation following dynamic social cues. *Journal of Eye Movement Research, 5*(5), 1–11. https://doi.org/10.16910/jemr.5.5.5

Hirstein, W., & Ramachandran, V.S. (1997). Capgras syndrome: A novel probe for understanding the neural representation of the identity and familiarity of persons. *Proceedings of the Royal Society of London B, 264*(1380), 437–444. https://doi.org/10.1098/rspb.1997.0062

Hosch, H.M., & Cooper, D.S. (1982). Victimization as a determinant of eyewitness accuracy. *Journal of Applied Psychology, 67*(5), 649–652. https://doi.org/10.1037/0021-9010.67.5.649

Hosch, H.M., Leippe, M.R., Marchioni, P.M., & Cooper, D.S. (1984). Victimization, self-monitoring, and eyewitness identification. *Journal of Applied Psychology, 69*(2), 280–288. https://doi.org/10.1037/0021-9010.69.2.280

Houck, M.M., Crispino, F., & McAdam, T. (2017). *The science of crime scenes.* Academic Press, Saint Louis, USA.

Jenkins, R., & Kerr, C. (2013). Identifiable images of bystanders extracted from corneal reflections. *PLoS ONE, 8*(12): 8–12. https://doi.org/10.1371/journal.pone.0083325

Jenkins, R., White, D., Van Montfort, X., & Burton, A.M. (2011). Variability in photos of the same face. *Cognition, 121*(3), 313–23. https://doi.org/10.1016/j.cognition.2011.08.001

Kane, H.S., McCall, C., Collins, N.L., & Blascovich, J.J. (2012). Mere presence is not enough: Responsive support in a virtual world. *Journal of Experimental Social Psychology, 48*(1), 37–44. https://doi.org/10.1016/j.jesp.2011.07.001

Kassin, S.M. (1984). Eyewitness identification: Victims versus bystanders. *Journal of Applied Social Psychology, 14*(6), 519–529. https://doi.org/10.1111/j.1559-1816.1984.tb02257.x

Keemink, J.R., Jenner, L., Prunty, J.E., Wood, N., & Kelly, D.J. (2021). Eye movements and behavioural responses to gaze-contingent expressive faces in typically developing infants and infant siblings. *Autism Research, 14*(5), 973–983. https://doi.org/10.1002/aur.2432

Kemp, R.I., Towell, N., & Pike, G. (1997). When seeing should not be believing: Photographs, credit cards and fraud. *Applied Cognitive Psychology, 11*(3), 211–222. https://doi.org/10.1002/(SICI)1099-0720(199706)11:3<211::AID-ACP430>3.0.CO;2-O

Kirby, M., & Sirovich, L. (1990). Application of the Karhunen-Loeve procedure for the characterization of human faces. *IEEE Transactions on Pattern Analysis and Machine Intelligence, 12*(1), 103–108. https://doi.org/10.1109/34.41390

Knapp, M.L., Hall, J.A., & Horgan, T.G. (2013). *Nonverbal communication in human interaction.* Wadsworth.

Lander, K., Bruce, V., & Hill, H. (2001). Evaluating the effectiveness of pixelation and blurring on masking the identity of familiar faces. *Applied Cognitive Psychology, 15*(1), 101–116. https://doi.org/10.1002/1099-0720(200101/02)15:1<101::AID-ACP697>3.0.CO;2-7

Lim, S., & Reeves, B. (2010). Computer agents versus avatars: Responses to interactive game characters controlled by a computer or other player. *International Journal of Human-Computer Studies, 68*(1–2), 57–68. https://doi.org/10.1016/j.ijhcs.2009.09.008

Loftus, E.F. (1976). Unconscious transference in eyewitness identification. *Law & Psychology Review, 2,* 93–98.

Longmore, C.A., Liu, C.H., & Young, A.W. (2008). Learning faces from photographs. *Journal of Experimental Psychology: Human Perception and Performance, 34*(1), 77–100. https://doi.org/10.1037/0096-1523.34.1.77

Loomis, J.M., Blascovich, J.J., & Beall, A.C. (1999). Immersive virtual environment technology as a basic research tool in psychology. *Behavior Research Methods, Instruments, & Computers, 31,* 557–564. https://doi.org/10.3758/BF03200735

McCaffery, J.M., & Burton, A.M. (2016). Passport checks: Interactions between matching faces and biographical details. *Applied Cognitive Psychology, 30*(6), 925–933. https://doi.org/10.1002/acp.3281

McCall, C., & Blascovich, J.J. (2009). How, when, and why to use digital experimental virtual environments to study social behavior. *Social and Personality Psychology Compass*, 3, 744–758. https://doi.org/10.1111/j.1751-9004.2009.00195.x

Megreya, A.M., & Burton, A.M. (2006). Unfamiliar faces are not faces: Evidence from a matching task. *Memory & Cognition*, 34(4), 865–876. https://doi.org/10.3758/BF03193433

Megreya, A.M., & Burton, A.M. (2008). Matching faces to photographs: Poor performance in eyewitness memory (without the memory). *Journal of Experimental Psychology: Applied*, 14(4), 364–372. https://doi.org/10.1037/a0013464

Meissner, C.A., & Brigham, J.C. (2001). Thirty years of investigating the own-race bias in memory for faces: A meta-analytic review. *Psychology, Public Policy, and Law*, 7(1), 3–35. https://doi.org/10.1037/1076-8971.7.1.3

Meissner, C.A., Tredoux, C.G., Parker, J.F., & MacLin, O.H. (2005). Eyewitness decisions in simultaneous and sequential lineups: A dual-process signal detection theory analysis. *Memory & Cognition*, 33, 783–792. https://doi.org/10.3758/BF03193074

Memon, A., Havard, C., Clifford, B., Gabbert, F., & Watt, M. (2011). A field evaluation of the VIPER system: A new technique for eliciting eyewitness identification evidence. *Psychology, Crime & Law*, 17(8), 711–729. https://doi.org/10.1080/10683160903524333

Moore, J.W. (2016). What is the sense of agency and why does it matter? *Frontiers in Psychology*, 7, 1272. https://doi.org/10.3389/fpsyg.2016.01272

Mori, M. (1970). The uncanny valley. *Energy*, 7, 33–35.

Nielsen, M.K., Slade, L., Levy, J.P., & Holmes, A. (2015). Inclined to see it your way: Do altercentric intrusion effects in visual perspective taking reflect an intrinsically social process?. *Quarterly Journal of Experimental Psychology*, 68(10), 1931–1951. https://doi.org/10.1080/17470218.2015.1023206

Nyman, T.J., Antfolk, J., Lampinen, J.M., Korkman, J., & Santtila, P. (2020). The effects of distance and age on the accuracy of estimating perpetrator gender, age, height, and weight by eyewitnesses. *Psychology, Crime & Law*. Advance online publication. https://doi.org/10.1080/1068316X.2020.1798425

O'Regan, J.K., & Noë, A.A. (2001). A sensorimotor account of vision and visual consciousness. *Behavioral and Brain Sciences*, 24(5), 939–973. https://doi.org/10.1017/s0140525x01000115

O'Toole, A.J., Jonathon Phillips, P., Weimer, S., Roark, D.A., Ayyad, J., Barwick, R., & Dunlop, J. (2011). Recognizing people from dynamic and static faces and bodies: Dissecting identity with a fusion approach. *Vision Research*, 51(1), 74–83. https://doi.org/10.1016/j.visres.2010.09.035

Oh, C.S., Bailenson, J.N., & Welch, G.F. (2018). Review of social presence: Definition, antecedents, and implications. *Frontiers in Robotics and AI*, 15(5):114. https://doi.org/10.3389/frobt.2018.00114

Pan, X., & Hamilton, A.F.C. (2018). Why and how to use virtual reality to study human social interaction: The challenges of exploring a new research landscape. *British Journal of Psychology*, 109(3), 395–417. https://doi.org/10.1111/bjop.12290

Pan, X., Gillies, M., Barker, C., Clark, D.M., & Slater, M. (2012). Socially anxious and confident men interact with a forward virtual woman: An experimental study. *PLoS One*, 7(4): e32931. https://doi.org/10.1371/journal.pone.0032931

Pan, X., Gillies, M., & Skater, M. (2008). The impact of avatar blushing on the duration of interaction between a real and a virtual person. *Proceedings of the 11th Annual International Workshop on Presence*, October 26–28 (Edinburgh). http://web4.cs.ucl.ac.uk/staff/S.Pan/avatarblushing.pdf

Peck, T.C., Seinfeld, S., Aglioti, S.M., & Slater, M. (2013). Putting yourself in the skin of a black avatar reduces implicit racial bias. *Consciousness and Cognition*, 22, 779–787. https://doi.org/10.1016/j.concog.2013.04.016

Phillips, P.J., Moon, H., Rizvi, S.A., & Rauss, P.J. (2000). The FERET evaluation methodology for face-recognition algorithms. *IEEE Transactions on Pattern Analysis and Machine Intelligence*, 22(10), 1090–1104. https://doi.org/10.1109/34.879790

Ramon, M., Bobak, A.K., & White, D. (2019). Super-recognizers: From the lab to the world and back again. *British Journal of Psychology*, 110(3), 461–479. https://doi.org/10.1111/bjop.12368

Reichherzer, C., Cunningham, A., Walsh, J., Kohler, M., Billinghurst, M., & Thomas, B.H. (2018). Narrative and spatial memory for jury viewings in a reconstructed virtual environment. *IEEE Transactions on Visualization and Computer Graphics* 24(11), 2917–2926. https://doi.org/10.1109/TVCG.2018.2868569

Reichherzer, C., Cunningham, A., Coleman, T., Cao, R., McManus, K., Sheppard, D., Kohler, M., Billinghurst, M., Thomas, B.H. (2021). Bringing the jury to the scene of the crime: Memory and decision-making in a simulated crime scene. *CHI '21: Proceedings of the 2021 CHI Conference on Human Factors in Computing Systems*, 709, 1–12. https://doi.org/10.1145/3411764.3445464

Ritchie, K.L., Mireku, M.O., & Kramer, R.S.S. (2020). Face averages and multiple images in a live matching task. *British Journal of Psychology*, 111(1), 92–102. https://doi.org/10.1111/bjop.12388

Ross, D.R., Ceci, S.J., Dunning, D., & Toglia, M.P. (1994). Unconscious transference and mistaken identity: When a witness misidentifies a familiar but innocent person. *Journal of Applied Psychology*, 79(6), 918–930. https://doi.org/10.1037/0021-9010.79.6.918

Rovira, A., Southern, R., Swapp, D., Campbell, C., Zhang, J.J., Levine, M., & Slater, M. (2021). Bystander affiliation influences intervention behavior: A Virtual Reality study. *SAGE Open*, 11(3). https://doi.org/10.1177/21582440211040076

Schweinberger, S.R., & Burton, A.M. (2003). Covert recognition and the neural system for face processing. *Cortex*, 39(1), 9–30. https://doi.org/10.1016/s0010-9452(08)70071-6

Shapiro, P.N., & Penrod, S. (1986). Meta-analysis of facial identification studies. *Psychological Bulletin*, 100(2), 139–156. https://doi.org/10.1037/0033-2909.100.2.139

Skarratt, P.A., Cole, G.G., & Kuhn, G. (2012). Visual cognition during real social interaction. *Frontiers in Human Neuroscience*, 6, 42979. https://doi.org/10.3389/fnhum.2012.00196

Slater, M. (2009). Place illusion and plausibility can lead to realistic behaviour in immersive virtual environments. *Philosophical Transactions of the Royal Society London B: Biological Sciences*, 364, 3549–3557. https://doi.org/10.1098/rstb.2009.0138

Slater, M., Rovira, A., Southern, R., Swapp, D., Zhang, J.J., Campbell, C., & Levine, M. (2013). Bystander responses to a violent incident in an immersive virtual environment. *PLoS One*, 8(1): e52766. https://doi.org/10.1371/journal.pone.0052766

Smith, S.M., & Vela, E. (1992). Environmental context-dependent eyewitness recognition. *Applied Cognitive Psychology*, 6(2), 125–139. https://doi.org/10.1002/acp.2350060204

Steblay, N.M. (1992). A meta-analytic review of the weapon focus effect. *Law and Human Behavior*, 16(4), 413–424. https://doi.org/10.1007/BF02352267

Tummon, H.M., Allen, J.A., & Bindemann, M. (2019). Facial identification at a virtual reality airport. *i-Perception*, 10, 2041669519863077. https://doi.org/10.1177/2041669519863077

Tummon, H.M., Allen, J.A., & Bindemann, M. (2020). Body language influences on facial identification at passport control: An exploration in virtual reality. *i-Perception*, 11, 2041669520958033. https://doi.org/10.1177/2041669520958033

Turing, A.M. (1950). Computing machinery and intelligence. *Mind*, 59, 433–460. https://www.cse.chalmers.se/~aikmitr/papers/Turing.pdf#page=442

Turk, M., & Pentland, A. (1991). Eigenfaces for recognition. *Journal of Cognitive Neuroscience*, 3(1), 71–86. https://doi.org/10.1162/jocn.1991.3.1.71

United States Government Accountability Office. (2010). Efforts to validate TSA's passenger screening behavior detection program underway, but opportunities exist to strengthen validation and address operational challenges (GAO Publication No. GAO-10-763). Retrieved from www.gao.gov/assets/310/304510.pdf

United States Government Accountability Office. (2013). TSA should limit future funding for behavior detection activities (GAO Publication No. GAO-14-159). Retrieved from www.gao.gov/assets/660/658923.pdf

Usoh, M., Catena, E., Arman, S., & Slater, M. (2000). Using presence questionnaires in reality. *Presence: Teleoperators and Virtual Environments*, 9, 497–503. https://doi.org/10.1162/105474600566989

von der Pütten, M., Krämer, N.C., Gratch, J., & Kang, S.H. (2010). "It doesn't matter what you are!" Explaining social effects of agents and avatars. *Computers in Human Behavior*, 26, 1641–1650. https://doi.org/10.1016/j.chb.2010.06.012

Wells, G.L., Memon, A., & Penrod, S.D. (2006). Eyewitness evidence: Improving its probative value. *Psychological Science in the Public Interest*, 7(2), 45–75. https://doi.org/10.1111/j.1529-1006.2006.00027.x

White, D., Kemp, R.I., Jenkins, R., Matheson, M., & Burton, A.M. (2014). Passport officers' errors in face matching. *PLoS ONE*, 9(8): e103510. https://doi.org/10.1371/journal.pone.0103510

Wilson, C.J., & Soranzo, A. (2015). The use of virtual reality in psychology: A case study in visual perception. *Computational and Mathematical Methods in Medicine*, 1–7. https://doi.org/10.1155/2015/151702

Witmer, B.G., & Singer, M.J. (1998). Measuring presence in virtual environments: a presence questionnaire. *Presence: Teleoperators and Virtual Environments*, 7, 225–240. https://doi.org/10.1162/105474698565686

9 Facial Composite Technology and Eyewitness Identification

Graham Pike

Introduction

Known by many names, the facial composite images recreated from the memory of a witness have fascinated psychologists for decades and psychology has played an important role in the development of the technology that produces them. Here we will refer to these images as "facial composites," or just "composites," where technology has been used to combine the characteristics of other faces, whether these be facial features or statistically derived features, and "sketches" where an artist has worked with no technology other than pencil and paper, or their equivalents.

The other names used tend to be those relating to the brand names of the technology employed, such as Identi-Kit, Photofit, EFIT and EvoFIT. Perhaps the most evocative and striking name is the Danish "fantombillede," meaning "phantom image"; a term indicative of the skepticism the Danish police tend to hold for facial composites. Indeed, one such phantom image is used on the cover of Fantombillede, Thomas Boberg's 2014 anthology of poetry (Boberg, 2014) that explores themes of memory. The image is an outline of a head obscured by charcoal, indicating that the detail has been lost to memory and cannot be trusted. Having discussed facial composites with a number of Danish police officers through the years, I think they would see Boberg's imagery as an apt summary of why composites have little to add to an investigation.

Officers from other jurisdictions would certainly disagree, seeing facial composites as a visual statement, worth a thousand words of written description, that can jog the memory of someone familiar with a potential suspect and generate an invaluable lead (Brace et al., 2008). Although it is worth stating that my own experience has very much been that composites have their advocates and detractors even within the same agency, so that it is not really possible to form a single opinion for any jurisdiction as a whole.

As well as whether composite systems produce accurate likenesses of the perpetrator and are a useful part of an investigation, there is also the question of how they interact with other investigative components, most importantly whether creating a composite might interfere with a witness's ability to identify the suspect in a lineup (Pike et al., 2019). Perhaps the most publicized view is that composites, like other forms of post-event information, are likely to disrupt the memory of a witness leading to them being less accurate when it comes to a subsequent identification task (Pike et al., 2019). Most worryingly, the view is that this inaccuracy can mean a witness is more likely to identify an innocent suspect. However, research on this topic has produced equivocal results, with studies as likely to find no effect or even that composite construction leads to greater identification accuracy (Tredoux et al., 2021). As Sporer et al. (2020) point out, research has tended to pay less attention to the fact that by producing an accurate composite the witness's memory of the perpetrator's appearance may be strengthened, making any subsequent identification at a lineup more likely to be accurate.

One key theme that emerges when it comes to most aspects of facial composites is that of differing opinions and results. There are practitioners and researchers that see composites as a valuable investigative aid that can assist witness memory, and those that see their problems as outweighing any possible benefits (Brace et al., 2008; Wells et al., 2005). These disagreements, and the psychological issues involved in composite construction, have led to a rich field in which psychology has had a considerable impact, and the issues with composite production have also been a significant force in driving more theoretical research on face perception (Davies & Young, 2017).

Role in an Investigation

One important point to understand regarding composites is the role they play within an investigation, a role that is more similar to the verbal description provided by an eyewitness than it is other *visual* evidence, particularly identification evidence. Indeed, composites are often referred to as a visual statement (e.g. Criminal Justice Act, 2003). Consequently, the primary reason for constructing a composite is to generate leads in a case and not to provide evidence regarding the potential guilt of an individual suspect. In other words, composites are used to identify possible suspects rather than to identify whether one particular suspect *is* the perpetrator.

However, composites can be and are presented in court. In the US, a composite can be ruled as admissible in order to rehabilitate an impeached identification (*People v. Maldonado*, 2002, cited in McQuiston-Surrett et al., 2008). In the UK, the Criminal Justice Act (2003, section 115 (2)) includes composites within the definition of a witness statement, namely: "A statement is any representation of fact or opinion made by a person by whatever means; and it includes a representation made in a sketch, Photofit or other pictorial form." However, the practice guidelines of the National Policing Improvement Agency (NPIA) covering composite production do also stress that a composite image is a *likeness* of a perpetrator and cannot be treated in the same way as a photograph (NPIA, 2009).

In the UK, investigating officers are reminded that when requesting a composite image, irrespective of the technique used, they are, in fact, asking for a pictorial statement from a witness.

In all cases, any notes and sketches made during the production of an image are subject to disclosure under the Criminal Procedure and Investigations Act 1996 (CPIA) and should be treated accordingly. Officers also are reminded that the prosecution must inform the defense of the existence of any composite image or unfinished image, irrespective of the technique used, as well as any notes made. The composite image and notes must, therefore, be retained and the witness may be called upon to produce them in any subsequent proceedings.

This means that in both the US and UK, a composite generated by a witness needs to be retained in the case file created by the investigating officers and made available to defense council, which means that the defense can use the composite image at trial. As a result, and although the primary purpose of a composite may be to generate leads rather than to provide identification evidence per se, composites do appear in some trials. Research using the mock-juror paradigm has found that a composite that resembles a defendant, results in jurors responding favorably towards the witness that produced it, and punitively toward the defendant, while a less accurate composite tends not to have any effect at all (McQuiston-Surrett et al., 2008).

Another important element concerns the target audience for the composite. Composites are only created by witnesses who are *unfamiliar* with the perpetrator. If a witness is familiar with the perpetrator, then they simply supply their name or other relevant information. The composite image is then shown to the public essentially by inclusion on a "Wanted Poster," or the analogue of this on social media or a TV show. The hope is that the image is seen by a member of the public, or indeed another officer, who is *familiar* with the perpetrator. The alternative would be for a member of the public who was *unfamiliar* with the perpetrator to first see the composite and later spot someone who looked like it, a process very unlikely to generate a useful lead given the problems of remembering and comparing unfamiliar faces (Pike et al., 2000).

History

Although psychological research has informed the development of contemporary, computer-based composite technology, the first composite systems had a very different beginning. For an in-depth history of the early years of facial compositing technology, see Paul Lawrence's article "Policing, 'Science' and the Curious Case of Photo-FIT" (Lawrence, 2020).

The first facial composite system, Identi-Kit, comprised line drawings of facial features that were printed on transparencies so they could be combined together (Home Office, 1969). Identi-Kit was developed by officers in the Los Angeles Police Department, who adopted it in 1959 (Lawrence, 2020). It also was used in the early 1960s in the UK where it enjoyed initial success and received positive media coverage (Lawrence, 2020). However, as well as not containing images of current hairstyles and head ware, the UK Home Office concluded that it was only effective in 5–10% of cases and was too resource intensive to be practical, taking more than half a day to construct a facial image (Home Office, 1969).

In the UK, Identi-Kit was replaced by Photofit which comprised grayscale photographs of facial features taken from the mugshot books of several police forces.[1] As Lawrence (2020) notes, although Photofit was, to some extent, developed by the Home Office's Police Scientific Development Branch (PSDB) in the late 1960s, its true development began sometime before this in decidedly non-scientific origins. Photofits "inventor," Jaques Penry, was an entrepreneur with no scientific or technological background and a firm belief in "character reading," discerning personality traits from physiognomy. He had previously produced a book (Penry, 1952) explaining how to interpret facial features (for example, a specific form of eyebrow would indicate the person to be unsociable with a self-centered disposition). He later turned this concept into a board game, titled "Physogs" in which players had to construct faces indicative of specific personality traits. It is no surprise then that he later contracted with Waddington Ltd. (i.e., the famous board game company) to be the suppliers of Photofit, which arose from the contacts he formed with the police and Home Office in an attempt to sell training to the police on how to read character through the face.

The first field test of Photofit, undertaken for the PSDB (King, 1971) revealed fairly poor results, with it contributing to the arrest of a suspect in approximately 8% of cases. Although a subsequent review by the Criminal Intelligence Branch was far more positive, this was not based on

---

[1] I have produced a free, online facial composite generator based on Photofit called PhotoFit Me, found at www.open.edu/openlearn/PhotoFitMe

any statistical analysis of case records, a problem that persists to this day making it very hard to judge the efficacy of composite systems in practice.

It was in the early 1970s that psychologists first became involved with facial composite technology (see Davies & Young, 2017, for an overview), when the famous Aberdeen research team of Ellis, Shepherd, and Davies evaluated a Photofit kit lent to them by the PSDB (Ellis et al., 1975). The results showed that participants were unable to recreate a Photofit image accurately even when they could see it and that when asked to make a Photofit of a real face, that no two participants selected the same feature. Further, independent judges were only able to match these Photofit images to the correct face on 1 in 8 attempts. As Davies and Young (2017) report, when the article was reported by *The Times*, the headline used of "Photofit 'useless' say scientists" led to threats of legal action from Jaques Penry.

This work on Photofit proved to be an important component in driving the development of psychological research and theory on face perception (Davies & Young, 2017). It also led to a more sustained program of research by the team at Aberdeen and collaboration with the PSDB to improve Photofit. This research included the finding that the accuracy of a Photofit was not improved by allowing the participant to view the target face during construction (Ellis et al., 1978), a result that has been replicated with a computerized system (Brace et al., 2006a).

A key finding in the early evaluation of Photofit was that it produced images no better than the sketches that were already in use by the police. For example, Ellis et al. (1978) found a slight advantage of Photofit over sketches done from memory, but that when the target face was present the sketches were more accurate. One surprising element to this result is that these sketches were produced by the participants themselves, rather than trained artists! The finding that sketches can be more accurate than composite images has been replicated even with more technologically advanced systems (Frowd et al., 2005b).

The research group at Aberdeen went on to map verbal descriptions to the individual features used within Photofit to produce the "Aberdeen Index" which was used at the time and later in the computerized composite system E-FIT (Davies & Young, 2017). They also worked further with the Home Office, including collaborating with the PSDB to survey police composite operators (Kitson et al., 1978) and were involved in designing and delivering composite training courses (Davies et al., 1986).

Thanks to the pioneering work of the Aberdeen group, from that point on, psychological research became the cornerstone of composite technological development, particularly in producing the computerized computer systems that were to replace Photofit and Identi-Kit. For example, with psychological research teams (Brace, Kemp, Pike, Turner, and others) working on E-FIT (e.g. Brace et al., 2000; Pike et al., 2000) and (Bruce, Frowd, Hancock, Ness, and others) working on PRO-fit (e.g. Bruce et al., 2002; Ness et al., 2015). Psychological research and knowledge also led to the development of the latest composite systems, such as EFIT 6 and EvoFit which will be described later, that employ a holistic construction method that is a far superior match to the cognition underpinning face perception than is the piecemeal construction used by older systems (Pike et al., 2005).

Recent Technological Developments

The most significant advantages involved in moving from paper-based systems, such as Photofit and Identi-Kit, to computerized systems such as E-FIT, which was developed with the involvement of the Aberdeen research group (Davies & Young, 2017) were arguably practical, because a single laptop replaced several large boxes and feature searching and placement could be conducted far more quickly.

Computerized systems also allowed features to be resized, re-oriented and, via the use of paint and photo manipulation software, for the addition of enhancements such as digitally editing hair and other features. These advances meant that more emphasis was placed on the configuration of facial features instead of just focusing on which features were selected, as well as facilitating the addition of artistic enhancements that had previously been shown to improve composite accuracy (Gibling & Bennett, 1994).

Despite the move to computers, the first composite systems essentially replicated the core psychological problem with the first systems in that they relied on databases of individual facial features; indeed, the Aberdeen Index was again used. This meant that construction was still essentially piecemeal, feature based and a poor match for the cognition involved in face memory (Pike et al., 2005). However, while Photofit involved initially looking through albums of individual features, E-FIT began by the operator asking the witness for a verbal description and then entering this into the system using the Aberdeen Index. Only once the system had produced an initial face was the screen shown to the witness. Although construction then, mainly, proceeded in a feature driven piecemeal fashion, the features were always seen within the context of a whole face. Based on research on the face superiority effect, whereby faces are more accurately recognized when their features are shown correctly within the context of a whole face (Purcell & Stewart, 1986), this development at least overcame the problem of needing to recognize individual facial features that were not part of a whole-face context that was undoubtedly a serious flaw with Photofit.

It was not until the development of the latest computerized composite systems, such as EvoFIT and the latest version and EFIT,[2] that are the primary systems used by many law enforcement agencies at the time of writing, that technology moved beyond the piecemeal approach (Brace et al., 2008). Although the cognition involved in face perception cannot simply be described as being based entirely on configural information and it is clear that featural cues do play a role (Collishaw & Hole, 2000), there exists a large body of research (e.g., Tanaka & Farah, 1993; Wilford & Wells, 2010) that has demonstrated the importance of configural information. It follows that if faces are not mentally represented by first decomposing them into their component features, that any composite system which relies on decomposing a face into component features will clash with the cognition of the witness.

The fundamental mismatch between early computerized composite systems and the cognition involved in face recognition led researchers to look for alternative methods of representing and constructing facial images. Research by Sirovich and Kirby (1987) had shown that principal component analysis (PCA), an image-based analysis technique, could be used to represent a set of facial images through a set of "eigenfaces" (essentially the facial images corresponding to the eigenvectors produced by the PCA). The success of this technique led to a large amount of subsequent research and the adoption of PCA as a leading technique in face recognition research as well as in face modelling (Blanz & Vetter, 1999).

The immediate advantage of PCA was that it was an inherently holistic method of representing faces. Critically, PCA also had been found to capture psychologically relevant information (Bruce et al., 1998). For example PCA-based systems were able to reliably categorize facial cues that would be meaningful to a human, such as those relating to identity, sex and race, and were also able to extract cues to do with expression. In addition, systems using PCA were also able to simulate key phenomena that had been well documented in the research on human's perception of faces, such as the own-race bias effect (Calder & Young, 2005), whereby people are usually more accurate at recognizing faces from their own ethnicity than they are faces from other ethnicities.

By combining the eigenfaces resulting from the PCA of a database of faces using the correct proportions, it is possible to recreate any of the facial images within that database. However, by varying these proportions, it is possible to synthesize entirely new facial images (O'Toole & Thompson, 1993). As a result, PCA began to be used in composite construction,

---

2 The initial prototype of this system was called "EigenFIT," before being renamed "EFIT-V" and then "EFIT 6," which is the name used at the time of writing.

initially employing "feature" based PCA (Brunelli & Mich, 1996), which by using PCA to examine variation within each facial feature replicated one of the main problems, namely representing a face as a set of individual features rather than more holistically, that had plagued existing feature-based composite systems (Gibson et al., 2003).

Hancock (2000) then developed a new method of PCA-based composite construction that used a genetic algorithm to evolve faces based on selections made by a user. Gibson et al. (2003) developed this technique further, combining an evolutionary algorithm with a facial appearance model that was able to make both global and local modifications to face images, allowing a potential witness to evolve photo-realistic images of a suspect. This research eventually led to the development of PCA-based composite systems that utilized genetic algorithms to evolve faces based on witness input, such as EvoFIT and EFIT 6 (Pike et al., 2019).

The move to PCA meant that a new interface was needed to facilitate composite construction. Rather than proceed by seeing a single facial image and attempting to improve it, contemporary systems use an array-based approach in which witnesses see a grid of 9 (EFIT 6) or 18 (EvoFit) faces. The witness is required to select the face they think is the best match for that of the perpetrator and the system will evolve a new array of faces. This means that many of the problems involved with older systems are avoided, including that a verbal description is not needed and there is no need to decompose the face into individual features.

It would have been possible for the interface to be no more complicated, and all the witness would need to do is point to the best match in iterative arrays. However, research conducted on how people interacted with the interface found that they often asked for more complex forms of interaction, including selecting multiple faces, selecting the worst match, and also making alterations to individual features (Pike et al., 2005). In addition, a survey of UK police composite operators found that they reported witnesses often mentioning holistic facial characteristics (e.g., attractiveness and distinctiveness) during construction, suggesting the need for future composite systems to be able to incorporate holistic manipulations (Brace et al., 2008). As a result, the interfaces of contemporary composite systems can accommodate holistic, configural, and featural alterations as well as multiple methods of selecting the best match, although importantly they never *require* a witness to engage in a task that they might find cognitively difficult.

Contemporary composite systems operate by combining PCA, genetic algorithms, and a more flexible interface. As Brace et al. (2008) pointed out, this interface is far more able to accommodate the human cognition involved in face perception by virtue of including holistic selection and manipulation methods, than were the older piecemeal composite systems.

In addition, the inclusion of multiple methods of selecting and manipulating the facial images means that contemporary composite systems are better able to respond to any requests made by a witness and, importantly, do not force them into one particular method of selection and construction, particularly that based on the manipulation of individual facial features which has been proven to be a cognitively difficult task (Brace et al., 2008).

Are Composites Accurate?

Determining the accuracy of composites used in a police investigation is problematic, as is any evaluation of investigative evidence, because of the issue of knowing for certain the identity of the perpetrator (Pike & Clark, 2018). The primary method of assessing composite accuracy has, therefore, involved psychological experiments in which the "ground-truth" of how the crime occurred and the identity of the perpetrator are known. Such experiments are similar to those conducted to explore most issues involving eyewitness memory and involve participants first seeing a staged crime (presented either live, on video or using static photos) before being asked to remember some aspect of that crime (for example by free-recalling what happened or by attempting to identify the perpetrator from a photo lineup). In composite research, it is usual for one group of participants to each create a facial composite and for a second group to each evaluate the accuracy of the image. This evaluation can involve attempting to match the composite to a face presented in a photo-lineup or a likeness rating produced by comparing the composite to the face it attempts to portray (Brace et al., 2006a).

As several researchers (e.g. Brace et al., 2006a; Frowd et al., 2005b) have pointed out, such evaluation methods are not a good match for how composites are used in a real investigation, where the witness is *unfamiliar* with the face of the perpetrator, but the hope is that the composite image will be seen by someone who *is familiar* with them. To appropriately recreate this situation it is necessary for the participants creating the composites to be unfamiliar with the perpetrator but for the group evaluating the composites to be familiar with them. This procedure then allows composite accuracy to be measured by whether these participants are able to both recognize and name the person depicted (Brace et al., 2006a; Frowd et al., 2005b).

As was previously stated, evaluations of both Photofit (Ellis et al., 1978) and even more technologically advanced systems such as E-FIT, PRO-fit, FACES, and EvoFIT (Frowd et al., 2005b) had found that the systems produced images that tended not to be as accurate as hand drawn sketches (Frowd et al., 2005b). Research conducted on the early, feature-based composite systems such as Identi-Kit (Laughery et al., 1977; Laughery & Fowler, 1980) and Photofit (Ellis et al., 1978) also tended to find that construction with a picture of the target face in view resulted in composites that were no more accurate than those constructed from memory. Similar research conducted on the first generation of computerized systems found more promising results. Cutler et al. (1988) found an improvement in accuracy for composites created with a picture present compared to those made from memory using the Mac-A-Mug Pro system, but these images were produced by an experienced operator rather than with a witness. Brace et al. (2000) found a similar superiority for images constructed by a participant-witness working with an operator and a picture of the target present using the E-FIT system. Thus, these systems seemed to offer an improvement in likeness accuracy over earlier systems, because construction using a picture of the target did improve quality, even when verbal descriptions and communication between operator and witness were involved.

Other research employing more realistic conditions painted a less positive picture. For example, Koehn and Fisher (1997) also used Mac-A-Mug Pro but employed an encoding task in which the participant interacted with an unfamiliar target. The resulting composites were given poor likeness ratings by independent judges and on average led to only a 40% hit rate on a photospread task. Kovera et al. (1997) used the same composite system but asked participants who were familiar with the targets to identify them from the composites produced, finding that identification rates were no better than chance and further that only 1.7% of the names generated by participants were correct. Frowd et al. (2005a) employed both a forensically relevant delay of 2 days between encoding and construction as well as using a naming task as a measure of accuracy, and found that naming rates for composites created using E-FIT, PRO-fit, FACES and EvoFIT (an earlier version still in development) was very low indeed at just 3% overall, with the rate for sketches being 8%.

Even though these early, computerized systems were sensitive enough to produce better quality composites when an image of the target was present during construction, the overall quality of the composites were relatively poor. Brace et al. (2006a) identified several possible sources of error in the composite construction process relating to the system itself, the memory of the witness, the ability of the witness to verbally describe the face to an operator and the ability of the operator to use the system. Previous research had shown the importance of this latter factor, with Davies et al. (1983) finding that experienced Photofit operators produced better quality composites than a novice, and Gibling and Bennett (1994) demonstrating that composites that had been artistically enhanced by trained operators were more likely to be identified than composites with no enhancement.

Building on this research, Brace et al. (2006a) used trained operators who combined E-FIT with graphics software in order to add artistic enhancement, and also employed from-memory and from-picture conditions, by manipulating whether the operator constructed a composite themselves or worked with a participant-witness. The composites were evaluated using a number of measures, including through naming rates, i.e. the number of participants familiar with the person depicted in the composite who were able to recognize and name the correct person. Their results showed that composites created directly by the operator were more accurate than those constructed with a participant-witness, and also that only the participant-witnesses showed an improvement in accuracy (using the data on naming rates) when working from a picture over working from memory. Based on these results, Brace et al. concluded that the principal limiting factor in composite quality lies in the ability of a witness to verbally describe a face, rather than their memory of what the face looks like or in the composite system itself.

It should follow then that because contemporary, PCA based composite systems use an interface and construction method that relies less on verbal description that they should tend to produce superior quality composites. However, such systems initially proved not to be effective (Skelton et al., 2020), with an evaluation of EvoFIT finding that it produced naming rates (10%) that were actually lower than for E-FIT (17%), with rates becoming comparable once alterations were made to the age of the target (Frowd et al., 2004).

The technological development of PCA composite systems has continued to involve psychological research and evaluations of the later versions of the systems have produced more positive results. For example, regression and meta-analyses of data from 23 studies revealed that the EvoFIT, PCA-based system, produced composites that were over four-times more identifiable than composites produced by PRO-fit and E-FIT, feature-based systems, or through sketching (Frowd et al., 2015).

As well as improvements to the systems, technological development has been augmented by other procedures based on psychological knowledge and research and together these have resulted in significant improvements in composite accuracy (Skelton et al., 2020). These procedures include the nature of the initial interview used. In the UK it is common to begin the process of composite construction by using a Cognitive Interview (Brace et al., 2008), which begins with the witness recalling all they can of the crime (see Fisher & Geiselman, 1992). Frowd et al. (2008) found that composite accuracy could be improved by using a Holistic Cognitive Interview, that employs a similar approach to the standard cognitive interview but includes questions that focus on holistic facial characteristics such as masculinity (Frowd et al., 2008). Research on the initial interview has also found that aligning the cognitive processes involved during the interview and construction process leads to more accurate composite images (Skelton et al., 2020).

Other methods for improving the accuracy of a composite have involved asking multiple witnesses to construct a composite of the same target, and then showing these multiple images together (Brace et al., 2006b) or morphing them together to produce a single image (Bruce et al., 2002), both of which can produce higher rates of naming and identification than showing a composite created by just a single witness. Research focusing on child witnesses, a sub-group of witnesses who might particularly struggle with verbal descriptions, successfully developed a visual interface that could be used to obtain information about individual facial features (Paine et al., 2008). In addition, Giannnou et al. (2021) found that embedding mindfulness instructions within the construction process of EvoFIT, which encouraged participants to focus their attention on the target and on the process of construction, led to more accurate composites than a control condition.

Do Composites Play a Role in Miscarriages of Justice?

Given that many of the empirical evaluations of composites, particularly those constructed using earlier systems, find that they tend not to produce a particularly accurate representation of a perpetrator, it is likely that they may not generate useful intelligence for an investigation. One obvious downside to this is opportunity cost, in that law enforcement agencies tend to have very limited personnel and other resources, which could be deployed in other areas of the investigation rather than creating a possibly poor likeness of the perpetrator. Although an interesting point of public management and forensic marketplaces, it is one that is beyond the scope of this chapter as it is more dependent on both the specific components of the crime and investigation and the views of the senior investigating officer, than it is either the technology or the cognition of the witness (see Bandy & Hartley, 2018, for more on forensic marketplaces).

The point I will focus on instead is that choosing to use investigative resources to create a composite is one thing if there are no adverse consequences, but quite another if doing so has a negative impact on other elements of the investigation. In particular, if creating a composite changes a witness's memory of the perpetrator, then it could result in a number of unwelcome outcomes if the witness is asked to attend a lineup, such as them being less likely to select a guilty suspect and at the same time more likely to select an innocent suspect.

One piece of compelling evidence from real investigations that composites can have a negative effect comes from the Innocence Project (the largely US based group that seeks to overturn miscarriages of justice, particularly using DNA based exoneration; https://innocenceproject.org), where 27% of eyewitness misidentifications involved a witness making a facial composite (Innocence Project, 2017a). As a result, the Innocence Project include composites as a potentially biasing type of investigative procedure. Moreover, the first case of an inmate on death row that was exonerated by the Innocence Project (Innocence Project, 2017b; Junkin, 2004) involved a facial composite: Kirk Bloodsworth became a suspect in the case of the rape and murder of a child because he resembled a composite created by an eyewitness. He was subsequently placed in a lineup and identified by three eyewitnesses.

On one hand, the Bloodsworth case appears to demonstrate the dangers of facial composites, as they led to an innocent man being investigated and subsequently identified in a lineup. However, this case also demonstrates the danger of drawing conclusions from archival analysis where it can be impossible to determine the precise impact of one specific form of evidence. That Bloodsworth became a suspect because of his similarity to the composite seems clear, but it does not follow that the witnesses selected Bloodsworth from the lineup because of this similarity. Even if the lineup was entirely fair and unbiased (e.g., all of the people in the lineup would be equally likely to be picked by someone who had simply read the witness's description of the perpetrator), there would be no way of knowing for sure whether the witness who constructed the composite would have still picked Bloodsworth even if they had not made the composite. There is simply no way of establishing this reliably without using controlled experimentation.

It is possible that the lineup used for Bloodsworth was not fair, meaning that Bloodsworth may have been the best match for the actual perpetrator and would have been picked out by the witnesses regardless of whether they had made a composite or not. However, although there is no way to know whether the source of error in this scenario was the composite creation altering the witness's memory of the perpetrator's appearance, it is still important to acknowledge that the composite was a contributing factor to a miscarriage of justice.

The key point is that the police suspected and investigated Bloodsworth because of his similarity to the composite. The possible inaccuracy of a composite could lead to an innocent person becoming a suspect and that can be a dangerous first step on the way to a later misidentification and miscarriage of justice. This is likely to be particularly problematic when an investigation uses adversarial and interrogative procedures based on assuming and proving the guilt of a suspect.

Do Composites Impact Eyewitness Identification Accuracy?

Although it is important to remember the potential dangers associated with any technique used to generate potential leads and suspects in an investigation, psychological research has focused on the question of whether creating, or indeed just viewing, a facial composite might alter a witness's memory to the extent that they make errors at a subsequent lineup.

One possibility is that composite construction could have an adverse effect on lineup performance because in creating the composite the memory of the witness regarding the appearance of the perpetrator becomes altered, making it harder for the eyewitness to make an accurate identification. Further, their memory may become contaminated, changing so that it becomes more similar to a different person—a particular danger if a suspect is arrested on the basis of their resemblance to the composite image. This problem can alternatively be seen as one of source monitoring failure (Johnson et al., 1993), in which the witness encodes both the face of the perpetrator and the face as seen in the composite image and is then unable to attribute which memory belongs to which source when attempting to identify the perpetrator from a lineup.

Although a great deal of applied cognitive research on eyewitness memory has focused on the problems associated with the witness encountering information after seeing the crime, known as post-event information (Loftus & Greene, 1980; Zaragoza et al., 2007), other research on memory (albeit not on memory for faces) has found that repetition and rehearsal tend to have a positive effect on recall and recognition (Ward, 2022), suggesting that composite construction could be potentially beneficial to a witness's memory for the perpetrator as it essentially provides an opportunity for repetition and rehearsal (Pike et al., 2019).

A similar dichotomy exists in research on the use of mugshot albums, with the majority of studies finding that viewing mugshots results in poorer accuracy at a lineup (Deffenbacher et al., 2006). In contrast, Lindsay et al. (1994) found that viewing mugshot albums (even those containing 500 images) had no effect on identification accuracy at a subsequent lineup. The authors suggest this result could have been because, unlike in previous research, they had included an image of the perpetrator in the mugshot album. It is possible that seeing this image could have refreshed the participant's memory of the perpetrator, thus preventing impairment in performance at the lineup.

While a mugshot can only be *viewed* by a witness, a composite has a dual impact in that it can be both *viewed* and *constructed*, with the latter process involving a gradual creation in which many iterations of composites are seen by the witness. Jenkins and Davies (1985) explored the possible interference effects of a witness *viewing* a Photofit on both subsequent verbal descriptions and identifications, by presenting participants with a composite that was either (largely) accurate or had been altered in an obvious way (e.g., different hair or an added moustache). The accuracy of both the descriptions and lineup identifications was poorer for the condition in which the altered composites were seen compared to the accurate composite condition and a control condition. Although other studies (Gibling & Davies, 1988; Sporer, 1996) produced similar results, Dekle (2006) found that viewing a biased composite (or indeed a more accurate one) did not impact lineup identification accuracy.

The above studies entailed participants simply viewing a composite, many more studies have been conducted in which participants actively construct a composite before viewing a lineup, and they too have produced mixed results. A number of studies have found that composite construction appears to have no impact on lineup accuracy (Davies et al., 1978; Davis et al., 2015; Pike et al., 2019, 2020; Yu & Geiselman, 1993), others that it adversely affects lineup accuracy (Comish, 1987; Kempen & Tredoux, 2012; Topp-Manriquez, McQuiston, & Malpass, 2014; Wells et al., 2005), and yet more that construction actually leads to an improvement in lineup accuracy (Davis, Gibson, & Solomon, 2014; Mauldin & Laughery, 1981; McClure & Shaw, 2002; Meissner & Brigham, 2001) compared to control conditions.

Unlike with mugshots, therefore, some research on composites has found that they can lead to an improvement in lineup identification accuracy, as well as studies showing either no or an adverse effect. Despite the decidedly equivocal results of the field in general, one of the studies finding that composite construction had an adverse effect on lineup identification accuracy, that of Wells et al. (2005), had a particularly significant impact. This included influencing recommendations to practitioners (e.g., Attorney General of the State of Wisconsin, 2005; Bockstaele, 2009), in law review articles (e.g., McNamara, 2009; Trenary, 2013) and also in the popular media (e.g., Munger, 2006; Roth, 2007).

In their first experiment, Wells et al. (2005) reported a very large reduction in identification accuracy for target-present lineups (target-absent lineups were not used) between those participants in the composite construction condition (10% correct identifications and 30% false identifications) and control conditions in which participants either viewed a composite or did no intervening task (84% correct identifications and 6% false identifications); and no impairment from just viewing the composite. Their second experiment not only contained target-absent lineups but also used a simulated crime video instead of a single photo of the target (that was also used in the lineup) and replicated the results of Experiment 1 for the target-present lineups but found no differences for the target-absent lineups.

Wells et al. explain the adverse effect that composite construction had on subsequent identification accuracy as resulting from the need to break the face down into its component features (as they used a piecemeal system). However, other studies using feature based compositing systems have found they can lead to an improvement in subsequent identification accuracy (E-FIT: Davis et al., 2014; Identi-Kit: Mauldin & Laughery, 1981).

A variation of Wells et al.'s suggestion was made in the discussion at two symposia (Pike, 2007, 2009) on facial composites and eyewitness identification at conferences of the Society for Applied Research in Memory and Cognition (SARMAC). The participants in Wells et al. (2005) study created the composites by themselves using an early version of the "Faces" software and it was suggested by researchers who were familiar with Faces that, in addition to the piecemeal, feature by feature construction method, it was possible that the screen layout and particularly the limited feature sets available were quite different to other systems such as E-FIT and PRO-fit, and could have had a differential effect on witness memory.

Since Wells et al.'s (2005) influential study, Sporer et al. (2020) reviewed the research that has been conducted on *viewing* a composite before attempting an identification at a lineup, and concluded that seeing a misleading composite can adversely affect identification accuracy but only if exposure to the target was short, occurred shortly before the lineup, and if the lineup was low-similarity (i.e. the foils in the lineup were not similar to the perpetrator).

In addition, Tredoux et al. (2021) conducted a meta-analysis of 23 studies (56 effects, 2276 participants) that had explored whether composite *construction* affected later identification accuracy. This analysis showed that creating a composite did *not* affect subsequent identification accuracy. More specifically, they state that rather than address a practical question, the studies in this area have tended to focus on the theoretical question of whether an identification made by a participant-witness in a laboratory will be affected by them first constructing a composite—to which the answer is that composite construction has little adverse consequence on subsequent identification accuracy.

As a result of these limitations, the authors note that this conclusion was necessarily tentative and did not allow for solid, evidence-based recommendations for law enforcement partly because the sample was relatively small and also because the ecological validity of the studies included was generally low. Although their study certainly had a significant impact in a number of settings, Wells et al. themselves actually concluded that they were "not yet prepared to argue that the use of composites should be significantly curtailed in criminal investigations" (Wells et al., 2005, p. 155). This is a conclusion that fits well with the results of subsequent reviews (Sporer et al., 2020) and meta-analyses (Tredoux et al., 2021), and is also very similar to the conclusion of Tredoux et al. (2021).

Ecological Validity

One important problem noted by Tredoux et al. (2021) in conducting their meta-analyses was that the studies conducted on composite construction and identification evidence were of generally low ecological validity. That is, the stimuli and procedures employed were very different to how composites are constructed and how lineups take place in practice. Sporer et al. (2020) also made recommendations for how future research could be conducted under ecologically valid conditions.

Criticisms of ecological validity have often been levelled at psychological research by law enforcement practitioners, who feel that the stimuli and procedures employed in a laboratory experiment are far too different to what happens in practice to provide useful conclusions. For example, Pike et al. (2021) reported that, on average, law enforcement practitioners felt that an experiment involving no delay between seeing a (staged) crime and a lineup or that did not use instructions and procedures as set out in relevant policing legislation would have a "generally negative effect" on their opinion of the study.

Although, as we saw with the Bloodsworth case, there are important counter-arguments to do with control, generalizability and (perhaps most importantly) establishing the ground truth, it is a point that has been acknowledged as an important limitation by many researchers. Pike et al. (2019) note a number of ways in which research on composite construction and identification accuracy is different to that of a real-world criminal investigation. These included that rather than working with an officer trained in the creation of a composite, participants in laboratory studies tend to either work by themselves or with a relatively inexperienced researcher. Creating the composite themselves would remove one potential source of error from the process concerning verbally communicating visual information to someone else (Brace et al., 2006a). A second difference involved showing participants either pictures (e.g., Wells et al., 2005, Experiment 1) or videos (e.g., Wells et al., 2005, Experiment 2) rather than a "live" crime event. This could be an issue as Ihlebæk et al. (2003) found that witnesses who viewed a live event provided less complete and less accurate statements than those who saw a video of the same event, meaning laboratory-based research may be overestimating eyewitness memory.

A third difference, and possibly the most important given the conclusion of Sporer et al. (2020), concerns the relative timelines of a laboratory experiment and a criminal investigation. It is common practice in laboratory experiments to have short (often no) delays between a participant encoding the face of the target, constructing a composite and attempting an identification. However, in real investigations the gap between seeing a crime is likely to be in the order of several days, while that between seeing a crime and attending a lineup is likely to be in the order of several weeks, approximately 4–6 weeks and possibly much longer (Pike et al., 2002).

Introducing ecologically valid delays poses a number of problems for researchers as spreading an experiment across several sessions spanning weeks, if not months, is likely to lead to a large number of participants dropping out. The increasing prevalence of online testing is likely to exacerbate this issue, as most online participant pools are not set up to cope with multiple sessions separated by long delays. Given these problems, and the extras costs, resources and time involved, it is not surprising that researchers have tended toward a much shortened approach.

Pike et al. (2019) did attempt to employ an ecologically valid approach to tackling the question of whether composite construction affects identification accuracy by using a live crime event witnessed by participants who worked with a trained officer to create a composite and then attempted (either a target-present or -absent) lineup 4 weeks later. The results of this study showed no significant effect of composite construction on identification accuracy compared to a control group, with the trend being for participants in the composite construction condition to be more likely to identify the target and less likely to make a misidentification. These results were replicated in a second, laboratory-based experiment.

Within the necessary constraints of modern frameworks of research ethics, it is almost impossible to match the consequentiality involved in a real investigation, but that does not mean this element should simply be overlooked. For example, Pike et al. (2019) suggest that using live events and real officers working with participants in a policing facility not only increases ecological validity but could lead to greater consequentiality too, simply because the situation might be perceived by participants as being more realistic and that there is more at stake.

The recommendations made by Pike et al. (2019), Sporer et al. (2020), and Tredoux et al. (2021) regarding the need for ecological validity in composite research appear to offer a useful next step for work in this area. In addition to filling gaps in existing research, more realistic methods are also likely to assist in translating results into practice. As well as ecological validity ensuring that research includes as many of the factors present in a police investigation as possible, it is also important for how the research is perceived by law enforcement practitioners. For example, Pike et al. (2021) found that policing practitioners tended to have a negative view of research which used a procedure that did not conform to relevant practice guidelines or that used immediate testing following a staged crime. In addition, they reported that practitioners who had been involved in research indicated that the main barrier to that research being applied to practice was that the research addressed academic, rather than practice, oriented questions.

Have Advances in Composite Technology Affected Eyewitness Identification?

Given the improvement in the facial image and the role of psychology in making the process more of a match for cognition, it seems logical that contemporary systems might interact with memory, and therefore identification accuracy, in a different way to older systems (Pike et al., 2005). For example, having to construct a face feature by feature, which is a poor match for cognition, could well impact memory in a different way to a more holistic construction method. Added to this is the suggestion from Wells et al. (2005) that the inaccuracies and contamination shown by their participants likely resulted "from the process of having to break the face down into individual features to perform the composite building task" (Wells et al., 2005, p. 151).

As well as whether contemporary composite systems designed to complement witness cognition produce better composites, whether they impact identification accuracy is also an important question. Several studies have explored this issue. Davis et al. (2014) compared construction using the latest version of a holistic composite system (EFIT-V) to construction using a piecemeal system (E-FIT) and found that subsequent accuracy on an identification task was superior for both conditions compared to a no-construction control. No significant difference was observed between the EFIT-V and E-FIT conditions. A second experiment also found an improvement in identification accuracy for the EFIT-V condition over a control condition, but a follow-up study (Davis et al., 2015) failed to replicate this effect.

Pike et al. (2020) also looked at whether piecemeal (E-FIT) and holistic (EFIT-V) systems impacted subsequent identification accuracy differentially but used more ecologically valid delays than in the Davis et al. studies, where a gap of 0 to 30 minutes was used between encoding and construction, while that between composite construction and identification was 5 minutes to 32 hours. Even introducing a delay of 2 days between viewing a video of a staged crime and constructing either an E-FIT or EFIT-V or providing a verbal description only (the control condition), and a delay ranging from 11 and 35 days between composite construction and a lineup task, resulted in no significant differences between conditions, although again the trend was for composite construction conditions to lead to greater identification accuracy rather than having a deleterious effect.

In some ways the results of Davis et al. (2015) and Pike et al. (2020) are surprising, given the very different approaches to composite generation that are involved in piecemeal and holistic systems. Moreover, Pike et al. (2020) also evaluated the quality of the composite images, finding that independent judges rated the EFIT-V images as being more accurate likenesses of the target face than the EFIT images. Given that the Davis et al. (2014) experiments did show improved identification accuracy for the composite conditions (albeit for both holistic and piecemeal construction) and used short delays between encoding and retrieval, one possible explanation is that composite construction does improve witness memory, thus leading to more accurate performance at lineup tasks, but only for a short-time period. Mauldin and Laughery (1981) provide some support for this suggestion as they found that the beneficial effect of composite construction on subsequent identification accuracy *decreased* as the delay between construction and lineup *increased*.

An explanation based on the length of delay between encoding and retrieval is also supported by the conclusion drawn by Sporer et al. (2020) that *viewing* a misleading composite can have a negative effect on identification accuracy but only if the composite is seen shortly before the lineup. Although, as Tredoux et al. (2021) state, there is currently insufficient research to offer an evidence-based recommendation for practice, from the studies available it does not look like the technological advances made in facial composite systems have led to an improvement in memory sufficient to impact lineup accuracy, at least not over the time periods that would be involved in a real investigation. As Brace et al. (2006a) concluded, the cognition of the witness (particularly face memory) may be the key limiting factor, and one that could prevent technological advances from making significant improvements to identification accuracy.

Are Composites Different from Other Forms of Post-Event Information

As well as being a question addressed by many psychological experiments, the potential contamination of asking a witness to provide multiple forms of evidence has also been a concern for policy makers. For example, in England and Wales the Police and Criminal Evidence Act (PACE) Codes of Practice state, "Where an eye-witness has previously made an identification by photographs, or a computerized or artist's composite or similar likeness, they must not be reminded of such a photograph or composite likeness once a suspect is available for identification by other means" (PACE, 1984, Code D, revised 2017, Annex A, Section 13). In addition to providing guidance regarding a witness who *creates* a composite and also attends a lineup, they also cover *showing* composite images to any witness involved in the investigation:

> When the use of a computerised or artist's composite or similar likeness has led to there being a known suspect who can be asked to participate in a video identification, appear on an identification parade or participate in a group identification, that likeness shall not be shown to other potential witnesses.
> (PACE, 1984, Code D, revised 2017, Annex E, Section 8)

Although the PACE Codes of Practice do make specific mention of composite images, they group them together with "identification by photographs," which implicitly assumes that creating a composite is a comparable task to that of searching an album of mugshots. Two meta-analyses conducted by Deffenbacher et al. (2006) demonstrate the dangers of an eyewitness seeing a mugshot album prior to a lineup, as exposure to a mugshot significantly increased the false alarm rate (selecting an innocent member of the lineup) as well as decreasing overall accuracy. Simply seeing the album, where neither the perpetrator nor anyone later seen in the lineup were present, did not significantly impair identification accuracy at the lineup and instead the result seems due to a commitment effect, whereby if a witness selects someone from the mugshot album they are likely to also select them in the lineup, regardless of whether they are actually guilty or innocent.

More than 25 years of psychological research has demonstrated the dangers of asking a witness to view a mugshot album and attempt an identification at a lineup, but are mugshot albums and facial composites really that similar? Even *viewing* a composite image is different to seeing a mugshot album for a number of reasons. First and most obvious is that the composite image is not an exact representation of the perpetrator, nor indeed of an innocent suspect seen in a lineup, so cannot lead to the same degree of commitment effect seen with actual photographic mugshots. Second, usually only one composite would be seen by a witness and even where multiple composites exist there would still be far fewer than the number of mugshots seen in an album. Third, the composite image will be a representation (albeit a likely inaccurate one) of the perpetrator seen by the witness, while by looking through a mugshot album a witness will see images of people who are definitely not the perpetrator, even if the guilty suspect is present. Again, this makes it unlikely that the commitment effects reported by Deffenbacher et al. (2006), which involve the veridical representation inherent in a photograph, would operate in the same way.

Although *viewing* composites and mugshots entail important differences, *construction* of a composite is a radically different process. Composite construction would also differ from a mugshot album because the images are based on the perpetrator seen by the witness and will not be exact representations of either guilty or innocent suspects, but there are other key differences.

These differences should lead to composites being less problematic than mugshots if the construction process is unbiased. In other words, even if composite construction does not have a negative impact on witness cognition, it does offer an opportunity for a law enforcement officer to bias that part of the investigation, whether consciously or unconsciously. The NPIA (2009) guidelines on composites acknowledge this possibility and offer suggestions for limiting the possibility of "operator contamination," primarily by stating that the operator (i.e., the officer assisting the witness to construct a composite) should not be given a detailed description of the suspect nor have seen CCTV recordings or other images. In practice this means that the operator cannot be an officer that is part of the investigating team, a practice that is routine in the UK. However, it does then follow that a composite that is created by an officer who has seen a description or image of the suspect should be considered to be biased/contaminated.

Conclusion

Psychological research has been an important component in developing facial composite technology, with contemporary systems using procedures that are a better match for human cognition than earlier approaches, and as a result producing images that are a more accurate likeness of the perpetrator. Research conducted to determine whether viewing or constructing a composite has any impact on subsequent performance on a lineup task has produced equivocal results, with studies as likely to find a positive effect as a negative one. Reviews and meta-analyses of this research have concluded that viewing a composite immediately prior to a lineup may have a negative effect if the lineup was low-similarity and that constructing a composite does not appear to impact lineup accuracy. Importantly, several researchers have also concluded that there is not yet a sufficient body of research, particularly using an ecologically valid approach, to make evidence-based recommendations for practice. This latter point is particularly important given potentially biased investigative methods can lead to misidentification and even a miscarriage of justice of a suspect who was initially investigated because of their similarity to a composite.

References

Attorney General of the State of Wisconsin. (2005). Model policy and procedure for eyewitness identification. Retrieved from https://media.law.wisc.edu/s/c_37/fdfky/ag_model_policy.pdf

Bandy, G., & Hartley, J. (2018). Debate: When spending less causes a problem. *Public Money & Management*, 38(1), 52–54.
Blanz, V., & Vetter, T. (1999, July). A morphable model for the synthesis of 3D faces. In *Proceedings of the 26th annual conference on Computer graphics and interactive techniques* (pp. 187–194).
Boberg, T. (2014). *Fantombillede*. Copenhagen: Gyldendal.
Bockstaele, M. (2009). *Handboek verhoren 2*. Antwerpen: Maklu.
Brace, N., Pike, G. & Kemp, R. (2000). Investigating E-FIT using famous faces. In A. Czerederecka, T. Jaśkiewicz-Obydzińska, & J. Wójcikiewicz (Eds.), *Forensic psychology and law*. Kraków: Institute of Forensic Research Publishers.
Brace, N.A., Pike, G.E., Allen, P. & Kemp, R.I. (2006a). Identifying composites of famous faces: Investigating memory, language and system issues. *Psychology, Crime and Law*, 12, 4, 351–366.
Brace, N., Pike, G., Kemp, R., Turner, J., & Bennett, P. (2006b). Does the presentation of multiple facial composites improve suspect identification? *Applied Cognitive Psychology*, 20(2), 213–226.
Brace, N.A., Pike, G.E., & Turner, J.A. (2008). Holistic facial composite systems: Are they compatible with witness recall? *Cognitive Technology Journal*, 13(2), 42–49.
Bruce, V., Ness, H., Hancock, P.J., Newman, C., & Rarity, J. (2002). Four heads are better than one: Combining face composites yields improvements in face likeness. *Journal of Applied Psychology*, 87(5), 894.
Bruce, V., Hancock, P.J., & Burton, A.M. (1998). Human face perception and identification. In H. Wechsler, P.J. Phillips, V. Bruce, F.F. Soulié, and T.S. Huang (Eds.), *Face recognition*, 51–72. Berlin: Springer.
Bruce, V., Ness, H., Hancock, P.J., Newman, C., & Rarity, J. (2002). Four heads are better than one: Combining face composites yields improvements in face likeness. *Journal of Applied Psychology*, 87(5), 894.
Brunelli, R., & Mich, O. (1996). SpotIt! an interactive identikit system. *Graphical Models and Image Processing*, 58(5), 399–404.
Calder, A.J., & Young, A.W. (2005). Understanding the recognition of facial identity and facial expression. *Nature Reviews Neuroscience*, 6(8), 641–651.
Collishaw, S.M., & Hole, G.J. (2000). Featural and configurational processes in the recognition of faces of different familiarity. *Perception*, 29(8), 893–909.
Comish, S.E. (1987). Recognition of facial stimuli following an intervening task involving the Identi-kit. *Journal of Applied Psychology*, 72(3), 488–491. (doi:10.1037/0021-9010.72.3.488)
Cutler, B.L., Stocklein, C.J. and Penrod, S.D. (1988). An empirical examination of a computerized facial composite production system. *Forensic Reports*, 1, 207–218.
Davies, G.M., Ellis, H.C., & Shepherd, J. (1978). Face identification: The influence of delay upon accuracy of photofit construction. *Journal of Police Science & Administration*, 6(1), 35–42.
Davies, G.M., Milne, A. & Shepherd, J.W., (1983). Searching for operator skills in face composite reproduction. *Journal of Police Science and Administration*, 11, 405–409.

Davies, G.M., & Young, A.W. (2017). Research on face recognition: The Aberdeen influence. *British Journal of Psychology*, *108*(4), 812–830.

Davies, G.M., Shepherd, J.W., Shepherd, J., Flin R., & Ellis, H.D. (1986). Training skills in police Photofit operators. *Policing*, 2, 35–46.

Davies, G., Van der Willik, P., & Morrison, L.J. (2000). Facial composite production: A comparison of mechanical and computer-driven systems. *Journal of Applied Psychology*, 85(1), 119.

Davis, J.P., Gibson, S., & Solomon, C. (2014). The positive influence of creating a holistic facial composite on video line-up identification. *Applied Cognitive Psychology*, 28(5), 634–639. doi:10.1002/acp.3045

Davis, J.P., Thorniley, S., Gibson, S., & Solomon, C. (2015). Holistic facial composite construction and subsequent lineup identification accuracy: Comparing adults and children. *The Journal of Psychology*, 1–20. (doi:10.1080/00223980.2015.1009867)

Deffenbacher, K.A., Bornstein, B.H., & Penrod, S.D. (2006). Mugshot exposure effects: Retroactive interference, mugshot commitment, source confusion, and unconscious transference. *Law and Human Behavior*, 30(3), 287–307.

Dekle, D.J. (2006). Viewing composite sketches: Lineups and showups compared. *Applied Cognitive Psychology*, 20(3), 383–395. (doi:10.1002/acp.1185)

Ellis, H. D., Davies, G. M., & Shepherd, J. W. (1978). A critical examination of the Photofit system for recalling faces. *Ergonomics*, 21(4), 297–307.

Ellis, H.D., Shepherd, J.W., & Davies, G.M. (1975). An investigation of the use of the Photofit technique for recalling faces. *British Journal of Psychology*, 66, 29–37.

Fisher, R.P., & Geiselman, R.E. (1992). *Memory enhancing techniques for investigative interviewing: The cognitive interview*. Charles C Thomas Publisher.

Frowd, C.D., Bruce, V., Smith, A., & Hancock, P.J.B. (2008). Improving the quality of facial composites using a holistic cognitive interview. *Journal of Experimental Psychology: Applied*, 14, 276–287. DOI: 10.1037/1076-898X.14.3.276

Frowd, C.D., Carson, D., Ness, H., McQuiston-Surrett, D., Richardson, J., Baldwin, H., & Hancock, P. (2005a). Contemporary composite techniques: The impact of a forensically-relevant target delay. *Legal and Criminological Psychology*, 10(1), 63–81.

Frowd, C.D., Carson, D., Ness, H., Richardson, J., Morrison, L., Mclanaghan, S., & Hancock, P. (2005b). A forensically valid comparison of facial composite systems. *Psychology, Crime & Law*, 11(1), 33–52.

Frowd, C.D., Erickson, W.B., Lampinen, J.M., Skelton, F.C., McIntyre, A.H., & Hancock, P.J. (2015). A decade of evolving composites: regression-and meta-analysis. *Journal of Forensic Practice*, 17, 319–334.

Frowd, C.D., Hancock, P.J., & Carson, D. (2004). EvoFIT: A holistic, evolutionary facial imaging technique for creating composites. *ACM Transactions on Applied Perception (TAP)*, 1(1), 19–39.

Frowd, C.D., Pitchford, M., Bruce, V., Jackson, S., Hepton, G., Greenall, M., McIntyre, A., & Hancock, P.J.B. (2010). "The psychology of face construction: giving evolution a helping hand." *Applied Cognitive Psychology*. 25(2): 195–203. (doi:10.1002/acp.1662)

Frowd, C.D., Skelton, F., Atherton, C., Pitchford, M., Hepton, G., Holden, L., McIntyre, A., & Hancock, P.J.B. (2012). "Recovering faces from memory: the distracting influence of external facial features." *Journal of Experimental Psychology: Applied.* 18 (2): 224–238. (doi:10.1037/a0027393)

Giannou, K., Frowd, C.D., Taylor, J.R., & Lander, K. (2021). Mindfulness in face recognition: Embedding mindfulness instructions in the face-composite construction process. *Applied Cognitive Psychology,* 35(4), 999–1010.

Gibling, F., & Bennett, P. (1994). Artistic enhancement in the production of Photo-FIT likenesses: An examination of its effectiveness in leading to suspect identification. *Psychology, Crime and Law,* 1(1), 93–100.

Gibling, F., & Davies, G. (1988). Reinstatement of context following exposure to post-event information. *British Journal of Psychology,* 79(1), 129–141. (doi:10.1111/j.2044-8295.1988.tb02278.x)

Gibson, S.J., Solomon, C.J. and Pallares-Bejarano, A. 2003. "Synthesis of Photographic Quality Facial Composites using Evolutionary Algorithms." In R. Harvey and J.A. Bangham (eds), *Proceedings of the British Machine Vision Conference 2003* 1: 221–230.

Hancock, P.J. (2000). Evolving faces from principal components. *Behavior Research Methods, Instruments, & Computers,* 32(2), 327–333.

Home Office (1969). *Use of Identikits. A Note on Facial Identification Techniques,* Aug. 1969, Home Office Police Research and Development Branch, Research Note 10/69, TNA, HO 377/73.

Ihlebæk, C., Løve, T., Eilertsen, D.E., & Magnussen, S. (2003). Memory for a staged criminal event witnessed live and on video. *Memory,* 11, 319–327. (doi:10.1080/09658210244000018)

Innocence Project. (2017a). *DNA Exonerations in the United States.* Retrieved from www.innocenceproject.org/dna-exonerations-in-the-united-states/

Innocence Project. (2017b). *Kirk Bloodsworth.* Retrieved from www.innocenceproject.org/cases/kirk-bloodsworth/

Jenkins, F., & Davies, G. (1985). Contamination of facial memory through exposure to misleading composite pictures. *Journal of Applied Psychology,* 70(1), 164–176. (doi:10.1037/0021-9010.70.1.164)

Johnson, M.K., Hashtroudi, S., & Lindsay, D. S. (1993). Source monitoring. *Psychological Bulletin,* 114(1), 3.

Junkin, T. (2004). *Bloodsworth: The true story of the first death row inmate exonerated by DNA.* Chapel Hill, NC: Algonquin Books.

Kempen, K., & Tredoux, C.G. (2012). "Seeing is believing": The effect of viewing and constructing a composite on identification performance. *South African Journal of Psychology,* 42(3), 434–444.

King, D. (1971). The use of Photo-FIT 1970–71: A progress report. *Police Research Bulletin,* 18, 40–45.

Kitson, A., Darnbrough, M., & Shields, E. (1978). Let's face it. Police Research Bulletin, no. 30, pp. 7–13.

Koehn, C.E. & Fisher, R.P. (1997). Constructing facial composites with the Mac-A-Mug Pro System. *Psychology, Crime and Law,* 3, 209–218.

Kovera, M.B., Penrod, S.D., Pappas, C. & Thill, D.L. (1997). Identification of computer-generated facial composites. *Journal of Applied Psychology,* 82, 235–246.

Laughery, K.R., Duval, G.C. & Fowler, R.H. (1977). An analysis of procedures for generating facial images. *Mug File Project Report Number UHMUG-2*. University of Houston, Texas.

Laughery, K.R. & Fowler, R.H., (1980). Sketch artist and Identikit procedures for recalling faces. *Journal of Applied Psychology*, 65, 307–316.

Lawrence, P. (2020). Policing, "Science" and the Curious Case of Photo-FIT. *The Historical Journal*, 63(4), 1007–1031.

Lindsay, R.C.L., Nosworthy, G.J., Martin, R., & Martynuck, C. (1994). Using mug shots to find suspects. *Journal of Applied Psychology*, 79(1), 121–130. (doi:10.1037/0021-9010.79.1.121)

Loftus, E.F., & Greene, E. (1980). Warning: Even memory for faces may be contagious. *Law and Human Behavior*, 4(4), 323–334. (doi:10.1007/BF01040624)

Mauldin, M.A., & Laughery, K.R. (1981). Composite production effects on subsequent facial recognition. *Journal of Applied Psychology*, 66(3), 351–357. (doi:10.1037/0021-9010.66.3.351)

McClure, K.A., & Shaw, J.S., III. (2002). Participants' free-hand drawings of a target face can influence recognition accuracy and the confidence–accuracy correlation. *Applied Cognitive Psychology*, 16(4), 387–405. (doi:10.1002/acp.802)

McNamara, J.M. (2009). Sketchy eyewitness-identification procedures: A proposal to draw up legal guidelines for the use of facial composites in criminal investigations. *Wisconsin Law Review*, 763–800.

McQuiston-Surrett, D., Douglass, A.B., & Burkhardt, S.G. (2008). Evaluation of facial composite evidence depends on the presence of other case factors. *Legal and Criminological Psychology*, 13(2), 279–298.

Meissner, C.A., & Brigham, J.C. (2001). A meta-analysis of the verbal overshadowing effect in face identification. *Applied Cognitive Psychology*, 15(6), 603–616. (doi:10.1002/acp.728)

Munger, D. (2006, September 27). When crime-fighting tools go bad: Problems with the face-composite system. *Cognitive Daily*. Retrieved from https://scienceblogs.com/cognitivedaily/2006/09/27/when-crimefighting-tools-go-ba

Ness, H., Hancock, P.J., Bowie, L., Bruce, V., & Pike, G. (2015). Are two views better than one? Investigating three-quarter view facial composites. *Journal of Forensic Practice*, 7(4), 291–306.

NPIA. (2009). Facial identification guidance. Retrieved from https://library.college.police.uk/docs/acpo/facial-identification-guidance-2009.pdf (accessed January 20, 2020).

O'Toole, A.J., & Thompson, J.L. (1993). An X Windows tool for synthesizing face images from eigenvectors. *Behavior Research Methods, Instruments, & Computers*, 25(1), 41–47.

PACE. (1984). *Police and Criminal Evidence Act, Code D, Revised 2017: Code of Practice for the identification of persons by Police Officers*. London: TSO.

Paine, C.B., Pike, G.E., Brace, N.A., & Westcott, H.L. (2008). Children making faces: the effect of age and prompts on children's facial composites of unfamiliar faces. *Applied Cognitive Psychology*, 22(4), 455–474.

Penry, J. (1952). *How to judge character from the face*. London: Hutchinson.

Pike, G. (2007). Suspect Identification in the 21st Century: New Issues but Old Problems? Symposium at *The 7th Conference of the Society for Applied Research in Memory and Cognition*, Maine.

Pike, G. (2009). Improving the accuracy of visual and eyewitness evidence. Symposium at *The 8th Biennial Conference of the Society for Applied Research in Memory and Cognition*, Kyoto, Japan.

Pike, G., Brace, N. & Kynan, S. (2002). *The visual identification of suspects: procedures and practice*. London: Policing and Reducing Crime Unit, Home Office Research, Development and Statistics Directorate.

Pike, G.E., Brace, N.A., Turner, J. & Kynan, S. (2005) Making faces with computers: Witness cognition and technology. *Pragmatics and Cognition, Special Issue: Cognition and Technology*, 13(3), 459–480.

Pike, G.E., Brace, N.A., Turner, J., & Vredeveldt, A. (2019). The effect of facial composite construction on eyewitness identification accuracy in an ecologically valid paradigm. *Criminal Justice and Behavior*, 46(2), 319–336.

Pike, G.E., Brace, N.A., Turner, J., & Vredeveldt, A. (2020). Advances in facial composite technology, utilizing holistic construction, do not lead to an increase in eyewitness misidentifications compared to older feature-based systems. *Frontiers in Psychology: Forensic and Legal Psychology*, 10.

Pike, G. & Clark, C. (2018). Identification Evidence. In A. Griffiths & R. Milne (Eds.), *The psychology of criminal investigation: From theory to practice*, pp. 133–153. Abingdon: Routledge.

Pike, G., Havard, C., Harrison, G., & Ness, H. (2021). Eyewitness identification procedures: Do researchers and practitioners share the same goals? *International Journal of Police Science & Management*, 23(1), 17–28.

Pike, G., Kemp, R. and Brace, N. (2000) The psychology of human face recognition. *IEE Electronics and Communications: Visual Biometrics*, 18, 12/1–12/6.

Purcell, D.G., & Stewart, A.L. (1986). The face-detection effect. *Bulletin of the Psychonomic Society*, 24(2), 118–120.

Roth, M. (2007, March 25). Why police composites don't always hit mark. *Pittsburgh Post-Gazette*. Retrieved from https://www.post-gazette.com/news/nation/2007/03/25/Why-police-composites-don-t-always-hit-mark/stories/200703250152

Sirovich, L., & Kirby, M. (1987). Low-dimensional procedure for the characterization of human faces. *Josa a*, 4(3), 519–524.

Skelton, F.C., Frowd, C.D., Hancock, P.J., Jones, H.S., Jones, B.C., Fodarella, C., ... & Logan, K. (2020). Constructing identifiable composite faces: The importance of cognitive alignment of interview and construction procedure. *Journal of Experimental Psychology: Applied*, 26(3), 507.

Sporer, S.L. (1996). Experimentally induced person mix-ups through media exposure and ways to avoid them. In G. Davies, S.M.A. Lloyd-Bostock, M. McMurran, & C.D. Wilson (Eds.), *Psychology, law, and criminal justice: International developments in research and practice*. Berlin: Walter de Gruyter.

Sporer, S.L., Tredoux, C.G., Vredeveldt, A., Kempen, K., & Nortje, A. (2020). Does exposure to facial composites damage eyewitness memory? A comprehensive review. *Applied Cognitive Psychology*, 34(5), 1166–1179.

Tanaka, J.W., & Farah, M.J. (1993). Parts and wholes in face recognition. *The Quarterly Journal of Experimental Psychology*, 46(2), 225–245.

Topp-Manriquez, L.D., McQuiston, D., & Malpass, R.S. (2014). Facial composites and the misinformation effect: How composites distort memory. *Legal and Criminological Psychology*, Advance online publication. doi:10.1111/lcrp.12054

Tredoux, C.G., Sporer, S.L., Vredeveldt, A., Kempen, K., & Nortje, A. (2021). Does constructing a facial composite affect eyewitness memory? A research synthesis and meta-analysis. *Journal of Experimental Criminology*, 17(4), 713–741.

Trenary, A.D. (2013). State v. Henderson: A model for admitting eyewitness identification testimony. *University of Colorado Law Review*, 84, 1257–1304.

Ward, G., (2022). Rehearsal Processes. In: *Oxford Handbook of Human Memory, Volume I: Foundations*. Editors: Kahana, MJ. and Wagner, AD., Oxford University Press

Wells, G.L., Charman, S.D., & Olson, E.A. (2005). Building face composites can harm lineup identification performance. *Journal of Experimental Psychology: Applied*, 11(3), 147–156. doi:10.1037/1076-898x.11.3.147

Wilford, M.M., & Wells, G.L. (2010). Does facial processing prioritize change detection? Change blindness illustrates costs and benefits of holistic processing. *Psychological Science*, 21(11), 1611–1615.

Yu, C.J., & Geiselman, R.E. (1993). Effects of constructing identi-kit composites on photospread identification performance. *Criminal Justice and Behavior*, 20(3), 280–292. doi:10.1177/0093854893020003005

Zaragoza, M.S., Belli, R.F., & Payment, K.E. (2007). Misinformation effects and the suggestibility of eyewitness memory. In M. Garry & H. Hayne (Eds.), *Do justice and let the sky fall: Elizabeth F. Loftus and her contributions to science, law, and academic freedom* (pp. 35–63). New Jersey: Erlbaum.

10 Technological Advances in the Administration of Lineups

Tia C. Bennett, Madeleine P. Ingham, Melissa F. Colloff, Harriet M. J. Smith, and Heather D. Flowe

Lineups are routinely used by police forces all over the world as a technique to collect identification evidence from an eyewitness (Fitzgerald et al., 2021). When someone witnesses a crime, they may be asked by the police to attempt to identify the perpetrator from a lineup. This lineup will contain the police suspect and multiple fillers. Fillers are individuals who look similar to the police suspect but who are known by the police to be innocent of the crime in question. The standard number of fillers varies across different countries (e.g., five fillers in the US: Technical Working Group for Eyewitness Evidence, 1999; eight fillers in the UK: Police and Criminal Evidence Act, 1984). Lineup methods employed by law enforcement vary globally; however, the overall process remains similar: eyewitnesses are shown a group of individuals, including a person suspected by the police of committing the crime. The witness must determine if the perpetrator is in the lineup and identify them if present. Accuracy depends on the perpetrator's presence and the witness's decision. In a target-present lineup, outcomes involve the witness correctly identifying the perpetrator, selecting a filler, or incorrectly rejecting the lineup (Clark et al., 2008). In a target-absent lineup, outcomes include the witness mistakenly identifying an innocent suspect or a filler, or correctly rejecting the lineup (Clark et al., 2008). An incorrect decision can result in the perpetrator remaining at large, or even a wrongful conviction of a mistakenly identified person. Incorrect decisions carry considerable human and financial costs, so it is essential to develop and enact lineup procedures that maximize discrimination accuracy, or the witness's ability to distinguish guilty from innocent suspects.

The Innocence Project is a US-based organization that aims to exonerate those who have been wrongfully convicted with the use of DNA evidence. They have worked to exonerate numerous individuals (Innocence Project, 2022b). Take Antonio Beaver, for example, who was sentenced to 18 years in prison for a carjacking he did not commit (Innocence Project, 2022c). The victim of the carjacking identified Antonio from an unfair live lineup.

DOI: 10.4324/9781003323112-12

The lineup was unfair because it contained four individuals—two of them police officers—and, crucially, Antonio was the only person in the lineup to have a distinctive feature like the one mentioned in the victim's description of the perpetrator. The victim recalled that the perpetrator had a gap between his teeth, and Antonio had chipped teeth. The victim also mentioned a baseball cap in their perpetrator description, and only two members of the lineup wore baseball caps—one of them was Antonio. Antonio was exonerated in 2007 after DNA testing proved that he was not the perpetrator, and the real perpetrator was identified as a man who was already incarcerated for other crimes. Antonio had served over 10 years in prison before he was exonerated. Unfortunately, Antonio Beaver is not a lone case. Around 70% of exoneree cases involve some form of eyewitness misidentification or misleading eyewitness evidence (Innocence Project, 2022a). It should be noted, however, that it is not possible to extrapolate from these cases the eyewitness identification accuracy rate or the conditions that affect accuracy. The cases were not randomly sampled. Further, to determine accuracy, we would have to know how often police lineups contain guilty suspects and how often witnesses make correct as well as incorrect identifications.

To better understand the conditions that affect identification accuracy, researchers conduct experiments with mock witnesses (i.e., participants acting as witnesses in research). Research suggests that participants make an incorrect identification decision (i.e., fail to identify the perpetrator when they are in the lineup *or* fail to reject the lineup when the perpetrator is not present in the lineup) around half of the time (Fitzgerald et al., 2018; Wells et al., 2016). In other words, the rate of accuracy in mock witness studies is around 50%, which exceeds chance performance, which is nearly 17% in a 6-person lineup. Importantly, laboratory studies vary in the extent to which they reflect real world witnessing conditions. Hence, accuracy rates from laboratory studies cannot be readily generalized to real world cases. For example, the median duration of exposure to the culprit is less than 30 seconds, and the median retention interval between the crime and the lineup test is 20 minutes in laboratory studies (Flowe, Carline, & Kragolu, 2018). These factors can affect memory strength and vary in real world cases. Nevertheless, the results of laboratory research indicate that people can make identification errors, and with accuracy being around 50%, research suggests there is much room for improvement. Therefore, it is imperative that researchers and police practitioners work together to improve eyewitness identification performance.

An optimal lineup procedure would be one that maximizes correct identifications of guilty suspects in target-present lineups while minimizing false identifications of innocent suspects in target-absent lineups. In other words, the procedure should maximize the witness's ability to tell the difference between innocent and guilty suspects, also known as *discriminability* (Wixted & Mickes, 2014). So, what are the different procedures, and which one is "optimal'? When thinking about police lineups, people usually picture a scene from a crime-related TV show or movie (*CSI* or *The Usual Suspects*, for example), with several individuals lined up in a row against a "mugshot wall," with the witness being asked to identify the perpetrator from the line of people. This traditional method of eyewitness identification, a "live" lineup, is rarely used in the US and UK in the present day.

Technology has advanced a long way since lineup procedures began, and lineup procedures have advanced with it, albeit to a limited extent. In the sections that follow, we discuss how the conduct of lineups has changed over time and the studies that have compared eyewitness performance across different procedures. We conclude by discussing what the next generation of police lineups might look like.

The History (and Future) of Police Lineups

Figure 10.1 offers an overview of the history of technological developments in the administration of eyewitness identification procedures. It is

Figure 10.1 Historical overview of technological developments in the administration of eyewitness identification procedures.

difficult to pinpoint the date and circumstance of the first police lineup in history, but in the UK, Home Office records dating back to 1905 describe guidelines for conducting lineups (termed "identification parades" in the UK) in England and Wales (Devlin, 1976). Further, the same report (the "Devlin" report) traces the first record of a police lineup conducted by the Metropolitan Police back to March 1860, indicating that they were occurring in the late 19th century, if not earlier. Appendix A of the Home Office report (Devlin, 1976) outlines that the original 1905 guidelines were amended in 1925, 1926, 1929, and 1969, and the procedural guidance presented in the Devlin report reflects the 1969 revisions in their final form. These 1969 guidelines specifically refer to live lineups, which involve in-person witness viewings, with the suspect (or multiple suspects, in some cases) standing in a line with fillers who match their physical description (Fitzgerald et al., 2018). Although live lineups were reported decades ago, 51 countries across the world still describe a live lineup procedure in official guidance, and 25 of those countries illustrate a preference for live lineups over other methods (Fitzgerald et al., 2021).

Alternatively, some police forces across the world use photographs rather than live procedures. In a photo lineup, static images of the suspect and fillers are presented, and lineup members are depicted in a frontal pose from the shoulders up (Fitzgerald et al., 2018). Photo lineups are the preferred identification procedure in the United States and are used by over 90% of police forces in the US (Police Executive Research Forum, 2013). In the US, these photo lineups typically contain one suspect along with five fillers, and the six static photographs are presented simultaneously, with witnesses able to make their identification decision at any time (Police Executive Research Forum, 2013).

Another method of identification that often involves using face photographs is a "showup," whereby the witness is presented with an image of a single individual who is the suspect (Steblay et al., 2003). Photographic showups are common practice in some places such as the US but are not permitted in England and Wales (Valentine et al., 2012). Instead, in England and Wales, showups take the form of a live identification task, also known as a "street identification." In these cases, the witness is typically driven around the area of the crime shortly after it has been committed to see if they are able to identify the perpetrator (Valentine et al., 2012).

In the UK, video lineups are typically used rather than photo lineups. Video lineups contain 15-second recordings of everyone in the lineup. In these clips, the lineup member looks straight ahead (frontal pose), then turns their head to the left (right profile), turns their head to the right (left profile), and finally, returns to frontal pose (Memon et al., 2011). In accordance with the Police and Criminal Evidence Act, Code D 2017 (Police and Criminal Evidence Act, 1984), video lineups typically contain eight fillers, and one police suspect, and each lineup member recording is presented sequentially, one at a time. Lineups with two suspects and 12 fillers are also permitted but appear to be less common in practice (Bennett et al., 2023). All eyewitnesses are presented with at least two viewing laps of the 9-person sequential lineup before making their final identification decision (Police and Criminal Evidence Act, 1984). There are two main systems used to facilitate the video recordings of suspects and fillers and enable the creation video lineups in the UK: the National VIPER Bureau system (www.viper.police.uk) and PROMAPS (www.promatenvision.co.uk). Each system has its own database of recordings; PROMAPS presents lineup members against a green background, while VIPER presents members against a grey background. Further, users of the VIPER service send in requests for a lineup to be created, but users of the PROMAPS system create the lineups themselves.

Although live, photo, and video procedures have been the primary ways in which lineups have been conducted for decades, lineups have been evolving over time and in line with research developments and, to some degree, with technological advancements. New techniques have been developed for adult eyewitnesses, such as the paired comparison procedure (Gepshtein et al., 2021), and the confidence judgement procedure (Brewer et al., 2020; Albright & Rakoff, 2020) as well as for child eyewitnesses, such as the elimination lineup procedure (Pozzulo & Lindsay, 1999). Alongside these advances, a suite of interactive lineup procedures has recently been developed. In an interactive lineup, the witness can interact with all lineup member images using their computer mouse to rotate and view the faces at any angle (Colloff et al., 2021). An interactive lineup can be administered sequentially, or simultaneously, with the witness able to move each face independently or all of the faces together in the same manner jointly. This procedure exemplifies how far technology has advanced in relation to lineup procedures, and despite its novelty, research to date suggests that the interactive lineup could provide a promising future in terms of increasing the accuracy of eyewitness identification. This procedure will be discussed in-depth later in the chapter.

Lineup Procedure Research

As explained above, there are various lineup types which differ in medium (e.g., live, photo, video, interactive) and in presentation (simultaneous, sequential, showup). But which procedure optimizes eyewitness performance? For decades, eyewitness memory researchers have used controlled laboratory experiments to investigate which lineup identification procedure is superior for eyewitness performance (for a review, see Flowe et al., 2018). This body of research has influenced current best practice lineup procedures, with multiple agencies and police forces striving for evidence-based guidelines to steer the creation and administration of police lineups (National Research Council, 2014).

Lineup research usually involves recruiting participants to act as mock-witnesses. Typically, participants will be asked to watch a mock crime video depicting a staged crime such as a theft or a robbery (this is the "encoding" stage). Once the crime has been viewed by the participant, there is often a break or filler task (e.g., a word search, maths questions, a short game, etc.) to create a delay between witnessing the crime and being presented with a lineup. The lineup task is also known as the "test" stage. The reason for the delay between the encoding and test stages is to emulate the journey of a real eyewitness who would also experience a delay between witnessing the crime and viewing a lineup. However, despite the attempt to replicate a witness's journey from the crime to the identification procedure, lineup research often uses much shorter delays than those that would occur in real life. Flowe et al. (2018) found that the median time between witnessing a real crime and attending a lineup in one jurisdiction in the US was 11 days, but the average (median) time delay in lineup research is 20 minutes. Similarly, Horry et al. (2012) conducted a field study to analyze the outcomes of 1039 lineups in the UK and found that there was a median delay of 31 days between the crime and the lineup viewing. Although this might seem concerning for the application of research to real procedures, some studies show that the length of delay between the mock-crime and the lineup viewing does not necessarily harm identification accuracy. For example, in a laboratory experiment, Valentine et al. (2012) compared identification accuracy (i.e., correct identifications and false identifications) between lineups conducted within one week of encoding (less than 7 days) and one month of encoding (between 7 and 28 days) and found that length of delay did not have a statistically significant effect on eyewitness performance in either target-present or target-absent lineups. Additionally, Wetmore et al. (2015) found that when mock eyewitnesses were presented with a lineup either immediately or 7 days after witnessing the crime video, retention interval (length of delay) had little effect on correct or false identification rates. Also, and perhaps most importantly, laboratory studies comparing different lineup procedures are typically interested in which procedure best improves witness performance (e.g., if video lineups are better than photo lineups), and there is often no theoretical reason to predict that a procedure which best enhances performance after a short delay would impair performance at a longer delay, though of course, that is an empirical question that could be tested.

Returning to the standard lineup research procedure, after a short delay, participants are then presented with either a target-present lineup (i.e., containing the guilty suspect), or a target-absent lineup (i.e., containing an innocent suspect), and are asked to identify the perpetrator from the lineup if they are present. It is standard procedure both in real police lineups and in research to include a statement in the lineup instructions which indicates to the witness (or participant) that the perpetrator may or may not be in the lineup (Malpass & Devine, 1981; National Research Council, 2014). This is known as an unbiased instruction and is designed to combat any preconceived notions that the witness may hold and prevent them from identifying someone simply because they think the real perpetrator must be present. As mentioned previously, target-present lineups can result in a correct identification, a filler identification, or an incorrect lineup rejection, and target-absent lineups can result in a false identification, a filler identification, or a correct lineup rejection.

Once the participant has made their lineup decision, they are typically asked to provide a confidence judgement for their decision, usually in the form of a Likert-type scale, for example, from 0% confident (i.e., guessing) to 100% confident (i.e., certain). Research has repeatedly demonstrated that there is typically a strong, positive relationship between confidence and eyewitness accuracy. That is, identification decisions made with high confidence are usually indicative of suspect guilt (for a summary of the confidence-accuracy relationship in eyewitness research, see Wixted & Wells, 2017).

Comparing Video, Photo, and Live Lineups

Using the experimental procedure above, many researchers have compared the accuracy of different lineup procedures. More specifically, research typically measures which procedure increases correct identification decisions (i.e., correct identifications of the perpetrator in target-present lineups and correct rejections in target absent lineups) and discriminability (i.e., the witnesses' ability to distinguish between innocent and guilty suspects). Interestingly, the results of these studies are inconsistent (for reviews see Cutler et al., 1994; Fitzgerald et al., 2018). Some researchers have found that video lineups are better than photo lineups for eyewitness performance (e.g., Cutler & Fisher, 1990; Sussman et al., 1972; Valentine et al., 2007), some find that photo lineups are better than video lineups (e.g., Darling et al., 2008), and others find that lineup performance is the same across both mediums (e.g., Beresford & Blades, 2006; Seale-Carlisle et al., 2019). Similarly, some researchers find that live presentations are superior to both photo lineups (Cutler & Fisher, 1990; Kerstholt et al., 2004) and video lineups (Kerstholt et al., 2004), and others find that there is no significant difference in performance between video versus live (Cutler et al., 1989; Cutler & Fisher, 1990; Rubínová et al., 2021) nor photo versus live (Rubínová et al., 2021). However, if these studies *did* find a benefit of one method, it was very often only a small difference. It is evident then that there is no overwhelming consensus about the "optimal" method of conducting lineups when looking across photo, video, and live lineup techniques.

Simultaneous vs Sequential (vs Showups)

Another way in which lineups can vary is the presentation style of the lineup members. In the case of US photo lineups, six static images of the lineup members are often presented all at once to the witness (i.e., simultaneous presentation). However, in some US jurisdictions the photos are presented one at a time (i.e., sequential presentation) and witnesses are asked to make a yes or no decision to each face (Technical Working Group for Eyewitness Evidence, 1999). A survey conducted in 2011-2012 revealed that around 30% of 547 police agencies in the US use a sequential photo lineup procedure (Police Executive Research Forum, 2013). While UK video lineups also use a sequential presentation, a different approach is adopted: the nine 15-second video clips are presented one after the other (i.e., sequential presentation), and once all nine lineup members have been presented, they are all presented again in a second viewing lap before the witness can make their identification decision (Code D—Police and Criminal Evidence Act, 1984). Photo showups present only one image to the witness and live shows present only one person, which is a different presentation style altogether since fillers are not used, which may affect how witnesses make their identification decision.

In more recent years, research about lineup presentation methods (i.e., simultaneous versus sequential) usually finds that the simultaneous presentation method is optimal for both eyewitness identification accuracy and discriminability compared to the sequential presentation method (e.g., simultaneous versus US sequential: Amendola & Wixted, 2015; Carlson & Carlson, 2014; Dobolyi & Dodson, 2013; simultaneous versus UK sequential: Seale-Carlisle et al., 2019). Despite this consensus, it is also important to discuss the opposing viewpoint that was dominant for some time—the sequential superiority argument. This argument is based on the finding that, while sequential lineups often reduce the number of correct guilty suspect identifications compared to simultaneous lineups, they reduce the false identification rate of innocent suspects to a greater extent (Steblay et al., 2011). However, laboratory research shows there are typically lower choosing rates in sequential lineups compared to simultaneous lineups (Steblay et al., 2001), and this may explain why there are fewer false (and correct) identifications in sequential lineups. Amendola and Wixted (2015) conducted a field study and found that choosing rates in both procedures are often similar in real life, and in this study, the sequential lineup resulted in a *higher* false identification rate than the simultaneous lineup. To summarize the simultaneous versus sequential argument, research seems to indicate that simultaneous lineups yield an increased ability for eyewitnesses to discriminate between guilty and innocent suspects (e.g., see Seale-Carlisle et al., 2019 for a mini meta-analysis). However, some researchers argue that since the sequential procedure can reduce false identifications (while also reducing correct identifications), it should be the preferred method.

Regarding the "showup" procedure, it is widely accepted within the literature that showups are suggestive and can lead to an increase in false identification rates and a decrease in discriminability compared to lineup procedures (Akan et al., 2020; Clark, 2012; Key et al., 2015; Mickes, 2015). More specifically, simultaneous lineups have been found to yield better lineup performance (i.e., enhanced discriminability) than showups (Colloff & Wixted, 2019; Gronlund et al., 2012; Neuschatz et al., 2016; Wooten et al., 2020), but research into sequential lineups versus showups has produced more mixed results. Some studies have found that there are no significant differences in overall performance between sequential lineups and showups (Gronlund et al., 2012; Wilson et al., 2019), while others find that there *is* a significant difference, but it is dependent upon suspect position in the lineup (Neuschatz et al., 2016). If a suspect is presented first in a sequential lineup, and witnesses are required to make a yes/no decision to each face, then this essentially becomes a showup for the first face. Position effects in sequential lineups are, however, complex (e.g., owing to similarity and shifts in response bias across the faces, see Wilson et al., 2019 for a discussion).

Theoretical Perspectives

One theory used to explain the superiority of simultaneous lineups compared to sequential lineups and lineups compared to showups is the diagnostic-feature-detection theory (Wixted & Mickes, 2014). This theory is based upon the notion that there are diagnostic and non-diagnostic features on the faces in a lineup. Diagnostic features are features which are unique to the perpetrator, and are therefore diagnostic of guilt, while non-diagnostic features are shared by either all members in the lineup (e.g., those features included in the witness description and used to select the lineup members), or by innocent and guilty suspects, and are therefore not useful for identifying the guilty suspect. When eyewitnesses have access to more diagnostic features, and rely less on non-diagnostic features, they should be better able to tell the difference between the perpetrator and the other lineup members (Wixted & Mickes, 2014; Wixted et al., 2018).

Simultaneous lineups show all lineup members at once, while sequential lineups show lineup members one after the other, in a sequence. Diagnostic-feature-detection theory (Wixted & Mickes, 2014) proposes that simultaneous lineups improve witnesses' ability to discriminate innocent from guilty suspects because they allow witnesses to compare across all faces and discount the non-diagnostic features (e.g., White male, brown hair, short hair, clean shaven), and therefore focus on the diagnostic features (e.g., wide nose, thick eyebrows, square face) to identify the perpetrator. Contrastingly, sequential lineups do not allow for a simultaneous comparison of features, so it is theoretically more difficult to discount non-diagnostic features in eyewitness decision making. Further, the diagnostic-feature-detection theory has also been used to explain why lineups (particularly simultaneous lineups) produce enhanced ability to discriminate between innocent and guilty suspects compared to showups. It has been argued that showups, unlike lineups, do not allow for comparison of features across faces, either diagnostic or non-diagnostic (Colloff & Wixted, 2019).

Can diagnostic-feature-detection theory also help to guide our thinking about the effect of different lineup procedures on eyewitness performance? As discussed in the previous section, discrimination accuracy (i.e., the ability to discriminate between innocent and guilty suspects) does not typically vary across video, photo, and live lineups. However, from a theoretical standpoint, this is a very surprising finding. Diagnostic-feature-detection theory posits that discrimination accuracy should be improved by adopting lineup procedures which reduce the number of non-diagnostic features and increase the number of diagnostic features available for the eyewitness to use. Since video lineups allow witnesses to view all angles of the face and therefore potentially more diagnostic features (frontal view and profile view), they should yield enhanced discrimination accuracy compared to photo lineups, which only allow for a frontal view of the lineup faces. The prediction that video lineups should yield enhanced performance compared to photo lineups is also supported by further research and theories within the field of face recognition.

The face recognition literature is useful for understanding how faces are encoded and remembered. Using this literature, three key insights have emerged which can be used to guide how lineups should be created and conducted to maximize eyewitness accuracy. Firstly, the representation enhancement hypothesis indicates that movement of faces is beneficial to memory retrieval since it helps to create a mental 3D representation of the structure of the face (O'Toole et al., 2002). Furthermore, when faces are learned during non-rigid motion (e.g., speaking or moving), participants perform better on face recognition tasks when they are tested with dynamic/moving faces rather than static faces (e.g., Buratto et al., 2009).

This is particularly relevant to eyewitness and lineup contexts because individuals who witness a real crime have observed a moving scene (e.g., the perpetrator moving around, interacting with objects, communicating with people). Therefore, it can be hypothesized that discrimination accuracy should be improved with the presence of motion cues within lineups compared to static lineups, since both "encoding" (the crime) and "test" include movement. It's important to note, however, that some face recognition researchers have provided an opposing suggestion and find that the presence of non-rigid motion cues during the test phase (i.e., the lineup) does *not* increase recognition accuracy for moving faces which have been encoded while carrying out a fluid act from a frontal pose (e.g., speaking) (Butcher et al., 2011). This line of research indicates that the benefit of motion cues at test may only be useful for specific kinds of encoded motions, and perhaps a more predictive factor of recognition accuracy relates to whether (and how) a face is encoded in motion rather than whether it is encountered in motion at test.

The second finding to emerge from the face recognition literature indicates that viewpoint is important for face recognition accuracy. More specifically, recognition accuracy increases when a face is presented from the same viewpoint at encoding and test (e.g., Bruce, 1982; Carbon & Leder, 2006). This idea is in line with the encoding specificity principle (Tulving & Thomson, 1973), which posits that the match between contextual cues at encoding and retrieval is important for accurate memory retrieval. Therefore, it can be hypothesized that when witnesses/participants are able to view lineup member faces in the same pose at encoding and test, performance on the lineup task should increase.

The third and final insight is that discrimination accuracy is improved when a testing procedure allows the test items to be actively explored, such when viewers can interact with a lineup member's face (e.g., view it from different angles). It is widely accepted that active exploration is more beneficial to recognition performance than passive viewing (e.g., Harman et al., 1999; Liu et al., 2007).

To summarize, findings from the face recognition literature indicate that—while not the *only* cues—there are three notable cues which represent promising avenues for aiding face memory retrieval. These three cues are motion, pose reinstatement, and active exploration. While these cues may be useful in a lineup scenario, they have not yet been widely studied within this context. Therefore, it is potentially difficult to generalize results from the face recognition literature to eyewitness memory contexts. Eyewitness studies typically do not control for the perpetrator's pose at encoding and test, and further, many do not report information about the extent to which mock witnesses saw the perpetrator in motion, nor do they mention the viewpoint of the witness. We are aware of only one study (besides our own work) that has researched active exploration in a lineup context (Bailenson et al., 2008). Bailenson and colleagues adopted an interactive eyewitness memory paradigm to investigate the potential benefits of active exploration using avatars presented in virtual reality. They found that identification accuracy improved when multiple facial angles of the avatars were viewed at test, but only in target-present lineups. However, the study was low powered statistically speaking, as very few participants took part. Further, the research did not employ real faces. Therefore, more research using more realistic eyewitness paradigms and larger samples is warranted.

What is more, the other research demonstrating the benefits of active exploration, motion, and pose reinstatement employed face recognition testing paradigms. For starters, legal officials will want to see empirical evidence that the benefits found for face recognition translate to lineups before adopting a new paradigm in practice. The generalizability of face recognition findings to eyewitness contexts may be hindered by differences in the experimental procedures. Face recognition studies usually involve presenting participants with unfamiliar faces sequentially, then, after a short delay, asking participants to make old/new judgments for a sequence of faces. On the other hand, eyewitness studies usually involve presenting participants with a mock crime video or a staged crime, and later asking them to identify the perpetrator from the mock crime using a lineup task. Therefore, face recognition studies typically do not involve episodic events. And, perhaps more importantly, lineup identifications (in the eyewitness context) and old/new judgements (in the face recognition context) have different requirements in terms of cognitive load—face recognition tasks involve only viewing one face at a time and deciding if that face has been seen before, but eyewitness tasks involve viewing multiple faces in a lineup and deciding whether or not the "seen-before face" (i.e., the perpetrator) is present in the array of faces. Ultimately, the presence of multiple faces compared to one face at test may alter the memory retrieval process (see Colloff & Wixted, 2019).

In conclusion, although the face recognition literature is useful for identifying key factors which may be beneficial for face memory retrieval generally, further research is needed to investigate how these retrieval cues (motion, pose reinstatement, active exploration) might operate in an eyewitness identification context.

Interactive Lineups

Considering the issues mentioned above, the novel and innovative interactive lineup procedure was developed to investigate whether the retrieval cues identified from face recognition research (i.e., motion, pose

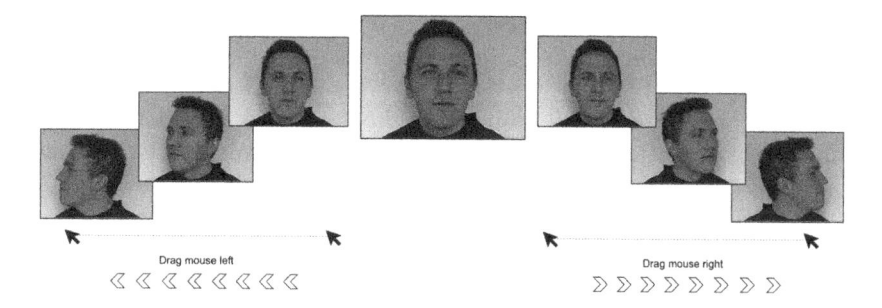

Figure 10.2 Illustration of viewing a single face in an interactive lineup procedure.

reinstatement, and active exploration) are also beneficial in eyewitness contexts (Colloff et al., 2021; Colloff et al., 2022; Meyer et al., 2023; Winsor et al., 2021). The interactive procedure allows participants (mock witnesses) to rotate the lineup members' faces using their computer mouse from left-profile to right-profile (see Figure 10.2 for example, and https://tinyurl.com/t4nc9gp for a demonstration). Mouse movements can be tracked using this procedure, so researchers are able to see *how* participants interact with each face, i.e., how long they hold each viewpoint for, how quickly they scroll through them, and whether they return to previously seen viewpoints.

This interactive procedure has been used by a number of researchers to investigate the benefits of motion, pose reinstatement, and active exploration as retrieval cues. For example, some researchers have adopted an eyewitness memory paradigm with large sample sizes to test the interactive procedure with adequate statistical power in both adults (Colloff et al., 2021, 2022; Meyer et al., 2023), and children (Winsor et al., 2021). Other researchers have examined the benefit of interactivity and motion on face perception in a face matching context (Smith et al., 2021), whereby participants view two faces and decide if they are the same or different people. All these studies used ROC analysis, or analyses based in signal-detection theory, to analyze the data. ROC analysis is widely used in fundamental memory research and has become increasingly popular in recent years as a primary analysis method for lineup studies, particularly because it can provide a measure of discriminability without relying on any theoretical assumptions about the distributions of the underlying data (sometimes termed a measure of empirical discriminability; Mickes et al., 2012; Wixted & Mickes, 2015). Despite the supporting evidence for ROC analysis, it is also important to note the counterpoint—some researchers prefer to use their own ROC-adjacent alternatives instead of the traditional method (e.g., Smith et al., 2020), but arguably, these novel alternatives are not tied to any models of memory or decision making and therefore, may result in misleading conclusions (e.g., for critiques see Wilson & Colloff, 2020; Starns et al., 2022).

Results of the interactive lineup studies show that discrimination accuracy (i.e., the ability to distinguish between innocent and guilty suspects) is significantly higher when facial viewing angle is matched at encoding and test (Colloff et al., 2021). Interestingly, it has also been found that when presented with an interactive lineup, participants actively recreate the facial angle that they saw at encoding, without prompting (Colloff et al., 2021). This demonstrates that pose reinstatement is indeed a useful tool for memory retrieval of faces in lineup scenarios. Furthermore, Colloff et al. (2022) found that interactive lineups increased eyewitness discrimination accuracy compared to static frontal photo lineups. For any possible false identification rate of innocent suspects, using sequential interactive lineups instead of sequential static photo lineups increased the correct identification rate of guilty suspects by 18%. Further, using simultaneous interactive lineups in which all the faces move together instead of sequential interactive lineups increased the correct identification rate of guilty suspects by a further 23%. Using simultaneous interactive lineups in which all the faces move together instead of simultaneous interactive lineups in which each face moved on its own improved discrimination accuracy, but this was not statistically significant. These findings were consistent across own-race and other-race identifications, which indicates that the interactive lineup may aid witnesses when they are identifying someone who is of the same race/ethnicity *or* a different race/ethnicity (see Meissner & Brigham, 2001 for a discussion of own-race bias).

A performance benefit when using the interactive procedure therefore appears to be a robust finding and has also been observed in other identity verification contexts. Smith et al. (2021) investigated the interactive procedure in forensic face matching situations, using a same/different matching paradigm that is closely related to the controlled face recognition literature which informed the design of the interactive lineup procedure. Participants were presented with one static photo on the left side of the screen and either an interactive image or a static frontal image on the right side of the screen and were asked whether or not the images were a match (i.e., depicted the same person). Results showed that overall face matching accuracy was higher for both superior face recognizers *and* typical face recognizers using an interactive procedure compared to the static photo. They also found that the interactive procedure improved performance compared to frontal static photos when one of the images involved in the face matching task was of low quality (e.g., pixelated). This suggests that the interactive performance advantage might even extend to cases where poor quality CCTV evidence is used and the task is to decide whether the suspect is or is not the person in the CCTV image.

Overall, the findings of all the research studies described here provide initial support for harnessing the use of retrieval cues when designing eyewitness testing procedures, and illustrate that the interactive lineup procedure is particularly beneficial for eyewitness identification performance. Future research has begun to test eyewitness performance on photo lineups, video lineups, and interactive lineups at different delays between encoding and lineup test to further examine if the substantial interactive benefit observed in existing research holds over time.

Conclusion

Eyewitness identification is a vital part of many criminal investigations, but eyewitness errors can have far-reaching extreme consequences. These consequences may extend far beyond an innocent suspect themselves, for example, to family and friends of the wrongfully convicted, and even to general society which bears the cost (financial and otherwise) of criminals being free to commit further crimes and legal systems which have inappropriately relied on weak eyewitness identification evidence. Therefore, it is crucial for researchers and practitioners to work together to create evidence-based best practice guidelines for police lineups to maximize eyewitness identification accuracy.

Lineup practices vary across the world, with some countries using video lineups, some using static photograph lineups, others using live lineups, and some using no lineup procedure at all. However, research into the "optimal" lineup procedure has produced mixed results thus far, and it is therefore difficult to draw explicit conclusions. Nevertheless, a novel procedure guided by theory and the basic face recognition literature—the interactive lineup procedure—has been developed and is currently being researched. Although research into this procedure is limited, early results are promising. Initial findings suggest that an interactive lineup procedure may be a way forward for policing to minimize false identifications of innocent suspects while also maximizing correct identifications of guilty suspects.

References

Akan, M., Robinson, M., Mickes, L., Wixted, J.T., & Benjamin, A.S. (2020). The effect of lineup size on eyewitness identification. *Journal of Experimental Psychology: Applied*, 27(2), 369–392. https://doi.org/10.1037/xap0000340

Albright, T.D. & Rakoff, J.S. (2020). The impact of the National Academy of Sciences report on eyewitness identification. *Judicature*, 104(1), 20–29.

Amendola, K.L. & Wixted, J.T. (2015). Comparing the diagnostic accuracy of suspect identifications made by actual eyewitnesses from simultaneous and sequential lineups in a randomized field trial. *Journal of Experimental Criminology*, 11, 263–284. https://doi.org/10.1007/s11292-014-9219-2

Bailenson, J.N., Davies, A., Blascovich, J., Beall, A.C., McCall, C., & Guadagno, R.E. (2008). The effects of witness viewpoint distance, angle, and choice on eyewitness accuracy in police lineups conducted in immersive virtual environments. *Presence: Teleoperators and Virtual Environments*, 17(3), 242–255. https://doi.org/10.1162/pres.17.3.242

Bennett, T.C., Flowe, H.D., Collins, W., Canham, R. & Colloff, M.F. (2023). How are identification parades constructed in the UK?: A survey of UK identification officers. [Manuscript in preparation]. Department of Psychology, University of Birmingham.

Beresford, J., & Blades, M. (2006). Children's identification of faces from lineups: The effects of lineup presentation and instructions on accuracy. *Journal of Applied Psychology*, 91(5), 1102–1113. https://doi.org/10.1037/0021-9010.91.5.1102

Brewer, N., Weber, N., & Guerin, N. (2020). Police lineups of the future? *American Psychologist*, 75(1), 76–91. https://doi.org/10.1037/amp0000465

Bruce, V. (1982). Changing faces: Visual and non-visual coding processes in face recognition. *British Journal of Psychology*, 73(1), 105–116. https://doi.org/10.1111/j.2044-8295.1982.tb01795.x

Buratto, L.G., Matthews, W.J., & Lamberts, K. (2009). When are moving images remembered better? Study-test congruence and the dynamic superiority effect. *The Quarterly Journal of Experimental Psychology*, 62(10), 1896–1903. https://doi.org/10.1080/17470210902883263

Butcher, N., Lander, K., Fang, H., & Costen, N. (2011). The effect of motion at encoding and retrieval for same-and other race face recognition. *British Journal of Psychology*, 102(4), 931–942. https://doi.org/10.1111/j.2044-8295.2011.02060.x

Carbon, C.C., & Leder, H. (2006). The Mona Lisa effect: Is "our" Lisa fame or fake? *Perception*, 35(3), 411–414. https://doi.org/10.1068/p5452

Carlson, C.A. & Carlson, M.A. (2014). An evaluation of lineup presentation, weapon presence, and a distinctive feature using ROC analysis. *Journal of Applied Research in Memory and Cognition*, 3(2), 45–53. https://doi.org/10.1016/j.jarmac.2014.03.004

Clark, S.E. (2012). Cost and benefits of eyewitness identification reform: Psychological science and public policy. *Perspectives on Psychological Science*, 7(3), 238–259. https://doi.org/10.1177/1745691612439584

Clark, S.E., Howell, R.T., & Davey, S.L. (2008). Regularities in eyewitness identification. *Law and Human Behavior*, 32, 187–218. https://doi.org/10.1007/s10979-006-9082-4

Colloff, M.F., Flowe, H.D., Smith, H.M.J., Seale-Carlisle, T.M., Meissner, C.A., Rockey, J.C., Pande, B., Kujur, P., Parveen, N., Chandel, P., Singh, M.M., Pradhan, S., & Parganiha, A. (2022). Active exploration of faces in police lineups increases discrimination accuracy. *American Psychologist*, 77(2), 196–220. https://doi.org/10.1037/amp0000832

Colloff, M.F., Seale-Carlisle, T.M., Karoğlu, N., Rockey, J.C., Smith, H.M.J., Smith, L., Maltby, J., Yaremenko, S. & Flowe, H.D. (2021). Perpetrator pose reinstatement during a lineup test increases discrimination accuracy. *Scientific Reports*, 11(1). https://doi.org/10.1038/s41598-021-92509-0

Colloff, M.F., & Wixted, J.T. (2019). Why are lineups better than showups? A test of the filler siphoning and enhanced discriminability accounts. *Journal* of *Experimental Psychology: Applied, 26*(1), 124–143. https://doi.org/10.1037/xap0000218

Cutler, B.L., Berman, G.L., Penrod, S.D., & Fisher, R.P. (1994). Conceptual, practical, and empirical issues associated with eyewitness identification test media. In D.F. Ross, J.D. Read, & M.P. Toglia (Eds), *Adult eyewitness testimony: Current trends and developments* (pp. 163–181). Cambridge University Press. https://doi.org/10.1017/CBO9780511759192.009

Cutler, B.L., & Fisher, R.P. (1990). Live lineups, videotaped lineups, and photoarrays. *Forensic Reports, 3*(4), 439–448.

Cutler, B.L., Fisher, R.P., & Chicvara, C.L. (1989). Eyewitness identification from live versus videotaped lineups. *Forensic Reports, 2*(2), 93–106.

Darling, S., Valentine, T., & Memon, A. (2008). Selection of lineup foils in operational contexts. *Applied Cognitive Psychology, 22*(2), 159–169. https://doi.org/10.1002/acp.1366

Devlin, L.P. (1976). *Report to the Secretary of State for the Home Department on the Departmental Committee on Evidence of Identification in Criminal Cases.* HMSO.

Dobolyi, D.G. & Dodson, C.S. (2013). Eyewitness confidence in simultaneous and sequential lineups: A criterion shift account for sequential mistaken identification overconfidence. *Journal of Experimental Psychology: Applied, 19*(4), 345–357. https://doi.org/10.1037/a0034596

Fitzgerald, R.J., Price, H.L., & Valentine, T. (2018). Eyewitness identification: Live, photo, and video lineups. *Psychology, Public Policy, and Law, 24*(3), 307–325. https://doi.org/10.1037/law0000164

Fitzgerald, R.J., Rubínová, E., & Juncu, S. (2021). Eyewitness identification around the world. In Smith, A.M., Toglia, M., & Lampinen, J.M. (Eds.), *Methods, measures, and theories in eyewitness identification tasks*. Taylor and Francis.

Flowe, H.D., Carline, A., & Karoğlu, N. (2018). Testing the reflection assumption: A comparison of eyewitness ecology in the laboratory and criminal cases. *International Journal of Evidence & Proof, 22*(3), 239–261. https://doi.org/10.1177/1365712718782996

Gepshtein, S., Wang, Y., He, F., Diep, D., & Albright, T.D. (2020). A perceptual scaling approach to eyewitness identification. *Nature Communications, 11*(1), 3380. https://doi.org/10.1038/s41467-020-17194-5

Gronlund, S.D., Carlson, C.A., Neuschatz, J.S., Goodsell, C.A., Wetmore, S.A., Wooten, A., & Graham, M. (2012). Showups versus lineups: An evaluation using ROC analysis. *Journal of Applied Research in Memory and Cognition, 1*(4), 221–228. https://doi.org/10.1016/j.jarmac.2012.09.003

Harman, K.L., Humphrey, G.K., & Goodale, M.A. (1999). Active manual control of object views facilitates visual recognition. *Current Biology, 9*(22), 1315–1318. https://doi.org/10.1016/S0960-9822(00)80053-6

Horry, R., Memon, A., Wright, D.B., & Milne, R. (2012). Predictors of eyewitness identification decisions from video lineups in England: A field study. *Law and Human Behavior, 36*(4), 257–265. https://doi.org/10.1037/h0093959

Innocence Project (2022a). DNA exonerations in the United States. Retrieved November 4, 2022, from https://innocenceproject.org/dna-exonerations-in-the-united-states/

Innocence Project (2022b). All cases. Retrieved December 19, 2022, from https://innocenceproject.org/all-cases/

Innocence Project (2022c). Antonio Beaver. Retrieved December 19, 2022, from https://innocenceproject.org/cases/antonio-beaver/

Kerstholt, J.H., Koster, E.R. & van Amelsvoort, A.G. (2004). Eyewitnesses: A comparison of live, video, and photo line-ups. *Journal of Police and Criminal Psychology*, 19(1) 15–22. https://doi.org/10.1007/BF02813869

Key, K.N., Cash, D.K., Neuschatz, J.S., Price, J., Wetmore, S.A., & Gronlund, S.D. (2015). Age differences (or lack thereof) in discriminability for lineups and showups. *Psychology, Crime & Law*, 21(9), 871–889. https://doi.org/10.1080/1068316X.2015.1054387

Liu, C.H., Ward, J., & Markall, H. (2007). The role of active exploration of 3D face stimuli on recognition memory of facial information. *Journal of Experimental Psychology: Human Perception and Performance*, 33(4), 895–904. https://doi.org/10.1037/0096-1523.33.4.895

Malpass, R.S., & Devine, P.G. (1981). Eyewitness identification: Lineup instructions and the absence of the offender. *Journal of Applied Psychology*, 66(4), 482–489. https://doi.org/10.1037/0021-9010.66.4.482

Meissner, C.A., & Brigham, J.C. (2001). Thirty years of investigating the own-race bias in memory for faces: A meta-analytic review. *Psychology, Public Policy, and Law*, 7(1), 3–35. https://doi.org/10.1037/1076-8971.7.1.3

Memon, A., Havard, C., Clifford, B., Gabbert, F., & Watt, M. (2011) A field evaluation of the VIPER system: a new technique for eliciting eyewitness identification evidence. *Psychology, Crime & Law*, 17(8), 711–729. https://doi.org/10.1080/10683160903524333

Meyer, M., Colloff, M.F., Bennett, T.C., Hirata, E., Stevens, L.M., Smith, H.M.J., Staudigl, T., & Flowe, H.D. (2023). Improving eyewitness discrimination accuracy: Comparing a novel interactive lineup procedure to photo and video lineups. [Manuscript in preparation].

Mickes, L. (2015). Receiver operating characteristic analysis and confidence–accuracy characteristic analysis in investigations of system variables and estimator variables that affect eyewitness memory. *Journal of Applied Research in Memory and Cognition*, 4(2), 93–102. https://doi.org/10.1016/j.jarmac.2015.01.003

Mickes, L., Flowe, H.D., & Wixted, J.T. (2012). Receiver operating characteristic analysis of eyewitness memory: Comparing the diagnostic accuracy of simultaneous versus sequential lineups. *Journal of Experimental Psychology: Applied*, 18(4), 361–376. https://doi.org/10.1037/a0030609

National Research Council (2014). *Identifying the culprit: Assessing eyewitness identification*. The National Academies Press. https://doi.org/10.17226/18891

Neuschatz, J.S., Wetmore, S.A., Key, K.A., Cash, D.K., Gronlund, S.D., & Goodsell, C.A. (2016). A comprehensive evaluation of showups. In M.K. Miller, B.H. Bornstein, M.K. Miller, & B.H. Bornstein (Eds.), *Advances in psychology and law* (pp. 43–69). Springer International Publishing.

O'Toole, A.J., Roark, D.A., & Hervé, A. (2002). Recognizing moving faces: A psychological and neural synthesis. *Trends in Cognitive Sciences*, 6(6), 261–266. https://doi.org/10.1016/S1364-6613(02)01908-3

Police and Criminal Evidence Act (1984). *Code D, Code of Practice for the identification of persons by Police Officers* (2017 edition). https://assets.publishing.service.gov.uk/government/uploads/system/uploads/attachment_data/file/903812/pace-code-d-2017.pdf

Police Executive Research Forum. (2013). *A national survey of eyewitness identification procedures in law enforcement agencies.* www.ncjrs.gov/pdffiles1/nij/grants/242617.pdf

Pozzulo, J.D., & Lindsay, R.C.L. (1999). Elimination lineups: An improved identification procedure for child eyewitnesses. *Journal of Applied Psychology, 84*(2), 167–176. https://doi.org/10.1037/0021-9010.84.2.167

Rubínová, E., Fitzgerald, R,J., Juncu, S., Ribbers, E., Hope, L., & Sauer, J.D. (2021). Live presentation for eyewitness identification is not superior to photo or video presentation. *Journal of Applied Research in Memory and Cognition, 10*(1), 167–176. https://doi.org/10.1016/j.jarmac.2020.08.009

Seale-Carlisle, T.M., Wetmore, S.A., Flowe, H.D., & Mickes, L. (2019). Designing police lineups to maximize memory performance. *Journal of Experimental Psychology: Applied, 25*(3), 410–430. https://doi.org/10.1037/xap0000222

Smith, A.M., Yang, Y., & Wells, G.L. (2020). Distinguishing between investigator discriminability and eyewitness discriminability: A method for creating full receiver operating characteristic curves of lineup identification performance. *Perspectives on Psychological Science, 15*(3) 1–19. https://doi.org/10.1177/1745691620902426

Smith, H.M.J., Andrews, S., Baguley, T., Colloff, M.F., Davis, J.P., White, D., Rockey, J.C., & Flowe, H.D. (2021). Performance of typical and superior face recognisers on a novel interactive face matching procedure. *British Journal of Psychology, 112*(4), 964–991. https://doi.org/10.1111/bjop.12499

Starns, J., Cohen, A.L., & Tuttle, M.D. (2022). A theory-based approach for constructing recognition Receiver Operating Characteristics (ROCs) in complex tasks, with an application to full lineup ROCs. PsyArXiv Preprints. https://doi.org/10.31234/osf.io/5wp7c

Steblay, N., Dysart, J., Fulero, S. & Lindsay, R.C.L. (2001) Eyewitness accuracy rates in sequential and simultaneous lineup presentations: A meta-analytic comparison. *Law and Human Behavior, 25*(5), 459–473. https://doi.org/10.1023/a:1012888715007

Steblay, N., Dysart, J., Fulero, S. & Lindsay, R.C.L. (2003) Eyewitness accuracy rates in police showup and lineup presentations: A meta-analytic comparison. *Law and Human Behavior, 27*(5), 523–540. https://doi.org/10.1023/A:1025438223608

Steblay, N.K., Dysart, J.E., & Wells, G.L. (2011). Seventy-two tests of the sequential lineup superiority effect: A meta-analysis and policy discussion. *Psychology, Public Policy, and Law, 17*(1), 99–139. https://doi.org/10.1037/a0021650

Sussman, E.D., Sugarman, R.C., & Zavala, A. (1972). A comparison of three media used in identification procedures. In A. Zavala & J.J. Paley (Eds.) *Personal appearance identification* (pp. 308–312). Charles C Thomas.

Technical Working Group for Eyewitness Evidence (1999). *Eyewitness evidence: A guide for law enforcement.* US Department of Justice. www.ojp.gov/pdffiles1/nij/178240.pdf

Tulving, E., & Thomson, D.M. (1973). Encoding specificity and retrieval processes in episodic memory. *Psychological Review*, 80(5), 352–373. https://doi.org/10.1037/h0020071

Valentine, T., Darling, S., & Memon, A. (2007). Do strict rules and moving images increase the reliability of sequential identification procedures? *Applied Cognitive Psychology*, 21(7), 933–949. https://doi.org/10.1002/acp.1306

Valentine, T., Davis, J.P., Memon, A., & Roberts, A. (2012). Live showups and their influence on a subsequent video line-up. *Applied Cognitive Psychology*, 26(1), 1–23. https://doi.org/10.1002/acp.1796

Wells, G.L., Memon, A., & Penrod, S.D. (2016). Eyewitness evidence: Improving its probative value. *Psychological Science in the Public Interest*, 7(2), 45–75. https://doi.org/10.1111/j.1529-1006.2006.00027.x

Wetmore, S.A., Neuschatz, J.S., Gronlund, S.D., Wooten, A., Goodsell, C.A., & Carlson, C.A. (2015). Effect of retention interval on showup and lineup performance. *Journal of Applied Research in Memory and Cognition*, 4(1), 8–14. https://doi.org/10.1016/j.jarmac.2014.07.003

Wilson, B.M., & Colloff, M.F. (2020). *Coherently creating full receiver operating characteristic curves of police lineups.* [Poster presentation]. 61st Annual Meeting of the Psychonomic Society (Virtual).

Wilson, B.M., Donnelly, K., Christenfeld, N., & Wixted, J.T. (2019). Making sense of sequential lineups: An experimental and theoretical analysis of position effects. *Journal of Memory and Language*, 104, 108–125. https://doi.org/10.1016/j.jml.2018.10.002

Winsor, A., Flowe, H.D., Seale-Carlisle, T.M., Kileen, I.M., Hett, D., Jores, T., Ingham, M.P., Lee, B., Stevens, L., & Colloff, M.F. (2021). Child witness expressions of certainty are informative. *Journal of Experimental Psychology: General*, 150(11), 2387–2407. https://doi.org/10.1037/xge0001049

Wixted, J.T., & Mickes, L. (2014). A signal-detection-based diagnostic-feature-detection model of eyewitness identification. *Psychological Review*, 121(2), 262–276. https://doi.org/10.1037/a0035940

Wixted, J.T. & Mickes, L. (2015). Evaluating eyewitness identification procedures: ROC analysis and its misconceptions. *Journal of Applied Research in Memory and Cognition*, 4(4), 318–323. https://doi.org/10.1016/j.jarmac.2015.08.009

Wixted, J.T., Mickes, L., & Fisher, R.P. (2018). Rethinking the reliability of eyewitness memory. *Perspectives on Psychological Science*, 13(3), 324–335. https://doi.org/10.1177/1745691617734878.

Wixted, J.T. & Wells, G.L. (2017). The relationship between eyewitness confidence and identification accuracy: A new synthesis. *Psychological Science in the Public Interest*, 18(1), 10–65. https://doi.org/10.1177/1529100616686966

Wooten, A.R., Carlson, C.A., Lockamyeir, R.F., Carlson, M.A., Jones, A.R., Dias, J.L. & Hemby, J.A., (2020). The number of fillers may not matter as long as they all match the description: The effect of simultaneous lineup size on eyewitness identification. *Applied Cognitive Psychology*, 34(3), 590–604. https://doi.org/10.1002/acp.3644

11 Using Body-Worn Camera Footage to Remember Use-of-Force Incidents

Craig Bennell, Simon Baldwin, Andrew Brown, and Ariane-Jade Khanizadeh

Using Body-Worn Camera Footage to Remember Use-of-Force Incidents

When police officers are involved in use-of-force events, they must typically complete a report following the incident to describe the encounter and articulate why they made the decisions they did. Such reports will involve an attempt by the officer to accurately recall information from memory about the interaction: What was the environment like? What behaviors was the subject exhibiting? What tactical issues did the officer consider? What risk factors were perceived? How did they respond, and why? Unfortunately, these recall attempts can be hindered by various factors, such as the stress officers likely experienced during the incident.

These use-of-force reports are used in various contexts to help determine what occurred in an incident and whether the officer's use of force was justified. In these situations, it is essential to have a report of the event that represents the officer's independent account of what transpired, one that is not influenced by factors that occurred following the event, including information that may be circulating about the incident. While a fuller description of the event, which is supplemented with information beyond the officer's initial account, may be useful in some contexts, it is the officer's individual account of their in-the-moment perceptions and risk assessment that is paramount when making decisions about the reasonableness of their use-of-force decisions (e.g., in a criminal trial).

A case has been made for using body-worn camera (BWC) footage from recorded use-of-force incidents to facilitate officer recall (e.g., Miller et al., 2014). Given the importance of an officer's account when determining the reasonableness of their force, critical questions must be asked about the impact that viewing BWC footage will have on use-of-force reports. For example, does viewing BWC footage of an event impact how officers articulate their use of force? If so, in what way? How would we determine if the resulting report accurately reflects what the officer perceived at the time of the incident?

DOI: 10.4324/9781003323112-13

In this chapter, we explore research related to the above questions. The chapter is divided into five sections. The first section briefly discusses BWCs and research related to their use. The second section describes how critical incident stress is likely to impact memory. The third section presents the rationale, advocated by some, for allowing officers to review BWC footage following their involvement in a use-of-force incident. The fourth section highlights concerns with adopting such a practice. We conclude the chapter by laying out some policy implications related to the issues raised in the previous sections.

Body-Worn Cameras

BWCs are small recording devices that police officers wear, typically mounted on their vest at chest level, to provide a first-person view of the events unfolding in a given incident. BWCs are often considered a tool that can contribute to police oversight and accountability, improve trust and transparency of police-citizen interactions, facilitate the collection of evidence, and help resolve complaints against the police (President's Task Force on 21st Century Policing, 2015). As a result, the use of this technology has been steadily growing. By 2016, approximately half of all police services in the United States had adopted BWCs (Nix et al., 2020), and that number continues to climb. In Canada, the rollout of BWCs has been slower. Still, numerous police services across the country now use BWCs, and the Royal Canadian Mounted Police (RCMP), Canada's largest police service, will soon be adopting the technology with a planned rollout in 2023.

Research examining the impact of BWCs is also steadily growing. This research has focused on the degree of support that the public and police officers have for BWCs, and factors that influence this support; whether BWCs reduce public complaints against the police, police use of force, and the time taken to resolve various types of proceedings (e.g., trials); and whether other outcomes are impacted by the presence of BWCs, such as subject and officer injuries, the frequency of arrests, or the probability of charges and convictions. A detailed discussion of this work is beyond the scope of the current chapter, but excellent reviews of this research are available elsewhere (e.g., Lum et al., 2020; Maskaly et al., 2017; White & Malm, 2020). In this chapter, we focus specifically on emerging research related to the impact of BWCs on officer report writing following their involvement in police-citizen interactions, specifically those that involve the use of force. Before doing so, however, we briefly review research on critical incident stress and memory.

Stress and Memory

Policing is, undisputedly, a highly stressful and potentially dangerous occupation that involves a complex set of environmental and psychosocial threats (Chopko & Schwartz, 2012; Pinizzotto et al., 2006; Violanti, 2014). During many real-world police encounters, including use-of-force incidents, officers exhibit highly elevated markers of stress physiology (Andersen et al., 2016; Baldwin et al., 2019). This is because, when presented with a threat, whether real or perceived, the body unconsciously engages in a series of physiological processes, colloquially known as the "fight-or-flight" response (LeDoux & Pine, 2016; Thayer & Sternberg, 2006). This adaptive survival response prepares the body's physiological and cognitive capacities to meet the demands of the situation.

Specifically, when encountering a threat, the autonomic nervous system is engaged, stimulating the sympathetic nervous system (SNS) and suppressing the parasympathetic nervous system (PNS; Berntson & Cacioppo, 2004; Fridman et al., 2019). When the SNS is stimulated, the hypothalamic-pituitary-adrenal axis is activated, and stress hormones such as cortisol, norepinephrine, and epinephrine (i.e., adrenaline) are released (De Kloet et al., 1998; Lovallo, 2016; Ness & Calabrese, 2016). Regions of the brain involved in the physiological stress response also become activated, particularly the hippocampus—a core memory structure in the brain—and the amygdala and prefrontal cortex—regions that extensively overlap with other brain structures critical to memory processes (Di Nota et al., 2020; Ness & Calabrese, 2016).

Memory is the capacity to encode, consolidate, and retrieve information that has been experienced (Ziotnik & Vansintjan, 2019). While there are various types of memory, our focus in this chapter will be on explicit declarative memory, specifically episodic memory. These personally experienced, event-based memories can be consciously recalled and are susceptible to bias and inaccuracy, especially under stress (Di Nota et al., 2020; Ness & Calabrese, 2016). While adaptive arousal that matches the demands of the situation can be beneficial to memory (Diamond et al., 2007; Mcgaugh, 2015), there is considerable evidence that elevated stress levels, like those experienced by officers during use-of-force incidents, negatively impact memory (Deffenbacher et al., 2004; Shields et al., 2017). Generally, stress can affect not only the number of details recalled but also the quality of memory (Ness & Calabrese, 2016).

The timing, type, and amount of stress one experiences can impact memory positively *or* negatively (Shields et al., 2017). For example, at the earliest stages of an event, stress-induced attentional and perceptual narrowing, including tunnel vision and diminished sound, can influence and distort what is initially encoded into memory (Davis & Loftus, 2009; Di Nota et al., 2020). While attentional and perceptual narrowing may enhance recall of the central features of an event, this may be at the expense of memory for peripheral details (Eysenck et al., 2007; Hope et al., 2016). Indeed, studies of officers involved in actual (e.g., Artwohl, 2002) and simulated (Baldwin et al., 2022;

Hope et al., 2016; Hope et al., 2012) shooting incidents have reported significant memory deficits, including memory loss and distortions (e.g., seeing, hearing, or experiencing something that did not happen).

The effects of stress on memory encoding are challenging to assess and are further confounded by consolidation and retrieval processes (Ness & Calabrese, 2016; Shields et al., 2017). For example, within the context of critical incidents, memory consolidation and retrieval may be affected by factors such as sleep deprivation (Diekelmann et al., 2008), sustained emotional arousal (Lewinski et al., 2016), memory contamination (Hope et al., 2013), rehearsal or rumination (Beehr et al., 2004; Porter et al., 2019; Yuille et al., 1994), the retrieval method used (e.g., cognitive interview: Memon et al., 2010; retention intervals: Grady et al., 2016; Porter et al., 2019). All this research makes clear that, through a constructive process, memories of stressful events can become contaminated by conscious and unconscious thoughts and social interactions. This can result in confabulations where gaps are filled to make personal sense (e.g., conformity with BWC footage or other officers' accounts of events), different events are blended, or imagined events become a memory.

Body-Worn Cameras as an "Aide-Mémoire"

Stress-induced cognitive and perceptual deficits mean that when presented with a threat, officers may be more prone to complex and wide-ranging memory issues. To compensate for memory deficits resulting from stress, BWC footage may act as an "aide-mémoire," similar to how contemporaneous officer notes (Cyr, 2014), or a "walk-through" of a crime scene (Geiselman, 2010; Honig & Lewinski, 2008), can enhance officers' ability to recall details about an incident (Dawes et al., 2015; Jennings et al., 2014). Some people have argued that this would be very helpful; when an officer watches their BWC footage, it may prompt them to more accurately remember what happened during an encounter so that a fuller account of what transpired can be generated (including their risk assessment; Dawes et al., 2015).

Research from outside of Policing

Outside the context of policing, it has certainly been shown that digitally recording and reviewing autobiographical events using cameras can significantly improve associated memories (e.g., Hodges et al., 2011; Hoisko, 2003; Silva et al., 2017). For example, various "lifelogging technologies" (e.g., cameras worn around an individual's neck) have been used by cognitively healthy individuals and those suffering from memory disorders (e.g., dementia, amnesia, brain injury) to record autobiographical events via digital images (Piasek et al., 2016). When viewed by the wearer, these captured images have been found to cue accurate memory recall (e.g., Berry et al., 2007; Browne et al., 2011; Hoisko, 2003). For example, in one of the first studies to research the memory-enhancing effect of this technology, Hoisko (2003) examined how these cameras can work as "episodic memory prostheses." He found that reviewing audio and visual images of past activities captured by these cameras enhances one's memories of previously lived experiences.

In similar studies, Berry et al. (2007) and Browne et al. (2011) examined the utility of a wearable camera called a SenseCam, which is worn around the neck at chest level to capture photographs every 30 seconds or when its microprocessors experience a fluctuation in the environment (i.e., changes in a room's lighting). Both studies requested participants experiencing memory deficits to wear the SenseCam and keep a personal diary to document their life experiences. Participants later took part in memory tests where they were asked to review their diary notes or SenseCam images before the test. Both studies found that participants exhibited greater memory scores when reviewing their SenseCam images compared to their diary notes. Additionally, both studies reported long-term improvements in SenseCam-facilitated memories following the initial memory tests. More recent research has confirmed the memory-enhancing impact of SenseCam (e.g., Mair et al., 2017, 2019; Silva et al., 2013, 2017; Van Teijilingen et al., 2021), although some studies have not found this effect (e.g., Seamon et al., 2014).

Research from within Policing

In the police setting, BWCs can be used similarly to lifelogging technologies. It has been argued that officers' memory recall can also improve after viewing BWC footage following a critical incident (e.g., Blaskovits & Bennell, 2020). In perhaps the earliest study to examine this issue, Dawes et al. (2015) studied 11 police officers who wrote statements after completing use-of-force training scenarios while equipped with BWCs. Some participants were given the opportunity to correct any errors in their initial statements after reviewing their BWC footage, whereas other officers were not. The study revealed that the accuracy of officers' use-of-force reports increased when they were able to review their BWC footage. This study even revealed that reviewing video footage could trigger memories of information that was not visibly present within the video footage itself (i.e., off-camera details).

More recently, Boivin and Gendron (2022) examined the impact of BWCs on event articulation. Three hundred and sixty-three participants, consisting of both new and experienced police officers, were asked to complete a live simulation involving a hostage situation in which a subject threatened the officer with a knife. The scenario ended when the officer discharged their firearm. Following the event, officers had to prepare a report. Participants were assigned to one of four conditions: (1) no BWC, (2) BWC, but not allowed to view their footage before writing their statement, (3) BWC, and asked to watch their footage before writing their statement, or (4) BWC, but asked to write an initial report before viewing their footage, and a supplementary report after viewing their footage.

The reports prepared by the officers were coded for various items (e.g., victim, subject, and scene descriptions). The researchers found that officers who were provided with a BWC and asked to view their footage before writing their report provided a slightly more accurate account of the incident. Moreover, they found that those who did not view their BWC footage before writing a statement were four times more likely to make at least one error in their report. Overall, the researchers determined that a two-step process, which involved (1) writing an initial report and (2) watching BWC footage and writing a supplementary report, resulted in the least number of errors.

This notion of a two-step process was also supported in a recent study by Vredreveldt et al. (2021). They recruited 102 officers from the Dutch National Police Force and had them complete a training scenario in pairs. The scenario consisted of a domestic dispute between neighbors in which the officers were tasked to arrest one of the individuals. One officer in each pair wore a BWC. Following the incident, one officer from the pair watched the BWC footage first and then wrote their post-incident report, whereas the other officer wrote their report first and then could revise it after watching the BWC footage. Surprisingly, the researchers found no significant difference in the amount of information reported by officers who watched their footage before or after writing their reports. However, individuals who wrote an initial report before viewing their footage, and then made amendments to it afterwards, provided more complete and more accurate reports post-viewing.

Finally, Pezdek et al. (2022) examined whether an officer's articulation of an incident changes after viewing BWC video footage of the incident (Experiment 1). Sixty-one officers from a single police department in Southern California participated in an experiment that had them participate in two live-action simulation scenarios sequentially. Prior to beginning the scenarios, officers were instructed to press the record button on their BWC. After completing the scenarios, officers were brought to an adjacent room to complete a 14-item survey to test their knowledge of several aspects of the scenario (Time 1). Officers were then assigned to one of two groups, where they were able to review their BWC footage in one and not in the other, and they completed the same 14-item survey again (Time 2).

The results from this experiment demonstrated that BWC footage could be a source of post-event information that may alter the memory of an original event (or at least the reporting of that event). For example, the researchers found that viewing BWC footage resulted in a higher proportion of information being changed in officer reports from Time 1 to Time 2. This was found to be the case for rates of commissions (i.e., information reported at Time 2 but not Time 1) and omissions (i.e., information reported at Time 1 but not Time 2), and for both the memory of the event (e.g., when the officer shot their gun) and memory for their state of mind at the time of the incident (e.g., how much danger the officer felt). In addition, the accuracy of their memory of the event improved from Time 1 to Time 2, and this change in accuracy was greater when officers viewed their BWC.

Cautions About Using Body-Worn Cameras as an "Aide-Mémoire"

Interestingly, the fact that officer reports are often revised if they are permitted to view BWC footage before preparing the report elicits two schools of thought (Boivin & Gendron, 2022). Some see this as a positive outcome and treat these findings as evidence that officers should be allowed to view their footage before writing their notes (e.g., Miller et al., 2014). For these people, the ultimate goal is to provide officers with the means to develop the most accurate account of the incident they were involved in; if viewing BWC footage can achieve this goal, then that is entirely acceptable. In contrast, others view these findings differently (e.g., Pezdek et al., 2022). For these individuals, what is important is to capture an officer's independent account of what happened during an incident, particularly concerning the reasons for using force. The fact that officers often change their account of what happened during an incident after viewing BWC footage means that the practice of viewing BWC footage before writing a report should be avoided.

These latter concerns are based largely on interpretations of what is required by courts of law (and other bodies)[1] when they are determining

---

1 For example, in an effort to avoid contaminating evidence, the independent investigation agencies of Canada that exist to examine allegations of officer wrongdoing asserted that video will be "presumptively treated as 'hold back' evidence in relation to the critical incident until such times as the investigative team determines otherwise" (Independent Investigation Agencies of Canada, 2016). In making this decision, the agencies acknowledged the frailties of human memory and that inconsistencies and mistakes of fact do *not* necessarily mean that the officer is lying. Despite this, the agencies considered a witness' perception of the incident as essential to their investigations. As a result, with the exception of "rare" circumstances, their position is that only once a "pure statement" has been taken, may an officer be able to refresh their memory with video of the incident for a subsequent interview. Their decision is underpinned by the principle of independence and equality, in that every witness, whether civilian or police, should be held to the same standard (i.e., prohibited from viewing video prior to a statement); otherwise, it may be perceived as preferential treatment.

whether a police officer's use of force was reasonable. Most relevant here is the US Supreme Court decision of *Graham v. Connor* (1989), which is the current standard in North America for determining whether an officer's use of force was justified. In its ruling, the court decided that the standard of "reasonableness" should be used when assessing the actions of police officers involved in use-of-force incidents. This standard was defined as being "judged from the perspective of a reasonable officer *on the scene*, rather than with the 20/20 vision of hindsight" (*Graham v. Connor*, 1989; emphasis added). Thus, if an officer's risk assessment process "on the scene" is to be used to determine what a "reasonable" officer would do, then it is essential to ensure that these in-the-moment memories are preserved and not distorted in any way.

Not only does the research cited above suggest that watching BWC footage following an event may contaminate an officer's memory for the event—memories that are critical for understanding the officer's in-the-moment perceptions and risk assessment, which might explain why they made the decisions they did—but research from the field of psychology more generally raises concerns about what might happen when officers are permitted to view their BWC footage when trying to recall what occurred during an incident, and their state of mind at the time. In this section, we describe some of these concerns.

Cognitive Offloading

Some research from outside the policing field suggests that the mere act of wearing a BWC could change how officers encode information during a use-of-force incident, especially if they know they will be able to view the footage from their BWC before writing their report (e.g., Henkel, 2014; Risko & Gilbert, 2016; Soares & Storm, 2018). In fact, recent research has found that, when possible, individuals often attempt to reserve limited cognitive resources by engaging in a process referred to as "cognitive offloading" (Risko & Gilbert, 2016), such as when we offload memory tasks to prosthetic devices like laptop computers or cell phones to remember important details (e.g., appointments and phone numbers).

Henkel (2014) was one of the first researchers to demonstrate this sort of "save-it-and-forget-it" type effect, where knowing that information is being saved in another manner impairs encoding of that information at the point of contact. In one of her experiments, she led participants on an art museum tour where they were exposed to 30 different artifacts. They were told to only observe half of the objects but to photograph the other half. In all cases, they were asked to pay attention to the objects and were informed that they would later be asked about them. Following the tour, Henkel had participants recall the objects and object details. She tested the participants' memory of the objects with free recall and then via an activity that asked them to name the objects, recognize them visually using a photograph, and report details about them using multiple-choice questions. The results demonstrated a "photo-taking impairment effect"—if participants had taken a photograph of the object, they were less likely to remember it and reported fewer details about it.

Cognitive offloading could have clear implications for officers wearing BWCs when involved in complex interactions with the public. For example, if officers believe they will be able to access information about an event later via their BWC footage, these officers may be less apt to encode information about the event, which is likely to hinder recall when they are preparing their report of the incident. This could prove especially problematic when BWC footage ends up being unavailable after the event, either because the camera was not recording due to human error or because of technological issues, the footage being of low quality, or the officer being restricted from viewing the video.

The only study we are aware of that has examined whether being equipped with a BWC negatively impacts memory encoding through cognitive offloading was conducted by our research team (Blaskovits et al., 2022). Fifty officers responded to a simulated domestic dispute that resulted in lethal force. Half the sample was provided a BWC and told their footage would be available to assist with post-event recall, but it was later feigned that there was a technological issue with the footage, so it could not be reviewed. The remaining officers were not equipped with a BWC and thus were aware they would not have any footage to rely on when reporting on the incident. The amount, accuracy, and type of details reported by officers on a use-of-force reporting form were coded and analyzed. The results revealed that wearing a BWC *did not* promote cognitive offloading. In fact, there were no significant differences between the two groups in the number of accurate details they recalled when contextual, subject, and officer details were examined.

This finding suggests that the training police officers receive (e.g., to carefully observe their surroundings) may mitigate the cognitive offloading effect observed in other contexts. Alternatively, the fact that BWCs remain a relatively new form of technology in policing, which officers may have reservations toward (Pelfrey & Keener, 2016), could explain the lack of an offloading effect. If participants assumed their BWC would be unreliable, this could explain why they did not offload to it (allowing their post-event report to be unaffected). This explanation may be particularly relevant in Blaskovits et al.'s (2022) study because the officers in that study came from an agency that did not employ BWCs at the time of the study; thus, the officers who participated would not have come to rely on BWC technology yet. Studies of police officers who do regularly wear BWCs on duty would be needed to test this hypothesis.

Misinformation-Type Effects

Beyond the potential for cognitive offloading, which may be shown in future research to influence the accuracy of reports following use-of-force events, BWCs could also cause other problems. For example, research suggests it might be possible to experience misinformation-type effects when viewing BWC footage while preparing a report, where details from the video are incorporated into an officer's "memory" of the event, even if those details were not encoded initially (Loftus, 2005). In contrast to typical misinformation studies, where the post-event information presented to research participants is often factually incorrect (Loftus et al., 1989), the information that may be incorporated into one's memory from BWC footage might be correct but simply not perceived and encoded by the responding officer during the initial incident. This could cause serious issues when figuring out what led an officer to use force (Grady et al., 2016).

The misinformation effect has been well-studied in laboratory settings, and much of this research leads us to believe that misinformation-type effects are distinctly possible in the police setting where BWCs are involved. Not only does it seem possible that officers could misremember important details of a use-of-force incident, but the environment within which they will be encoding aspects of these encounters is particularly conducive to misremembering. For example, Loftus (2005) suggests that misinformation is more likely to be internalized when the memory of the event in question is weak. This may accurately characterize many encounters involving the use of force because these encounters are often rapid, complex, and stressful events, which can result in weak memory traces of the incident (Artwohl, 2002; Klinger, 2004; Sharps, 2010).

The research cited above (e.g., Boivin & Gendron, 2022; Dawes et al., 2015; Pezdek et al., 2022) suggests that viewing BWC footage can influence the information contained in post-event statements. To the extent that an independent account of what transpired in a use-of-force incident is vital for determining why an officer used force and whether that force was reasonable, as it presumably would be in court cases surrounding allegations of excessive force, this would pose a problem. In those cases, it is important to ensure that an officer's memory of their risk assessment process is preserved and not altered by the act of viewing their BWC footage (Pezdek et al., 2022).

Retrieval-Induced Forgetting

Another memory-related concern that may be associated with BWCs, especially in cases where officers are permitted to view their BWC footage prior to providing a statement about an incident, is that watching the footage may foster retrieval-induced forgetting (RIF). Commonly studied by psychologists with interests in memory, RIF refers to the phenomenon where remembering part of an event prompts other aspects of the event to be forgotten (Grady et al., 2016).

Retrieval-induced forgetting has been consistently demonstrated via the retrieval-practice paradigm (Anderson et al., 1994; Camp et al., 2012; Murayama et al., 2014). Using this paradigm, individuals learn a list of word pairs (e.g., fruits–banana, drinks–coffee) and practice retrieval on half of them (e.g., drinks–coffee). They then receive a test where they are asked to recall all word pairs. Not surprisingly, retrieval practice tends to improve recall of the practiced material (drinks–coffee). However, the retrieval practice also appears to impair recall of the unpracticed material (fruits–banana) when compared to conditions where no retrieval practice occurred (Johansson et al., 2006).

Currently, the available evidence suggests that RIF occurs as a result of an inhibitory mechanism (Anderson, 2003; Levy & Anderson, 2002; Storm & Levy, 2012). According to this view, when an individual attempts to retrieve a certain item, multiple related items are activated. This creates competition such that an individual must inhibit the related items in order to selectively retrieve the to-be-remembered item from their memory. Consequently, the inhibited items are less accessible. In other words, inhibition reduces interference from competing memories, resulting in enhanced recall of practiced items but a loss of unpracticed items.

When officers watch their BWC footage, they are re-exposed to a to-be-remembered event, which is comparable to someone receiving additional retrieval practice on specific word pairs. However, BWCs do not necessarily capture details of an entire incident, including details that an officer may have attended to. An officer who reviews their BWC footage before providing their post-event statement may be able to document what is in the footage but could experience worsened recall for anything not captured by the BWC, including information outside the camera's view, the officer's internal perceptions, or obstructed items (Grady et al., 2016). If officers who review their footage accurately report aspects of the incident captured in the recording, but fail to report uncaptured portions of the event, this would be a concern; one that might be prevented by not allowing officers to watch their BWC footage before completing their use-of-force report.

One study that has examined what happens when research participants view BWC footage has raised concerns about RIF-type phenomena. Adams et al. (2020) had student participants wear BWCs as they viewed a theft in virtual reality. After a one-week delay, half the students were asked to recall the events in an initial statement, whereas the other half of the sample were not. Participants then viewed either the BWC footage or a control video. After viewing these videos, those participants who wrote an initial statement could amend their statement if they wished, while participants who did not provide an initial statement provided their first recall statement about the theft.

According to Adams and her colleagues (2020), the results of their study demonstrated that viewing BWC footage enhanced the completeness and accuracy of recall statements. However, while reviewing the footage allowed participants to exclude any errors they had included in their initial statement, they also excluded accurate details of the event that were uncorroborated by the camera footage (i.e., details that individuals might have experienced but that their camera did not record). Whether these details were truly forgotten or were left out of statements for some other reason is unclear. At the very least, these results evidence some form of camera conformity (i.e., statements were revised to align them with BWC footage). Interestingly, other research has failed to find the same sort of RIF-type effect after watching BWC footage (e.g., Vredreveldt et al., 2021, which was discussed above), raising questions about the conditions under which it is likely to surface.

Implications for Policy and Practice

BWCs are not a panacea; they are another tool that police can use to enhance investigations and potentially improve trust, transparency, and oversight. Their benefits and drawbacks must be considered with caution, particularly when used to facilitate memory for stressful encounters. Based on the research we have cited throughout this chapter, we make the following recommendations for police policy and practice related to collecting statements from police officers following their involvement in use-of-force incidents.

First, despite current practices in the US that generally allow officers to view their BWC footage before writing their report (e.g., White et al., 2019), we recommend that police officers provide their initial report (i.e., pure version statement) of what transpired, including their reasons for using the force they did, before watching their footage of the event. This is the only way to ensure that an independent account of the officer's in-the-moment perceptions and risk assessment while on the scene is captured to determine the reasonableness of their use of force. Once BWC footage is reviewed, it will be impossible to disentangle original memories from information that is included in officer reports based on the viewed footage.

Second, given that there are likely to be significant discrepancies between initial officer accounts and BWC footage of the incidents, an effort will need to be invested in educating the public and triers of fact (e.g., members of a jury) to ensure they do not automatically assume that discrepancies are due to officer deception (or incompetence). BWC footage should be seen as complementary to officer recollection, not competitive, with both being examined with a healthy dose of credibility and skepticism. There are a variety of reasons why discrepancies are likely, including the effects of stress highlighted above and differences that exist between BWCs and the visual system (e.g., the ability to perceive depth, pick up on subtle tactile threat cues, and register detail in low light conditions; Force Science Institute, 2013). Such educational efforts will be critical given research from our lab, which has shown that people often interpret discrepancies between officer testimony and BWC footage as deliberate attempts on the officer's part to be deceptive rather than considering alternative explanations (Schultheis et al., 2015).

Third, in light of existing research that supports the memory-enhancing effects of watching BWC footage, it may be helpful for officers to review their BWC footage following their pure version statement in order to develop a more complete and accurate picture of what transpired. Such elaborated accounts might be useful in a variety of contexts. If this is done, supplemental reports should be labelled as such, and any revisions officers make to their initial report should be clearly marked in the revised report. This is consistent with the two-step report writing process that other researchers have recommended (e.g., Boivin & Grendon, 2022; Vredreveldt et al., 2021). In addition to properly documenting amendments to a statement or report, it is essential that officers clearly articulate why those amendments were made (e.g., while I recalled the subject doing X then Y, after reviewing the video, I now see that the subject did Y then X). However, given people's interpretation of these types of discrepancies (discussed above) and the significant legal and professional jeopardy officers face if suspected of wrongdoing or if they are involved in particularly serious use-of-force incidents, a "hybrid approach" may be prudent in certain circumstances. This approach would involve an officer completing a "pure version" statement with their attorney, then watching the video and consolidating any amendments into one statement. This approach can prevent discrepancies between an officer's initial statement and BWC footage while preserving their pure version account under client-solicitor privilege if required later.

Fourth and finally, education and awareness interventions should be put in place to try and mitigate the effects of cognitive offloading, the inclusion of post-event misinformation in reports, and RIF. More specifically, police officers who use BWCs should be reminded about the potential risks of offloading memory tasks to their cameras so that they invest the appropriate cognitive resources to encode important information while on scene. Not only will this be critical if they are restricted from viewing their BWC footage before preparing their post-incident report, but it will also be important given common issues that occur with BWCs (e.g., officers failing to activate cameras, images on camera being obstructed, low-quality footage, etc.). Specific strategies to deal with the misinformation effect and RIF should also be explored. Concerning the misinformation effect, post-event warnings may be a useful way to minimize the chance that officers unintentionally (and erroneously) conform their memory of what they perceived during an encounter with what was depicted in their BWC footage (e.g., by explicitly highlighting for officers the possibility that this can occur; Blank & Launay, 2014). In an attempt to reduce RIF, there is some evidence that introducing a 24-hour delay between the retrieval practice and the final recall counteracts the effect (Macleod, 2002). Thus, introducing sufficient time between when officers view their BWC footage and when they provide a statement may mitigate the effects of RIF.

References

Adams, D., Paterson, H.M., & MacDougall, H.G. (2020). Law and (rec) order: Updating memory for criminal events with body-worn cameras. *Plos One*, 15(12), e0243226.

Andersen, J.P., Papazoglou, K., & Collins, P. (2016). Reducing robust health-relevant cardiovascular stress responses among active-duty special forces police. *General Medicine: Open Access*.

Anderson, M.C. (2003) Rethinking interference theory: Executive control and the mechanisms of forgetting. *Journal of Memory and Language*, 49(4), 415–445.

Anderson, M.C., Bjork, R.A., & Bjork, E.L. (1994). Remembering can cause forgetting: Retrieval dynamics in long-term memory. *Journal of Experimental Psychology: Learning, Memory, and Cognition*, 20(5), 1063–1087.

Artwohl, A. (2002). Perceptual and memory distortion during officer-involved shootings. *FBI Law Enforcement Bulletin*, 71(10), 18–24.

Baldwin, S., Bennell, C., Andersen, J.P., Semple, T., & Jenkins, B. (2019). Stress-activity mapping: Physiological responses during general duty police encounters. *Frontiers in Psychology*, 10, 2216.

Baldwin, S., Bennell, C., Blaskovits, B., Brown, A., Jenkins, B., Lawrence, C., McGale, H., Semple, T., & Andersen, J.P. (2022). A reasonable officer: Examining the relationships among stress, training, and performance in a highly realistic lethal force scenario. *Frontiers in Psychology*, 12.

Beehr, T.A., Ivanitskaya, L., Glaser, K., Erofeev, D., & Canali, K. (2004). Working in a violent environment: The accuracy of police officers' reports about shooting incidents. *Journal of Occupational and Organizational Psychology*, 77(2), 217.

Berntson, G.G., & Cacioppo, J.T. (2004). Heart rate variability: Stress and psychiatric conditions. In M. Malik and A.J. Camm (Eds.), *Dynamic electrocardiography* (pp. 57–64). Blackwell Publishing.

Berry, E., Hampshire, A., Rowe, J., Hodges, S., Kapur, N., Watson, P., ... & Owen, A.M. (2009). The neural basis of effective memory therapy in a patient with limbic encephalitis. *Journal of Neurology, Neurosurgery, and Psychiatry*, 80(11), 1202–1205.

Blank, H., & Launay, C. (2014). How to protect eyewitness memory against the misinformation effect: A meta-analysis of post-warning studies. *Journal of Applied Research in Memory and Cognition*, 3(2), 77–88.

Blaskovits, B., & Bennell, C. (2020). Exploring the potential impact of body worn cameras on memory in officer-involved critical incidents: A literature review. *Journal of Police andCcriminal Psychology*, 35(3), 251–262.

Blaskovits, B., Jenkins, B., Brown, A., Baldwin, S., & Bennell, C. (2022). Misplacing memory: Examining the phenomenon of cognitive offloading during an officer-involved use-of-force scenario. *Journal of Police and Criminal Psychology*, 37(1), 49–67.

Boivin, R., & Gendron, A. (2022). An experimental study of the impact of body-worn cameras on police report writing. *Journal of Experimental Criminology*, 18(4), 747–764.

Browne, G., Berry, E., Kapur, N., Hodges, S., Smyth, G., Watson, P., & Wood, K. (2011). SenseCam improves memory for recent events and quality of life in a patient with memory retrieval difficulties. *Memory*, 19(7), 713–722.

Camp, G., Wesstein, H., & Bruin, A.B. (2012). Can questioning induce forgetting? Retrieval-induced forgetting of eyewitness information. *Applied Cognitive Psychology*, 26(3), 431–435.

Chopko, B.A., & Schwartz, R.C. (2012). Correlates of career traumatization and symptomatology among active-duty police officers. *Criminal Justice Studies*, 25(1), 83–95.

Cyr, K. (2014). Rethinking police testimony: Notes, lies, and videotape. *Criminal Law Quarterly*, 60(4), 522.

Davis, D., & Loftus, E.F. (2009). Expectancies, emotion, and memory reports for visual events. In J.R. Brockmole (Ed.), *The visual world in memory* (pp. 178–214). Psychology Press.

Dawes, D., Heegaard, W., Brave, M., Paetow, G., Weston, B., & Ho, J.D. (2015). Body-worn cameras improve law enforcement officer report writing accuracy. *The Journal of Law Enforcement*, 4(6).

De Kloet, E.R., Vreugdenhil, E., Oitzl, M.S., & JoëLs, M. (1998). Brain corticosteroid receptor nalance in health and disease. *Endocrine Reviews*, 19(3), 269–301.

Deffenbacher, K.A., Bornstein, B.H., Penrod, S.D., & Mcgorty, E.K. (2004). A meta-analytic review of the effects of high stress on eyewitness memory. *Law and Human Behavior*, 28(6), 687–706.

Di Nota, P.M., Stoliker, B.E., Vaughan, A.D., Andersen, J.P., & Anderson, G.S. (2020). Stress and memory: A systematic state-of-the-art review with evidence-gathering recommendations for police. *Policing: An International Journal*, 44(1), 1–17.

Diamond, D.M., Campbell, A.M., Park, C.R., Halonen, J., & Zoladz, P.R. (2007). The temporal dynamics model of emotional memory processing: A synthesis on the neurobiological basis of stress-induced amnesia, flashbulb and traumatic memories, and the Yerkes-Dodson law. *Neural Plasticity*, 2007, 60803–60833.

Diekelmann, S., Landolt, H.-P., Lahl, O., Born, J., & Wagner, U. (2008). Sleep loss produces false memories. *PloS One*, 3(10), e3512.

Eysenck, M.W., Derakshan, N., Santos, R., & Calvo, M.G. (2007). Anxiety and cognitive performance: Attentional control theory. *Emotion, 7*(2), 336–353.

Force Science Institute. (2013). *10 limitations of body cams you need to know for your protection.* Retrieved from: https://static.spokanecity.org/documents/police/accountability/bodycamera/force-science-body-cameras.pdf

Fridman, J., Barrett, L.F., Wormwood, J.B., & Quigley, K.S. (2019). Applying the theory of constructed emotion to police decision making. *Frontiers in Psychology, 10*(1946).

Geiselman, R.E. (2010). Rest and eyewitness memory recall. *American Journal of Forensic Psychology, 28*(2), 65–69.

Grady, R.H., Butler, B.J., & Loftus, E.F. (2016). What should happen after an officer-involved shooting? Memory concerns in police reporting procedures. *Journal of Applied Research in Memory and Cognition, 5*(3), 246–251.

Graham v Connor. (1989). 490 US 386.

Henkel, L.A. (2014) Point-and-shoot memories: The influence of taking photos on memory for a museum tour. *Psycholocal Science, 25*(2), 396–402.

Hodges, S., Berry, E., & Wood, K. (2011). SenseCam: A wearable camera that stimulates and rehabilitates autobiographical memory. *Memory, 19*(7), 685–696.

Hoisko, J. (2003). Early experiences of visual memory prosthesis for supporting episodic memory. *International Journal of Human-Computer Interaction, 15*(2), 209–230.

Honig, A.L., & Lewinski, W.J. (2008). A survey of the research on human factors related to lethal force encounters: Implications for law enforcement training, tactics, and testimony. *Law Enforcement Executive Forum, 4*(4), 129–152.

Hope, L., Blocksidge, D., Gabbert, F., Sauer, J.D., Lewinski, W.J., Mirashi, A., & Atuk, E. (2016). Memory and the operational witness: Police officer recall of firearms encounters as a function of active response role. *Law and Human Behavior, 40*(1), 23–35.

Hope, L., Gabbert, F., & Fraser, J. (2013). Postincident conferring by law enforcement officers: Determining the impact of team discussions on statement content, accuracy, and officer beliefs. *Law and Human Behavior, 37*(2), 117–127.

Hope, L., Lewinski, W., Dixon, J., Blocksidge, D., & Gabbert, F. (2012). Witnesses in action: The effect of physical exertion on recall and recognition. *Psychological Science, 23*(4), 386–390.

Independent Investigation Agencies of Canada. (2016). *Model independent investigation agency policy—Handling of incident video.* Independent Investigation Agencies of Canada.

Jennings, W.G., Fridell, L.A., & Lynch, M.D. (2014). Cops and cameras: Officer perceptions of the use of body-worn cameras in law enforcement. *Journal of Criminal Justice, 42*(6), 549–556.

Johansson, M., Aslan, A., Bäuml, K.H., Gäbel, A., & Mecklinger, A. (2006). When remembering causes forgetting: Electrophysiological correlates of retrieval-induced forgetting. *Cereb Cortex, 17*(6), 1335–1341.

Klinger, D. (2004). *Into the kill zone: A cop's eye view of deadly force.* Jossey-Bass.

LeDoux, J.E., & Pine, D.S. (2016). Using neuroscience to help understand fear and anxiety: A two-system framework. *American Journal of Psychiatry, 173*(11), 1083–1093.

Levy, B.J., & Anderson, M.C. (2002). Repression can (and should) be studied empirically. *Trends in Cognitive Science*, 6(12), 502–503.

Lewinski, W.J., Dysterheft, J.L., Priem, M.M., & Pettitt, R.W. (2016). Police officers' actual vs. recalled path of travel in response to a threatening traffic stop scenario. *Police Practice and Research*, 17(1), 51–67.

Loftus, E.F. (2005). Planting misinformation in the human mind: A 30-year investigation of the malleability of memory. *Learning and Memory*, 2(4), 361–366.

Loftus, E.F., Donders, K., Hoffman, H.G., & Schooler, J.W. (1989). Creating new memories that are quickly accessed and confidently held. *Memory and Cognition*, 17(5), 607–616.

Lovallo, W.R. (2016). *Stress & health: Biological and psychological interactions* (Third ed.). Sage.

Lum, C., Koper, C.S., Wilson, D.B., Stoltz, M., Goodier, M., Eggins, E., Higginson, A., & Mazerolle, L. (2020). Body-worn cameras' effects on police officers and citizen behavior: A systematic review. *Campbell Systematic Reviews*, 16(e1112), 1–40.

MacLeod, M. (2002). Retrieval-induced forgetting in eyewitness memory: Forgetting as a consequence of remembering. *Applied Cognitive Psychology*, 16(2), 135–149.

Mair, A., Poirier, M., & Conway, M.A. (2017). Supporting older and younger adults' memory for recent everyday events: A prospective sampling study using SenseCam. *Consciousness and Cognition*, 49, 190–202.

Mair, A., Poirier, M., & Conway, M.A. (2019). Memory for staged events: Supporting older and younger adults' memory with SenseCam. *Quarterly Journal of Experimental Psychology*, 72(4), 717–728.

Maskaly, J., Donner, C., Jennings, W.G., Ariel, B., & Sutherland, A. (2017). The effects of body-worn cameras (BWCs) on police and citizen outcomes: A state-of-the-art review. *Policing: An International Journal of Police Strategies & Management*, 40(4), 672–688.

Mcgaugh, J. L. (2015). Consolidating memories. *Annual Review of Psychology*, 66(1), 1–24.

Memon, A., Meissner, C.A., & Fraser, J. (2010). The cognitive interview: A meta-analytic review and study space analysis of the past 25 years. *Psychology, Public Policy, and Law*, 16(4), 340–372.

Miller, L., Toliver, J., & Police Executive Research Forum. (2014). *Implementing a body-worn camera program: Recommendations and lessons learned*. Office of Community Oriented Policing Services.

Murayama, K., Miyatsu, T., Buchli, D., & Storm, B.C. (2014). Forgetting as a consequence of retrieval: A meta-analytic review of retrieval-induced forgetting. *Psychological Bulletin*, 140(5), 1383–1409.

Ness, D., & Calabrese, P. (2016). Stress effects on multiple memory system interactions. *Neural Plasticity*, 2016, 1–20.

Nix, J., Todak, N., & Tregle, B. (2020). Understanding body-worn camera diffusion in US policing. *Police Quarterly*, 23(3), 396–422.

Pelfrey Jr, W.V., & Keener, S. (2018). Body-worn cameras and officer perceptions: A mixed-method pretest posttest of patrol officers and supervisors. *Journal of Crime and Justice*, 41(5), 535–552.

Pezdek, K., Shapland, T., & Barragan, J. (2022). Memory outcomes of police officers viewing their body-worn camera video. *Journal of Applied Research in Memory and Cognition, 11*(3), 392–404.

Piasek, P., Irving, K., & Smeaton, A.F. (2016). Exploring boundaries to the benefits of lifelogging for identity maintenance for people with dementia. In I. Management Association (Ed.), *Psychology and mental health: Concepts, methodologies, tools, and applications* (pp. 213–227). IGI Global.

Pinizzotto, A.J., Davis, E.F., & Miller III, C.E. (2006). *Violent encounters: A study of felonious assaults on our nation's law enforcement officers.* US Department of Justice.

Porter, L.E., Ready, J., & Alpert, G.P. (2019). Officer-involved shootings: Testing the effect of question timing on memory accuracy for stressful events. *Journal of Experimental Criminology, 15*(1), 1–28.

President's Task Force on 21st Century Policing. (2015). *Final report of the President's task force on 21st century policing.* Retrieved from www.ojp.gov/ncjrs/virtual-library/abstracts/final-report-presidents-task-force-21st-century-policing

Risko, E.F., & Gilbert, S.J. (2016). Cognitive offloading. *Trends in Cognitive Science, 20*(9), 676–688

Schultheis, E., Ellingwood, H., & Bennell, C. (2015). *Is seeing believing? Public perception of the use of body worn video by police.* Poster presented at the annual meeting of the Society for Police and Criminal Psychology, Atlanta, Georgia, United States.

Seamon, J.G., Moskowitz, T.N., Swan, A.E., Zhong, B., Golembeski, A., Liong, C., Narzikul, A.C., & Sosan, O.A. (2014). Sensecam reminiscence and action recall in memory-unimpaired people. *Memory, 22*(7), 861–866.

Sharps, M.J. (2010). *Processing under pressure: Sress, memory, and decision-making in law enforcement.* Looseleaf Law Publications.

Shields, G.S., Sazma, M.A., McCullough, A.M., & Yonelinas, A.P. (2017). The effects of acute stress on episodic memory: A meta-analysis and integrative review. *Psychological Bulletin, 143*(6), 636–675.

Silva, A.R., Pinho, S., Macedo, L.M., & Moulin, C.J. (2013). Benefits of SenseCam review on neuropsychological test performance. *American Journal of Preventive Medicine, 44*(3), 302–307.

Silva, A.R., Salome Pinho, M., Macedo, L., & Moulin, J.A. (2017). The cognitive effects of wearable cameras in mild Alzheimer disease—An experimental study. *Current Alzheimer Research, 14*(12), 1270–1282.

Soares, J.S., & Storm, B.C. (2018). Forget in a flash: A further investigation of the photo-taking impairment effect. *Journal of Applied Research in Memory and Cognition, 7*(1), 154–160.

Storm, B.C., & Levy, B.J. (2012). A progress report on the inhibitory account of retrieval-induced forgetting. *Memory and Cognition, 40*(6), 827–843.

Thayer, J.F., & Sternberg, E. (2006). Beyond heart rate variability: Vagal regulation of allostatic systems. *Annals of the New York Academy of Sciences, 1088*(1), 361–372.

Van Teijlingen, T., Oudman, E., & Postma, A. (2021). Lifelogging as a rehabilitation tool in patients with amnesia: A narrative literature review on the effect of lifelogging on memory loss. *Neuropsychological Rehabilitation*, 1–27.

Violanti, J.M. (2014). *Dying for the job: Police work exposure and health.* Charles C. Thomas Publisher, Ltd.

Vredeveldt, A., Kesteloo, L., & Hildebrandt, A. (2021). To watch or not to watch: When reviewing body-worn camera footage improves police reports. *Law and Human Behavior, 45*(5), 427–439.

White, M.D., & Malm, A. (2020). *Cops, cameras, and crisis: The potential and the perils of police body-worn cameras.* NYU Press.

White, M.D., Flippin, M., & Malm, A. (2019). *Key trends in body-worn camera policy and practice: A four-year policy analysis of US Department of Justice-funded law enforcement agencies.* Office of Justice Programs, US Department of Justice.

Yuille, J.C., Davies, G., Gibling, F., Marxsen, D., & Porter, S. (1994). Eyewitness memory of police trainees for realistic role plays. *Journal of Applied Psychology, 79*(6), 931–936.

Zlotnik, G., & Vansintjan, A. (2019). Memory: An extended definition [Perspective]. *Frontiers in Psychology, 10.* https://doi.org/10.3389/fpsyg.2019.02523

12 "Super-recognizers" and the Legal System

Emma Portch, Janice Attard-Johnson, Alejandro J. Estudillo, Natalie Mestry, and Sarah Bate

The twenty-first century has seen a notional shift in the human face recognition literature. Whereas face recognition skills have traditionally been regarded as absolute (with people from the typical population possessing intact skills and those with certain patterns of brain damage experiencing an abrupt loss of the ability), it is now acknowledged that face recognition proficiency can vastly differ in the typical population (e.g., Bindemann et al., 2012; White & Burton, 2022; Wilmer, 2017). As such, a small proportion of people at the bottom end of this continuum appear to naturally exhibit face recognition impairments that match the severity of those acquired via brain injury (developmental prosopagnosia; Bate & Tree, 2017; Bowles et al., 2009), and an equivalent population at the top end display unusually accurate face recognition skills. The latter individuals have been dubbed "super-recognizers" (Russell et al., 2009).

Interest in super-recognizers has quickly escalated from a small number of theoretical investigations in the Cognitive Psychology literature to real-world deployment of police officers who appear to possess these skills (e.g., Davis, 2019, 2020; Davis et al., 2016; Robertson et al., 2016). While research examining super-recognition has increased at a steady rate, the operational deployment of these individuals has far outpaced theoretical developments (e.g., Ramon et al., 2019). As such, the involvement of super-recognizers in forensic and policing settings has naturally led to the question of whether they can provide expert testimony in a court of law. This chapter examines this issue in the context of our theoretical understanding of super-recognition. We initially provide contextual and theoretical background about super-recognizers and their role in applied settings before critically assessing their suitability and efficacy as potential expert witnesses in legal cases.

Super-recognition in Research, Real-World, and Legal Settings

The term "super-recognizer" first appeared in the academic literature in 2009, when Russell et al. probed the self-professed exceptional face memory abilities of four participants. This small-scale investigation appeared to support the notion that the super-recognizers sampled were as good at face recognition as people with developmental prosopagnosia were bad (Russell et al., 2009, p.256). Much subsequent work has attempted to examine whether super-recognizers' disparate placement on the face recognition continuum is driven by qualitative or merely quantitative differences in face-processing strategy utilization, relative to typical and impaired performers (e.g., Bobak et al., 2017; Tardif et al., 2019). An array of experimental and applied face-processing tasks have been conducted with larger samples, the results of which pose important questions for the drivers, limitations, and heterogeneities of super-recognizer performance (e.g., Bate et al., 2018, 2019a, 2019b, 2020a; Belanova et al., 2018; Bobak et al., 2016a, 2016b, 2016c, 2016d; Fysh et al., 2020; Ramon, 2021; Robertson et al., 2020).

Despite concerns that external interest has outpaced progression in the academic literature, various police departments report current and previous operational deployment of officers they consider to be "super-recognizers" (e.g., London, Munich, Stuttgart, and Berlin; Davis, 2019, 2020; Ramon et al., 2019; Thielgen et al., 2021). Reportedly these individuals familiarize themselves with large databases of photographic images to aid live suspect apprehension at events or match current and historical images of familiar offenders to facilitate crime linkage (e.g., Davis, 2020; Edmond & Wortley, 2016). Apparent success in these tasks suggests that super-recognizer identifications may have investigative value, prompting further consideration of whether their evidence might be admissible in court, and whether they could be considered "expert" witnesses (see also Edmond & Wortley, 2016; Edmon et al., 2021; Moreton, 2020; Roberts, 2020).

To our knowledge, super-recognizers have thus far played a very limited role in the courtroom (e.g., Davis, 2020; Edmond & Wortley, 2016; Edmond et al., 2021; Roberts, 2020). Identifications in judicial settings typically require an individual to attempt to match an unfamiliar face across multiple static and/or dynamic images (e.g., Roberts, 2020; Edmond et al., 2021). The courts recognize that the (presumably) typical perceivers comprising a jury are unlikely to be able to perform this type of "facial mapping" with a high degree of accuracy (e.g., Moreton, 2020). Thus, the ability to offer this type of opinion evidence as *fact* falls only to those with evidenced expertise (*R v Turner*, 1975; US Government Publishing Office, 2019), particularly in cases where image quality is questionable (*R v Clarke*, 1995; *R v Stockwell*, 1993). In the past 25 years, courts within common law jurisdictions (including the USA and UK) have typically accepted this "facial mapping" evidence from trained forensic face examiners (Edmond et al., 2013; *R v Clarke*, 1995; *R v Stockwell*, 1993; US Government Publishing Office, 2019). While in some cases this evidence has substantially contributed towards conviction (*R v Hookway*, 1999), courts have sometimes adopted a more cautious approach whereby experts forego opining about the possibility that two unfamiliar faces match in identity and simply provide the jury with their assessment of feature-based similarities between two images (e.g., Edmond et al., 2013; *R v Gray*, 2003). Human-verified outputs from computer algorithms may also be admissible, given significant improvements in machine accuracy since the advent of Deep Convolutional Neural Networks (DCNNs). These systems used a multi-layered approach to face encoding wherein various facial attributes and dimensions are processed and pooled to create a progressively more complex and specific facial representation (e.g., Moreton, 2021; Noyes & Hill, 2020; O'Toole et al., 2018).

Exceptions to expert admissibility rules in common law jurisdictions apply only when a witness can evidence personal familiarity with the target (e.g., when police officers involved in the investigation recognize current perpetrators from past incidents; Ministry of Justice, 2015a, 2015b; *R v Leung and Wong*, 1999, though see *R v Smith*, 2001). This departure tallies with the academic face recognition literature, which firmly asserts that familiar face processing is far less error-prone than unfamiliar face matching and can be performed with high levels of accuracy, even by typical perceivers (e.g., Bruce et al., 2001; Johnston & Edmond, 2009). Despite historically demonstrating a disproportionate advantage in unfamiliar face recognition (e.g., Russell et al., 2009), reports suggest that super-recognizers have also only provided familiar identifications in the courtroom (Edmond & Wortley, 2016) and only on an incidental basis when they are already involved in that particular investigation (e.g., Davis, 2019, though see Davis et al., 2019 for an exception[1]). This mirrors the reported nature of super-recognizer identifications in operational settings, which typically rely on officers' ability to recognize local, known offenders from photographic databases or CCTV captures (e.g., Evision, 2015). However, Edmond and Wortley (2016) note a potentially problematic caveat. Relative to typical perceivers, super-recognizers may engage in more robust face encoding processes, meaning that they can rapidly build comparatively stable face representations across limited image exposures (Dunn et al., 2022). As such, while some operational work may allow

---

1 In Davis et al. (2019) a group of super-recognisers matched a post-mortem photograph of an individual to an ante-mortem photograph of a suspected target, presented within a line-up of appropriately matched foils. Combined with other evidence, this identification led a coroner to issue a death certificate for the individual. Forensic face examiners had declined the task based on insufficient image quality. Moreton (2021) suggests that this practice is unlikely to be common given that ante- to post-mortem image matching is typically insufficient to confirm identification (Caplova et al., 2017).

super-recognizers to derive familiarity via brief exposures to static images of a face when housed in photographic databases (see also Davis, 2020), legally, the ability to match this memory-based representation to subsequent captures of the individual may occupy a grey area between familiar and unfamiliar face recognition (e.g., Moreton, 2020). While it is unclear whether and how often super-recognizers may have provided this "ad-hoc" form of expert evidence (Davis, 2019), in the UK the Forensic Science Regulator (2018) takes heed of such concerns. They ultimately discourage attempts to redefine super-recognizers as expert witnesses, noting that the methods they employ may not adhere to the reliability standards or safeguards required of forensic scientists within common law jurisdictions (e.g., *Daubert v Merrell Dow Pharmaceuticals Inc.* 1993; *R v Bonython*, 1984; US Government Publishing Office, 2019).

However, several researchers note that this position may be reversed in the future. Compared to forensic face examiners and algorithms, super-recognizers may be less cost- and labor-intensive to deploy (e.g., Edmond & Wortley, 2016; Edmond et al., 2021; Towler et al., 2020; see a further critical comparison of group accuracy below). Indeed, as face recognition abilities appear largely fixed from middle adulthood (e.g., Germine et al., 2011), forensic face examiners must engage in considerable training to exploit a different route to expertise, suppressing naturalistic, holistic strategies to match unfamiliar faces, and instead adopting piecemeal, feature-based analytical methods (e.g., Towler et al., 2017, 2020). Research shows that expertise may be effectively developed via this route (e.g., White et al., 2015b; but see Edmond et al., 2015; Moreton, 2020), but that processing transitions can be lengthy, with the ability to identify and analyze the most diagnostic features honed through extensive on-the-job experience, mentoring and feedback (Towler et al., 2019). While there is some indication that these skills translate to speeded face-matching decisions (e.g., White et al., 2015b; Moreton, 2021), accuracy typically improves linearly to task duration, and examiners must use the tools of their trade to deliver expert evidence, particularly for poor-quality images, which necessitate a lengthy approach (White et al., 2015b). To achieve high accuracy, DCNNs still require extensive input of training images that ideally include multiple naturally varying images of the same individual (Noyes & Hill, 2020; O'Toole et al., 2018) as well as individuals of different ethnicities (Phillips et al., 2011). While algorithms can deliver matching results quickly, the labelling of training images and the verification of output still require extensive human interaction, delaying the process (e.g., Grother et al., 2019).

Conversely, super-recognizers are thought to exploit naturalistic, holistic pathways to perform both face memory and matching tasks (Bobak et al., 2017; Towler et al., 2020; see below for further discussion), rendering costly training unnecessary and expediting identifications (Nador et al., 2022; Towler et al., 2020; though rigorous screening to select top innate performers may also entail costs e.g., Bate et al., 2020b). While legally the matching of images that become familiar through simple image-based exposure may present a grey area (Edmond & Wortley, 2016), super-recognizers may possess the skills to complete a more diverse set of facial recognition tasks than facial examiners, which could be operationally advantageous (e.g., Davis, 2019; White et al., 2020).

In response to these observations, the remainder of this chapter uses empirical evidence to critically assess whether a future role exists for super-recognizers in the courtroom. Legislation regulating the provision of unfamiliar face mapping evidence typically requires the witness to have developed demonstrable expertise through rigorous accredited training in robust and communicable techniques; a process both undertaken by and applicable to those who currently provide admissible evidence in court (i.e., forensic face examiners; e.g., Ministry of Justice, 2015a; *Daubert v Merrell Dow Pharmaceuticals Inc.* 1993; *R v Bonython*, 1984; US Government Publishing Office, 2019; President's Council of Advisors on Science and Technology, 2016; though see Edmond et al., 2015 and Roberts, 2020, for caveats). However, some legal guidelines acknowledge differential routes to expertise based on experience (*R v Luttrell*, 2004); a conceptualization that would accommodate the proposed naturalistic mechanisms that are thought to be exploited in super-recognition (Roberts, 2020; Towler et al., 2020). Crucially, in accordance with facets of the relevance principle, the use of these mechanisms should allow the individual to reach conclusions that a typical perceiver, or juror, would be incapable of independently arriving at with any certainty of accuracy. The expert should thus be able to inform judicial disputes about identity through the provision of *opinion* evidence as *fact* (*R v Turner*, 1975; US Government Publishing Office, 2019).

To assess whether super-recognizers meet these specifications, we first probe literature that examines the mechanisms that underpin their superior abilities, critically exploring whether they differ qualitatively or quantitatively from those utilized by typical perceivers. We then consider whether super-recognizers consistently perform at an exceptional level relative to statistical benchmarks and typical perceiver baselines, critically recognizing how these attempts may be severely compromised by (a) the screening techniques used to initially identify superior performers, and (b) the tests used to further probe their abilities. These same contemporary issues will be relevant to our final discussion of how super-recognizer ability compares to that demonstrated by alternative and admissible expert witnesses (e.g., forensic face examiners and algorithms).

Why Are Super-recognizers So Good at Face Recognition?

Much theoretical research into super-recognition has aimed to understand the underpinnings of the ability (e.g., Abudarham et al., 2021; Bobak et al., 2016a, 2017; Dunn et al., 2022; Russell et al., 2012; Tardif et al., 2019). Researchers typically agree that two possible alternative accounts may apply (e.g., Bate et al., 2020b; Noyes et al., 2017). According to one view, super-recognizers may possess qualitatively different face recognition mechanisms that go beyond the typical processes employed by the rest of the population (e.g., they may preferentially attend to a facial feature or collection of features that are not the typical focus of the average perceivers). If this account is true then a strong operationalized definition of super-recognition can emerge, which would clearly suggest that super-recognizers have the ability to successfully make identifications that a standard juror could not (i.e., a facet of the relevance principle; *R v Turner*, 1975; US Government Publishing Office, 2019). If instead super-recognizers are quantitatively superior at using the same face-processing strategies employed by the rest of the population, then the relevance criterion may only be met if their performance is consistently at a statistically distinguishable level from typical perceivers, who reside separately on a normally distributed spectrum of face recognition ability (see below for further discussion).

A full understanding of the cognitive mechanisms underpinning super-recognition begin with a consideration of heritability—a factor known to underpin individual differences in face recognition across the spectrum (e.g., McKone et al., 2012; Shakeshaft & Plomin, 2015). Indeed, various studies report that developmental prosopagnosia, a profound impairment in familiar face recognition, runs in families (e.g., Kennerknecht et al., 2008; Schmalzl et al., 2008), with little evidence that these impairments could be attributed to shared variance in other general cognitive factors, such as IQ and visual processing capability (e.g., Duchaine et al., 2007; Lee et al., 2010). Similarly, monozygotic twins show more similar domain-specific face recognition performance than dizygotic twins (e.g., Wilmer et al., 2010); an asymmetry that may be underpinned by shared variance in holistic processing ability (e.g., Zhu et al., 2010). Reports of heritability are also supported by the limited success of face identification training programs, particularly for "face reviewers," who regularly perform face-matching tasks in operational roles (e.g., passport control officers, White et al., 2014, 2015a; police officers, Bruce et al., 1999). While training may be more efficacious for forensic face examiners (Towler et al., 2019; but see Edmond et al., 2015; Moreton, 2020), gains are linked explicitly to the development of atypical face-processing strategies and thus evidenced only in face mapping tasks, with no commensurate improvement in everyday face recognition ability (Towler et al., 2019, 2020). Together, this evidence suggests that naturalistic face recognition mechanisms are likely biologically predisposed and at least somewhat resilient to improvement via training or experience.

Further work has examined whether super-recognizer ability is domain-specific, critically assessing whether superior face recognition and face matching abilities generalize to other classes of stimuli that are thought to be processed in a qualitatively different way (i.e., objects, Farah, 1995). While all six super-recognizers in Bobak et al.'s (2016a) study demonstrated superior face memory performance, only two showed some selective facilitation, relative to controls, in tests of either object matching or memory. In one case facilitation appeared to be linked to matching of a specific class of object (hands) and, in another, a general memory-based advantage. However, it is unlikely that the super-recognizer advantage can be attributed to a general memory enhancement: Ramon et al. (2016) found typical face memory and matching scores in two participants who held Guinness World Records for generalized memory at the time of testing. Similar to Bobak et al. (2016a), Bennetts et al. (2017) also found no conclusive evidence of facilitated object recognition or matching performance when adopting a thorough case study approach with an adolescent super-recognizer (O.B.). In sum, work appears to support the notion that super-recognizers show face-specific proficiencies.

Faces are sometimes considered "special" because they are thought to be processed in a different way to other classes of stimuli e.g., objects; while faces are processed "holistically," as a single and decomposable whole, objects are processed in a piecemeal fashion, as a collection of isolated features (e.g., Diamond & Carey, 1986; Farah, 1995; Farah et al., 1998; Maurer et al., 2002). As holistic processing ability is predictive of variance in the face recognition performance of typical perceivers (e.g., DeGutis et al., 2013; Wang et al., 2012), differential strategy application and/or efficiency may similarly underpin the selective advantage observed in super-recognizers. Although many measures of holistic processing have been proposed (e.g., Rezlescu et al., 2017; Tanaka & Simonyi, 2016; Wong et al., 2021), typical demonstrations comprise (a) inversion effects, whereby recognition of faces (versus objects) are disproportionately affected when presented upside down (McKone & Yovel, 2009; Yin, 1969), and (b) composite effects, that are evidenced by a difficulty to match identity across two face halves when they are presented aligned, rather than separate (Hole, 1994; Rossion, 2013; Young et al., 1987). The super-recognizers reported by Russell et al. (2009) showed larger inversion effects in a face perception task compared to controls, with effects of a similar magnitude shown by 83% of the super-recognizers sampled in Bobak et al. (2016a) and O.B. (Bennetts et al., 2017). However, inversion effects may not only reflect disruption to holistic processing, but to stimulus-specific local feature extraction (McKone & Yovel, 2009), thus Bobak et al. (2016a) extended their investigation to include an atypical composite task that adopted the "partial" design of Robbins and McKone (2007). Here, participants assessed whether the top-halves of two sequentially presented faces matched in identity. Bobak et al. (2016a) found no difference in the size of the composite effect across super-recognizers and controls; while these results may suggest that the holistic processing enhancement in super-recognition is specific to those mechanisms tapped by the inversion effect (Lee et al., 2022a; Rezlescu et al., 2017), they may alternatively reflect the methodological decision to use a partial rather than complete composite task (e.g., Rossion, 2013). Thus, further behavioral investigation of holistic processing in super-recognizers are required to reconcile the available literature.

The monitoring of eye movements also provides a way to assess holistic and feature-based contributions to face identification (e.g., Lee et al., 2022b; Rossion, 2008). In typical perceivers, holistic processing has been associated with longer fixations to the central region of the face (Blais et al., 2008; van Belle et al., 2010). Bobak et al. (2017) replicated this finding and reported that super-recognizers specifically spend more time looking at the nose. At first glance this finding appears indicative of a qualitative difference in processing strategy; however, a common linear relationship was exhibited between face recognition ability and proportion of time spent fixating on the nose in both super-recognizers and controls, suggesting that their strategy utilization differed only in degree, and not type.

Results consistent with the existence of only quantitative (versus qualitative) processing differences come from experiments that use selective information-sampling techniques. Dunn et al. (2022) presented unfamiliar, to-be-learnt faces to their participants through gaze-contingent "spotlight" apertures of different sizes. Super-recognizers were later more accurate at recognizing these faces than controls, even when sampling from small apertures. While this result may suggest that super-recognizers can effectively use feature-based processing strategies to encode faces, the researchers also found a more widely distributed fixation pattern in their information sampling; a technique that may cumulatively build a strong holistic representation of the face. Mirroring the findings of Bobak et al. (2017), there was evidence that control participants also engaged in widespread sampling that was strongly predictive of task performance. Tardif et al. (2019) similarly found that they could predict 65% of the variance in their top-end (super-recognizers) and bottom-end performers (people with developmental prosopagnosia) by modelling the behavior of control participants in a task of familiar face recognition. Using the bubbles technique (Gosselin & Schyns, 2001), they found more accurate recognition of famous faces in all participant groups when the eyes, eyebrows, and mouth were randomly sampled at a higher rate than other facial regions. Interestingly, characteristics within the eye region (eye color, shape, and eyebrow size) were also disproportionately important in Abudarham et al.'s (2021) study, where famous face recognition ability in typical perceivers, super-recognizers and people with prosopagnosia diminished when localized alterations or substitutions were made to these features. These findings suggest that all three groups regard similar features as diagnostic for identification and that accuracy fluctuations arise due to differences in the efficacy with which these regions are sampled.

In conclusion, the limited literature that examines the underpinning mechanisms of super-recognition appears to support the existence of a normally distributed face recognition continuum wherein superior and typical performers differ only quantitatively in their strategy utilization. While evidence of qualitative differences would help to convince a court of law that super-recognizers' possess skills over and above those of typical jurors, quantitative accounts could only meet this criterion if super-recognizers can consistently show exceptional performance relative to typical perceivers. We discuss this possibility in the section below.

How Can We Demonstrate that Someone Is Genuinely a Super-recognizer?

A definitive assessment of performance consistency requires two preliminary conditions to be met (e.g., Bate et al., 2020b, 2021; Ramon et al., 2019; Ramon, 2021). First, that implemented screening methods are sufficient to accurately identify those who are genuinely superior performers, and second, that the additional tests used to further probe the abilities of these individuals are equally and reliably calibrated to allow continued performance differentiation. Below, we critically evaluate whether these conditions have been met in both experimental and applied settings.

Methods of Identification

Different approaches underpin the classification of super-recognizers, including on-the-job performance metrics, self-report ratings, and objective assessment tools. While all three methods have been used in both research and operational attempts, precise screening criteria are often ill-defined. For instance, it appears that on-the-job performance metrics (e.g., high perpetrator identification rates from photographic, circulated "Caught on Camera" resources) may have driven early identification in UK police forces, prior to the development of the Metropolitan Police Service's dedicated Super-recognizer Unit (Davis, 2020).[2] However, these indices arguably provide a poor measure of true ability as they may be influenced by extraneous factors such as feedback, training and motivation (Bate et al., 2021; White et al., 2020), or inflated by the instances of familiar perpetrator recognition that are reportedly common within investigations (i.e., where a police or custody officer recognizes an image of a known offender with whom they have had previous contact, rather than identifying two instances of the same unfamiliar person across multiple image captures, Davis, 2019, 2020; Evision, 2015). Importantly, proficiency in (comparatively easy) familiar face recognition tasks are unlikely to translate to traditional, unfamiliar face mapping (e.g., Bruce et al., 2001; Johnston & Edmond, 2009). In support, when sampling is based solely or partially on unit membership and/or number of operational identifications, "super-recognizers" show highly variable performance on objective tests of unfamiliar face recognition, only exceeding the performance of controls at a group level (e.g., Davis et al., 2016; Robertson et al., 2016; see similar observations in Edmond et al., 2021, and Ramon, 2021).

Further, assessment of on-the-job metrics requires that an individual is already employed and performing operational tasks. However, this post-hoc approach does not accommodate assessment of face recognition ability in new recruits. Other approaches are thus required, with self-reported face recognition ability being attractive due to its simplicity. However, accurate self-report relies on the ability to flexibly temper our confidence estimates in line with the difficulty of a face recognition task, which may fluctuate according to characteristics of the to-be-matched or -memorized images (e.g,. lighting, pose). This awareness appears limited even in top-performers (Bate & Dudfield, 2019; Bobak et al., 2019) where self-assessment remains susceptible to feedback and external influence (Bindemann et al., 2014). Validated tests likely offer opportunity for objective comparison between the performance of typical perceivers and super-recognizers, however, they are not without their limitations, as discussed below.

The Quality of Objective Tests

Objective tests must be of sufficient difficulty to facilitate identification of cut-off scores that allow statistical differentiation between typical and

---

2 While Davis (2019) describes the application of more objective and comprehensive screening protocols for subsequent recruitment to the Metropolitan Police Service's dedicated unit, it is difficult to ascertain their appropriateness as, to our best knowledge, normative data are only available for some tests (e.g., Davis et al., 2018, 2020).

superior perceivers, with sufficient room from ceiling also necessary to further probe possible performance heterogeneity among top performers (Bate et al., 2020b, 2021; Bobak et al., 2016d; Ramon, 2021). It is now recognized that some tests are only appropriate for probing low and typical face-recognition abilities (e.g., Bate et al., 2021), with high control baselines and associated ceiling effects precluding their suitability for assessment of superior skill (e.g., the Glasgow Face Matching Test, GFMT: (Burton et al., 2010; the Cambridge Face Perception Test, CFPT: Duchaine et al., 2007; and the short-version of the Cambridge Face Memory Test, CFMT; Duchaine & Nakayama, 2006). Currently, the laboratory-based criteria to qualify as a super-recognizer is predominantly based on the extended version of the CFMT (CFMT+; Russell et al., 2009). Here participants have a time-limited opportunity to encode six target faces and then attempt to select these target faces from among sequentially presented triads that contain two unfamiliar fillers. To increase task difficulty, images vary according to pose and lighting, with heavy pixelation applied in later blocks. The CFMT+ is used in 80% of super-recognizer studies and is considered reliable ($\alpha = 0.89$) and sufficiently sensitive for detecting superior performance (Bate et al., 2021).

While tightly controlled laboratory-style tests such as the CFMT+ underpin theoretical assessment, correlations between performance on these and more ecologically valid tests are highly variable (e.g., Davis et al., 2018; Nador et al., 2022; Noyes et al., 2018; Thielgen et al., 2021). Indeed, data simulations suggest only mild-to-moderate predictive power (Baldson et al., 2018; Ramon et al., 2019), resulting in calls for interdisciplinary efforts to develop tasks that mirror occupational demands according to process and stimulus type (e.g., Nador et al., 2022; Ramon et al., 2019; Ramon, 2021; Thielgen et al., 2021). This approach was adopted by Davis et al. (2018), whose "Spotting the Face in a Crowd" test requires participants to match instances of an unfamiliar individual across static photographs and naturalistic whole-body footage from active CCTV units across London (as might be the case in a missing person's investigation). Critically, this and other user-inspired screening tasks integrate target-absent and target-present trials (e.g., Balsdon et al., 2018; Bate et al., 2018; Davis et al., 2016), which facilitate the exploration of response biases that may carry differential consequences at an operational level (e.g., Devue, 2019; Robertson & Bindemann, 2019). It is also recommended that tasks integrate extrinsic occupational factors (e.g., Bate et al., 2019c; Moreton et al., 2019), such as time pressure and repetition (Robertson & Bindemann, 2019), and that outcome measures carefully merge indices of accuracy and reaction time to assess whether personnel can continue to work consistently and efficiently when these pressures are present (Nador et al., 2022).

Consistency of Performance

To ensure that single-point screening attempts reliably identify truly superior performers and produce results to support matching of these individuals to the tasks in which they are likely to excel, they should include multiple tests that (a) assess the *same* sub-processes (e.g., different tests assessing face memory), and (b) measure *different* sub-processes (e.g., face matching and face memory; Bate et al., 2021; Lander et al., 2018; Ramon et al., 2019; Ramon, 2021; Young & Noyes, 2019). To ensure consistency in ability after varying delays, later assessment of the same individuals must necessarily implement the same or similar testing formats (Ramon et al., 2019; Ramon, 2021). To reduce the potential for stimulus-specific inflations to accuracy, alterations may be made to the identity, pose, age or featural characteristics of the faces sampled (e.g., Bate et al., 2019b).

A similar pattern of results are obtained in post-screening studies which aim to assess multi-test performance consistency: while super-recognizers as a group tend to outperform the control baseline, not all individuals therein will exceed this benchmark, with heterogenous performance profiles observed and few individuals demonstrating exceptional performance across the board (e.g., Bate et al., 2018, 2019b; Bobak et al., 2016b, 2016c; Davis et al., 2016; Fysh et al., 2020). These patterns are commonly observed in batteries that include tests that tap the *same* face-recognition component. For example, a group of police officers who met exceptional performance cut-offs on the CFMT+ did not all achieve this criterion when tested on the Models Memory Test (MMT; Bate et al., 2018); a similarly constructed paradigm which differs only in the type of stimuli used and presence of target-absent, as well as target-present, trials (Bate et al., 2019b). Bobak et al. (2016b) similarly compared the performance of super-recognizers on two simultaneous face-matching tests, the GFMT and the Models Face Matching Test (Dowsett & Burton, 2015), with performance heterogeneities underpinning the failure of some participants to exceed the control baseline across both tests. However, these results may be attributed to differences in difficulty calibration, with the GFMT generally considered unsuitable for the assessment of superior performers (e.g., Bate et al., 2020b, 2021). In a more robust assessment, which explored performance consistency across three equally calibrated blocks of the more difficult simultaneous Pairs Matching Task (PMT; Bate et al., 2018), Bate et al. (2019b) similarly reported that only 15% of their police super-recognizers statistically outperformed the control baseline across the board.

Inconsistencies are also observed when comparing super-recognizer performance across tests that tap *different* face-processing components.

Bate et al. (2018) found that fewer than half of their sample were able to attain cut-off scores to denote exceptional performance on 75% of a battery that comprised multiple appropriately calibrated tests of face memory (the CFMT+ and MMT) and matching (PMT). Bobak et al. (2016c) noted similar performance heterogeneities, particularly when they conducted single-case comparisons between individual super-recognizer scores ($n = 6$) and respective control baselines. While all comparisons at this level were significant for the CFMT+, only four super-recognizers reached this statistical cut-off on the simultaneous 1-in-10 face-matching array task (Bruce et al., 1999), and only one on a separate ecologically valid test of face memory. Despite finding positive correlations between CFMT+ and matching performance, asymmetrical data rankings revealed that those who performed worst on the CFMT+ were among the highest performers on the 1-in-10 task. Similar performance asymmetries were noted in a study that sampled CFMT+-screened civilian super-recognizers and police "identifiers," who had been selected based on the number of successful suspect identifications they had made in a 12-month period (Davis et al., 2016). Here, many participants within these "specialist" groups failed to statistically outperform the control mean on the GFMT, with the two highest performers on the CFMT+ performing poorly both on this task and other tests of familiar (Bruce et al., 1999) and unfamiliar face memory (Lander et al., 2001).

Observed performance inconsistencies in multi-component batteries may suggest that super-recognition has a complex, multi-faceted presentation, with some individuals excelling only in tests of face memory, and others in matching (e.g., Bate et al., 2018; Bobak et al., 2016a, 2016c). Both same- and multi-component performance inconsistencies have practical implications as they suggest that screened super-recognizers may be unable to replicate their exceptional performance when assigned to operational work. Given the evidence of heterogeneous presentation, this may particularly be the case when screening and applied demands differ (e.g., Bate et al., 2021; Fysh et al., 2020). Applied tasks performed by officers and expert witnesses almost exclusively rely on unfamiliar face mapping; thus, current screening protocols, which typically focus heavily on outcomes from a difficult test of face memory (the CFMT+), may select individuals whose skills cannot generalize to this work, and fail to identify those whose might (Bate et al., 2018, 2021). Taken together, until screening protocols exist that include appropriately calibrated and ecologically valid tests, designed to comprehensively explore the potentially multi-faceted nature of super-recognition, we cannot be sure that identified individuals show truly superior abilities in face-memory, matching, or both processes. The results of consistency testing, important both for operational deployment and legally relevant assessments of the possession of atypical skill level, are severely compromised when this first condition goes unmet.

Comparing Facial Mapping Accuracy against Typical and Expert Witnesses

Limitations associated with super-recognizer screening preclude use of performance consistency findings to reliably address whether super-recognizers can deliver face-mapping conclusions beyond the reach of typical perceivers. To alternatively assess the relevance principle, we explore whether super-recognizers exhibit perceptual biases, widely evidenced in typical perceivers, that make them more effective perceivers of some faces than others. If these perceptual biases are shared, this may again suggest that super-recognizers differ only quantitatively (versus qualitatively) in their approach to face-processing, and will have operational significance, suggesting that tailoring may need to accommodate both type of task (memory or matching) and type of face stimulus, to ensure generalizability of skill. Having assessed throughout whether super-recognizers can reliably be expected to deliver more accurate identifications than a standard juror, we finally examine whether they can match the performance of those currently permitted to provide expert face mapping evidence in court (i.e., forensic face examiners and algorithms).

The Impact of Perceptual Bias on Super-recognizers

The literature recognizes that face recognition performance asymmetries in typical perceivers are sometimes driven by perceptual characteristics that differ between themselves and those they observe. Indeed, the own-race bias (ORB) asserts that individuals show superior processing for own-race than other-race faces; an effect demonstrated in both tasks of face memory (e.g., Meissner & Brigham, 2001) and unfamiliar face matching, with differences in holistic processing thought to underpin the separate inversion effects observed for each type of face (e.g., Megreya et al., 2011).

Two recent studies investigated the ORB in super-recognizers. Bate et al. (2019a) sampled eight Caucasian super-recognizers who had obtained exceptional scores on two screening tests of face memory that utilized own-race targets and asked them to complete two equally calibrated versions of the PMT; one comprising Caucasian faces and the other Asian faces. Super-recognizer performance was compared to separate control groups of Caucasian and Asian participants (Experiment 2). While at a group level super-recognizers outperformed Caucasian controls on the Asian matching task (mean accuracy = 86.46% and 68.27%, respectively), heterogeneities in super-recognizer performance meant that the size of the ORB, assessed via accuracy differences between performance in the Caucasian and Asian matching task, was similar across the two groups. Similar findings were obtained by Robertson et al. (2020), who compared Caucasian super-recognizer ($n = 35$) and control performance across the short-version of the Egyptian Face Matching Task; a simultaneous face-matching task, similar in construction to the GFMT, in which participants must discriminate between pairs of Egyptian vs. Caucasian faces (EFMT-short; Megreya et al., 2011). However, these researchers noted that the size of the ORB, evidenced here via differences in performance across the EFMT-short and the GFMT, was only of similar magnitude in super-recognizers and controls when the latter group were highly motivated to perform well. Here, motivated controls showed a 5% difference in mean accuracy across the GFMT (91%) and EFMT-short (86%), where super-recognizers showed a 3% difference ($M^{GFMT} = 97\%$; $M^{EFMT\text{-}short} = 94\%$). Super-recognizers evidenced a comparatively smaller ORB when compared to more typical controls (7% difference in accuracy; $M^{GFMT} = 81\%$, $M^{EFMT\text{-}short} = 74\%$). Crucially, only Bate et al.'s investigation implemented a fully crossed design, wherein super-recognizer performance on the other-race matching task could be compared to the performance of respective groups of same-ethnicity observers (Asian observers in Experiment 2 and Black and Arabian observers in Experiment 3). Here, single-case statistics revealed that no super-recognizer outperformed same-ethnicity performers. The researchers thus concluded that, while Caucasian super-recognizers may exceed the other-race matching performance of Caucasian controls, they are still subject to the ORB and could not be expected to surpass the performance of same-ethnicity observers.

The own-age bias (OAB) contends that we are better at recognizing faces from our own age group compared to those of another age group (e.g., Rhodes & Anastasi, 2012). In support, findings show that typical adult perceivers are more accurate to match pairs of unfamiliar adult faces than faces of infants, children, and adolescents (e.g., Kramer et al., 2018; White et al., 2015a). Two recent studies suggest that the OAB impacts super-recognizer performance on tasks of sequential (Belanova et al., 2018) and simultaneous face-matching (Bate et al., 2020a). Mirroring findings from typical perceivers, Belanova et al. (2018) and Bate et al. (2020a) found that super-recognizers ($M^{age} = 32.67$ and 39, respectively), none of whom had extensive contact with children, performed better on tasks of adult-face matching ($M^{accuracy} = 88\%$ and 94%, respectively) than on tasks that utilized infants' or children's faces ($M^{accuracy} = 79\%$ and 90%, respectively). Belanova et al. (2018) found that super-recognizers outperformed controls ($M^{age} = 32.20$), who had similarly low exposure to children, at a group-level on both tasks of adult (mean control accuracy = 80%) and infant face-matching (mean control accuracy = 71%). However, not all super-recognizers in Bate et al.'s (2020a) study demonstrated superiority when single-case statistics were used to compare their performance to controls (M^{age} = 32) with high and low contact with children on the child-matching task (mean pooled control accuracy = 67.82%; mean super-recognizer accuracy = 90%). Interestingly, Bate et al. (2020a) found that the difference between adult- and child-face matching performance was larger for super-recognizers (4%) than controls (<1%), suggesting that their comparatively exceptional performance with adult faces may increase the magnitude of the OAB. Implicating the role of holistic mechanisms, Belanova et al. (2018) found that, while inversion effects were similarly noted across adult and infant face recognition for controls, super-recognizers only showed these effects for adult faces. Given that superior holistic processing is sometimes thought to underpin super-recognition (e.g., Bobak et al., 2016a, 2017), this may suggest that super-recognizers find it difficult to apply their innate skillset to classes of stimuli to which they have had relatively little exposure.

These results suggest that perceptual biases are shared by super-recognizers and typical perceivers—an observation that is theoretically important because it suggests only a quantitative (and not a qualitative) difference drives superiority. While most investigations suggest that super-recognizers surpass own-group controls when matching other-group faces, these differences are typically only observed at a group-level. Further, these observations stem predominantly from work which defined super-recognition according to exceptional performance on difficult tests of face memory (e.g., the CFMT+; Bate et al., 2019a, 2020a; Belanova et al., 2018) and/or insufficiently calibrated tests of face-matching (e.g., the GFMT; Robertson et al., 2020). Given observed heterogeneities in the performance profiles of super-recognizers it will be important to assess whether similar findings are obtained when sampling those who predominantly or exclusively excel at face-matching (e.g., Bate et al., 2018, 2019b). Screening batteries should also include tasks that probe other-group recognition, and only those who excel at such tasks should be assigned to similar operational work. While this work continues, existing findings suggest that super-recognizers cannot consistently be relied upon to provide other-group face mapping conclusions that are beyond the reach of a standard juror.

Comparing Accuracy across Super-recognizers and Expert Face-mappers

Earlier in this chapter we outlined practical reasons why super-recognizers might be preferred as expert witnesses (cf. forensic face examiners and algorithms; here we critically compare these groups on performance accuracy. Phillips et al. (2018) provide the most comprehensive example, testing 57 trained forensic face examiners, 13 super-recognizers, and four modern DCNNs. All groups performed a simultaneous face-matching task comprising 20 algorithm-and-human-determined challenging face pairs, responding to each on a 7-point Likert scale anchored from +3 (high confidence that the pair matched in identity) to −3 (high confidence that the pair mismatched in identity), easing comparison of human-to-machine responses. Both human groups were given three months to complete the task using methods and tools of their choice. This method arguably provides a true test of forensic face examiner ability as it mirrors the circumstances of their work (White et al., 2020). However, suboptimal screening methods preclude the same test for super-recognizers. No additional screening information was provided for the single super-recognizer hailing from the Metropolitan Police Service, and the remaining 12 were screened using only the insufficiently calibrated GFMT. These limitations impact the strength of comparison, below.

Consulting "area under the receiver operating characteristic curve" (AUC) medians, the most recently developed algorithm achieved the highest accuracy (AUC = 0.96). Although no performance differences were statistically significant, forensic face examiners (AUC = 0.93) outperformed super-recognizers (AUC = 0.83). While variability was noted in both human groups, numerical accuracy differences may have been disproportionately driven by the performance of forensic face examiners. Accuracy ranged from 50–100% in this group, with seven examiners producing ceiling performance and a further seven committing errors on 30% of trials (Edmond et al., 2021; Moreton, 2021). Similar variability-induced skew was also noted in Moreton's (2021, Experiment 3) small-scale comparison of face-matching ability across three forensic face examiners and police "super-matchers"; the latter selected according to occupational role and performance on only single screening and verification tests of unfamiliar face-matching. When applied to data from the verification test, single-case statistics revealed that numerical group differences were predominantly driven by the exceptional score of one forensic face examiner, who outperformed all five other face recognition professionals. This pattern of performance variability is of particular concern when all forensic face examiners have been accredited by appropriate bodies and are using prescribed methods and tools (Edmond et al., 2021), as was the case in Phillips et al. (2018).

Further differences in the response profiles of super-recognizers and forensic face examiners were noted by Hahn et al. (2022) in their examination of Phillips et al.'s (2018) data. Compared to super-recognizers, who frequently utilized the scale end-points in their determinations, forensic face examiners used the full response scale and demonstrated more conservative and consistent modal response profiles at a group level. Indicators of metacognitive awareness, evidenced here via adjustments of confidence to reflect both perceived task difficulty and diagnosticity, were noted in both groups. However, when errors were made, they were more likely to be accompanied by high confidence for super-recognizers versus forensic face examiners (see also Moreton, 2021). The latter group may be specifically trained to express conservatism (Norell et al., 2015) as high decision confidence, particularly when expressed by an expert, can be extremely persuasive to triers of fact (Cramer et al., 2009).

The "wisdom of the crowds" approach may provide an alternative way to monopolize on the enhanced face recognition accuracy of specialist groups (e.g., White et al., 2015b; Balsdon et al., 2018). Here the independent decisions of several individuals working on the same task are amalgamated (e.g., Jeckeln et al., 2018; White et al., 2015a). Typically, amalgamated responses are more accurate than those made by the contributing individuals themselves, with gains attributed to nullification of individual response biases (e.g., Towler et al., 2017), possibly because each individual uses diverse cognitive strategies to form their decision (e.g., Hong & Page, 2004). This conceptualization first allows exploration of the potential accuracy benefits accrued by high-ability human performers working together, and second may present an alternative, fused way to approach tasks in which human performers verify algorithm-generated identifications (e.g., O'Toole et al., 2007). A linear approach is typically taken to such tasks across forensic and security settings, whereby algorithms may search large, automated databases to locate potential persons of interest whom human operators may match to identity documentation or CCTV stills (e.g., Grother et al., 2019; Towler et al., 2017). Errors often occur when human operators are given end-stage veto power and are attributed to the emergence of response biases which may increase as a function of the number of images and/or comparisons that the human operator must make (e.g., White et al., 2015a; Heyer et al., 2018).

Phillips et al. (2018) and Moreton (2021) examined both proposals. When focusing on human performers, both researchers found that larger accuracy boosts could be achieved by the amalgamation of a smaller number of super-recognizers (or matchers; Moreton, 2021), than forensic face examiners. While pairs of super-matchers always exceeded the performance of the top super-matcher (Moreton, 2021), the top forensic face examiner, working alone, outperformed groups comprised of the same. This likely reflects the group's high degree of performance variability, as well as their potential application of trained strategies, which reduced diversity in decision-making strategy (Moreton, 2021).

When examining a fused human-computer approach, data from Phillips et al. (2018) and Moreton (2021) suggest that human and computer contributions equally influence efficacy, with performance asymmetries indicative of different strategy utilization and perceptions of difficulty. Indeed, for matching trials deemed comparatively more challenging by humans than algorithms, fused accuracy rates surpassed the algorithm's baseline in

~40% of cases, with only one human surpassing this score when working alone (Moreton, 2021). Of note, Moreton (2021) sampled a fuller range of human face recognition abilities and found that, while fusion allowed all top-performing humans to surpass the algorithm's baseline, fusion-induced boosts were most modest for this group than for moderate or lower performers. In support, Phillips et al. (2018) found that examination of the benefits of fusion were somewhat hampered as ceiling and near-ceiling performance rates rate were attained when they fused their most accurate algorithm with a single face examiner and super-recognizer, respectively. Conversely, for matching trials deemed comparatively more challenging by algorithms than humans, fusion did not always result in heightened accuracy relative to algorithm and human baselines. In particular, fusion led to asymmetrical results when applied to the highest human performers; accuracy was higher than the algorithm's baseline, but lower than the human performer working alone (Moreton, 2021). Similarly, when Phillips et al. (2018) sampled lower-performing algorithms, pairs of both super-recognizers and forensic face examiners outperformed both the algorithm working alone, and fused scores.

In sum, suboptimal screening measures in both Phillips et al. (2018) and Moreton (2021) make it difficult to assess whether they sampled true super-recognizers or simply those who were above average at face recognition. Adopting a diluted comparison, performers relying on innate mechanisms appear to attain similar group-level accuracy to those employing trained methods. Interestingly, innate performers may implement a wider range of strategies to achieve these consistent accuracy rates, making this group more suited to a "wisdom of crowds" implementation; an approach that, teamed with non-face-specific forensic training in conservatism, may nullify the worrying high-confidence errors sometimes evidenced in their determinations (e.g., Hahn et al., 2022). The results also suggest that the Criminal Justice System should exercise greater caution when accepting the testimony of forensic face examiners and algorithms as both show considerable variability in their performance, which may negatively impact their independent or fused judgments.

Overall Conclusion

While evaluating the suitability of super-recognizers to act as expert witnesses in court, this chapter has presented a critical overview of the contemporary challenges facing theoretical and applied work involving these individuals. Further, thorough critiques of some of the same issues are available elsewhere (e.g., Bate et al., 2020b, 2021; Ramon et al., 2019; Ramon, 2021), which similarly highlight that a definition of super-recognition is currently limited by the protocols that are used to identify truly superior performers and further probe the consistency of their abilities. Crucially then, until definitions can be consolidated via the design and implementation of psychometric-standard screening and testing batteries, it is unlikely that the relevance principle can be definitively met as the comparative "expertise" of any given super-recognizer can readily be challenged. This is further complicated by (a) the absence of any biological marker of super-recognition, and (b) the arguable arbitrariness of current thresholds for statistical differentiation of superior and typical performers. As such, it seems prudent to currently limit the role of super-recognizers to (a) providing identifications of potential investigative value in rapidly developing live cases (e.g., Davis, 2020), and (b) acting only as civilian versus expert witnesses in court, where they may identify familiar identities with whom they have demonstrable previous contact (e.g., Edmond & Wortley, 2016). If future research can alleviate the concerns discussed above, then we agree that the delivery of expert testimony by super-recognizers should be negotiated very carefully (see Edmond & Wortley, 2016; Edmond et al., 2021). Potential bias should be mitigated by recruiting super-recognizers who have not previously been involved in the case in an operational capacity. Further, to overcome the inherent limitations when a super-recognizer attempts to describe and defend their use of innate mechanisms for identification, cross-examination should be tackled by a cognitive psychologist with relevant knowledge both of super-recognizer ability in general and, more crucially, that individual's screening test scores.

References

Abudarham, N., Bate, S., Duchaine, B., & Yovel, G. (2021). Developmental prosopagnosics and super recognizers rely on the same facial features used by individuals with normal face recognition abilities for face identification. *Neuropsychologia*, 160, 107963. https://doi.org/10.1016/j.neuropsychologia.2021.107963

Balsdon, T., Summersby, S., Kemp, R.I., & White, D. (2018). Improving face identification with specialist teams. *Cognitive Research: Principles and Implications*, 3(1), 1–13. https://doi.org/10.1186/s41235-018-0114-7

Bate, S., Bennetts, R., Hasshim, N., Portch, E., Murray, E., Burns, E., & Dudfield, G. (2019a). The limits of super recognition: An other-ethnicity effect in individuals with extraordinary face recognition skills. *Journal of Experimental Psychology: Human Perception and Performance*, 45(3), 363–377. https://doi.org/10.1037/xhp0000607

Bate, S., Bennetts, R., Murray, E., & Portch, E. (2020a). Enhanced matching of children's faces in "super-recognisers" but not high-contact controls. *i-Perception*, 11(4), https://doi.org/10.1177/2041669520944420

Bate, S., & Dudfield, G. (2019). Subjective assessment for super recognition: an evaluation of self-report methods in civilian and police participants. *PeerJ*, 7, e6330. https://doi.org/10.7717/peerj.6330

Bate, S., Frowd, C., Bennetts, R., Hasshim, N., Murray, E., Bobak, A.K., Wills, H. & Richards, S. (2018). Applied screening tests for the detection of superior face recognition. *Cognitive Research: Principles and Implications, 3*(1), 1–19. https://doi.org/10.1186/s41235-018-0116-5

Bate, S., Frowd, C., Bennetts, R., Hasshim, N., Portch, E., Murray, E., & Dudfield, G. (2019b). The consistency of superior face recognition skills in police officers. *Applied Cognitive Psychology, 33*(5), 828–842. https://doi.org/10.1002/acp.3525

Bate, S., Mestry, N. & Portch, E. (2020b). Individual differences between observers in face matching. In M. Bindemann (Eds.), *Forensic Face Matching: Research and Practice* (pp. 118–146). Oxford University Press. https://doi.org/10.1093/oso/9780198837749.003.0006

Bate, S., Portch, E., & Mestry, N. (2021). When two fields collide: Identifying "super-recognisers" for neuropsychological and forensic face recognition research. *Quarterly Journal of Experimental Psychology, 74*(12), 2154–2164. https://doi.org/10.1177/17470218211027695

Bate, S., Portch, E., Mestry, N., & Bennetts, R.J. (2019c). Redefining super recognition in the real world: Skilled face or person identity recognizers? *British Journal of Psychology, 110*(3), 480–482. https://doi.org/10.1111/bjop.12392

Bate, S., & Tree, J.J. (2017). The definition and diagnosis of developmental prosopagnosia. *Quarterly Journal of Experimental Psychology, 70*(2): 193–200. https://doi.org/10.1080/17470218.2016.1195414

Belanova, E., Davis, J.P., & Thompson, T. (2018). Cognitive and neural markers of super-recognisers' face processing superiority and enhanced cross-age effect. *Cortex, 108,* 92–111. https://doi.org/10.1016/j.cortex.2018.07.008

Bennetts, R.J., Mole, J., & Bate, S. (2017). Super-recognition in development: A case study of an adolescent with extraordinary face recognition skills. *Cognitive Neuropsychology,* 1–20. https://doi.org/10.1080/02643294.2017.1402755

Bindemann, M., Attard, J., & Johnston, R.A. (2014). Perceived ability and actual recognition accuracy for unfamiliar and famous faces. *Cogent Psychology, 1*(1), 986903. https://doi.org/10.1080/23311908.2014.986903

Bindemann, M., Avetisyan, M., & Rakow, T. (2012). Who can recognize unfamiliar faces? Individual differences and observer consistency in person identification. *Journal of Experimental Psychology: Applied, 18*(3), 277–291. https://doi.org/10.1037/a0029635

Blais, C., Jack, R.E., Scheepers, C., Fiset, D., & Caldara, R. (2008). Culture shapes how we look at faces. *PloS One, 3*(8), e3022. https://doi.org/10.1371/journal.pone.0003022

Bobak, A.K., Bennetts, R.J., Parris, B.A., Jansari, A., & Bate, S. (2016a). An in-depth cognitive examination of individuals with superior face recognition skills. *Cortex, 82,* 48–62. https://doi.org/10.1016/j.cortex.2016.05.003

Bobak, A.K., Dowsett, A.J., & Bate, S. (2016b). Solving the border control problem: Evidence of enhanced face matching in individuals with extraordinary face recognition skills. *PloS one, 11*(2), e0148148. https://doi.org/10.1371/journal.pone.0148148

Bobak, A.K., Hancock, P.J., & Bate, S. (2016c). Super-recognisers in action: Evidence from face-matching and face memory tasks. *Applied Cognitive Psychology, 30*(1), 81–91. https://doi.org/10.1002/acp.3170

Bobak, A.K., Pampoulov, P., & Bate, S. (2016d). Detecting superior face recognition skills in a large sample of young British adults. *Frontiers in Psychology*, 7, 1378. https://doi.org/10.3389/fpsyg.2016.01378

Bobak, A.K., Parris, B.A., Gregory, N.J., Bennetts, R.J., & Bate, S. (2017). Eye-movement strategies in developmental prosopagnosia and "super" face recognition. *Quarterly journal of experimental psychology*, 70(2), 201–217. https://doi.org/10.1080/17470218.2016.1161059.

Bobak, A.K., Mileva, V.R., & Hancock, P.J. (2019). Facing the facts: Naive participants have only moderate insight into their face recognition and face perception abilities. *Quarterly Journal of Experimental Psychology*, 72(4), 872–881. https://doi.org/10.1177/1747021818776145

Bowles, D.C., McKone, E., Dawel, A., Duchaine, B., Palermo, R., Schmalzl, L., Rivolta, D., Wilson, C.E. & Yovel, G. (2009). Diagnosing prosopagnosia: Effects of ageing, sex, and participant–stimulus ethnic match on the Cambridge Face Memory Test and Cambridge Face Perception Test. *Cognitive Neuropsychology*, 26(5), 423–455. https://doi.org/10.1080/02643290903343149

Bruce, V., Henderson, Z., Greenwood, K., Hancock, P.J., Burton, A.M., & Miller, P. (1999). Verification of face identities from images captured on video. *Journal of Experimental Psychology: Applied*, 5(4), 339–360. https://doi.org/10.1037/1076-898X.5.4.339

Bruce, V., Henderson, Z., Newman, C., & Burton, A.M. (2001). Matching identities of familiar and unfamiliar faces caught on CCTV images. *Journal of Experimental Psychology: Applied*, 7(3), 207–218. https://doi.org/10.1037/1076-898X.7.3.207

Burton, A.M., White, D., & McNeill, A. (2010). The Glasgow face matching test. *Behavior Research Methods*, 42(1), 286–291. https://doi.org/10.3758/BRM.42.1.286

Caplova, Z., Obertova, Z., Gibelli, D.M., Mazzarelli, D., Fracasso, T., Vanezis, P., Sforza, C. & Cattaneo, C. (2017). The reliability of facial recognition of deceased persons on photographs. *Journal of Forensic Sciences*, 62(5), 1286–1291. https://doi.org/10.1111/1556-4029.13396

Cramer, R.J., Brodsky, S.L., & DeCoster, J. (2009). Expert witness confidence and juror personality: Their impact on credibility and persuasion in the courtroom. *Journal of the American Academy of Psychiatry and the Law Online*, 37(1), 63–74.

Davis, J.P. (2019). The worldwide impact of identifying super-recognisers in police and business. *The Cognitive Psychology Bulletin*, 4, 17–22.

Davis, J.P. (2020). CCTV and the super-recognisers. In C. Stott, B. Bradford, M. Radburn, and L. Savigar-Shaw (Eds.), *Making an Impact on Policing and Crime: Psychological Research, Policy and Practice* (pp 34–67). Routledge. https://doi.org/10.4324/9780429326592

Davis, J.P., Bretfelean, L.D., Belanova, E., & Thompson, T. (2020). Super-recognisers: Face recognition performance after variable delay intervals. *Applied Cognitive Psychology*, 34(6), 1350–1368. https://doi.org/10.1002/acp.3712

Davis, J.P., Forrest, C., Treml, F., & Jansari, A. (2018). Identification from CCTV: Assessing police super-recogniser ability to spot faces in a crowd and susceptibility to change blindness. *Applied Cognitive Psychology*, 32(3), 337–353. https://doi.org/10.1002/acp.3405

Davis, J.P., Lander, K., Evans, R., & Jansari, A. (2016). Investigating predictors of superior face recognition ability in police super-recognisers. *Applied Cognitive Psychology*, 30(6), 827–840. https://doi.org/10.1002/acp.3260

Davis, J.P., Maigut, A., & Forrest, C. (2019). The wisdom of the crowd: A case of post-to ante-mortem face matching by police super-recognisers. *Forensic Science International*, 302, 109910. https://doi.org/10.1016/j.forsciint.2019.109910

DeGutis, J., Wilmer, J., Mercado, R.J., & Cohan, S. (2013). Using regression to measure holistic face processing reveals a strong link with face recognition ability. *Cognition*, 126(1), 87–100. https://doi.org/10.1016/j.cognition.2012.09.004

Devue, C. (2019). Breaking face processing tasks apart to improve their predictive value in the real world: a comment on Ramon, Bobak, and White (2019). *British Journal of Psychology*, 110(3), 483–485. https://doi.org/10.1111/bjop.12391

Diamond, R., & Carey, S. (1986). Why faces are and are not special: an effect of expertise. *Journal of Experimental Psychology: General*, 115(2), 107–117. https://doi.org/10.1037/0096-3445.115.2.107

Dowsett, A.J. & Burton, A.M. (2015). Unfamiliar face matching: Pairs outperform individuals and provide a route to training. *British Journal of Psychology*, 106, 433–445. https://doi.org/10.1111/bjop.12103

Duchaine, B.C. & Nakayama, K. (2006). The Cambridge Face Memory Test: Results for neurologically intact individuals and an investigation of its validity using inverted face stimuli and prosopagnosic participants. *Neuropsychologia*, 44, 576–585. https://doi.org/10.1016/j.neuropsychologia.2005.07.001

Duchaine, B., Germine, L., & Nakayama, K. (2007). Family resemblance: Ten family members with prosopagnosia and within-class object agnosia. *Cognitive Neuropsychology*, 24, 419–430. https://doi.org/10.1080/02643290701380491

Dunn, J.D., Varela, V.P., Nicholls, V.I., Papinutto, M., White, D., & Miellet, S. (2022). Face-Information Sampling in Super-Recognizers. *Psychological Science*, 33(9), 1615–1630. https://doi.org/10.1177/09567976221096320

Edmond, G., Cole, S., Cunliffe, E., & Roberts, A. (2013). Admissibility compared: the reception of incriminating expert evidence (i.e., forensic science) in four adversarial jurisdictions. *University of Denver Criminal Law Review*, 3(1), 31–109.

Edmond, G., Davis, J.P., & Valentine, T. (2015). Expert analysis: Facial image comparison. In T. Valentine & J.P. Davis (Eds.), *Forensic facial identification: Theory and practice of identification from eyewitnesses, composites, and CCTV* (pp. 239–262). Wiley-Blackwell. https://doi.org/10.1002/9781118469538

Edmond, G., White, D., Towler, A., San Roque, M., & Kemp, R. (2021). Facial recognition and image comparison evidence: Identification by investigators, familiars, experts, super-recognisers and algorithms. *Melbourne University Law Review*, 45, 99–160.

Edmond, G., & Wortley, N. (2016). Interpreting image evidence: Facial mapping, police familiars and super-recognisers in England and Australia. *Journal of International and Comparative Law*, 3(2), 1–50.

Evison, M.P. (2015) The Third Forensics—images and allusions. *Policing and Society: An International Journal of Research and Policy*, 25, 521–539. https://doi.org/10.1080/10439463.2014.895347

Farah, M.J. (1995). Dissociable systems for visual recognition: A cognitive neuropsychology approach. In *Visual cognition: An Invitation to Cognitive Science* (Vol. 2, 2nd ed., pp. 101–119). The MIT Press.

Farah, M.J., Wilson, K.D., & Tanaka, J.N. (1998). What Is "Special" About Face Perception? *Psychological Review*, 105(3), 482–498. https://doi.org/10.1037/0033-295X.105.3.482

Forensic Science Regulator (2018). *Annual Report November 2016–November 2017.* https://assets.publishing.service.gov.uk/government/uploads/system/uploads/attachment_data/file/674761/FSRAnnual_Report_2017_v1_01.pdf.

Fysh, M.C., Stacchi, L., & Ramon, M. (2020). Differences between and within individuals, and subprocesses of face cognition: Implications for theory, research and personnel selection. *Royal Society Open Science*, 7(9), 200233. https://doi.org/10.1098/rsos.200233

Germine, L.T., Duchaine, B., & Nakayama, K. (2011). Where cognitive development and aging meet: Face learning ability peaks after age 30. *Cognition*, 118(2), 201–210. https://doi.org/10.1016/j.cognition.2010.11.002

Gosselin, F., & Schyns, P.G. (2001). Bubbles: a technique to reveal the use of information in recognition tasks. *Vision Research*, 41(17), 2261–2271. https://doi.org/10.1016/S0042-6989(01)00097-9

Grother, P., Ngan, M., & Hanaoka, K. (2019). Face Recognition Vendor Test (FRVT) Part 3: Demographic Effects. *National Institute of Science and Technology (NIST) NISTIR*, 8280. https://doi.org/10.6028/NIST.IR.8280.

Hahn, C.A., Tang, L.L., Yates, A.N. & Phillips, P.J. (2022). Forensic facial examiners versus super-recognisers: Evaluating behaviour beyond accuracy. *Applied Cognitive Psychology*, 1–10, https://doi.org/10.1002/acp.4003

Heyer, R., Semmler, C., & Hendrickson, A.T. (2018). Humans and algorithms for facial recognition: The effects of candidate list length and experience on performance. *Journal of Applied Research in Memory and Cognition*, 7(4), 597–609. https://doi.org/10.1016/j.jarmac.2018.06.002

Hole, G.J. (1994). Configurational factors in the perception of unfamiliar faces. *Perception*, 23(1), 65–74. https://doi.org/10.1068/p230065

Hong, L., & Page, S.E. (2004). Groups of diverse problem solvers can outperform groups of high-ability problem solvers. *Proceedings of the National Academy of Sciences*, 101(46), 16385–16389. https://doi.org/10.1073/pnas.0403723101

Jeckeln, G., Hahn, C.A., Noyes, E., Cavazos, J.G., & O'Toole, A.J. (2018). Wisdom of the social versus non-social crowd in face identification. *British Journal of Psychology*, 109(4), 724–735. https://doi.org/10.1111/bjop.12291

Johnston, R.A., & Edmonds, A.J. (2009). Familiar and unfamiliar face recognition: A review. *Memory*, 17(5), 577–596. https://doi.org/10.1080/09658210902976969

Kennerknecht, I., Pluempe, N., & Welling, B. (2008). Congenital prosopagnosia–a common hereditary cognitive dysfunction in humans. *Frontiers in Bioscience*, 13(8), 3150–3158. https://doi.org/10.2741/2916.

Kramer, R.S., Mulgrew, J., & Reynolds, M.G. (2018). Unfamiliar face matching with photographs of infants and children. *PeerJ*, 6, e5010. https://doi.org/10.7717/peerj.5010

Lander, K., Bruce, V., & Bindemann, M. (2018). Use-inspired basic research on individual differences in face identification: Implications for criminal investigation and security. *Cognitive Research: Principles and Implications*, 3(1), 1–13. https://doi.org/10.1186/s41235-018-0115-6

Lander, K., Bruce, V. & Hill, H. (2001). Evaluating the effectiveness of pixelation and blurring on masking the identity of familiar faces. *Applied Cognitive Psychology*, 15(1), 101–116. https://doi.org/10.1002/1099-0720(200101/02)15:1<101::AID-ACP697>3.0.CO;2-7

Lee, Y., Duchaine, B., Wilson, H.R., & Nakayama, K. (2010). Three cases of developmental prosopagnosia from one family: Detailed neuropsychological and psychophysical investigation of face processing. *Cortex*, 46(8), 949–964. https://doi.org/10.1016/j.cortex.2009.07.012

Lee, J.K.W., Janssen, S.M.J., & Estudillo, A.J. (2022a). A featural account for own-face processing? Looking for support from face inversion, composite face, and part-whole tasks. *I-Perception*, 13(4), 1–22. https://doi.org/10.1177/20416695221111409

Lee, J.K.W., Janssen, S.M.J., & Estudillo, A.J. (2022b). A more featural based processing for the self-face: An eye-tracking study. *Consciousness and Cognition*, 105, 103400. https://doi.org/10.1016/j.concog.2022.103400

Maurer, D., Grand, R.L., & Mondloch, C.J. (2002). The many faces of configural processing. *Trends in Cognitive Sciences*, 6(6), 255–260. https://doi.org/10.1016/S1364-6613(02)01903-4

McKone, E., Crookes, K., Jeffery, L., & Dilks, D.D. (2012). A critical review of the development of face recognition: Experience is less important than previously believed. *Cognitive Neuropsychology*, 29(1–2), 174–212. https://doi.org/10.1080/02643294.2012.660138

McKone, E., & Yovel, G. (2009). Why does picture-plane inversion sometimes dissociate perception of features and spacing in faces, and sometimes not? Toward a new theory of holistic processing. *Psychonomic Bulletin & Review*, 16(5), 778–797. https://doi.org/10.3758/pbr.16.5.778

Megreya, A.M., White, D., & Burton, A.M. (2011). The other-race effect does not rely on memory: Evidence from a matching task. *Quarterly Journal of Experimental Psychology*, 64(8), 1473–1483. https://doi.org/10.1080/17470218.2011.575228

Meissner, C.A., & Brigham, J.C. (2001). Thirty years of investigating the own race bias in memory for faces: A meta-analytic review. *Psychology, Public Policy, and Law*, 7(1), 3–35. https://doi.org/10.1037/1076-8971.7.1.3

Ministry of Justice. (2015a). Criminal practice directions. Retrieved from www.justice.gov.uk/courts/procedure-rules/criminal/docs/2015/crim-practice-directions-V-evidence-2015.pdf.

Ministry of Justice. (2015b). Criminal procedure rules. Retrieved from www.justice.gov.uk/courts/procedure-rules/criminal/docs/2015/criminal-procedure-rules-practice-directions-april-2019.pdf.

Moreton, R. (2020). Forensic face matching: Procedures and application. In M. Bindemann (Eds.), *Forensic Face Matching: Research and Practice* (pp. 147–176). Oxford University Press. https://doi.org/10.1093/oso/9780198837749.003.0007

Moreton, R. (2021). *Expertise in applied face matching: training, forensic examiners, super matchers and algorithms* [PhD Thesis, The Open University, UK]. https://doi.org/10.21954/ou.ro.00013240

Moreton, R., Pike, G., & Havard, C. (2019). A task-and role-based perspective on super-recognizers: Commentary on "Super-recognizers: From the lab to the world and back again". *British Journal of Psychology, 110*(3), 486–488. https://doi.org/10.1111/bjop.12394

Nador, J.D., Vomland, M., Thielgen, M.M., & Ramon, M. (2022). Face recognition in police officers: Who fits the bill? *Forensic Science International: Reports, 5*, 100267. https://doi.org/10.1016/j.fsir.2022.100267

Norell, K., Läthén, K.B., Bergström, P., Rice, A., Natu, V., & O'Toole, A. (2015). The effect of image quality and forensic expertise in facial image comparisons. *Journal of Forensic Sciences, 60*(2), 331–340. https://doi.org/10.1111/1556-4029.12660

Noyes, E. & Hill, M.Q. (2020). Automatic recognition systems and human computer interaction in face matching. In M. Bindemann (Eds.), *Forensic Face Matching: Research and Practice* (pp. 64–90). Oxford University Press. https://doi.org/10.1093/oso/9780198837749.003.0009

Noyes, E., Hill, M.Q., & O'Toole, A.J. (2018). Face recognition ability does not predict person identification performance: Using individual data in the interpretation of group results. *Cognitive research: Principles and Implications, 3*(1), 1–13. https://doi.org/10.1186/s41235-018-0117-4

Noyes, E., Phillips, P.J., & O'Toole, A.J. (2017). What is a super-recogniser? In Markus. Bindemann & A.M. Megreya (Eds.), *Face Processing: Systems, Disorders and Cultural Differences* (pp. 173–201). Nova Science Publishers Inc.

O'Toole, A.J., Abdi, H., Jiang, F., & Phillips, P.J. (2007). Fusing face-verification algorithms and humans. *IEEE Transactions on Systems, Man, and Cybernetics, Part B (Cybernetics), 37*(5), 1149–1155. https://doi.org/10.1109/TSMCB.2007.907034

O'Toole, A.J., Castillo, C.D., Parde, C.J., Hill, M.Q., & Chellappa, R. (2018). Face space representations in deep convolutional neural networks. *Trends in Cognitive Sciences, 22*(9), 794–809. https://doi.org/10.1016/j.tics.2018.06.006

Phillips, P.J., Jiang, F., Narvekar, A., Ayyad, J., & O'Toole, A.J. (2011). An other-race effect for face recognition algorithms. *ACM Transactions on Applied Perception (TAP), 8*(2), 1–11. https://doi.org/10.1145/1870076.1870082

Phillips, P.J., Yates, A.N., Hu, Y., Hahn, C.A., Noyes, E., Jackson, K., Cavazos, J.G., Jeckeln, G., Ranjan, R., Sankaranarayanan, S., Chen, J-C., Castillo, C.D., Chellappa, R., White, D. & O'Toole, A.J. (2018). Face recognition accuracy of forensic examiners, superrecognizers, and face recognition algorithms. *Proceedings of the National Academy of Sciences, 115*(24), 6171–6176. https://doi.org/10.1073/pnas.1721355115

President's Council of Advisors on Science and Technology (2016). *Forensic science in criminal courts: Ensuring scientific validity of feature-comparison methods*. https://obamawhitehouse.archives.gov/sites/default/files/microsites/ostp/PCAST/pcast_forensic_science_report_final.pdf.

Ramon, M. (2021). Super-Recognizers–a novel diagnostic framework, 70 cases, and guidelines for future work. *Neuropsychologia, 158*, 107809. https://doi.org/10.1016/j.neuropsychologia.2021.107809

Ramon, M., Bobak, A.K., & White, D. (2019). Super-recognizers: From the lab to the world and back again. *British Journal of Psychology, 110*(3), 461–479. https://doi.org/10.1111/bjop.12368

Ramon, M., Miellet, S., Dzieciol, A.M., Konrad, B.N., Dresler, M., & Caldara, R. (2016). Super-Memorizers Are Not Super-Recognizers. *PLOS ONE, 11*(3), e0150972. https://doi.org/10.1371/journal.pone.0150972

Rezlescu, C., Susilo, T., Wilmer, J.B., & Caramazza, A. (2017). The inversion, part-whole, and composite effects reflect distinct perceptual mechanisms with varied relationships to face recognition. *Journal of Experimental Psychology: Human Perception and Performance, 43*(12), 1961–1973. https://doi.org/10.1037/xhp0000400

Rhodes, M.G., & Anastasi, J.S. (2012). The own-age bias in face recognition: a meta-analytic and theoretical review. *Psychological Bulletin, 138*(1), 146–174. https://doi.org/10.1037/a0025750

Robbins, R., & McKone, E. (2007). No face-like processing for objects-of-expertise in three behavioural tasks. *Cognition, 103*(1), 34–79. https://doi.org/10.1016/j.cognition.2006.02.008

Roberts, A. (2020). Forensic face matching: A legal perspective. In M. Bindemann (Eds.), *Forensic Face Matching: Research and Practice* (pp. 177–195). Oxford University Press.

Robertson, D.J., & Bindemann, M. (2019). Consolidation, wider reflection, and policy: Response to "Super-recognisers: From the lab to the world and back again". *British Journal of Psychology, 110*(3), 489–491. https://doi.org/10.1111/bjop.12393

Robertson, D.J., Black, J., Chamberlain, B., Megreya, A.M., & Davis, J.P. (2020). Super-recognisers show an advantage for other race face identification. *Applied Cognitive Psychology, 34*(1), 205–216. https://doi.org/10.1002/acp.3608

Robertson, D.J., Noyes, E., Dowsett, A.J., Jenkins, R., & Burton, A.M. (2016). Face recognition by metropolitan police super-recognisers. *PloS one, 11*(2), e0150036. https://doi.org/10.1371/journal.pone.0150036

Rossion, B. (2008). Picture-plane inversion leads to qualitative changes of face perception. *Acta Psychologica, 128*(2), 274–289. https://doi.org/10.1016/j.actpsy.2008.02.003

Rossion, B. (2013). The composite face illusion: A whole window into our understanding of holistic face perception. *Visual Cognition, 21*(2), 139–253. https://doi.org/10.1080/13506285.2013.772929

Russell, R., Chatterjee, G., & Nakayama, K. (2012). Developmental prosopagnosia and super-recognition: No special role for surface reflectance processing. *Neuropsychologia, 50*(2), 334–340. https://doi.org/10.1016/j.neuropsychologia.2011.12.004

Russell, R., Duchaine, B., & Nakayama, K. (2009). Super-recognizers: People with extraordinary face recognition ability. *Psychonomic Bulletin & Review, 16*(2), 252–257. https://doi.org/10.3758/PBR.16.2.252

Schmalzl, L., Palermo, R., & Coltheart, M. (2008). Cognitive heterogeneity in genetically based prosopagnosia: A family study. *Journal of Neuropsychology*, 2(1), 99–117. https://doi.org/10.1348/174866407X256554

Shakeshaft, N.G., & Plomin, R. (2015). Genetic specificity of face recognition. *Proceedings of the National Academy of Sciences*, 112(41), 12,887–12,892. https://doi.org/10.1073/pnas.1421881112

Tanaka, J.W., & Simonyi, D. (2016). The "parts and wholes" of face recognition: A review of the literature. *The Quarterly Journal of Experimental Psychology*, 69(10), 1876–1889. https://doi.org/10.1080/17470218.2016.1146780

Tardif, J., Morin Duchesne, X., Cohan, S., Royer, J., Blais, C., Fiset, D., Duchaine, B. & Gosselin, F. (2019). Use of face information varies systematically from developmental prosopagnosics to super-recognizers. *Psychological science*, 30(2), 300–308. https://doi.org/10.1177/0956797618811338

Thielgen, M.M., Schade, S., & Bosé, C. (2021). Face processing in police service: the relationship between laboratory-based assessment of face processing abilities and performance in a real-world identity matching task. *Cognitive Research: Principles and Implications*, 6(1), 1–18. https://doi.org/10.1186/s41235-021-00317-x

Towler, A., Kemp, R.I., Burton, A.M., Dunn, J.D., Wayne, T., Moreton, R., & White, D. (2019). Do professional facial image comparison training courses work? *PloS one*, 14(2), e0211037. https://doi.org/10.1371/journal.pone.0211037

Towler, A., Kemp, R.I., & White, D. (2017). Unfamiliar face matching systems in applied settings. In M. Bindemann & A.M. Megreya (Eds.), *Face processing: Systems, Disorders and Cultural Differences* (pp. 21–40). Nova Science Publishers

Towler, A., Kemp, R.I., & White, D. (2020). Can face identification ability be trained? Evidence for two routes to expertise. In M. Bindemann (Eds.), *Forensic Face Matching: Research and Pratice* (pp. 91–117). Oxford University Press. https://doi.org/10.1093/oso/9780198837749.003.0005

US Government Publishing Office. (2019). US Federal rules of evidence. Retrieved from www.uscourts.gov/sites/default/files/federal_rules_of_evidence_-_dec_1_2019_0.pdf

van Belle, G., Ramon, M., Lefèvre, P., & Rossion, B. (2010). Fixation patterns during recognition of personally familiar and unfamiliar faces. *Frontiers in Psychology*, 10. https://doi.org/10.3389/fpsyg.2010.00020

Wang, R., Li, J., Fang, H., Tian, M., & Liu, J. (2012). Individual differences in holistic processing predict face recognition ability. *Psychological Science*, 23(2), 169–177. https://doi.org/10.1177/0956797611420575

White, D., & Burton, A.M. (2022). Individual differences and the multidimensional nature of face perception. *Nature Reviews Psychology*, 1(5), 287–300. https://doi.org/10.1038/s44159-022-00041-3

White, D., Dunn, J.D., Schmid, A.C., & Kemp, R.I. (2015a). Error rates in users of automatic face recognition software. *PloS one*, 10(10), e0139827. https://doi.org/10.1371/journal.pone.0139827

White, D., Kemp, R.I., Jenkins, R., Matheson, M., & Burton, A.M. (2014). Passport officers' errors in face matching. *PloS One*, 9, e103510. https://doi.org/10.1371/journal.pone.0103510

White, D., Phillips, P.J., Hahn, C.A., Hill, M., & O'Toole, A.J. (2015b). Perceptual expertise in forensic facial image comparison. *Proceedings of the Royal Society B: Biological Sciences*, 282(1814), 20151292. https://doi.org/10.1098/rspb.2015.1292

White, D., Towler, A. & Kemp, R.I. (2020). Understanding professional expertise in unfamiliar face matching. In M. Bindemann (Eds.), *Forensic face matching: Research and practice* (pp. 64–90). Oxford University Press. https://doi.org/10.1093/oso/9780198837749.003.0004

Wilmer, J.B. (2017). Individual Differences in Face Recognition: A Decade of Discovery. *Current Directions in Psychological Science*, 26(3), 225–230. https://doi.org/10.1177/0963721417710693

Wilmer, J.B., Germine, L., Chabris, C.F., Chatterjee, G., Williams, M., Loken, E., Nakayama, K. & Duchaine, B. (2010). Human face recognition ability is specific and highly heritable. *Proceedings of the National Academy of Sciences*, 107(11), 5238–5241. https://doi.org/10.1073/pnas.0913053107

Wong, H.K., Estudillo, A.J., Stephen, I.D., & Keeble, D.R.T. (2021). The other-race effect and holistic processing across racial groups. *Scientific Reports*, 11(1), 8507. https://doi.org/10.1038/s41598-021-87933-1

Yin, R.K. (1969). Looking at upside-down faces. *Journal of Experimental Psychology*, 81(1), 141–145. https://doi.org/10.1037/h0027474

Young, A., Hellawell, D., & Hay, D. (1987). Configural information in face perception. *Perception*, 16, 747–759. https://doi.org/10.1068/p160747

Young, A.W., & Noyes, E. (2019). We need to talk about super-recognizers Invited commentary on: Ramon, M., Bobak, AK., & White, D. "Super-recognizers: From the lab to the world and back again". *British Journal of Psychology*, 110(3), 492–494. https://doi.org/10.1111/bjop.12395

Zhu, Q., Song, Y., Hu, S., Li, X., Tian, M., Zhen, Z., Dong, Q., Kanwisher, N. & Liu, J. (2010). Heritability of the specific cognitive ability of face perception. *Current Biology*, 20(2), 137–142. https://doi.org/10.1016/j.cub.2009.11.067

Cases

Daubert v Merrell Dow Pharmaceuticals Inc. [1993] 509 U.S. 579
R v Bonython [1984] 38 SASR 45
R v Clarke [1995] 2 Cr App R 425
R v Gray [2003] EWCA Crim 1001
R v Hookway [1999] Crim LR 750
R v Leung and Wong [1999] NSWCCA 287
R v Luttrell [2004] EWCA Crim 1344.
R v Smith [2001] HCA 50
R v Stockwell [1993] 97 Cr. App. R. 260.
R v Turner [1975] 1 All ER 70.

Part III

Technology in the Courtroom: Social Media, Citizen Crime Sleuths, Virtual Court, and Child Witnesses

13 Digitally Networked Sleuthing

Online Platforms, Netizen Detectives, and Bottom-Up Investigations

James P. Walsh

Introduction

From communication and surveillance to forensics and records management, technological innovation has significantly shaped modern law enforcement. While scholars have rigorously detailed the operational and symbolic effects of various advancements on police services and personnel, considerably less attention has been devoted to technology's role in expanding the policing landscape. Such neglect is unfortunate as the development of web-based platforms and related digital tools offers unprecedented opportunities for thick, bottom-up participation. Since the start of the twenty-first-century, online communities composed of private civilians have leveraged breakthroughs in information-gathering and analysis to independently share evidence, generate intelligence, and investigate various criminal justice issues.

To broaden analysis and illuminate significant, but less-noticed, trends, this chapter surveys emergent alignments between citizens, technology, and law enforcement. In doing so, it presents the sensitizing concept of "digitally networked sleuthing" to capture instances where groups of citizens have employed digitally networked communications and analogous advances to collectively augment police investigations. While a handful of incisive works have employed terms like "digilantism," "websleuthing," "crowdsourced investigations," and "citizen-led digital policing" to accentuate particular aspects of the phenomenon (for example, see Estelles-Arolas, 2022; Gray & Benning, 2019; Hadjimatheou, 2021; Ireland, 2023; Kennett, 2019; McMahon, 2021; Myles et al., 2020; Nhan et al., 2017; Pantumsinchai, 2018; Trottier, 2012), knowledge remains fragmentary and organized around case studies of discrete platforms, communities, and investigative techniques. In an effort to offer a synoptic, wide-angled assessment, the following paragraphs synthesize the insights of existing work and delimit digitally networked sleuthing's defining features, diverse manifestations, and wider consequences.

DOI: 10.4324/9781003323112-16

After reviewing research on policing and digital platforms, this chapter presents the essential properties of digitally networked sleuthing and assesses the technical, cultural, and political forces underpinning its emergence. Leading examples of the phenomenon and their distinctive methods, goals, and organizational structure are then detailed. To orient future research, the chapter concludes by discussing digital sleuthing's benefits and limitations, whether practical or normative, and how potential harms can be assuaged.

The Rise of Digitally Networked Sleuthing

While technological change has fueled police innovation since modern law enforcement's emergence in the early nineteenth century, its effects are distinctly conspicuous within the current *information* era (Hooper, 2014). Digital tools like body-worn cameras, biometric registries, license plate scanners, predictive analytics, and mobile data terminals, ensure that, more than crime fighters, officers constitute knowledge workers devoted to collating, analyzing, and disseminating crime-related information. As web-based venues for creating, circulating, and consuming content, interactive digital platforms represent the latest addition to law enforcement's technological toolkit. In interrogating their effects, criminologists have largely assessed how, by offering unprecedented opportunities for monitoring and engaging publics, digital platforms enhance police services' image and operations (Walsh & O'Connor, 2019).

In foregrounding the activities and experiences of government agents and institutions, received scholarship has neglected other developments. Specifically, the ubiquity of digital platforms has facilitated a double movement in which technological changes have broadened policing's institutional boundaries, allowing citizens to substantively participate in governing security and detecting, analyzing, and resolving crime-related events. Despite some recent attention to these developments, digitally networked sleuthing represents a diminutive research field as scholars have tended to prioritize either state-orchestrated and superficial patterns of participation or extra-legal activities that are entirely disconnected from formal policing.

On one hand, analysts have documented the use of digital communications to "responsibilize" citizens and enlist them in legal enforcement. To promote legal compliance and self-help, police utilize platforms like Twitter, Facebook, and YouTube to broadcast public service announcements that admonish citizens about enforcement, punishment, and the harms of illicit activities or educate them on preventing victimization (Crump, 2011; Aitken et al., 2023). Authorities also employ digital platforms to solicit information about unsolved crimes, missing persons, wanted offenders, and general law-breaking, regularly posting virtual "wanted" posters, disseminating Amber alerts, promoting tiplines, and livestreaming CCTV footage (Fielding, 2023; Walsh et al., 2022). Despite broadening the scope of regulation, such arrangements reinforce authorities investigate primacy as police hierarchically identify problems, orchestrate information-sharing networks, and lead investigations, while citizens complete narrowly defined tasks and play a passive, subsidiary role. Moreover, citizens are mobilized as isolated informants rather than an active community of investigators, inhibiting collective action.

Scholars have also explored the phenomenon of digital vigilantism. Here, citizens collectively "weaponize" online visibility (Trottier, 2017) and use digital platforms to expose and condemn behavior (e.g., animal cruelty, adultery, racism, fraud, trolling, misogyny) deemed morally reprehensible, if not illegal, by publicly sharing perpetrators' personal details and identities (Chang et al., 2018; Ingraham & Reeves, 2016). As a form of retributive folk justice that relies on informal sanctions such as loss of employment, status, and credibility, digital vigilantism is invested in enforcing moral, rather than legal, order.

Overlooked in much of the existing literature is digitally networked sleuthing: collaborative, bottom-up efforts that actively contribute to legal enforcement. In recent years, a growing number of individuals have taken to social media and related online forums to autonomously assist police investigations by scouring the web for information, sharing open-source intelligence (e.g., documents, images, audio files), verifying evidence, iteratively discussing cases and investigations, building and managing databases, conducting undercover stings, offering investigative advice, and sharing potential leads with police and other pertinent agencies.

As a phenomenon, digitally networked sleuthing displays distinctive contours that require systematic evaluation. In contrast to responsibilization which entails formal "state anchoring" (Crawford, 2006) and passive assistance, it involves self-deputization and substantive involvement. Digital sleuths are active policing agents who, beyond providing auxiliary support, define security agendas, take initiative, appeal to others directly, and develop surveillance and investigative techniques and infrastructures. Moreover, despite operating at arms-length of authorities and frequently criticizing government inaction, unlike vigilantes, digital sleuths seek to strengthen, rather than wrest, state authority and control. They depend on criminal justice institutions to resolve cases, initiate legal proceedings, and, when necessary, punish wrongdoing (see Table 13.1).

As its name suggests, digitally networked sleuthing leverages the participatory, collaborative, and analytic affordances of digital platforms. While armchair detectives and citizen sleuths have long populated the policing landscape (Soothill, 1998), technological advances in computing, data

Table 13.1 Forms of digitally mediated citizen involvement.

Activity	Leading agents	Mode of action	Primary objectives	Relationship with criminal justice agencies
Responsibilization	Police	Individual	Legal enforcement and security governance	Complementary
Vigilantism	Citizens	Collective	Social control and moral regulation	Combative
Digitally networked sleuthing	Citizens	Collective	Legal enforcement and security governance	Complementary

analytics, and networked media have lowered barriers to entry, prompting an explosion in amateur investigations.

Decentralized, free, and user-friendly, digital platforms empower end-users to publicly create, share, connect, and discuss crime-related information, inspiring "vernacular creativity" (Burgess, 2006) and reallocating investigative knowledge and capacity (Horeck, 2019). Moreover, the hyperconnectivity and "aggregative functionalities" (Gerbaudo, 2018) of online platforms—the ability to rapidly mobilize sprawling webs of individuals—have converted amateur sleuthing from a solitary pursuit into a conjoint endeavor, allowing netizens to seek out like-minded others, build community, and orchestrate investigations involving networked interaction, collective intelligence, and distributed problem-solving.

Digitally networked sleuthing also exploits the "new visibility" (Thompson, 2005) produced by conditions of information abundance and technologies of "dataveillance" (Lyon, 2007). Accompanying multifarious records and data-sources that are remotely accessible online (e.g., satellite imagery, leaked databases, arrest reports, environmental data), the glut of user-generated content on digital platforms presents an untapped repository of crime and security-related intelligence. With the ability to record and share content no longer hoarded by major media outlets, end-users' documentation of daily life fosters social transparency, allowing formerly private details to be mined for potential evidence (Harcourt, 2015).

Lastly, lay actors possess considerable computing-power and new investigative tools (e.g., digital forensics, facial recognition, image-enhancement software, big data analytics, and geographic information systems) that boost the scale, scope, and speed of data-gathering and analysis, ensuring anyone with the requisite technological resources and literacy can undertake activities formerly monopolized by law enforcement, state militaries, and intelligence agencies (Slobogin, 2022).

Digitally networked sleuthing is irreducible to technological advancement. While digital platforms transform knowledge production and facilitate new forms of participatory policing, the ascendance of true-crime infotainment and neoliberal restructuring have created a popular willingness, if not perceived obligation, to contribute to policing efforts.

When combined with the long-standing cultural prominence of amateur sleuths and eccentric outsiders (e.g., Sherlock Holmes, Miss Marple, Nancy Drew), true-crime infotainment—media content featuring factual yet heavily stylized and sensational accounts of criminal acts (Murley, 2008)—has increased interest in private justice-seeking. Accompanying reality-based shows like *Crimewatch UK* and *America's Most Wanted* which solicit public assistance (Jermyn, 2007), new immersive, on-demand formats, including podcasts and video-streaming sites, have produced passionate fandom communities interested in investigative techniques, legal transgression, and broader "cultures of detection" (Horeck, 2019).[1] In nurturing fascination with crime-solving and instilling intense desire to obtain the sorts of dramatic results showcased in popular culture, resurgent interest in true-crime programming has stimulated collaborative efforts from energized and concerned citizens to resolve particular cases and unsolved crimes generally (Yardley et al., 2018).

Digitally networked sleuthing also reflects current political trends. While law enforcement has always relied on societal involvement, patterns of co-production, public-private partnership, and plural, multilateral policing have accelerated under neoliberalism (Loader, 2000). Reflecting the contemporary climate of retrenchment, lean government, and networked regulation, public order and security have become duties shared with and effectuated by a patchwork of non-police actors, including firms, communities, and citizens (Walsh, 2019b). Despite being instigated by citizens, rather than authorities, digitally networked sleuthing reflects governmental templates that promote active citizenship, entrepreneurialism, and delegation over centralized planning and command-and-control (Garland, 2001). Accordingly, for many, the value of bottom-up investigations is palpable, a civic-duty and moral responsibility.

Netizen Detectives: The Varieties of Digitally Networked Sleuthing

This section discusses exemplary cases of digitally networked sleuthing. Rather than exhaustive, it is illustrative and devoted to delineating the phenomenon's central tendencies and myriad forms. While digitally

---

1 Examples include followers of the series: *Serial*, *My Favorite Murder*, *Making a Murderer*, and *The Tiger King*.

networked sleuthing necessarily involves non-police employing digital platforms, whether as communicative infrastructures, data sources, or investigative domains, to collectively govern crime and insecurity, it is tactically and organizationally eclectic. Tactically, it displays varied targets, methods, technological underpinnings, and scales of participation. Alongside addressing a diverse array of domestic and international issues (e.g., missing persons, homicide, sexual abuse, terrorism, war crimes, human rights violations), the practice involves distinct investigative techniques (e.g., visual analysis, bioinformatics, geolocation), levels of sophistication (e.g., manual versus automated analysis), and degrees of involvement (e.g., smaller tight-knit efforts versus colossal crowdsourced campaigns). Organizationally, citizen-led investigations vary widely in their longevity, coordination, and institutionalization. In certain instances, digitally networked sleuthing is spontaneous, ephemeral, and organically surfaces to address emergent, extraordinary events, while, in others, it is the province of sustained movements and formal organizations displaying core memberships, standard operating procedures, and explicit codes of conduct.

Unsolved Mysteries and Cold Cases

Online communities devoted to resolving high-profile mysteries and cold cases provide a leading expression of digitally networked sleuthing. In recent years, mainstream social media platforms have emerged as popular meeting points and communications hubs for millions of users to access virtual evidence, assess potential clues, and pursue their Sherlockian fantasies.[2] An emblematic case is the Reddit Bureau of Investigation, a loose collective of over 625,000 cyber-detectives. As stated on its landing-page, the forum or subreddit employs "the power of Reddit to solve crimes" and invites visitors to request the community's help in investigating criminal offenses (e.g., murder, robberies, hit-and-runs, identity theft) and other matters concerning public safety (Myles et al., 2020). Visitors seeking assistance can ask questions, provide information, and, when present, upload photos and videos featuring crime-related events which are then used to establish the identities of people and things through technical analysis (e.g., sharpening the blurry image of a license plate), personal knowledge (e.g., determining a clothing brand, logo, or vehicle's make-and-model), or manual searches (e.g., identifying suspects using social media posts).

---

2 Regarding Facebook and Reddit, the former contains several public and private groups, including "Cold Cases," "Unsolved Crimes: Missing, Murdered, and Cold Cases," "Unsolved Mysteries," and "Canada Unsolved," while the latter features r/UnresolvedMysteries and numerous subreddits concerning specific cases (e.g., r/DelphiMurders).

To distance themselves from retributive vigilantism, forum members frame their activities as extensions of institutionalized policing. Alongside featuring an emblem resembling the FBI, the subreddit reminds posters to always contact law enforcement and is thoroughly moderated to ensure threads do not devolve into witch-hunts involving doxing and the release of personal information about suspects and other individuals.

Collaborative justice-seeking is also facilitated by purpose-built forums like Websleuths.com. Created in 1999 amid participatory media's nascent stage, the site, which presently features over 200,000 members and millions of posts, provides an interactive space where registered users can share, obtain and discuss information about crimes, trials, and cold cases which they attempt to clear (Loveluck, 2020).[3] While much of its traffic concerns discussion of highly publicized mega-cases, a distinctly animated subset of users, many of whom report spending over forty-hours of their spare time per week, investigates and pores over evidence about unsolved crimes neglected by the press, politicians, and police (Halber, 2014).[4] According to its owner Tricia Griffith, a retiree who also hosts a weekly podcast, maintains a YouTube channel, and is fully immersed in the field of true-crime infotainment, Websleuths.com represents the "21st-century version of America's Most Wanted" and permits individuals possessing varied backgrounds and experiences to congregate and "unravel real-life mysteries":

> [L]aw enforcement ... [gives us] a cold case ... [or] some piece of evidence ... that just sucks up the time of their detectives ... [and] we're looking at it fresh and we're excited ... Thousands of fresh eyes looking at it for nothing ... we can do all kinds of things for them and they can take all the credit.
>
> (Gane, 2018)

As nodes in a global web of digital sleuths, participants are potentially one web search or mouse click away from exposing vital leads, with several cases being cleared due to their efforts (Weintraub, 2023).

Accompanying immense forums like Websleuths.com, are smaller niche communities devoted to cases involving missing and unidentified persons which, in the US, presently exceed 50,000 (National Institute of Justice, 2023).

---

3 While anyone with an email account can participate, those with knowledge or backgrounds relevant to investigations (e.g., psychologists, cartographers, computer scientists, graphologists) can opt to have their credentials verified by the site's administrators.
4 Two of the leading discussion threads on Websleuths.com, for instance, concern the murders of Caylee Anthony (1.2 million messages) and JonBenet Ramsey (225,000 messages).

A prominent example is the Doe Network, which, since 1999, has maintained a centralized databank containing virtual dossiers for missing and unidentified persons from North America, Europe, and Australia. Each entry features descriptions of the individual, the circumstances surrounding their disappearance, digitized case files, and, when available, other relevant content (e.g., crime scene and post-mortem photos, coroner's reports, artist- and computer-generated facial reconstructions) that users are encouraged to methodically scour and cross-reference with other public records (e.g., yearbook photos, news clippings, missing person's reports). When important clues or potential matches are uncovered, users are required to contact the site's administrators who assess their strength and credibility before alerting authorities. Despite lacking formal training in policing or forensics, many participants have developed distinctive heuristics through years of experience that they openly share with others. Accordingly, the website contains detailed advice on conducting systematic web-based investigations, whether "reading" clues from visual evidence, using advanced search operators, or accessing newspaper archives, public records, and other data-sources (Stow, 2023; Yardley et al., 2018).

Through its efforts, the organization has helped revive long-dormant investigations, raising the possibility that what doubles as a macabre pastime can extend a sense of selfhood to the unidentified and offer closure to friends and family. In ensuring case files and other records previously relegated to filing cabinets or evidence lockers are accessible to far-flung virtual audiences, the community: broadens public awareness; presents a unified means of information-sharing; and transforms neglected cases and bodies into crowdsourcing data. While, at times, criticized by police for submitting irrelevant tips, the Doe Network has helped resolve over 100 cases and publicize thousands more. Consequently, several local police services have approached the organization with evidence and high-profile members have been hired to coordinate federal law enforcement initiatives (Murray et al., 2018).[5]

The most recent iteration of such efforts is the DNA Doe Project. A web-based volunteer network of genetic genealogists, the group utilizes advances in biometrics and big data to assist in resolving cases featuring unidentified individuals, whether as offenders, victims, or missing persons. Founded in 2017, the group accepts requests for assistance from

---

5 Alongside being hired by CBS, the Discovery Channel, and other nationwide outlets to provide expert commentary, Todd Matthews, a founding member of website, was recruited by the US Department of Justice in 2007 to help create and co-direct NamUs (the National Missing and Unidentified Persons System) an online registry featuring records regarding the missing and unidentified.

jurisdictions unable to afford crucial tasks like laboratory work, forensic anthropology, or genealogical research. Once a suitable case is identified, the DNA Doe Project purchases DNA sequencing and, employing techniques of bioinformatics, translates the resulting sequence into digital data that is submitted to GEDmatch—a publicly accessible repository housing genetic records sourced from commercial databanks like Ancestry.com and 23andMe (Scudder et al., 2020). If no immediate relatives (e.g., parents or siblings) are identified, group members try to locate distant ancestors through meticulous cross-referencing, and, if successful, construct potential family trees to unveil genetic relationships between known and unknown individuals within the present-day (Kennett, 2019). As a form of genetic crime-solving that pools public and private resources, the organization's activities greatly broaden police intelligence. By trawling and matching genetic records, it has helped unearth the identities of over 75 individuals whose DNA is missing in government databanks.

Pedophile Hunters

Accompanying retrospective analysis, digitally networked sleuthing is also proactive and oriented towards facilitating earlier interventions in law-breaking. A prominent example is online activist groups colloquially known as "pedophile hunters." Informed by sensational media reporting, the mass-accessibility of social media has ignited moral panics about computer-mediated child sexual predation, transforming the issue into a leading site of social anxiety and ostensibly intractable threat (Marwick, 2008; Campbell, 2016).[6] To address perceived rifts in security provision, non-police actors throughout the world, which include organizations like Perverted-Justice, Creep Catcher, Predator Poachers, Letzgo Hunting, and Dark Justice, have appropriated the very technologies that empower offenders to expose their identities, document their crimes, and facilitate their prosecution.[7]

While many pedophile hunting groups represent vigilantes devoted exclusively to administering gratuitous, extra-judicial sanctions—harassment, stigmatization, and (sometimes fatal) violence (Kasra, 2017; Favarel-Garrigues, 2020)—the following considers a notable subset whose first-order objectives are monitoring and flagging illicit online behavior to facilitate criminal prosecution. Even as their conduct is frequently denounced by police, such groups defer to extant penal arrangements and

---

6 Rather than strangers met online, research suggests 80–90% of child sexual abuse cases involve individuals known to the victim (Kohm, 2009).
7 Over 75 such groups operate the UK alone (Holmes, 2021).

operate within the confines of the law. Accordingly, they arguably resemble police in miniature as, to build the strongest case possible and pre-empt more serious harm and criminality, they screen and train recruits, demonstrate detailed knowledge of criminal law, maintain respectful comportment when confronting suspects, and are conscientious of the importance of different types of evidence and proper investigative conduct (Hadjimatheou, 2021).

Like many of the individuals they pursue and entrap, pedophile hunters exploit the anonymity of cyberspace to assume fictitious identities and befriend and communicate with others under false pretenses. Group members stage sting operations in which they pose as children in online venues (e.g., chatrooms, dating sites, social networks) to ferret out and engage potential offenders in incriminating conversations where they are informed of the decoy's underage status. Alongside compiling screenshots of explicit images and inappropriate communications, group members typically arrange real-world meetings where offenders are confronted before being reported or handed over to police. Besides preserving virtual evidence and fostering "suspicionless data collection" (Slobogin, 2022, p. 186), platforms like Facebook, YouTube, and TikTok are frequently used to post, and sometimes livestream, footage from in-person meetings, with several organizations amassing millions of views in the process (Ireland, 2023).[8] While broadcasting encounters constitutes surplus punishment involving spectacles of humiliation (Kohm, 2009), rather than inciting persecution, doing so is typically justified through references to the criminal justice goals of risk communication and deterring illegal conduct through the prospect of retribution (Tippett, 2022). Operationally, pedophile hunters have made demonstrable contributions to policing efforts, and, given the extent of moral outrage surrounding pedophilia, have garnered considerable media coverage and public support.[9]

Even in its more professional expressions, pedophile hunting occupies a legal borderland. By publicly disseminating footage of accused individuals, its practitioners facilitate, if not implicitly encourage, harassment and

---

8 While the overwhelming majority of groups stage and record public meetings, there is considerable variation in whether and how footage is publicly shared. Certain groups refuse to post footage entirely, while others refrain from livestreaming encounters or posting content before an arrest or conviction occurs (Hadjimatheou, 2021).
9 According to the American organization Perverted-Justice, as of October 2018, its operations had facilitated 623 convictions, with over 200 individuals still awaiting trial. In Scotland, pedophile hunters contributed to 55% of reported grooming cases in 2018–2019 (Holmes, 2021). Additionally, alongside being featured in national news reports and reality-based programs, 58% of respondents to a British survey expressed support for pedophile hunting if it facilitates more offenders being caught (Smith, 2017).

abuse which can consume police attention and has resulted in cases of mistaken identity, as well as suspects taking their own lives (Button, 2019). Moreover, when improperly orchestrated, sting operations may give offenders the opportunity to destroy vital evidence or inadvertently divert police resources from high-risk offenders towards "low-hanging fruit" who may never have offended were it not for pedophile hunters' efforts (Hadjimatheou, 2021). Finally, more than operating at arms-length of law enforcement, the available evidence suggests many pedophile hunters are animated by private agendas including amassing attention online, profiting financially, pursuing revenge fantasies, and achieving catharsis associated with confronting personal histories of victimization (Holmes, 2021; Kohm, 2009).

Nonetheless, unlike strong forms of vigilantism that seek to displace public policing and usurp sovereign power, the effectiveness of more professionalized pedophile hunting groups is thoroughly dependent upon the machinery and power of government. Even as their activities resemble informal justice-seeking, they are primarily oriented towards legal enforcement rather than moral censure, and, thus, rely on policing agencies' authority to detain and charge offenders. This ambiguous relationship is, in many respects, bidirectional. Even as police openly emphasize the harms of pedophile hunting, several services have provided advice and support. Moreover, while they may not engage pedophile hunters directly, by responding to requests for assistance, utilizing evidence they provide, and punishing perpetrators, law enforcement readily accept and tacitly promote their investigations (Purshouse, 2020).

Violent Disorder and High-Intensity Events

While digitally networked sleuthing generally focuses on traditional crimes involving small numbers of individuals and occurring away from the public eye, citizens have also mobilized to investigate high-intensity events, like riots and terrorist attacks, associated with mass-gatherings. Reflecting the chaos and cacophony of the incidents they target, such investigations are typically emergent, unregulated, and involve leaderless, rhizomatic participation where multitudes of non-professionals spontaneously converge to circulate content, scrutinize information, and assist police. Two early, and particularly notorious, examples of organic crowdsourcing are the 2011 Vancouver Hockey riots and 2013 Boston Marathon bombing.

Almost immediately after the Vancouver Canucks lost game seven of the Stanley Cup Finals in June 2011, a riot erupted in the city's downtown core. During the public disturbance, several cars were overturned and set ablaze, commercial properties were vandalized and looted, and at least 140 individuals, including nine police officers, were injured, resulting in

$4.2 million in damages (Bailey, 2011). As one of the first riots in Canada to occur in the age of smartphones and social media, it was extensively documented by participants and onlookers, with the resulting footage reverberating widely online. Outraged citizens flocked to Facebook, YouTube, and other platforms to post, gather, and share photos and videos of suspected rioters. In one instance, a Facebook group devoted to amassing visual evidence, attracted over 100,000 users, five million views, and a wide array of content in under five days (Trottier, 2012).

While the extent of community support was unprecedented and helped authorities identify and prosecute several participants, absent centralized coordination or planning, it frequently interfered with police efforts (Schneider & Trottier, 2012). Lacking reliable systems for verifying digital content and separating "signal" from "noise," police were overwhelmed by the sheer volume of submitted information (Hume, 2011). Crowdsourced efforts further taxed police resources as they rapidly degenerated into online shaming campaigns involving the release of rioters' personal identities, as well as harassment and threats of violence (Trottier, 2012). Also troubling was the fact many of those identified were minors whose names would ordinarily be banned in the legal system, resulting in violations of their Charter Rights and the Youth Criminal Justice Act (Hui, 2011).

In April 2013, two homemade bombs detonated near the finish line of the Boston Marathon, killing three individuals and injuring over one hundred more. In its efforts to bring the perpetrators to justice, the FBI appealed directly to citizens, asking for bystander photos and videos and, once images of the suspects were discovered, requesting help in establishing their identities (Marx, 2013). Citizens also took matters into their own hands as digital sleuths affiliated with the hacktivist collective Anonymous, the content aggregation site Reddit, and other social platforms, launched parallel investigations. Utilizing the affordances of networked media, users assembled and analyzed an extensive virtual archive of footage from near the scene of the bombing to uncover the perpetrators' identities and the type of explosive device employed (Tapia et al., 2014).

While highlighting the promise of crowdsourcing as throngs of netizens possessing diverse skills and experiences converged to evaluate relevant information (Nhan et al., 2017), such efforts also exposed its limitations as the supposed "wisdom of the crowd" quickly mutated into the atavism of the mob (Surowiecki, 2005). As users collectively scanned the massive corpus of images from the incident, many deployed gazes clouded by popular stereotypes and racialized depictions of terrorism featured in media reporting (Nacos, 2016; Walsh, 2017), resulting in the misidentification of several individuals. Accompanying two Moroccan running enthusiasts photographed near the finish line, Reddit users mistakenly identified Sunil Tripathi, a missing university student who it was later revealed had committed suicide before the attacks, resulting in his distraught family receiving threats and verbal abuse (Kang, 2013).

While police identified the actual perpetrators shortly thereafter, the incident demonstrated how the confluence of unvetted evidence, faulty analysis, untrained amateurs, and social networks' "feral and viral" qualities (Goldsmith, 2010, p. 930) generated powerful feedback loops which allowed unfounded claims to emerge as incontrovertible truth. Similar dynamics were witnessed following terrorist attacks in Bangkok (2015) and London (2017) as rampant speculation and rumor-mongering on social media resulted in the widespread propagation of specious claims and information pollution (Pantumsinchai, 2018). Together, such examples underscore the risks of crowdsourced justice in the wake of critical, emotionally potent events as, more than deficient, the generation of collective intelligence proved harmful and counter-productive.

Witnessed in the recent efforts of self-styled "sedition hunters," crowdsourced investigations have become more organized and sophisticated. Following the January 6 insurrection where a mob of supporters of Donald Trump attacked the US Capitol, amateur investigators mobilized online to gather content including photos, videos, and livestreams from various platforms (e.g., Instagram, Twitch, Parler, Facebook) and help authorities identify those responsible for storming the building, destroying property, and assaulting members of law enforcement. What initially represented a relatively small community, quickly evolved into an expansive movement as thousands of individuals assembled to dissect evidence on Twitter and private-run websites [e.g., seditionhunters.org, jan6evidence.com, facesoftheriot.com (site no longer accessible)] featuring photo galleries of participants, as well as interactive maps linking visual content to particular locations on the Capitol grounds. Intended to bolster the FBI's official inquiry, volunteers combed through thousands of images to unmask rioters using unique identifiers, whether tattoos, clothing, or facial features, facilitating hundreds of arrests within two months of the incident (Reilly, 2021). As a collaborative undertaking, volunteers' efforts were imbricated and interlocking, with one participant claiming, "[Everyone] brings a piece of the puzzle together. People are only able to ... hone in on somebody based on the work that everyone else is doing" (Yaffe-Bellany, 2021).

Cognizant of the potential pitfalls of crowdsourcing, central figures within the sedition hunting movement have counseled discipline and restraint, urging volunteers to avoid speculation and to only share information with law enforcement (Yaffe-Bellany, 2021). Nonetheless, false accusations have occurred, with many being attributable to the use of new techniques of surveillance. Unlike past investigations, sedition-hunting is partly automated and machine-led. In their quest to identify rioters, many participants have employed PimEyes, a facial recognition application that uses artificial intelligence to compare submitted photos against a massive cache of images scrapped from online platforms (Harwell, 2021). While increasing the circumference and celerity of investigative efforts and uncovering matches that, otherwise, would have likely gone unnoticed, the use of such "smart" technologies has sparked civil liberties-based concerns. Accompanying anxieties about insufficient oversight, as, unlike police investigations, facial recognition data is not required to undergo human review, are issues of mislabeling and erroneous inclusion. Several websites and social media accounts featuring images of suspected rioters have been found to contain pictures from previous, non-violent rallies, as well as, photos of bystanders, journalists, and those who only attended protests outside the Capitol, raising the possibility innocent parties might experience significant reputational damage and abuse (Gillespie, 2021; Greenberg, 2021).

Intelligence Gathering and Transnational Policing

The maturation of digitally networked communications has not only accelerated lay participation in security provision, but transformed it. While bottom-up involvement has historically addressed domestic crimes governed by conventional police services, digitally networked sleuthing often entails activities that, until recently, were monopolized by shadowy military and intelligence. Specifically, the utter ubiquity and accessibility of information and media evidence that is produced and hosted online has unleashed an era of open-data where governments and their organs of surveillance are no longer the exclusive purveyors of security-related intelligence. Consequently, global security and crimes against humanity and the international order are increasingly governed by private actors employing new types of evidence assembled and distributed from the ground-up.

A key participant within the incipient field of open-source intelligence is Bellingcat, an online community that employs digital forensics to "identify, verify, and amplify" evidence concerning war crimes, human rights violations, and other offenses perpetrated by states and violent extremists (Higgins, 2021).[10] Unlike the highly secretive cloak-and-dagger techniques of high-policing agencies, Bellingcat valorizes transparent methods and publicly available sources. Deemed "an intelligence agency for the people" and collection of "online sleuths" devoted to "solving global crimes" by "finding evidentiary needles in the haystack of free online information" (Eilstrup-Sangiovanni & Sharman, 2022, p. 39), the organization, which

---

10 Organizations employing similar methods include: Forensic Architecture, the Citizen Lab, Airwars, and Syrian Archive.

was founded in 2014, currently maintains eighteen full-time staff, a four-member management team, and a transnational network of volunteers who are rigorously vetted, receive significant training, and sign non-disclosure forms before accessing sensitive materials (Higgins, 2021).

Despite benefiting from the expertise of core staff and sophisticated algorithmic tools (e.g., acoustic modelling, facial recognition software, image distance calculators, automated map searches), Bellingcat's success largely rests on the labor of lay actors. Specifically, volunteers engage in distributed sense-making as they manually gather and sift through various information available online and compare it with other data sources to build factual knowledge and render situations that have traditionally been rife with uncertainty intelligible agencies. A prime example is the organization's favored investigative method: crowdsourced visual analysis or geolocation. Here, crime or atrocity-related footage (e.g., selfies, dashcam recordings, livestreams) is sourced from social media or other public websites and carefully scrutinized to ascertain the reality of events. In the latter instance, geo-tagged metadata, satellite imagery, road and topographical maps, and *in situ* data (photos and "street-view" images) are frequently consulted to reveal an incident's location, while meteorological conditions, astronomical data, and shadow length and direction are employed to determine its temporal parameters. Content analysis of buildings, vehicles, clothing, weapons, insignia, landmarks, street signs, and other phenomena featured in online content is also performed to identify participants and further verify information. Accordingly, beyond providing a crucial source of open-data, digital platforms allow Bellingcat to exploit the speed and scale of networked crowds and investigate incidents in settings that were previously inaccessible, whether due to conflict, geography, or financial constraints.

Bellingcat's activities straddle the boundaries between citizen journalism and law enforcement. Facing conditions of "post-truth," "alternative facts," and "fake news" (McIntyre, 2018), the organization not only produces open-source intelligence, but arbitrates truth and exposes, corrects, and inoculates against misinformation. Accordingly, much of its operations involve considerable debunking, whether unmasking fake social media accounts, identifying doctored or mislabeled photos, or refuting specious, conspiratorial claims. To these ends, Bellingcat employs exacting standards when confirming the provenance and authenticity of any evidence it gathers. Alongside documenting a clear, uncorrupted chain of custody, the organization archives and triangulates its data sources, and regularly consults with subject-matter experts to confirm their accuracy and significance. Bellingcat also preserves, organizes, and frames evidence for the purposes of legal intervention at the domestic and international levels. Discrete bits of information are assembled into larger media artifacts—architectural reconstructions, virtual simulations, photo galleries—are carefully curated to facilitate prosecution and avoid overwhelming formal inquires as massive data dumps often exceed authorities' processing capacity (Brodeur, 2010).

The organization's first substantial investigation involved the downing of Malaysia Airlines Flight 17, which crashed in Ukraine in 2014, killing 298 individuals. By combining, among others, satellite imagery, social media posts, photographs, phone logs, handwriting samples, and military records, group members were able to document the movement of a Russian Buk surface-to-air missile system through rebel-held territory in Eastern Ukraine, revealing that, contra the insistence of Russian authorities who blamed Ukrainian troops and promulgated forged images and false narratives to sow confusion, the aircraft was shot down by pro-Russian separatists who likely mistook it for a military plane. Alongside being corroborated by a Dutch-led international investigation team, these findings are presently being used by victims' relatives in their case against Russia before the European Court of Human Rights (Eilstrup-Sangiovanni & Sharman, 2022).

Since then, Bellingcat has investigated numerous atrocities. Utilizing local reports and visual analysis of the weaponry, uniforms, and topography featured in a grainy cell-phone video, the organization helped expose extra-judicial killings perpetrated by Cameroonian troops, resulting in their eventual arrest. By analyzing photographic evidence and consulting catalogues of military ordnance, it has also determined the origins of bombs used in airstrikes targeting civilians in Syria and Yemen (McMahon, 2021). Following Russia's invasion of Ukraine in 2022, Bellingcat has created an online database to document war crimes involving, among others, the use of cluster munitions, the killing of non-combatants, and destruction of civilian infrastructure (e.g., schools, hospitals, cultural sites) in the hopes it will be used in future criminal trials (Suarez, 2023). Finally, accompanying state crime, Bellingcat has orchestrated crowdsourced investigations of terrorist activity. Alongside using remote-sensing to identify ISIS training camps, its network of volunteers employed social media content and related data to trace the movements and activities of the white supremacist Brendan Tarrant, with New Zealand authorities using their work when investigating his attack on two Christchurch mosques (Macklin, 2019).

Unlike the opaque and cloistered world of traditional intelligence work, the public nature of Bellingcat's sources, investigations, and findings, not only means its conclusions are easily confirmed, but ensures its activities double as powerful forms of witnessing, advocacy, and consciousness-raising. In compiling evidence about state and transnational crimes that are often disregarded by governments and the international community, Bellingcat fills a legal vacuum, rendering "unseen" events visible and providing an alternative economy of information. Besides publishing incident reports that have influenced public opinion, news coverage, legal proceedings, and government decision-making (McMahon, 2021), the organization has released several guides on online investigations (e.g., "A Beginner's Guide to Social Media Verification," "How to Scrape Interactive Geospatial Data") and hosted workshops on open-source intelligence for journalists, human rights workers, and law enforcement personnel. Accordingly, it is part of an emerging digital public sphere or "networked fourth estate" that utilizes information technologies and web-based platforms to monitor governments, expose injustice, and reconfigure public knowledge, opinion, and sentiment (Benkler, 2011). Evincing Bellingcat's sociopolitical impact, its founder Elliot Higgins presently serves on the Technology Advisory Board of the International Criminal Court, and several established institutions, including media outlets (*The New York Times*), non-governmental organizations (Amnesty International), think-tanks (The Atlantic Council), and university research centers (UC Berkeley's Human Rights Investigations Lab), have emulated its investigative techniques (Ahmad, 2019).

The Virtues and Vices of Digitally Networked Sleuthing

Through contributions of their time and capabilities, web-based communities seek to enhance police investigations and deepen understanding of security-related issues and events. Despite participants' enthusiasm and desire to help, digitally networked sleuthing has generally experienced an ambivalent, if not antagonistic, reception from authorities. While often utilizing information provided by digital sleuths, reflecting the insular "siege mentality" that pervades police culture, civilians are frequently perceived as uninformed, untrustworthy, and lacking, among others, formal experience and training, objective distance, expertise in evidence-gathering, and knowledge of procedural standards (Crank, 2014). Bottom-up initiatives, therefore, tend to be viewed through a jaundiced eye and framed as jeopardizing police work and public safety (Siegel & Worrall, 2018). As a result, law enforcement has regularly denounced digital sleuths, refused their assistance, and, in extreme instances, threatened prosecution (Carbonaro, 2022; Yardley et al., 2018).

Since official reticence is largely derived from cultural mythologies, rather than dispassionate assessment, it is vital to assess digitally networked sleuthing's benefits and hazards, whether operational or normative. While more systematic evaluations are required, the following maps the phenomenon's potential effects on police investigations, as well as security, equity, and democratic arrangements. Doing so can help identify and initiate broader conversations about the specific modalities and circumstances through which digitally connected individuals can augment police efforts and obtain justice without attenuating rights, inflicting trauma, or perpetuating disadvantage.

Virtues

In general, netizens' investigative efforts offer an inexpensive force multiplier that bolsters the stock of knowledge and human and technological resources available to police. By providing additional eyes, ears, and skill-sets, digital sleuths improve authorities' acuity and field of vision. Moreover, when thousands, if not millions, of individuals collaborate, scale effects reduce the transaction costs of intelligence-gathering. While expert investigators' experience and expertise exceeds ordinary citizens, networked crowds possess superior processing-capacity and can mobilize, classify, and interpret impressive quantities of information more adroitly. In providing a vast reservoir of intelligence that supplements police's finite resources, digitally networked sleuthing therefore promises to elevate the speed and efficacy of problem-solving, producing "long tail" effects where, "the power of probabilities ... [and] numeric wherewithal of the masses" increase "the chances of investigative success" (Logan, 2020, p. 148).

Since authorities readily admit they cannot unilaterally govern issues like online child sexual abuse, missing and unidentified persons, terrorism, and human rights violations (Eilstrup-Sangiovanni & Sharman, 2022; Halber, 2014; Holmes, 2021; Walsh, 2020), external assistance, so long as it remains strictly tethered to legal enforcement, strengthens security provision. Beyond improving personal protection and communal safety, which represent public goods, if not human rights (Zedner, 2009), by allowing authorities to address more pressing matters and quell mounting demands for service, digitally networked sleuthing can also enhance police legitimacy.

Digital sleuthing's value is not merely additive, but synergistic. The connectedness, cooperation, and variegated insights of ordinary end-users is purported to foster more comprehensive situational awareness, providing a source of untapped "security capital" (Nhan et al., 2017, p. 345). Further, unorthodox actors with fresh eyes and open minds can facilitate creative, "outside-the-box" problem-solving that would likely be avoided by authorities (Brabham, 2013). Finally, alongside possessing access to and knowledge of otherwise unmonitored environments, the collaborative efforts of far-flung individuals nurture more effective information-sharing. By pursuing open-source investigations, digitizing case files, or merging information into accessible, searchable databases, digital sleuths streamline investigative work and transcend the resource limitations, interorganizational frictions, and jurisdictional turf-wars that often constrain law enforcement agencies (Manning, 2010).

Beyond its instrumental contributions, digitally networked sleuthing promises to correct historical inequities in policing while strengthening democratic citizenship's participatory and solidaristic dimensions. On one hand, it can help draw attention and resources to cases and victims overlooked or forgotten by authorities, journalists, and citizens, promoting greater inclusivity. Additionally, bottom-up participation embodies the values of direct democracy, including empowerment, engagement, and self-determination. Thus, by cultivating more responsible, resilient, and civically potent communities, participatory justice-seeking possesses the ability to build social capital and collective efficacy (Hadjimatheou, 2021; Skogan, 2006).

Hazards

Since legal enforcement and related powers of arrest and detention represent leading expressions of coercion and sovereign power, the involvement of private parties who represent unqualified arbiters of individual rights, legal protections, or investigatory procedure, displays significant practical and moral hazards.

Instrumentally, it is often argued that digitally networked sleuthing is ineffective and, without substantial oversight or accountability, threatens police operations. Whether concerning the scale of data-gathering, disrupted investigations, false leads, or groupthink, many contend that the actions of digital sleuths are more hazardous than the inaction of terrestrial bystanders.

In cases involving large-scale collaboration, irrespective of its importance or veracity, crowdsourcing can produce a crippling overabundance of data (Andrejevic, 2013). As the scale of participation and availability of open-source intelligence continue to expand unabated, police will likely be required to devote greater time to filtering information. Accordingly, the surfeit, rather than dearth, of evidence is problematic as the resources required to cleave information and discern meaningful connections can impede investigations.

Furthermore, when digital sleuths fail to employ exacting evidentiary standards, the presence of additional eyes and ears may produce inaccurate, unspecific, or unconfirmed information, corroding the quality of police intelligence. Without significant training or supervision, citizens are less likely to conduct meticulous, even-handed investigations, and prone to unflinchingly accept second-hand evidence, adopt conspiratorial orientations, and relay erroneous leads (Marx, 2013). As the Boston Marathon bombing and similar examples reveal, lay intelligence is often deeply flawed and "cannot qualify as knowledge under any rigorous understanding of the word" (Brodeur, 2010, p. 245).

Digitally networked sleuthing is also prone to misrecognition and bias. When evidence is gathered online, computer-mediated communications are often ambiguous and lack the contextual clues available in offline interactions (Suler, 2016). Consequently, benign activities may be erroneously designated suspicious and, more concerning, innocent parties mislabeled suspects. Citizen-led efforts, both manual and automated, can also disproportionately target non-dominant groups. Facial-recognition apps, which are widely used and readily accessible online, are less accurate in classifying darker-skinned faces (Ferguson, 2017), raising the possibility private actors may levy false accusations and deepen racialized injustice. Further, as crowdsourced investigations of terrorism, for instance, reveal, citizens' judgements are often guided by associations between social difference and criminality. Whether due to prejudice or impropriety, such instances suggest digitally networked sleuthing may foster investigations "run amok" (Tapia et al., 2014), promoting conjectural interventions and environments where rumor replaces rigor and innuendo passes as intelligence. Consequently, law enforcement will likely be forced to expend valuable personnel and resources correcting misinformation and policing the facts.

Finally, despite facilitating unprecedented participation and connectivity, digital platforms' affordances organize and encourage patterns of engagement and interaction that inhibit creativity. Commenting on Reddit as an information source in the immediate aftermath of the Boston Marathon bombing, one journalist claimed the site's tendency to endow popular, heavily upvoted posts with outsized visibility blunted innovation while promoting echo-chambers and conformation bias:

> Instead of offering ... lots of diverse, independent opinions ... Redditors [tended] to herd together, taking their cues from the conclusions that others before them had reached ... It was a process that ended up fostering groupthink more than collective intelligence.
> (Surowiecki, 2013)

The tendency to winnow information and crowd-out unconventional, minority views is also present on other platforms (e.g., Facebook, Instagram, TikTok, Twitter) where, despite their nodal configuration, influence remains highly stratified (Vaidyanathan, 2018).

In normative terms, digitally networked sleuthing creates situations where citizens double as agents and objects of suspicion and surveillance, and, thus, displays potentially deleterious consequences for legal rights, democratic accountability, and social cohesion.

Despite representing willing appendages of state power, as non-police, digital sleuths are unencumbered by privacy protections, allowing them to circumvent the procedural safeguards that constrain police investigations (Logan, 2020). Consequently, lateral forms of surveillance and investigative work contain the potential to considerably expand the government's power and reach into society through the backdoor. Because online venues allow such activities to occur on unprecedented scales, the possibility of subverting due process and attenuating civil liberties is distinctly pronounced (Slobogin, 2022). More broadly, empowering an army of citizen spies reinforces cultures of informing and suspicion which threaten to fragment societies and diminish the trust and reciprocity that underpin democratic citizenship (Walsh, 2019a).

The more lay actors become involved in crime control, the greater the tendency for untrained citizens to act autonomously, outcomes that may nurture vigilantism and generate unpredictability in the law's application and enforcement (Chang et al., 2018; Walsh, 2014). Absent regulatory regimes that promote transparency, accountability, and the rule-of-law, citizens operate in a legal void or twilight zone and, accordingly, may possess non-consensual values, objectives, and problem-definitions. While many are undoubtedly animated by public-mindedness, the available evidence suggests a significant portion are driven by self-interest and private desire for, among others, pleasure, notoriety, profits, revenge, or social exclusion. Accompanying prior experiences of victimization and the exhilaration that accrues from cracking a case and outsmarting authorities, amateur investigators are often inspired by commercial considerations as many represent influencers or content creators (Favarel-Garrigues, 2020; Ireland, 2023). Consequently, in seeking to acquire fame and "clicks" online, citizens may resort to extreme measures and intrusions off-limits to police. Moreover, by permitting overzealous citizens to influence legal enforcement, digitally networked sleuthing allows private actors to wield state power when exerting control over despised others. In the US, for example, pedophile hunting groups have recently been partly infiltrated by followers of the QAnon movement, a far-right conspiracy theory claiming political and cultural elites are secretly grooming children and operating a global sex-trafficking ring (Ireland, 2023). As this example suggests, without thorough screening or regulation, digitally networked sleuthing may help advance extremist agendas by subterfuge, increasing the likelihood of witch-hunts and biased, politicized enforcement.

Together, such scenarios imply citizens' emotional investment in policing may produce a loss of perspective and stimulate injudicious interventions. Accordingly, rather than suturing control gaps, digitally networked sleuthing may, instead, foster pernicious disjuncture between policing's formal objectives and practical consequences. To the extent, police are perceived as tolerating, if not encouraging, private acts of questionable legality, their legitimacy and moral authority may be compromised (Tyler & Fagan, 2008).

Finally, while online communities have helped reignite unresolved investigations, digitally networked sleuthing does not appear to correct historical imbalances in popular awareness and concern. Like the media representations and true-crime content that inspire many participants, amateur investigators tend to favor and fetishize crimes featuring "ideal victims" associated with youth, whiteness, and femininity, ensuring their efforts may sharpen, rather than mitigate, existing inequities (Halber, 2014; Jeanis et al., 2021). A recent example is found in the disappearance of Gabby Petito, a 22-year-old white woman who was killed by her fiancé in Wyoming as the two were travelling across the US. While her case triggered a massive crowdsourced investigation on TikTok and other platforms, equivalent cases involving marginalized populations were scarcely registered.[11] Accordingly, it is entirely probable, digitally networked sleuthing will entrench disparities in investigative attention, ensuring that, rather than a universal public good, justice is unevenly apportioned.

Discussion and Conclusion

Digitally networked sleuthing, like social media, open-data, and related information technologies, is certain to become more prevalent and complex in its applications and influence. The full implications of these developments have only recently begun to be appreciated and remain partly adumbrated. As this chapter reveals, in light of its varied expressions, digital sleuthing's effects are not pre-ordained, but contingent upon the intentions, methods, and regulatory regimes that shape its effectuation. Accordingly, a leading task for future research is identifying the conditions that will maximize its potential while minimizing, if not averting, its risks.

While space constraints have precluded an exhaustive assessment, the preceding analysis implies that, much like the information environments in which it occurs, digitally networked sleuthing requires muscular gatekeeping and moderation to rein in its potential for error, abuse, and harm. Since the majority of hazards—misinformation, bias, overzealousness, and co-optation—are typically linked to cases involving mass-participation from actors that are insufficiently regulated, vetted, and trained, citizen involvement should occur under public auspices and within coherent and

---

11 On TikTok alone, the hashtag #GabbyPetito was viewed over two hundred million times in the week following her disappearance, while the cases of numerous indigenous people reported missing near the same location sparked comparatively little interest online (Rosman, 2021).

robust institutional arrangements. To these ends, police and other relevant authorities should proactively incorporate online communities into their investigative efforts. Governments must, therefore, go further in: creating and administering platforms where citizens can submit, share, and evaluate information; enumerating best practices, quality standards, and ethical guidelines; developing formal training protocols; and sanctioning irresponsible and injurious behavior. Such efforts are distinctly important as digitally networked sleuthing shows no signs of subsiding and is likely to attract new participants lacking expertise and ethics of responsibility. This chapter, it is hoped, has helped illuminate the phenomenon's merits and deficiencies, as well as chart fruitful pathways forward.

References

Ahmad, M. (2019, June 10). Bellingcat and How Open Source Reinvented Investigative Journalism. *The New York Review of Books*. www.nybooks.com/online/2019/06/10/bellingcat-and-how-open-source-reinvented-investigative-journalism/

Aitken, A., Ralph, L., & Robinson, P. (2023). Police use of Twitter during a sporting mega-event. *Policing*. Advance online publication. https://doi.org/10.1093/police/paad016.

Andrejevic, M. (2013). *Infoglut*. London: Routledge.

Bailey, I. (2011, June 20). Bill for damages to be much higher than for the 1994 Stanley Cup. *Globe and Mail*.

Benkler, Y. (2011). A free irresponsible press: Wikileaks and the battle over the soul of the networked fourth estate. *Harvard Civil Rights-Civil Liberties Law Review*, 46(2), 311–397.

Brabham, D.C. (2013). *Using crowdsourcing in government*. Washington, DC: IBM Center for the Business of Government.

Brodeur, J.P. (2010). *The policing web*. Oxford: Oxford University Press.

Burgess, J. (2006). Hearing ordinary voices: Cultural studies, vernacular creativity and digital storytelling. *Continuum*, 20(2), 201–214.

Button, M. (2019). *Private policing*. London: Routledge.

Campbell, E. (2016). Policing paedophilia: Assembling bodies, spaces and things. *Crime, Media, Culture*, 12(3), 345–365.

Carbonaro, G. (2022, December 10). Idaho police warn internet sleuths of criminal charges over "harassment." *Newsweek*. www.newsweek.com/idaho-police-warn-internet-sleuths-criminal-charges-harassment-1766098

Chang, L., Lena, Y.C., Zhong, Y., & P.N. Grabosky (2018). Citizen co-production of cyber security: Self-help, vigilantes, and cybercrime. *Regulation & Governance*, 12(1), 101–114.

Crank, J. (2014). *Understanding police culture*. London: Routledge.

Crawford, A. (2006). Networked governance and the post-regulatory state? *Theoretical Criminology* 10(4), 449–479.

Crump, J. (2011). What are the police doing on Twitter? Social media, the police and the public. *Policy & Internet*, 3(4), 1–27.

Eilstrup-Sangiovanni, M. & Sharman, J.C. (2022). *Vigilantes beyond borders: NGOs as enforcers of international law*. Princeton: Princeton University Press.

Estellés-Arolas, E. (2022). Using crowdsourcing for a safer society: When the crowd rules. *European Journal of Criminology*, 19(4), 692–711.

Favarel-Garrigues, G. (2020). Digital vigilantism and anti-paedophile activism in Russia. Between civic involvement in law enforcement, moral policing and business venture. *Global Crime*, 21(3-4), 306–326.

Ferguson, A.G. (2017). *The rise of big data policing*. New York: NYU Press.

Fielding, N.G. (2023). Police communications and social media. *European Journal of Criminology*, 20(1), 316–334.

Gane, T. (2018, August 13) Should police turn to crowdsourced online sleuthing? *OZY*, https://perma.cc/YVS7-GZKV.

Garland, D. (2001). *The culture of control*. Oxford: Oxford University Press.

Gerbaudo, P. (2018). Social media and populism: an elective affinity? *Media, Culture & Society*, 40(5), 745–753.

Gillespie, E. (2021, January 21). FBI, rioters and social media: The pitfalls of online vigilantism. *SBS*, www.sbs.com.au/news/the-feed/article/fbi-rioters-and-social-media-the-pitfalls-of-online-vigilantism/c4jr1g3su

Goldsmith, A.J. (2010). Policing's new visibility. *British Journal of Criminology*, 50(5), 914–934.

Greenberg, A. (2021, January 28). This site published every face from Parler's Capitol riot videos. *Wired*, www.wired.com/story/faces-of-the-riot-capitol-insurrection-facial-recognition/

Grey, G. & Benning, B. (2019). Crowdsourcing criminology: Social media and citizen policing in missing person cases. *Sage Open*, 9(4).

Hadjimatheou, K. (2021). Citizen-led digital policing and democratic norms: The case of self-styled paedophile hunters. *Criminology & Criminal Justice*, 21(4), 547–565.

Halber, D. (2014). *The skeleton crew*. New York: Simon and Schuster.

Harcourt, B.E. (2015). *Exposed*. Cambridge, MA: Harvard University Press.

Harwell, D. (2021, May 14). This facial recognition website can turn anyone into a cop—or a stalker. *Washington Post*. www.washingtonpost.com/technology/2021/05/14/pimeyes-facial-recognition-search-secrecy/

Higgins, E. (2021). *We are Bellingcat*. New York: Bloomsbury.

Holmes, A.M. (2022). Citizen-Led Policing in the Digital Realm: Paedophile Hunters and Article 8 in the case of Sutherland v Her Majesty's Advocate. *The Modern Law Review*, 85(1), 219–231.

Hooper, M.K. (2014). Acknowledging existence of a fourth era of policing: The information era. *Journal of Forensic Research and Crime Studies*, 1, 1–4.

Horeck, T. (2019). *Justice on demand*. Detroit: Wayne State University Press.

Hui, S. (2011, June 20). UBC student apologizes for role in Vancouver riot, criticizes social media mob. *The Georgia Straight*. www.straight.com/blogra/ubc-student-apologizes-role-vancouver-riot-criticizes-social-media-mob.

Hume, C. (2011, June 16). Vancouver riots could have happened anywhere. *Toronto Star*. www.thestar.com/news/gta/2011/06/16/hume_vancouver_riots_could_have_happened_anywhere.html

Ingraham, C. & Reeves, J. (2016). New media, new panics. *Critical Studies in Media Communication 33*(5), 455–467.

Ireland, L. (2023). The acquisition of legitimacy for civilian policing: A case study of pedophile hunting groups. *Crime, Law and Social Change, 79*(2), 195–216.

Jeanis, M.N., Powers, R.A., Miley, L.N., Shunick, C.E., and Storms, M. (2021). The new milk carton campaign: An analysis of social media engagement with missing persons' cases. *Social Forces, 100*(2), 454–476.

Jermyn, D. (2007). *Crime watching*. London: IB Taurus.

Kang, J. (2013, July 28). Should Reddit be blamed for the spreading of a smear? *New York Times Magazine*. Retrieved from www.nytimes.com/2013/07/28/magazine/should-reddit-be-blamed-for-the-spreading-of-a-smear.html?pagewanted=all&_r=2&.

Kasra, M. (2017). Vigilantism, public shaming, and social media hegemony. *The Communication Review, 20*(3), 172–188.

Kennett, D. (2019). Using genetic genealogy databases in missing persons cases and to develop suspect leads in violent crimes. *Forensic Science International, 301*, 107–117.

Kohm, S.A. (2009). Naming, shaming and criminal justice: Mass-mediated humiliation as entertainment and punishment. *Crime, Media, Culture, 5*(2), 188–205.

Loader, I. (2000). Plural policing and democratic governance. *Social & Legal Studies, 9*(3), 323–345.

Logan, W.A. (2020). Crowdsourcing crime control. *Texas Law Review, 99*, 137–163.

Loveluck, B. (2020). The many shades of digital vigilantism. A typology of online self-justice. *Global Crime, 21*(3–4), 213–241.

Lyon, D. (2007). *Surveillance studies*. Cambridge: Polity.

Macklin, G. (2019). The Christchurch attacks. *CTC Sentinel, 12*(6), 18–29.

Manning, P.K. (2010). *Policing contingencies*. Chicago: University of Chicago Press.

Marwick, A. (2008). To catch a predator? The MySpace moral panic. *First Monday, 13*(6).

Marx, G.T. (2013). The public as partner? Technology can make us auxiliaries as well as vigilantes. *IEEE Security and Privacy, 11*(5), 56–61.

McIntyre, L. (2018). *Post-truth*. Cambridge: MIT Press.

McMahon, F. (2021). Digital sleuthing. In H. de Burgh & P. Lashmar (eds.), *Investigative journalism*, London: Routledge, pp. 57–72.

Murley, J. (2008). *The rise of true crime*. London: Praeger.

Murray, E.A., Anderson, B.E., Clark, C.S., and Hanzlick, R.L. (2018). The history of use of the national missing and unidentified persons system (NamUs) in the identification of unknown persons. In K.E. Latham, E.J. Bartelink and M. Finnegan (Eds.), *New perspectives in forensic skeletal identification*, pp. 115–126. Cambridge, MA: Academic Press.

Myles, D., Benoit-Barné, C. and Millerand, F. (2020). "Not your personal army!" Investigating the organizing property of retributive vigilantism in a Reddit collective of websleuths. *Information, Communication & Society, 23*(3), 317–336.

Nacos, B.L. (2016). *Mass-mediated terrorism*. Washington, DC: Rowman and Littlefield.

Nhan, J., Huey, L. & Broll, R. (2017). Digilantism: An analysis of crowdsourcing and the Boston marathon bombings. *The British Journal of Criminology*, 57(2), 341–361.

National Institute of Justice. (2023). Monthly NamUs case reports. https://namus.nij.ojp.gov/library/reports-and-statistics

Pantumsinchai, P. (2018). Armchair detectives and the social construction of falsehoods: an actor–network approach. *Information, Communication & Society*, 21(5), 761–778.

Purshouse, J. (2020). "Paedophile hunters," criminal procedure, and fundamental human rights. *Journal of Law and Society*, 47(3), 384–411.

Reilly, R.J. (2021, June 30). "Sedition hunters": Meet the online sleuths aiding the FBI's Capitol manhunt. *Huffington Post*, www.huffpost.com/entry/sedition-hunters-fbi-capitol-attack-manhunt-online-sleuths_n_60479dd7c5b6530400 34f749.

Rosman, K. (2021, October 20). How the case of Gabrielle Petito galvanized the Internet. *The New York Times*, www.nytimes.com/2021/09/20/style/gabby-petito-case-tiktok-social-media.html

Schneider, C.J. & Trottier, D. (2012). The 2011 Vancouver riot and the role of Facebook in crowd-sourced policing. *BC Studies*, 175(Autumn), 93–109.

Scudder, N., Robertson, J., Kelty, S.F., Walsh, S.J., and McNevin, D. (2020). Crowdsourced and crowdfunded: the future of forensic DNA? *Australian Journal of Forensic Sciences*, 52(2), 235–241.

Siegel, L.J. & Worrall J.L. (2018). *Essentials of criminal justice*. Boston: Cengage Learning.

Skogan, W.G. (2006). The promise of community policing. In: Weisburd, D. and Braga, A. (eds.) *Police Innovation*. Cambridge: Cambridge University Press, pp. 27–43.

Slobogin, C. (2022). *Virtual searches*. New York: NYU Press.

Smith, M. (2017, September 18). Most say police and paedophile-hunters should link up if it puts more behind bars. *YouGov*. https://yougov.co.uk/topics/politics/articles-reports/2017/09/18/most-brits-say-police-working-vigilante-paedophile.

Soothill, K. (1998). Armchair detectives and armchair thieves. *Police Journal*, 71, 155–159.

Stow, N. (2023). *The real-life murder clubs: Citizens solving true crimes*. London: Ad Lib.

Suarez, E. (2023, February 21). How Bellingcat collects, verifies and archives digital evidence of war crimes in Ukraine. *Reuters Institute for the Study of Journalism*, https://reutersinstitute.politics.ox.ac.uk/news/how-bellingcat-collects-verifies-and-archives-digital-evidence-war-crimes-ukraine

Suler, J.R. (2016). *Psychology of the digital age*. Cambridge: Cambridge University Press.

Surowiecki, J. (2005). *The wisdom of crowds*. New York: Anchor.

Surowiecki, J. (2013, April 23). The wise way to crowdsource a manhunt. *The New Yorker*. Retrieved from www.newyorker.com/news/daily-comment/the-wise-way-to-crowdsource-a-manhunt

Tapia, A.H., N. LaLone, & H.W. Kim, (2014). Run amok: Group crowd participation in identifying the bomb and bomber from the Boston Marathon bombing.

Proceedings from the International Conference on Information Systems for Crisis Response and Management, pp. 265–274.

Thompson, J.B. (2005). The new visibility. *Theory, Culture & Society*, 22(6), 31–51.

Tippett, A. (2022). The rise of paedophile hunters: To what extent are cyber-vigilante groups a productive form of policing, retribution and justice? *Criminology & Criminal Justice*. https://doi.org/10.1177/17488958221136845

Trottier, D. (2012). Policing social media. *Canadian Review of Sociology*, 49(4), 411–425.

Trottier, D. (2017). Digital vigilantism as weaponisation of visibility. *Philosophy & Technology*, 30(1), 55–72.

Tyler, T. R. and Fagan, J. (2008). Legitimacy and cooperation: Why do people help the police fight crime in their communities. *Ohio State Journal of Criminal Law*, 6(1), 231–275.

Vaidhyanathan, S. (2018). *Antisocial media*. Oxford: Oxford University Press.

Walsh, J. (2014). Watchful citizens: Immigration control, Surveillance and Societal Participation. *Social & Legal Studies*, 23(2), 237–252.

Walsh, J.P. (2017). Moral panics by design: The case of terrorism. *Current Sociology* 65(5), 643–662.

Walsh, J.P. (2019a), Countersurveillance. In Deflem, M. (ed.) *The handbook of social control*. Oxford: Blackwell, pp. 374–388.

Walsh, J.P. (2019b). Education or enforcement? Enrolling universities in the surveillance and policing of migration. *Crime, Law and Social Change*, 71(4), 325–344.

Walsh, J. (2020). Report and deport: Public vigilance and migration policing in Australia. *Theoretical Criminology*, 24(2), 276–295.

Walsh, J.P. & O'Connor, C. (2019). Social media and policing: A review of recent research. Sociology Compass, 13(1), 1–14.

Walsh, J.P., Baker, V. & Frade, B. (2022). Policing and social media: The framing of technological use by Canadian newspapers (2005–2020). *Criminology & Criminal Justice*. https://doi.org/10.1177/17488958221114254.

Weintraub, A. (2023, January 19) How amateur web sleuths helped solve the case of missing lottery winner Abraham Shakespeare. *ABC News*. https://abcnews.go.com/US/amateur-web-sleuths-helped-solve-case-missing-lottery/story?id=96079852.

Yaffe-Bellany, D. (2021, June 7). The sedition hunters. *Bloomberg*, www.bloomberg.com/features/2021-capitol-riot-sedition-hunters/

Yardley, E., Lynes, A.G.T., Wilson, D., & Kelly, E. (2018). What's the deal with "websleuthing"? News media representations of amateur detectives in networked spaces. *Crime, Media, Culture*, 14(1), 81–109.

Zedner, L. (2009). *Security*. London: Routledge.

14 The Virtual Court
Implications for Eyewitnesses and Beyond

Eryn J. Newman, Bethany Muir, and Nericia Brown

Since the start of 2020, there has been an overwhelming increase in the number of court cases heard remotely—where people are not physically in the courtroom but joining in the same online location—on Zoom, Microsoft Teams, or similar platforms. In the UK, for instance, an estimated 990,000 hearings took place remotely between 2020–2021 (Spinney, 2022). In Texas, an estimated 1.1 million remote hearings took place over that same one-year period (Rickard et al., 2021; see also Wienrich et al., 2022). In these contexts, people listen to, or provide evidence online from distant locations, drawing on a variety of different online tools and hardware. The use of remote platforms has significant potential—during the pandemic they helped to maintain momentum in addressing significant caseloads at an incredibly difficult time where people were unable to enter a shared physical space to make collective decisions (for a review see Song & Legg, 2021).

Across jurisdictions many embraced this remote justice potential and moved to online formats by early 2020. For example, Australian and UK courts had closed all in-person courtrooms by March 2020 and moved all (except jury) trials online (Song & Legg, 2021). Similar, but slower shifts were made in the US (Denney, 2020), with 38 states mandating virtual hearings by 2021 (Ariturk et al., 2020). Forecasts on the reliance of remote courts going forward suggest continued use of and investment into digital infrastructure (e.g., Bender, 2021; Susskind, 2019). Initial caseload data align with this digital investment. During the pandemic, caseloads in the UK were reduced by up to 22% compared to pre-covid (Criminal Justice Joint Inspection, 2022), with virtual court proceedings having a positive impact on caseload management and resource allocation. The move to remote communications gave people flexibility and protection during a public health crisis.

Notably, the concept and implementation of the virtual court did not directly emerge from the pandemic with countries like the UK and Australia having already begun trials and empirical research on implementation

DOI: 10.4324/9781003323112-17

of the virtual court pre-pandemic (Rossner & McCurdy, 2020; Wallace et al., 2019; see also Sanders, 2020, for European review). However, the widespread online shift—with over 160 countries flipping to some form of remote proceedings in early 2020—demonstrated at scale, an advantage for digital criminal justice capabilities at times of crisis. This rapid shift also illuminated gaps and vulnerabilities in policy, technology, and empirical research regarding the impact of virtual hearings for human decision-making. In this chapter we briefly review the history of the virtual court and how it has been implemented thus far. We identify sources of disparity and procedural hurdles that have emerged over the last three years and consider implications for decision-making and human memory. Given that this is an emerging field of research, we identify areas for future empirical research and consider implications for the legal system and social justice.

Emerging Virtual Courts

The use and entry of remote evidence in the form of audio-visual links (AVL) has had a presence in court systems throughout the world over the last three decades (Smith et al., 2021). The entry of such evidence is typically utilized for expert or vulnerable witnesses and in some instances for an accused who may be appearing from a custodial environment (see Fobes, 2020, for a discussion on entry of remote testimony). Thus, existing courtrooms are often set up to host digital appearances in a physical courtroom space, typically from one individual at any one moment. In 2020, however, the COVID-19 pandemic social distancing requirements necessitated not one, but many members of a given hearing to join the court remotely and collectively. Countries (and states within countries) varied significantly in how remote hearings were managed. In some cases, all actors moved online. In other cases, the judge remained in the court while other participants joined from homes, offices, and other locations—depending on means, advice from one's counsel, and policies and procedures implemented by the specific court (e.g., Song & Legg, 2021). For example, some people joined video platforms from phones, others used audio only, some sat in awkward spaces in family homes, and some sat at PCs with built-in cameras in private offices (Song & Legg, 2021). While jury trials paused in some jurisdictions (see Thornburg, 2020), others continued in remote spaces, or even in cinemas where the trial—held on a remote video conferencing platform—was live-streamed to jurors placed physically distant from each other in the same room (see Spinney, 2022). Thus, over the last three years there has been wide variability in the presentation of evidence and manner of participation in remote courts.

While the move away from a shared physical space creates a significant departure in court rituals and formality, it also, incidentally, introduces several extra-legal factors that have the potential to impact decision-making and recall. This impact may have quite broad consequences for legal decision-making more generally, but the focus of this current chapter is to consider how these extra-legal factors may work to influence people's perceptions of eyewitnesses and one's ability to recall information as an eyewitness presenting evidence in an online environment. In the next sections, we identify and review key extra-legal factors such as variation in access to high quality digital experience, variation in the context in which people appear in the virtual court, and how online platforms may impact general cognitive processing. Throughout, we turn to psychological literature to help contextualize the possible impact of these factors on impressions of eyewitnesses and their memory.

The Digital Divide and Impact on Perceptions of Eyewitnesses

While digital and remote communication has promise in facilitating justice at times of crisis, access and experience of communicating online is not distributed equally. A digital divide exists, with access to high-speed internet (and high-quality mobile data plans) systematically varying with socio-economic status (SES) and location, such that those with lower incomes or living in more rural communities may be disadvantaged (Park, 2017; Reddick et al., 2020; Thomas et al., 2021; see also Eruchalu et al., 2021). As governments and global initiatives work to close the digital gap (Federal Communications Commission, 2017; World Health Organization, 2021), research suggests that other sources of digital inequality will persist (see Napoli & Obar, 2014; Tsetsi & Rains, 2017) in the form of variation in hardware.

People living in higher SES communities typically have greater access to PCs and more modernized technology than those in lower SES communities (Tsetsi & Rains, 2017). This instantiation of the digital divide in the form of device divide matters. Notably, there are broad discrepancies in the content availability, processing speed, storage capacity, and interface functionality between mobile devices and PCs (Napoli & Obar, 2014; Tsetsi & Rains, 2017). And although remote communications and video conferencing platforms are often accessible through mobile devices (World Health Organization, 2016), fundamental constraints including sub-optimal interfaces, smaller screen sizes, and lower-quality audio (Mossberger et al., 2012; Napoli & Obar, 2014), may result in a compromised communication experience compared to using a PC.

While increasing access to the internet increases the chances that one can have *a* seat at the digital table, research in cognitive and social psychology suggests that if one is on the wrong side of the digital divide, one may not have an *equal* seat at the table. Emerging psychological research suggests that poor connections, drop out and difficult audio quality may do more than simply interrupt a communication, but may impact people's perceptions of a speaker. Although caused by technology and tools outside of a speaker's control, digital disruptions may work to negatively impact people's perceptions of a speaker, and disproportionately impact those with poor internet or reduced access to advanced digital technology.

Interruptions in Cognitive Processing and Implications for Eyewitness Evidence

Legal scholars have noted the presence of, and difficulties in, navigating unreliable internet or other digital interruptions in testimony, where witnesses have been asked to repeat themselves, or lean towards the microphones to be heard (Song & Legg, 2021; McKay, 2020). While these interruptions can lengthen proceedings, they may also harm witnesses and their evidence. If the witness drops out significantly when sharing evidence, decision-makers may be missing content that might work to impact the perceived or objective coherence and accuracy of witness reports. When people encounter information that has degraded semantic context, they have lower comprehension and worse memory for that information later (e.g., Bransford & Johnson, 1972). Moreover, coherence is one of several key criteria people draw on in assessing the truth of information they encounter (Schwarz et al., 2016). But these significant digital interruptions—complete drop out—should readily be identified by the court and addressed by pausing proceedings until the witness has a reliable connection (reviews see Song & Legg, 2021; McKay, 2022).

But more subtle digital interruptions—ongoing echo or background noise that persists throughout witness testimony—may be endured without explicit awareness, leading to a lack of action in addressing such disruption. This form of digital disruption is a cause for concern, not only because a simple ongoing echo can produce psychophysiological markers of distress (see Arlinger et al., 2009; Wilson & Sasse, 2000), but also because emerging research suggests that when a speaker has low quality audio, listeners tend to evaluate the speaker less favorably. In one study, people listened to snippets of scientists presenting research in high (crisp, clear) audio or low (with an echo and static) quality audio. Listeners evaluated the scientist with low quality audio as less likeable, less smart, and the research they were sharing as less important (Newman & Schwarz, 2018; see also Dragojevic & Giles, 2016). This pattern held even when listeners heard an introduction—in clear audio—that the speakers were professors from top-tier research intuitions and were being interviewed for recent research successes. The preference for speakers with high quality audio also held when speakers were compared against themselves: the same speaker was rated as more intelligent and likeable, and their research seemed more important when people heard the same content, from the same speaker in high quality audio (Newman & Schwarz, 2018). Parallel patterns have been found in job interview contexts. When people listened to job candidates with disrupted audio-visual quality, people evaluated the job candidates less favorably (Fiechter et al., 2018).

Recently, these impacts of audio quality on people's impressions of speakers was investigated in the context of remote eyewitness testimony (Bild et al., 2021). In a series of experiments, people listened to testimony in high or low audio quality and then evaluated how reliable, credible, and trustworthy the witnesses seemed. Across all experiments, whether people were listening to two children or two adults providing testimony, people evaluated the witness with higher audio quality more favorably. This pattern held when we controlled for whether people remembered key details in the testimony—where one can be more certain that the effect of audio quality was not due to significant dropout of content. Bild et al. also found initial evidence that people made final guilt judgements in line with the speaker with high quality audio, though this effect should be replicated in future research.

Why would audio quality impact people's perceptions of the witness in this way? One possibility is that people perceive the speaker to be less organized or prepared if their digital devices and internet are not optimized for the presentation of evidence in formal proceedings. While this would be a non-diagnostic assessment of evidence—people may not have access to high quality devices or internet due to socio-demographic disadvantage—this nonetheless may be one route through which people may arrive at a negative impression about a witness due to audio quality. We examined that possibility in recent research: when we explicitly told people that both witnesses were using the same technology, from the local police station, the impact of audio quality on people's impressions of the witnesses remained the same (Brown et al., in preparation). That is, the witness with high quality audio was evaluated more favorably even when people were told that both witnesses were using the same technology and in the same environment, ruling out a causal link between audio quality and personal responsibility for the technology (Brown et al., in preparation).

Another explanation for the impact of audio quality on people's impressions of the witness is that the difficulty in listening to the speaker served as a metacognitive cue that informed people's social impressions of the witness. Indeed, there is a large body of literature showing that when people encounter information in their daily experience, they are sensitive to not only the content of a given message, but also the metacognitive ease or fluency of processing the message (Alter & Oppenheimer, 2009; Schwarz et al., 2021). People use this fluency or ease of processing to make inferences about the quality of the message or messenger. For example, when trivia claims are presented in a foreign accent, people find those claims less likely to be true than when the same claims are presented in a native accent (Lev-Ari & Keysar, 2010; see also Dragojevic & Giles, 2016). Beyond audio cues, when claims are difficult to visually perceive people are less likely to endorse them. In one study, people rated claims presented in low color contrast (e.g., written in yellow font on a white background) as less true than when claims were presented in high color contrast (e.g., dark blue font on a white background; Reber & Schwarz, 1999). Ease of pronunciation can have a similar impact. When people have difficulty in pronouncing a source's name, people find that person less trustworthy, less familiar, more risky, and less inclined to believe the claims they share (Laham et al., 2012; Newman et al., 2014; Silva et al., 2017). This pattern holds even when people are provided with more diagnostic information about the person's prior behavior (Silva et al., 2017). Thus, a variety of cognitive factors can influence impressions of messages and messengers in a similar way. Regardless of the source that creates the difficulty in processing—whether difficulty is due to audio, visual perceptual, or linguistic factors—people use the metacognitive experience of general difficulty in processing as an informative cue to make inferences about information around them (for a review see Schwarz et al., 2021).

Depleted Social Cognitive Cues and Implications for Eyewitness Impressions

The research on cognitive fluency suggests broader implications for virtual courts that reach beyond the impact of an interrupted signal (e.g., Schwarz et al., 2021). Online communications may be impeded by a variety of social-cognitive factors that make it more difficult to process incoming information. In virtual environments, we lose many cues that are typically present in face-to-face settings that would usually facilitate social communication and trust (Bailenson, 2021; see e.g., role of body language and facial expression, Meeren et al., 2005). For example, non-verbal cues such as gesturing would typically work to facilitate communication and comprehension (Goldin-Meadow et al., 2001; Hostetter, 2011). In virtual environments many non-verbal cues are degraded or absent and thus may mean that communication is disrupted relative to in-person settings. While the loss of non-verbal cues might be considered a consistent factor impacting all witnesses, research suggests that there is individual variation in the reliance of gesturing in communication (Gillespie et al., 2014; Marstaller & Burianová, 2013), which may work to disproportionately hurt some people's ability to communicate evidence (possibly through increased working memory load) and potentially harm perceptions of them as witnesses. The impact of these variables on comprehension and social impressions are all questions for future research and may warrant attention. Mismatching facial expressions or minor gestures due to lag is another factor that may work to introduce novel forms of disruption in social-cognitive processing of evidence. In recent research by ten Brinke and Weisbuch (2020), people who heard video communications where the audio was slightly lagged and unaligned with the visual information judged the speaker as less truthful than when audio-visual information aligned. Like audio quality, interruptions of facial cues may systematically impact those who have less stable digital connections to the virtual court, raising significant questions about equity, access to justice, and policy and procedure.

Visual Context and Impact on Perceptions of Eyewitnesses

Beyond instances where people mistakenly clicked digital filters (e.g., the judge that appeared as a cat on Zoom; Spinney, 2022), or had people walking through their backgrounds, court participants were able to view people's personal spaces—the environment from which they joined a video conference. In a traditional courtroom space, court participants share a consistent physical space, one that provides cues to history, court rituals—good and bad—and collective decision-making in the context of a jury (Rossner, 2021). In the virtual courtroom, procedural requirements for joining the virtual court varied greatly and across jurisdictions many did not require a universal background shared by all. Depending on available technology and personal or professional space, people were joining with effective (or unreliable) virtual backgrounds, professional office spaces, and home environments—all of which allowed for a variety of socio-demographic cues to enter the courtroom in an uncontrolled manner. While decision-makers are instructed to attend to the content of evidence shared by a given witness, how might the witness's background impact perceptions and impression formation regarding them and their evidence?

Impact of Semantic Context on Impressions of Eyewitnesses

While very limited psychological research has examined this question directly, initial research in our own lab suggests that simple variation in the tidiness of a witnesses' background (at work, or at home) can alter people's impressions of a witness. In one study, people were asked to read testimony attributed to witnesses who appeared from messy or clean backgrounds and then rate their impressions of the witnesses (Muir et al., 2022). Those witnesses who appeared from messy backgrounds were rated as less diligent and less credible. While a messy background is non-diagnostic of an eyewitnesses' memory accuracy (or their organization when they were required to present evidence from work settings), people nonetheless were influenced by background context when they formed impressions. These findings are consistent with research from impression formation research more generally (see Devine & Caughlin, 2014, for a review). When we evaluate others, we draw on tangential cues to make social evaluations. Classic psychological studies show that, for example, when people are primed with hostile words, they are more inclined to make negative inferences about a target person they read about in a subsequent, but unrelated task (Srull & Wyer, 1979). In more recent work, Silva et al. (2019) showed that when participants viewed photographs of faces on dating websites, their evaluations of those same faces differed depending on the type of website they were presented on. If the faces were presented on a "hook-up" website, those faces were judged as less trustworthy than if presented on "long-term dating" or social websites. That is, people unwittingly draw on tangential information in forming social judgement.

While there is limited empirical evidence for the impact of backgrounds on impressions of witnesses, there are at least two other literatures that support the possibility that backgrounds may matter. Research on comprehension and human memory shows that adding semantic context can systematically impact people's memory for content they have encountered and impressions of that content in the moment. For example, when people encounter complex verbal descriptions, adding a contextually related picture can help to increase comprehension and memory for the descriptions (Bransford & Johnson, 1972; Carney & Levin, 2002). In other research, when pictures activate a specific schema, the addition of pictures to a piece of text can lead people to misremember elements of a story that were not present, but are consistent with a schema (Garry et al., 2007; Henkel, 2012). From this schema perspective, it is possible that backgrounds can prime a schema that could shape the way decision-makers view and remember evidence. While listening to witness evidence is different to reading a piece of text, the existing research in memory and cognition suggests that semantic information in the form of visual context may impact people's memory for content they encounter.

In a recent study, photos that related to forensic science evidence, but provided no diagnostic value for the credibility of that evidence (e.g., a generic photo of broken glass paired with a claim that pieces of glass were a match) increased people's belief in the forensic science testimony (Sanson et al., 2020). This finding is consistent with broader research on the impact of related photos on people's perceptions of associated claims—when people see a claim like "Magnesium is the liquid metal inside a thermometer" with a photo of a thermometer, they are more inclined to believe the claim. This *truthiness effect* is particularly pronounced when people are judging unfamiliar information (see Newman et al., 2012; for a review see Newman & Zhang, 2020). Considered together, existing research suggests that visual semantic context can not only shape people's memory for associated text but can impact people's perceptions of truth for associated claims. An important question to examine in the context of virtual court backgrounds is the extent to which these effects extend to visual semantic context in the form of video backgrounds and witness claims.

Another literature that may bear on possible impacts of background on witness perception is research from environmental psychology. This body of work examines how people make social inferences after reviewing another person's space, typically a home environment or workspace. A key finding in this literature is that people draw conclusions about others after viewing their spaces. For example, in one study, viewing an individual's living space shaped impressions about the occupant's character (Gosling et al., 2002). Cues within an occupant's room, such as how it is organized or decorated, correlated to perceived personality traits of the occupant, such as openness and agreeableness. In another study, photographs of the same office in a cluttered and uncluttered state led to different evaluations of personality, where the more organized the space, the more conscientious and agreeable the occupant was perceived to be (Horgan et al., 2019). As already noted, there is a lack of empirical research that has focused explicitly on eyewitnesses in virtual environments. But the literature reviewed thus far highlights the importance of considering backgrounds as an extra-legal factor that people may unwittingly draw on in decision-making.

Distance and Eye Contact and Perceptions of Eyewitnesses

Beyond introducing background context, the virtual environment also allows for other variations in visual and spatial experience between witnesses and the decision-makers that may impact impressions and later judgement (Leach et al., 2022). Research in shared physical spaces shows that increasing the distance between a pair of participants reduces positive evaluations of the other—with increasing distance, people are evaluated as less likeable (e.g., Shin et al., 2019; see also Scherer, 1974). In online spaces, this distance effect may further vary due to camera angles which position people's faces closer or further from the camera, impacting eye gaze and perceived eye contact. These factors may influence interpersonal experience with the possibility that those who are closer to the camera are perceived as at a relatively close distance (Bailenson, 2021). Further, variations in perceived eye contact may influence the extent to which people feel socially included (see Hietanen, 2018, for a review on impacts of eye contact). Indeed, eye contact can signal attention and people infer social characteristics such as sincerity and trust with increasing eye contact (see Hietanen, 2018; Kleinke et al., 1973; Mason et al., 2005; see also Macrae et al., 2002). In video-based communications eye contact facilitation is considered a fundamental digital target for high quality communication (see Bohannon et al., 2013; Mühlbach et al., 1995). While these visual spatial variations are driven by technology and perhaps digital literacy, they represent extra-legal factors that may have insidious effects on the way eyewitnesses are perceived and their evidence received.

While many of the variables discussed thus far have yet to be systematically examined in psychology and law contexts, some are the focus of recommendations in early trials of virtual court presentation formats. Indeed, Rossner and McCurdy (2020) recommend that remote participants should appear with effective lighting and framing, use external microphones for best audio input, and incorporate messages that signal when audio or video inputs fail. Other researchers provide suggestions to adjust cameras to eye level, place speaker notes near the camera to achieve eye contact, including instructions to decision-makers, using headphones, and implementing virtual backgrounds (Sternlight & Robbennolt, 2022). Again, while existing research suggests these factors may impact person perception, the specific impact for eyewitnesses is less clear and further research is warranted to inform effective policy and procedure.

Cognitive Load and Eyewitness Evidence

The current chapter has largely focused on *perceptions* of eyewitnesses and how virtual court contexts may work to influence other people's impressions of eyewitness accounts. But the *experience* of being an eyewitness and ability to effectively recollect information in a virtual court context may also be impacted by features inherent in virtual court spaces. Eyewitnesses are tasked with providing accurate evidence for the court in the form of memory representations of past events. This task is already challenging given features of our cognitive systems that mean event memory is reconstructed, rather than simply played back (Loftus, 2005). In many of the current virtual court environments, eyewitnesses have joined video conferencing meetings and provided evidence in an environment that may create further challenges for memory recall. We examine those factors here, with a focus on the variables that may work to increase cognitive load, highlighting opportunities for future research.

Cognitive Load In Remote Communications?

The digital interface on platforms like Zoom introduces variables not typically present in the physical court, and like other digital contexts, may produce higher cognitive load and fatigue (see Bailenson, 2021; Bennett et al., 2021; see also Skulmowski & Xu, 2022). For example, while communicating online, a speaker may encounter popup notifications. While chat functions may be disabled, warnings about internet quality may capture the attention of the speaker. Digital interruptions are not innocuous, they can work to disrupt performance on an ongoing task and lead to negative affect and anxiety (Bailey et al., 2001; see also Couffe & Michael, 2017). Moreover if the notification alerts the speaker to poor internet quality, that may add an ongoing concern and burden to working memory with the speaker not only having difficulty in processing the questions they are asked, but also worrying about whether others can sufficiently hear what they are saying (see DiGiovanni et al., 2017). Another variable that may introduce a cognitive load in video conferencing interactions is the management of non-verbal cues in communication. For instance, while eye contact would often occur without much thought in in-person settings, on video platforms—depending on how sophisticated the digital set up is—people have to monitor and deliberately engage in simulated eye-contact by looking into the camera, sometimes at the cost of looking away from the person we are responding to (Bohannon et al., 2013). This is an ongoing task where one must override the default tendency to look at the person on the screen, rather than the camera. The gaze of other participants in a gallery style view may also be a source of distraction, given it is a rich source of social information (e.g., Conty et al., 2010; Burra et al., 2019). Further, on Zoom, someone's gaze to another video participant—or side glance—may be encoded negatively by the speaker, and thus may create yet another source of social distraction (Bailenson, 2021). Bailenson has further suggested that people may engage in more active non-verbal communication on Zoom by engaging in more pronounced facial expressions and nodding. Having a self-camera view may further magnify digital communication burden through constant regulation of self-presentation. Indeed, research suggests that camera-on setups increase fatigue more so than camera-off and this effect may be greater for some populations than others. For instance, more junior female faculty members suffered from greater fatigue after camera-on meetings than did their male more senior counterparts (Hockley et al., 2021).

Cognitive Load and Impact for Eyewitness Memory

The additional cognitive load that may arise from video conferencing platforms may have impacts for memory recall. Research shows that when people are attempting to accurately recall information, having a higher cognitive load during retrieval, reducing available cognitive resources, can negatively impact memory (e.g., Jacoby et al., 1989). This pattern holds true at an individual differences level too: those with lower cognitive resources or working memory capacity—the ability to hold onto and manipulate information, while inhibiting distraction—are more susceptible to memory distortions (e.g., Battista et al., 2020; Gerrie & Garry, 2007; Leding, 2012; Unsworth & Brewer, 2010; Watson et al., 2005; Zhu et al., 2010). For instance, a recent study showed that those who had lower cognitive resources recalled a recent event less accurately—remembering fewer accurate details and reporting more false information—than those with higher cognitive resources (Battista et al., 2020). Lower cognitive resources are thought to impact memory through difficulty in maintaining accurate memory representations, and a reduced ability to ignore interference or irrelevant, but related information that has the potential to distort memory. A reduced ability to manage interference may make it particularly challenging at retrieval when one is tasked with sorting through mental experiences that are the result of true memory, imagination, post event suggestion, or semantically related ideas activated at the time of retrieval (see Battista et al., 2020; Gerrie & Garry, 2007; Unsworth & Brewer, 2010).

Considered together, these different literatures suggest that with an increasing burden on cognitive resources, factors inherent in remote communications platforms may work to impact the ability to recall accurate information and susceptibility to memory distortion. However, again as in other sections, more applied research is needed focusing specifically on digital communications. A related literature on audience communication also highlights the perils of cognitive load for a speaker. With increased cognitive load people are worse at effectively communicating, even when memory ability is held constant (the target to be described is in front of them, readily available for description). In a study by Navarro et al. (2020) people were asked to explain the position of pegs in a visual display while under high or low cognitive load (tasked with remembering 6 or 3 digits respectively during the communication task). When people had high load, they produced more errors in their communication than those with low or no load. This effect of high load was more pronounced for people who had lower working memory capacity, likely due to an increased cognitive demand compared to their higher working memory counterparts (Navarro et al., 2020).

Considered together, while there is converging evidence that high cognitive load may jeopardize the accuracy of eyewitness memory, these questions are yet to be considered in simulated virtual court settings. Do video conferencing contexts influence eyewitness memory accuracy by increasing cognitive load? To what extent do video conferencing platforms affect eyewitnesses in courtroom contexts? The existing body of literature raises concerns about testimony provided under these conditions but does not directly address these questions by quantifying impact in virtual courts.

Implications for Policy, Research, and Social Justice

The virtual court offers promise in the ability to process high caseloads and keep people safe during times of crisis. Moreover, this digital development arguably increases access to justice, reducing the burden of transport and increasing flexibility in one's ability to participate in court proceedings (e.g., Criminal Justice Joint Inspection, 2022). However, the virtual court introduces new extra-legal factors that may work to systematically bias perceptions of witnesses and reduce quality of memory, impacting evidence in a given trial. As we have outlined in the current chapter, there is a significant gap in the existing research regarding the extent to which virtual proceedings exert these effects. Thus, there is a need for more research in this area to understand the social cognitive factors that are unique to virtual justice settings and their bearing on judgment and decision-making and human memory. From a policy and social justice perspective, some extra-legal factors may be mitigated by procedural considerations. Ensuring that participants have access to high quality connections and devices would increase the chances of achieving digital equity and may work to reduce the psychological impacts of digital disruption. But digital literacy is an additional target, which can contribute to an experienced digital divide for a communicator (e.g., World Health Organization, 2021). Discomfort or poor understanding in operating devices and platforms may have similar consequences for a speaker as having poor audio quality. Indeed, closing the digital education and confidence gap is another consideration in digital justice contexts. Further, developing guidelines and opportunity for consistent visual participation—similar backgrounds, camera angles, eye contact practices—may work to reduce the potential impact of these factors. Instructions for visual consistency may not be enough, training or simulations may afford further equity. Again, these are questions worthy of pursuing in future work.

While our current analysis has focused on current technology—Zoom, Webex, Teams— innovative digital justice technology is emerging with increasing momentum (Rossner & Tait, 2023). The opportunity to simulate in-person experience through virtual reality courtrooms may, in the future, work to address many of the factors we have raised here (simulating eye-contact and providing high quality directional audio cues). Going forward, combining psychological science with digital development positions virtual courtrooms with a unique opportunity. Digital courts of the future might not only address extra-legal factors in videoconferencing spaces, but perhaps even eliminate biases that emerge in physical courtroom environments (e.g., Rossner et al., 2017).

References

Alter, A.L., & Oppenheimer, D.M. (2009). Uniting the tribes of fluency to form a metacognitive nation. *Personality and Social Psychology Review*, 13(3), 219–235. https://doi.org/10.1177/1088868309341564

Ariturk, D., Crozier, W.E., & Garrett, B.L. (2020, November). Virtual criminal courts. *The University of Chicago Law Review Online*. Retrieved from https://lawreviewblog.uchicago.edu/2020/11/16/covid-ariturk/

Arlinger, S., Lunner, T., Lyxell, B., & Kathleen Pichora-Fuller, M. (2009). The emergence of Cognitive Hearing Science. *Scandinavian Journal of Psychology*, 50(5), 371–384. https://doi.org/10.1111/j.1467-9450.2009.00753.x

Bailenson, J.N. (2021). Nonverbal overload: A theoretical argument for the causes of Zoom fatigue. *Technology, Mind, and Behavior*, 1(3), 1–13. https://doi.org/10.1037/tmb0000030

Bailey, B.P., Konstan, J.A., & Carlis, J.V. (2001). The effects of interruptions on task performance, annoyance, and anxiety in the user interface. In M. Hirose (Ed.), *Proceedings of IFIP TC.13 International Conference on Human–Computer Interaction* (pp. 593–601). Amsterdam: IOS Press. www.interruptions.net/literature/Bailey-Interact01.pdf

Battista, F., Otgaar, H., Lanciano, T., & Curci, A. (2020). Individual differences impact memory for a crime: A study on executive functions resources. *Consciousness and Cognition*, 84, 103000. https://doi.org/10.1016/j.concog.2020.103000

Bender, M. (2021). Unmuted: Solutions to safeguard constitutional rights in virtual courtrooms and how technology can expand access to quality counsel and transparency in the criminal justice system. *Villanova Law Review*, 66(1), 1–61. https://digitalcommons.law.villanova.edu/vlr/vol66/iss1/1

Bennett, A.A., Campion, E.D., Keeler, K.R., & Keener, S.K. (2021). Videoconference fatigue? Exploring changes in fatigue after videoconference meetings during COVID-19. *Journal of Applied Psychology*, 106(3), 330–344. https://doi.org/10.1037/apl0000906

Bild, E., Redman, A., Newman, E.J., Muir, B.R., Tait, D., & Schwarz, N. (2021). Sound and credibility in the virtual court: Low audio quality leads to less favorable evaluations of witnesses and lower weighting of evidence. *Law and Human Behavior*, 45(5), 481–495. https://doi.org/10.1037/lhb0000466

Bohannon, L.S., Herbert, A.M., Pelz, J.B., & Rantanen, E.M. (2013). Eye contact and video-mediated communication: A review. *Displays*, 34(2), 177–185. https://doi.org/10.1016/j.displa.2012.10.009

Bransford, J.D., & Johnson, M.K. (1972). Contextual prerequisites for understanding: Some investigations of comprehension and recall. *Journal of Verbal Learning and Verbal Behavior*, 11(6), 717–726. https://doi.org/10.1016/S0022-5371(72)80006-9

Brown, N., Newman, E., McLennan, D., & Smithson, M. (in preparation). Virtual courts and digital disruption: Can instructions ward off bias from audio quality? Manuscript in preparation.

Burra, N., Massait, S., & Vrtička, P. (2019). Differential impact of trait, social, and attachment anxiety on the stare-in-the-crowd effect. *Scientific Reports*, 9(1), 1–11. https://doi.org/10.1038/s41598-019-39342-8

Carney, R.N., & Levin, J.R. (2002). Pictorial illustrations still improve students' learning from text. *Educational Psychology Review*, 14(1), 5–26. https://doi.org/10.1023/A:1013176309260

Conty, L., Gimmig, D., Belletier, C., George, N., & Huguet, P. (2010). The cost of being watched: Stroop interference increases under concomitant eye contact. *Cognition*, 115(1), 133–139. https://doi.org/10.1016/j.cognition.2009.12.005

Couffe, C., & Michael, G.A. (2017). Failures due to interruptions or distractions: A review and a new framework. *The American Journal of Psychology*, 130(2), 163–181. https://doi.org/10.5406/amerjpsyc.130.2.0163

Criminal Justice Joint Inspection. (2022, May 17). The impact of the Covid-19 pandemic on the criminal justice system—A progress report. Crown. www.justiceinspectorates.gov.uk/cjji/

Denney, A. (2020, April 28). 3 New York judges died from coronavirus, almost 170 court workers infected. *New York Post*. Retrieved from https://nypost.com/2020/04/28/coronavirus-in-ny-3-judges-die-almost-170-court-workers-infected/

Devine, D.J., & Caughlin, D.E. (2014). Do they matter? A meta-analytic investigation of individual characteristics and guilt judgments. *Psychology, Public Policy, and Law*, 20(2), 109–134. https://doi.org/10.1037/law0000006

DiGiovanni, J., Riffle, T.L., Lynch, E.E., & Nagaraj, N.K. (2017, June). Noise characteristics and their impact on working memory and listening comprehension performance. In *Proceedings of Meetings on Acoustics 173EAA* (Vol. 30, No. 1, p. 050007). Acoustical Society of America.

Dragojevic, M., & Giles, H. (2016). I don't like you because you're hard to understand: The role of processing fluency in the language attitudes process. *Human Communication Research*, 42(3), 396–420. https://doi.org/10.1111/hcre.12079

Eruchalu, C.N., Pichardo, M.S., Bharadwaj, M., Rodriguez, C.B., Rodriguez, J.A., Bergmark, R.W., ... & Ortega, G. (2021). The expanding digital divide: digital health access inequities during the COVID-19 pandemic in New York City. *Journal of Urban Health*, 98(2), 183–186. https://link.springer.com/article/10.1007/s11524-020-00508-9

Federal Communications Commission. (2017, July 27). Bridging the digital divide for all Americans. Retrieved 16 September, 2020, from https://www.fcc.gov/news-events/blog/2017/07/13/bridging-digital-divide.

Fiechter, J.L., Fealing, C., Gerrard, R., & Kornell, N. (2018). Audiovisual quality impacts assessments of job candidates in video interviews: Evidence for an AV quality bias. *Cognitive Research: Principles and Implications*, 3(1), 1–5. https://cognitiveresearchjournal.springeropen.com/articles/10.1186/s41235-018-0139-y

Fobes, C. (2020). Rule 43(a): Remote witness testimony and judiciary resistant to change. *Lewis & Clark Law Review*, 24(1), 299–324. https://law.lclark.edu/live/files/29604-lcb241article7fobespdf

Garry, M., Strange, D., Bernstein, D.M., & Kinzett, T. (2007). Photographs can distort memory for the news. *Applied Cognitive Psychology*, 21(8), 995–1004. https://doi.org/10.1002/acp.1362

Gerrie, M.P., & Garry, M. (2007). Individual differences in working memory capacity affect false memories for missing aspects of events. *Memory, 15*(5), 561–571. https://doi.org/10.1080/09658210701391634.

Gillespie, M., James, A.N., Federmeier, K.D., & Watson, D.G. (2014). Verbal working memory predicts co-speech gesture: Evidence from individual differences. *Cognition, 132*(2), 174–180. https://doi.org/10.1016/j.cognition.2014.03.012

Goldin-Meadow, S., Nusbaum, H., Kelly, S.D., & Wagner, S. (2001). Explaining math: gesturing lightens the load. *Psychological Science, 12*(6), 516–522. https://doi.org/10.1111/1467-9280.00395

Gosling, S.D., Ko, S.J., Mannarelli, T., & Morris, M.E. (2002). A room with a cue: Personality judgments based on offices and bedrooms. *Personality Processes and Individual Differences, 82*(3), 379–398. https://doi.org/10.1037//0022-3514.82.3.379

Henkel, L.A. (2012). Seeing photos makes us read between the lines: The influence of photos on memory for inferences. *Quarterly Journal of Experimental Psychology, 65*(4), 773–795. https://doi.org/10.1080/17470218.2011.628400

Hietanen, J.K. (2018). Affective eye contact: an integrative review. *Frontiers in Psychology, 9*, 1587. https://doi.org/10.3389/fpsyg.2018.01587

Hockley, K.M., Gabriel, A.S., Robertson, D., Rosen, C.C., Chawla, N., Ganster, M.L., & Ezerins, M.E. (2021). The fatiguing effects of camera use in virtual meetings: A within-person field experiment. *Journal of Applied Psychology, 106*(8), 1137–1155. https://doi.org/10.1037/apl0000948

Horgan, T.G., Herzog, N.K., & Dyszlewski, S.M. (2019). Does your messy office make your mind look cluttered? Office appearance and perceivers' judgments about the owner's personality. *Personality and Individual Differences, 138*, 370–379. https://doi.org/10.1016/j.paid.2018.10.018

Hostetter, A.B. (2011). When do gestures communicate? A meta-analysis. *Psychological Bulletin, 137*(2), 297–315. https://doi.org/10.1037/a0022128

Jacoby, L.L., Woloshyn, V., & Kelley, C. (1989). Becoming famous without being recognized: Unconscious influences of memory produced by dividing attention. *Journal of Experimental Psychology: General, 118*(2), 115.

Kleinke, C.L., Bustos, A.A., Meeker, F.B., & Staneski, R.A. (1973). Effects of self-attributed and other-attributed gaze on interpersonal evaluations between males and females. *Journal of Experimental Social Psychology, 9*(2), 154–163. https://doi.org/10.1016/0022-1031(73)90007-3

Laham, S.M., Koval, P., & Alter, A.L. (2012). The name-pronunciation effect: Why people like Mr. Smith more than Mr. Colquhoun. *Journal of Experimental Social Psychology, 48*(3), 752–756. https://doi.org/10.1016/j.jesp.2011.12.002

Leach, A.M., Woolridge, L.R., Cutler, B.L., Neuschatz, J.S., & Jenkins, B.D. (2022). COVID-19 and the courtroom: How social and cognitive psychological processes might affect trials during a pandemic. *Psychology, Crime & Law, 28*(8), 731–762. https://doi.org/10.1080/1068316X.2021.1962867

Leding, J.K. (2012). Working memory predicts the rejection of false memories. *Memory, 20*(3), 217–223. https://doi.org/10.1080/09658211.2011.653373

Lev-Ari, S., & Keysar, B. (2010). Why don't we believe non-native speakers? The influence of accent on credibility. *Journal of Experimental Social Psychology, 46*(6), 1093–1096. https://doi.org/10.1016/j.jesp.2010.05.025

Loftus, E.F. (2005). Planting misinformation in the human mind: A 30-year investigation of the malleability of memory. *Learning & Memory, 12*(4), 361–366.

Macrae, C.N., Hood, B.M., Milne, A.B., Rowe, A.C., & Mason, M.F. (2002). Are you looking at me? Eye gaze and person perception. *Psychological Science, 13*(5), 460–464. https://doi.org/10.1111/1467-9280.00481

Marstaller, L., & Burianová, H. (2013). Individual differences in the gesture effect on working memory. *Psychonomic Bulletin & Review, 20*(3), 496–500. https://link.springer.com/article/10.3758/s13423-012-0365-0

Mason, M.F., Tatkow, E.P., & Macrae, C.N. (2005). The look of love: Gaze shifts and person perception. *Psychological Science, 16*(3), 236–239. https://journals.sagepub.com/doi/pdf/10.1111/j.0956-7976.2005.00809.x

McKay, C. (2020). Glitching justice: Audio visual links and the sonic world of technologised courts. *Law Text Culture, 24*, 364–404. https://search.informit.org/doi/abs/10.3316/informit.363393170884992

Meeren, H.K.M., van Heijnsbergen, C.C.R.J., & de Gelder, B. (2005). Rapid perceptual integration of facial expression and emotional body language. *Proceedings of the National Academy of Sciences, 102*(45), 16518–16523. https://doi.org/10.1073/pnas.0507650102

Mossberger, K., Tolbert, C.J., & Hamilton, A. (2012). Measuring digital citizenship: mobile access and broadband. *International Journal of Communication, 6*, 2492–2528. https://ijoc.org/index.php/ijoc/article/view/1777/808

Mühlbach, L., Böcker, M., & Prussog, A. (1995). Telepresence in videocommunications: A study on stereoscopy and individual eye contact. *Human Factors, 37*(2), 290–305. https://doi.org/10.1518/001872095779064582

Muir, B.R., Newman, E.J., Schwarz, N. (2022, November 17–20). Messy background, messy mind: Consequences of background on perceptions of witnesses [Poster presentation]. Psychonomics Society, Boston, MA, United States. https://cdmcd.co/B7A4KB

Napoli, P.M., & Obar, J.A. (2014). The emerging mobile internet underclass: A critique of mobile internet access. *The Information Society, 30*(5), 323–334. https://doi.org/10.1080/01972243.2014.944726

Navarro, E., Macnamara, B.N., Glucksberg, S., & Conway, A.R. (2020). What influences successful communication? An examination of cognitive load and individual differences. *Discourse Processes, 57*(10), 880–899. https://doi.org/10.1080/0163853X.2020.1829936

Newman, E.J., & Schwarz, N. (2018). Good sound, good research: How audio quality influences perceptions of the research and researcher. *Science Communication, 40*(2), 246–257. https://doi.org/10.1177/1075547018759345

Newman, E.J., Garry, M., Bernstein, D.M., Kantner, J., & Lindsay, D. S. (2012). Nonprobative photographs (or words) inflate truthiness. *Psychonomic Bulletin & Review, 19*(5), 969–974. https://link.springer.com/article/10.3758/s13423-012-0292-0

Newman, E.J., Sanson, M., Miller, E.K., Quigley-McBride, A., Foster, J.L., Bernstein, D.M., & Garry, M. (2014). People with easier to pronounce names promote truthiness of claims. *PloS ONE, 9*(2), e88671. https://doi.org/10.1371/journal.pone.0088671

Newman, E.J., & Zhang, L. (2020). Truthiness: How non-probative photos shape belief. In R. Greifeneder, M.E. Jaffé, E.J. Newman, & N. Schwarz (Eds.), The psychology of fake news: Accepting, sharing, and correcting misinformation (pp. 90–114). Routledge.

Park, S. (2017). Digital inequalities in rural Australia: A double jeopardy of remoteness and social exclusion. *Journal of Rural Studies*, 54, 399–407. https://doi.org/10.1016/j.jrurstud.2015.12.018

Reber, R., & Schwarz, N. (1999). Effects of perceptual fluency on judgments of truth. *Consciousness and Cognition*, 8(3), 338–342. https://doi.org/10.1006/ccog.1999.0386

Reddick, C.G., Enriquez, R., Harris, R.J., & Sharma, B. (2020). Determinants of broadband access and affordability: An analysis of a community survey on the digital divide. *Cities*, 106, 102904. https://doi.org/10.1016/j.cities.2020.102904

Rickard, E., Bird, L., White, D., Naqui, Q., Godfrey, S., Lewis, A., Chiappetta, C., & Khwaja, N. (2021). How courts embraced technology, met the pandemic challenge, and revolutionized their operations. The PEW Charitable Trusts. www.pewtrusts.org/-/media/assets/2021/12/how-courts-embraced-technology.pdf

Rossner, M. (2021). Remote rituals in virtual courts. *Journal of Law and Society*, 48(3), 334–361. https://doi.org/10.1111/jols.12304

Rossner, M., & McCurdy, M. (2020). Video Hearings Process Evaluation (Phase 2): Final Report (Ministry of Justice). London School of Economics. Retrieved from https://assets.publishing.service.gov.uk/government/uploads/system/uploads/attachment_data/file/905603/HMCTS391_Video_hearings_process_evaluation__phase_2__v2.pdf

Rossner, M., & Tait, D. (2023). Presence and participation in a virtual court. *Criminology & Criminal Justice*, 23(1), 135–157.

Rossner M, Tait D, McKimmie B, et al. (2017) The dock on trial: Courtroom design and the pre- sumption of innocence. *Journal of Law and Society*, 44(3), 317–344.

Sanders, A. (2021). Video-Hearings in Europe before, during and after the COVID-19 Pandemic. *International Journal for Court Administration*, 12(2), 1–21. https://doi.org/10.36745/ijca.379

Sanson, M., Crozier, W. E., & Strange, D. (2020). Court case context and fluency-promoting photos inflate the credibility of forensic science. *Zeitschrift für Psychologie*, 228(3), 221–225. https://doi.org/10.1027/2151-2604/a000415

Scherer, S.E. (1974). Influence of proximity and eye contact on impression formation. *Perceptual and Motor Skills*, 38(2), 538–538. https://journals.sagepub.com/doi/pdf/10.2466/pms.1974.38.2.538

Schwarz, N., Jalbert, M., Noah, T., & Zhang, L. (2021). Metacognitive experiences as information: Processing fluency in consumer judgment and decision making. *Consumer Psychology Review*, 4(1), 4–25. https://doi.org/10.1002/arcp.1067

Schwarz, N., Newman, E., & Leach, W. (2016). Making the truth stick & the myths fade: Lessons from cognitive psychology. *Behavioral Science & Policy*, 2(1), 85–95. https://doi.org/10.1353/bsp.2016.0009

Shin, J., Suh, E.M., Li, N.P., Eo, K., Chong, S.C., & Tsai, M.-H. (2019). Darling, get closer to me: Spatial proximity amplifies interpersonal liking. *Personality and Social Psychology Bulletin*, 45(2), 300–309. https://doi.org/10.1177/0146167218784903

Silva, R.R., Chrobot, N., Newman, E., Schwarz, N., & Topolinski, S. (2017). Make it short and easy: Username complexity determines trustworthiness above and beyond objective reputation. *Frontiers in Psychology*, 8, 2200. https://doi.org/10.3389/fpsyg.2017.02200

Silva, R.R., Koch, M.-L., Rickers, K., Kreuzer, G., & Topolinski, S. (2019). The Tinder™ stamp: Perceived trustworthiness of online daters and its persistence in neutral contexts. *Computers in Human Behavior*, 94, 45–55. https://doi.org/10.1016/j.chb.2018.12.041

Skulmowski, A., & Xu, K.M. (2022). Understanding cognitive load in digital and online learning: A new perspective on extraneous cognitive load. *Educational Psychology Review*, 34(1), 171–196. https://doi.org/10.1007/s10648-021-09624-7

Smith, R., Savage, R., & Emami, C. (2021). *Benchmarking the use of audiovisual link technologies in Australian criminal courts before the pandemic* (No. 23). Australian Institute of Criminology. https://doi.org/10.52922/rr78191

Song, A., & Legg, M. (2021). The courts, the remote hearing and the pandemic: From action to reflection. *University of New South Wales Law Journal*, 44(1), 126–166. https://search.informit.org/doi/pdf/10.3316/agispt.20210421044944

Spinney, L. (2022, 19 February). Zoom trials and kitten lawyers: Inside the e-justice revolution. The New Statesman. shorturl.at/cmnoB

Srull, T.K., & Wyer, R.S. (1979). The role of category accessibility in the interpretation of information about persons: Some determinants and implications. *Journal of Personality and Social Psychology*, 37(10), 1660–1672. https://doi.org/10.1037/0022-3514.37.10.1660

Sternlight, J.R., & Robbennolt, J.K. (2022). In-person or via technology?: Drawing on psychology to choose and design dispute resolution processes. *DePaul Law Review*, 71, 701–776. https://papers.ssrn.com/abstract=3896021

Susskind, R. (2019). *Online Courts and the Future of Justice*. Oxford University Press, Incorporated. http://ebookcentral.proquest.com/lib/anu/detail.action?docID=6006830

ten Brinke, L., & Weisbuch, M. (2020). How verbal-nonverbal consistency shapes the truth. *Journal of Experimental Social Psychology*, 89, 103978. https://doi.org/10.1016/j.jesp.2020.103978

Thomas, J., Barraket, J., Parkinson, S., Wilson, C., Holcombe-James, I., Kennedy, J., Mannell, K., & Brydon, A. (2021). *Australian Digital Inclusion Index: 2021*. RMIT, Swinburne University of Technology, and Telstra. https://drive.google.com/file/d/1syBRxCAg3KQSFMb-wtZYLwL55BNb-jos/view

Thornburg, E.G. (2020). Observing online courts: Lessons from the pandemic. *Family Law Quarterly*, 54(3), 181–244. https://doi.org/10.2139/ssrn.3696594

Tsetsi, & Rains, S.A. (2017). Smartphone Internet access and use: Extending the digital divide and usage gap. *Mobile Media & Communication*, 5(3), 239–255. https://doi.org/10.1177/2050157917708329

Unsworth, N., & Brewer, G.A. (2010). Individual differences in false recall: A latent variable analysis. *Journal of Memory and Language*, 62(1), 19–34. https://doi.org/10.1016/j.jml.2009.08.002.

Wallace, A., Roach Anleu, S., & Mack, K. (2019). Judicial engagement and AV links: Judicial perceptions from Australian courts. *International Journal of the Legal Profession*, 26(1), 51–67. https://doi.org/10.1080/09695958.2018.1490294

Watson, J.M., Bunting, M.F., Poole, B.J., & Conway, A.R.A. (2005). Individual differences in susceptibility to false memory in the Deese-Roediger-McDermott paradigm. *Journal of Experimental Psychology: Learning, Memory, and Cognition*, 31(1), 76–85. https://doi.org/10.1037/0278-7393.31.1.76.

Wienrich, C., Fries, L., & Latoschik, M.E. (2022). Remote at court. In *International Conference on Human-Computer Interaction* (pp. 82–106). Cham: Springer. https://doi.org/10.1007/978-3-031-05014-5_8

Wilson, G.M., & Sasse, M.A. (2000). Investigating the impact of audio degradations on users: Subjective vs. objective assessment methods. In *Proceedings of the Annual Conference of CHISIG, OZCHI 2000: Inter-facing reality in the new millennium* (pp. 135–142). The Computer Human Interaction Special Interest Group of the Ergonomics Society of Australia. https://core.ac.uk/download/pdf/1785691.pdf

World Health Organization (2016). *Global diffusion of eHealth: Making universal health coverage achievable: Report of the third global survey on eHealth*. World Health Organization.

World Health Organization (2021). *Global strategy on digital health 2020–2025*. World Health Organization. Retrieved from www.who.int/docs/default-source/documents/gs4dhdaa2a9f352b0445bafbc79ca799dce4d.pdf

Zhu, B., Chen, C., Loftus, E.F., Lin, C., He, Q., Chen, C., He, L., Xue, G., Lu, Z., & Dong, Q. (2010). Individual differences in false memory from misinformation: Cognitive factors. *Memory*, 18(5), 543–555. https://doi.org/10.1080/09658211.2010.487051

15 The Impact of Technology on Jurors' Decisions

Emma Rempel and Tara Burke

After a lengthy jury selection process, you now sit shoulder-to-shoulder alongside your fellow jurors—twelve strangers united by a shared purpose. In just a few short weeks, you will be tasked with rendering a verdict that may alter the course of the defendant's life. Your eyes dart anxiously across the courtroom, scanning the eager faces of the trial observers who have organized themselves neatly in rows on either side of the courtroom. Your attention shifts to the foreground, where you catch a glimpse of your reflection in the glossy, black screen of an HD monitor– one of several mounted directly at eye level in the jury box. As you begin to acclimate to your new surroundings, you notice several other pieces of modern equipment, juxtaposed against the otherwise timeless Neoclassical architecture of the courtroom. On a wooden lectern directly opposite the judge's bench sits an evidence camera—a projector used to convert paper documents and physical exhibits into a digital format. Perched squarely in each corner of the courtroom you observe a set of surround-sound speakers, deliberately angled toward the jury box to ensure witness testimony—both live and virtual—is conveyed clearly. Directly adjacent to the bench you recognize the familiar borders of a witness stand that you've seen countless times in your favorite primetime legal dramas—a wireless tablet discretely affixed to one corner. As you begin to contemplate what it may be used for, the ambient whispers of the courtroom are stifled suddenly as the judge enters the courtroom. The judge takes a few moments to settle into her designated spot, a stately chair perched on a raised platform. She swipes her hand across a switchboard, activating the evidence display system and bringing the courtroom equipment to life: a projection screen emits a mechanical hum as it slowly descends from the ceiling; the monitors in the jury box light up in sequence as they power on. The judge strikes her gavel twice, commanding the courtroom as her voice resonates from each of its four corners: "Court is now in session."

DOI: 10.4324/9781003323112-18

Overview

The right to a trial by a jury is a pillar of the justice system and every year, thousands of criminal defendants have their cases tried in front of a jury (as cited in Dufraimont, 2008; Devine et al., 2001). In Canada and the US, defendants who are accused of a serious criminal offense (i.e., in Canada, defined as an offense punishable by 5 years or more of imprisonment, or 6 months in the US) are granted the right to a trial by jury (Canadian Charter of Rights and Freedoms, 1982; US Const. amend. VI). Juries that try these cases are typically composed of a group of twelve laypersons who act as the triers of fact and are therefore tasked with weighing the case evidence and coming to a unanimous decision, or verdict (Bala & Anand, 2012). Defendants may face a number of punitive outcomes if they are convicted, not least of which being a loss of their personal liberty and freedoms, and thus a jury's final verdict is consequential.

Since the adversarial legal system was established in the late eighteenth century, trial practices—including the jury selection process, opening, and closing statements, witness examination and evidence introduction—have changed remarkably little over time (Lederer, 2021). Over the last 30 years, however, the rapid proliferation of digital technologies—including the internet, personal computers, mobile phones, and smart devices—have become increasingly integrated into our everyday lives, marking a paradigm shift into this digital age. The same technologies that have revolutionized the way we work, learn, and socialize have now permeated the legal system, resulting in courtrooms that are equipped with digital infrastructure, and accommodate new forms of multimedia evidence that have not yet been encountered by factfinders within the justice system.

The current chapter will provide an updated account of the current technological landscape within American courtrooms, including the emergent types of digital and computer-generated evidence that jurors may expect to be exposed to at trial. While there is no shortage of speculation about the potential effects of technology on jurors' cognition, there have been relatively few empirical studies which have formally evaluated these claims. This chapter will provide a review of this emergent body of literature, with a specific emphasis on the established effects of technology, both positive and negative, on jurors' decision-making processes and ultimate judgments. Finally, the chapter will conclude with a discussion of the legal, social, and ethical implications that the judiciary may wish to consider in order to ensure technology is used in a way that upholds a defendant's due process rights.

352 Emma Rempel & Tara Burke

Cyberjustice: How Emerging Technologies are Transforming the Legal Landscape

In light of the significant digital reform that has swept the North American court system, legal scholars have begun to contemplate the intersection of technology and justice, and how to merge the two domains in a way that upholds the constitutional values the justice system was pioneered to uphold (US Const. Amend. V). "Cyberjustice" is a term that has emerged to describe the incorporation of technology into the justice system through the electronic *delivery* of court services (i.e., virtual hearings or trials), or the *integration* of technology within the courtroom itself (i.e., the electronic courtroom; Mizrahi, 2016). The rationale underlying the cyberjustice initiative is simple: by leveraging the power of digital technologies, the court system can begin to reduce the backlogs and expenses associated with trials, thereby making justice more accessible (Donoghue, 2017; Mizrahi, 2016).

In the United States alone, there are at least five independent bodies dedicated to testing cyberjustice initiatives, and countless more entities dedicated to this purpose globally (see Mizrahi, 2016). One of the most notable of these initiatives is the Courtroom 21 project, which originally launched in 1993 as a collaboration between the William & Mary Law School and the National Centre for State Courts. As part of this project, the McGlothin Courtroom—a state-of-the-art courtroom and testing ground for emergent technologies—was constructed as a platform for legal researchers and professionals to study and experience the impact of technology on judicial proceedings (Lederer, 2002, 2004). In Canada, the Cyberjustice Laboratory based at the University of Montreal includes an international team of researchers exploring ways to integrate technology within the justice system. Their facilities include a state-of-the-art technologically advanced courtroom, as well as a mobile courtroom, to study videoconferencing and remote information exchange.

The Electronic Courtroom

In 1998, the United States Judicial Conference declared courtroom technologies as "necessary and integral," thereby prompting efforts to incorporate digital technology into courtroom facilities, both old and new (DeSario, 2002). As part of the movement toward "electronic courtrooms," public funds were allocated toward retrofitting select courtrooms across America with advanced technologies including monitors, document cameras, video-conferencing capabilities, and Internet connections (Kuchler & O'Toole, 2008). What began as a pilot project quickly became a movement across the United States; as early as 2002, over half of U.S. districts had at least one courtroom containing evidence presentation equipment, and over 70% had access to video conferencing equipment (DeSario, 2002).

At present, there is no central registry that records their existence, nor is there a single definition of what constitutes an "electronic courtroom." Therefore, we can only speculate about the degree to which technology has become a fixture within today's justice system (Lederer, 2021). As of 2000, it was estimated that there were approximately 500 functional electronic courtrooms in the United States; however, with the use of digital technology in North American courtrooms steadily rising over the past two decades, it is reasonable to assume that their prevalence is much greater today, perhaps by several orders of magnitude (Lederer, 2002). Regardless of specific number of courtrooms that are outfitted with technology, the percentage of lawyers *using* courtroom technology is on the rise: as of 2020, 83% of lawyers report using technology in the courtroom, compared to only 46% in 2014 (Embry, 2020).

Given the rapid pace of technological advancement both in and outside of the courtroom, it would be short-sighted to attempt to anchor definitions of an "electronic courtroom" to the transient technologies that are currently available. Rather, it is more pragmatic to enumerate courtroom technologies by grouping them on their intended purpose or use (Salyzyn, 2016). One such definition proposed by Lederer (2005) conceptualizes courtroom technology as the following: (i) remote appearances, (ii) court record, (iii) assistive technology, (iv) information (i.e., evidence) presentation, and (v) jury deliberations.

Remote Appearances

Remote appearances involve the use of video-conferencing technology as a means of facilitating off-site participation by witnesses and other parties when they cannot be physically present in the courtroom (Dixon, 2017; Rowden & Wallace, 2013). Videoconferencing is most often considered a dynamic two-way process, whereby a witness or witnesses appear virtually on monitors within the courtroom, and the courtroom and its live proceedings are videocasted back to the witness in the real-time (Mizrahi, 2016). The efficacy of videoconferencing relies on several sophisticated technologies, including HD video cameras, codecs (i.e., a device that converts audiovisual displays into a digital signal), speakers, and an adequate broadband connection, as well as enterprise-level video conferencing software such as Lifesize, Polycom and Cisco (United States Court of Federal Claims, n.d.; Administrative Conference of the United States, 2014).

While remote participation in trials is not a new phenomenon, the COVID-19 pandemic has acted as a catalyst for the more widespread adoption and acceptance toward this practice. With the onset of social distancing requirements and other safety measures engendered by the pandemic, videoconferencing represented a viable means of resolving cases while preserving public safety (Lederer, 2021). While initially borne out of necessity, the use of videoconferencing technologies as a means of resolving cases has quietly gained traction and is now being routinely used by attorneys as a means of expediting routine bureaucratic processes, such as first appearances, motion, status and review hearings and arraignments (Lederer, 2021). While still used to a lesser degree, videoconferencing is a practical alternative for more elaborate judicial matters, including within civil or criminal trials. For example, videoconferencing allows for witnesses to provide their testimony from a remote location if they are unwilling, or unable, to testify in person. It can also be used to deliver the testimony of an expert witness, thereby reducing costs by eliminating the need to compensate an expert for travel expenses in addition to paying for the preparation and presentation of their opinions (Salyzyn, 2016). As aptly explained by Lederer (2021), in a matter of a few short years, discussions in this area have evolved from "How [might we] best conduct a hearing with one or more remote participants?" (p. 315) to "How might we conduct entirely remote hearings in which no two people are in the same physical space?" (p. 316).

Court Record

In its most basic sense, a "court record" is a written transcript of court proceedings that is documented primarily for appellate review. Prior to the late nineteenth century, the court record primarily relied on handwritten notes which were manually transcribed by a court reporter. The first major advance for the court record came in the late 1800s, with the introduction of a shorthand typewriter called a stenotype machine, which allowed court stenographers to transcribe dialogue with greater speed and accuracy (Lederer, 1999). Later, this advance was eclipsed by digital recording and computer-aided transcription (CAT) software, which enables stenographers to translate keystrokes into comprehensible text in real-time (Mizrahi, 2016). With the recent emergence of real-time reporting technology, transcriptions of audio dialogue can be displayed on monitors within the courtroom almost instantaneously, allowing legal actors to follow along as the trial unfolds (Kuchler & O'Toole, 2008). In the last few years, the courts have begun to leverage AI-driven, speech-to-text software such as *For the Record*, which automates the transcription process by capturing audio from multiple courtroom speakers and converts it to a time-stamped transcript with up to 90% accuracy (Lederer, 2017, 2021; For the Record, 2019). While the technology underlying FTR, and related AI-transcription tools is still imperfect, given the exponential rate of machine learning, it is not unreasonable to expect that AI is poised to overtake the role of a human stenographer in the coming years.

Looking ahead, the court record must continue to evolve to accommodate multimedia exhibits and evidence that are increasingly becoming the norm across American courtrooms. Organizations such as the Center for Legal and Court Technology (CLCT) have begun to test new initiatives, such as a "multimedia court record" which captures multiple streams of input, including written transcription, digital visual displays, as well as a comprehensive audiovisual recording of the trial and merges them into a single multimodal record (Moyeda, 2014; Lederer, 2010). As of 2018, the CLCT is also in the process of testing a VR-based court record, which allows for an observer to wear a virtually immersive headset that allows them to fully relive the trial experience from start to finish (Lederer, 2017). Evidently, the evolution of the court record is a timely example of how the progression of one technology necessitates change in another; with evidence presentation technology increasingly going digital, the court record must also adapt if it is to be considered a comprehensive and accurate record of courtroom proceedings.

Assistive Technology

The composition of a jury is intended to reflect a diverse cross-section of society, including individuals who represent a variety of demographic factors such as race, gender, age, religion, and ability (Greenstein, 2016). In line with this supposition, the Americans with Disabilities Act (1990) stipulates that citizens with disabilities, defined as self-reported difficulty in hearing, vision, cognition, ambulation, self-care, and/or independent living must also be afforded an equal opportunity to partake in jury service.

Assistive technologies (AT) have played a fundamental role in enabling individuals with disabilities to participate on a jury (Lederer, 2010, 2021). AT consists of specialized equipment (i.e., for temporary use by individuals or permanently installed into the courtroom) and software programs that are used to increase, maintain, or improve the functional capability of individuals with disabilities (World Health Organization, 2023). There are many accommodations available for those who are deaf or hard of hearing, including access to a remote American Sign Language interpreter (via videoconferencing), real-time transcription for courtroom audio interpretation, as well as assistive listening devices which are used to enhance audio volume and quality (Lederer, 2010, 2021; Mizrahi, 2016; Smith & Hurley, 2018). Those with limited vision or blindness may be provided with computerized screen readers and braille note-taking devices, optical magnifiers/electronic enlargement devices, and special scanners that can read physical documents aloud (Lederer, 2017). Electronic communication devices, such as UbiDuo or CART, allow for communication by those with speech disorders (Smith & Hurley, 2018). Most courtrooms today are designed to be fully accessible to those using wheelchairs and scooters by way of ramps, wheelchair lifts, and dedicated space for wheelchairs within the jury box (Lederer, 2017, 2021). Finally, the implementation of bariatric seating can facilitate a comfortable jury experience for bodies of all shapes and sizes (Smith & Hurley, 2018).

Evidence Presentation Systems

The evidence presentation system has been described as the "heart" of the electronic courtroom (Kuchler & O'Toole, 2008; Moyeda, 2014). Visual presentation technology enables lawyers to display evidence and other documentary information to the jury in a highly compelling way (Lederer, 2021). In the early days of technology-augmented courtrooms, document cameras—which convert physical or paper exhibits into electronic images and magnify or reduce certain details—were extremely popular, allowing observers to view evidence via a projection screen or monitor (Mizrahi, 2016; National Center for State Courts, 2023; Lederer, 2021). More recently, lawyers have begun to use high-tech or "smart" whiteboards (aka "SMART Boards") for evidence presentation. One advantage of these whiteboards is that they allow for lawyers to mark-up, highlight or otherwise interact with the image, and these annotations will automatically be documented and saved within court record (Mizrahi, 2016).

Perhaps the most preeminent courtroom technology is the inclusion of laptops and, to a lesser extent, tablets (Embry, 2020). As of 2020, 57% of lawyers reported using laptops in the courtroom as a means of accessing email, court documents and other critical evidence. Laptops can be connected to flatscreen monitors, which are located throughout the courtroom (i.e., within the witness and jury box, judges' bench, witness stands, counsel tables etc.), allowing for information to be visible to all observers no matter their position within the courtroom (Kuchler & O'Toole, 2008). Approximately 25% of lawyers report using specialized presentation software, such as PowerPoint, Summation, TrialDirector, and TrialPad, for the purposes of presenting arguments and case information to the jury (Embry, 2020). Finally, the system controller in the courtroom provides the judge with control over the evidence presentation system. Using this switchboard, the judge can control individual aspects of the visual presentation system, such as turning specific monitors on or off, or to shut off the entire system using a "kill-switch" should they need to suddenly limit the jury's exposure to inadmissible evidence (Dixon, 2017; National Center for State Courts, 2023).

Jury Deliberation Technology

Jurors' exposure to courtroom technologies does not necessarily end when a trial adjourns (Lederer, 2004; Moyeda, 2014). Upon retiring to the deliberation room, juries are often provided with materials that are relevant to their discussions, including written copies of the judge's instructions, verdict forms, notepads and physical copies of exhibits or evidence (Lederer, 2002). With evidence increasingly being generated or created in a digital format, there has been a corresponding shift from physical to digital materials being disseminated to jurors within the deliberation room (Lederer, 2017). While the specific technology that is accessible by jurors varies by jurisdiction, deliberation technologies can loosely be categorized as (i) input technology, which converts physical exhibits into a digital format (e.g., a document camera), (ii) display technology (e.g., HD monitors), (iii) annotation technology, which allows jurors to write/mark-up exhibits (e.g., SMART boards), and (iv) assistive technologies (Lederer, 2002). Undoubtedly, the technologies that are available to jurors during deliberation are constantly changing and will continue to evolve alongside associated trial technologies.

Early research by Lederer (2002), conducted as part of the Courtroom 21 project, explored whether allowing jurors access to technologies during deliberations, including document cameras, computers, plasma displays, and rear-projection displays, would facilitate their decision-making process. Across two experiments, mock-jurors participated as fact-finders in a personal injury trial (i.e., *Matthews v. Morton*) in a traditional courtroom (Experiment 1) and an electronic courtroom (Experiment 2). Results demonstrated that, regardless of whether a courtroom was technologically augmented or not, mock-jurors made appropriate use of the available technologies, and described them as being "highly useful" to their deliberation process. In a follow up study conducted with actual jurors from the United States District Court for the District of Oregon, jurors similarly responded that the technology provided during deliberation was very useful, furthered their understanding of the evidence, and that it contributed to the speed of their deliberations (Lederer, 2002).

A recent Australian study by McDonald and colleagues (2015) explored whether the use of tablets during jury deliberations influenced jurors' verdicts and perceptions of a case compared to when the same information was presented on paper. Mock-jurors viewed a 60-minute simulated criminal trial on video which featured a defendant charged with conspiracy to commit a terrorist act, before deliberating with a group of their peers.

Results showed that juries who reviewed the prosecution's evidence via an iPad did not differ from those who received the evidence in paper form regarding the quality of their deliberations or their ultimate verdicts. These preliminary findings support the conclusion that the tablets may represent a viable alternative to paper documents, as they are expected to result in time and cost savings (i.e., expenses associated with manually photocopying documents), without compromising the quality of jury deliberations and subsequent verdicts (McDonald et al., 2015).

Digital and Computer-Generated Evidence

As the courtroom presentation mediums evolve over time, so too do the types of evidence they were designed to accommodate. Advanced evidence presentation systems are equipped to handle even the most contemporary forms of digital and computer-generated evidence, allowing for a highly progressive courtroom experience for jurors. Computer-generated evidence (CGE) can be understood as any evidence that is generated by a computer system, whereas digital evidence encompasses any evidence that is stored, transmitted, or processed in a digital form (Moussa, 2021; Norris, 2015). For the purposes of brevity, the coupling of digital and computer-generated evidence will be referred to as "multimedia evidence" throughout this chapter. While by no means exhaustive, a selection of emergent, multimedia evidence will be reviewed below.

Digital Device Data

Digital devices, such as laptops, tablets, smartphones, and smartwatches have become nearly ubiquitous in the twenty-first century. These devices harbor huge repositories of personal information and, in criminal investigations, these data are often used as evidence to establish the location and/or time a crime occurred, or the context, motivation and means of a suspect or defendant (Mylonas et al., 2012). Perhaps unsurprisingly, digital evidence has become a factor in most criminal cases (i.e., up to 90% of cases contain digital evidence; Overill & Collie, 2020), and is therefore increasingly being represented in judicial proceedings (Goodison et al., 2015).

The emergence of digital evidence has precipitated the specialized discipline of digital forensics, which describes the extraction, preservation, and analysis of digital evidence (Harrill & Mislan, 2007). The results of a proper digital forensics analysis can unearth a wealth of personal evidence from any digital device (often referred to as "artifacts"), including browser history, emails, text messages, geolocation data, photos, and videos that can be used as inculpatory evidence against a defendant (Casey et al., 2022).

During trial, digital forensic evidence is often handled similarly to other forms of physical evidence, with a forensics expert testifying to the authenticity and reliability of the findings and using the evidence presentation system to display the evidence to the fact-finders. There are numerous high-profile cases which serve as examples of digital evidence being used to establish a defendant's guilt. Take for instance the highly publicized case of *SC v. Murdaugh* (2023), where video footage found on the victim's phone, as well as GPS data embedded in Murdaugh's cell phone and vehicle placed him at the scene at the time his wife and son were murdered (Chappell & Hansen, 2023).

Police Body-Worn Camera Footage

Between 2013 and 2019, the prevalence of body-worn cameras (BWC) by American police has nearly doubled, securing their place as one the most rapidly adopted technologies in the law enforcement sector today (Lum et al., 2019). Canada, by comparison, was much slower to sign on (Laming, 2019). The Royal Canadian Mounted Police (RCMP) only recently agreed to allow some of their officers to wear the technology, previously citing the cost as a major impediment to their adoption. As of 2018, about 60% of local police departments and 49% of sheriff's offices had acquired and deployed BWCs, and these numbers are only increasing (Hyland, 2018). This increase is largely driven by several highly publicized instances of violence toward unarmed Black individuals at the hands of White police officers, such as in the tragic cases of George Floyd, Trayvon Martin, Michael Brown, Breonna Taylor and countless other innocents (Braga et al., 2022; Lum et al., 2019). Considering these flagrant instances of injustice, body-worn cameras theoretically represent a means of recording an objective account of police-citizen encounters, with the intention of improving the civility and lawfulness of these encounters, deterring police misconduct, and increasing public trust in law enforcement (Braga et al., 2022).

The interactions between the police and the public captured via body-worn camera footage can be shared with relative ease within an electronic courtroom. A lawyer may admit video footage of a police-citizen interaction captured on a BWC as evidence to justify or condemn a police officer's use of force in a criminal case, or as a means of arguing the validity of a police misconduct allegation in a civil case. In either instance, this audio-visual footage can be displayed to jurors within courtroom monitors or a projection screen, affording them a first-hand perspective to the encounter in question. Although the courts have traditionally conceptualized visual evidence—such as photographs and videos—as a medium which can deliver the "absolute truth," (Ellingwood, 2019) it is important to acknowledge that the version of events captured on BWCs is often incomplete as a result of officer movements or other stimuli obstructing the camera's position or angle, or when the lighting or noise in the environment disrupts the audiovisual quality (McCluskey & Uchida, 2023; Suss et al., 2018; Terrill & Zimmerman, 2022). Finally, because humans are active observers, whose pre-existing knowledge and experiences influence the way they perceive and interpret visual evidence, it is debatable whether visual imagery can ever *truly* offer direct evidence of an external "reality" which is inherently subjective (Butler & Sontag, 2007; Feigenson, 2014). These factors should be considered when assessing the probative value of BWC footage and other real-time video recording technologies, such as police dashboard cameras or CCTV surveillance footage.

Computer-Generated Animations and Simulations

One particularly notable innovation in the digital landscape are computer-generated animations (CGA) and simulations (CGS), which are digital visual productions that represent the operation of some scientific principle or the recreation of events at issue in a case (Rempel & Burke, 2022; Wiggins, 2004). While computer-generated animations and simulations are similar, insofar as they both rely on computer-technology to visually represent how a crime or accident occurred, simulations typically rely on technical data and scientific principles to *model* a real-world phenomena or process, animations are reserved for the purposes of *illustration* (Rempel & Burke, 2022). For example, a CGS could be used to model how a mechanical or electrical issue affected an airplane's trajectory causing it to crash, whereas an animation would be better suited to visualize how the plane crash might have looked from the perspective of a witness on the ground. CGAs are most often used as visual aids, instead of true substantive evidence with probative value (i.e., the ability to prove facts at issue in a case; Walker, 2018).

Virtual Reality and 3D Evidence

In addition to the aforementioned types of evidence, which are already widely circulated across American courtrooms, virtual reality (VR) and 3D projection technologies are believed to represent the future of multimedia evidence presentation. Using a headset, VR technology allows an observer to view and navigate within a scene (often referred to a fully immersive environment or IVE; Leonetti & Bailenson, 2010) as if they were physically present (Kuchler & O'Toole, 2008). Holographic, or 3D evidence, serves a similar purpose, but involves the use of laser beams to create three-dimensional images which appear to artificially "hang" in the air in front of a viewer. It may come as a surprise that the use of VR and holographic evidence has been documented as early as 2002, although these technologies have yet to become mainstream (Lederer, 2004).

Using data derived from methods such as surface scanning and photogrammetry, forensic engineers can fuse data from multiple sources of data to create 3D images of crime scenes, objects, or the injuries inflicted on a victim (Buck et al., 2013; Sieberth et al., 2019). In a simulated case conducted by the National Centre for State Courts in Baltimore, a 3D hologram was used to show jurors a bloody brick, and blood-spattered baseball bat that were key pieces of evidence in the case. In a recent case in Florida, a defense attorney motioned the court to allow the use of virtual reality headsets, which would put jurors "in the driver's seat" in an attempted murder case involving a man who was accused of running over his neighbor. While the motion was ultimately unsuccessful, had the technology been allowed into court, jurors would have been able to experience the scenario from the first-hand perspective of the defendant (Pumphrey, Jr., 2022; Weiss, 2023). Owing to recent advancements by forensic companies such as Explico Inc. and High Impact, jurors are now able to have a fully immersive, first-hand experience at a crime scene without having to leave the courtroom (Jacinto et al., 2019; High Impact, 2022; Varjo, 2023).Three-dimensional evidence presence systems allow jurors the opportunity to test competing hypotheses and "what if" scenarios to determine whether a defendant or witness's version of events is supported by data, and to observe transient evidence recovered from an actual crime scene long after it has been removed (Schofield, 2012). While there have not been any documented instances of virtual reality or 3D evidence in *real* American trials, their ability to effectively communicate highly complex scenarios to a jury certainly set them apart from other presentation technologies that are commercially available today.

The Anticipated Benefits of Courtroom Technology:
Anecdotal and Subjective Accounts

According to Lederer (2004), presentation technologies can reduce the duration of a trial by 25–50% in any given case, thereby reducing the potentially exorbitant costs that are associated with lengthy trials. As mentioned in the previous section, the use of videoconferencing as an alternative to in-person testimony is expected to garner significant time and cost savings for legal teams, which translates into reduced costs for those individuals in need of legal representation. The digital presentation of evidence is intended to reduce the time it takes for attorneys to locate physical exhibits during trial and assist them with maintaining jurors' attention and directing them to relevant portions of the evidence (Carney & Feigenson, 2004; Wiggins, 2004). As a result, the use of digital presentation technologies should, theoretically, enhance attorneys' ability to explain complex evidence, such as highly technical simulations or scientific concepts, in turn making it easier for jurors to understand this evidence (Aronson & McMurtrie, 2007).

These descriptive claims about the hypothesized benefits of courtroom technologies are supported by subjective accounts by judges, jurors and lawyers who have direct experience with courtroom technologies. A 1998 survey by the Judicial Conference Committee on Automation and Technology reported that a vast majority of judges believed that multimedia evidence presentation technologies enhanced their understanding of witness testimony, ability to question witnesses, and overall management of judicial proceedings. This positive sentiment was echoed by jurors, who indicated that evidence-presentation technology encouraged them to remain focused on the testimony and evidence presented to them at trial (as cited by Salyzyn, 2016).

While these early subjective impressions are somewhat outdated, a more recent survey by the DC Superior Court (as cited in Dixon, 2011) yielded similar results: 86% of jurors who had participated in a trial in an electronic courtroom felt that the audiovisual presentation technology helped them to better understand the information, and 96% expressed that these technologies enhanced their ability to serve as a juror during trial. Finally, a 2022 survey conducted by the American Bar Association showed that the percentage of lawyers using technology continues to rise. As of 2020, 83% of lawyers self-reported that they are using one or more courtroom technologies, compared to only 46% in 2014 (Embry, 2020). While not a direct measure of their attitudes toward technology, lawyers' increasing adoption of technologies is a reasonable indicator of the extent to which they are willing to rely on and use the technologies that are available to them. In summary, in the twenty-first century, those who have become accustomed to interactive digital communication in their daily lives expect an equally progressive experience in court.

Controlled Experimental Research Evaluating the Effects of Technology on Jurors

The willingness of the judiciary to routinely expose jurors to emergent technologies within the courtroom suggests that these technologies are considered a medium that at best facilitates jurors' comprehension and judgments, and at worst has a neutral effect that is more or less equivalent to the way evidence would traditionally be received by jurors. However, emergent experimental research predicts that the high-tech infrastructure and evidence which is increasingly being used in modern courtrooms may have unintended cognitive effects on jurors—both positive and negative—that have not yet been accounted for by the legal system. Therefore, before forming premature conclusions about their expected utility based solely on anecdotal and subjective accounts, it is important to assess the rigor of these claims by comparing them with empirical research that has formally evaluated the effects of technology on jurors.

To date, there have been a handful of studies that have explored the effects of computer-generated evidence on jurors' judgments. Early research by Kassin and Dunn (1997) tested the hypothesis that animations can either facilitate or prejudice jurors' comprehension of evidence and subsequent judgments depending on the manner of presentation. In the first of two experiments, participants viewed a simulated trial video involving a contested slip-and-fall incident, in which the plaintiff was arguing that the victim had slipped and fallen, and the defendant was arguing that he had intentionally jumped. Participants were presented with either a *proplaintiff* version of the case (in which the body was found 5–10 feet away, consistent with a fall) or a *pro-defendant* version of the case (in which the body was found 15–20 feet away, consistent with a jump). Within each condition, the testimony was presented either orally or with a computer-generated animation illustrating the scenario. Participants who viewed the evidence within an animation rendered verdicts which more closely aligned with the physical evidence (i.e., the location of the body from the building) compared to those who heard oral testimony. In Experiment 2, researchers presented the animation in a suggestive way that depicted either party's opposing theories about the nature of his death, but contradicted the physical evidence. In the pro-defendant version, for example, the victim was shown running and jumping off of the building, whereas in the pro-plaintiff version he was shown slipping and falling to his death. This time, participants were more likely to render judgments which aligned with each party's partisan theories, even when these theories were largely inconsistent with the physical evidence.

While this study was conducted several decades ago, these results were later replicated by Rempel and Burke (2022) in a mock second-degree murder trial. Participants were presented with a trial transcript which featured a police officer who had shot and killed an unarmed black teen, arguing that he had shot and killed the victim in self-defense. Across the three modality conditions participants were presented with an audio recording of the defendant's testimony, and viewed static visual images illustrating his testimony, a dynamic computer-generated animation or did not view any additional imagery. Participants were significantly more likely to acquit the defendant when his testimony was accompanied by an animation compared to static visual imagery or no imagery. This effect was observed whether or not other key pieces of evidence in the case supported his self-defense version of events. In sum, the results of this study provide further support for the facilitation and prejudice hypotheses (Kassin & Dunn, 1997) and suggest that computer-generated animations may have a disproportionate impact on jurors' judgments compared to more traditional forms of visual evidence or oral testimony.

With regards to courtroom technology, even seemingly "minor" alterations to how information is presented can dramatically affect the way that jurors process information and the outcome of their judgments (Gilovich et al., 2002). Emergent evidence suggests that digital technologies may prompt jurors to evaluate case evidence in a superficial manner, consistent with a "Type 1" or "peripheral" style of processing, ultimately compromising their ability to render impartial verdicts (Petty & Cacioppo, 1986). In a study examining the effects of PowerPoint on jurors' liability judgments, Park and Feigenson (2013) presented opening statements to mock jurors' either orally, or accompanied by a PowerPoint presentation. While the use of PowerPoint was shown to enhance their recall for the evidence which was presented, and sensitized their responsibility judgments to this evidence, it also functioned as a peripheral cue whereby those who were exposed to the PowerPoint were more likely to rely on factors that were unrelated to the content of the evidence, such as the lawyer's perceived preparedness, competence and credibility. In a later study by Rempel et al. (2019) which examined the effects of PowerPoint in a mock criminal case, participants who were exposed to the case evidence within a PowerPoint did not significantly differ from those who received the evidence in written form in terms of their understanding of the evidence. However, participants who viewed the PowerPoint were significantly more likely to convict the defendant than those who received the evidence in written form. These findings are somewhat concerning, given that participants were exposed to the exact same content across conditions, and suggests that the use of PowerPoint may have led jurors to focus on factors other than the content of the information, thereby biasing their verdicts.

In addition to the aforementioned studies which explored the effects of *visual* presentation mediums on mock-jurors, researchers have also begun to evaluate the emergent effects of remote testimony on judgment. Across three experiments conducted by Bild et al. (2021), participants listened to audio clips of witnesses describing an event, with either high-quality audio or low-quality audio. Results demonstrated that, when witnesses heard low-quality audio testimony, they rated the witnesses as less credible, reliable and trustworthy (Exp. 1), had poorer memory for the relevant information provided by the witness (Exp. 2) and were less likely to integrate the evidence into their final guilt judgments (Exp. 3). While the researchers do not specifically implicate peripheral processing as the mechanism underlying these effects, the results are consistent with the elaboration likelihood model, which would predict that the audio quality was used as a cue to make inferences about the reliability of the information. In a study by Jones et al. (2022), researchers explored whether the modality in which an expert delivered their testimony would affect perceptions of the expert's testimony or the weight the testimony received in participants' judgments. In the context of a contested competency hearing, a forensic psychologist provided their opinion via phone, videoconference or in-person within the courtroom. The findings of the study were inconsistent with the aforementioned research, as the researchers did not observe any differences in ratings of efficacy, credibility or social presence across the various presentation mediums. Thus, the study somewhat assuages concerns about unforeseen effects of remote appearances as an alternative to in-person testimony.

While these early findings represent an important start for an emergent area of research pertaining to technology in the courtroom, at present we do not have sufficient empirical evidence to form reliable predictions about the presence, direction, and magnitude of the effects of technologies on jurors' perceptions and judgments during trial. Given the potential applied significance of this work, this area of research would benefit from continued experimental research, across a range of technologies, to help advance the current understanding of the effects of multimedia evidence on legal decision-makers.

The Legal, Social and Ethical Impact of Technological Innovation

The use of high-tech evidence and infrastructure has, and will continue to, disrupt the traditional administration of justice (Dixon, 2013). Historically, the judicial response to the dynamic state of technological innovation has been reactive rather than proactive; that is, the real-world use of multimedia evidence has often outpaced the establishment of evidentiary regulations and policies which adequately govern their use (Legate, 2006). While technology as a medium has been referred to as "morally neutral," it can certainly be used in a way that is ethically dubious (Donoghue, 2017). Accordingly, it is important to take a moment to pause and reflect on the legal, social, and ethical quandaries related to the widespread and pervasive use of technology within the justice system.

Admissibility Considerations for Digital and Computer-Generated Evidence

Evidentiary issues and concerns surrounding the admissibility of multimedia evidence can be divided into three categories: substantive, procedural, and discretionary determinations (DeSario, 2002). Substantive determinations involve the application of legal rules, principles and standards to the evidence that is being admitted into trial. The party proffering the evidence must satisfy basic evidentiary requirements, including FRE 901, which governs the *authentication* and *chain of custody* of proffered evidence, and FRE 401 which establishes its *relevance*. Authentication involves establishing that the item is genuine, and is what it claims to be. For example, if a prosecutor were to admit as evidence a photo or video of a victim found on the defendant's phone, they would be responsible for establishing that the individual in question is in fact the victim, and that the video was truly captured by the defendant and found on his/her phone. Maintaining the chain of custody involves maintaining proper documentation surrounding where, when, and how (i.e., by which means) the evidence was collected, where it was stored after seizure and who had access to it. Finally, relevance relates to whether the evidence makes a fact of consequence more or less probable and, in other words, is relevant to the case. While the evidentiary requirements mentioned above are applicable to *all* forms of evidence, the application of substantive law can become more complicated when considering increasingly complex forms of digital and computer-generated evidence.

Federal Rule of Evidence 702 and 703 govern the testimony of expert witnesses and bases of an expert's opinion, respectively. FRE 702 requires that the principles and methods underlying scientific expert testimony are, whereas FRE 703 ensures that the expert's opinion is reliant on facts or data that are generally accepted in the field, and that the expert appropriately applied these data to the facts of the case. While FRE 702 and 703 have traditionally been reserved for matters involving physical evidence (e.g., DNA, fingerprint, or ballistics analysis), these evidentiary rules are increasingly being applied to digital and computer-generated evidence. Given the speed at which digital evidence and software is advancing, the standard of "general acceptance" for the particular programs and methods that are employed by an expert are constantly changing, making it more difficult to ensure that FRE 702 and 703 are satisfied (Goodison et al., 2015). Particularly when a technology or methodology has just emerged, there may be a dearth of applicable case law available to a judge, making it difficult to form educated opinions on the admissibility of evidence based on the absence of previously established standards. Take for example the case of computer-generated simulations, which rely on state-of-the-art software programs which make calculations based on case data and scientific/physical laws to form an output (Louie et al., 2007). It would reasonably be much more difficult for a judge to make a determination as to whether a particular simulation violates FRE 702 or 703 than it would be for one that is more established, such as in the case of toxicology or other matters of physical or applied science.

Procedural determinations are a means of ensuring that various aspects of the justice system—such as the established procedures governing appeals, discovery, and motions—are being followed. Procedural law is also relevant to decisions of evidence admissibility, including the procedure underlying pretrial motion, objections, and application of the Federal Rules of Evidence to admissibility decisions. Regarding the latter, a procedural determination would govern which evidentiary rule(s) should be applied to a particular type of evidence and when (e.g., *In what circumstances should digital evidence be exempt from hearsay objections?*) or how to categorize the nature of a particular exhibit. At present, there is some debate as to whether computer-generated evidence represents a form of demonstrative evidence—akin to less advanced illustrative aids such as maps, charts, 3D models, and diagrams used for the purpose of illustration (DeSario, 2002)—or whether it possesses inherent probative value, and should therefore be subject to the more rigorous evidentiary rules governing substantive evidence (e.g., FRE 702/703). While the courts appear to have recently arrived at a consensus that computer-generated *animations* are typically demonstrative (and are therefore more readily accepted by the courts) whereas *simulations* are typically substantive (Walker, 2018) the classification and admissibility criteria governing CGE has historically led to inconsistent rulings and a lack of consistency in terms of their admissibility at trial (Dahir, 2011; Legate, 2006; see Rempel & Burke, 2022 for specific cases).

Finally, it is worth mentioning that there is no "one-size-fits-all" approach to judicial decision-making; as such, admissibility decisions involve a uniquely human element of discretion. Accordingly, discretionary determination refers to a judge's ability to exercise their own judgment, within the bounds of the law, when making decisions about evidence admissibility (DeSario, 2002). Given the highly persuasive nature of dynamic, visual evidence—such as CGEs, crime-scene reconstructions and the like—multimedia evidence may be subject to a greater number of reliability issues and objections on the grounds that they have a disproportionate capacity to bias, or prejudice, jurors (Goodison et al., 2015; Kuchler & O'Toole, 2008). FRE 403 (i.e. the "balancing test") provides judges with a metric to weigh the probative value of evidence (i.e. its utility to prove facts at issue in a case) against the danger of unfair prejudice, confusion of the issues, or misleading the jury (Federal Rules of Evidence, 2019). When a judge feels that the probative value of an exhibit is outweighed by its potential for prejudice, they are afforded the discretion to bar its admission into trial, even when the evidence fulfills other basic evidentiary rules. While the balancing test serves as an important purpose as a judicial safeguard, without reliable empirical data quantifying the influence of technological evidence on jurors' judgments, judges will lack the necessary information to make informed decisions about their probative and prejudicial potential (Rempel & Burke, 2022). In the meantime, while this area of research develops, judges may wish to exercise additional caution when making discretionary decisions about multimedia evidence.

Social Policy Implications

Since their emergence, technology-augmented courtrooms have been lauded for their purported ability to enhance the transparency and accountability of legal proceedings and increase access to justice. As mentioned earlier, several of the initiatives that are now routinely implemented into the electronic courtroom, including advanced court-reporting technology and, in certain jurisdictions, the ability to live-stream court proceedings allows for more thorough documentation and visibility of court proceedings by observers who are not physically present in the courtroom. Affording the general public the opportunity to actively monitor and scrutinize the inner workings of the judiciary should, at least theoretically, increase public trust in a system that is built on the tenets of fairness, impartiality and equal access.

The integration of videoconferencing and assistive technologies is in line with judicial efforts to promote an inclusive and democratic experience for individuals who are directly participating in legal proceedings. For example, the ability to remotely appear in the courtroom benefits those who live in remote or marginalized communities, or who are physically or financially unable to appear in person (Bailey et al., 2013). Assistive technologies, such as mobility, visual, hearing aids are designed to lessen the burden on individuals who may otherwise experience significant challenges with communication or comprehension when serving as a juror or witness. Perhaps most importantly, prior to the widespread distribution of technology into American courtrooms, these expensive technologies and software would need to be purchased in-house by the law firms who wish to employ them. Historically, the exorbitant costs of technology proffered a competitive advantage to the legal teams who could afford them. In a civil context, this advantage is most often afforded to a client who is represented by a larger, more-established firm who has more expendable resources available to them (DeSario, 2002); in a criminal case, this is the prosecution, which is backed by government resources (Huff, 2004). With these technologies now accessible to either legal party, there is a sense that electronic courtrooms have "leveled the playing field" so to speak, thus promoting fairness and equitability at trial regardless of financial standing (DeSario, 2002).

With this being said, the integration of technology into the justice system is not without controversy. Even prior to their inception, legal scholars have documented concerns related to courtroom technology being incompatible with certain maxims of social and public policy. While on one hand, the increased access to technology afforded by electronic courtrooms has abated concerns about financial disparities between opposing legal parties, some have argued that these technological inequities remain, and have simply become less obvious. A timely example of this issue is the use of computer-generated evidence. While two opposing lawyers may, in theory, have equal access to the technology that is required to *present* an animation or simulation to a jury, these visualizations are extremely expensive to create and these expenses are incurred by the defendant or plaintiff; therefore, having equal access to evidence presentation technologies is rendered irrelevant, if an individual cannot independently afford to fund the production of this evidence (Moyeda, 2014). This pervasive disparity is certainly important to consider, especially in light of research demonstrating that visual presentation mediums tend to have the greatest impact on jurors' culpability judgments when their use is differential. In other words, when only one legal team leverages technology and the other does not, jurors tend to be particularly punitive toward the party who presented their argument with less advanced means (e.g., Dunn, et al., 2006; Kassin & Dunn, 1997; Park & Feigenson, 2013).

Finally, scholars have contended that some degree of humanity and solemnity of a trial has been lost in the transition from "justice" to "cyberjustice." According to Lederer (1999), when technology is at the forefront of judicial proceedings, it may detract from the innately *human* elements of a trial. When jurors are presented with evidence through the confines of a monitor—no matter how sophisticated—the evidence may no longer be tangible to them in the same way it would have been had it been viewed or handled first-hand. The same applies to witness testimony—it is not unreasonable to expect that a juror may feel detached from a witness who is testifying remotely, and could feasibly be thousands of miles away rather than in a juror's immediate vicinity. This "immediacy" in time and space is part of the reason juries are sometimes afforded the opportunity to visit crime scenes in person: there is something to be said about being able to directly observe and experience a setting than hearing about it or being shown it through a screen.

Closely related to this issue is the question of whether remote proceedings could have intended impacts on participatory justice (Donoghue, 2017). As technology becomes increasingly embedded into the justice system, are there unforeseen, and potentially negative, implications for the perceived legitimacy of justice? This issue has become a recent focus of legal and sociolegal scholars who contend that the grandeur of the courthouse itself serves an important symbolic function, conveying a message about the sanctity of the institution of law, and the gravity of the events that unfold within its walls (Donoghue, 2017; Ferguson, 2022; Juszczyk, 2021). When technology inevitably evolves the point where entire trials are hosted online, with a defendant never coming face-to-face with the counsel who is representing them or the jury who is deciding their fate, concerns have been raised that public confidence in the justice system may erode, and the legitimacy of the institution of law may never rebound back to its former state (Donoghue, 2017).

Legal Ethics

While electronic courtrooms provide trial attorneys with generalized access to evidence presentation technology, in the majority of cases the decision of whether or not to make use of the available technology is typically left to legal counsel. In light of the significant advantages that courtroom technologies can afford a defendant, technological proficiency is certainly a significant consideration when choosing legal representation (Lederer, 1999; Quigley, 2010). In 2012, the American Bar Association recognized technological competence as an extension of a lawyer's ethical obligations to provide competent representation to their clients. Comment 8 under Rule 1.1, of the Model Rules of Professional Conduct competence now reads:

> To maintain the requisite knowledge and skill, a lawyer should keep abreast of changes in the law and its practice, including the benefits and risks associated with relevant technology, engage in continuing study and education and comply with all continuing legal education requirements to which the lawyer is subject.
> (ABA, 2023)

The rationale underlying this provision is twofold: first, a client may be severely disadvantaged in a court case should their lawyer decline or be unable to make use of the tools that are available to them, and second, a lawyer requires at least a baseline level of technological knowledge to be able to recognize and respond to technological malfeasance exhibited by opposing parties (Salyzyn, 2016). With regard to the latter, it is the lawyer's responsibility to appropriately object to potentially prejudicial use of technology—such as using PowerPoint as a means to display overly graphic visual content which could prejudice a jury—as this use of technology could violate their defendant or client's right to a fair trial, and may constitute grounds for an appeal should a case be lost. With this mandate now in effect in a majority of American jurisdictions, failure to make reasonable efforts to keep up with contemporary technological advancements could constitute professional misconduct (Webb, 2023).

Although the American Bar Association has declared that technological competence is a requirement of practicing law, recent data would suggest that this is a skill that many lawyers have yet to acquire. In response to the 2022 *ABA Legal Technology Survey*, while nearly 75% of lawyers reported having access to technology training at their firms, only 30% expressed "strong agreement" that the training that they had received was adequate (Rosch, 2022). Interestingly, while 93.6% of attorneys from large firms (i.e., 100–499 attorneys) were significantly *more* likely to indicate having training available to them compared to only 31.8% of solo attorneys, attorneys from large firms were significantly *less* likely to report feeling comfortable with these technologies (i.e., 33.3% of attorneys from large firms, compared to 61.8% of solo attorneys). Perhaps most concerningly, just over 2/3 of attorneys who responded to this survey acknowledged that they were required to stay abreast of the benefits and risks of technology as part of the rules of professional conduct, compared to 10% who answered "*No*" and 21% who answered "*I don't know*" (Rosch, 2022).

The importance of comprehensive judicial training, which properly educated lawyers about the capabilities, limitations and costs associated with courtroom technology, cannot be understated. According to Lederer (2010), training is the single largest obstacle to the effective use of technology in the courtroom. Indeed, judges are quick to report that the difficulty with courtroom technology arises not from the technology itself, but from its ineffective operation by counsel (Lederer, 2004). Despite "technological competence" being considered a requisite of professional conduct for attorneys, to date, there has been no formal attempt to operationalize what constitutes a sufficient degree of "competence," nor has there been any standardized guidance as to the specific praxis one might take in order to arrive at this ambiguous threshold. As of 2022, at least three states (i.e., North Carolina, Florida, and New York) have mandated regular technology training as part of their bar requirements to participate in continuing legal education (Webb, 2023; Weiss, 2023). While this is certainly a step in the right direction, a more formalized system of education and training—one which adequately equips lawyers with the skills they need to effectively practice in the electronic courtroom—is needed in order promote standardization and ethical use of courtroom technologies across the United States.

Summary and Conclusion

In conclusion, the advent of courtroom technology has engendered a profound transformation in the justice system as we know it today. Technology holds the potential to enhance the efficiency of legal processes, streamline evidence presentation and deliberations, and increase access to justice due to greater access to remote participation and assistive technology. Within the electronic courtroom, advanced evidence presentation systems have ushered in a new era of digital and computer-generated evidence, revolutionizing the way juries receive and evaluate case information. While this chapter focused on a handful of contemporary evidence types, namely VR/3D evidence, computer-generated animations and simulations, body-worn camera footage and digital device data, these represent only a fraction of those that are currently available. Like all technology, courtroom technology will continue to change and improve over time, and the justice system will undoubtedly embrace the latest technological advancements as they arrive.

The opportunities that have been afforded by recent technological innovation should be considered alongside new challenges and considerations. The rapid emergence of new technologies raises questions about the need to refine or elaborate on existing evidentiary standards to ensure their proper governance and admissibility. As noted by Rowden and Wallace (2013), the promise of a digital courtroom may not yet live up to its billing, in terms of either the quality of the technology currently available, or its use in the court process itself.

The widespread integration of courtroom technology has significant implications for social and public policy. It is imperative that these technologies are employed in a manner that minimizes existing disparities in the legal system, while at the same time, preserving the integrity of judicial procedures. Finally, technology is undoubtedly a helpful resource, but it is only a tool. As lawyers adapt to technological change, they must remain vigilant in updating their knowledge and training to fulfill their professional obligations to their clients.

Looking ahead, the future of the American justice system remains uncertain. The pace of technological advancement shows no signs of slowing down, and discussions are already underway regarding highly advanced decision-support and automation systems that rely on machine learning and artificial intelligence. It is conceivable that in the not-so-distant future, these systems may provide precise estimates about an offender's likelihood of re-offending, and natural language processing may assist in determining whether a defendant or witness is lying on the stand (Dixon, 2013; Zalnieruite & Bell, 2020). As technologies become increasingly sophisticated, it is imperative that we, as a society, take a proactive and multidisciplinary approach to develop evidence-based frameworks and regulations designed to manage these technologies while safeguarding the rights of citizens whom the justice system was designed for. By doing so, the justice system can harness the full potential of technology while upholding the core values upon which our legal system is built.

References

ABA (2023). *Rule 1.1. Competence—Comment.* American Bar Association. www.americanbar.org/groups/professional_responsibility/publications/model_rules_of_professional_conduct/rule_1_1_competence/comment_on_rule_1_1/

Administrative Conference of the United States (2014) Recommendation 2014-7, Best Practices for Using Video Teleconferencing for Hearings, 79, Fed. Reg. 75114.

Americans with Disabilities Act of 1990, 42 USC §12101 (1990). www.ada.gov/pubs/adastatute08.htm

Aronson, R.H., & McMurtrie, J. (2007). The use and misuse of high-tech evidence by prosecutors: Ethical and evidentiary issues. *Fordham Law Review*, 76(3), 1453–1492.

Bailey, J., Burkell, J., & Reynolds, G. (2013). Access to justice for all: Towards an "expansive vision" of justice and technology. *Windsor Yearbook of Access to Justice*, 31(2), 181–207. https://doi.org/10.22329/wyaj.v31i2.4419

Bala, N.C., & Anand, S. (2012). *Youth criminal justice law* (3rd ed.). Irwin Law.

Bild, E., Redman, A., Newman, E.J., Muir, B.R., Tait, D., & Schwarz, N. (2021). Sound and credibility in the virtual court: Low audio quality leads to less favorable evaluations of witnesses and lower weighting of evidence. *Law and Human Behavior*, 45(5), 481–495. https://doi.org/10.1037/lhb0000466

Bornstein, B.H. & Greene, E. (2011). Jury decision making: Implications for and from psychology. *Current Directions in Psychological Science*, 20(1), 63–67. https://doi.org/10.1177/0963721410397282

Braga, A.A., MacDonald, J.M., & McCabe, J. (2022). Body-worn cameras, lawful police stops, and NYPD officer compliance: A cluster randomized controlled trial. *Criminology*, 60(1), 124–158. https://doi.org/10.1111/1745-9125.12293

Buck, U., Naether, S., Räss, B., Jackowski, C., & Thali, M.J. (2013). Accident or homicide–virtual crime scene reconstruction using 3D methods. *Forensic Science International*, 225(1–3), 75–84. https://doi.org/10.1016/j.forsciint.2012.05.015

Butler, J. (2007). Torture and the ethics of photography. *Environment and Planning D: Society and Space*, 25(6), 951–966. https://doi.org/10.1068/d2506jb

Carney, B. & Feigenson, N. (2004), Visual persuasion in the Michael Skakel trial: enhancing advocacy through interactive media presentations, *Criminal Justice Magazine*, 19(1), 22–35.

Casey, E., Nguyen, L., Mates, J., & Lalliss, S. (2022). Crowdsourcing forensics: Creating a curated catalog of digital forensic artifacts. *Journal of Forensic Sciences*, 67(5), 1846–1857. https://doi.org/10.1111/1556-4029.15053

Chappell, B. & Hansen, V. (2023, March 23). Here are 8 big revelations from the Alex Murdaugh murder trial. National Public Radio. www.npr.org/2023/03/01/1160319398/alex-murdaugh-murder-trial-revelations

Dahir, V.B. (2011). Digital Visual Evidence. In C.E. Henderson & J. Epstein (Authors), *The Future of Evidence: How Science and Technology Will Change the Practice of Law* (pp. 77–112). American Bar Association, ABA Section of Science & Technology Law.

DeSario, N.J. (2002). Merging technology with justice: How electronic courtrooms shape evidentiary concerns. *Cleveland State Law Review, 50*, 57–72.

Devine, D.J., Clayton, L.D., Dunford, B.B., Seying, R., & Pryce, J. (2001). Jury decision making: 45 years of empirical research on deliberating groups. *Psychology, Public Policy, and Law, 7*(3), 622–727. https://doi.org/10.1037/1076-8971.7.3.622

Dixon, H.B. (2011). The evolution of a high-technology courtroom. *National Center for State Courts, Future Trends in State Courts, 1*(6), 28–32. http://ncsc.contentdm.oclc.org/cdm/ref/collection/tech/id/769

Dixon, H.B. (2013). Technology and the courts: A futurist view. *Judges Journal, 52*(3), 36–38.

Dixon, H.B. (2017). The basics of a technology-enhanced courtroom. *American Bar Association.* www.americanbar.org/groups/judicial/publications/judges_journal/2017/fall/basics-technologyenhanced-courtroom/

Donoghue, J. (2017). The rise of digital justice: Courtroom technology, public participation and access to justice. *The Modern Law Review, 80*(6), 995–1025. https://doi.org/10.1111/1468-2230.12300

Dufraimont, L. (2008). Evidence law and the jury: a reassessment. *McGill Law Journal, 53*, 199–242.

Dunn, M.A., Salovey, P., & Feigenson, N. (2006). The jury persuaded (and not): computer animation in the courtroom. *Law and Policy, 28*(2), 228–248. https://doi.org/10.1111/j.1467-9930.2006.00225.x

Ellingwood, H.A. (2019). Vantage points: Mock juror perception of body-worn camera video evidence in cases involving police use of force (Doctoral dissertation, Carleton University). Carleton Institutional Repository. https://doi.org/10.22215/etd/2019-13594

Embry, S. (2020). *2020 Litigation and Tar Report.* American Bar Association. www.americanbar.org/groups/law_practice/publications/techreport/2020/litigationtar/

Federal Rules of Evidence. (2019). Grand Rapids, MI: Michigan Legal Publishing.

Feigenson, N. (2014). The visual in law: some problems for legal theory. *Law, Culture and the Humanities, 10*(1), 13–23. https://doi.org/10.1177/1743872111421126

Ferguson, A.G. (2022). Courts without court. *Vanderbilt Law Review, 75*(5), 1461–1522.

For the Record (2019). The sound and sight of justice. Retrieved from https://fortherecord.com/

Gilovich, T., Griffin, D., & Kahneman, D. (Eds.). (2002). *Heuristics and biases: The psychology of intuitive judgment.* Cambridge University Press. https://doi.org/10.1017/CBO9780511808098

Goodison, S.E., Davis, R.C., & Jackson, B.A. (2015). Digital evidence and the US criminal justice system: Identifying technology and other needs to more effectively acquire and utilize digital evidence. *RAND Corporation.* 1–32. www.rand.org/pubs/research_reports/RR890.html

Greenstein, M.N. (2016). The challenge of maintaining confidence in a judiciary lacking in Diversity. *Judges Journal, 55*(2), 40.

Harrill, D.C., & Mislan, R.P. (2007). A small scale digital device forensics ontology. *Small Scale Device Forensics Journal, 1*(1), 1–7.

High Impact, LLC. (2022). About us. www.highimpact.com/about/

Huff, G.R. (2004). Wrongful convictions: The American experience. *Canadian Journal of Criminology and Criminal Justice*, 46(2), 107–120. https://doi.org/10.3138/cjccj.46.2.107

Hyland, S. (2018). *Body-worn cameras in law enforcement agencies, 2016*. US Department of Justice, Office of Justice Programs, Bureau of Justice Statistics. NCJ 251775.

Jacinto, R.F., Sproule, D., Williams, J., Perlmutter, S., Arndt, S., & Rundell, S. (2019). Application of Stereoscopic Head-Mounted Displays and Interactive Virtual Reality Environments to an "Optical Illusion" Misstep and Fall Case. Proceedings of the Human Factors and Ergonomics Society Annual Meeting, 63(1), 552–556. https://doi.org/10.1177/1071181319631495

Jones, A.C.T., Batastini, A.B., Patel, M.B., Sacco, D.F., & Warlick, C.A. (2023). Does Convenience Come with a Price? The Impact of Remote Testimony on Perceptions of Expert Credibility. *Criminal Justice and Behavior*, 50(2), 197–215. https://doi.org/10.1177/00938548221087177

Juszczyk, G. (2021). Power on a pedestal: How architecture creates, reinforces, and reflects power structures in the legal system. *ANU Undergraduate Research Journal*, 11(1), 39–57. https://studentjournals.anu.edu.au/index.php/aurj/article/view/722

Kassin, S.M., & Dunn, M.A. (1997). Computer-animated displays and the jury: Facilitative and prejudicial effects. *Law and Human Behavior*, 21(3), 269–281. https://doi.org/10.1023/A:1024838715221

Kuchler, D.D., & O Toole, L.C. (2008). How technological advances in the courtroom are changing the way we litigate. *Quarterly-Federation of Defense and Corporate Counsel*, 58(2), 205–217.

Laming, E. (2019). Police use of body worn cameras. *Police Practice and Research*, 20(2), 201–216. https://doi.org/10.1080/15614263.2018.1558586

Lederer, F.I. (1999). The road to the virtual courtroom? A consideration of today's—and tomorrow's—high technology courtrooms. *Faculty Publications*, 50, 800–844.

Lederer, F.I. (2002). Empirical research report: The use of technology in the jury room to enhance deliberations. Retrieved from https://scholarship.law.wm.edu/cgi/viewcontent.cgi?article=1557&context=facpubs

Lederer, F.I. (2004). Courtroom technology: For trial lawyers the future is now. *Criminal Justice*, 41, 14–21.

Lederer, F.I. (2005). Courtroom technology: A status report. In K.N. Agarwala & M.D. Tiwardi (Eds). *Electronic Judicial Resource Management* (pp. 179–180). Macmillan Publishers.

Lederer, F.I. (2010). Wired: What we've learned about courtroom technology. *Criminal Justice*, 24, 19–25.

Lederer, F.I. (2017). Technology-augmented and virtual courts and courtrooms. In *The Routledge handbook of technology, crime and justice* (pp. 518–531). Routledge.

Lederer, F.I. (2021). The evolving technology-augmented courtroom before, during and after the pandemic. *Vanderbilt Journal of Entertainment and Technology Law*, 23(2), 301–340.

Legate, B.L. (2006). The admissibility of demonstrative evidence in jury trials: Applying the principled approach to the law of evidence. *Advocates' Quarterly*, *31*, 316–346.

Leonetti, C., & Bailenson, J. (2009). High-tech view: the use of immersive virtual environments in jury trials. *Marquette Law Review*, *93*(3), 1073–1120.

Louie, D.M., Rincon, C., Anderson, V.R., & Kayfetz, P. (2007). Use and admissibility of high definition video visibility studies, computer animations and computer simulations. *Quarterly-Federation of Defense and Corporate Counsel*, *58*(1), 87–107.

Lum, C., Stoltz, M., Koper, C.S., & Scherer, J.A. (2019). Research on body-worn cameras: What we know, what we need to know. *Criminology & Public Policy*, *18*(1), 93–118. https://doi.org/10.1111/1745-9133.12412

McCluskey, J.D., & Uchida, C.D. (2023). Video data analysis and police body-worn camera footage. *Sociological Methods & Research*, online ahead of print. https://doi.org/10.1177/00491241231156968

McDonald, L.W., Tait, D., Gelb, K., Rossner, M., & McKimmie, B.M. (2015). Digital evidence in the jury room: The impact of mobile technology on the jury. *Current Issues in Criminal Justice*, *27*(2), 179–194. https://doi.org/10.1080/10345329.2015.12036040

Mizrahi, S. (2016). Cyberjustice: An Overview. *Laboratoire de Cyberjustice*. www.cyberjustice.ca/files/sites/102/WP15.pdf

Moussa, A.F. (2021). Electronic evidence and its authenticity in forensic evidence. *Egyptian Journal of Forensic Sciences*, *11*(1), 1–10. https://doi.org/10.1186/s41935-021-00234-6

Moyeda, J. (2014). Courtroom technology. *Cornell Law School J.D. Student Research Papers*, *30*, 1–5.

Mylonas, A., Meletiadis, V., Tsoumas, B., Mitrou, L., & Gritzalis, D. (2012, June). Smartphone forensics: A proactive investigation scheme for evidence acquisition. In *IFIP International Information Security Conference* (pp. 249–260). Springer.

National Center for State Courts (2023). *Trial court technology in courthouses: Evidence display camera*. www.ncsc.org/courthouseplanning/courthouse-technology/evidence-display-camera

Norris, G. (2015). Judgement heuristics and bias in evidence interpretation: The effects of computer generated exhibits. *International Journal of Law and Psychiatry*, *42–43*, 121–127. https://doi.org/10.1016/j.ijlp.2015.08.016

Overill, R.E., & Collie, J. (2021). Quantitative evaluation of the results of digital forensic investigations: a review of progress. *Forensic Sciences Research*, *6*(1), 13–18. https://doi.org/10.1080/20961790.2020.1837429

Park, J., & Feigenson, N. (2013). Effects of a visual technology on mock juror decision making. *Applied Cognitive Psychology*, *27*(2), 235–246. https://doi.org/10.1002/acp.2900

Petty, R.E., & Cacioppo, J.T. (1986). *Communication and persuasion: Central and peripheral routes to attitude change*. Springer-Verlag.

Pumphrey, D. Jr. (2022, March 12). How the metaverse could change criminal defense forever. Retrieved from www.pumphreylawfirm.com/blog/how-the-metaverse-could-change-criminal-defense-forever/

Quigley, M.L. (2010). Courtroom technology and legal ethics: considerations for the ABA commission on ethics 20/20. *Professional Lawyer, 20*(3), 18–21.

Rempel, E., Hamovitch, L., Zannella, L., & Burke, T.M. (2019). The power of technology: Examining the effects of digital visual evidence on jurors' processing of trial information. *Applied Cognitive Psychology, 33*(6), 1288–1295. https://doi.org/10.1002/acp.3598

Rempel, E. & Burke, T.M. (2022). Technology on trial: facilitative and prejudicial effects of computer-generated animations on jurors' legal judgments, *Psychology, Crime & Law*, online ahead of print. https://doi.org/10.1080/1068316X.2022.2041014

Rosch (2022). 2022 technology training report. Retrieved from www.americanbar.org/groups/law_practice/publications/techreport/2022/

Rowden, E., & Wallace, A. (2018). Remote judging: The impact of video links on the image and the role of the judge. *International Journal of Law in Context, 14*(4), 504–524. doi:10.1017/S1744552318000216

Salyzyn, A. (2016). The case for courtroom technology competence as an ethical duty for litigators. In K. Benyekhlef, J. Bailey, J. Burkell, & F. Gélinas (Eds.), *eAccess to Justice* (pp. 211–240). University of Ottawa Press.

Schofield, D. (2012). Virtual evidence in the courtroom. In H. Yang & S. Yuen (Eds.), *The handbook of research on practices and outcomes in virtual worlds and environments* (pp. 200–216). IGI Global. https://doi.org/10.4018/978-1-60960-762-3

Sieberth, T., Dobay, A., Affolter, R., & Ebert, L.C. (2019). Applying virtual reality in forensics: A virtual scene walkthrough. *Forensic Science, Medicine, and Pathology, 15*(1), 41–47. https://doi.org/10.1007/s12024-018-0058-8

Smith, D., & Hurley, G. (2018). Jurors with disabilities. National Center for State Courts. www.ncsc-jurystudies.org/__data/assets/pdf_file/0014/7340/juror-with-disabilities-final-report.pdf

Suss, J., Raushel, A., Armijo, A., & White, B. (2018). Design considerations in the proliferation of police body-worn cameras. *Ergonomics in Design, 26*(3), 17–22. https://doi.org/10.1177/1064804618757686

Terrill, W., & Zimmerman, L. (2022). Police use of force escalation and de-escalation: The use of systematic social observation with video footage. *Police Quarterly, 25*(2), 155–177. https://doi.org/10.1177/10986111211049145

United States Court of Federal Claims (n.d.) Guidance on use of videoconferencing in court. Retrieved from www.uscfc.uscourts.gov/video-conferencing-guidance

Varjo (2023). Case Explico: how mixed reality helps forensic engineers educate jurors in the courtroom. Retrieved from https://varjo.com/case-studies/how-mixed-reality-helps-forensic-engineers-educate-jurors-in-the-courtroom/

Walker, C. (2018). Using computer-generated animation and simulation evidence at trial: what you should know. Retrieved from www.americanbar.org/groups/litigation/committees/products-liability/practice/2018/using-computer-generated-animation-simulation-evidence-at-trial/

Webb, J. (2023). The lawyer's duty of tech competence post-COVID: Why Georgia needs a new professional role now—more than ever. *Georgia State University Law Review, 39*(2), 551–604.

Weiss, D.C. (2023, March 14). May jurors see 3D defense reenactment of alleged crime? Judge appears reluctant to allow it. Retrieved from www.abajournal.com/news/article/may-jurors-see-3-d-reenactment-of-alleged-attempted-murder-judge-appears-reluctant-to-allow-it

Wiggins, E.C. (2004). What we know and what we need to know about the effects of courtroom technology. *William and Mary Bill of Rights Journal, 12,* 731–743.

World Health Organization (2023, May 15). Assistive technology. Retrieved from www.who.int/news-room/fact-sheets/detail/assistive-technology

Zalnieriute, M., & Bell, F. (2020). Technology and the Judicial Role. In G. Appleby & A. Lynch (Eds.), *The judge, the judiciary and the court: Individual, collegial and institutional judicial dynamics in Australia* (pp. 116–142). Cambridge University Press. http://dx.doi.org/10.2139/ssrn.3492868

16 The CSI Effect and its Impact on the Legal System, Policy, and Practice

Kimberley Schanz

An 18-year-old man is on trial for murder. Prosecutors outline their case: the man met the victim at a bar, followed the victim home, murdered the victim in their home, and then disposed of the victim's body in a forest ten miles from the victim's home. Prosecutors present eyewitness evidence confirming that the defendant and victim spent time together at the bar, that they were seen entering the victim's home together, and the defendant was seen leaving the victim's home alone, but with a very large suitcase. Security footage can additionally confirm those actions. However, the fingerprint and DNA evidence that was presented could not conclusively be linked to the defendant. Additional witness evidence was presented, stating that the defendant was bragging about his crime at the same bar the next night. Lastly, the prosecution presented evidence from the police's interrogation of the defendant that he knew details about the victim's injuries that were not released to the public. The prosecution was convinced that the case was a slam dunk; a guaranteed conviction. However, after three days of deliberation, the jury found the defendant not guilty.

How is that possible? What led the jury to make that decision? How did they evaluate the evidence provided in the case? What other evidence could the jury have possibly wanted?

This case example would likely be considered a "quintessential CSI Effect case". Ever since the introduction and consequential proliferation of crime dramas on television and now streaming sites, scholars from the legal, psychological, and criminological fields have been concerned regarding the impact of the shows' content on the general public, and therefore, potential jurors (e.g., Cather, 2004; Cooley, 2007; Durnal, 2010; Shelton et al., 2007). This impact, also known as the "CSI Effect" (e.g., Cole and Dioso-Villa, 2007), has spurned much debate, particularly between scholars who are trying to test its impact and practitioners who are simultaneously trying to mitigate its influence. This chapter will describe the various facets of the CSI Effect, evaluate the currently available empirical research on its main impacts, and discuss the policy and practice changes that have been implemented as mitigation strategies thus far.

What Is the CSI Effect?

The CSI Effect is a wide-reaching theory that argues crime dramas and crime-related television are influencing the knowledge and/or behavior of specific subsets of the public in a way that impacts the operation of the criminal justice and legal systems (e.g., Cole & Dioso-Villa, 2007; Ley et al., 2012; Preuß & Labudde, 2022; Schanz & Salfati, 2016; Stinson et al., 2007). Crime dramas and crime-related television are generally created and produced for entertainment purposes, which requires a level of poetic license. Because television is time and content limited, these shows cannot and do not portray the legal and criminal justice systems accurately (Cooley, 2007; Forensic Science Initiative, 2011; Nolan, 2007; Pratt et al., 2006). However, the CSI Effect argues that those who are watching these shows, and particularly those who are watching these shows frequently, are learning from and developing expectations of the legal and criminal justice systems as a result (e.g., Cole & Dioso-Villa, 2007; Schanz & Salfati, 2016).

Resulting from viewers learning from crime shows, Cole and Dioso-Villa (2007) argue that there are six manifestations of the CSI Effect, all varying by potential behavioral outcome (see Table 16.1). Of these six, the two that have seen the most controversy and debate are the strong prosecutor's effect and the defendant's effect (as summarized in Figure 16.1).

These two manifestations argue that, among people who watch many hours of crime dramas and/or crime-related television, unrealistically heightened expectations of forensic evidence develop and become engrained in their knowledge. These unrealistic expectations include that forensic evidence is always present at the crime scene, that forensic evidence is always tested, that forensic evidence is tested quickly, and that forensic evidence is infallible. As a result, forensic evidence presented in a trial is weighted more heavily than other types of evidence because it is seen as the most valid type of evidence. These expectations then become the knowledge framework through which the potential jurors evaluate the evidence presented in a trial when they are serving as jurors. Therefore, when forensic evidence is present, those people will vote to convict the defendant, given they believe the evidence accurately and conclusively determines that the defendant is guilty. However, when forensic evidence is absent, they will vote to acquit the defendant given the absolute decider of guilt (i.e., forensic evidence) is absent, that opens up any conclusions about the defendant to doubt. In fact, most research that examines the CSI Effect has evaluated one or both of those manifestations and its impact on juror

Table 16.1 The six manifestations of the CSI Effect.

Manifestation	Explanation
Strong Prosecutor's Effect	Jurors are giving more credibility to forensic scientists and forensic science, and therefore, are (wrongfully) acquitting defendants as a result of a lack of forensic evidence (despite other evidence)
Weak Prosecutor's Effect	Prosecutors are forced to modify their courtroom practices to mitigate the influence of crime shows
Defendant's Effect	Jurors are giving more credibility to forensic scientists and forensic science, and therefore, convicting defendants in the presence of forensic evidence (despite other evidence)
Producer's Effect	Crime shows have increased public awareness of forensic science and therefore, jurors are more educated and can better evaluate forensic evidence.
Professor's Version	Crime shows have increased interest in forensic science and enrollment in forensic science programs has significantly increased, as has attrition, once the enrollees' expectations of forensic science are not met.
Police Chief's Version	Crime shows are educating people who commit crime on the best methods to avoid detection by law enforcement.

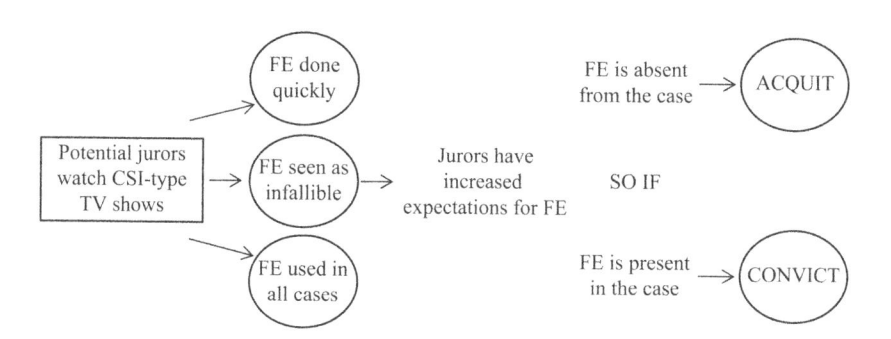

Figure 16.1 Combination of strong prosecutor's effect and defendant's effect of the CSI Effect theory. "FE" is an abbreviation for "forensic evidence."

Source: reprinted from Schanz & Salfati (2016); reprinted by permission of the publisher (Taylor & Francis Ltd, www.tandfonline.com)

verdicts (e.g., Hawkins & Scherr, 2017, 2018; Ling et al., 2021; Schanz & Salfati, 2016; Shelton et al., 2007).

Social psychology argues that this manifestation of the CSI Effect occurs through mechanisms outlined in both cultivation theory and social cognitive theory. Cultivation theory (Gerbner et al., 1980) argues that shows on television represent a depiction of social reality for viewers, so the more viewers watch, the more they are likely to incorporate what they see into their personal social reality. They then use that television-informed social reality as a basis to inform their future behavior. Since crime shows portray the criminal justice and legal systems, cultivation theory argues that those who watch many of these crime shows create a personal social reality of the criminal justice and legal systems in line with what is portrayed in the shows. As a result, the CSI Effect occurs when in a relevant situation themselves (e.g., a courtroom, a police station, a witness to a crime), the viewers apply their social reality developed from the crime shows to inform what they expect to happen and how they should behave. For example, if the shows they watch repeatedly find DNA evidence at the crime scene, the viewers will begin to expect DNA to be found at every crime scene.

The social cognitive theory (Bandura, 2001) similarly argues that what is portrayed on television can serve as a social model for those who watch, pay attention, and are able to remember and recall what they see. For those that watch crime shows, social cognitive theory argues that what is portrayed in those shows becomes the social model for viewers for all relevant criminal justice and/or legal-related situations. As long as the viewer is engaged in the show and paying enough attention to it so that they are able to recall it later, then that show can serve as a model for the viewer's future behavior. Therefore, the CSI Effect occurs when the viewers of crime shows are engaging in behaviors they have previously seen on television when they find themselves in a relevant legal- or criminal justice-related situation. For example, if the shows portray confidence by practitioners in all kinds of forensic evidence, then, when presented with forensic evidence when serving as a juror, the viewer will imitate that confidence.

Despite a solid theoretical explanation, the existence of the CSI Effect in all of its manifestations has resulted in much debate in the empirical literature (e.g., Cole & Dioso-Villa, 2007; Hawkins & Scherr, 2017, 2018; Ling et al., 2021; Schanz & Salfati, 2016; Shelton, 2010; Shelton et al., 2007; Shelton et al., 2009; Tyler, 2006). When focusing on the CSI Effect's impact on verdict decision-making, the empirical results are mixed (Hawkins & Scherr, 2017, 2018; Ling et al., 2021; Schanz & Salfati, 2016; Shelton et al., 2007). However, what is clear is that there is a growing area of research showing how the legal and criminal justice systems are changing their policies and practices out of fear that the CSI effect is negatively impacting the intended operations of the systems (e.g., Durnal, 2010; Maricopa County Attorney's Office, 2005; Stinson et al., 2007).

The CSI Effect's Impact on Evaluation of Evidence

How the public in general, and potential jurors specifically, evaluate and use forensic evidence in verdict decisions as a result of what they watch on television is a significant concern for those in the criminal justice and legal systems (Stinson et al., 2007). However, the empirical research on the CSI Effect and its impact on verdict decision-making is limited and what has been done is mixed on whether watching crime shows have any impact at all. As a result, the research on this phenomenon will be discussed in two ways: first, how watching crime shows impacts people's perceptions of evidence, and second, how watching crime shows impacts people's verdict decision making behavior. Lastly, a second explanation besides the CSI Effect for changing perceptions and verdicts is discussed.

Impact on Perceptions of Evidence

There is significant evidence that illustrates watching crime shows impacts what evidence people expect to be presented and how they evaluate that evidence in a trial setting. This is especially evident when potential jurors are examining forensic evidence specifically. Potential jurors who watch a significant amount of crime shows have reported that they expect to see forensic evidence presented at trial to support the prosecution's argument (Biju et al., 2021; Fedorek, 2015; Groscup, 2015; Holmgren & Fordham, 2011; Kinsey, 2012; Ley et al., 2012; Ley et al., 2012; Mancini, 2011; Kim et al., 2009; Schanz & Salfati, 2016; Schweitzer & Saks, 2007; Shelton et al., 2007; Sutton & Byrd, 2017). This expectation of jurors to present forensic evidence also has been perceived by lawyers from the prosecution and the defense (Alderden et al., 2018; Brickell, 2008; Maricopa County Attorney's Office, 2005; Robbers, 2008; Stevens, 2008) and more recently, by judges (Cole & Dioso-Villa, 2021). It is clear that, by watching television shows in which forensic evidence is always present, tested quickly, and always useful (Lam, 2015; Pratt et al., 2006), potential jurors are incorporating those unrealistic expectations into their expectations for all real-world cases. This shows that jurors are expecting the real-world to meet their television-based expectations by presenting forensic evidence in most, if not all, criminal court cases.

Potential jurors who watch crime shows also have reported that they expect forensic evidence to be reliable (Baskin & Sommers, 2010; Ley et al., 2012; Smith et al., 2007), valid (Smith et al., 2007), and objective (Ghoshray, 2006). Since crime shows rarely show forensic evidence being inaccurate or subject to human bias, viewers incorporate this perception of infallibility into their reality. In fact, jurors have even reported weighing forensic evidence as more reliable and valid than other types of evidence in general (Alldredge, 2015; Ling et al., 2021; Maeder & Corbett, 2015; Sutton & Byrd, 2017), and specifically, eyewitness testimony (Robbers, 2008; Harvey & Derksen, 2009; Hawkins & Scherr, 2018; Sutton & Byrd, 2017). However, the National Academy of Sciences (2009) has definitively stated that the only form of forensic evidence that is based in science and about which judgements on validity and reliability can be made is DNA evidence. The remaining types of forensic evidence (e.g., fingerprints, blood splatter analysis, bite mark impressions, etc.) lack baseline information and error rates, making them of an unknown reliability and validity (National Academy of Sciences, 2009). Clearly, viewers of crime shows are learning inaccurate information about forensic evidence and incorporating that into their knowledge frameworks. These heightened expectations of the presence and quality of forensic evidence in general implies a mentality among crime show viewers that forensic evidence trumps all; that in the absence of forensic evidence, they may perceive that there is not enough evidence to convict the defendant.

Impact on Verdict Decisions

Despite there being extensive research that perceptions of evidence are influenced by learning from crime shows, there is mixed evidence regarding whether watching crime shows impacts how people vote when asked to give their verdict in a trial. There is some evidence to suggest that those who watch crime shows make different verdict decisions than those who do not (Baskin & Sommers, 2010; Ewanation et al., 2017; Harvey & Derksen, 2009; Hawkins & Scherr, 2017; Kim et al., 2009; Ling et al., 2021; Mancini, 2011; Mancini, 2013; Schanz & Salfati, 2016). Generally, research has shown that those who watch more crime shows tend to vote in line with their unrealistic expectations. Multiple studies have shown that those who watch crime shows are less likely to convict when forensic evidence is not presented (Baskin & Sommers, 2010; Harvey & Derksen, 2009; Kim et al., 2009; Ling et al., 2021; Mancini, 2011; Mancini, 2013). This has been shown particularly when the viewers perceived the crime shows as accurate to real-life (Ewanation et al., 2017). When viewers perceive the crime shows on television as more real than not, they are more likely to vote in line with the CSI Effect. This implies that they are learning from the crime shows they are watching and applying that knowledge to potential real-life cases. This evidence suggests that there is a direct influence of the content of crime shows on television and real-world behavior related to guilt decision.

Multiple studies also highlight that those who watch crime shows are more confident in their verdicts (Ling et al., 2021; Schweitzer & Saks, 2007). Therefore, not only are potential jurors voting based on what they have viewed on television, but they are also confident in the knowledge that they learned from the crime shows on television. This implies that combating the guilt-based decisions formed by those who watch crime shows may be more difficult. Additionally, an emerging research study found that, when considering crime show watching and gender of the victim of a sexual assault, only crime show watching had a significant impact of perceptions of blame and deservingness of punishment of the victim and the offender (Schanz & Jones, 2023). While these were not guilt-based decisions in the form of verdict decisions, this study does imply that the crime shows someone watches on television can inform the perceptions directly relevant to verdict decisions: blame and punishment. Therefore, not only are people educating themselves on what guilt looks like and what people should be held responsible for, but they are also using that knowledge to inform their decision making.

However, there are also a similar number of studies that show that whether a person watches crime shows or not does not impact on their verdict decision-making process (Alejo, 2016; Brickell, 2008; Davis & Brooke, 2021; Hui & Lo, 2015; Shelton et al., 2007). These studies show that, regardless of how much or how often people watch crime shows, verdict decisions do not vary. This implies that there is similar likelihood that crime show watching makes no difference when it comes to verdict decision-making. While a recent small sample meta-analysis (Schanz & Salfati, 2016) did find a small, but significant, impact of crime show watching habits on verdict decisions, given the small sample size and the small effect size, there is the potential that other factors (e.g., individual differences, previous knowledge, suggestibility, etc.) are more influential than crime show watching. Additionally, in one recent study, jury deliberation was shown to eliminate any presence and/or influence of the CSI Effect, particularly when DNA evidence was presented (Klentz et al., 2020). This implies that, while there may be an impact on individual's decisions on guilt, the group dynamics of jury deliberation do not allow the individual to dictate the group's decision. This, then, could explain the mixed results found in the empirical literature. The majority of empirical literature looking at the CSI Effect measures individual verdict decisions. However, Klentz et al. (2020) shows that jury deliberations negate or eliminate any impact that the CSI Effect may have on verdict decisions, making the real-world impact of the CSI Effect very small. Consequently, there is still a very limited amount of empirical research examining the impact of the CSI Effect on verdict decisions. Therefore, whether there is a definitive impact on verdicts as a result of watching crime shows is still very much up for debate.

Alternate explanation to the CSI Effect's impact

Recent theoretical and empirical research has suggested that it is not crime show watching solely that is impacting how people perceive and act on evidence presented in a court case. Instead, some literature has argued that the proliferation of technology and its showcasing in the media in our society in general can best explain both jurors' increased expectations of forensic science and their verdict decision-making processes (Cole, 2015; Cole & Porter, 2017; Eatley et al., 2016; Lodge & Zloteanu, 2020; Shelton et al., 2009; Shelton, 2010). This perspective argues that the general knowledge that our society has advanced technology is enough for the general public to have high expectations for science and its outcomes. Consequently, that knowledge of advanced technology increases the expectations of forensic evidence specifically as well, regardless of what television shows a person watches regularly (Shelton et al., 2009; Eatley et al., 2016). Additionally, this perspective argues that, as a result, expectations of all evidence presented in the courtroom are increased and subject to increased scrutiny (LaRose & Maddan, 2016; Ribeiro et al., 2019). These increased expectations and heightened scrutiny then serve as the basis of voting behavior. While there is empirical evidence to support this perspective, it currently is not examined or tested in a way that disproves an independent effect of the CSI effect.

The CSI Effect's Impact on the Legal and Criminal Justice Systems

Across the literature, there is one thing that is clear: those that are involved in the criminal justice and legal systems are concerned about the potential impacts of the CSI effect on the systems themselves. Despite mixed empirical evidence on the actual impact of the CSI Effect, there is widespread evidence for a sound belief among legal and criminal justice practitioners that the CSI Effect exists and is negatively impacting the operations of the legal and criminal justice systems (Alderden et al., 2018; Alejo, 2016; Brickell, 2008; Byers & Johnson, 2009; Chin & ibaviosa, 2022; Chin & Workewych, 2016; Davis & Brooke, 2021; Maricopa County Attorney's Office, 2005; Podlas, 2017; Scanlan & Morreale, 2018; Stephens, 2007; Stevens, 2008; Stinson et al., 2007; Sutton & Byrd, 2017). Overall, the belief is that jurors are demanding and requiring more forensic evidence to be presented at trial, and therefore, in order to satisfy them, police and prosecutors must meet those demands. When that demand is not met, the belief is that defense attorneys can and do exploit the lack of evidence, or the presence of only circumstantial evidence, as part of their argument in favor of the defendant. As a result, many individuals working within the legal and criminal justice systems have made significant changes to their operations as a way to mitigate the potential impact of the CSI Effect.

These changes will be discussed in two main areas: changes in practices and changes in policy.

Changes in Practice

Overall, in terms of the types of changes in practice that have been reported, all of them stem from the belief that jurors expect forensic evidence to be presented at every trial. As a result, when it comes to evidence collection, police have reported spending more time and effort collecting more evidence than they would previously deem necessary (Houck, 2006). Since they believe that, in order to convict the defendant a jury requires some kind of forensic evidence, crime scene investigators feel the need and the pressure to produce more evidence from the crime scene than they have previously. This increased need or pressure in forensic evidence collection may also be a direct response to heightened demands from prosecutors themselves. Multiple studies surveying prosecutors have found that, overall, prosecutors report requesting more forensic evidence to be tested as a way to ensure they have some type of scientific evidence to present to the jury (Alderden et al., 2018; Kinsey, 2012; Maricopa County Attorney's Office, 2005; Wise, 2010). This implies that prosecutors believe that, in order to get a conviction, they need to present the jury with definitive forensic evidence that ties the defendant to the crime scene; that, without that, their case is significantly weaker. As a result, prosecutors are changing their practices and engaging in significant efforts to meet the demands of jurors and therefore, perpetuate the impacts of the CSI Effect.

Interestingly, one survey of defense attorneys also reported requesting more forensic evidence to be tested (Kinsey, 2012). This may be an attempt to find independent forensic evidence indicative of innocence, or it may be an attempt to provide alternate, non-definitive forensic evidence findings to the jury. Defense attorneys also have reported spending more time educating jurors on forensic science and its lack of 100% accuracy when forensic evidence is present (Durnal, 2010) as a tactic to insert potential doubt among jurors. Defense attorneys also report spending much discussion in their opening and closing statements discussing the differences between television and reality (Robbers, 2008), potentially as a way to highlight the possible errors in which forensic evidence could result. This suggests that, when forensic evidence is present, that defense attorneys are changing their practices to focus more time and effort into dismantling the CSI Effect among jurors.

It is apparent that all parties, regardless of legal "side", are seeking out and discussing as much forensic evidence from the crime scene as possible, albeit for different purposes. It is also clear that this is taking place regardless of what other, non-scientific evidence is available. This implies that, not only are jurors devaluing non-scientific evidence (Alldredge, 2015; Harvey & Derksen, 2009; Hawkins & Scherr, 2018; Ling et al., 2021; Maeder & Corbett, 2015; Robbers, 2008; Sutton & Byrd, 2017), but legal and criminal justice professionals are as well. As a result of the belief that forensic evidence is necessary to meet the demands of the jury, gathering forensic evidence has taken priority over gathering other types of circumstantial evidence. This has a clear impact on resources: instead of using resources to source witness statements or background information on potential suspects, those resources are being re-directed towards collecting and testing scientific evidence. This means that forensic laboratories require more employees to complete the increased demand in testing and that police departments require more crime scene investigators to meet the increased demand to collect evidence to test. As a result, some argue that the CSI Effect is a major contributor to the significant backlog that exists at forensic labs across the U.S (Scanlan & Morreale, 2018). That, without the increased demand for forensic evidence for jurors, and without the police, prosecution, and defense trying to meet that demand, the backlog would not exist nor would it be as exacerbated as it is.

More commonly, however, forensic evidence is either not found at the scene or the evidence lacks definitive conclusions. In these situations, practices within the trial change in order to mitigate the jurors' expectations that forensic evidence will be presented. Prosecutors have reported, in the absence of forensic evidence, spending more time explaining to jurors why that forensic evidence is missing and/or is not relevant to the case at hand (Durnal, 2010; Maricopa County Attorney's Office, 2005). Prosecutors report achieving this through bringing in negative witnesses, who are expert witnesses who are brought in to explain the absence (as opposed to the presence) of evidence (Cather, 2004; Hansen, 2005; Maricopa County Attorney's Office, 2005; Robbers, 2008; Wise, 2010). These witnesses are put on the stand to discuss the prevalence of certain types of evidence from certain types of crime scenes, why forensic evidence was not found at the crime scene, and/or why forensic evidence would not be probative in the given case. Prosecutors achieve this by asking the witness questions about the appropriate applications and methods of forensic science and discussing the differences between the reality of forensic science and forensic science portrayed on television (Durnal, 2010; Robbers, 2008). For example, in Hennepin, MN, prosecutors report explaining to jurors that, unlike in crime shows on television, DNA is not required for a conviction and forensic evidence is not always indicative of conclusive proof of guilt or innocence (Stevens, 2008). Additionally, prosecutors report asking judges to modify jury instructions for cases in which there is no forensic evidence presented. These instruction modifications usually request that the jurors be instructed that the burden of proof not be informed by expectations gained from television (Hansen, 2005) and/or that the lack of forensic evidence or testing of that evidence not be held against the prosecution (Kinsey, 2012). This suggests that, when forensic evidence is present, prosecutors are engaging in practices aimed towards dismantling the CSI Effect in jurors. The defense, similarly, report spending more time discussing the lack of forensic evidence, but their aim is to highlight why it is necessary to present that forensic evidence (Durnal, 2010; Hansen, 2005). Therefore, when forensic evidence is absent, defense attorneys are using the potential impact of the CSI Effect to their advantage and using tactics to perpetuate it.

Regardless of the presence of forensic evidence in the trial, both prosecutors and defense attorneys have reported spending a significant amount of time trying to limit the impact of the CSI Effect through *voir dire*, or the process through which the jurors for a trial are selected (Cather, 2004; Durnal, 2010; Hansen, 2005; Kinsey, 2012; Maricopa County Attorney's Office, 2005; Robbers, 2008). During *voir dire*, both sets of lawyers ask questions of potential jurors to highlight any potential bias that may impact the jurors' abilities to be impartial in their listening to the evidence, interpreting that evidence, and coming to a decision regarding guilt as a result. When it comes to concerns regarding mitigating the impact of the CSI Effect, lawyers from the prosecution and defense have reported spending more time asking potential jurors additionally about their television watching habits and their beliefs about the accuracy of those television portrayals (Maricopa County Attorney's Office, 2005; Robbers, 2008). How a potential juror answers those questions then determines whether they should be kept on or struck from the jury, just as they would be based on other types of more typical biases that lawyers ask about in *voir dire*. The goal here is to mitigate the impact of the CSI Effect (i.e., the jurors' expectations that forensic evidence will be presented in the trial) before the trial even starts.

Overall, clearly those in the criminal justice and legal systems are significantly concerned about the potential impacts of the CSI Effect and are increasingly modifying their behavior to combat it. Both prosecutors as well as defense attorneys report changing their *voir dire* approach and questioning as well as their witness lists in order to ensure that jurors' expectations are met or, when they cannot be met, explained appropriately. As a result, prosecutors and defense attorneys argue that they can ensure that the legal and criminal justice systems are not producing inaccurate results in their cases.

Changes in Policy

Despite the many changes that prosecutors and defense attorneys have reported making in order to mitigate the impact of the CSI Effect, only a few jurisdictions have implemented these practice changes as administrative policies. However, practitioners have suggested additional policy implementations as the potential be-all-end-all solutions to the CSI Effect.

On the state level, Illinois, Arizona, and California have formally implemented policy that allows for and encourages the use of negative witnesses (Stevens, 2008; Kinsey, 2012). The policy states that these negative witnesses should be used in cases in which forensic evidence is not available. As a result, the goal of the testimony of these witnesses would be to inform the jury why forensic evidence is missing and why it is not unusual for forensic evidence not to be found at a crime scene (Stevens, 2008; Kinsey, 2012). This is a mitigation strategy in which jurors are given credible information to combat their unrealistic expectations of forensic evidence. Therefore, when the jury leaves the courtroom to deliberate, they can rely on the evidence of the negative witness to eliminate any doubt that is relevant to the absence of forensic evidence. Additionally, by explaining why forensic evidence was unnecessary, the jury can then focus more accurately and appropriately on the other types of evidence that were presented in the case.

On the jurisdiction level, Maricopa County, Arizona is one of the few jurisdictions that have implemented a CSI Effect specific policy. In 2005, Maricopa County conducted a county-wise investigation into the impact of the CSI Effect in the jurisdiction. As a result of the investigation, the county made both policy changes and policy suggestions as a way to mitigate the impact of the CSI Effect (Maricopa County Attorney's Office, 2005). The changes boiled down to one major policy change that formally directed prosecutors to fully address the techniques used by defense attorneys who, they argue, use the CSI Effect to sway juries. Within that policy, prosecutors are instructed to achieve this goal through tactics within *voir dire*, opening and closing statements, and presentation of other evidence and testimony through negative witnesses. They argued that this policy was necessary because the defense tactics of questioning the work of investigators and pointing out the absence of forensic evidence was creating an imbalance in the criminal justice system that required addressing. Essentially, this policy dictates to prosecutors that (a) the CSI Effect is a serious issue, (b) the defense is taking advantage of it, and (c) it needs to be counteracted as pervasively as possible. As a result, this policy serves as a directive to all prosecutors in the jurisdiction to engage in as many practice changes as possible to ensure that the defense does not use the CSI Effect to their advantage. This has implications on resources, both human and financial, as these changes require extra time for the prosecutor as well as extra money to pay the negative witnesses, should one be brought into court. While there has been no follow-up investigation to determine the effectiveness of this policy implementation, it is clear that Maricopa

County has invested a significant amount of its resources in combatting any anti-prosecutorial impact of the CSI Effect.

While there are few formal policies that are CSI Effect specific currently implemented within the criminal justice and legal systems, practitioners argue for a number of additional policies to combat jurors' unrealistic expectations of forensic evidence. Within the courtroom, practitioners have argued that there should be standard jury instructions that dictate that outside standards like those portrayed on television crime shows are not applicable to real-life court cases (Maricopa County Attorney's Office, 2005). While these types of changes to jury instructions have been implemented in individual cases (as discussed in Hansen, 2005; Kinsey, 2012), the practitioners argue that including these instructions in the standard jury instructions in every case provides wide-reaching protection from the CSI Effect. This type of policy would address the potential impact of the CSI Effect in all cases, even if television habits were not addressed in *voir dire* and regardless of whether forensic evidence was presented in the case or not. As a result, practitioners argue that it could serve as an all-encompassing mitigation strategy for the case.

Outside of the courtroom, practitioners argue that jurors' unrealistic perceptions of forensic evidence could be addressed at the source: the crime shows themselves. Practitioners argue that crime shows should be required to provide a disclaimer at the start of each of the show's episodes highlighting the potential for inaccuracies to be portrayed throughout the show (Maricopa County Attorney's Office, 2005). This disclaimer would highlight the dramatization and poetic license used when portraying real-world systems and their interaction with science. Consequently, this would essentially provide potential jurors with appropriate expectations from the beginning of the show instead of allowing them to come to their own (inaccurate) conclusions about the legal and criminal justice systems. Practitioners also argue that crime shows should be required to highlight the process and outcome of the CSI Effect in their storylines (Maricopa County Attorney's Office, 2005). The argument here is that, if potential jurors see the impact of the CSI Effect from the source of the CSI Effect, then they will be less likely to engage in the process of the CSI Effect themselves. Essentially, jurors would be learning about the errors inherent in the CSI Effect and therefore, act in accordance with the opposite of the modeled behavior. Obviously, these policy changes would require cooperation from television producers and their backing companies which so far have yet to acknowledge the CSI Effect as an issue that they contribute to.

While the implementation of CSI Effect specific policy is rare, it is evident that, given a continuation of the belief that the CSI Effect is negatively impacting the operations of the criminal justice and legal systems, it could become more common. Should currently implemented policies be shown to be effective in eliminating the perceived impacts of the CSI Effect, it is likely that more jurisdictions will move to implement similar measures.

Conclusion

With the proliferation of the crime drama genre, crime shows have become more popular and potentially more influential than ever. Consequently, concern regarding the CSI Effect has become more pronounced as well. While there is little doubt that viewers of crime shows are learning inaccurate information regarding forensic evidence and incorporating it into their knowledge frameworks, it is still up for debate as to whether that knowledge is impacting their behavior. It is very evident, however, that those in the legal and criminal justice professions are convinced of the CSI Effect's impact and are actively changing their practices to mitigate its impact. Both prosecutors and defense attorneys are modifying their approaches to jury selection as well as to which witnesses they will bring to court. A few jurisdictions are implementing changes in practice as policies for all lawyers under the jurisdiction to follow. As a result, even if the CSI Effect as discussed here is not impacting juror behavior, it is absolutely impacting lawyers' behavior. Thus, even if it cannot be empirically and definitively determined whether the CSI Effect exists, its perceived existence is actively changing both the legal and criminal justice systems.

Acknowledgements

Significant appreciation goes to my graduate assistant, Samantha Holder, whose efforts to organize and update my wide collection of literature relevant to this chapter allowed me to put this together as effectively and efficiently as possible.

References

Alderden, M., Cross, T.P., Vlajnic, M., & Siller, L. (2018). Prosecutors' perspectives on biological evidence and injury evidence in sexual assault cases. *Journal of Interpersonal Violence*, 36(7–8), 3880–3902. https://doi.org/10.1177/0886260518778259

Alejo, K. (2016). The CSI effect: Fact or fiction? *Themis: Research Journal of Justice Studies and Forensic Science*, 4(1), 1–20. https://doi.org/10.31979/THEMIS.2016.0401

Alldredge, J. (2015). The "CSI effect" and its potential impact on juror decisions. *Themis: Research Journal of Justice Studies and Forensic Science*, 3(1), 114–125. https://doi.org/10.31979/themis.2015.0306

Bandura, A. (2001). Social cognitive theory of mass communications. In J. Bryant, & D. Zillman (Eds.). *Media effects: Advances in theory and research* (2nd ed., 121–153). Hillsdale, NJ: Lawrence Erlbaum.

Baskin, D.R., & Sommers, I.B. (2010). Crime-show-viewing habits and public attitudes toward forensic evidence: The "CSI effect" revisited. *Justice System Journal*, 31(1), 97–113. https://doi.org/10.1080/0098261x.2010.10767956

Biju, A., Hambly, K., & Joshi, A. (2021). The complexity of forensic science in criminal investigations: Is there a gold standard? In M. Clayton & N. Abbas (Eds.), *Voices of forensic science* (pp. 7–26). University of Toronto Mississauga.

Brickell, W. (2008). Is it the CSI effect or do we just distrust juries? *Criminal Justice*, 23(2), 10–17.

Byers, M., & Johnson, V.M. (2009). *The CSI effect: Television, crime, and governance*. Lexington Books.

Cather, K.H. (2004). The CSI effect: Fake TV and its impact on jurors in criminal cases. *Prosecutor*, 38(9), 9–15.

Chin, J.M., & Ibaviosa, C.M. (2022). Beyond CSI: Calibrating public beliefs about the reliability of forensic science through openness and transparency. *Science & Justice*, 62(3), 272–283. https://doi.org/10.1016/j.scijus.2022.02.006

Chin, J. & Workewych, L. (2016). The CSI effect. In M. Dubber (Ed.), *Oxford handbooks online* (pp. 2–39). Oxford University Press. http://dx.doi.org/10.2139/ssrn.2752445

Cole, S.A. (2015). A surfeit of science: The "CSI effect" and the media appropriation of the public understanding of Science. *Public Understanding of Science*, 24(2), 130–146. https://doi.org/10.1177/0963662513481294

Cole, S.A., & Dioso-Villa, R. (2007). CSI and its effects: Media, juries, and the burden of proof. *New England Law Review*, 41(3), 435–470.

Cole, S.A., & Dioso-Villa, R. (2021). Should judges worry about the "CSI" effect? *Court Review*, 47, 16–27.

Cole, S.A. & Porter, G. (2017). The CSI effect. In Q. Rossy, D. Décary-Hétu, O. Delémont, & M. Mulone (Eds.), *The Routledge international handbook of forensic intelligence and criminology* (pp. 112–124). Routledge. https://www.routledgehandbooks.com/doi/10.4324/9781315541945-10

Cooley, C.M. (2007). The CSI Effect: Its impact and potential concerns. *New England Law Review*, 41, 471–501.

Davis, B.K., & Brooke, E.J. (2021). Making better offenders? Exploring the perception of the CSI effect among college students. *Journal of Criminal Justice Education*, 32(4), 446–463. https://doi.org/10.1080/10511253.2021.1912128

Durnal, E.W. (2010). Crime scene investigation (as seen on TV). *Forensic Science International*, 199(1–3), 1–5. doi:10.1016/j.forsciint.2010.02.015

Eatley, G., Hueston, H.H., & Price, K. (2016). A meta-analysis of the CSI effect: The impact of popular media on jurors' perception of forensic evidence. *Politics, Bureaucracy, and Justice*, 5(2), 1–10.

Ewanation, L.A., Yamamoto, S., Monnink, J., & Maeder, E.M. (2017). Perceived realism and the CSI-effect. *Cogent Social Sciences*, 3(1), 1–13. https://doi.org/10.1080/23311886.2017.1294446

Fedorek, B. (2015). "I want to be like the police on CSI": Does crime-related television impact perceptions of police and investigative procedures? *International Journal of Education and Social Science*, 2(1), 1–16.

Forensic Science Initiative. (2011). *Project FORESIGHT Annual Report, 2011–2012*. Morgantown, WV: College of Business & Economics, West Virginia University.

Retrieved from https://business.wvu.edu/files/d/0e133632-0c47-4d65-8f0a-6d493f0ba6d1/fy2012examplereport-1.pdf.

Gerbner, G., Gross, L., Morgan, M., & Signorielli, N. (1980). The "mainstreaming" of America: Violence profile no. 11. *Journal of Communication*, *30*, 10–29.

Ghoshray, S. (2006). Untangling the CSI effect in criminal jurisprudence: Circumstantial evidence, reasonable doubt, and jury manipulation. *New England Law Review*, *41*, 533–562.

Groscup, J. (2015). Media and the law. In B.L. Citler & P.A. Zapf (Eds.), *APA handbook of forensic psychology: Criminal investigation, adjudication, and sentencing outcomes*. American Psychological Association. http://dx.doi.org/10.1037/14462-011

Hansen, M. (2005). The uncertain science of evidence. *ABA Journal*. Retrieved from www.abajournal.com/magazine/article/the_uncertain_science_of_evidence

Harvey, E., & Derksen, L. (2009). Science fiction or social fact?: An exploratory content analysis of popular press reports on the CSI effect. In M. Byers & V. Johnson (Eds.), *The CSI Effect: Television, Crime, and Governance*. (pp. 3–28). Lexington Books.

Hawkins, I., & Scherr, K. (2017). Engaging the CSI effect: The influences of experience-taking, type of evidence, and viewing frequency on juror decision-making. *Journal of Criminal Justice*, *49*(1), 45–52. https://doi.org/10.1016/j.jcrimjus.2017.02.003

Hawkins, I., & Scherr, K. (2018). Corrigendum to "Engaging the CSI effect: The influences of experience-taking, type of evidence, and viewing frequency on juror decision-making". *Journal of Criminal Justice*, *57*, 126. https://doi.org/10.1016/j.jcrimjus.2018.03.002

Holmgren, J.A., & Fordham, J. (2011). The CSI effect and the Canadian and the Australian jury, *Journal of Forensic Sciences*, *56*(1), 63–71. https://doi.org/10.1111/j.1556-4029.2010.01621.x

Houck, M.M. (2006). CSI: Reality. *Scientific American*, *295*(1), 84–89.

Hui, C.Y., & Lo, T.W. (2015). Examination of the "CSI effect" on perceptions of scientific and testimonial evidence in a Hong Kong Chinese sample. *International Journal of Offender Therapy and Comparative Criminology*, *61*(7), 819–833. https://doi.org/10.1177/0306624x15611874

Kim, Y.S., Barak, G., & Shelton, D.E. (2009). Examining the "CSI-effect" in the cases of circumstantial evidence and eyewitness testimony: Multivariate and path analyses. *Journal of Criminal Justice*, *37*(5), 452–460. https://doi.org/10.1016/j.jcrimjus.2009.07.005

Kinsey, C.L. (2012). CSI: From the television to the courtroom. *Virginia Sports and Entertainment Law Journal*, *11*(2), 313–361.

Klentz, B.A., Winters, G.M., & Chapman, J.F. (2020). The CSI effect and the impact of DNA evidence on mock jurors and jury deliberations. *Psychology, Crime & Law*, *26*(6), 552–570. https://doi.org/10.1080/1068316x.2019.1708353

Lam, A. (2015). Televisual waiting: Images of time and waiting in CSI. *Time & Society*, *27*(3), 275–294. https://doi.org/10.1177/0961463x15604517

LaRose, A.P. & Maddan, S. (2016) Crime in primetime: The CSI effect and student expectations. *National Social Science Journal*, *46*(2), 48–60.

Ley, B.L., Jankowski, N., & Brewer, P.R. (2012). Investigating CSI: Portrayals of DNA testing on a forensic crime show and their potential effects. *Public Understanding of Science, 21*(1), 51–67. https://doi.org/10.1177/0963662510367571

Ling, S., Kaplan, J., & Berryessa, C.M. (2021). The importance of forensic evidence for decisions on criminal guilt. *Science & Justice, 61*(2), 142–149. https://doi.org/10.1016/j.scijus.2020.11.004

Lodge, C., & Zloteanu, M. (2020). Jurors' expectations and decision-making: Revisiting the CSI effect. *The North of England Bulletin, 2020*(2), 19–30.

Maeder, E.M., & Corbett, R. (2015). Beyond frequency: Perceived realism and the CSI effect. *Canadian Journal of Criminology and Criminal Justice, 57*(1), 83–115. https://doi.org/https://doi.org/10.3138/cjccj.2013.E44

Mancini, D.E. (2011). The CSI effect reconsidered: Is it moderated by need for cognition? *North American Journal of Psychology, 13*(1), 155–174.

Mancini, D.E. (2013). The "CSI effect" in an actual juror sample: Why crime show genre may matter. *North American Journal of Psychology, 15*(3), 543–564.

Maricopa County. (2005). The CSI Effect and its real-life impact on justice: A study by the Maricopa County Attorney's Office (June 30, 2005). Retrieved from www.maricopacountyattorney.org/Press/PDF/CSIReport.pdf.

National Academy of Sciences. (2009). *Strengthening Forensic Science in the United States: A Path Forward.* Washington, DC: National Academies Press

Nolan, T. W. (2007). Depiction of the "CSI" effect in popular culture: Portrait in domination and effective affection. *New England Law Review, 41*, 575–589.

Podlas, K. (2017). The "CSI effect." *Oxford Research Encyclopedia of Criminology and Criminal Justice,* 1–20. https://doi.org/10.1093/acrefore/9780190264079.013.40

Pratt, T.C., Gaffney, M.J., Lovrich, N.P., & Johnson, C.L. (2006). This isn't CSI: Estimating the national backlog of forensic DNA cases and the barriers associated with case processing. *Criminal Justice Policy Review, 17*(1), 32–47. https://doi.org/10.1177/0887403405278815

Preuß, S. & Labudde, D. (2022). A pipeline for analysing image and video material in a forensic context with intelligent systems. *Informatik, 2022,* 109–118. https://doi.org/10.18420/inf2022_09

Ribeiro, G., Tangen, J.M., & McKimmie, B.M. (2019). Beliefs about error rates and human judgment in forensic science. *Forensic Science International, 297*(1), 138–147. https://doi.org/10.1016/j.forsciint.2019.01.034

Robbers, M.L. (2008). Blinded by science: The social construction of reality in forensic television shows and its effect on criminal jury trials. *Criminal Justice Policy Review, 19*(1), 84–102. https://doi.org/10.1177/0887403407305982

Scanlan, T.P. & Morreale, S.A. (2018). Influence of CSI effect, Daubert ruling, and NAS report on forensic science. *International Journal of Education and Social Science, 5*(2), 48–61.

Schanz, K., & Jones, E.E. (2023). The impact of media watching and victim gender on victim and offender blameworthiness and punishment. *Violence Against Women,* online ahead of print. https://doi.org/10.1177/10778012231170862

Schanz, K., & Salfati, C.G. (2016). The CSI effect and its controversial existence and impact: A mixed methods review. *Crime Psychology Review, 2*(1), 60–79. https://doi.org/10.1080/23744006.2016.1260276

Schweitzer, N.J., & Saks, M.J. (2007). The CSI effect: Popular fiction about forensic science affects the public's expectations about real forensic science. *Jurimetrics*, 47(3), 357–364.

Shelton, D.E. (2010). Juror expectations for scientific evidence in criminal cases: Perceptions and reality about the "CSI effect" myth. *Thomas M. Cooley Law Review*, 27(1), 1–35.

Shelton, D.E., Kim, Y.S., & Barak, G. (2007). A study of juror expectations and demands concerning scientific evidence: Does the CSI effect exist? *Vanderbilt Journal of Entertainment and Technology Law*, 9(2), 331–368.

Shelton, D.E., Kim, Y.S., & Barak, G. (2009). An indirect-effect model of mediated adjudication: The CSI myth, the tech effect, and metropolitan jurors' expectations for scientific evidence. *Vanderbilt Journal of Entertainment and Technology Law*, 12(1), 1–43.

Smith, S.M., Patry, M.W., & Stinson, V. (2007). But what is the CSI effect? How crime dramas influence people's beliefs about forensic evidence. *The Canadian Journal of Police & Security Services*, 5(3–4), 187–195.

Stephens, S.L. (2007). The "CSI effect" on real crime labs. *New England Law Review*, 41, 591–607.

Stevens, D.J. (2008). Forensic science, wrongful convictions, and American prosecutor discretion. *The Howard Journal of Criminal Justice*, 47(1), 31–51. https://doi.org/10.1111/j.1468-2311.2008.00495.x

Stinson, V., Patry, M. W., & Smith, S. M. (2007). The CSI effect: Reflections from police and forensic investigators. *The Canadian Journal of Police & Security Services*, 5(3–4), 125–133.

Sutton, L., & Byrd, J. (2017). CSI culture: The evolution and influences of forensic science. *Forensic Research & Criminology International Journal*, 4(3), 76–77. https://doi.org/10.15406/frcij.2017.04.00112

Tyler, T.R. (2006). Viewing CSI and the threshold of guilt: Managing truth and justice in reality and fiction. *The Yale Law Journal*, 115(5), 1050–1085. https://doi.org/10.2307/20455645

Wise, J. (2010). Providing the CSI treatment: Criminal justice practitioners and the CSI effect. *Current Issues in Criminal Justice*, 21(3), 383–399. https://doi.org/10.1080/10345329.2010.12035856

17 Is Facial Recognition Software a Solution to the Negative Effects of Social Media on Eyewitness Testimony?

Heather M. Kleider-Offutt and Beth B. Stevens

This chapter investigates the impact of social media on (1) eyewitness memory, (2) trial outcomes in criminal cases, (3) novice investigators "websleuthing," and (4) police investigations. Face recognition software is a potential solution to some of the memory contamination issues that plague human memory, but it is not infallible. The advantages and disadvantages of technology-based suspect searching and related ethical issues for legal system policy are discussed.

Background and Eyewitness Memory

The Innocence Project has facilitated the release of over 300 people falsely convicted (Innocence Project, n.d.). Eyewitness misidentification is found to be a contributing factor in over 70% of these known wrongful conviction cases. Mistaken identification is rooted in the fact that human memory is malleable, it updates with new information, regardless of how salient or traumatic the to-be-remembered event may be (Albright, 2017; Morgan et al., 2012; Wixted et al., 2016). This is an adaptive feature of the memory system but works against recalling specific detailed information from an episode along with the source of the information (Chan et al., 2012; Gordon & Thomas, 2017; Paterson et al., 2011).

The scientific community and legal experts have published best practices policy papers to inform law enforcement and triers-of-fact about the nuances of memory contamination (Department of Justice Programs, 2017; Smalarz & Wells, 2015; Wells et al., 2020). These papers focus on systems variables, which are procedures within the legal system that can influence the validity and reliability of eyewitness memory (Wells, 1978). Some of these variables include interview techniques that avoid leading questions, lineup procedures that are fair to the suspect, and ensuring that there is substantial evidence to warrant putting a photo in a lineup (Wells et al., 2020). The later new addition is related to media searches. Law enforcement may have the idea that someone was involved in a crime or, based on a social media search, a witness is led to believe that someone found in the search was involved. However, these hunches or suspicions without other evidence serve to "muddy the waters" when trying to ensure photos of people presented for lineup identification are connected to the crime—once presented in a lineup, a witness cannot easily disconnect lineup presentation from assumptions of involvement in the crime.

The ubiquitous nature of social media and the seemingly immediate accessibility of almost any information, be it valid or not, has created a situation wherein law enforcement and triers-of-fact may be unsure of the source of reported information from eyewitnesses. The influence of extraneous information on eyewitness reports and police procedures, and juror decisions has been the focus of literature attempting to define and prevent memory error in a legal context (Frenda et al., 2011 for review; Wells, 2020; Wells & Quigley-McBride, 2016). The advent of social media has created a new set of issues in an attempt to thwart memory errors and maintain the integrity of legal system decisions.

Repeated Exposure Effect on Confidence and Accuracy

Recent research suggests that when a witness makes a lineup identification quickly (5 seconds or less is optimal) and with high confidence, that identification is more likely to be accurate than one made with less confidence and that is slower, even when tested on real eyewitnesses in police stations (Seale-Carlisle et al., 2019). This recent work builds upon earlier research that suggested a boundary of a few seconds "10–12 second rule" was more likely to indicate an accurate identification than slower identifications (Dunning & Perretta, 2002) but that other factors related to the crime context made the speed of identification more or less reliable (Weber et al., 2004). That is, confidence and accuracy are linked with the caveat that memory contamination has not occurred (Brewer & Wells, 2006; Wixted & Wells, 2017). Ultimately speed and confidence are indicators of the strength of the memory signal which is tied to how well the witness could record information into memory during the crime (Seale-Carlisle et al., 2019; Weber et al., 2004). This is important as crafting best practices policy needs to be something measurable and useable in a police station. Having a policy to video record the lineup procedure and indicate confidence at the time of selection, can be used to ascertain whether the witness remembers the perpetrator. For these indicators to be valid and useful, however, the witness' memory must be non-contaminated with post-crime information, which could influence the strength of the original memory signal.

For example, it is well established that if a witness peruses mugshot books and someone in the mugshots looks familiar, even if he is not the perpetrator, he now will be linked to the crime in the witness' memory; this is known as the mugshot commitment effect (Dysart et al., 2001). This also occurs when a witness is shown multiple lineups or the same lineup repeatedly, as witnesses may mentally commit to a person who is familiar from an earlier lineup (Dysart et al., 2001; Steblay & Dysart, 2016; Wixted & Mickes, 2022). Research suggests that multiple lineups contribute to memory confusion, however, social media searches create the same confusion, but unlike lineups and mugshot perusal that occur with police supervision, the searches are undocumented. The repeated presentation of a suspect creates mis-placed familiarity. Because the suspect was seen multiple times, increasing the familiarity with the suspect, witness confidence is bolstered that they are choosing the perpetrator when the familiar suspect is presented in the lineup. As such, using speed and confidence of the lineup identification as an indicator of accurate identification (of the perpetrator) is now invalid, as the familiarity is for the innocent suspect. Thus, a speed of response tool that could serve useful for law enforcement and triers-of-fact, does not serve its purpose when there is exposure to possible suspects, via any medium, post-crime (Dunning & Perretta, 2002; Wixted et al., 2015).

How can a witness not remember whom they saw at a crime? This relates to how well the original memory was recorded. If a witness sees a perpetrator for a brief period or under poor viewing conditions, the face of the perpetrator is not stored in memory with sufficient detail to be accurately remembered later (Vallano et al., 2019). If the original memory is poor, and the witness is shown a lineup without intervening information, the witness should calibrate their identification. Meaning, if they do not have a good memory of the perpetrator, they will either be unable to make an identification, or if they do make an identification, the confidence should be low, and indicative of the poor memory. This is how the confidence and speed indicator in lineup identification should work. Social media searches are especially damaging when the original memory is poor, and the witness should not make an identification, but the search "fills in" the memory with a potential face of a person who is later misidentified (Loftus, 2005; Smith, 2020; Smith et al., 2019). Alternatively, if the original memory for the perpetrator is retrievable, but becomes confused with memory for the searched innocent suspect, this misidentification is called a *source monitoring error* (Johnson et al., 1993). Both situations are problematic and occur when witness memory for the perpetrator is not distinct and tied to context.

Source Monitoring

When encountering new information, people, conversations, articles read, and events witnessed, the information becomes familiar. Familiarity is not specific to a live episode, it is more like knowing that something has been experienced before, but it is not tied to time, place or source (Haw et al, 2007; Johnson et al., 1993; Memon et al., 2002). Knowing that something is familiar can be a cue to a previous experience, or something can feel familiar because it is similar to something previously encountered but not the same. For example, when hiking the Grand Canyon for the first time, it feels familiar, as would retrieval of a memory, because it is similar to other canyons I have hiked, but there is no real memory of the Grand Canyon. Familiarity can also lead to source misattribution (Johnson et al., 1993; Memon et al., 2002). A legal-system example of source monitoring error is when a juror who is part of an ongoing trial, hears testimony from a witness about a gun present at the crime, and this juror is also following a blog online about the trial, and reads that there was no gun. Later, when weighing evidence during deliberation, if the juror recalls that the witness did not report a gun being present at the scene, that is a source monitoring error that has an applied consequence. The recalled information about the gun was attributed to the wrong source—the blog information was attributed to the witness testimony. Source error plays out as a misidentification when the witness misattributes the familiarity of the person seen in a social media search to the perpetrator in the lineup (Dysart et al., 2001; Steblay & Dysart, 2016; Wixted & Mickes, 2022).

Misinformation Effect

To fully understand the mechanisms behind source confusion based on familiarity, one should be versed in the classic *misinformation effect* (Loftus, 1979) wherein post-event information influences how an event is remembered, such that new information modifies the original memory. This highly replicated phenomenon is typically tested in stages:

1 Participants view an event or crime; this can be a video, slides or live.
2 After some delay, some misleading information is presented; this can be pictures of faces, lineups, or written information with changed details.
3 The participant tries to determine what was presented during stage 1; they recall event information or attempt lineup identification if they viewed a crime.

Participants often include information presented in stage 2 and are confident of this information. For example, if a participant saw a video of an armed robbery and read about details that were inconsistent with what they saw (misinformation), they tend to report the errant details as having come from the actual event; this is memory contamination. This error is more likely to occur when the original memory is weak due to memory fade, high emotion, poor lighting, and the misinformation is recent, people incorporate the new information into the poorly remembered original memory (Manning & Loftus, 1996). Because memory updates with new information, misinformation, or social media searches, are incorporated into memory for the original event. What can be done to guard against misinformation effects?

Best-practice procedures suggest that a witness should see at most one lineup, and the identification should be made as soon as possible after the event (Wixted et al., 2021). In this case, the lineup and the conditions are considered "pristine," meaning that the witness identification is likely based on their memory for the perpetrator rather than another source, and speed and confidence are indicators of accuracy (Wixted et al., 2021). However, making this happen in a real-world situation is difficult as lineup identification is often delayed until a suspect can be identified, sometimes years, after the event (Brewer et al., 2019; for review see Gettleman et al., 2021).

Social Media as a Show-up

Moreover, other aspects of the lineup identification that are in place to protect the suspect from misidentification are compromised with social media searching. That is, a lineup that is considered fair, wherein all the photos match the description of the perpetrator, requires the witness to retrieve the memory of whom they saw at the crime and match that to the lineup pictures. When social media is searched, this is akin to a showup, wherein one person is presented to the witness, who then determines if that person is the perpetrator (Steblay et al., 2003). Showups are notoriously biased (Smith et al., 2017; Steblay et al., 2003; Wells et al., 2015), but are still used in some circumstances, such as when the suspect is apprehended quickly after the crime and/or is in close proximity to the crime scene. In these situations, the showup is conducted by police, rather than by a witness. Finding ways to shore up witness memory is essential not only for the triers-of-fact to know an identification is reliable, but also for juries, such that they can calibrate witness testimony when factors that degrade memory are present.

Efforts to ensure reliable witness memory are upended by social media. Checks and balances put in place to guard against memory contamination during the investigation process are not viable if witnesses can conduct their own search within minutes of a crime. By definition, finding a suspect via a social media search after a crime will be a more recent memory for the found "suspect" than who was seen at the crime. When put into a lineup, the picture of the searched suspect will likely result in a familiarity cue that can be interpreted as memory for the actual perpetrator. The *recency effect*, wherein newer information is easier to retrieve and thus interpreted as more familiar than older information, works against a witness's calibration of their retrieval cues (Butt et al., 2020). In a recent paper, Butt and colleagues (2020) found that when participants read information about the inaccuracy of eyewitness memory before watching a mock crime, they were less confident in their memory and reported fewer details about the crime than participants who were told that memory is accurate. This suggests that given information about memory fallibility or factors that influence memory accuracy, people will consider the weight they give to the reported event recollection (Butt et al., 2020). If witnesses or potential jurors are unaware of intervening information searches that took place post-crime, then details reported by the witness are likely to be considered valid.

Problems in the Courtroom

Whether or not a person is found guilty of a crime may hinge on eyewitness identification (Laney & Loftus, 2018). However, given the ease with which pictures of potential suspects are circulated, can triers-of-fact ever know whether a witness is basing their identification on memory for the perpetrator? It may be impossible. When procedures used by law enforcement are documented and follow protocol, all parties can review the process and evidence, and evaluate whether something occurred that influences the validity of the identification or reporting of case facts. Concern over consistent documentation and incomplete reporting of case-related information by witnesses, knowingly or not, has made it such that the legal system has lost control of identification procedures (Eisen et al., 2020).

Kleider-Offutt first became aware of this issue in 2015 when public defenders that she consulted with as an eyewitness identification expert, said that witnesses were doing searches of suspects which falsely implicated their clients. Moreover, in some cases the witnesses were not truthful about the extent or content of the searches.

Below are examples of court cases, from Dekalb county, Atlanta GA, wherein social media searches had a bearing on the trial's outcome.

Scenario 1

In a recent murder trial (— *vs Georgia*; 2022) involving several individuals in a drug-deal-gone-wrong, the local newspaper published an online story describing the crime, the location and showing a picture of the suspect two days after the crime. The story was easily searched online as it was associated with the name of the apartment complex where the crime took place. The only witness to the murder, was shown a lineup four months after the crime, the suspect's picture presented in the newspaper was also in the lineup—the suspect was identified by the witness with high confidence. Attorneys were concerned that the witness' memory was contaminated by the newspaper article and that regardless of who he remembered from the crime, he was biased to remember the online picture. However, the witness stated he did not conduct an online search, and without his admittance, memory contamination was not established. The defendant was convicted. It is noteworthy that the online presence of a person presented with a crime creates a bias in memory such that the person may be associated with negative information (Skorniko & Spellman, 2013; Dixon & Azocar, 2007). If the suspect was seen in an article about a murder and was later shown in a lineup, the witness may be biased in identifying him and may be confused by where the face was previously seen.

Similar cases and discussions with attorneys, motivated our recent publication wherein we tested the influence of negative social media context on memory for a crime scene, we manipulated whether the person in the social media feed was the perpetrator or innocent foil (Kleider-Offutt et al., 2021). We found that that after seeing an innocent person in a social media feed, regardless of the content, people were less likely to accurately identify the actual perpetrator when he was in the lineup, suggesting the social media had created memory confusion at identification (Figure 17.1 shows the study design). Although this study was lab-based without the typical delays encountered in an actual crime, participants were influenced by the social media presentation.

Scenario 2

In another murder case (— *vs Georgia*; 2016), during an apartment party, two guests who were attempting to make a drug deal, got into an altercation with the party host and shot him. The two accomplices immediately fled the scene. The party was well attended so several eyewitnesses conducted a social media search soon after the event took place. The witnesses were familiar with one of the perpetrators and used his identity to guide their search for the other accomplice. By the time the police arrived, the witnesses had identified a possible accomplice they did not identify/ see at the event or remember. Based on this speculation, the suspect was put in a lineup and identified by the witnesses. At trial, it was established that the search had led to the subsequent lineup identification rather than

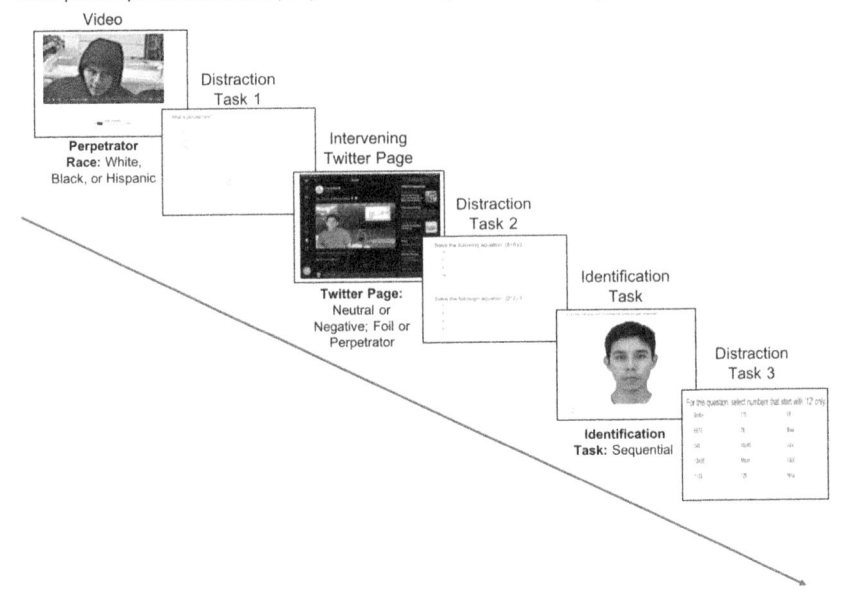

Figure 17.1 Example of eyewitness memory experimental design with intervening contextual information. Screen captures of the experimental progress/procedure of the study are show.

Source: Kleider-Offutt et al. (2021)

the witnesses remembering the suspect from the crime. In this case, the searched suspect was found not guilty on all counts.

These different cases are described to demonstrate that it is difficult to establish whether a witness has conducted a suspect search, and whether they will admit to the search. Once a witness has contaminated their memory for the perpetrator, the initial memory trace is tainted and unreliable (Loftus & Greene, 1980; Wells et al., 2005). The loss of control over identification procedures by law enforcement, when it comes to searches that confuse memory, makes it such that triers-or-fact, must do their due diligence to ascertain whether a search was conducted and, to the extent possible, determine the content of the search and explain to a jury why a search could be problematic.

Police Use of Social Media

Police departments use social media for a variety of reasons, including community relations and outreach, finding missing persons, Amber alerts, and communicating information about crime-related concerns, including crime solving (Walsh, 2020). Social media can be a vehicle for police departments to communicate with the community, build trust and rapport, and control their image via what information is released. This is considered positive for police departments, as officers generally feel that the news media can portray them negatively (Brodeur, 2010). Thus, police departments who use social media can interact directly with the community and avoid the filters imposed by information presented via news outlets. In addition, when police departments post on social media, they control the narrative, communicating crime related concerns while the news media may instill an unwarranted or exaggerated fear of crime for some individuals (Lieberman et al., 2013; Walsh, 2020). Crime solving efforts include posting be-on-the-look-out-for (BOLO) information and suspects related to specific crimes and related details. Law enforcement also use social media to cast a wide net when identifying suspects. Social media can be a powerful tool for law enforcement, assisting in broad communication to the community without media bias.

However, in the same way, that memory is contaminated by witnesses looking for suspects, law enforcement may similarly contaminate memory with a showup identification, as stated above, this occurs when social media photos of a possible suspect are shown without comparison faces that are present in a lineup (e.g., Smith et al., 2017) or several suspects may be pulled from social media and presented without corroborating evidence. Law enforcement also uses social media to identify suspects; in some instances, the alleged crime is posted along with the suspect's photo (Huey et al., 2013). Although this activity may be helpful in some cases, it also may bias public opinion of the alleged suspect's guilt before case facts are reviewed and contaminate the memory of potential witnesses (Ganga, 2021). One real-world example of using social media for disseminating information about crime-related events pre-maturely, was the highly publicized Boston Marathon bombing (see National Public Radio, 2016). Following the 2013 bombing, the FBI released a series of photographs of the suspect on multiple social media outlets. One user on Twitter falsely identified one of the suspects as Sunil Tripathi and spread this information on another popular social media site, Reddit (National Public Radio, 2016). Following this identification, the FBI later released the actual names of the suspects, and Sunil was not named. Even though Sunil Tripathi was never arrested or convicted of the Boston bombing, this instance does exemplify how disseminating information on social media by police departments can lead to false accusations that have the potential to turn into wrongful arrests and convictions (see National Public Radio, 2016). This taps into two psychological concepts related to memory retrieval.

Memory Plausibility and Conformity

When people in the community see that law enforcement have posted a picture of a suspect, along with crime details, the suspect is now associated with the crime in the mind of community members. Thus, it becomes plausible that this person committed the crime if he matches the original description of the perpetrator. For example, if police post the details of a drug-related crime along with possible suspects who are part of a gang known to be involved with drug dealing, the community may see the posted pictures as plausible suspects. In addition, posting the suspect's picture with crime details, suggests that the police believe he is the perpetrator (Eisen et al., 2020). It becomes difficult for police to gather remembered information from actual witnesses when they live in a community wherein case facts are openly discussed on social media. This is a similar scenario to what was described in the murder case earlier in the chapter, once the witness discusses information with their co-witnesses or community memory is contaminated with possible misinformation, the witness' memory for the perpetrator is no longer reliable (Skagerberg & Wright, 2008). Legislation is now being considered to prevent law enforcement from posting mugshots of suspects on social media as part of their suspect search (Cabanatuan, 2021).

In some scenarios, on a small scale, police use of social media can be an expedient way to locate a suspect without biasing witnesses. For example, if a witness reports that Joe, their neighbor, committed a robbery, police then have cause to search social media for incriminating social media posts that tie them to the crime. A picture of Joe then can be placed in a lineup for the witness to identify. Best practice policy suggests that before putting someone in a lineup, there must be evidence regarding their involvement (Wells et al., 2020). This is to guard against repeated exposure to an innocent person leading to misplaced familiarity and increasing the likelihood of a false identification (Wells et al., 2020).

What can Facial Recognition Software Bring to the Equation?

The rapid expansion of technology within recent years has granted police officers access to previously unavailable human biometric data using facial recognition software (FRS). While FRS is a highly tested system, and research has revealed that the majority of US adults view its use by police officers as beneficial when aiding missing person cases and identifying perpetrators of a crime (see Rainie et al., 2022), the established reliability of such biometric security systems is uncertain when considering the extant external factors it's accurate performance relies on, such as *estimator variables* (i.e., those variables/factors influencing accurate eyewitness performance that are not under the direct control of the criminal justice system, such as the stress of the eyewitness or lighting at the scene of the crime; see Wells, 1978) and human memory. Estimator variables influence the accuracy of human eyewitnesses such that people are better at identifying people of their own race, when the perpetrator is seen in daylight and from a close distance, and when a weapon is not present (Brigham et al., 2007; Kramer et al., 1990; Wells, 1978). However, whether these variables influence eyewitnesses and FRS in the same way is unclear. Witnesses remember what they attend to and accurately record into memory—a detailed initial memory bodes well for remembering that information later. Thus, a poor initial memory would not result in detailed information at retrieval. Whether FRS can return an accurate match despite poor stimuli quality (i.e., unclear surveillance footage) has not been tested. Potentially, FRS is vulnerable to the same encoding or perceptual challenges that befall eyewitnesses.

To test this idea, we conducted a study that established the reliability and accuracy of FRS compared to actual eyewitnesses when considering video clarity and perpetrator race—two estimator variables (Kleider-Offutt et al., under review). Eyewitnesses viewed a series of six crime videos that varied in video clarity (i.e., clear versus unclear) and race of perpetrator (i.e., White, Black, and Hispanic). After viewing each video, the eyewitnesses made perpetrator identifications while viewing a lineup containing 6 suspects, presented simultaneously. The performance of the eyewitnesses was then compared to that of a highly rated FRS. While the authors agreed to a non-disclosure agreement regarding the system's name (see Cino et al., 2022; Kleider-Offutt et al., under review), the FRS algorithm is one commonly utilized by security companies and the Department of Defense (see Cino et al., 2022; Kleider-Offutt et al., under review). It utilizes proprietary algorithms that have been submitted to the National Institute of Standards and Technology's (NIST) for accuracy testing (see Cino et al., 2022; Kleider-Offutt et al., under review), and operates using a one-to-many identification system that takes an unknown face and compares it to the databases of known faces to make an identification (US Government Publishing Office, 2020).

During the study, this FRS system was given the same videos and lineups as the eyewitnesses and tried to identify the target. Overall, results indicated that the discriminability and reliability of the FRS system was superior to that of eyewitnesses when considering perpetrator race and clarity of the video. Specifically, there was only one instance in which the FRS could not match the perpetrator (i.e., a White perpetrator, unclear video condition). On the other hand, the human eyewitnesses made misidentifications 23% of the time across all video condition trials and only made correct identifications 39% of the time. It is noteworthy that while the FRS did not correctly match the perpetrator in the one video condition, it did not provide a false identification of an innocent suspect. The eyewitnesses, however, misidentified an innocent suspect 14% of the time during this video condition. This suggests an even greater accuracy of the FRS as the program did not make a false identification when it could not discern the perpetrator of the crime. The eyewitnesses, however, still attempted to identify the perpetrator and made a false identification 14% of the time (Kleider-Offutt et al., under review).

Given that the first study served as a control to establish how FRS performs when given the same parameters as eyewitnesses wherein, they both were only given 6 individuals to make an identification from for each video, a follow-up study was conducted to test the accuracy of the FRS when given an additional 10,000 foil/filler faces. This follow-up study allowed us to establish the accuracy of FRS given more real-world parameters, as when police officers utilize FRS to make suspect identifications; the FRS searches for a match within a more extensive database that contains thousands of facial images. Results revealed that the software returned similar matches as in Study 1 and only misidentified innocent individuals in the unclear video condition containing the Hispanic perpetrator (Kleider-Offutt et al., under review). The follow-up results suggested that the FRS still performs well when given real-world parameters to search for suspects within a very large database.

However, in one instance wherein the video quality was poor, and the perpetrator was Hispanic, the software returned seven possible matches that were not the perpetrator (Kleider-Offutt et al., under review). While the person conducting the FRS search (typically a police officer) would make the final decision about whether the returned identification matches were of the actual perpetrator, the fact that the software returned possible misidentifications when the video quality was poor, and the perpetrator was Hispanic, raises a common concern with FRS about reliability for identification of people of color.

FRS systems are reported to perform less accurately when searching for the faces of Black individuals, females, and younger people. Research conducted by Klare and colleagues (2012) revealed that these inaccuracies based on race, age, and gender sometimes occur regardless of the amount of algorithm training an FRS system had. In some instances, proper algorithmic training can eliminate these disparities for inaccurate face recognition; however, regular testing of FRS is not required for law enforcement officials that use them (Bacchini & Lorusso, 2019). Therefore, there is no guarantee that the FRS algorithms are free of race, gender, and age biases.

Additionally, the current procedures required for FRS use guarantee that the possibility of human bias and error is never entirely removed. Like the procedures guiding the use of other forensic technologies, such as Automated Fingerprint Identification Systems (AFIS), results returned by an FRS are often reviewed by an individual (see Dror et al., 2011; Lynch, 2020). In some instances, a trained facial recognition expert may determine whether the matches returned by the system accurately identify the perpetrator. In the context of the criminal justice system, however, police officers or FBI agents are often the ones reviewing the system results (for example, see Hamann & Smith, 2019; Lynch, 2020). While research has yet to address how accurately officers can evaluate the returned FRS matches, research has suggested that human error is not eliminated when forensic machine technology, such as AFIS or FRS, is employed (see Dror et al., 2011). Human experts that evaluate human biometric and machine-based data can make false alarms that threaten the validity of the results (see Dror et al., 2011). Therefore, the accuracy of FRS identifications may depend upon how well the officer can evaluate the FRS results.

As such, three concerns surround the future and continued use of FRS in police proceedings. First, while some FRS systems utilize highly rated, trained, and tested algorithms, others do not. Results from our study do suggest the superior performance of a highly rated and tested software in comparison to actual eyewitnesses, but it is not guaranteed that every instance in which police officers formally utilize FRS has the benefit of a highly regarded system. It is also not certain that the FRS software can accurately match target faces from all racial and gender groups.

Secondly, regardless of the accuracy of the system's algorithm, the evidentiary and investigative use of facial recognition technology within the criminal justice system remains heavily unregulated, despite the racial disparities in its accurate identification (see Cino et al., 2022). Currently, rather than utilizing FRS instead of eyewitnesses, the two are applied in conjunction with one another during the initial investigation phase. Specifically, police officers utilize FRS to identify persons of interest that they include within the lineup. Eyewitnesses are then employed to view the lineup to confirm the identifications made by the FRS, and the eyewitnesses' identifications are provided as evidentiary support during the trial. This procedure is inherently problematic as it removes and directly avoids the admissibility concerns of FRS evidence during trials.

Additionally, this procedure reveals the final concern of utilizing FRS formally during an investigation, and that is, the accuracy of the FRS hinges on the accurate memory and recall of the human eyewitness. While relying on artificial intelligence systems to identify perpetrators for lineup construction alleviates some malleability issues, as noted above, the human factor of FRS is never entirely removed because officers review the FRS matches and make the final decision about which suspects to include in the lineup. Additionally, as described above, eyewitnesses are sometimes called to make the final lineup identification. As the current chapter has already established, human memory is susceptible to errors due to source monitoring, repeated exposure, and misinformation effects (Dysart et al., 2001; Loftus, 1979; Steblay & Dysart, 2016; Wixted & Mickes, 2022). Of additional concern is that when police utilize FRS to identify suspects and construct lineups, eyewitnesses may be aware of which suspects the FRS identified as a match (Jackson, 2019). This is problematic as it may lead to biasing of the eyewitness, wherein the eyewitness assumes the guilty suspect is within the lineup and consequently make a misidentification with high confidence. Moreover, given that our study (see Kleider-Offutt et al., under review) revealed that even a highly rated software makes misidentifications when the video quality is poor, and the perpetrator is a minority, it is possible for FRS to identify an innocent suspect as a match. In this situation an eyewitness may misidentify the innocent person because the suspect's appearance resembles the perpetrator.

Therefore, for law enforcement to successfully implement and reduce eyewitness misidentifications utilizing FRS systems in conjunction with traditional eyewitness procedures, policies will need to be developed and implemented by officers to ensure an uncontaminated identification made by the eyewitness when utilizing FRS. Additionally, proper regulations guiding its use will need to be implemented to ensure that police officers are utilizing highly rated FRS systems trained in recognizing and identifying different suspects that vary in physical characteristics. Thus, with proper training, FRS can be a tool to aid police in suspect identification.

Beyond FRS systems as a vehicle in suspect identification, is the untrained community member who tries to aid law enforcement in suspect identification helpful? It is unknown whether this novice involvement in technology-based identification gathering is an advantage or a hinderance to law enforcement.

Websleuthing and Community Policing

In September of 2021, the *New York Times* posted an article suggesting a group of "amateur detectives" aided in the national investigation of the recent sensationalized missing person case of Gabby Petito (Rosman, 2021). The article detailed how a well-known comedian and writer, Paris Campbell, utilized a popular networking site, TikTok, to disseminate information about the missing person case to help reunite Gabby with her family. Similarly, other news outlets reported instances wherein novice individuals documented, through YouTube, their attempts to canvas areas looking for Gabby's van and clues to aid officers in their investigation (Spencer, 2021). Widespread media reports suggested combined efforts of these individuals and others across various networking sites notably aided in the successful location of Gabby's vehicle and her bodily remains (Rosman, 2021; Salo, 2021; Spencer, 2021).

Even more recently, an American news broadcasting program, *Inside Edition*, reported on the November 2022 murders of four University of Idaho students. The report highlighted the story of one victim's sister, Aleiva Goncalves, who was conducting her own investigation in hopes of identifying her sister's murderer (Inside Edition, 2022). Notably, Goncalves discussed utilizing online platforms to access ring and security camera footage and delve into phone records to piece together the events preceding her sister's murder (Inside Edition, 2022). *Inside Edition* (2022) reported that Goncalves and others pursued their amateur investigations regarding the case because of the lack of answers provided by law enforcement to the public and the lack of an identified suspect.

The sensationalized efforts put forth by individuals across the web to aid in the Idaho and Gabby Petito investigations exemplify a newly and vastly emerging phenomenon known as *websleuthing,* wherein individuals take to social networking sites to assist police through amateur detective work by searching for case-related information, engaging in conversations regarding the case details, canvasing areas of interest, and even engaging in online communication with detectives (Yardley et al., 2018).

While research has revealed that individuals conduct most websleuthing practices with good intentions, most notably to achieve justice, assist victims and families of crime, and help police identify important information (see Yardley et al., 2018), as was the case in Idaho and Gabby Petito investigations, websleuthing is not immune to human fallibility and biases. Acts of websleuthing commonly fall prey to, and are plagued by, human expectations and biases (Huey et al., 2013; Nhan et al., 2015; Pantumsinchai, 2018; Yardley et al., 2018). Like the Boston Marathon bombing, following the 2015 Bangkok bombing, websleuths took to social media sites to identify the bomber(s) (Pantumsinchai, 2018). The websleuths wrongly named several individuals on various online platforms, but as in the Boston Marathon bombing case, the websleuths never correctly identified the bomber. While no innocent suspects were ever wrongfully arrested or convicted, in this case, or the Boston Marathon bombing, both represent the most concerning issues surrounding the practices of websleuthing. That is, improper websleuthing can hinder criminal investigations by releasing private information to the public and facilitating the misidentification of innocent suspects (Huey et al., 2013; Nhan et al., 2015).

Beyond suspect misidentifications, recent research has revealed a new area of concern surrounding websleuthing—the distribution of body-worn camera (BWC) footage is a possible memory contaminant that can lead to the public dissemination of biased information (Pezdek et al., 2022). In a recent study by Pezdek and colleagues (2022), police officers participated in a police-suspect interaction during a simulation of a domestic dispute. In a two-part experiment, officers were either not allowed to view their BWC footage, view it once, or view it multiple times following participation in the simulation. Results indicated that officers' memory for the event was altered after viewing their BWC footage as it facilitated (in most instances) more accurate memory recall for the simulated events. While the results do not suggest BWC footage facilitates inaccurate memory recall by officers, it does raise concerns about how perceptions of BWC footage may influence websleuthing efforts (Pezdek et al., 2022).

Specifically, the authors suggest that because officers wear BWC devices on their chests, the footage can provide a vastly different perspective than what the officers observe (Pezdek et al., 2022). For example, the footage may be angled in a way that does not reveal every event within the officer's line of sight. Additionally, camera footage may not capture emotional contexts or threats that inform the use of force by officers. Because legislation allows public access to BCW in some US states (see Reporters Committee, n.d.), and given that research has suggested the biggest activity websleuths engage in is analyzing content that can include BWC footage (see Yardley et al., 2018), it is possible websleuths may utilize BWC footage to inform the information they broadcast to the public regarding police-suspect interactions.

If websleuths analyze BWC footage that is high in quality and captures an accurate portrayal of the police and suspects' interactions, then the information disseminated based on the footage may rightfully inform the public's knowledge about the case. However, if the context of the provided footage is not high quality and provides an altered, inaccurate portrayal of the scene, websleuths may utilize the footage to unknowingly distribute biased and even false information regarding high-profile cases throughout Reddit communities and social networking sites. Websleuth dissemination of misinformation based on BWC footage is of great societal importance. It can hinder police investigations by casting doubt around police officers' intentions and may lead to mistrust of officers.

Before the rising popularity of social media, the biggest concern regarding the contamination of police investigations and criminal trials was juror access to pre-trial publicity through news media sites (see Bertrand, 2000; Steblay et al., 1999). Today this threat of pre-trial publicity has not been eliminated. Instead, jurors' access to pre-trial publicity has been further complicated by the actions of websleuths, as they have a reputation for facilitating the spread of biased and false information throughout online social-media communities before criminal trials or investigations take place (Frampton, 2022; Huey et al., 2013; Nhan et al., 2015). As a result, ensuring an uncontaminated juror pool is becoming increasingly more complicated.

Furthermore, websleuths spread of biased and false information has contributed to law enforcement officers' general mistrust of them and the information they bring forth (see Huey et al., 2013; Nhan et al., 2015). This developed mistrust, while sometimes warranted, can cause officers to dismiss information that may benefit criminal investigations. For instance, in 2006, one websleuth discovered evidence that a man, William Melchert-Dinkle, was utilizing online platforms to lure and aid individuals in suicide attempts (see Nhan et al., 2015). Police initially dismissed this evidence brought by the websleuth, but after the websleuth's continual investigation and attempts to inform the police, the websleuth led police to the rightful arrest of Melchert-Dinkle (Nhan et al., 2015).

The successful amateur investigations of the websleuths in the cases of Melchert-Dinkle and Gabby Petito for example, represent how technology can aid and benefit the criminal justice system. However, there have been similar instances, as seen in the Boston and Bangkok bombing incidents, in which websleuths' amateur attempts to aid in police investigations have hindered the investigative process. While the impact of this form of cyber-vigilantism is ambivalent, the rise of technology and the popularity of "true crime culture" almost guarantee that practices of websleuthing are not disappearing anytime soon. Therefore, moving forward, best practices must consider how officers can work in tandem with websleuths to ensure unbiased and unobstructed criminal investigations and criminal trials.

Ethical Considerations for the Future Use of Technological Advances by the Criminal Justice System

The widespread use of technology by the criminal justice system, has revealed several ethical concerns surrounding the privacy and protection of individuals.

First, beyond concerns of facilitating misidentifications, FRS allows biometric data use without consent. As already noted, FRS must be heavily trained and tested to perform accurately. This algorithm training requires the implementation of large datasets displaying facial stimuli in varying conditions (i.e., lighting, angles, and contexts; see Van Noorden, 2020). Individuals' faces may be easily obtained through various outlets (such as social media) and included within these databases for training FRS algorithms without the individual's knowledge. While some companies, such as Clearview AI, have noted that they only obtain photos in searches of publicly available data and information, other companies have utilized facial photographs from non-public data without consent (Van Noorden, 2020). For instance, the US-based social media site, Facebook, was recently sued in a class-action lawsuit wherein the Facebook administrators utilized non-publicly available facial stimuli from users without their consent in a tagging system powered by facial recognition technology (see Van Noorden, 2020). This class-action lawsuit raises an essential ethical consideration regarding the general use of FRS; Should facial recognition companies be allowed to utilize individuals' faces in FRS algorithm training without consent and when the data is not publicly available? Given this concern and the fact that police officers should utilize highly trained FRS algorithms to reduce innocent suspect misidentifications, the question then becomes how ethical the police utilization of FRS is when the large quantity of biometric data used to train the algorithm may or may not be obtained through proper consenting procedures.

Second, facial recognition technology used by police officers poses a threat to individuals belonging to marginalized and underrepresented groups. Specifically, Black individuals are disproportionately arrested and incarcerated in the US criminal justice system (see Bacchini & Lorusso, 2019). In fact, in the US, Black individuals are incarcerated at a rate five times more than that of White individuals (see Nellis, 2021). As a result of the disproportionate incarceration of Black individuals, Black men are overrepresented in facial recognition databases. This bolsters and reinforces the racial disparities within criminal justice because the overrepresentation of Black men within FRS databases results in increased true and false identifications (see Bacchini & Lorusso, 2019). Therefore, Black individuals may be more likely to be falsely identified simply due to their overrepresentation in FRS databases, regardless of the algorithm's accuracy.

Third, as already noted, there are no rules or guidelines concerning the regulation of FRS use by police officers; therefore, there are no protections in place to prevent the overrepresentation of Black men within these databases (see Bacchini & Lorusso, 2019). Police officers may utilize any FRS algorithm and any FRS database without concern for what demographic of individuals the algorithm was trained upon or includes. Given the potential for the reinforcement of systemic racial disparities based on biased FRS, the protection of marginalized individuals is of ethical concern when employing the use of FRS formally within the criminal justice system.

Fourth, the implementation of technology within the criminal justice system facilitates privacy violations, especially in the context of websleuthing. Many amateur websleuths participate in sleuthing practices because of the misconception that officers are not investigating their cases correctly or to their full ability (see Campbell, 2016). This misconception, however, is fueled by the time-consuming legal regulations that officers must formally follow during their investigations which creates a false perception that officers are not investigating or obtaining information quickly enough (Campbell, 2016). Given that websleuths utilize social media and chat platforms (see Yardley et al., 2018), the nature of these online communities is not always formally guided by the same legal regulations that officers are therefore, websleuths can obtain case and perpetrator information more freely than officers can in the absence of formal laws and regulations. This lack of websleuthing regulation highlights two ethical concerns regarding privacy. The first is that websleuths can share private information regarding individuals that would not reasonably be released to the public otherwise through a process known as *doxing* (see Merriam-Webster, n.d.). Websleuths exemplified this process of *doxing* during the 2017 Delphi murder case when Ron Logan was wrongly implicated in the murders of Libby German and Abby Williams based on Snapchat footage of the potential murder suspect. In this case, Websleuths used social media outlets to dox and shame Ron Logan, by releasing personal information about him online and providing information about him to law enforcement (see Ubiera, 2022; Wilkins, 2022). The second privacy concern surrounding websleuthing is that revealing private information may lead to safety concerns for various individuals. Yardley and colleagues (2018) suggest that websleuths utilize their practices to engage with suspects and even bait and lure them. Although only small percentages of sleuths participate in such activities, this generates safety concerns for the suspects and the websleuths. A lack of laws and regulations guiding sleuthing behavior does not prevent sleuths from accosting potential suspects, threatening the physical safety of all involved.

Based on these concerns, the future implementation of technology by the criminal justice system should ethically consider the consenting procedures in which facial recognition companies obtain their facial databases. Additionally, the justice system must consider how it can reasonably protect the privacy of individuals, given the rise of websleuthing practices. Finally, the justice system will need to implement protections for underrepresented groups to eliminate the disproportionate treatment of marginalized individuals, especially in the overlooked context of facial recognition technology.

Conclusion

The internet and social media have created a situation where law enforcement can access information quickly. Social media can offer a means for law enforcement to communicate with the community for public relations purposes and to disseminate information. With a highly rated FRS, rapid suspect identification is made possible via social media. However, there are disadvantages to a system that facilitates rapid and broad-reaching information, especially for suspect identification, wherein possible misidentifications and jury pool contamination can occur.

Given the malleability of memory and the tenuous nature of episodic retrieval of crime-related details, law enforcement must exercise caution about which information they disseminate to the community. Recent best practices guidelines (Department of Justice Programs, 2017; Wells et al., 2020) for police procedure suggest that physical evidence or other corroborating evidence must be established before including someone in a lineup; it is not sufficient to include someone in a lineup based on social media information alone. If these guidelines are used as a rule to disseminate information or create a lineup, this would mitigate some of the concern over misidentifications stemming from police communications. However, controlling what witnesses do on their own to search for suspects is beyond the control of law enforcement. Unfortunately, law enforcement and triers-of-fact must rely on the accuracy of the eyewitness to determine whether identifications are reliable, since witnesses are not obligated to adhere to procedures even if law enforcement asks them to avoid conducting their own suspect search. Technology has expanded the reach of suspect search activity and shows promise as a helpful tool in subsequent identification with the caveat that the lineup is "pristine" and witness memory is non-contaminated by post-event information.

Internet resources heighten active community interest in crime solving. Websleuthing allows the public to assist police in unearthing case facts or identifying possible suspects. However, this assistance is not always helpful and, in cases such as the Boston Bombing, can lead to the rapid dissemination of misinformation which is more deleterious to crime-solving than it is helpful. Moreover, the ethics and personal privacy of individuals are threatened by many aspects of crime-solving via the internet. People generally seem to be habituated to personal information and photos being widely dispersed, likely due to the ubiquitous nature of social media and one's level of activity on such sites. However, when law enforcement uses photos that one may consider private because they are posted on their social media page, or FRS is used to identify someone after accessing social media pictures, this raises the question of what is private? The court system will address this question as more cases use social media and FRS in suspect identification (Cino et al., 2022). Taken together, the internet is not going away; the legal system must create laws and procedures to reduce biased outcomes facilitated by social media, whether at the time of arrest or at the time of sentencing. In all segments of the legal system, professional guidelines for dealing with social media content is an essential next step.

References

Albright, T.D. (2017). Why eyewitnesses fail. *Proceedings of the National Academy of Sciences, 114*(30), 7758–7764. https://doi.org/10.1073/pnas.1706891114

Bacchini, F., & Lorusso, L. (2019). Race, again: How face recognition technology reinforces discrimination. *Journal of Information, Communication & Ethics in Society, 17*(3). https://doi.org/10.1108/JICES-05-2018-0050

Bertrand, C.J. (2000). *Media ethics and accountability systems.* Transaction Publishers.

Brewer, N., Weber, N., & Guerin, N. (2019). Police lineups of the future? *American Psychologist, 75,* 76–91. http://dx.doi.org/10.1037/amp0000465

Brewer, N., & Wells, G.L. (2006). The confidence-accuracy relationship in eyewitness identification: Effects of lineup instructions, foil similarity, and target-absent base rates. *Journal of Experimental Psychology: Applied, 12,* 11–30. https://doi.org/10.1037/1076-898X.12.1.11

Brigham, J.C., Bennett, L.B., Meissner, C.A., & Mitchell, T.L. (2007). The influence of race on eyewitness memory. In *The handbook of eyewitness psychology: Volume II* (pp. 271–296). Psychology Press.

Brodeur, J.P. (2010). *The policing web.* Oxford University Press.

Butt, M.M., Colloff, M.F., Magner, E., & Flowe, H.D. (2020). Eyewitness memory in the news can affect the strategic regulation of memory reporting. *Memory, 30*(6), 763–774. https://doi.org/10.1080/09658211.2020.1846750

Cabanatuan, M. (2021, July 24). Newsom signs bill banning police from posting mug shots of nonviolent suspects on social media. *San Francisco Chronicle.* Retrieved from www.sfchronicle.com/crime/article/Bay-Area-lawmaker-wants-to-keep-mugshots-of-16335621.php

Campbell, E. (2016). Policing paedophilia: Assembling bodies, spaces and things. *Crime, Media, Cultuer: An International Journal, 12*(3), 345–365. https://doi.org/10.1177/1741659015623598

Chan, J.C.K., Wilford, M.M., & Hughes, K.L. (2012). Retrieval can increase or decrease suggestibility depending on how memory is tested: The importance of source complexity. *Journal of Memory and Language, 67*(1), 78–85. https://doi.org/10.1016/j.jml.2012.02.006

Cino, J.G., Kleider-Offutt, H.M., Stevens, B.B., Albrecht, K., Evans, R., & Riedley, E. (2022). The oracle testifies: Facial recognition technology as evidence in criminal courtrooms. *University of Louisville Law Review, 61*(1).

Department of Justice Programs (2017). Eyewitness Identification: Procedures for Conducting Photo Arrays. Retrieved from www.justice.gov/archives/opa/press-release/file/923201

Dixon, T.L., & Azocar, C.L. (2007). Priming crime and activating Blackness: Understanding the psychological impact of the overrepresentation of Blacks as lawbreakers on television news. *Journal of Communication, 57*(2), 229–253. https://doi.org/10.1111/j.1460-2466.2007.00341.x.

Dror, I.E., Wetheim, M., Frazer-Mackenzie, P., & Walajtys, J. (2011). The impact of human-technology cooperation and distributed cognition in forensic science: Biasing effects of AFIS contextual information on human experts. *Journal of Forensic Science, 57*(2), 343–352. https://doi.org/10.1111/j.1556-4029.2011.02013.x

Dunning, D., & Perretta, S. (2002). Automaticity and eyewitness accuracy: A 10- to 12-second rule for distinguishing accurate from inaccurate positive identifications. *Journal of Applied Psychology, 87*(5), 951–962. https://doi.org/10.1037/0021-9010.87.5.951

Dysart, J.E., Lindsay, R.C.L., Hammond, R., & Dupuis, P. (2001). Mug shot exposure prior to lineup identification: Interference, transference, and commitment effects. *Journal of Applied Psychology, 86*(6), 1280–1284. https://doi.org/10.1037/0021-9010.86.6.1280

Eisen, M., Frenda, S., Jones, J. & Williams, T. (2020). How exposure to social media affects eyewitness memory. *The Champion, Jan/Feb*, 46. Retrieved from www.nacdl.org/Article/JanFeb2020-HowExposuretoSocialMediaAffectsEyewitne

Frampton, L. (2022). Paedophile hunters: Implications for police courts and probation. *British Journal of Community Justice, 18*(1), 59–72. https://doi.org/10.48411/dxzk-jw27

Frenda, S.J., Nichols, R.M., & Loftus, E.F. (2011). Current issues and advances in misinformation research. *Current Directions in Psychological Science, 20*(1), 20–23. https://doi.org/10.1177/0963721410396620

Ganga, M.L. (2021, June 29). Police take "wanted" posters onto social media, nabbing suspects and ruining lives. Los Angeles Times. Retrieved from www.latimes.com/california/story/2021-06-29/police-social-media-wanted-posts-help-cases-ruin-lives

Gettleman, J.N., Grabman, J.H., Dobolyi, D.G., & Dodson, C.S. (2021). A decision processes account of the differences in the eyewitness confidence-accuracy relationship between strong and weak face recognizers under suboptimal exposure and delay conditions. *Journal of Experimental Psychology: Learning, Memory, and Cognition, 47*(3), 402–421. https://doi.org/10.1037/xlm0000922.supp (Supplemental)

Gordon, L.T., & Thomas, A.K. (2017). The forward effects of testing on eyewitness memory: The tension between suggestibility and learning. *Journal of Memory and Language, 95*, 190–199. https://doi.org/10.1016/j.jml.2017.04.004

Hamann, K., & Smith, R. (2019). Facial recognition technology. *Criminal Justice, 34*(1), 9–13.

Haw, R.M., Dickinson, J.J., & Meissner, C.A. (2007). The phenomenology of carryover effects between show-up and line-up identification. *Memory, 15*(1), 117–127. https://doi.org/10.1080/09658210601171672

Huey, L., Nhan, J., & Broll, R. (2013). "Uppity civilians" and "cyber-vigilantes": The role of the general public in policing cyber-crime. *Criminology & Criminal Justice, 13*(1). https://doi.org/10.1177/1748895812448086

Innocence Project. (n.d.). Eyewitness memory reform. Retrieved from https://innocenceproject.org/eyewitness-misidentification/.

Inside Edition. (2022, November 18). Slain University of Idaho student's sister is searching for her killer herself. Inside Edition. Retrieved from www.insideedition.com/slain-university-of-idaho-students-sister-is-searching-for-her-killer-herself-78117?amp

Jackson, K. (2019, July). Challenging facial recognition software in criminal court. The Champion. Retrieved December 2, 2021, from www.nacdl.org/getattachment/548c697c-fd8e-4b8d-b4c3-2540336fad94/challenging-facial-recognition-software-in-criminal-court_july-2019.pdf.

Johnson, M.K., Hashtroudi, S., & Lindsay, D.S. (1993). Source monitoring. *Psychological Bulletin, 114*(1), 3–28. https://doi.org/10.1037/0033-2909.114.1.3

Klare, B.F., Burge, M.J., Klontz, J.C., Bruegge, R.W.V. and Jain, A.K. (2012). Face recognition performance: role of demographic information. *IEEE Transactions on Information Forensics and Security, 7*(6), 1789–1801. https://doi.org/10.1109/TIFS.2012.2214212

Kleider-Offutt, H.M., Stevens, B.B., & Capodanno, M. (2021). He did it! Or did I just see him on Twitter? Social media influence on eyewitness identification, *Memory*. https://doi.org/10.1080/09658211.2021.1953080

Kleider-Offutt, H.M., Stevens, B.B., & Cino, J.G. (under review). Who is the best eyewitness? A comparison of identification accuracy between human eyewitnesses and face recognition software. *Journal of Applied Research in Memory & Cognition*.

Kramer, T.H., Buckhout, R., & Eugenio, P. (1990). Weapon focus, arousal, and eyewitness memory. *Law and Human Behavior*, 14, 167–184. https://doi.org/10.1007/BF01062971

Laney, C., & Loftus, E.F. (2018). Eyewitness memory. In R.N. Kocsis (Ed.), *Applied criminal psychology: A guide to forensic behavioral sciences*, 2nd ed. (pp. 199–228). Charles C Thomas Publisher, Ltd.

Lieberman, J.D., Koetzle, D., & Sakiyama, M. (2013). Police departments' use of Facebook: Patterns and policy issues. *Police Quarterly*, 16(4), 438–462. https://doi.org/10.1177%2F1098611113495049

Loftus, E.F. (2005). Planting misinformation in the human mind: A 30-year investigation of the malleability of memory. *Learning and Memory*, 12, 361–366. 10.1101/lm.94705

Loftus, E.F. (1979). Reactions to blatantly contradictory information. *Memory & Cognition*, 7(5), 368–374. https://doi.org/10.3758/BF03196941

Loftus, E.F., & Greene, E. (1980). Warning: Even memory for faces may be contagious. *Law and Human Behavior*, 4, 323–334. https://doi.org/10.1007/BF01040624

Lynch, J. (2020). Face off: Law Enforcement use of face recognition technology. Electronic Frontier Foundation. Retrieved from www.eff.org/wp/law-enforcement-use-face-recognition

Manning, C.G., & Loftus, E.F. (1996). Eyewitness testimony and memory distortion. *Japanese Psychological Research*, 38(1), 5–13. https://doi.org/10.1111/j.1468-5884.1996.tb00003.x

Memon, A., Hope, L., Bartlett, J., & Bull, R. (2002). Eyewitness recognition errors: The effects of mugshot viewing and choosing in young and old adults. *Memory & Cognition*, 30(8), 1219–1227. https://doi.org/10.3758/BF03213404

Merriam-Webster. (n.d.). Dox. Retrieved November 27, 2022, from www.merriam-webster.com/dictionary/dox

Morgan, C.A., Southwick, S.M., Steffian, G., Hazlett, G., (2012). Misinformation can influence memory for recently experienced, highly stressful events. *International Journal of Law and Psychiatry*, 36(1). 10.1016/j.ijlp.2012.11.002

National Public Radio. (2016, April 18). How social media smeared a missing student as a terrorism suspect. Retrieved from www.npr.org/sections/codeswitch/2016/04/18/474671097/how-social-mediasmeared-a-missing-student-as-a-terrorism-suspect

Nellis, A. (2021, October 13). The color of justice: Racial and ethnic disparity in state prisons. The Sentencing Project. Retrieved from www.sentencingproject.org/reports/the-color-of-justice-racial-and-ethnic-disparity-in-state-prisons-the-sentencing-project/

Nhan, J., Huey, L., & Broll, R. (2015). Digilantism: An analysis of crowdsourcing and the Boston Marathon bombings. *British Journal of Criminology*, 57(2), 341–361. https://doi.org/10.1093/bjc/azv118

Pantumsinchai, P. (2018). Armchair detectives and the social construction of falsehoods: An actor-network approach. *Information, Communication, & Society*, 21(5), 761–778. https://doi.org/10.1080/1369118X.2018.1428654

Paterson, H.M., Kemp, R.I., & Ng, J.R. (2011). Combating co-witness contamination: Attempting to decrease the negative effects of discussion on eyewitness memory. *Applied Cognitive Psychology*, 25(1), 43–52. https://doi.org/10.1002/acp.1640

Pezdek, K., Shapland, T., & Barragan, J. (2022). Memory outcomes of police officers viewing their body-worn camera video. *Journal of Applied Research in Memory and Cognition*, 11(3), 392–404. https://doi.org/10.1037/mac0000013

Rainie, L., Funk, C., Anderson, M. & Tyson, A. (2022, March). AI and human enhancement: Americans' openness is tempered by a range of concerns. Retrieved from www.pewresearch.org/internet/2022/03/17/ai-and-human-enhancement-americans-openness-is-tempered-by-a-range-of-concerns/

Reporters Committee. (n.d.). Access to police body-worn camera video. Retrieved from www.rcfp.org/resources/bodycams/

Rosman, K. (2021, September 20). How the case of Gabrielle Petito galvanized the internet. *The New York Times*. Retrieved from www.nytimes.com/2021/09/20/style/gabby-petito-case-tiktok-social-media.html

Salo, H. (2021, September 20). Gabby Petito case: Tips that may have led to discovery of body. *New Yok Post*. Retrieved from https://nypost.com/2021/09/20/gabby-petito-case-tips-that-may-have-led-to-discovery-of-body/?utm_campaign=iphone_nyp&utm_source=mail_app

Seale-Carlisle, T.M., Colloff, M.F., Flowe, H.D., Wells, W., Wixted, J.T., & Mickes, L. (2019). Confidence and response time as indicators of eyewitness identification accuracy in the lab and in the real world. *Journal of Applied Research in Memory and Cognition*, 8(4), 420–428. https://doi.org/10.1016/j.jarmac.2019.09.003

Skagerberg, E.M., & Wright, D.B. (2008). The co-witness misinformation effect: Memory blends or memory compliance? *Memory*, 16(4), 436–442. https://doi.org/10.1080/09658210802019696

Skorinko, J.L., & Spellman, B.A. (2013). Stereotypic crimes: How group-crime associations affect memory and (sometimes) verdicts and sentencing. *Victims & Offenders*, 8(3), 278–307. https://doi.org/10.1080/15564886.2012.755140

Smalarz, L., & Wells, G.L. (2015). Contamination of eyewitness self-reports and the mistaken-identification problem. *Current Directions in Psychological Science*, 24(2), 120–124. https://doi.org/10.1177/0963721414554394

Smith, A.M. (2020). Why do mistaken identification rates increase when either witnessing or testing conditions get worse? *Journal of Applied Research in Memory and Cognition*, 9(4), 495–507. https://doi.org/10.1016/j.jarmac.2020.08.002

Smith, A.M., Wilford, M., Quigley-McBride, A., & Wells, G.L. (2019). Mistaken eyewitness identification rates increase when either witnessing or testing conditions get worse. *Law and Human Behavior*, 43, 358–368. https://doi.org/10.1037/lhb0000334

Smith, A.M., Wells, G.L., Lindsay, R.C.L., & Penrod, S.D. (2017). Fair lineups are better than biased lineups and showups, but not because they increase underlying discriminability. *Law and Human Behavior*, 41(2), 127–145. https://doi.org/10.1037/lhb0000219

Spencer, C. (2021, September 21). How amateur detective on social media helped crack the Gabby Petito case. *The Hill.* Retrieved from https://thehill.com/changing-america/respect/equality/573248-how-amateur-detectives-on-social-media-helped-crack-the/#:~:text=Gabby%20Petito's%20disappearance%20has%20people,Petito's%20boyfriend%2C%20who%20was%20hitchhiking.

Steblay, N.M., Besirevic, J., Fulero, S.M., & Jimenez-Lorente, B. (1999). The effects of pretrial publicity on juror verdicts: A meta-analytic review. *Law and Human Behavior, 23*(2), 219–235. https://doi.org/10.1023/A:1022325019080

Steblay, N.K., & Dysart, J.E. (2016). Repeated eyewitness identification procedures with the same suspect. *Journal of Applied Research in Memory and Cognition, 5*(3), 284–289. https://doi.org/10.1016/j.jarmac.2016.06.010

Steblay, N.M., Dysart, J., Fulero, S., & Lindsay, R.C.L. (2003). Eyewitness accuracy rates in police showup and lineup presentations: A meta-analytic comparison. *Law and Human Behavior, 27*(5), 523–540. https://doi.org/10.1023/A:1025438223608

Ubiera, C.R. (2022, May 29). Delphi Snapchat murder update-Inside violent past of Ron Logan after 2 girls bodies found 1,400ft from his home. Retrieved from www.the-sun.com/news/5449055/delphi-murders-new-details-ron-logan/

US Government Publishing Office. (2020). About face: Examining the Department of Homeland Security's use of facial recognition and other biometric technologies, part II. 116 Congress. Retrieved from www.congress.gov/event/116th-congress/houseevent/LC65455/text?q=%7B%22search%22%3A%5B%22Charles+romine%22%2C%22Charles+romine%22%5D%7D&s=1&r=5

Vallano, J.P., Pettalia, J., Pica, E., & Pozzulo, J. (2019). An examination of mock jurors' judgments in familiar identification cases. *Journal of Police and Criminal Psychology, 34*(2), 121–133. https://doi.org/10.1007/s11896-018-9266-0

Van Noorden, R. (2020). The ethical questions that haunt facial-recognition research. *Nature, 587*(7834), 354–358. http://dx.doi.org/10.1038/d41586-020-03187-3

Walsh, J.P. (2020). Social media and border security: Twitter use by migration policing agencies. *Policing & Society, 30*(10), 1138–1156. https://doi.org/10.1080/10439463.2019.1666846

Weber, N., Brewer, N., Wells, G.L., Semmler, C., & Keast, A. (2004). Eyewitness Identification Accuracy and Response Latency: The Unruly 10-12-Second Rule. *Journal of Experimental Psychology: Applied, 10*(3), 139–147. https://doi.org/10.1037/1076-898X.10.3.139

Wells, G.L. (1978). Applied eyewitness-testimony research: System variables and estimator variables. *Journal of Personality and Social Psychology, 36*(12), 1546–1557. https://doi.org/10.1037/0022-3514.36.12.1546

Wells, G.L. (2020). Psychological science on eyewitness identification and its impact on police practices and policies. *American Psychologist, 75*(9), 1316–1329. https://doi.org/10.1037/amp0000749

Wells, G.L., Charman, S.D., & Olson, E.A. (2005). Building face composites can harm lineup identification performance. *Journal of Experimental Psychology: Applied, 11*(3), 147–156. https://doi.org/10.1037/1076-898x.11.3.147

Wells, G.L., & Quigley-McBride, A. (2016). Applying eyewitness identification research to the legal system: A glance at where we have been and where we could go. *Journal of Applied Research in Memory and Cognition, 5*(3), 290–294. https://doi.org/10.1016/j.jarmac.2016.07.007

Wells, G.L., Kovera, M.B., Douglass, A.B., Brewer, N., Meissner, C.A., & Wixted, J.T. (2020). Policy and procedure recommendations for the collection and preservation of eyewitness identification evidence. *Law and Human Behavior, 44*(1), 3–36. https://doi.org/10.1037/lhb0000359

Wells, G.L., Yang, Y., & Smalarz, L. (2015). Eyewitness identification: Bayesian information gain, base-rate effect equivalency curves, and reasonable suspicion. *Law and Human Behavior, 39*(2), 99–122. https://doi.org/10.1037/lhb0000125

Wilkins, R. (2022, May 18). Possible suspect in Delphi murders on police radar since the killings. Journal & Courier. Retrieved from www.jconline.com/story/news/crime/2022/05/18/delphi-murders-suspect-indiana-state-police-search-warrant-killings-victims/9821164002/

Wixted, J.T., & Mickes, L. (2022). Eyewitness memory is reliable, but the criminal justice system is not. *Memory, 30*(1), 67–72. https://doi.org/10.1080/09658211.2021.1974485

Wixted, J.T., & Wells, G.L. (2017). The relationship between eyewitness confidence and identification accuracy. A new synthesis. *Psychological Science in the Public Interest, 18*(1). 10–65. http://dx.doi.org/10.1177/1529100616686966

Wixted, J.T., Mickes, L., Clark, S.E., Gronlund, S.D., & Roediger, H.L., III. (2015). Initial eyewitness confidence reliably predicts eyewitness identification accuracy. *American Psychologist, 70*(6), 515–526. https://doi.org/10.1037/a0039510

Wixted, J.T., Mickes, L., Dunn, J.C., Clark, S.E., & Wells, W. (2016). Estimating the reliability of eyewitness identifications from police lineups. *PNAS Proceedings of the National Academy of Sciences of the United States of America, 113*(2), 304–309. https://doi.org/10.1073/pnas.1516814112

Wixted, J.T., Wells, G.L., Loftus, E.F., & Garrett, B.L. (2021). Test a witness's memory of a suspect only once. *Psychological Science in the Public Interest, 22*(1, Suppl), 1S–18S. https://doi.org/10.1177/15291006211026259

Yardley, E., Lynes, A.G.T., Wilson, D., & Kelly, E. (2018). What's the deal with "websleuthing"? News media representations of amateur detective in networked spaces. *Crime, Media, Culture, 14*(1), 81–109. https://doi.org/10.1177/1741659016674045

18 Developmental Psychology and Law in the Digital Era
Emerging Trends, Challenges, and Opportunities

I-An Su and Stephen J. Ceci

Introduction

The use of children's testimonies in legal proceedings has posed a significant challenge for scholars and practitioners (Ceci & Bruck, 1993; Goodman & Melinder, 2007). As early as the end of the nineteenth century, researchers such as Binet and Henri (1894) recognized that various factors might influence children's narratives and their ability to resist suggestions. A number of early researchers recognized that these factors are particularly relevant in the forensic context, given that children may serve as crucial witnesses, victims, and even perpetrators in legal cases. In alleged cases of sexual abuse, for example, children are often the sole source of testimonial evidence, as such allegations typically occur in the absence of a third party. The accuracy of children's narratives is of paramount importance in such situations, as the veracity of forensically relevant details may significantly impact the outcome of the case. During the 1980s, a series of high-profile child sexual abuse allegations, such as the McMartin Preschool trial (Garven et al., 1998; Schreiber et al., 2006) and the Wee Care Nursery School trial (Schreiber et al., 2006), drew nationwide attention to the importance of the process of retrieving children's testimonies in such high-stake situations. These cases were often built on children's testimonies obtained through what came to be recognized as problematic interviewing procedures. This recognition alerted scholars, practitioners, and the general public to the need for scientifically validated forensic child interviewing protocols. Consequently, the development of science-based best practices for eliciting children's testimonies has emerged as a key concern in the field of forensic developmental psychology (Poole & Lamb, 1998; Lamb et al., 2018). In contemporary times, technology in diverse forms has emerged as a significant subject of discussion with regard to the formulation of science-based interviewing protocols for children.

Child Witnesses: An Overview

Before delving into a discussion of technologies utilized to aid in the testimonies of children, we first provide a brief background of child witnesses for the benefit of those who may not be familiar with related research and practices. We will provide a brief overview of the factors that can potentially impact children's ability to testify. Following that, we will briefly introduce the current science-based guidelines for interviewing children. If you have prior knowledge on this topic, you may skip this section and proceed to the next.

Factors Affecting Children's Testimony

There is a myriad of factors that can potentially affect the testimonial abilities of children. For ease of exposition, we can distinguish between dispositional and situational factors, which together encompass the range of influences that children may encounter during forensic interviews.

Dispositional Factors

Dispositional factors refer to individual differences among children, such as variations in demographic background, cognitive, social, neurobiological, and emotional development, as well as language and communication skills. Providing verbal accounts of events through interviews is a highly intricate form of conversation for children, especially considering the potential stress that may be involved. Child interviewees are expected to exhibit a range of competencies simultaneously, including interacting cooperatively with an unfamiliar adult, engaging in sustained dialogue, and accurately comprehending and responding to questions posed by the interviewer. Variations in children's cognitive, social, linguistic, and communicative abilities can pose significant challenges for young children during the interview process. To ensure constructive communication in child forensic interviews, it is crucial to consider children's limitations, which can vary due to their *age* (the typical level of performance and the constraints commonly observed within a specific age group) and other *individual differences* (the real performance and the constraints that are specific to an individual case).

Specifically, researchers have noted that children's testimony is closely related to their ability to remember personally experienced or witnessed events associated with a particular time and place) and their *suggestibility* (i.e., "the degree to which children's encoding, storage, retrieval, and reporting of events can be influenced by a range of social and psychological factors", Ceci & Bruck, 1993). This definition notably includes "reporting" to signal that suggestibility goes beyond cognitive mechanisms associated with encoding, storage, and retrieval and explicitly includes non-cognitive factors that may affect how children report an event in the absence of cognitive impairment, such as factors that might relate to children's social, emotional, and language development.

Children's episodic memory and suggestibility may be significantly influenced by age. Research has consistently demonstrated a normative pattern where older children exhibit superior performance on measures of eyewitness memory, both quantitatively (in terms of the number of details provided) and qualitatively (in terms of the type of the details provided), as well as their ability to resist suggestions (Bruck & Ceci, 1999). In addition, some researchers have reported that variations in children's eyewitness memory and suggestibility may be attributed to differences in their children's intelligence, executive functioning, language ability, creativity, and self-concept/self-efficacy (see Bruck & Melnyk, 2004, for a review, and Klemfuss & Olaguez, 2020, for an updated review). However, some have found these relationships to be complicated. It is worth noting that children with varying degrees of *intellectual disabilities* constitute a disproportionately high percentage of child sexual abuse victims, and their legal treatment and accommodations may need to be tailored accordingly, as Bruck and Melnyk (2004) did find strong suggestibility-proneness among intellectually impaired individuals.

Before conducting forensic interviews with children, interviewers should be mindful of dispositional factors that could impact or hinder a child's ability to provide a meaningful account of the events in question. In addition to examining psychological factors such as cognitive, social, emotional, linguistic, and communicational variables, demographic factors such as culture, parenting style, and socioeconomic status should also be considered by interviewers.[1]

Situational Factors

The second category pertains to situational factors, encompassing extraneous influences such as environmental factors not obtained from the child interviewee. These factors include the type of interview questions, the repetition of questioning and interviews, the demeanor of the interviewer, the physical setting, and the overall structure of the interview protocol.

---

[1] Although the focus of this chapter is on young children's perceived credibility, it deserves mention that older adults, particularly those aged 79+, are known to have their own difficulties in eyewitness situations and perceptions of their credibility and accuracy are colored by stereotypes (e.g., Mueller-Johnson et al., 2007).

For instance, regarding the type of interview questions, numerous studies have consistently shown that *open-ended questions* are a highly effective means of prompting children to recall a specific event without compromising the reliability of their responses (Orbach et al., 2000). Children of all ages tend to provide more accurate accounts when asked open-ended questions (Lamb & Fauchier, 2001). Open-ended questions, such as *free recall* prompts that encourage the child to provide a detailed account of a targeted event from beginning to end, or *cued recall* prompts that use the child's previous responses to elicit further details, have been demonstrated to be highly effective in eliciting accurate information across a range of situations (Wilson & Pipe, 1989). Another instance that external factors might affect children's testimonial abilities is that the interviewer's demeanor can influence children's responses to interview questions. Consistent findings indicate that the interviewer's supportiveness positively influences the quality and quantity of children's reports, as well as reducing their vulnerability to suggestions during the interview process (Saywitz et al., 2019). Excessive interruptions by the interviewer can have adverse effects on a child's ability to provide precise testimony, underscoring the significance of the interviewer's demeanor in the interview process (Teoh & Lamb, 2013).

In summary, as these studies suggest, situational factors, much like dispositional factors, can affect a child's performance during the interview process. However, unlike dispositional factors, situational factors can largely be controlled by the interviewer and other professionals involved, which creates an opportunity for scholars and practitioners to develop evidence-based best practices for conducting forensic interviews with children.

Science-Based Child Forensic Interviewing Guidelines

Researchers have spent decades developing science-based guidelines for conducting investigative interviews with children (Ceci & Hembrooke, 1998; Faller, 2014). These guidelines are designed to account for children's developmental abilities and limitations while ensuring their performance is not compromised during the interview process.

The NICHD Investigative Interview Protocol

One example of a successful interview protocol is the NICHD Investigative Interview Protocol (the NICHD Protocol), developed by Michael Lamb and his colleagues (Lamb et al., 2011; Lamb et al., 2018). This semi-structured protocol places emphasis not only on the *substantive phase* but also on the *pre-substantive* and *post-substance* phases. These non-substantive phases, unlike the substantive phase that directly asks forensically relevant questions, are often overlooked but are essential to ensure the quality of the interview.

During the pre-substantive phase of the interview, the research team emphasizes the development of *rapport-building, narrative training, explaining and practicing ground rules*, and *episodic memory training*. Various of these elements have been found to be helpful in the pre-substantive phase of the interview, including self-introductions and conversing with the child interviewee about non-forensically related topics, ground-rule instructions that encourage truth-telling and reassuring children that it is acceptable to say "I don't know" or challenge the interviewer when necessary (Lamb et al., 2011, 2018; Earhart et al., 2014). During the post-substantive phase of the interview, the research team emphasizes the importance of a proper closure that allows the interviewer and interviewee to reflect on the interview. All these practices improve the performance of children's eyewitness memory and help prevent them from succumbing to misleading questions, ultimately leading to more accurate testimony in the event the child is later summoned to testify (Brown et al., 2013; La Rooy et al., 2015).

The NICHD Protocol has become a widely used tool in forensic interviews with children and has been translated into dozens of languages and used worldwide. Numerous studies have been conducted to examine its effectiveness, and it has consistently been shown to be one of the most reliable methods for eliciting narratives from children for forensic purposes (La Rooy et al., 2015; Benia et al., 2015).

The Narrative Elaboration Technique

The Narrative Elaboration Technique (NET) interview protocol involves a training session to help children provide detailed descriptions of past events by simultaneously addressing children's cognitive limitations, such as a lack of knowledge about the listener's expectations and ineffective search strategies (Saywitz & Snyder, 1996; Saywitz & Camparo, 2013). The training includes teaching children about the necessary level of detail and providing four *cue cards* as reminders to talk about the *participants, setting, actions*, and *conversation/affect* associated with the event. This training helps children structure their reports and provides additional details to improve the accuracy and completeness of their narratives. Children interviewed by NET demonstrated a huge improvement in their recall performance without compromising accuracy.

In summary, these empirically supported methods have shown advantages for children in the forensic interview process (Goodman & Melinder, 2007). Although they may vary in their approaches and emphases, they all provide science-based guidelines for conducting interviews, emphasizing the use of open-ended questions and rapport-building while discouraging the use of aids such as anatomical dolls, hypothesis-posing, and drawings. Despite being a longstanding concern at the intersection of psychology and law, child forensic interviewing is a field in its own right, one that continues to evolve. Researchers and practitioners seek to optimize interview processes for different legal and non-legal contexts, including asylum-seeking scenarios, and for children from diverse backgrounds with varying cultures and socioeconomic statuses.

Trends in Video Technology and Child Witnesses

Now that we have discussed the background of child witnesses in a legal context, let's shift our focus to how technological advancements have impacted research and practices related to child witnesses. This has been especially significant in the past few decades. In this section, we will briefly provide background about how video technology influenced the norms in child forensic interviewing, such as closed-circuit television (CCTV) and videotaped evidence.

Closed-Circuit Television

CCTV is a secure television system that transmits signals from video cameras to a designated monitor. It has been utilized in courtrooms to enable child witnesses to participate in legal proceedings without being physically present in the same room as the alleged perpetrators. The CCTV system is available in two formats, namely one-way and two-way. The former involves a single camera and monitor, while the latter employs two sets of cameras and monitors, enabling face-to-face-like communication. In contrast to the videotaped evidence, which we will discuss later, CCTV maintains a formality for synchronous conversation. This allows the audience in the courtroom to retain the opportunity to pose follow-up questions for the child about the narrated event if needed. Additionally, the child typically appears in a separate room within the same courthouse. Nevertheless, the viewers of the televised audience still feel a sense of proximity, and the procedure using CCTV does not differ significantly from standard legal practices.

The Landmark Supreme Court Cases

The legal debate over the use of CCTV was mainly between the need to protect children in open court from the trauma engendered by facing the defendant versus the defendant's right to confrontation. The Sixth Amendment's Confrontation Clause ensures that a person accused of a crime has the right to face-to-face confront their accuser in court. However, there are only a few limited exceptions that could prevent the defendant from exercising this right. There have been debates about whether the risk of harm to a child witness falls into the narrow exceptional cases where a defendant may have to give up their constitutionally protected right. The Supreme Court of the United States (SCOTUS) has held different views at different times on this issue.

Coy v. Iowa (1988)

Although the case of *Coy v. Iowa* did not directly address CCTV, it raised similar questions about whether a shielded live conversation between the defendant and the accuser would be legally permissible under certain conditions. In this case, John Coy was tried in an Iowa court for sexually assaulting two 13-year-old girls. During the trial, a large screen was set up in front of John Coy to prevent the two 13-year-old girls from having to see him. However, Coy was able to see the girls dimly and hear their testimony. After the trial, Coy was found guilty by the jury. Nonetheless, Coy argued that his Sixth Amendment right to confront his accusers face-to-face was violated by the use of the screen, which was allowed under Iowa Code 910A for cases involving child sexual abuse. He also claimed that his right to due process was violated because the use of the screen created an appearance of guilt arguing that the backlit screen placed in front of him connoted that he was a dangerous person. Despite his objections, the trial court dismissed his claims, and the Iowa Supreme Court upheld the decision. The US Supreme Court's decision in *Coy v. Iowa* (1988), with 4:5 votes, ruled that placing a screen between child victims/witnesses of sexual abuse and the defendant in the courtroom violated the confrontation clause. The decision, which emphasized the importance of confrontation in ensuring fairness, has faced criticism for flawed reasoning and inconsistency with previous cases and modern views of confrontation clauses. Fortunately, its impact on the use of similar protective measures for child and teenage witnesses has been minimal, as it conflicts with mainstream scholarly discussions and real-life practices. Later in 1990, the *Maryland v. Craig* case reinstated the significance of preventing children from confronting defendants directly, even if it meant that the defendant's right to confrontation was outweighed.

Maryland v. Craig (1990)

In *Maryland v. Craig* (1990), Sandra Ann Craig was accused of sexually abusing a six-year-old child who was unable to testify in court due to severe emotional trauma. Despite Craig's objections, the trial court allowed the child to testify via a one-way CCTV in another room. The judge and jury viewed the testimony in the courtroom, while Craig could communicate with her lawyer and make objections. After the trial, Craig was found guilty by the trial court, but the Maryland high court overturned the decision. The SCOTUS justices later ruled that the utilization of one-way CCTV would be deemed lawful if a child witness possessed the potential to undergo significant psychological trauma when testifying in the presence of the defendant. The court determined that the alleged victim and other children who were witnesses and allegedly abused would experience severe emotional distress if they were compelled to testify in open court, to the point where they would be unable to communicate effectively. Despite finding that the children were competent to testify, the court allowed their testimony to proceed using alternative procedures. Consequently, child sexual abuse victims may provide their testimony via one-way CCTV under such circumstances.

The Benefits and Challenges of CCTV

The case of *Maryland v. Craig* sparked a debate in legal literature about balancing the defendant's right to confrontation and the protection of children in the 1990s. The admissibility of CCTV testimonies in cases involving child witnesses has become widespread as a result. This has led psychologists to investigate the potential effects of CCTV on child forensic interviews.

Based on laboratory and clinical findings, it has been consistently shown that CCTV could be beneficial for children when giving testimony. This is because it can decrease their suggestibility and anxiety compared to traditional face-to-face open-court settings, where they may feel stressed and intimidated, especially when facing the accused (Cashmore, 2002; Goodman et al., 1998; Landström & Granhag, 2010). In addition, using CCTV may allow children to provide more accurate and comprehensive information when answering forensic questions related to events of interest. Overall, CCTV can improve children's testimonial performance while reducing emotional discomfort (Cashmore, 2002).

Even though CCTV is a science-based measure that can enhance children's testimonial performance, the presentation of CCTV testimony without direct examination or cross-examination might diminish its credibility compared to other traditional forms of testimonial evidence. For instance, while using CCTV may not affect the factfinders' ability to detect deception in children's reports or create a bias towards the accused, it could potentially create bias against child witnesses among jurors (Goodman et al., 1998). Anecdotally, it has been suggested that jurors are less likely to feel empathy for a child victim who is screened because it results in less emotion than one might expect from someone claiming to have been assaulted. Furthermore, Ross et al. (1994) found that the common belief that employing protective shields such as CCTV to safeguard child witnesses would lead to increased conviction rates was unfounded. On the contrary, their research revealed that the use of such measures had the opposite effect—conviction rates actually decreased when children were protected compared to when they testified in open court.

After years of research and practice, many state and federal regulations have now allowed the use of CCTV in cases involving child witnesses in juvenile and family law proceedings in the United States and other countries. However, there are specific restrictions, such as the age of the child witness, the nature of the offense being tried, and the procedures involved, that govern its use. Nonetheless, it has become a standard practice in legal proceedings involving children in many countries.

Videotaped Evidence

Another way that video technology has impacted children's testimony in the courtroom, in addition to CCTV, is through videotaped interviews used as testimonial evidence. The key distinction between videotaped evidence and CCTV is that CCTV preserves the live video link that allows for live communications during the trial between factfinders, the accused, and the child witness. In contrast, pre-videotaped evidence is solely in the form of a video and may be considered hearsay evidence, which makes its admissibility controversial. Furthermore, as we previously discussed when examining the CCTV debate, pre-videotaped evidence also eliminates the defendant's right to confrontation. Hence, similarly to the use of CCTV, the use of videotaped evidence in the courtroom is subject to legislative limitations that vary depending on factors such as the age of the child and the type of case, both in the United States and worldwide.

The Use of Videotaped Evidence

The methods used to videotape children's initial reports of alleged offenses vary across states in the United States and around the globe. These interviews typically occur before trial and are recorded in less formal settings, such as child-friendly rooms or hospital settings where victims of child sexual abuse or domestic violence are often identified for the first time. The interviewers may include certified forensic child interviewers, social workers, police officers, prosecutors, and other professionals experienced in working with vulnerable populations. Interdisciplinary professionals, such as case investigators and medical professionals, are often involved to ensure that all necessary questions are asked. The videotaped interviews occur soon after the initial report, and the questions asked are tailored to the needs of follow-up investigations and treatment. Depending on the jurisdiction, the videotaped evidence may be presented in court as an exception to the hearsay rule.

The Benefits of Videotaped Evidence

Videotaped evidence offers child witnesses a different experience compared to testifying in open court or through CCTV, and there are several advantages to using this form of evidence. One benefit is that pre-trial interviews can occur in a less stressful environment than in the courtroom. Depending on the jurisdiction, the accused may or may not be present during the interview, and children may be shielded from seeing or hearing the accused. This can lead to higher-quality reports from children about the events in question compared to traditional open court settings. In a more relaxed setting, child witnesses may be more confident, and their narratives may appear more convincing. Another advantage is that videotaped evidence enables child witnesses to provide their testimonies in a timely manner compared to testifying in court, which can take months or even years after the alleged offense. Testimony retrieved shortly after the event is considered more reliable than testimony retrieved after a long delay, and immediate testimony is perceived as more trustworthy by judges and juries (Miller et al., 2022). Additionally, videotaped evidence can minimize repeated interviews by providing the initial interview at the beginning of the legal proceedings. Repeated interviews can be mentally taxing, stressful, and traumatic for child witnesses, and they can harm the perceived credibility of child witnesses by creating potential discrepancies across interviews, which are often challenged by the defense.

To summarize, the use of videotaped evidence has become a widespread practice globally to safeguard children in legal contexts. Its implementation prevents repetitive questioning of children about the same event and leads to a more compelling report, which can assist in supporting their allegations. Overall, the effectiveness of videotaped evidence is well-established in this regard (Vandervort, 2005).

Trends in Digital Technology and Child Witnesses

Technology revolutionized forensic interviewing involving children in the 1990s, and during the COVID-19 pandemic, it has regained significance. Tele-forensic interviewing (tele-FI) has become a major focus, which involves remote interviewing through computer-mediated videoconferencing tools such as Zoom, Skype, and Teams. It is important to note that while the use of such tools for forensic interviews involving child witnesses was discussed and studied before the pandemic, the urgent adoption of tele-FI during the pandemic has brought this issue to the forefront. The effects of pandemic-induced shutdowns and changes have impacted the use of these tools, and it is expected to continue even after the pandemic ends. This section presents empirical studies on tele-FI with children and how they inform current practices, particularly in the context of COVID-19. Finally, we discuss the benefits, challenges, and ethical concerns of tele-FI.

Tele-FI in Research

Two studies directly compared face-to-face and online interviewing on children's reporting of an episode in the context of child forensic interviewing before the onset of the COVID-19 pandemic. The first study by Doherty-Sneddon and McAuley (2000) involved 64 children, with an equal split of six-year-olds and ten-year-olds. These children were interviewed about a staged event, either in a video-mediated communication (VMC) or face-to-face setting. Their results reported no significant differences in the total correct information, relevant information given during narrative recall, and the style of questioning required between the two interview formats. However, the face-to-face interviews resulted in significantly more incorrect information during specific questioning, and younger children were found to be more resistant to leading questions in the online condition. Moreover, older children produced more information during free narrative recall in face-to-face interviews. According to their findings, Doherty-Sneddon and McAuley (2000) suggest that although there may be differences in evidential quality, the VMC condition may enhance children's confidence levels, and the potential risks of informational loss outweigh any benefits.

In a similar vein, Hamilton and colleagues (2017) examined the impact of live video-feed interviews compared to face-to-face interviews on the measures of children's memory in a mock child forensic interviewing setting. A hundred child participants between the ages of five and twelve were interviewed by an experienced interviewer about an innocuous event with a one or two-day delay. The results showed that live video-feed interviews were as effective as face-to-face interviews regarding the accuracy and informativeness in retrieving children's reports. However, video-feed interviews required more clarification prompts than face-to-face interviews. Doherty-Sneddon and McAuley (2000) as well as Hamilton and colleagues (2017) arrived at the same conclusion that video-mediated interviews are comparable to face-to-face interviews and might be a secure means of questioning children about a harmless event.

Unlike aforementioned studies that examined the effect of computer or internet-mediated forensic interviews on typically developing children, Hsu and Teoh (2017) concentrated on children with neurological differences, particularly those with autism spectrum disorder (ASD), to explore whether non-human interviews could be effective in eliciting responses from children who struggle with communication when interacting with humans. Thirty children participated in a target event, including an equal number of typically developing children and children with ASD. A week later, they were interviewed by either an avatar or a human interviewer. The analysis revealed that both groups of children interviewed by the avatar demonstrated an improvement in memory performance, with a more significant effect for children with ASD. These results suggest promising implications for future applications, particularly regarding the most effective accommodation for children with special needs in forensic contexts.

Following Hsu and Teoh (2017), Brown, Walker, and Godden (2021) were among the first to address the issue of tele-forensic interviewing at the onset of the pandemic. In response to this crisis, they published a review paper that examined past relevant studies and predicted the potential opportunities and challenges, along with ethical considerations, of using tele-FI in real-world settings, especially in the context of the COVID-19 lockdowns. Their article suggested that tele-FI may be as good as or even better than traditional methods of interviewing children. However, more scientific evidence is required to support this claim. Although acknowledging the advantages of remote interviewing, such as increased accessibility, equity, cultural responsiveness, and reduced delay, the authors cautioned remote interviewers to be mindful of potential changes in questioning strategies and engagement with children. They stressed the importance of considering that a shift in interviewing mode might undermine the reliability of children's responses.

Following Brown et al.'s (2021) call for empirical research on the effects of tele-FI, Dickinson, Lytle, and Poole (2021) published a timely article supporting tele-FI as a practical alternative to face-to-face interviews for questioning child witnesses during the COVID-19 pandemic. Two hundred sixty-one children participated in an event where a character violated a non-touching policy. Subsequently, the children were provided with a piece of misinformation from their parents. After a two-week delay, they were interviewed about the original event. The results revealed that regardless of the interview mode, the children reported similar touch events and demonstrated comparable accuracy on challenging source-monitoring and detail questions. Therefore, they conclude that tele-FI is a viable substitute for traditional in-person interviewing of child witnesses.

Klassen et al.'s (2023) ongoing study intends to explore how tele-FI might affect children by examining the impact of environmental factors in virtual investigative interviews on children's reports of an event. Their study involves 107 children between the ages of 9 to 11 and utilizes a 2 × 2 design with two independent variables: the complexity of the interviewer's virtual background (simple or complex) and video feed visibility, which determines whether the child interviewee can see themselves on the screen (visible or hidden). The study's three dependent variables are accuracy, completeness, and disclosure. Their preliminary results show that children who viewed a complex background were more accurate in their responses when compared to those who viewed simple backgrounds. However, the interviewer's background did not have an impact on the completeness of the responses. The video feed did not distract the children during the interview, but they were likelier to admit wrongdoing when they could see their own faces. To improve the relationship between the interviewer and children, it is recommended to provide child-friendly items in the virtual background, which can lead to better interview results. Nonetheless, more research is necessary to determine the most effective techniques for conducting tele-forensic interviews with children.

In general, there is still a need for further research to explore the impact of tele-forensic interviews on children. However, current evidence suggests that tele-forensic interviews could be a viable substitute for in-person interviews. In some cases, tele-forensic interviews may even be a better option for eliciting accurate accounts from children with special needs regarding a target forensic event.

Tele-FI in Practice

Practitioners in governments and organizations developed preliminary guidelines for tele-forensic interviewing in response to the COVID-19 pandemic to make it feasible and address potential technological and logistical challenges (e.g., Vieth et al., 2020; State of Michigan Governor's Task Force on Child Abuse and Neglect and Department of Health and Human Services, 2020; National Children's Alliance, 2022). These guidelines were beneficial in the early stages of the pandemic when there was widespread uncertainty about how to conduct virtual investigative interviews involving children, especially when there was a surge in alleged child maltreatment during the lockdowns (Lawson et al., 2020). Scholars collaborated in creating some of these guidelines, ensuring that research and practice were aligned on this topic (Vieth et al., 2020; National Children's Alliance, 2022). The initial tele-FI guidelines were based on modifying existing FI guidelines discussed in previous sections and focused on preparing child forensic interviewers to become familiar with hardware and software for videoconferencing and using virtual interviewing aids instead of physical ones. The later versions of the guidelines became more complicated, such as the decision tree developed by the National Children's Alliance (2022) for front-line practitioners to follow before conducting tele-FIs. Although there is limited knowledge about the perspectives of front-line practitioners on tele-FI, there have been hundreds of tele-FIs executed during the past few years with no significant concerns about using tele-FIs in practice (Dickinson et al., 2023). Still, it would be beneficial to gather more comprehensive feedback from practitioners on the use of tele-FI. Based on the latest research and practice, there are currently no science-based guidelines for best practices of tele-forensic interviewing that we are aware of from either practitioners or researchers. Therefore, further research and practice are needed to identify the necessary information to create science-based guidelines for tele-FI.

Benefits of Tele-FI

Despite limited data and experiences shared, both researchers and practitioners have shown support for using tele-FI because of its various benefits.

Geographic Flexibility

The use of tele-FI enables children to access experienced interviewers without being limited by geography. This is particularly useful for children in remote areas who may have experienced alleged adverse incidents and require timely assistance. Additionally, telecommunication tools that are affordable and widely available can help bridge the geographical divide, addressing the issue of inequality that is often overlooked or impossible to address otherwise when children must travel long distances to be interviewed at a regional center.

Neurodiversity and Cultural Responsiveness

The flexibility and convenience of tele-forensic interviewing are particularly important for children with special needs and cultural considerations. For instance, in cases of alleged child sexual abuse involving children with diverse cultural backgrounds or neurodiversity, it may be challenging to find local interviewers with specialized training or proficiency in the child's language. In such cases, the accessibility of tele-forensic interviews becomes especially vital for potentially vulnerable groups. Additionally, as demonstrated by Hsu and Teoh (2017), tele-FI might be helpful for children with special needs.

Environmental Accommodations

Tele-FI can help reduce the stress and anxiety experienced by children by avoiding the need to transport them to an unfamiliar location for a face-to-face interview with unfamiliar individuals. This is particularly relevant in cases of alleged child sexual abuse where the child has been relocated. Tele-forensic interviewing offers greater flexibility in planning the child's interview, allowing it to be conducted in more hospitable locations. Unlike traditional interviews that often occur in institutional settings, such as hospitals or legal offices, tele-forensic interviewing can be conducted in places where the child feels comfortable or familiar, such as their own homes, communities, schools, or other suitable settings. This feature can be particularly beneficial in situations where external factors, such as epidemics, weather disruptions, or war, make transportation or relocation unsafe.

Shielded Interviews

Tele-FI functions similarly to CCTV in terms of minimizing the presence of an unfamiliar individual in a potentially stressful environment, thus helping to alleviate anxiety experienced by the child during the interview process. This aspect may be particularly relevant for children with special needs, as previous research (Hsu & Teoh, 2013) has shown that the presence of an unfamiliar adult can cause stress for child interviewees and impede children's ability to report a witnessed or experienced event.

Digital Familiarity

Additionally, children may be more comfortable with the digital tools used in tele-forensic interviewing due to their familiarity with them. Many communication tools are now a part of daily life, and children are no longer unfamiliar with them. This familiarity has been further increased by the COVID-19 pandemic, during which these tools were widely used in educational and family settings. The use of familiar tools during tele-forensic interviews may reduce children's nervousness and facilitate rapport building, potentially leading to higher quality interviews.

Overall, the various advantages of tele-FI provide the possibility of considering it as a standard method for forensic interviews.

Risks of Tele-FI

While the potential benefits of tele-forensic interviewing are promising, there are still lingering concerns that need to be addressed. However, due to the currently widespread and continued use of tele-FI during and after the COVID-19 pandemic, it is imperative that these issues are acknowledged, and solutions are collaboratively developed.

More Challenging Rapport Building

One of the most significant concerns surrounding tele-FI is the challenge of establishing rapport in a virtual setting. Physical and social distancing prevent a sense of proximity between the interviewer and the child interviewee. Therefore, early research suggests that children participating in tele-FI may need more prompts than their counterparts interviewed in a traditional face-to-face setting (Hamilton et al., 2017). The consensus among the interviewer community is that building rapport enhances children's testimonial abilities and protects them from falling prey to suggestions. However, it is crucial to develop and implement digital-accommodating strategies based on the best scientific evidence to build rapport effectively.

More Unwanted Interruptions

The nature of conversations between interviewers and interviewees can differ significantly in in-person versus online settings. For example, it is reasonable to anticipate that more technological support, such as check-in questions and instructions, may be necessary for online interviews, which could result in more interruptions. While non-forensic communication may be more prevalent in tele-forensic interviews than in-person interviews, we must also consider that excessive verbal interruptions can hinder children's performance in the interview process (Teoh & Lamb, 2013).

Limited Non-Verbal Behavioral Cues

In addition, screen-mediated conversations restrict the transmission of non-verbal gestural information between the interviewer and the child interviewee. This limitation could potentially lead to the misinterpretation of communicative information and pose a threat to effective communication. The digital transformation of images and videos, as well as the potential time delay associated with internet-transmitted communications, may not accurately capture the subtle facial micro-expressions that are crucial for forensic interviews involving potentially deceptive behaviors. Similarly, the absence of the physical presence of both parties eliminates the possibility for the interviewer to observe and notice some case-relevant details (e.g., bruises on the child's skin), which could at times be crucial for relevant forensic investigations.

Unknown Perceptions of Tele-FI Children's Testimony

There is currently limited understanding regarding the perceived credibility of children's testimonies obtained through tele-FI in the context of evidentiary considerations in courtrooms. Given that both potential advantages and disadvantages are associated with using tele-FI with children, the ultimate objective of obtaining children's testimonies is to ensure that it fulfills its forensic function of conveying the child's truthful report of the alleged event. Therefore, the perception of judges, juries, and other investigative professionals is crucial. However, there is currently no research investigating how professionals or the general public view children's testimonies when they are obtained in an online setting. We believe that, as with earlier debates about how CCTV and videotaped child testimonial evidence may be perceived in court, the protective nature of tele-FI may prevent adversarial questioning and cross-examination of the child, potentially reducing the risk of secondary trauma on children who might have adverse experiences. However, the child's increased ease and comfort may also lead to a deviation from stereotypical responses of child victims or witnesses, which could have negative implications for their credibility in the courtroom. While keeping the issue of bias in mind, it is challenging to find the optimal angle for tele-FI interviews. On the one hand, we want to maintain a centralized perspective that provides an unbiased view of the child interviewee, but on the other hand, we want to ensure that the child's facial expressions and verbal and non-verbal reactions can be seen clearly, such as through a close-up view.

Other Challenges

To sum up, the behavior of children during extended videoconferencing conversations is not well understood. Su and Ceci (2021) discussed the challenges that may arise in home-based videoconferencing conversations involving children in research settings, and some of these concerns may also apply to forensic interview settings. These include short attention spans, the "Zoom Fatigue" phenomenon (Wiederhold, 2020), and the lack of seriousness in the setting, where children may not be aware that the videoconferencing conversation is an official interview and hence do not treat it seriously.

Therefore, it is crucial to understand the potential impact of these changes in dynamics on children's responses to digital interviews, as tele-FI is expected to remain a prominent tool even after the COVID-19 pandemic. Moreover, given that tele-FI may be frequently used with underprivileged populations, including those residing in remote areas, with special needs, or from diverse cultural and socioeconomic backgrounds, some of which may be related to immigration or asylum-seeking scenarios, it is essential to ensure that tele-FI serves to assist child witnesses without creating additional barriers to accessing legal justice.

Ethical and Legal Concerns of Tele-FI

The application of internet-based technology like tele-FI has brought forth relatively new and unprecedented ethical and legal concerns in the digital era.

Cyber Security

The security and confidentiality of data storage and distribution related to digital tools like tele-fi are now a concern. Synchronous communication technologies, such as Zoom, Google Meet, Microsoft Teams, and Webex, developed and supported by major tech companies, pose risks in discussing sensitive topics (John, 2020). Despite the recognition that digital communication services may not be safe for such discussions, there is insufficient consideration of the potential compromise of expected privacy in the legal context. In cases involving highly sensitive information, like alleged sexual abuse or domestic violence, interviewers must carefully manage file security before opting for this less regulated and innovative form of interviewing. If privacy cannot be guaranteed, the risks may outweigh the benefits, and traditional interview methods may be the safer option.

Politics of Digital Surveillance

In addition, tele-FI involving asylum-seeking or immigration matters can also be sensitive due to the involvement of technology providers from certain countries. For instance, the use of Zoom by Western governments has raised concerns about the software's potential vulnerability to discussions of sensitive information due to its lack of end-to-end encryption (Molloy & Tidy, 2020). Therefore, evaluating online conferencing and storage tool providers is crucial as it can impact the level of security for tele-FI, particularly when the service providers may have a potential conflict of interest with the users' countries.

In conclusion, safeguarding the confidentiality of tele-FI necessitates interviewers and stakeholders to adopt security measures not only for traditional data collection methods but also for digital formats such as video and audio recordings of children's testimonies. While storing data in a secure space on a disconnected computer can offer protection in non-digital formats, interviewers must also consider multiple layers of cyber security concerns when using innovative interviewing methods in real-life forensic scenarios. As both researchers and practitioners, we urge governments and organizations to regulate tele-FI as a digitally assisted interviewing tool for child victims and witnesses in forensic proceedings.

Current Challenges and Future Directions

As of writing, the recent explosion in the latest generation of artificial intelligence (AI) since November 2022 has significantly impacted people's daily lives, especially those who work with writing in both academic and non-academic settings. This trend was not foreseen just six months ago. While we have discussed the current challenges that need to be addressed with the use of tele-FI in child interviews, it is important to acknowledge that continuous advancements in technology will impact the future of child interviews. With AI becoming more prevalent, how will it reshape the practice and research of child witnesses? It is crucial for the field to remain proactive and adaptable to these changes to ensure that the use of digital technology in child interviews benefits the child while simultaneously not hindering the pursuit of justice.

Incorporating the latest digital technology is crucial for professionals, as it provides them with intelligent tools to enhance the quality and efficiency of collecting testimonial evidence from vulnerable witnesses in a legal context. Additionally, understanding these new digital tools allows legal professionals to utilize them in combating cybercrime that exploits vulnerable populations, particularly children. For instance, recognizing the use of Deep Fakes technology in creating child pornography and brainstorming solutions to combat its illegal usage can aid in protecting child victims (Ratner, 2021). It is essential to acknowledge the potential negative impact of technology on children and explore safe ways to utilize its potential opportunities to achieve justice.

Advice for Researchers

It's crucial to promptly evaluate and integrate technological advancements into reliable methods for child forensic interviewing through research. For instance, using AI-generated faces for child-friendly avatars could be efficient in accommodating children with special needs and tailoring the situation of the case (e.g., using the face of the police officer in charge as an avatar). Another example is that AI-automated transcription can efficiently monitor interview quality, detect any misuse of suggestive questions, and aid in interviewer training. As a community, it is our responsibility to promptly scientifically evaluate how new technology may affect children's responses in the context of forensic investigative interviews. Despite its rapidly evolving nature, evaluation of technology's impact on child forensic interviewing in laboratory settings is necessary. Ethical and safe implementation of technology with science-based testing is important while exploring new possibilities.

Advice for Practitioners

In the fast-paced world of forensic interviews with children, it is essential to proceed with caution when implementing technology. While staying abreast of the latest technological advances, it is crucial to carefully introduce untested tools in situations as sensitive as child forensic interviews and investigations. Although the allure of new technology may be strong, especially in high-pressure scenarios with limited time and resources, it is vital to wait for scientific validation before employing untested tools, such as the accuracy of Zoom word-to-text conversion software. Collaborating with researchers to generate insights and research questions can aid in determining whether new technologies have value in forensic settings involving children. A thorough framework for testing new technology should be established before considering implementation.

Conclusion

The use of technology, such as CCTV, videotaped evidence, and tele-FI, has shown promise in litigating crimes involving child victims and improving the well-being of children involved in legal conflicts. While legislation regarding CCTV and videotaped testimonies has matured over the past decades, research and legislation for the ongoing use of tele-FI are still needed. Limited existing research suggests that tele-FI may be a feasible alternative to traditional face-to-face interviews for innocuous events in laboratory settings, but its effects on interviews in real-world scenarios involving potentially stressful or traumatic events are largely unknown, as is the accuracy of auto-transcriptions of Zoom interviews. Furthermore, the influence of technology-assisted interviews on children with diverse levels of technological literacy is yet to be determined. Despite the growing popularity of tele-FI, with hundreds of cases already tested with this new technology, more scientific evidence is necessary to ensure that it is feasible to elicit children's narratives about forensic-relevant episodes.

In conclusion, a balanced and mindful approach will be important when it comes to embracing the progress of digital technology, especially those backed by third-party service providers, and their potential use in forensic settings. It is also important to thoroughly test any new technology before implementing it in real-world situations while also being willing to take risks and explore uncharted territories in laboratory settings. It is advisable to encourage top-down rather than bottom-up usage when it comes to the application of digital technology in child forensic interviews and to prioritize the safety and well-being of children above all else.

References

Benia, L.R., Hauck-Filho, N., Dillenburg, M., & Stein, L.M. (2015). The NICHD investigative interview protocol: A meta-analytic review. *Journal of Child Sexual Abuse*, 24(3), 259–279.

Binet, A., & Henri, V. (1894). De la suggestibilité naturelle chez les enfants. *Revue Philosophique de la France et de l'Etranger*, 38, 337–347.

Brown, D.A., Lamb, M.E., Lewis, C., Pipe, M.E., Orbach, Y., & Wolfman, M. (2013). The NICHD investigative interview protocol: an analogue study. *Journal of experimental psychology: Applied*, 19(4), 367.

Brown, D., Walker, D., & Godden, E. (2021). Tele-forensic interviewing to elicit children's evidence—Benefits, risks, and practical considerations. *Psychology, Public Policy, and Law*, 27(1), 17–29.

Bruck, M., & Ceci, S.J. (1999). The suggestibility of children's memory. *Annual Review of Psychology*, 50(1), 419–439.

Bruck, M., & Melnyk, L. (2004). Individual differences in children's suggestibility: A review and synthesis, *Applied Cognitive Psychology*, 18, 947–996. DOI: 10.1002/acp.1070

Cashmore, J. (2002). Innovative procedures for child witnesses. In H.L. Westcott, G.M. Davies, and R.H.C. Bull (eds.), *Children's testimony: A handbook of psychological research and forensic practice*, pp. 203–218. John Wiley & Sons.

Ceci, S.J., & Bruck, M. (1993). Suggestibility of the child witness: A historical review and synthesis. *Psychological Bulletin*, 113(3), 403–439.

Ceci, S.J. & Hembrooke, H. (Eds.) (1998). *What can (and should) be said in court?: Expert witnesses in child abuse cases*. Washington, DC: APA Books.

Dickinson, J.J., Lytle, N.E., & Poole, D.A. (2021). Tele-forensic interviewing can be a reasonable alternative to face-to-face interviewing of child witnesses. *Law and Human Behavior*, 45(2), 97–111. https://doi.org/10.1037/lhb0000443

Dickinson, J.J., Lytle, N.E., & Poole, D.A. (2023). The 26 emerging investigative practice of tele-forensic interviewing: Implications for children's testimony. In D. DeMatteo & K.C. Scherr (Eds.), *The Oxford handbook of psychology and law*, pp. 449–463. Oxford: Oxford University Press.

Doherty-Sneddon, G., & McAuley, S. (2000). Influence of video-mediation on adult–child interviews: implications for the use of the live link with child witnesses. *Applied Cognitive Psychology: The Official Journal of the Society for Applied Research in Memory and Cognition*, 14(4), 379–392.

Earhart, B., La Rooy, D.J., Brubacher, S.P., & Lamb, M.E. (2014). An examination of "don't know" responses in forensic interviews with children. *Behavioral Sciences & the Law*, 32(6), 746–761.

Faller, K.C. (2014). Forty years of forensic interviewing of children suspected of sexual abuse, 1974–2014: Historical benchmarks. *Social Sciences*, 4(1), 34–65.

Garven, S., Wood, J.M., Malpass, R.S., & Shaw III, J.S. (1998). More than suggestion: the effect of interviewing techniques from the McMartin Preschool case. *Journal of Applied Psychology*, 83(3), 347–359.

Goodman, G.S., & Melinder, A. (2007). Child witness research and forensic interviews of young children: A review. *Legal and Criminological Psychology*, 12(1), 1–19.

Goodman, G.S., Tobey, A.E., Batterman-Faunce, J.M., Orcutt, H., Thomas, S., Shapiro, C., & Sachsenmaier, T. (1998). Face-to-face confrontation: Effects of closed-circuit technology on children's eyewitness testimony and jurors' decisions. *Law and Human Behavior*, 22, 165–203.

Hamilton, G., Whiting, E.A., Brubacher, S.P., & Powell, M.B. (2017). The effects of face-to-face versus live video-feed interviewing on children's event reports. *Legal and Criminological Psychology*, 22(2), 260–273.

Hsu, C.W., & Teoh, Y.S. (2017). Investigating event memory in children with autism spectrum disorder: Effects of a computer-mediated interview. *Journal of Autism and Developmental Disorders*, 47, 359–372.

John, A.S. (2020, April 30). It's not just Zoom. Google Meet, Microsoft Teams, and Webex have privacy issues too. *Consumer Reports*. Retrieved from www.consumerreports.org/video-conferencing-services/videoconferencing-privacy-issues-google-microsoft-webex-a7383469308/

Klassen, N.R., Price, H.L., & Connolly, D.A. (March 16–18, 2023). The impact of environmental distractions in tele-forensic interviews with children [Themed presentation session]. American Psychology-Law Society, Philadelphia, PA.

Klemfuss, J.Z., & Olaguez, A.P. (2020). Individual differences in children's suggestibility: An updated review. *Journal of Child Sexual Abuse*, 29(2), 158–182.

Lamb, M.E., & Fauchier, A. (2001). The effects of question type on self-contradictions by children in the course of forensic interviews. *Applied Cognitive Psychology*, 15(5), 483–491.

Lamb, M.E., Hershkowitz, I., Orbach, Y., & Esplin, P.W. (2011). *Tell me what happened: Structured investigative interviews of child victims and witnesses* (Vol. 56). John Wiley & Sons.

Lamb, M.E., Brown, D.A., Hershkowitz, I., Orbach, Y., & Esplin, P.W. (2018). *Tell me what happened: Questioning children about abuse*. John Wiley & Sons.

Landström, S., & Granhag, P.A. (2010). In-court versus out-of-court testimonies: Children's experiences and adults' assessments. *Applied Cognitive Psychology*, 24(7), 941–955.

La Rooy, D., Brubacher, S.P., Aromäki-Stratos, A., Cyr, M., Hershkowitz, I., Korkman, J., Myklebust, T., Naka, M., Peixoto, C.E., Roberts, K., Stewart, H., & Lamb, M.E. (2015). The NICHD protocol: A review of an internationally-used evidence-based tool for training child forensic interviewers. *Journal of Criminological Research, Policy and Practice*, 1(2), 76–89.

Lawson, M., Piel, M.H., & Simon, M. (2020). Child maltreatment during the COVID-19 pandemic: Consequences of parental job loss on psychological and physical abuse towards children. *Child Abuse & Neglect*, 110, 104709.

Miller, Q.C., Call, A.A., & London, K. (2022). Mock jurors' perceptions of child sexual abuse cases: Investigating the role of delayed disclosure and relationship to the perpetrator. *Journal of Interpersonal Violence*, 37(23–24), NP23374–NP23396.

Molloy, D. & Tidy, J. (2020, April 3). Zoom "unsuitable" for government secrets, researchers say. *BBC*. Retrieved from www.bbc.com/news/technology-52152025

Mueller-Johnson, K., Toglia, M., Sweeney, C., & Ceci, S.J. (2007). The perceived credibility of older adults as witnesses and its relation to ageism. *Behavioral Science and the Law*, 25, 355–375.

National Children's Alliance (2022, April 26). Emergency tele-forensic interview guidelines. Retrieved from https://learn.nationalchildrensalliance.org/telefi

Orbach, Y., Hershkowitz, I., Lamb, M.E., Sternberg, K.J., Esplin, P.W., & Horowitz, D. (2000). Assessing the value of structured protocols for forensic interviews of alleged child abuse victims. *Child Abuse & Neglect, 24*(6), 733–752.

Poole, D.A. & Lamb, M.E. (1998). *Investigative interviews of children*. Washington DC: APA Books.

Ratner, C. (2021). When "sweetie" is not so sweet: Artificial intelligence and its implications for child pornography. *Family Court Review, 59*(2), 386–401.

Ross, D.F., Hopkins, S., Hanson, E., Lindsay, R.C.L., Hazen, K., & Eslinger, T. (1994). The impact of protective shields and videotape testimony on conviction rates in a simulated trial of child sexual abuse. *Law and Human Behavior, 18*(5), 553–566.

Saywitz, K.J., & Camparo, L.B. (2013). *Evidence-based child forensic interviewing: The developmental narrative elaboration interview*. Oxford University Press.

Saywitz, K.J., & Snyder, L. (1996). Narrative elaboration: Test of a new procedure for interviewing children. *Journal of Consulting and Clinical Psychology, 64*(6), 1347–1357.

Saywitz, K.J., Wells, C.R., Larson, R.P., & Hobbs, S.D. (2019). Effects of interviewer support on children's memory and suggestibility: Systematic review and meta-analyses of experimental research. *Trauma, Violence, & Abuse, 20*(1), 22–39.

Schreiber, N., Bellah, L.D., Martinez, Y., McLaurin, K.A., Strok, R., Garven, S., & Wood, J.M. (2006). Suggestive interviewing in the McMartin Preschool and Kelly Michaels daycare abuse cases: A case study. *Social influence, 1*(1), 16–47.

State of Michigan Governor's Task Force on Child Abuse and Neglect and Department of Health and Human Services. (June, 2020). Provisional tele-forensic interview guidelines. Retrieved from www.michigan.gov/-/media/Project/Websites/mdhhs/Folder3/Folder93/Folder2/Folder193/Folder1/Folder293/Provisional_Tele-Forensic_Interview_Guidelines.pdf?rev=8ee237db420a4345affa99f8b3c76695

Su, I.A., & Ceci, S. (2021). "Zoom developmentalists": Home-based videoconferencing developmental research during COVID-19. PsyArXiv. Retrieved from https://psyarxiv.com/nvdy6/

Teoh, Y.S., & Lamb, M. (2013). Interviewer demeanor in forensic interviews of children. *Psychology, Crime & Law, 19*(2), 145–159.

Vandervort, F.E. (2005). Videotaping investigative interviews of children in cases of child sexual abuse: One community's approach. *Journal of Criminal Law & Criminology, 96*, 1353.

Vieth, V., Farrell, R., Johnson, R., & Peters, R. (2020). Conducting and defending a pandemic-era forensic interview. *Zero Abuse Project-National District Attorneys Association*.

Wiederhold BK (2020) Connecting through technology during the coronavirus disease 2019 pandemic: Avoiding "Zoom Fatigue". *Cyberpsychology, Behavior, and Social Networking, 23*, 437–438. https://doi.org/10.1089/cyber.2020.29188.bkw

Wilson, J.C., & Pipe, M.E. (1989). The effects of cues on young children's recall of real events. *New Zealand Journal of Psychology, 18*, 65–70.

Index

3D evidence 360–361, 372
"10-12 second rule" 398
23andMe 311

Aberdeen Index 209, 210
Abudarham, N. 280
accusatorial interviews 4–7
ACFE *see* Association of Certified Fraud Examiners (ACFE)
active exploration 243–244
Adams, D. 263–264
ADDS *see* Automated Deception Detection Systems (ADDS)
affective realism 185–187
AFIS *see* Automated Fingerprint Identification Systems (AFIS)
AFR *see* Automated Facial Recognition (AFR)
AI *see* artificial intelligence (AI)
alcohol myopia theory 144
ALPRs *see* automated license plate readers (ALPRs)
Althoff, R. R. 149
amateur detectives 410, 411
amateur sleuthing 306
Amber alerts 305, 404–405
Amendola, K. L. 240
American Bar Association 362, 370–371
American Psychiatric Association 101
American Sign Language 355
Americans with Disabilities Act 355
America's Most Wanted 307
Ancestry.com 311
Anthony, Caylee 309
AOI *see* area of interest (AOI)
area of interest (AOI) 144, 156
Arenzon, Valerie 3

Aristotle 94
Armstrong, G. 85
artificial intelligence (AI) 3, 42, 441; defined 117–119; interviewing 13–14; South Africa 111
ASD *see* autism spectrum disorder (ASD)
assistive technology 355–356, 368
Association of Certified Fraud Examiners (ACFE) 114, 122, 128, 131
Attard, J. 144, 272
Attempted Behavioral Control Theory 16–17
audio quality 334–335
audio-visual links (AVL) 331
auditory-phonetic and acoustic (AuPhA) analysis 125
Australia 330
authentication 366
autism spectrum disorder (ASD) 434
Automated Border Control electronic gates (E-gates) 82
Automated Deception Detection Systems (ADDS) 25–26
Automated Facial Recognition (AFR): disguises affects 65–66; filler selection 62–65; history 58–59; identification evidence 60–65; law enforcement 59–60; lead generation 61–62; privacy issues 66–68; similarity rating 60
Automated Fingerprint Identification Systems (AFIS) 409
automated interrogation 3
automated interviewing systems *see* virtual interviewing

automated license plate readers (ALPRs) 41
automatic speaker recognition system 125
avatars 176; benefits and challenges 12–13; of real people 181–185
AVL *see* audio-visual links (AVL)

Bailenson, J. N. 244, 340
BAI *see* behavior analysis interview (BAI)
balancing test 367
Baldwin, Simon 253
Bangkok 315
Baskin, J. H. 105
Bate, S. 283–285, 286–287
Bate, Sarah 272
Beaver, Antonio 233–234
Bedouin tribe of Arabia 116
behavioral cues 4–5, 438
behavior analysis interview (BAI) 4
Beland, R. V. 20–21
Belanova, E. 81, 286–287
Bellingcat 316–318
Bennell, Craig 253
Bennett, P. 214
Bennett, Tia C. 73, 233
Bennetts, R. J. 278
Benson, Bernadine Carol 111
be-on-the-look-out-for (BOLO) information 405
Bernard, C. 104
Berry, E. 257
Bertillon, Alphonse 58
Bertillonage system 58
between-person variability 78
Bild, E. 334, 364
Bindemann, M. 144, 173
Binet, A. 423
biometric identification 59, 68
biometric registries 304
biometric systems 85, 119–120
BioPac 160
bipolar disorder 101
Birmingham Six 8
bite mark 119, 384
Black people: eye tracking on 148, 151; FRS systems 408; incarceration of 414; misidentification 67, 75; tragic cases 359

Blais, C. 147, 151
Bland, Sandra 44
Blaskovits, B. 261
Bledsoe, Woodrow 58
blood splatter analysis 384
Bloodsworth, Kirk 217
Bobak, A. K. 278–279, 283–284
Boberg, Thomas 205
body language 13, 116, 190, 335
body-worn cameras (BWCs) 45–46, 304, 359–360, 411–412; as *Aide-Mémoire* 256–264; cognitive offloading 260–261; implications for policy and practice 264–266; misinformation-type effects 262, 266; outside of policing 256–257; within policing 257–259; retrieval-induced forgetting (RIF) 262–264, 265; stress and memory 254–256; use-of-force incidents 253
bogus-pipeline effect 124
Boivin, R. 257
BOLO information *see* be-on-the-look-out-for (BOLO) information
Bond, C. F. 17, 28
borderline personality disorders 101–102
Boston Marathon bombing (2013) 75, 313, 314, 321, 405, 411, 416
bottom-up investigations 307, 316
Brace, N. A. 212, 214, 224
Brain Defense, The 97
Brown, Andrew 253
Brown, D. 434
Brown, Michael 45, 359
Brown, Nericia 330
Browne, G. 257
Bruce, V. 77–78, 85
Bruck, M. 425
Bulger, James 73
burden of proof 116, 129, 388–389
Burgund, E. D. 148
Burke, Tara 350, 363
Burton, A. M. 85
Busby, L. P. 103
Butt, M. M. 402
BWCs *see* body-worn cameras (BWCs)

CAD *see* computer-aided dispatch (CAD)
Cahill, B. S. 100
calibration 162–163, 283
Cambridge Face Memory Test (CFMT) 282, 284
Cambridge Face Perception Test (CFPT) 282
cameras, and policing 45–46
Campbell, A. C. 145
Campbell, Paris 410
Canada: AFR technology 59–60; BWC footage 254; cyberjustice 352; polygraph tests 20; Royal Canadian Mounted Police (RCMP) 254, 359; Vancouver Hockey riots (2011) 313–314
Capgras syndrome 185
CART 356
Castells, M. 44, 47, 52
CAT software *see* computer-aided transcription (CAT) software
CBCA *see* criteria-based content analysis (CBCA)
CCTV *see* closed-circuit television (CCTV)
Ceci, S. 423, 439
Center for Legal and Court Technology (CLCT) 355
Certified Fraud Examiner (CFE) 114, 133
CFMT *see* Cambridge Face Memory Test (CFMT)
CFPT *see* Cambridge Face Perception Test (CFPT)
CGA *see* computer-generated animations (CGA)
CGE *see* computer-generated evidence (CGE)
CGS *see* computer-generated simulations (CGS)
chain of custody 317, 366
character creator engines 180
ChatGPT 53
children, avatar-based interviewing 12–13
children's witnesses/testimonies 423, 424; CCTV 428–431; digital technology and 432–433; dispositional factors affecting 424–425; interviewing guidelines 426–428; Narrative Elaboration Technique (NET) 427–428; NICHD protocol 426–427; situational factors affecting 425–426; videotaped evidence 428, 431–432; *see also* tele-FI
China: CCTV cameras 57; facial recognition technology 42; rice powder technique 18, 116
Cisco 353
citizen-led digital policing 303
citizen-led investigations 308
CLCT *see* Center for Legal and Court Technology (CLCT)
Clearview AI 413
closed-circuit television (CCTV) 57–58, 61, 428–431; benefits and challenges 430–431; *Coy v. Iowa (1988)* 429; and crime prevention 74–76; livestreaming 305; *Maryland v. Craig (1990)* 429–430; SCOTUS 428–429; smart systems 84
cognitive load 17, 244; and eyewitness evidence 339–342; and eyewitness memory 145–146, 340–342; pupil dilation 144; in remote communications 339–340; role on deception detection 157
cognitive offloading 260–261
Cohen, N. J. 149
cold cases 308–311
Cole, S. A. 380
Coleman, Savanna 94
collaborative justice-seeking 309
Colloff, M. F. 233, 246
composites *see* facial composite technology
computer-aided dispatch (CAD) 41, 44
computer-aided transcription (CAT) software 96, 354
computer-generated animations (CGA) 360, 367
computer-generated evidence (CGE) 358–362; admissibility considerations 365–368; body-worn camera 359–360; CGA/CGS 360, 366, 367;

courtroom technology benefits 361–362; digital device 358–359; virtual reality and 3D evidence 360–361
computer-generated simulations (CGS) 10, 360, 366
computer voice stress analysis (CVSA) 111, 121, 122–123, 129–131
confabulations 256
confidence judgement procedure 237
confidentiality 12
conformity 256, 264, 406
Content Complexity Theory 16–17
control question test (CQT) 18–19
cooperative eyewitnesses: gaze during encoding 144–149; gaze during retrieval 149–155
Cottrell, G. W. 152
Courtier, J. L. 103
court record 354–355
Courtroom 21 project 352
Couzens, Wayne 75
COVID-19 pandemic 10, 129, 133, 331, 353, 432, 434
Coy, John 429
Coy v. Iowa (1988) 429
CPIA *see* Criminal Procedure and Investigations Act 1996 (CPIA)
CQT *see* control question test (CQT)
Craig, Sandra Ann 429
Creswell's Data Analysis Spiral 126
crime dramas 379, 380
crime prevention, and CCTV 74–76
crime-scene reconstructions 193–194, 367
Crimewatch UK 307
Criminal Interrogation and Confessions (Reid) 4
Criminal Procedure and Investigations Act 1996 (CPIA) 207
criteria-based content analysis (CBCA) 24
cross-cultural interviews 27
cross-race effects 146–148, 151–152
crowdsourcing 303, 313–315, 321
CSI Effect 380–383; legal and criminal justice systems impacts 386–392; perceptions of evidence 383–384; verdict decisions 384–385
cued recall prompts 426

cultivation theory 382
cultural responsiveness 436
Curtis, Ashley 3
Cutler, B. L. 214
CVSA *see* computer voice stress analysis (CVSA)
cybercrime 441
cyber-detectives 308
cyberjustice 352
cyber security 440

D'Amico, J. 46
Dando, C. J. 12
dashcams 45–46
dataveillance 306
Daubert v Merrell Dow Pharmaceuticals Inc. 276
Davies, G. 209, 214, 218
Davis, J. P. 79, 223–224, 274, 281–282
Dawes, D. 257
DCNNs *see* Deep Convolutional Neural Networks (DCNNs)
de Almeida, Hannah 3
deception cues 5, 15, 28
deception detection 3; Automated Deception Detection Systems (ADDS) 25–26; cognitive theories 16–17; emotional theories 14–16; evolution of 14–26; future research 27–28; during Medieval ages 14; nonverbal cues 17; physiological cues 18–21; reality monitoring 23; Statement Validity Assessment (SVA) 23–24; strategic use of evidence (SUE) 24–25; unanticipated questions 22; verbal cues 21–22; verifiability approach 23
Deep Convolutional Neural Networks (DCNNs) 274, 275
Deep Fakes technology 441
defense attorneys 386–387, 389, 390, 392
Deffenbacher, K. A. 225
Degner, J. 148
Dekle, D. J. 219
DePaulo, B. M. 17
deprivation, of human necessities 3

de Ruyter, A. M. 112
De Sola, I. S. 152
Devlin, L. P. 236
diagnostic-feature-detection theory 242
diagnosticity 5–6
diagnostic value 5, 337
Diamond, Shari S. 100
Dick, Philip K. 51
Dickinson, J. J. 434
Diges, M. 152
digilantism 303
digital communications 304
digital devices 358–359
digital disruption 333
digital evidence 358–362
digital familiarity 437
digital interruptions 333, 340
digital literacy 339, 342
digitally networked sleuthing 303–304; discussion 324–325; hazards 321–324; intelligence gathering and transnational policing 316–319; netizen detectives 307–319; pedophile hunters 311–313; rise of 304–307; unsolved mysteries and cold cases 308–311; violent disorder and high-intensity events 313–316; virtues 320–321
digital recording 354
digital surveillance 440
digital vigilantism 305–306
Dioso-Villa, R. 380
discriminability 235, 240, 245
discrimination accuracy 242–243, 246
DNA Doe Project 310–311
DNA evidence 59, 61, 66, 68, 116, 119, 216, 382, 384, 388
DNA sequencing 6, 311
Doherty-Sneddon, G. 433
domestic violence 12, 46, 431, 440
doxing 414
drift correction 162–163
Drummond, Edward 95
Dunn, J. D. 279
Dunn, M. A. 363
Dutch National Police Force 258

ecological valid approach 221–223
edge aversion 154
Edmond, G. 274

EFF *see* Electronic Frontier Foundation (EFF)
E-FIT 205, 210, 213
EFIT 6 210, 212
EFIT-V 211, 223–224
EFMT *see* Egyptian vs. Caucasian faces (EFMT)
E-gates *see* electronic gates (E-gates)
Egyptian *vs.* Caucasian faces (EFMT) 286
Ekman, P. 14–16
electronic courtroom 352–353
Electronic Frontier Foundation (EFF) 42
electronic gates (E-gates) 82
elimination lineup procedure 237
Ellis, H. D. 209
Elphick, C. E. 151
EMIs *see* Environmental Management Inspectors (EMIs)
EMME *see* eye-movement-based memory effect (EMME)
emotional responses 14–15
empathy 11, 430
English Medieval courts 14
environmental accommodations 436–437
Environmental Management Inspectors (EMIs) 113
Enzinger, E. 125
episodic memory 255
Eskom 112
estimator variables 406–407
Estudillo, Alejandro J. 272
European Union (EU) 26, 57
Evans, J. R. 9
Everard, Sarah 75
evidence presentation systems 356–357
EvoFIT 205, 210, 212, 213
exoneration 234
explicit deal 5–6
Explico Inc. 361
eye contact 338
EyeLink 1000 159
eye-movement-based memory effect (EMME) 149, 156–157
eye tracking: calibration and drift correction 162–163; cooperative eyewitnesses 144–155; data collection 163–164; data quality 160–161;

Index 451

environment 161–162; experimental design and stimuli 163; gaze data processing 164–165; measurement 143–144; reporting 165; resolution and cost of hardware 159–160; uncooperative eyewitnesses 155–158

eyewitness: accuracy 145, 173–178, 187, 193, 239, 242; cognitive load 339–342; digital divide 332–333; distance and eye contact 338–339; evidence 333–335; impressions 335–338; misidentification 216, 234, 397, 410; perceptions 332–333, 336, 338–339; policy, research, and social justice 342–343; procedures 62–63

eyewitness identification 144, 174, 240, 247; *vs.* composites 217–220, 223–224; *see also* lineups

eyewitness memory: "10-12 second rule" 398; background and 397–402; of children 425; confidence & accuracy exposure effect 398–399; misinformation effect 400–401; social media as show-up 401–402; source monitoring 400

eyewitness testimony 116, 173, 177, 334; and eye tracking 158; and VR 191, 193, 197

Facebook 413
face matching 58, 76; automated face recognition 82–85; of avatars 183; erroneous identification 75–76; and eyewitness accuracy 187 *vs.* machine performance 85–86; identity challenges 77–79; individual differences 79–80; interactive 81–82; mismatch prevalence 78–79; recognizing perpetrators 76–77; training 80–81
face memory 224, 243–244, 284
faceprint 60, 83
FACES 213
face-to-face interviews 12, 133, 433–434, 437, 442

facial composite technology: accuracy of 213–216; cognitive interview 215; ecological validity 221–223; history 208–210; miscarriages of justice 216–217; role in investigation 206–207; technological developments 210–213; as visual statement 206; *vs.* eyewitness identification 217–220, 223–224; *vs.* other post-event information 206, 224–226
facial disguises 65–66
facial expressions 15, 78, 147, 335, 340, 439
facial identification 56, 60, 66
facial mapping 273, 285
Facial Recognition Software (FRS) 406–410; background and eyewitness memory 397–402; ethical considerations 413–415; police use of social media 404–406; trial outcomes 402–404; websleuthing and community policing 410–413
facial recognition technologies (FRTs) 42, 119, 272; demographic bias 67; and lineups accuracy 242–243; PimEyes 315–316; *see also* Automated Facial Recognition (AFR); super-recognizers
facial verification 56
false confessions 4–7, 21
false identifications 62–63, 65, 67, 146, 149, 219, 240–241, 246, 408
familiarity 155, 157, 274–275, 399–400
fantombillede (phantom image) 205
Farahany, N. A. 97
FBI *see* Federal Bureau of Investigation (FBI)
FE *see* forensic evidence (FE)
featural comparison 80
Federal Bureau of Investigation (FBI) 57, 314–315, 405
Federal Rule of Evidence (FRE) 366, 367
Feigenson, N. 364
Fiedler, S. 144
"fight-or-flight" response 18, 255

fillers 233; background 62–64; use of AFR 64–65
fingerprints 58, 78, 119, 384
First, M. 102
Fisher, R. P. 214
fixation duration 149, 155, 159, 161, 163
Flight 17 (Malaysia Airlines) 318
Flowe, H. 73, 152, 153, 233, 238
Floyd, George 359
fMRI *see* functional MRI (fMRI)
Fong, C. T. 5
forensic evidence (FE) 177, 359, 380–383, 387–392
forensic face matching 76–77
Forensic Science Regulator 275
forensic voice comparison (FVC), 111, 121, 124–125, 129–131, 134
see also voice biometrics
Four-Factor Theory of Deception 16
Fourth Industrial Revolution (4IR) 117
free recall prompts 426
FRE *see* Federal Rule of Evidence (FRE)
Friesen, W. V. 14–15
Frowd, C. D. 214, 215
FRS *see* Facial Recognition Software (FRS)
FRTs *see* facial recognition technologies (FRTs)
Frye v. United States 20
Fu, G. 146
functional MRI (fMRI) 96
FVC *see* forensic voice comparison (FVC)
Fysh, Matthew C. 173

gang crimes 175
gaze behavior 144; cross-race effects 146–148, 151–152; eyewitness memory 145–146; lineup decision processes 152–153; lineup fairness and construction 153–154; lineup performance 149–151; weapon focus 148
GazePoint 159, 162
Gedeon, T. 157
GEDmatch 311
Gelfand, M. J. 27
Gendron, A. 257
geographic flexibility 436

geographic information systems (GIS) 41
German, Libby 415
Germany 58
GFMT *see* Glasgow Face Matching Test (GFMT)
Giannou, K. 216
Gibling, F. 214
Gibson, S. J. 212
GIS *see* geographic information systems (GIS)
GKT *see* guilty knowledge test (GKT)
Glasgow Face Matching Test (GFMT) 189, 282, 283, 286
Glendale, Arizona 41
Godden, E. 434
Goldinger, S. D. 146, 147
Goncalves, Aleiva 411
Google Meet 440
Graham v. Connor 260
Granhag, P. A. 24–25
Great Britain 57
Greely, H. T. 97
Greene, C. M. 145
Greene, E. 100
Griffith, Tricia 309
Guildford Four 8
guilt-based decisions 385
guilty knowledge test (GKT) 19–20
gunshot-detection audio devices 41
Gurley, J. R. 100

Hachey, Joshua 3
Hahn, C. A. 288
hair sample 119
Hamilton, G. 433
Hancock, P. J. 156, 212
hand geometry 119
Hannula, D. E. 149
harassment 13, 50, 311–312, 314
Hartwig, M. 24–25, 28
Harvey, A. J. 145
He, Y. 146
Henderson, T. A. 102
Henkel, L. A. 260
Henri, V. 423
heritability 277
Higgins, Elliot 319
High Impact 361
high-intensity events 313–316
Hills, P. J. 147

Hillstrom, A. P. 156
Hinckley, John Jr. 96, 103
Hoisko, J. 257
Hole, G. J. 151
holistic features 80
holistic processing 278–279, 287
Holmes, M. E. 151
Holmqvist, K. 159–162, 164–165
hologram 361
Holt, G. A. 154
Home Office 236
home security cameras 74
honesty 14, 116
Hoover, Herbert 4
Hope, L. 156
Horne, Juanida Suzatte 111
Horry, R. 238
Hsu, C. W. 433–434, 436
humanitarian interviewing 8–10
human rights 9, 84, 316, 320
human voices 120

iBorderCtrl 26
ICFP *see* Institute of Commercial Forensic Practitioners (ICFP)
identification evidence 56, 60–65, 68, 206, 221, 233, 247
identification parades 236
Identi-Kit 205, 208, 213
ignorance 94
Ihlebæk, C. 221
Inbau, F. E. 6
incorrect decisions 233
Independent Police Investigative Directorate (IPID) 113
Industry 4.0 *see* Fourth Industrial Revolution (4IR)
information-gathering 9–10, 303
Ingham, Madeleine P. 233
Innocence Project 6, 216–217, 233, 397
insanity defense: and clinical diagnoses 100–102; history 94–96; neurohype and pseudoscience 104–105; neuroimaging 98–104; neuroscience, in courts 96–97; unreliable evaluations 97–98
Inside Edition 410
Institute of Commercial Forensic Practitioners (ICFP) 114, 128, 131
intellectual disabilities 425
intelligence gathering 9, 316–319
interactive lineup 237, 244–247
intergroup violence 191–193
internet quality 332–333, 340
interrogation: 19th century 3–4; accusatorial interviews 4–7; artificial intelligence interviewing 13–14; avatar-based interviewing 12–13; evolution of 3–14; false confessions 6–7; humanitarian interviews 8–10; PEACE Model of Investigative Interviewing 8–10; third degree practices 3–4; virtual interviewing 10–12
inversion effects 278–279
investigative interviewing 3, 8, 10, 14
IPID *see* Independent Police Investigative Directorate (IPID)
iris 59, 61, 66, 68, 119–120, 164
irrelevant questions 19
isolation 3, 62, 187

Januszewski, J. 145
Japan 58
Jeffreys, Alec 6
Jenkins, F. 218
Jones, A. C. T. 365
Jones, Gideon 111
Jordan, S. R. 15
Josephson, S. 151
Judicial Conference Committee on Automation and Technology 362
jurors', and technological impacts 350–372; assistive technology 355–356; computer-generated evidence (CGE) 358–362; controlled experimental research 362–365; court record 354–355; cyberjustice 352; electronic courtroom 352–353; evidence presentation systems 356–357; jury deliberation technology 357–358; legal, social and ethical impacts 365–371; remote appearances 353–354

454 Index

Kassin, S. M. 5, 7, 21, 363
Keeler, Leonard 18
Kelling, G. 43
Kent Face Matching Test (KFMT) 189
Khanizadeh, Ariane-Jade 253
Khan, M. J. 65
Kirby, M. 211
Klare, B. F. 408
Klassen, N. R. 434
Kleider-Offutt, Heather M. 397, 402, 404
Kleinberg, B. 25–26
Klentz, B. A. 385
Kneller, W. 145
knowledge workers 44, 47, 52, 304
Koehn, C. E. 214
Kovera, M. B. 214
Kusma, Robert Alexander 61

laboratory experiments 28, 174, 189, 221, 237–238
Lamb, Michael 426
Landmark Supreme Court Cases 428–429
laptops 356
Lariviere, Dion C. 11
Larson, John 18, 121
Laughery, K. R. 224
Lawrence, P. 208
layered voice analysis (LVA) 111, 121, 123–124, 129–131
lead generation 56, 60, 61–62, 65
Lederer, F. I. 353, 354, 357, 361, 369, 371
legal ethics 370–371
license plate recognition 41, 44, 47, 51, 77, 304
lie detection 15, 123, 128–129
lifelogging technologies 256, 257
Lifesize 353
Lilienfeld, S. O. 104
Lindsay, R. C. L. 218
lineups 62, 145, 233–234, 398, 401; decision processes 152–153; elimination procedure 237; fairness and construction 153–154; history and future 235–237; interactive 237, 244–247; live 234–236, 239; performance 149–151; photo 236, 239; procedural research 237–241; sequential 240–241, 246; simultaneous 240–242, 246; target-absent 149–150, 151, 154, 219, 234, 238–239; target-present 145, 151, 219, 234, 238–239; test stage 238; theoretical perspectives 241–244; video 236, 239
Linguistic Inquiry and Word Count (LIWC) software 25
live crime event 221–222
live facial recognition 42, 84–85
live lineup 234–236, 239
live video-feed interviews 433
LIWC software see Linguistic Inquiry and Word Count (LIWC) software
Loftus, E. F. 148–149, 262
Loftus, G. R. 148–149
Logan, Ron 415
Lombrosso, Cesare 18
London 42, 315
London Riots (2011) 76, 79
Lundy, Jessica 3
Luther, Kirk 3
LVA see layered voice analysis (LVA)
lying 16
Lykken, D. T. 19
Lynch, A. J. 104
Lytle, N. E. 434

Mac-A-Mug Pro system 214
machine learning 25–26, 42, 118–119, 157
Mackworth, N. H. 148
magnetic resonance imaging (MRI) 96
major depression 101
Malaysia (Flight 17 crash) 318
Mansour, J. K. 143, 150
Marcus, D. K. 100
Marshall, J. 100
Marston, William 18
Martin, Trayvon 359
Maryland v. Craig (1990) 429–430
mass-gatherings 313
match-to-description strategy 62
match-to-suspect strategy 62–63
Matthews, Todd 310
Mauldin, M. A. 224
McAuley, S. 433
McCarthy, John 117–118

McCurdy, M. 339
McDonald, Laquan 45
McDonald, L. W. 357–358
McDonnell, G. P. 146–147
McGlothin Courtroom 352
McMartin Preschool trial 423
MDS see memory distrust syndrome (MDS)
MDTs see Mobile Data Terminals (MDTs)
Medieval ages (deception detection) 14
Megreya, A. M. 152, 154
Meissner, C. A. 9
Melchert-Dinkle, William 413
Melnyk, L. 425
memory contamination 218, 256, 397, 398, 401, 403, 405
memory distrust syndrome (MDS) 7
memory-enhancing effect 257, 265
memory plausibility 406
mental health disorders 101
Messo, J. 148–149
Mestry, Natalie 272
METT see micro-expression training tool (METT)
micro-expression training tool (METT) 15
Microsoft Teams 330, 342, 432, 440
microtremor detection 123
Millen, A. E. 155–156
mindfulness 216
minimization techniques 5–6
Minsky, Marvin 118
misidentification 67, 75, 144, 216–217, 314, 397, 399–400, 407–408, 410
misinformation 4, 262, 266, 317, 400–401, 406, 412
Mitchell, Major 96
mitigation strategies 380, 390–391
MMT see Models Memory Test (MMT)
M'Naghten, Daniel 95
M'Naghten test 95
Mobile Data Terminals (MDTs) 44–45, 304
mock-juror paradigm 207
mock witness 234
Models Memory Test (MMT) 283
Mohamed, F. B. 16
Montgomery, Lisa 99
Moore, M. 43

Moreton, R. 274, 288, 289–290
Morrison, G. S. 125
motion cues 243
motion detection algorithms 77
MRI see magnetic resonance imaging (MRI)
mugshot commitment effect 399
mugshots 56, 76, 79, 218, 225, 399, 406
Muir, Bethany 330
multimedia court record 355
multimedia evidence 351, 358, 360, 362; procedural determinations 367–368; substantive determinations 365–366
Murdaugh, Alex 359
Murphy, G. 145

Nahari, T. 157
Narrative Elaboration Technique (NET) 427–428
National Academy of Sciences 384
National Centre for State Courts 352, 361
National Commission on Law Observance and Enforcement 4
National Institute of Standards and Technology (NIST) 67, 407
National Policing Improvement Agency (NPIA) 207, 226
National Real Time Crime Center Association (NRTCCA) 52
National Registry of Exonerations 6
Navarro, E. 341
netizen detectives 307; intelligence gathering and transnational policing 316–319; pedophile hunters 311–313; unsolved mysteries and cold cases 308–311; violent disorder and high-intensity events 313–316
NET see Narrative Elaboration Technique (NET)
neurodiversity 436
neurofallacies 104–105
neurohype 104–105
neuroimaging: case examples 98–99; findings 100–102; insanity evaluations 95, 98–99; and juries 99–100; limitations 102–104

456 *Index*

neurolaw 97
neuroscience 96–97, 104
neutral questions 19
Newman, Eryn J. 330
New Scotland Yard Super-Recognition Unit 79
Next Generation Identification (NGI) system 57, 59
NGI *see* Next Generation Identification (NGI) system
Nhan, Johnny 41
NICHD protocol 426–427
Nicomachean Ethics 94
Niehorster, D. C. 160
Nimmerhoudt, Bruce 125
NIST *see* National Institute of Standards and Technology (NIST)
nodding 12, 186, 340
nonverbal behaviors/cues 6, 14, 17, 186, 190, 335, 340, 438
nonverbal leakage theory 15
Norris, C. 85
NPIA *see* National Policing Improvement Agency (NPIA)
NRTCCA *see* National Real Time Crime Center Association (NRTCCA)
Nyathi v Special Investigating Unit 122, 131

OAB *see* own-age bias (OAB)
objective tests 281–282
one-to-many face matching 78
one-to-one face matching 76
online platforms 306
open-ended questions 426
open-source intelligence 305, 316–317
ORB *see* own-race bias (ORB)
Orquin, J. L. 164
other-race effect 146–148, 151, 193, 246, 286
own-age bias (OAB) 286
own ethnicity effect 193
own-race bias (ORB) 146–147, 151, 211, 246, 285–286

PACE Codes of Practice *see* Police and Criminal Evidence Act (PACE) Codes of Practice
Packer, I. K. 95

paired comparison procedure 237
Pake, J. M. 147
Palmer, M. A. 154
Papesh, M. H. 146
parasympathetic nervous system (PNS) 255
Park, J. 364
Paterson, H. M. 153
PCA *see* principal component analysis (PCA)
PEACE Model of Investigative Interviewing: account 9; closure 9; engage and explain 8; evaluation 9–10; planning and preparation 8
pedophile hunters 311–313, 323
Penry, Jaques 208
Pentland, S. J. 15
Perez-Mata, N. 152
Perlin, M. L. 104
personality disorders 101–102
Petito, Gabby 324, 410–411, 413
Pezdek, K. 258, 411
Phillips, P. J. 287–290
photo databases 57, 275
Photofit 205, 208–209, 213
photo lineup 236, 239
photo showups 236, 240–241
photo-taking impairment effect 261
phrenology 96
physiological responses 14, 17
Pike, G. 151, 205, 221–223
PimEyes 315–316
Piza, E. L. 75
place illusion 178
Plato 94
plausibility illusion 178
PNS *see* parasympathetic nervous system (PNS)
Police and Criminal Evidence Act (PACE) Codes of Practice 224–225, 236
police and technology 42–47; cameras and policing 45–46; MDTs, databases, and information age 44–45; police car and two-way radios 43–44; Real-Time Crime Centers (RTCCs) 46–47; *reform era* 43
police cars 43–44
Police Executive Research Forum 63

Police Scientific Development Branch (PSDB) 208–209
policing 45–46, 256
Polycom 353
polygraphs 14, 18, 20–21, 111, 116, 121–122
Pompedda, F. 13
Poole, D. A. 434
pop-out effect 152, 154
Portch, Emma 272
Porter, S. 15
pose reinstatement 243, 246
post-event information 206, 218, 224–226, 258
potential jurors 379, 380, 383, 389, 391, 402
PowerPoint 356, 364, 370
predictive analytics 304
principal component analysis (PCA) 85, 183, 211–212
privacy issues 66–68
Private Security Regulating Authority (PSiRA) 113–114, 127–128
PRO-fit 210, 213, 216
PROMAPS 237
PSDB *see* Police Scientific Development Branch (PSDB)
PSE *see* psychological stress evaluator (PSE)
pseudoscience 96, 104–105
PSiRA *see* Private Security Regulating Authority (PSiRA)
psychological stress evaluator (PSE) 121–122
psychopathy 99, 101–102
pupillometry 160
pupil size 151
Putin, Vladimir 83

Qin, Z. 157

racial bias 45, 193, 407–408; AI-based tools 119; cross-race effects 146–148, 151–152; eyewitness memory 146–148; within facial recognition technology 75; other-race effect 146–148, 151, 193, 246, 286; own-race bias (ORB) 146–147, 151, 211, 246, 285–286
Rahal, R. M. 144

Ramon, M. 278
Ramsey, JonBenet 309
rapport building 11, 438
RCMP *see* Royal Canadian Mounted Police (RCMP)
Reagan, Ronald 96
reality monitoring (RM) 23
Real Time Crime Centers (RTCCs) 41–42; discussion 52–53; improved community policing 51; increase in officer efficiency 48–49; managing risks and minimizing danger 47; methods of inquiry 47; police and technology history 42–47; privacy and current limitations 49–50; training and policies 51–52
reasonableness 260
recency effect 402
Reddit 308, 314, 322, 405
reference voiceprint 120
region of interest (ROI) 144
rehearsal 11, 218, 256
Reid, John E. 4
Reid Model of Interrogation 4–6
relevant evidence 366
relevant questions 19, 427
remote appearances 353–354, 365
remote hearings 330, 331, 354
Rempel, Emma 350, 363–364
responsibilization 305
retinal scanning 119
retributive vigilantism 309
retrieval cues 244–245, 247
retrieval-induced forgetting (RIF) 262–264, 265
retrieval-practice paradigm 263
RIF *see* retrieval-induced forgetting (RIF)
riots 76, 313–314
RM *see* reality monitoring (RM)
Robertson, D. J. 79, 286
Robinson, Devon 61
ROC analysis 245
ROI *see* region of interest (ROI)
Rommel, M. 148
Ross, D. F. 431
Rossner, M. 339
Rowden, E. 372
Royal Canadian Mounted Police (RCMP) 254, 359

RTCCs *see* Real Time Crime Centers (RTCCs)
rumination 256
Russano, M. B. 5
Russell, R. 272–273, 278
Russia 318
R. v. Béland 20
Ryan, J. D. 149, 155

Saks, M. J. 100
SANDF *see* South African National Defence Force (SANDF)
Sandra Bland Act 44
SAPS *see* South African Police Service (SAPS)
SARMAC *see* Society for Applied Research in Memory and Cognition (SARMAC)
Satel, S. 104
Sauer, J. D. 154
"save-it-and-forget-it" type effect 260
Scarpazza, C. 98
Schanz, Kimberley 379
Schizophrenia 100, 101, 185
Schwab, Klaus 117
Schwedes, C. 155
Schweitzer, N. J. 100
SCOTUS *see* Supreme Court of the United States (SCOTUS)
Screening Passengers by Observation Technique (SPOT) program 16, 190
SC v. Murdaugh 359
sedition hunting 315–316
SEIs *see* statement evidence inconsistencies (SEIs)
self-disclosure 10, 11
SenseCam 257
sensorimotor contingency 178
sequential lineups 240–241, 246
SES *see* socio-economic status (SES)
sexual abuse, in children 12, 311, 320, 423, 429, 431, 436–437, 440
Shepherd, J. W. 209
Sherlock Holmes 115, 134, 307–308
shielded interviews 437
showups 150–151, 236, 240–241, 401
siege mentality 319
signature verification 119
Silva, R. R. 337
similarity rating 60

simultaneous lineups 240–242, 246
Singh, M. 66
Sirovich, L. 211
sketches 205
Skype 432
sleep deprivation 256
smart doorbells 74
Smith, Harriet M. J. 73, 82, 233, 246
Smith, T. 21
Snapchat 415
SNS *see* sympathetic nervous system (SNS)
Snyder, A. A. 99–100
social cognitive theory 382
social distancing 331, 354
social media 305, 398, 399, 415; Facial Recognition Software (FRS) 406–410; future advances for criminal justice system 413–415; police usage of 404–406; as showups 401; trial outcomes 402–404; websleuthing and community policing 410–413
social policy implications 368–370
social presence (co-presence) 186–187, 365
social psychology 191, 193, 332, 382
Society for Applied Research in Memory and Cognition (SARMAC) 220
socio-economic status (SES) 332
source monitoring 399–401
South Africa: artificial intelligence 117–119, 129; Association of Certified Fraud Examiners (ACFE) 114, 122; biometrics and voice biometrics 119–121; computer voice stress analysis (CVSA) 121, 122–123, 129–131; discussion and recommendations 127–133; evidence and rules of evidence 114–115; forensic voice comparisons 121, 124–125, 129–131, 132; Fourth Industrial Revolution (4IR) 117, 129; Institute of Commercial Forensic Practitioners (ICFP) 114; investigative and legislative

landscape 111–112; investigative standards in 114; layered voice analysis (LVA) 121, 123–124, 129–133; legislative parameters of investigations 112–113; methodological framework 125–127; polygraph 121–122; Private Security Regulating Authority (PSiRA) 113–114; psychological stress evaluator (PSE) 121; skilled investigator 115–117
South African National Defence Force (SANDF) 113
South African Police Service (SAPS) 111, 113, 127
speaker recognition 124
speech-to-text software 354
Sporer, S. L. 206, 220–222, 224
Spot (misconduct reporting tool) 13–14
SPOT program *see* Screening Passengers by Observation Technique (SPOT) program
SR Research's EyeLink II 159
Stanko, Stephen 99
statement evidence inconsistencies (SEIs) 24
Statement Validity Assessment (SVA) 23–24
Stelter, M. 148
stenotype machine 354
Stevens, Beth 397
stigmatization 311
Stinnett, Bobbie Jo 99
strategic use of evidence (SUE) 24–25
street identification 236
stress, and memory 254–256
structural neuroimaging 98
Su, I. A. 423, 439
SUE *see* strategic use of evidence (SUE)
suggestibility 424–425
Summation 356
super-recognizers 79–81; comparing accuracy across face-mappers and 287–290; demonstration 280–285; face recognition ability 277–280; identification methods 280–281; objective tests 281–282; perceptual bias on 285–287; performance consistency 283–285; in research, real world, and legal settings 272–276
Supreme Court of the United States (SCOTUS) 429–430
surveillance 41, 74 *see also* closed-circuit television (CCTV)
suspicionless data collection 312
sustained emotional arousal 256
SVA *see* Statement Validity Assessment (SVA)
sympathetic nervous system (SNS) 255

Tardif, J. 279
target-absent lineups 149–150, 151, 154, 219, 234, 238–239
target-present lineups 145, 151, 219, 234, 238–239
Tarrant, Brendan 318
Taylor, Breonna 359
Taylor, D. 12
technological competence 370–371
technological issues, during virtual interviews 11–12
tele-forensic interviewing (tele-FI) 432; benefits 436–437; ethical and legal concerns 440; in practice 435–436; in research 433–435; risks 437–439
ten Brinke, L. 15, 336
Teoh, Y. S. 433–434, 436
terrorist attacks 313
Terry stop 48
Texas 330
text-chat 13
third degree practices 3–4
Thompson, Lauren E. 56
Tiemens, Robert 153
TikTok 312, 324, 410
Tobii's machines 160
Towler, A. 80
transnational policing 316–319
Tredoux, C. G. 221–222, 224
TrialDirector 356
TrialPad 356
triers-of-fact 397–399, 401, 416
Tripathi, Sunil 314–315, 405
true-crime infotainment 307, 309
Trump, Donald 315
truthiness effect 337

Truworths Ltd v CCMA and others 122, 131
Tsarnaev, Dzhokhar 75
Tsarnaev, Tamerlan 75
Turing, Alan 117, 186–187
Turing test 186
twins 277
two-way radios 43–44

UbiDuo 356
UK College of Policing 85
Ukraine 318
UK *see* United Kingdom (UK)
unanticipated questions 22
unbiased instruction 239
Uncanny Valley phenomenon 186
uncooperative eyewitnesses: countermeasures 156–157; detection 155–156
United Kingdom (UK): AuPhA approach 125; CCTV cameras 58; Criminal Justice Act (2003) 207; facial databases 84; Home Office 208; polygraph tests 20; remote hearings 330
United States (US): BWC footage 254; Capitol (mob attack) 315; CCTV cameras 57–58; cyberjustice 352; electronic courtrooms 353; eyewitness identifications 144; facial databases 84; *M'Naghten* test 95; polygraph tests 20; Screening of Passengers by Observation Techniques program 190
United States Judicial Conference 352
Unreal Character Creator 180
unsolved mysteries 308–311
unwanted interruptions, in tele-FI 438
use-of-force events 253–254 *see also* body-worn cameras (BWCs)
US *see* United States (US)

Valentine, T. 238
Vallano, Jonathan P. 143
Vancouver Hockey riots (2011) 313–314
verbal behaviors 14, 17
verbal cues 12, 21–22
verdict decisions 384–385

verifiability approach 23
vernacular creativity 306
Verschuere, B. 25–26
video clarity 407
video conferencing 331–332, 353–354, 368
video lineups 236, 239
video-mediated communication (VMC) 433
videotaped evidence 428, 431–432
viewpoints 243
vigilantism 305–306
violent disorder 313–316
VIPER 237
virtual courts 330; cognitive load and eyewitness evidence 339–342; cognitive processing interruptions 333–335; digital divide 332–333; distance and eye contact 338–339; emerging 331–332; implications for policy, research, and social justice 342–343; perceptions of eyewitnesses 332–333; semantic context 336–338; social cognitive cues 335–336; visual context 336
virtual environments 176–179; background context 336–337; in-person interviews 11–12; for interviewing 10; visual and spatial variations 338
virtual hearings 330
virtual interviewing 10–12
virtual people 179–180
virtual reality (VR) 10, 175–176, 195–196, 360–361, 372; affective realism 185–187; crime scenes and jury decision-making 193–195; face matching and eyewitness accuracy 187–191; intergroup violence 191–193; real people avatars 180–185; virtual objects and environments 176–179; virtual people 179–180
Vitacco, Michael J. 94
VMC *see* video-mediated communication (VMC)
voice biometrics 111, 120–121, 124, 132–133

Index   461

voice stress analyzer 14
Voice Stress Detection (VSD) 123
voir dire 389
Vollmer, August 43, 53
voluntary false confessions 7
Vredeveldt, A. 258
Vrij, A. 22
VR *see* virtual reality (VR)
VSD *see* Voice Stress Detection (VSD)

Walker, D. 434
Wallace, A. 372
Walsh, James P. 303
war crimes 308, 316, 318
watchlist database 82
weapon focus effect 148, 177, 178
web-based investigations 310, 319
Webex 342, 440
websleuthing 303, 410–413, 414–415
Websleuths.com 309
Wee Care Nursery School trial 423
Weinstein, Herbert 97
Weisbuch, M. 336
Wells, G. L. 219–220, 223
Wentura, D. 155
Wetmore, S. A. 238
whistle-blowers 112
White, D. 80–81
Whitman, Charles 96–97

Wild Beast Test 94
William & Mary Law School 352
Williams, Abby 415
Williams, Robert Julian-Borchak 75
Wilson, O. W. 43, 53
Winchester County, New York 41
"wisdom of the crowds" 289, 314
within-person variability 78, 82
within-statement inconsistencies (WSIs) 24
witness testimony 126, 333, 362, 369, 400–401
Wittwer, T. 147, 153
Wixted, J. T. 240
workplace harassment 13
Wortley, N. 274
Wright, D. 74
WSIs *see* within-statement inconsistencies (WSIs)
Wu, E. X. W. 151

Yardley, E. 415
Young, A. W. 209
YouTube 410

Zoom 330, 340, 342, 432, 440
"Zoom Fatigue" phenomenon 439
Zuckerman, M. 16
Zuo, J. 157